BLEU
1b

Deuxième
partie

TEACHER'S
EDITION

Discovering FRENCH
Nouveau!

Jean-Paul Valette
Rebecca M. Valette

McDougal Littell
A HOUGHTON MIFFLIN COMPANY
Evanston, Illinois • Boston • Dallas

From the Authors

DEDICATION

On June 6, 1944, shortly after 6:30 a.m., Private John Nedelka of the 16th Regiment, First Division (the Big Red One), came ashore on a stretch of the Normandy Coast now known as Omaha Beach. Pinned down under a deluge of fire, he spent the next hour crawling his way to the relative safety of a seawall just one hundred yards inland. As he scrambled up the cliffs off the beach later that afternoon, he suddenly realized that he was one of the few survivors of his company.

This book is dedicated to our friend John Nedelka, to the hundreds of thousands of young Americans who, like him, risked their lives, and, above all, to the tens of thousands who lost theirs in the liberation of France.

IN MEMORIAM

Roger Coulombe (*1940–2001*)

We would like to dedicate *Discovering French, Nouveau!* to the memory of our long-time associate, Roger Coulombe. For twenty-five years, he provided his editorial guidance and focused his artistic flair on the production and design of our language books—books which have encouraged millions of American young people to discover the beauty of French language and culture. May his commitment to quality and education inspire new generations of foreign language editors.

Jean-Paul Valette   Rebecca M. Valette

Printed in the United States of America

ISBN: 0-618-03218-5   2 3 4 5 6 7 8 9 10 - VJM - 07 06 05 04 03

Dear French Teachers,

We take this opportunity to welcome you to **Discovering French, Nouveau!** In fact, this is really your program, for it has been revised and expanded thanks to the suggestions, critiques, and encouragement we have received from the many hundreds of secondary school teachers who have enjoyed success getting their students to communicate with *Discovering French*.

Discovering French, Nouveau! emphasizes communication with accuracy and stresses meaningful cultural contexts. With **Discovering French, Nouveau!** your students will:

- **Experience France and the Francophone world**
- **Communicate with confidence**
- **Extend and enhance their learning through integrated technology**

As you look through the book you will discover new features, such as the end-of-unit *Tests de contrôle* and the addition of thematic vocabulary lists.

In conclusion, we would like to stress that our program is a flexible one, which allows teachers to take into account the needs of their students and build their own curriculum focusing on specific skills or topics.

We wish you the best of success with **Discovering French, Nouveau!** It is our hope that for you and your students, teaching and learning French with this program will be an enjoyable as well as a rewarding experience.

Jean-Paul Valette *Rebecca M. Valette*

Contents

Program Consultants

- Dan Battisti
- Dr. Teresa Carrera-Hanley
- Bill Lionetti
- Patty Murguía Bohannan
- Lorena Richins Layser

Discovering FRENCH *Nouveau!*

Discovering French *Nouveau!*

Explore French-speaking cultures with the proven leader.
A program that offers:

Culture
• Experience France and the Francophone World

Skills and Strategies
• Communicate with confidence

Integrated Technology
• Extend and enhance learning

Discovering FRENCH *Nouveau!*

Explores France and the distinctive French-speaking cultures

- Photos and illustrations reflect the cultural diversity of the French-speaking world.

- *Connexions* offer real-world activities that promote cultural awareness.

- *En bref* features familiarize students with the wide variety of countries in the French-speaking world.

- *Notes culturelles* provide more in-depth cultural information about France and the French-speaking world.

Builds skills and develops strategies for more accurate communication

- Strategies for developing reading and writing skills are included in each unit.

- Writing hints provide further support to help students write accurately in French.

- Learning about Language features provide strategies for communication and help students understand how language functions.

Integrates technology for engaging, real-world instruction

- Extensive video program presents and practices vocabulary and grammar in authentic cultural contexts.

- Online *Activités pour tous* Workbook offers leveled practice on the Internet.

- EasyPlanner CD-ROM and Test Generator CD-ROM give teachers the flexibility of having all ancillaries available in an electronic format.

- ClassZone.com presents a variety of engaging resources, from WebQuests to test preparation tools, all correlated to *Discovering French, Nouveau!*

Program Resources

Extensive resources tailored to the needs of today's students!

TEACHER'S RESOURCE PACKAGE ‑‑ ●

Unit Resource Books

Per Lesson -
Workbook TE
Activités pour tous TE
Lesson Plans
Block Scheduling Lesson Plans
Absent Student Copymasters
Family Involvement
Video Activities
Videoscripts
Audioscripts
Lesson Quiz

Per Unit -
Family Letter
Communipak
Activités pour tous TE Reading
Workbook TE Reading and Culture Activities
Lesson Plans for *Images*
Block Scheduling Lesson Plans for *Images*

Assessment Options
Portfolio Assessment
Unit Test Form A
Unit Test Form B
Unit Test Part III (Alternate) Cultural Awareness
Listening Comprehension Performance Test
Speaking Performance Test
Reading Comprehension Performance Test
Writing Performance Test
Multiple Choice Test Items
Test Scoring Tools
Audioscripts
Answer Keys

Block Scheduling Copymasters

Teacher to Teacher Copymasters

TEACHER'S EDITION

ADDITIONAL RESOURCES

Overhead Transparencies & Copymasters

Student Workbooks
• **Workbook**
• *Activités pour tous*

INTERNET RESOURCES

• **Online Workbook**
  leveled, self-scoring practice
• **eTest Plus Online**
  Complete Test Generator functionality, plus
  administer tests online
• **EasyPlanner Plus Online**
  Complete EasyPlanner functionality, plus
  view or print standards with each lesson
• **ClassZone.com**
  WebQuests, test preparation, flashcards
  and more

MIDDLE SCHOOL RESOURCES

• **Middle School Bridging Packet**
  • Reprise Workbook TE
  • Reprise Audioscript
  • Middle School Copymasters
  • Middle School Audio CD

TECHNOLOGY RESOURCES

• **Audio CD Program**
• *Chansons* **Audio CD**
• **Video Program (videotape / DVD)**
• **Test Generator CD-ROM**
• **EasyPlanner CD-ROM**
• **Power Presentations CD-ROM**

Easy Articulation

▶ *Discovering French, Nouveau!* is a carefully articulated three-level sequence of French instruction. Each level has its own special focus, which builds a spiraling progression across levels.

	CONVERSATION	DESCRIPTION	NARRATION	EXPLANATION
BLEU	Basic communication with learned phrases; simple questions and answers	Simple descriptions of people and things	Simple narration in the present; introduction to past narration	Simple explanations as to why something is done
BLANC	Creative conversation; asking and answering questions	More detailed descriptions, including simple comparisons	Basic narration in the past (*passé composé* and imperfect) and future	Expression of personal wishes and needs
ROUGE	Extended conversation using complex sentences and appropriate pronouns	More complex comparisons of people, things and actions	Extended narration of past, present and future events and corresponding conditions	Expression of emotions, wishes and hypotheses in complex sentences

▶ This chart shows the articulation of basic communication themes and topics across levels. (Only the major entry and reentry points are shown.) These themes and topics are recycled throughout the program in the various exercises, readings and communication activities.

THEMES AND TOPICS	BLEU *première partie* and *deuxième partie*	BLANC	ROUGE
Greeting and meeting people	Unit 1 *première partie*	Reprise: Rappel 1	–
Time and weather	Unit 2 *première partie*	Reprise: Rappel 1	Unit 3
Family and friends; Family relationships	Unit 1 *première partie*	Unit 1	Reprise A; Unit 9
Food and restaurants	Unit 2 *première partie* Unit 8 *deuxième partie*	Units 1, 3	Reprise A
Money and shopping	Unit 2 *première partie* Unit 6 *deuxième partie*	Reprise: Rappel 2	Reprise B; Unit 4
School and education	Images: À l'école en France *première partie*	Reprise: Faisons connaissance	Unit 10
Daily activities	Unit 3 *première partie*	Reprise: Rappel 3	Reprise A
Getting around the city	Unit 3 *première partie* Unit 5 *deuxième partie*	Unit 2	Unit 8
Describing oneself	Unit 4 *première partie*	Units 1, 7	Unit 1
Home and furnishings	Unit 4 *première partie* Unit 5 *deuxième partie*	Unit 6	Unit 6
Possessions and their description	Unit 4 *première partie*	Reprise: Rappel 2 Unit 2	Reprise A; Unit 2
Sports, fitness, daily routine	Unit 5 *deuxième partie*	Units 5, 8	Unit 1
Medical and dental care	–	Unit 5	Unit 7
Clothing and personal appearance	Unit 6 *deuxième partie*	Unit 7	Reprise A; Unit 4
Leisure activities, music, entertainment	Unit 7 *deuxième partie*	Unit 4	Interlude 4
Vacation and travel	Unit 7 *deuxième partie*	Unit 8	Reprise B; Unit 3
Transportation	Unit 7 *deuxième partie*	Units 8, 9	Unit 5
Jobs and professions	–	Unit 1	Units 2, 10
Helping around the house	–	Unit 2	Unit 2
Nature and the environment	–	Unit 2	Unit 3
Services and repairs	–	–	Unit 4
Hotel accommodations	–	–	Unit 6

FUNCTION	BLEU	BLANC	ROUGE
Greeting people and socializing	Units 1, 2 *première partie*	Reprise: Rappel 1	–
Talking about the present Asking and answering questions Describing people, places and things Describing future plans (Simple description)	Units 3, 4, 5, 6 *première partie, deuxième partie*	Reprise: Rappels 2, 3; Unit 1	Reprise A
Narrating past events (Simple narration)	Unit 7 *deuxième partie*	Unit 2	Reprise B
Discussing daily routines (Simple narration)	–	Unit 5	Unit 1
Describing people, places, things (Extended description)	Unit 8 *deuxième partie*	Units 3, 4, 5	Reprise C Units 2, 4
Describing past conditions and narrating past events (Extended narration)	–	Unit 6	Reprise B Units 3, 7
Comparing and discussing people, things and actions (Complex description)	–	Unit 7	Units 6, 9
Discussing future events (Extended narration)	–	Unit 8	Units 5, 8
Discussing hypothetical conditions and events (Complex discussion)	–	Unit 8	Units 5, 8
Expressing wishes and obligations (Direct statements)	–	Unit 9	Unit 2
Expressing doubts and emotions (Complex discussion)	–	–	Unit 7
Expressing cause and purpose (Complex discussion)	–	–	Unit 10

Book Organization
Discovering French, *Nouveau!* BLEU Deuxième partie

Basic Structure The Student Text contains a *Reprise* review section, four units and an *Images* photo essay. The *Reprise* reviews material taught in *Bleu-Première partie*. Units 5 & 6 form the core of study, and focus on the formal development of language for accurate communication. Units 7 & 8 introduce somewhat more complex language functions.

REVIEW

This section reviews the basic communicative structures contained in the Core Material of *Discovering French, Nouveau! – Bleu Première partie.* In addition there is some expansion of thematic vocabulary.

REPRISE · *Bonjour!*

Rappel 1	Être; nouns, articles, adjectives
Rappel 2	Avoir; objects
Rappel 3	Faire; -er verbs; negative and interrogative constructions
Rappel 4	Numbers, time and date, weather expressions; ordering in a café
Le savez-vous?	Cultural discovery and enrichment

COMMUNICATIVE FOCUS:
Asking and answering questions about oneself, one's friends, and one's daily activities

COMMUNICATIVE THEMES:
School, daily life, making phone calls, introducing people, inviting friends

CORE MATERIAL

These units provide the linguistic base needed for basic communication skills.
Emphasis is on asking and answering questions. (Students should complete these units.)

UNITÉ 5 · *En ville*

 IMAGES *À Paris*

UNITÉ 6 · *Le shopping*

TOPICS COVERED
• getting around town
• describing where one lives
• shopping for clothes

FURTHER DEVELOPMENT

Units 7 and 8 introduce somewhat more complex language functions. (It is not critical to finish these units since the material is reviewed and expanded in the first part of *Discovering French, Nouveau! – Blanc.*)

UNITÉ 7 · *Le temps libre*

UNITÉ 8 · *Les repas*

TOPICS COVERED
• describing weekend activities   • planning meals
• talking about vacation plans   • shopping for food

INVITATION AU FRANÇAIS

UNITÉ 1 Faisons connaissance • CULTURAL CONTEXT Meeting people

PREMIÈRE PARTIE

COMMUNICATION: FUNCTIONS AND ACTIVITIES COMPREHENSION AND SELF-EXPRESSION	COMMUNICATION TOPICS THEMATIC VOCABULARY	LINGUISTIC GOALS ACCURACY OF EXPRESSION
Meeting people • Introducing oneself (**Leçon 1A**) • Spelling one's name (**Leçon 1A**) • Asking someone's name (**Leçon 1A**) • Saying where you are from (**Leçon 1B**)	• Adjectives of nationality (**Leçon 1B**)	• **L'alphabet (Leçon 1A)** • **Français / française (Leçon 1B)**
Greeting people • Saying hello (**Leçon 1A**) • Asking how people feel (**Leçon 1C**) • Saying good-bye (**Leçon 1C**)	• Expressions with **ça va (Leçon 1C)** • Counting 0 to 10 (**Leçon 1A**) • Counting 10 to 20 (**Leçon 1B**) • Counting 20 to 60 (**Leçon 1C**)	
Talking about other people • Pointing people out (**Leçon 2A**) • Finding out someone's name (**Leçon 2B**) • Saying where a person is from (**Leçon 2B**)	• People (**Leçon 2A**)	• **Un garçon / une fille (Leçon 2A)** • **Le garçon / la fille (Leçon 2B)**
Introducing one's family • Giving their names (**Leçon 2B**) • Giving their ages (**Leçon 2C**)	• Family members (**Leçon 2C**) • Counting 60 to 79 (**Leçon 2A**) • Counting 80 to 100 (**Leçon 2B**)	• **Mon cousin / ma cousine (Leçon 2C)** • **Ton cousin / ta cousine (Leçon 2C)**

UNITÉ 2 La vie courante • CULTURAL CONTEXT Having a snack in France

PREMIÈRE PARTIE

Saying you are hungry • Offering a friend something to eat (**Leçon 3A**) • Asking a friend for something to eat (**Leçon 3A**)	• Foods (**Leçon 3A**)	• **Un sandwich / une pizza (Leçon 3A)**
Saying you are thirsty • Ordering a beverage in a café (**Leçon 3B**) • Asking an adult for something to eat or drink (**Leçon 3B**)	• Beverages (**Leçon 3B**)	• **S'il te plaît / s'il vous plaît (Leçon 3B)**
Paying at a café in France • Asking what something costs (**Leçon 3C**) • Asking a friend to lend you money (**Leçon 3C**)		
Talking about time • Asking for the time (**Leçon 4A**) • Indicating the time (**Leçon 4A**) • Saying when certain events are scheduled (**Leçon 4A**)	• Expressions of time (**Leçon 4A**)	
Talking about dates • Asking the day of the week (**Leçon 4B**) • Giving the date (**Leçon 4B**) • Talking about birthdays (**Leçon 4B**)	• Days of the week (**Leçon 4B**) • Months of the year (**Leçon 4B**)	
Talking about the weather	• Weather expressions (**Leçon 4C**) • Seasons (**Leçon 4C**)	

UNITÉ 3 Qu'est-ce qu'on fait? • CULTURAL CONTEXT Daily activities at home, at school, on weekends

PREMIÈRE PARTIE

COMMUNICATION: FUNCTIONS AND ACTIVITIES COMPREHENSION AND SELF-EXPRESSION	COMMUNICATION TOPICS THEMATIC VOCABULARY	LINGUISTIC GOALS ACCURACY OF EXPRESSION
Describing daily activities • What people do and don't do (**Leçon 5**) • What people like to do and don't like to do (**Leçon 5**) • What you want and don't want to do (**Leçon 5**)	• Daily activities (**Leçon 5**) • Expressions with **faire** (**Leçon 8**)	• Subject pronouns (**Leçon 6**) • The negative **ne… pas** (**Leçon 6**) • Verb + infinitive (**Leçon 7**) • Regular **-er** verbs (**Leçon 7**) • The verb **faire** (**Leçon 8**)
Talking about where people are	• Places (**Leçon 6**)	• The verb **être** (**Leçon 6**)
Finding out what is going on • Asking yes/no questions (**Leçon 6**) • Asking information questions (**Leçon 8**)	• Question words (**Leçon 8**)	• Yes/no questions with **est-ce que** (**Leçon 6**) • Information questions with **est-ce que** (**Leçon 8**) • Questions with inversion (**Leçon 8**)
Inviting friends to do things with you • Extending an invitation (**Leçon 5**) • Accepting an invitation (**Leçon 5**) • Turning down an invitation (**Leçon 5**)		• Verb + infinitive (**Leçon 7**)
Expanding one's conversational skills • Answering yes/no questions (**Leçon 6**) • Expressing approval or regret (**Leçon 7**) • Expressing mild doubt or surprise (**Leçon 8**)	• Affirmative and negative expressions (**Leçon 6**)	

UNITÉ 4 Le monde personnel et familier • CULTURAL CONTEXT People and their possessions

PREMIÈRE PARTIE

Describing yourself and others • Physical appearance (**Leçon 9**) • Age (**Leçons 9, 10**) • Character traits (**Leçon 11**) • Nationality (**Leçon 11**)	• People (**Leçon 9**) • Adjectives of physical description (**Leçon 9**) • Adjectives of personality (**Leçon 11**) • Adjectives of nationality (**Leçon 11**) • Adjectives of aspect (**Leçon 12**)	• Singular and plural nouns (**Leçon 10**) • Definite and indefinite articles (**Leçon 10**) • The expression **avoir… ans** (**Leçon 10**) • Adjective formation (**Leçon 11**) • Adjective position (**Leçons 11, 12**) • Use of **c'est** and **il est** (**Leçon 12**)
Describing your room • What is in it (**Leçon 9**) • Where things are located (**Leçon 9**)	• Room furnishings (**Leçon 9**) • Prepositions of place (**Leçon 9**)	• The expression **il y a** (**Leçon 9**)
Talking about possessions • Things that one owns and doesn't own (**Leçons 9, 10**) • Whether they work or not (**Leçon 9**) • Where they were made (**Leçon 11**) • What they look like (**Leçon 12**)	• Everyday objects (**Leçon 9**) • Color (**Leçon 12**) • Aspect (**Leçon 12**)	• The verb **avoir** (**Leçon 10**) • The negative article **pas de** (**Leçon 10**)
Expanding one's conversational skills • Getting someone's attention (**Leçon 12**) • Making generalizations (**Leçon 10**) • Expressing opinions (**Leçon 12**) • Talking about regular events (**Leçon 10**) • Contradicting a negative statement or question (**Leçon 10**) • Introducing a conclusion (**Leçon 11**)	• Attention getters (**Leçon 12**) • Expressions of opinion (**Leçon 12**)	• Use of the definite article: in general statements to indicate repeated events (**Leçon 10**) • Impersonal **c'est** (**Leçon 12**)
optional: Talking about past events (**Leçons 10, 11, 12**)		• Conversational introduction: answering questions in the **passé composé** (**Leçons 10, 11, 12**)

REPRISE Bonjour! • CULTURAL CONTEXT Getting reacquainted

COMMUNICATION: FUNCTIONS AND ACTIVITIES COMPREHENSION AND SELF-EXPRESSION	COMMUNICATION TOPICS THEMATIC VOCABULARY	LINGUISTIC GOALS ACCURACY OF EXPRESSION
Talking about school and classes (Bonjour: Et vous) **Talking about self and family (Bonjour and Et vous)**	Personal and family characteristics School subjects **(Faisons connaissance!)**	
Expressing oneself on familiar topics • Giving the date **(R-4)** • Telling time **(R-4)** • Describing the weather **(R-4)**	• Review: numbers 1-100 **(App. A)** • Review: days, months **(App. A)** • Review: times of day **(App. A)** • Review: weather **(App. A)**	
Talking about places and things • Describing things you own **(R-2)** • Saying where things are **(R-2)** • Pointing things out **(R-2)** • Expressing preferences **(R-3)**	• Review: place names **(App. A)**	• Review: possessive adjectives **(App. A)**
Carrying out simple conversations • Asking and answering questions **(R-1)** • Talking about daily activities **(R-1)** • Talking about places where you go **(R-3)** • Saying what you like **(R-3)**	• Review: question words **(R-3)** • Review: common verbs **(App. A)**	• Review: present tense of regular verbs **(App. A)** • Review: interrogative and negative constructions **(App. A)**

UNITÉ 5 En ville • CULTURAL CONTEXT City life—the home, the family and urban activities

Describing your city • Streets and public buildings **(Leçon 13)** • Places you often go to **(Leçon 14)** • How you get around **(Leçon 14)**	• City places and buildings **(Leçon 13)** • Transportation **(Leçon 14)**	• The verb **aller (Leçon 14)** • Contractions with **à (Leçon 14)**
Finding your way around • Asking and giving directions **(Leçon 13)** • Indicating the floor **(Leçon 16)**	• Giving directions **(Leçon 13)**	• Ordinal numbers **(Leçon 16)**
Describing your home and your family • Your address **(Leçon 13)** • The inside and outside of your home **(Leçon 13)** • Your family **(Leçon 16)**	• Neighborhood **(Leçon 13)** • Rooms of the house **(Leçon 13)** • Family members **(Leçon 16)**	• The expression **chez (Leçon 14)** • Stress pronouns **(Leçon 15)** • The construction noun + **de** + noun **(Leçon 15)** • Possession with **de (Leçon 16)** • Possessive adjectives **(Leçon 16)**
Making plans to do things in town • What you are going to do **(Leçon 14)** • Asking others to come along **(Leçon 15)** • Saying where you have been **(Leçon 15)**	• Activities: sports, games, etc. **(Leçon 15)**	• **Aller** + infinitive **(Leçon 14)** • The verb **venir (Leçon 15)** • Contractions with **de (Leçon 15)**
Expanding one's conversational skills: • Contradicting someone **(Leçon 15)** • Expressing doubt **(Leçon 16)** • Expressing surprise **(Leçon 15)**		
optional: Talking about past events **(Leçons 13, 14, 15, 16)**		• Conversational introduction: answering questions in the **passé composé (Leçons 13, 14, 15, 16)**

UNITÉ 6 Le shopping • CULTURAL CONTEXT Buying clothes

Talking about clothes • What people are wearing **(Leçon 17)** • Whether the clothes fit **(Leçon 17)** • What they look like **(Leçons 17, 19)** • What one's preferences are **(Leçon 17)**	• Clothing and accessories **(Leçon 17)** • Descriptive adjectives **(Leçon 17)** • Adjectives **beau, nouveau, vieux (Leçon 19)** • Expressions of opinion **(Leçon 17)**	• The verb **mettre (Leçon 18)** • The verb **préférer (Leçon 18)** • The demonstrative **ce (Leçon 18)** • The interrogative **quel? (Leçon 18)**
Discussing shopping plans • Where to go **(Leçons 17, 20)** • What to buy **(Leçon 18)**	• Stores that sell clothes **(Leçon 17)** • Verbs like **vendre (Leçon 20)**	• The verb **acheter (Leçon 18)** • Regular **-re** verbs **(Leçon 20)** • The pronoun **on (Leçon 20)**

DEUXIÈME PARTIE

UNITÉ 6 *(continued)*

	COMMUNICATION: FUNCTIONS AND ACTIVITIES COMPREHENSION AND SELF-EXPRESSION	COMMUNICATION TOPICS THEMATIC VOCABULARY	LINGUISTIC GOALS ACCURACY OF EXPRESSION
DEUXIÈME PARTIE	**Buying clothes** • Asking for help **(Leçon 17)** • Finding out prices **(Leçons 17, 20)** • Deciding what to choose **(Leçon 19)** • Comparing items **(Leçon 19)** • Talking about what you need and what you like **(Leçon 20)** • Giving advice **(Leçon 20)**	• Numbers 100–1000 **(Leçon 17)** • Money-related expressions **(Leçon 20)** • Verbs like **choisir (Leçon 19)** • Expressions **avoir besoin de** and **avoir envie de (Leçon 20)**	• Regular **-ir** verbs **(Leçon 19)** • The verb **payer (Leçon 20)** • Comparisons **(Leçon 19)** • The imperative **(Leçon 20)**
	Expanding one's conversational skills • Emphasizing a remark **(Leçon 18)** • Indicating approval **(Leçon 20)** • Introducing an opinion **(Leçon 19)**		
	optional: Talking about past events **(Leçons 17, 18, 19, 20)**		• Conversational introduction:answering questions in the **passé composé (Leçons 17, 18, 19, 20)**

UNIT 7 Le temps libre • CULTURAL CONTEXT Leisure-time activities

DEUXIÈME PARTIE	**Discussing leisure activities** • Going out with friends **(Leçon 21)** • Sports **(Leçon 21)** • Helping around the house **(Leçon 21)** • How you and others feel **(Leçon 22)** • Things you never do **(Leçon 24)**	• Common weekend activities **(Leçon 21)** • Individual summer and winter sports **(Leçon 21)** • Household chores **(Leçon 21)**	• **Faire de** + sport **(Leçon 21)** • Expressions with **avoir (Leçon 22)** • **Ne … jamais (Leçon 24)**
	Describing vacation travel plans • Travel dates **(Leçons 21, 24)** • How to travel **(Leçon 21)** • How long to stay **(Leçons 21, 23)** • What to see **(Leçon 23)**	• Means of transportation **(Leçon 21)** • Divisions of time **(Leçon 21)** • Periods of future time **(Leçon 23)** • Verbs of movement **(Leçon 24)**	• The verb **voir (Leçon 23)**
	Narrating what happened • What you did and didn't do **(Leçons 22, 23)** • Where you went and when you returned **(Leçon 24)** • The sequence in which you did these things **(Leçon 22)** • Remaining vague about certain details **(Leçon 24)**	• Adverbs of sequence **(Leçon 22)** • Periods of past time **(Leçon 23)**	• **Passé composé** of **-er** verbs **(Leçon 22)** • **Passé composé** of **-ir** verbs **(Leçon 23)** • **Passé composé** of **-re** verbs **(Leçon 23)** • **Passé composé** of irregular verbs **(Leçon 23)** • **Passé composé** with **être (Leçon 24)** • **Quelqu'un, quelque chose** and their opposites **(Leçon 24)**

UNITÉ 8 Les repas • CULTURAL CONTEXT Food and meals

DEUXIÈME PARTIE	**Talking about your favorite foods** • What you like and don't like **(Leçon 25)** • What you can, should and want to eat **(Leçons 25, 26, 27)**	• Names of foods and beverages **(Leçon 25)** • Verbs of preference **(Leçon 25)**	• The verb **vouloir (Leçon 26)** • The verbs **pouvoir** and **devoir (Leçon 27)**
	Shopping for food • Making a shopping list **(Leçon 25)** • Interacting with vendors **(Leçon 25)** • Asking prices **(Leçon 25)**	• Quantities **(Leçon 25)** • Fruits and vegetables **(Leçon 25)**	• Partitive article **(Leçon 26)**
	Planning a meal • Asking others to help you **(Leçon 27)** • Setting the table **(Leçon 25)**	• Meals **(Leçon 25)** • Verbs asking for service **(Leçon 27)** • Place setting **(Leçon 25)**	• Pronouns **me, te, nous, vous (Leçon 27)** • Pronouns with commands **(Leçon 27)**
	Eating out with friends • Ordering food **(Leçon 25)** • Asking the waiter/waitress to bring things for others **(Leçon 28)** • Talking about people you know **(Leçon 27)** • Talking about what others have said or written **(Leçon 28)**	• Verbs using indirect objects **(Leçon 28)**	• The verb **prendre (Leçon 26)** • The verb **boire (Leçon 26)** • The verb **connaître (Leçon 28)** • The verbs **dire** and **écrire (Leçon 28)** • Pronouns **le, la, les, lui, leur (Leçon 28)**

LEVEL 2 SCOPE AND SEQUENCE

COMMUNICATION: FUNCTIONS AND ACTIVITIES COMPREHENSION AND SELF-EXPRESSION	**COMMUNICATION TOPICS** THEMATIC VOCABULARY	**LINGUISTIC GOALS** ACCURACY OF EXPRESSION
Talking about school and classes (Faisons connaissance!)	• School subjects **(Faisons connaissance!)**	
Expressing oneself on familiar topics • Giving the date **(Rappel-1)** • Telling time **(Rappel-1)** • Describing the weather **(Rappel-1)**	• Review: numbers 1-100 **(Appendix A)** • Review: days, months **(Appendix A)** • Review: times of day **(Appendix A)** • Review: weather **(Appendix A)**	
Talking about places and things • Describing things you own **(Rappel-2)** • Saying where things are **(Rappel-2)** • Pointing things out **(Rappel-2)** • Expressing preferences **(Rappel-2)**	• Review: common objects and items of clothing **(Appendix A)** • Prepositions of location **(Rappel-2)** • Review: place names **(Appendix A)**	• Review: articles and contractions, **ce** and **quel** **(Appendix A)** • Review: possessive adjectives **(Appendix A)**
Carrying out simple conversations • Asking and answering questions **(Rappel-3)** • Talking about daily activities **(Rappel-3)** • Talking about places where you go **(Rappel-3)** • Saying what you like **(Rappel-3)**	• Review: question words **(Rappel-3)** • Review: common **–er, -ir, -re** verbs **(Appendix A)**	• Review: present tense of regular verbs **(Appendix A)** • Review: interrogative and negative constructions **(Appendix A)** • Review: subject pronouns and stress pronouns **(Rappel-3)** • Review: the imperative **(Appendix A)**

Presenting oneself and others • Providing personal data **(Leçon 1)** • Identifying one's family **(Leçon 1)** • Talking about professions **(Leçon 1)**	• Adjectives of nationality **(Leçon 1)** • Family and friends **(Leçon 1)** • Professions **(Leçon 1)**	• The verb **être (Leçon 2)** • **C'est** and **il est (Leçon 2)**
Interacting with others • Introducing people **(Leçon 1)** • Making phone calls **(Leçon 1)** • Reading birth and wedding announcements **(Leçon 1)**		
Talking about oneself and others • Describing looks and personality **(Leçon 2)** • Talking about age **(Leçon 3)** • Describing feelings and needs **(Leçon 3)**	• Descriptive adjectives **(Leçon 2)** • Expressions with **avoir (Leçon 3)** • Expressions with **faire (Leçon 3)**	• Regular and irregular adjectives **(Leçon 2)** • The verb **avoir (Leçon 3)** • The verb **faire (Leçon 3)** • Inverted questions **(Leçon 3)**
Describing one's plans • Saying where people are going and what they are going to do **(Leçon 4)** • Saying where people are coming from **(Leçon 4)** • Saying how long people have been doing things **(Leçon 5)**	• Expressions with **depuis (Leçon 4)**	• The verb **aller (Leçon 4)** • The construction **aller** + infinitive **(Leçon 4)** • The verb **venir (Leçon 4)** • The present with **depuis (Leçon 4)**

READING Getting the gist

UNITÉ 2 Le week-end, enfin! • CULTURAL CONTEXT Weekend activities

COMMUNICATION: FUNCTIONS AND ACTIVITIES COMPREHENSION AND SELF-EXPRESSION	COMMUNICATION TOPICS THEMATIC VOCABULARY	LINGUISTIC GOALS ACCURACY OF EXPRESSION
Talking about weekend plans • Describing weekend plans in the city **(Leçon 5)** • Planning a visit to the country **(Leçon 5)**	• Going out with friends **(Leçon 5)** • Helping at home **(Leçon 5)** • The country and the farm **(Leçon 5)** • Domestic and other animals **(Leçon 5)** • Expressions of present and future time **(Leçon 7)**	• The verbs **mettre**, **permettre**, and **promettre (Leçon 6)** • The verb **voir (Leçon 7)** • The verbs **sortir**, **partir**, and **dormir (Leçon 8)**
Getting from one place to another • Getting around in Paris **(Leçon 5)** • Visiting the countryside **(Leçon 5)**	• Getting around by subway **(Leçon 5)**	• The verb **prendre (Leçon 6)**
Narrating past weekend activities • Talking about where one went **(Leçons 7, 8)** • Talking about what one did and did not do **(Leçons 6, 7, 8)**	• Expressions of past time **(Leçon 6)**	• The **passé composé** with **avoir (Leçons 6, 7)** • The **passé composé** with **être (Leçons 7, 8)** • Impersonal expressions: **quelqu'un, quelque chose, personne, rien (Leçon 7)** • **Il y a** + elapsed time **(Leçon 8)**

READING Recognizing word families

UNITÉ 3 Bon appétit! • CULTURAL CONTEXT Meals and food shopping

Planning a meal • Talking about where to eat **(Leçon 9)** • Setting the table **(Leçon 9)**	• Meals **(Leçon 9)** • Place setting **(Leçon 9)**	
Going to a café • Ordering in a café **(Leçon 9)**	• Café foods and beverages **(Leçon 9)**	• The verb **boire (Leçon 11)**
Talking about favorite foods • Discussing preferences **(Leçon 9)** • Expressing what one wants **(Leçon 12)**	• Mealtime foods and beverages **(Leçon 9)** • Fruits and vegetables **(Leçon 9)**	• The verb **préférer (Leçon 11)** • The verb **vouloir (Leçon 10)**
Shopping for food at a market • Interacting with vendors and asking prices **(Leçon 9)** • Asking for specific quantities **(Leçon 9)** • Discussing what one can get **(Leçon 12)** • Talking about what one should buy or do **(Leçon 12)**	• Common quantities **(Leçon 12)** • Expressions of quantity **(Leçon 12)**	• Partitive article **(Leçon 10)** • The verbs **acheter** and **payer (Leçon 11)** • Expressions of quantity with **de (Leçon 12)** • The adjective **tout (Leçon 12)** • The verbs **devoir** and **pouvoir (Leçon 10)** • The expression **il faut (Leçon 12)**

READING Reading by phrase groups

UNITÉ 4 Loisirs et spectacles! • CULTURAL CONTEXT Free time and entertainment

COMMUNICATION: FUNCTIONS AND ACTIVITIES COMPREHENSION AND SELF-EXPRESSION	COMMUNICATION TOPICS THEMATIC VOCABULARY	LINGUISTIC GOALS ACCURACY OF EXPRESSION
Planning one's free time • Going out with friends (**Leçon 13**) • Extending, accepting, and turning down invitations (**Leçon 13**) • Talking about concerts and movies (**Leçon 13**)	• Places to go and things to do (**Leçon 13**) • Types of movies (**Leçon 13**)	
Talking about your friends and your neighborhood • Describing people and places you know (**Leçon 15**)		• The verb **connaître** (**Leçon 15**) • Object pronouns **le, la, les** (**Leçon 15**) • The verb **savoir** (**Leçon 16**)
Discussing relations with others • Asking others for assistance (**Leçon 14**) • Describing services of others (**Leçon 16**)	• Verbs asking for a service (**Leçon 14**) • Verbs using indirect objects (**Leçon 16**)	• Object pronouns **me, te, nous, vous** (**Leçon 14**) • Object pronouns **lui, leur** (**Leçon 16**) • Object pronouns in commands (**Leçon 14**) • Double object pronouns (**Leçon 16**)
Reading and writing about daily events • Writing a letter to a friend (**Leçon 14**) • Discussing what you like to read (**Leçon 16**) • Talking about what others have written or said (**Leçon 16**)	• Expressions used in letters (**Leçon 14**) • Reading materials (**Leçon 16**)	• The verbs **écrire, lire,** and **dire** (**Leçon 16**)
Narrating what happened • Talking about losing and finding things (**Leçon 15**)	• Verbs used to talk about possessions (**Leçon 15**)	• Object pronouns in the **passé composé** (**Leçon 15**)

READING Inferring meaning

UNITÉ 5 Vive le sport! • CULTURAL CONTEXT Sports and health

Discussing sports • Finding out what sports your friends like (**Leçon 17**) • Talking about where you practice sports and when (**Leçon 18**) • Giving your opinion (**Leçon 18**)	• Individual sports (**Leçon 17**) • Adverbs of frequency (**Leçon 18**) • Expressions of opinion (**Leçon 18**)	• The verb **courir** (**Leçon 17**) • The expression **faire du** (**Leçon 17**) • The pronouns **en** and **y** (**Leçon 18**)
Discussing fitness and health • Describing exercise routines (**Leçon 17**) • Describing common pains and illnesses (**Leçon 17**)	• Parts of the body (**Leçon 17**) • Health (**Leçon 17**)	• The expression **avoir mal à** (**Leçon 17**) • Definite article with parts of the body (**Leçon 19**)
Talking about one's daily activities • Describing the daily routine (**Leçon 19**) • Caring for one's appearance (**Leçon 19**) • Giving others advice (**Leçon 20**) • Asking about tomorrow's plans (**Leçon 20**)	• Daily occupations (**Leçon 19**) • Hygiene and personal care (**Leçon 19**)	• Reflexive verbs: present tense (**Leçon 19**) • Reflexive verbs: imperative (**Leçon 20**) • Reflexive verbs: infinitive constructions (**Leçon 20**)
Narrating past activities • Describing one's daily routine in the past (**Leçon 20**)	• Common activities (**Leçon 20**)	• Reflexive verbs: **passé composé** (**Leçon 20**)

READING Recognizing prefixes

UNIT 6 Chez nous • CULTURAL CONTEXT House and home

COMMUNICATION: FUNCTIONS AND ACTIVITIES COMPREHENSION AND SELF-EXPRESSION	COMMUNICATION TOPICS THEMATIC VOCABULARY	LINGUISTIC GOALS ACCURACY OF EXPRESSION
Discussing where you live • Describing the location of your house or apartment (**Leçon 21**) • Explaining what your house or apartment looks like (**Leçon 21**)	• Location of one's home (**Leçon 21**) • Rooms of the house (**Leçon 21**) • Furniture and appliances (**Leçon 21**)	• The verb **vivre** (**Leçon 22**)
Renting an apartment or house • Reading classified ads (**Leçon 21**) • Asking about a rental (**Leçon 21**) • Giving more complete descriptions (**Leçon 22**)		• Relative pronouns **qui** and **que** (**Leçon 22**)
Talking about the past • Explaining what you used to do in the past and when (**Leçon 23**) • Describing ongoing past actions (**Leçon 23**) • Giving background information about specific past events (**Leçon 24**)	• Prepositions of time (**Leçon 23**) • An accident (**Leçon 24**)	• The imperfect (**Leçon 23**) • Contrasting the imperfect and the **passé composé** (**Leçons 23, 24**)

READING Recognizing partial cognates

UNITÉ 7 Soyez à la mode! • CULTURAL CONTEXT Clothes and accessories

Talking about clothes • Saying what people are wearing (**Leçon 25**) • Describing clothes and accessories (**Leçon 25**)	• Clothes and accessories (**Leçon 25**) • Colors (**Leçon 25**) • Fabric, design, materials (**Leçon 25**)	
Shopping for clothes • Talking with the sales clerk (**Leçon 25**) • Expressing opinions (**Leçon 25**)	• Types of clothing stores (**Leçon 25**) • Sizes, looks, and price (**Leçon 25**) • Numbers 100-1,000,000 (**Leçon 26**) • Adjectives **beau, nouveau, vieux** (**Leçon 26**)	
Comparing people and things • Ranking items in a series (**Leçon 26**) • Expressing comparisons (**Leçon 27**) • Saying who or what is the best (**Leçon 27**) • Referring to specific items (**Leçon 28**)	• Descriptive adjectives (**Leçon 27**)	• Ordinal numbers (**Leçon 26**) • Comparisons with adjectives (**Leçon 27**) • Superlative constructions (**Leçon 27**) • Pronouns **lequel?** and **celui** (**Leçon 28**)
Talking about how things are done • Describing how things are done (**Leçon 26**) • Comparing how things are done (**Leçon 27**)	• Common adverbs (**Leçon 27**)	• Adverbs ending in **-ment** (**Leçon 26**) • Comparisons with adverbs (**Leçon 27**)

READING Understanding the context

UNITÉ 8 Bonnes vacances • CULTURAL CONTEXT Travel and summer vacations

COMMUNICATION: FUNCTIONS AND ACTIVITIES COMPREHENSION AND SELF-EXPRESSION	COMMUNICATION TOPICS THEMATIC VOCABULARY	LINGUISTIC GOALS ACCURACY OF EXPRESSION
Discussing summer vacations • Talking about vacation plans (**Leçon 29**) • Planning a camping trip (**Leçon 29**)	• Destinations, lodging, travel documents (**Leçon 29**) • Foreign countries (**Leçon 29**) • Camping equipment (**Leçon 29**)	• Prepositions with names of countries (**Leçon 30**) • The verbs **recevoir** and **apercevoir** (**Leçon 30**)
Making travel arrangements • Buying tickets (**Leçon 29**) • Checking schedules (**Leçon 29**) • Expressing polite requests (**Leçon 32**)	• At the train station, at the airport (**Leçon 29**)	• The use of the conditional to make polite requests (**Leçon 32**)
Talking about what you would do under various circumstances	• Verbs followed by infinitives (**Leçon 30**)	• The constructions verb + **à** + infinitive, verb + **de** + infinitive (**Leçon 30**)
Making future plans • Talking about the future (**Leçon 31**) • Setting forth conditions (**Leçon 31**)		• The future tense (**Leçon 31**) • The future with **si**-clauses (**Leçon 31**) • The future with **quand** (**Leçon 31**)
Talking about what one would do under certain circumstances • Discussing what would occur (**Leçon 32**) • Describing conditions (**Leçon 32**)		• The conditional (**Leçon 32**) • The conditional with **si**-clauses (**Leçon 32**)

READING Recognizing false cognates

UNITÉ 9 Bonne route • CULTURAL CONTEXT Getting around by car

Talking about cars • Describing cars (**Leçon 33**) • Having one's car serviced (**Leçon 33**) • Getting one's license (**Leçon 33**) • Rules of right of way (**Leçon 33**)	• Types of vehicles (**Leçon 33**) • Parts of a car (**Leçon 33**) • Car maintenance (**Leçon 33**)	• The verbs **conduire** and **suivre** (**Leçon 33**)
Expressing how one feels about certain events		• Adjective + **de** + infinitive (**Leçon 34**)
Talking about past and present events • Describing purpose and sequence (**Leçon 34**) • Describing simultaneous actions and cause and effect (**Leçon 34**)	• Prepositions **pour, sans, avant de**, and **en** (**Leçon 34**)	• Preposition + infinitive (**Leçon 34**) • Present participle constructions (**Leçon 34**)
Discussing what has to be done • Expressing necessity and obligation (**Leçon 35**) • Letting others know what you want them to do (**Leçon 36**)	• **Il faut que** (**Leçon 35**) • **Je veux que** (**Leçon 36**)	• Present subjunctive: regular forms (**Leçon 35**) • Present subjunctive: irregular forms (**Leçon 36**)

READING Recognizing figures of speech

Discovering FRENCH *Nouveau!*

REPRISE • OBJECTIVE Light Review of Basic Material (from Levels One and Two)

BASIC REVIEW		CULTURE AND READING
STRUCTURES	**VOCABULARY**	**VACATION OPTIONS** Travel, sports, archaeology, helping others
A. La vie courante Describing the present • Present of regular verbs • **Être, avoir, aller, faire, venir** and expressions used with these verbs • Other common irregular verbs • Use of present with **depuis** • Regular and irregular adjectives • Use of the partitive article	• Daily activities • Food and beverages	The French-speaking world: Its people
B. Hier et avant Describing the past • **Passé composé** with **avoir** and **être** • Imperfect and its basic uses	• Clothes	The French-speaking world: Cultural background
C. Nous et les autres Referring to people, things, and places • Object pronouns • Negative expressions • **Connaître** and **savoir** • Other irregular verbs		**Lecture:** *Les trois bagues*

UNITÉ 1 Au jour le jour • MAIN THEMES Looking good; one's daily routine

COMMUNICATION OBJECTIVES		READING AND CULTURAL OBJECTIVES		Interlude Culturel 1
COMMUNICATION: FUNCTIONS AND CONTEXTS LE FRANÇAIS PRATIQUE	**LINGUISTIC GOALS** LANGUE ET COMMUNICATION	**DAILY LIFE** INFO MAGAZINE	**READING** LECTURE	*Le monde des arts* GENERAL CULTURAL BACKGROUND
Describing people • Their physical appearance **Caring for one's appearance** • Personal care and hygiene • Looking good **Describing the various aspects of one's daily routine** **Expressing how one feels and inquiring about other people**	**Describing people and their ailments** • The use of the definite article **Describing what people do for themselves** • Reflexive verbs **Explaining one's daily activities** • Reflexive verbs: different tenses and uses	**How important is personal appearance for French young people and what do they do to enhance it?** • The importance of **le look** • Clothing and personal style **How have artists expressed their concept of beauty?** **How do people begin their daily routine?**	Ionesco, *Conte pour enfants de moins de trois ans*	**French modern art** • **Impressionism** and impressionist artists: **Monet, Degas, Renoir, Manet, B. Morisot** • Artists of the **post-impressionist** era: **Van Gogh, Gauguin, Matisse, Rousseau, Toulouse-Lautrec** • **Surrealism** as an artistic and literary movement: **Magritte** **Poems** • Desnos, *La fourmi* • Prévert, *Pour faire le portrait d'un oiseau*

UNITÉ 2 Soyons utiles! • MAIN THEME Being helpful around the house

COMMUNICATION OBJECTIVES		READING AND CULTURAL OBJECTIVES		Interlude Culturel 2 Les grands moments de l'histoire de France (jusqu'en 1453)
COMMUNICATION: FUNCTIONS AND CONTEXTS LE FRANÇAIS PRATIQUE	**LINGUISTIC GOALS** LANGUE ET COMMUNICATION	**DAILY LIFE** INFO MAGAZINE	**READING** LECTURE	
Helping around the house • In the house itself • Outside **Asking for help and offering to help** • Accepting or refusing help • Thanking people for their help **Describing an object** • Shape, weight, length, consistency, appearance, etc. • The material it is made of	**Explaining what has to be done** • **Il faut que +** subjunctive **Telling people what you would like them to do** • **Vouloir que +** subjunctive	Why do French people enjoy do-it-yourself activities? • What is **bricolage**? • What is **jardinage**? How should you take care of your plants? How do French young people earn money by helping their neighbors?	*La Couverture (Une fable médiévale)*	GENERAL CULTURAL BACKGROUND **Early French history** • Important events The Roman conquest The Holy Roman Empire The Norman Conquest of England The Hundred Years War • Important people **Vercingétorix Charlemagne Guillaume le Conquérant Aliénor d'Aquitaine Jeanne d'Arc** Literature: *La Chanson de Roland*

UNITÉ 3 Vive la nature! • MAIN THEMES Vacation and outdoor activities; the environment and its protection

				Interlude Culturel 3 Les grands moments de l'histoire de France (1453-1715)
Talking about outdoor activities • What to do • What not to do **Describing the natural environment and how to protect it** **Talking about the weather and natural phenomena** **Relating a sequence of past events** **Describing habitual past actions**	**Talking about the past** • The **passé composé** • The imperfect • The **passé simple** • Contrastive uses of the **passé composé** and the imperfect **Narrating past events** • Differentiating between specific actions (**passé composé**) and the circumstances under which they occurred (imperfect) • Providing background information (imperfect)	How do the French feel about nature and their land? • What is **le tourisme vert**? • What is an **éco-musée**? How do the French protect their environment? • What rules to observe on camping trips • What young people do to protect the environment • Who was **Jacques-Yves Cousteau**? Why do the French people love the sun?	Sempé / Goscinny, *King*	GENERAL CULTURAL BACKGROUND **The classical period of French history** • Important periods: **la Renaissance, le Grand Siècle** • Important people: **François I**er**, Louis XIV** • French castles, as witnesses of French history **Literature** • **La Fontaine,** *Le Corbeau et le renard* • **Prévert,** *Soyons polis* **Film: Rostand,** *Cyrano de Bergerac*

UNITÉ 4 Aspects de la vie quotidienne • MAIN THEME Going shopping and asking for services

COMMUNICATION OBJECTIVES		READING AND CULTURAL OBJECTIVES		Interlude Culturel 4
				Vive la musique!
COMMUNICATION: FUNCTIONS AND CONTEXTS LE FRANÇAIS PRATIQUE	**LINGUISTIC GOALS** LANGUE ET COMMUNICATION	**DAILY LIFE** INFO MAGAZINE	**READING** LECTURE	GENERAL CULTURAL BACKGROUND
Shopping for various items • in a stationery store • in a pharmacy • in a convenience store **Buying stamps and mailing items at the post office** **Having one's hair cut** **Asking for a variety of services** • at the cleaners • at the shoe repair shop • at the photo shop	**Answering questions and referring to people, things, and places using pronouns** • Object pronouns • Two-pronoun sequence **Talking about quantities** • The pronoun **en** • Indefinite expressions of quantity **Describing services that you have done by other people** • The construction **faire + infinitive**	**How are certain aspects of daily life different in France?** • Shopping on the Internet • Shopping in a supermarket • Services at the post office • When to tip and not to tip	*Histoire de cheveux*	**The musical landscape of France and the French-speaking world** • Classical musicians: **Lully, Chopin, Bizet, Debussy** • Historical overview of French songs • Famous French singers of yesterday and today • The multicultural aspect of music from the francophone world: **zouk** (Antilles); **raï** (North Africa); **cajun, zydéco** (Louisiana) **Song: Vigneault,** *Mon pays* **Opera: Bizet,** *Carmen*

UNITÉ 5 Bon voyage! • MAIN THEME Travel

				Interlude Culturel 5
				Les grands moments de l'histoire de France (1715-1870)
				GENERAL CULTURAL BACKGROUND
Planning a trip abroad **Going through customs** **Making travel arrangements** • Purchasing tickets **Travel in France** • at the train station • at the airport	**Making negative statements** • Affirmative and negative expressions **Describing future plans** • Future tense • Use of future after **quand** **Hypothesizing about what one would do** • Introduction to the conditional	**What are the advantages of visiting France by train?** • The **TGV** • The **Eurotunnel** **Why do French people like to travel abroad and what do they do on their vacations?** • Impressions of young people visiting the United States	*Le mystérieux homme en bleu*	**The historical foundation of modern France** • Important periods the **French Revolution** the **Napoleonic era** • Important contemporary French institutions • Important people **Louis XVI et Marie-Antoinette Napoléon** **Song: Rouget de Lisle,** *La Marseillaise* **Literature: Victor Hugo,** *Les Misérables*

UNITÉ 6 Séjour en France • MAIN THEME Hotels and other places to stay when traveling

COMMUNICATION OBJECTIVES		READING AND CULTURAL OBJECTIVES		Interlude Culturel 6
COMMUNICATION: FUNCTIONS AND CONTEXTS LE FRANÇAIS PRATIQUE	LINGUISTIC GOALS LANGUE ET COMMUNICATION	DAILY LIFE INFO MAGAZINE	READING LECTURE	Les grands moments de l'histoire de France (1870 au présent) GENERAL CULTURAL BACKGROUND

Deciding where to stay when traveling
Reserving a room in a hotel
Asking for services in a hotel
	Comparing people, things, places and situations
	• The comparative
	• The superlative
	Asking for an alternative
	• The interrogative pronoun **lequel?**
	Pointing out people or things
	• The demonstrative pronoun **celui**
	Indicating possession
	• The possessive pronoun **le mien**
		What inexpensive accommodations are available to students?
		• **Auberges de jeunesse**
		• **Séjour à la ferme**
		How does one use the *Guide Michelin* when traveling in France?
		• To find a hotel
		• To choose a restaurant
			Une étrange aventure	France in the 20th century
				• Important events
				  the two World Wars
				  the economic union of Europe
				• Important people
				  Marie Curie
				  Charles de Gaulle
				  Simone Veil
				Literature: ÉT26luard, *Liberté*
				Film: L. Malle, *Au revoir, les Enfants*

UNITÉ 7 La forme et la santé • MAIN THEME Health and medical care

				Interlude Culturel 7 Les Français d'aujourd'hui GENERAL CULTURAL BACKGROUND
Going to the doctor's office • Describing your symptoms • Explaining what is wrong • Giving information about your medical history • Understanding the doctor's prescriptions Going to the dentist Going to the emergency ward	Expressing how you and others feel about certain facts or events • Use of the subjunctive after expressions of emotion Expressing fear, doubt or disbelief • Use of the subjunctive after expressions of doubt and uncertainty Expressing feelings or attitudes about past actions and events • The past subjunctive	How do the French take care of their health? • How does the French health system work? • What is the **Sécurité sociale?** • Why do the French consume so much mineral water? • What is **thermalisme?** How do French doctors participate in humanitarian missions around the world? • What is **Médecins sans frontières?**	Maupassant, *En voyage*	Modern France as a multi-ethnic and multi-cultural society • The French as citizens of Europe • The new French mosaic: the impact of immigration on French society • The **Maghrébins** – their culture and their religion • **SOS Racisme** • Two French humanitarians: **L'abbé Pierre** and **Coluche** Song: *Éthiopie*

UNITÉ 8 En ville • MAIN THEME Cities and city life

				Interlude Culturel 8 Les Antilles francophones GENERAL CULTURAL BACKGROUND

Making a date and fixing the time and place
Explaining where one lives and how to get there
Discussing the advantages and disadvantages of city life
	Narrating past actions in sequence
	• The pluperfect
	Formulating polite requests
	• The conditional
	Hypothesizing about what one would do under certain circumstances
	• The conditional and its uses
	• The past conditional
	• Sequence of tenses in si-clauses
		What does a typical French city look like?
		• Its historical development
		• Its various neighborhoods
		• Its buildings
		• The **villes nouvelles**
		Why do French people love to stroll in the streets?
		• Various street shows
		• Sculptures to view while walking in Paris
			Theuriet, *Les Pêches*	The French-speaking Caribbean islands
				• Historical background
				• Important people
				  Toussaint Louverture
				  Joséphine de Beauharnais
				  Aimé Césaire
				• Haitian art as an expression of life
				Literature: Césaire, *Pour saluer le Tiers-Monde*
				Film: Palcy, *Rue Cases-nègres*

UNITÉ 9 Les relations personnelles • MAIN THEME Personal relationships, friendships, and family life

COMMUNICATION OBJECTIVES		READING AND CULTURAL OBJECTIVES		Interlude Culturel 9
COMMUNICATION: FUNCTIONS AND CONTEXTS LE FRANÇAIS PRATIQUE	**LINGUISTIC GOALS** LANGUE ET COMMUNICATION	**DAILY LIFE** INFO MAGAZINE	**READING** LECTURE	L'Afrique dans la communauté francophone
Describing degrees of friendship **Expressing different feelings towards other people** **Discussing the state of one's relationship with other people** **Congratulating, comforting, and expressing sympathy for other people** **Describing the various phases of a person's life**	**Describing how people interact** • Reciprocal use of reflexive verbs **Describing people and things in complex sentences** • Relative pronouns • Relative clauses	**How important are friends and family to French people?** • The meaning of friendship • Family relationships **How socially concerned are French young people and what type of social outreach do they do?** **What is a typical French wedding like?** • Where French spouses meet one another • Planning the wedding • A French wedding ceremony	**M. Maurois,** *Le Bracelet*	GENERAL CULTURAL BACKGROUND **The place of Western and Central Africa in the francophone world** • Historical periods and events: prehistory, the **African empires**, colonization, and independence • Basic facts about Western Africa language and culture religions and traditions • **African art** and its influence on European art **African Fable:** *La Gélinotte et la Tortue* **Literature** • D. Diop, *Afrique* • Dadié, *La légende baoulé*

UNITÉ 10 Vers la vie active • MAIN THEME University studies and careers

				Interlude Culturel 10
				La France et le Nouveau Monde
Deciding on a college major • University courses **Planning for a career** • Professions • The work environment • Different types of industries **Looking for a job** • Preparing a résumé • Describing one's qualifications at a job interview	**Describing simultaneous actions** • The present participle **Explaining the purpose of an action** • **Pour** + infinitive • **Pour que** + subjunctive **Explaining the timing, conditions, and constraints of an action** • The use of the infinitive or the subjunctive after certain prepositions and conjunctions	**How important is academic success to French young people?** • The French school system: high schools and universities • **Le bac:** its history and its importance **What does one do after graduation?** • Choosing a profession • **Le service militaire** **How does one interview for a job?** • Preparing for the interview • Writing a résumé in French	**Thériault,** *Le Portrait*	GENERAL CULTURAL BACKGROUND **The French presence in North America** • Historical background The French in Canada and Louisiana • Important people **Jacques Cartier, Jeanne Mance, Cavelier de La Salle** • Why certain American cities have French names **Song:** Richard, *Réveille* **Literature:** La Fayette, *Lettre à sa femme*

Setting the Stage for Communication

The Unit Opener presents the unit theme and communicative objectives.

REPRISE
Bonjour!

RAPPEL 1
Les personnes

RAPPEL 2
Les choses de la vie courante

RAPPEL 3
Les activités

RAPPEL 4
Expressions de tous les jours

LE SAVEZ-VOUS?

THÈME ET OBJECTIFS

Getting Reacquainted

In **Reprise**, you will become reacquainted with the French-speaking world: its people, its culture, its language.

In this opening unit, you will have the opportunity to brush up on your French skills. In particular, you will practice . . .

- describing yourself and others
- talking about your possessions and your room
- asking and answering questions about what people are doing
- expressing your preferences
- extending and accepting (or turning down) invitations
- ordering food in a café

In addition, you will review . . .

- how to count
- how to give the date and tell time
- how to talk about the weather

WEBQUEST
CLASSZONE.COM

2 deux
Reprise

UNITÉ 5

En ville

LEÇON 13 LE FRANÇAIS PRATIQUE
La ville et la maison

LEÇON 14 Week-end à Paris

LEÇON 15 Au Café de l'Univers

LEÇON 16 Mes voisins

THÈME ET OBJECTIFS

Visiting a French city

There are many things to do in a city: place concerts to attend, sports to play.

In this unit, you will learn . . .

- to describe your city, its public buildings of interest
- to ask for and give directions
- to talk about the various places you go the week and on weekends
- to describe your house or apartment

You will also be able . . .

- to discuss your future plans and say wh going to do
- to talk about your friends and their fam

WEBQUEST
CLASSZONE.COM

192 cent quatre-vingt-douze
Unité 5

○ There are **four thematically-linked lessons** in each unit. Vocabulary presented in the first lesson (*Le français pratique*) is then used throughout the next three lessons as structure is taught, reinforcing the unit theme.

○ **Unit Theme and Objectives** preview for the students what they will be able to do at the end of the unit.

cent quatre-vingt-treize **193**
Unité 5

Discovering FRENCH *Nouveau!*

The unique structure of the *Reprise* section allows students to personalize their review of previously learned material.

Vocabulary, coded in yellow, is introduced by function.

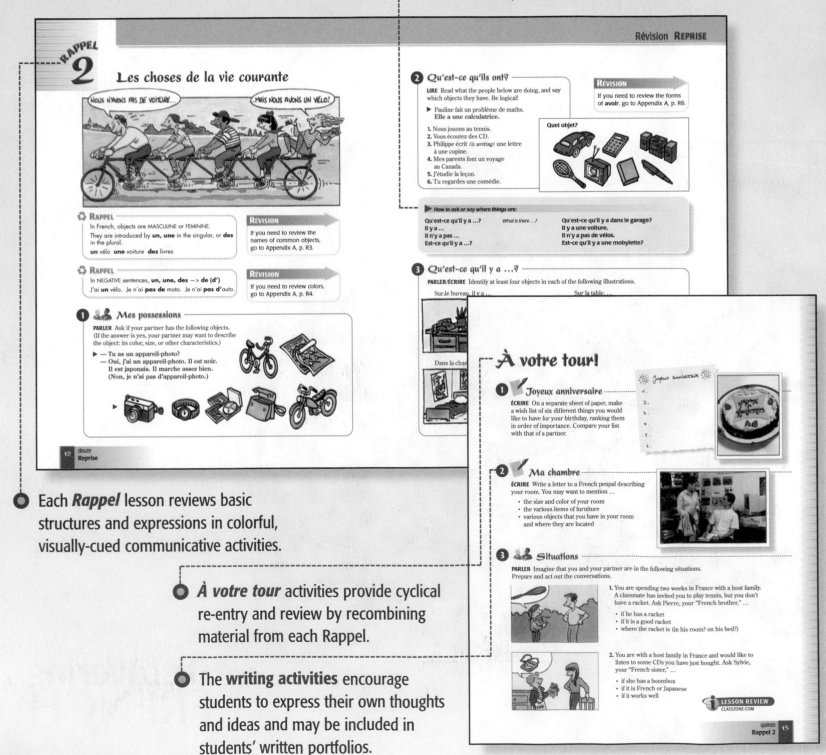

Each *Rappel* lesson reviews basic structures and expressions in colorful, visually-cued communicative activities.

À votre tour activities provide cyclical re-entry and review by recombining material from each Rappel.

The **writing activities** encourage students to express their own thoughts and ideas and may be included in students' written portfolios.

Student-centered *Rappel/Révision*: Students who need further review are directed to Appendix A for additional material.

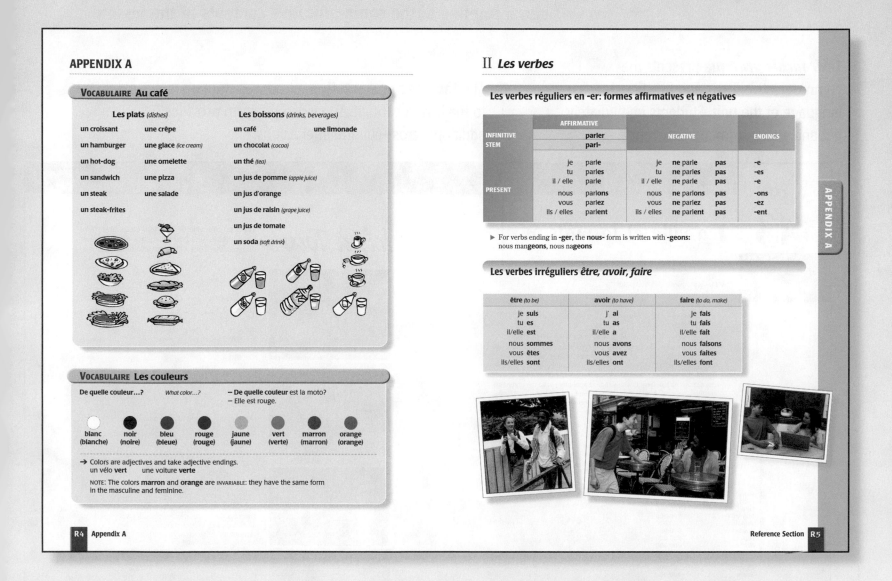

APPENDIX A

VOCABULAIRE Au café

Les plats *(dishes)*

un croissant	une crêpe
un hamburger	une glace *(ice cream)*
un hot-dog	une omelette
un sandwich	une pizza
un steak	une salade
un steak-frites	

Les boissons *(drinks, beverages)*

un café	une limonade
un chocolat *(cocoa)*	
un thé *(tea)*	
un jus de pomme *(apple juice)*	
un jus d'orange	
un jus de raisin *(grape juice)*	
un jus de tomate	
un soda *(soft drink)*	

VOCABULAIRE Les couleurs

De quelle couleur...?   *What color...?*   **– De quelle couleur** est la moto?
                                        – Elle est rouge.

blanc (blanche)	noir (noire)	bleu (bleue)	rouge (rouge)	jaune (jaune)	vert (verte)	marron (marron)	orange (orange)

→ Colors are adjectives and take adjective endings.
    un vélo **vert**   une voiture **verte**

NOTE: The colors **marron** and **orange** are INVARIABLE: they have the same form in the masculine and feminine.

II *Les verbes*

Les verbes réguliers en -er: formes affirmatives et négatives

	AFFIRMATIVE		NEGATIVE		ENDINGS
INFINITIVE	parler				
STEM	parl-				
PRESENT	je parle		je ne parle pas		-e
	tu parles		tu ne parles pas		-es
	il / elle parle		il / elle ne parle pas		-e
	nous parlons		nous ne parlons pas		-ons
	vous parlez		vous ne parlez pas		-ez
	ils / elles parlent		ils / elles ne parlent pas		-ent

▶ For verbs ending in **-ger**, the **nous-** form is written with **-geons:**
nous man**geons**, nous na**geons**

Les verbes irréguliers *être, avoir, faire*

être *(to be)*	avoir *(to have)*	faire *(to do, make)*
je **suis**	j' **ai**	je **fais**
tu **es**	tu **as**	tu **fais**
il/elle **est**	il/elle **a**	il/elle **fait**
nous **sommes**	nous **avons**	nous **faisons**
vous **êtes**	vous **avez**	vous **faites**
ils/elles **sont**	ils/elles **ont**	ils/elles **font**

Strengthen proficiency

After completing the Reprise review unit, students move into the core material. The Lesson Opener provides cultural and linguistic background through text and photos from the video, and a visual briefing of the communicative contents of the lesson.

● *Le français pratique* presents the communicative focus and functional language of the unit. Students immediately get and give information in French.

● The **thematic presentation** introduces students to the lesson content. The video program provides additional cross-cultural interactions.

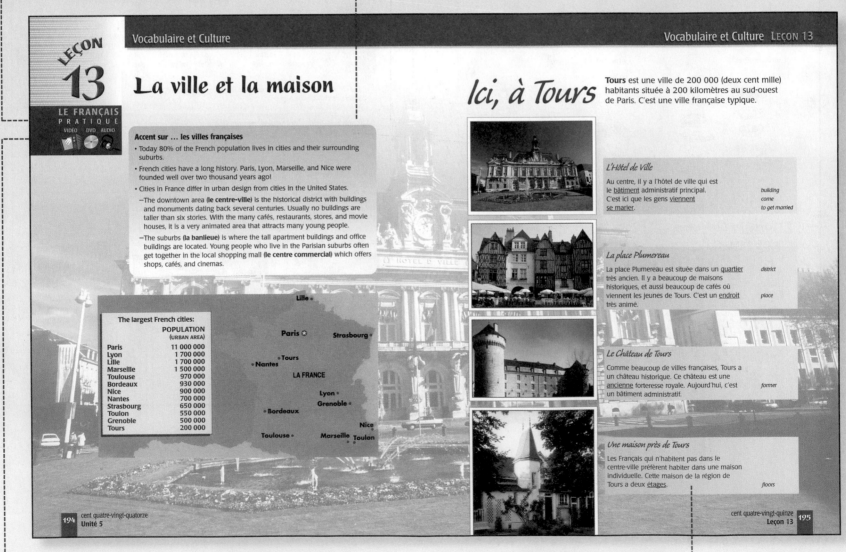

LEÇON 13

LE FRANÇAIS PRATIQUE
VIDEO · DVD · AUDIO

Vocabulaire et Culture

La ville et la maison

Accent sur ... les villes françaises

• Today 80% of the French population lives in cities and their surrounding suburbs.
• French cities have a long history. Paris, Lyon, Marseille, and Nice were founded well over two thousand years ago!
• Cities in France differ in urban design from cities in the United States.
  —The downtown area (**le centre-ville**) is the historical district with buildings and monuments dating back several centuries. Usually no buildings are taller than six stories. With the many cafés, restaurants, stores, and movie houses, it is a very animated area that attracts many young people.
  —The suburbs (**la banlieue**) is where the tall apartment buildings and office buildings are located. Young people who live in the Parisian suburbs often get together in the local shopping mall (**le centre commercial**) which offers shops, cafés, and cinemas.

The largest French cities:

	POPULATION (URBAN AREA)
Paris	11 000 000
Lyon	1 700 000
Lille	1 700 000
Marseille	1 500 000
Toulouse	970 000
Bordeaux	930 000
Nice	900 000
Nantes	700 000
Strasbourg	650 000
Toulon	550 000
Grenoble	500 000
Tours	200 000

Lille · Paris ⊙ Strasbourg · Tours · Nantes · LA FRANCE · Lyon · Grenoble · Bordeaux · Nice · Toulouse · Marseille · Toulon

cent quatre-vingt-quatorze
194 Unité 5

Vocabulaire et Culture LEÇON 13

Ici, à Tours

Tours est une ville de 200 000 (deux cent mille) habitants située à 200 kilomètres au sud-ouest de Paris. C'est une ville française typique.

L'Hôtel de Ville

Au centre, il y a à l'hôtel de ville qui est le bâtiment administratif principal. C'est ici que les gens viennent se marier.
— building
— come
— to get married

La place Plumereau

La place Plumereau est située dans un quartier très ancien. Il y a beaucoup de maisons historiques, et aussi beaucoup de cafés où viennent les jeunes de Tours. C'est un endroit très animé.
— district
— place

Le Château de Tours

Comme beaucoup de villes françaises, Tours a un château historique. Ce château est une ancienne forteresse royale. Aujourd'hui, c'est un bâtiment administratif.
— former

Une maison près de Tours

Les Français qui n'habitent pas dans le centre-ville préfèrent habiter dans une maison individuelle. Cette maison de la région de Tours a deux étages.
— floors

cent quatre-vingt-quinze 195
Leçon 13

● **Video, DVD and audio** icons indicate the variety of resources that support lesson content.

● Students are introduced to the **language** patterns of the unit **in context**.

The *Vocabulaire et communication* sections of *Le français pratique* lessons present new conversational patterns by function.

● *Notes culturelles,* coded in blue throughout the program, expand on the cultural content of the lesson opener.

● New vocabulary and related conversational patterns are introduced in **thematic context**. All vocabulary is coded in yellow; functions are highlighted with a red triangle and darker yellow band.

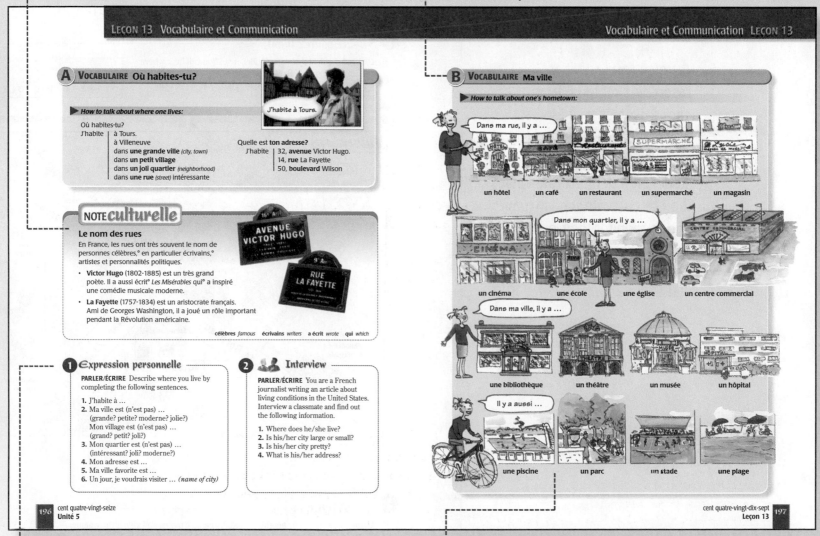

● **Student-centered activities** practice new vocabulary in contexts ranging from structured to open-ended self-expression.

● **Art-cued vocabulary** is used to help the visual learner and provide a functional cultural context. Since the artists used in *Discovering French, Nouveau!* are actually French, students are exposed to authentic cultural detail in every drawing. All visuals are also available in overhead transparencies.

Each *Le français pratique* lesson moves through functional introduction of language, practice activities, and culminates in the *À votre tour* review section.

Objectifs remind students of what they've learned and why.

À votre tour activities recombine material from each lesson as well as previous units. These open-ended activities allow students to demonstrate what they can do with the language and to monitor their own progress.

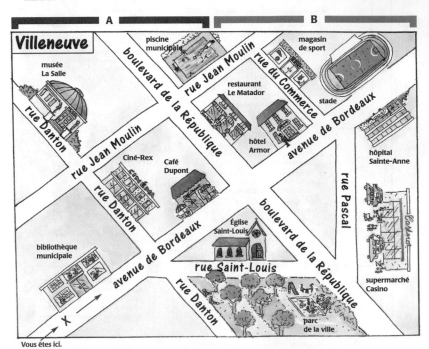

À votre tour!

OBJECTIFS

Now you can …
• describe your town and your neighborhood
• ask and give directions

1 Écoutez bien!

ÉCOUTER Look at the map of Villeneuve. You will hear where certain people are. If they are somewhere on the left side of the map, mark A. If they are on the right side of the map, mark B.

	1	2	3	4	5	6	7	8
A								
B								

Villeneuve

Vous êtes ici.

2 Mon quartier

ÉCRIRE Describe your neighborhood, listing five places and giving their names.

▶ Dans mon quartier, il y a un supermarché. C'est le supermarché Casino.

202   deux cent deux
Unité 5

3  Créa-dialogue

PARLER You have just arrived in Villeneuve, where you will spend the summer.
Ask a pedestrian where you can find the places represented by the symbols.
He (She) will give you the location of each place, according to the map.

▶ —Pardon, monsieur
(madame). Où est-ce
qu'il y a <u>un hôtel</u>?
—Il y a <u>un hôtel avenue
de Bordeaux.</u>
—Est-ce que c'est loin?
—<u>Non, c'est près</u>.
—Merci beaucoup!

▶

4  Où est-ce?

PARLER Now you have been in
Villeneuve for several weeks
and are familiar with the city.
You meet a tourist on the **avenue
de Bordeaux** at the place indicated by an X
on the map. The tourist asks you where certain
places are and you indicate how to get there.

Pardon, monsieur. Où est
l'hôpital Sainte-Anne?

C'est tout droit,
mademoiselle.

Merci bien,
monsieur.

▶ l'hôpital Sainte-Anne

1. le musée La Salle
2. le supermarché Casino
3. l'hôtel Armor
4. le restaurant Le Matador
5. l'église Saint-Louis

5 Composition: La maison idéale

ÉCRIRE Briefly describe your dream house. You may use the
following adjectives to describe the various rooms: **grand,
petit, moderne, confortable, joli,** as well as colors. If you
wish, sketch and label a floor plan.

▶

La maison
idéale est
grande et
moderne. Le
salon est …

LESSON REVIEW
CLASSZONE.COM

- - - - - - **Web icons** guide students to relevant
online materials at ClassZone.com

deux cent trois 203
Leçon 13

The **writing activities** encourage students to
express their own thoughts and ideas and may
be included in students' writing portfolios.

Build accuracy

Conversation et culture lesson openers present conversation and culture as they re-cycle the communicative functions of *Le français pratique* vocabulary and provide grammar support and explanation.

● The opening **reading and/or video dialog** provides a context for the communicative functions and presentation of linguistic structures. You may vary your presentation of the new language according to the needs of your students, addressing a variety of learner types.

LEÇON
15

Conversation et Culture

Au Café de l'Unive...

LEÇON
14

Conversation et Culture

Week-end à Paris AUDIO

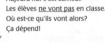

Aujourd'hui c'est samedi.
Les élèves <u>ne vont pas</u> en classe. *are not going*
Où est-ce qu'ils vont alors?
Ça dépend!

Thomas <u>va</u> au café. *is going*
Il a un <u>rendez-vous</u> avec une copine. *date*

Florence et Karine vont aux Champs-Élysées.
Elles vont regarder les <u>vêtements</u> dans les magasins. *clothes*
<u>Après</u>, elles vont <u>aller</u> au cinéma. *Afterward / to go*

Daniel va <u>chez</u> <u>son</u> copain Laurent. *to the house of / his*
Les garçons vont jouer aux jeux vidéo.
Après, ils vont aller au musée des sciences de la Villette.
Ils vont jouer avec les machines électroniques.

Béatrice a un grand sac et des <u>lunettes de soleil</u>. *sunglasses*
Est-ce qu'elle va à un rendez-vous secret?
Non! Elle va au Centre Pompidou.
Elle va regarder les acrobates.
Et après, elle va aller à un concert.

Et Jean-François? Qu'est-ce qu'il va faire aujourd'hui?
Est-ce qu'il va visiter le Centre Pompidou?
Est-ce qu'il va regarder les acrobates?
Est-ce qu'il va aller à un concert?
<u>Hélas</u>, non! *Alas (Unfortunately)*
Il va <u>rester</u> à la maison. *to stay*
Pourquoi? Parce qu'il est <u>malade</u>. *sick*
<u>Pauvre</u> Jean-François! *Poor*
Il fait <u>si</u> beau <u>dehors</u>! *so / outside*

Compréhension

1. Quel jour est-ce aujourd'hui?
2. Pourquoi est-ce que Thomas va au café?
3. Avec qui est-ce que Florence va au cinéma?
4. Où va Daniel? Qu'est-ce qu'il fait avec Laurent?

5. O...
6. Po... pa...
7. Q...

NOTE *culturelle*

À Paris
Paris offre beaucoup d'attractions diverses pour les jeunes.

Les Champs-Élysées
Les Champs-Élysées sont une très longue et très large° avenue avec beaucoup de cafés, de restaurants, de cinémas et de boutiques élégantes.

Le Centre Pompidou
Le Centre Pompidou est un grand musée d'art moderne. C'est aussi un centre culturel avec un grand nombre de salles° multimédia pour les jeunes. Devant le musée, il y a une place où les acrobates, les mimes, les jongleurs° et les musiciens démontrent leurs° talents. Ici, le spectacle est permanent.

Le Parc de la Villette
Le Parc de la Villette est un musée scientifique pour les jeunes. À la Géode, ils peuvent° voir° des films sur un grand écran panoramique Omni. Au Zénith, ils peuvent assister à° des concerts de rock et de musique techno.

large *wide* **salles** *large rooms* **jongleurs** *jugglers* **leurs** *their* **peuv...**

204 deux cent quatre
Unité 5

LEÇON 16

Conversation et Culture

Mes voisins AUDIO

Bonjour!
Je m'appelle Frédéric Mallet.
J'habite à Paris avec ma famille.

Conversation et Culture LEÇON 15

Compréhension

1. Où va Valérie après les cours?
2. Avec qui est-ce qu'elle va au café?
3. Qu'est-ce que les filles font au café?
4. Est-ce qu'elles parlent de l'école?
5. Est-ce qu'elles parlent des activités du week-end?
6. De quelle *(which)* personne parlent-elles aujourd'hui?
7. De quelle nationalité est le professeur d'anglais?
8. Comment est-il?

---

n et Culture LEÇON 14

...u do by completing the following sentences.

...rès les cours,

• à la bibliothèque	• au café
• chez mes *(my)* copains	• directement chez moi

...ins,

e Jean-François ne va

...

...ujourd'hui?

• de la classe de français	• des examens
• du prof de français	• du week-end

...nts,

...

• de l'école	• de mes notes *(grades)*
• de la classe de français	• de mes copains

...e ou ma soeur,

• de mes copains	• de mes problèmes
• du week-end	• des vacances

...ris

...lturelle

...beaucoup de choses différentes dans un
...On peut manger un sandwich. On peut
...n jus de fruits. On peut étudier. On peut
...électroniques. Dans les cybercafés, on
...r sur l'Internet. Les jeunes Français vont
...alement pour retrouver° leurs° copains et
... moment avec eux.°

...is est divisé en deux parties: l'intérieur et
...printemps et en été, les Français
...eoir° à la terrasse. Là, ils peuvent° profiter
...garder les gens qui passent dans la rue.

commander *order* **retrouver** *meet* **leurs** *their* **passer** *spend* **eux** *them*
...(outdoor section of a café) **s'asseoir** *to sit* **peuvent** *can* **profiter du soleil** *enjoy the sun*

deux cent dix-sept
Leçon 15 217

...ee **assister à** *attend*

deux cent cinq 205
Leçon 14

Conversation et Culture LEÇON 16

Compréhension

1. Où habite Frédéric Mallet?
2. Combien *(How many)* d'étages a son immeuble?
3. Qui habite à chaque *(each)* étage?
4. Quelle est la profession des Lacroche?
5. Selon toi *(In your opinion)*, est-ce que Mademoiselle Ménard est une personne bizarre ou intéressante? Pourquoi?

COMPARAISONS CULTURELLES

The floors of buildings are numbered differently in France and in the United States. Compare:

• **rez-de-chaussée**	*ground floor or first floor*
• **premier étage (1er étage)**	*second floor*
• **deuxième étage (2ème étage)**	*third floor*

NOTE: In the older downtown areas of French cities, apartment houses have a maximum of six stories. This is because until the twentieth century there were no elevators and people had to use the stairs.

NOTE culturelle

Les animaux domestiques en France
La France a une population de 60 millions d'habitants et de 42 millions d'animaux domestiques.° Les Français adorent les animaux. Une famille sur deux° a un animal domestique. Par ordre de préférence, les principaux animaux domestiques sont les chiens (39%: trente-neuf pour cent), les chats (35%), les poissons (12%), les oiseaux (5%) et les hamsters (4%). Il y a aussi un certain nombre de serpents, de tortues et de lapins.

un hamster

un lapin

un poisson

une tortue

un poisson rouge

un oiseau

animaux domestiques *pets* **une ... sur deux** *one out of two*

deux cent vingt-sept
Leçon 16 227

● ***Comparaisons culturelles*** engage students in critical thinking and promote cultural awareness.

● **Comprehension checks** allow students to self-check their comprehension (both reading and listening) as receptive skills are developed.

Langue et communication pages present grammatical structures in a variety of formats, including model sentences, visual representations, cartoons, summary boxes, and charts.

Listening icons highlight the listening strand in the student books.

Coded in green, the **structure sections** clearly and concisely summarize essential grammar points. Sample sentences are provided to present material in meaningful context.

Supplementary vocabulary, coded in yellow, offers students communicative functions for immediate implementation in dialogs.

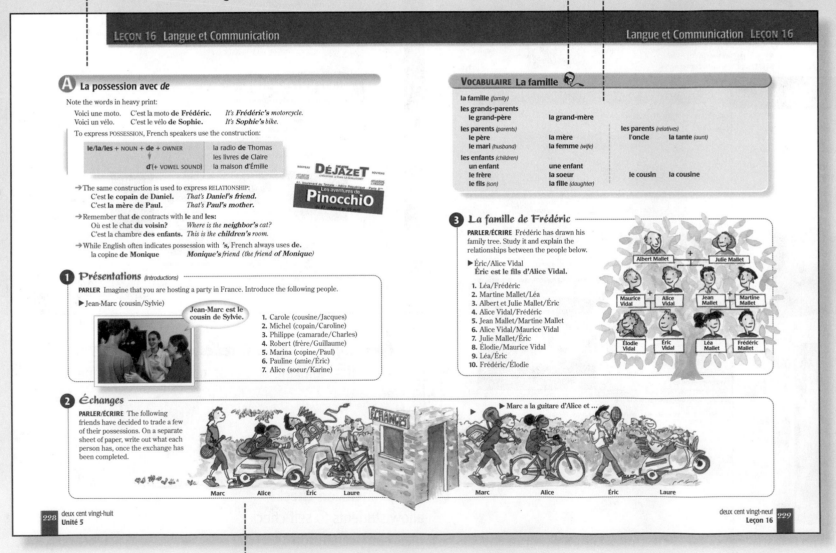

LEÇON 16 Langue et Communication

Langue et Communication LEÇON 16

A   La possession avec de

Note the words in heavy print:

Voici une moto.   C'est la moto **de Frédéric.**   *It's **Frédéric's** motorcycle.*
Voici un vélo.   C'est le vélo **de Sophie.**   *It's **Sophie's** bike.*

To express POSSESSION, French speakers use the construction:

le/la/les + NOUN + **de** + OWNER	la radio **de** Thomas
	les livres **de** Claire
d'(+ VOWEL SOUND)	la maison **d'**Émilie

→ The same construction is used to express RELATIONSHIP:
C'est **le copain de Daniel.**   *That's **Daniel's** friend.*
C'est **la mère de Paul.**   *That's **Paul's** mother.*

→ Remember that **de** contracts with **le** and **les:**
Où est le chat **du voisin?**   *Where is the **neighbor's** cat?*
C'est la chambre **des enfants.**   *This is the **children's** room.*

→ While English often indicates possession with **'s,** French always uses **de.**
la copine **de Monique**   ***Monique's** friend (the friend of Monique)*

NOUVEAU PARIS NOUVEAU
DÉJAZET
Les aventures de
PinocchiO

1   Présentations *(Introductions)*

PARLER Imagine that you are hosting a party in France. Introduce the following people.

▶ Jean-Marc (cousin/Sylvie)

Jean-Marc est le cousin de Sylvie.

1. Carole (cousine/Jacques)
2. Michel (copain/Caroline)
3. Philippe (camarade/Charles)
4. Robert (frère/Guillaume)
5. Marina (copine/Paul)
6. Pauline (amie/Éric)
7. Alice (soeur/Karine)

2   Échanges

PARLER/ÉCRIRE The following friends have decided to trade a few of their possessions. On a separate sheet of paper, write out what each person has, once the exchange has been completed.

ÉCHANGES

▶ Marc a la guitare d'Alice et ...

Marc   Alice   Éric   Laure

Marc   Alice   Éric   Laure

VOCABULAIRE La famille

la famille *(family)*
les grands-parents
   le grand-père   la grand-mère
les parents *(parents)*   **les parents** *(relatives)*
   le père   la mère   l'oncle   la tante *(aunt)*
   le mari *(husband)* la femme *(wife)*
les enfants *(children)*
   un enfant   une enfant
   le frère   la soeur   le cousin   la cousine
   le fils *(son)*   la fille *(daughter)*

3   La famille de Frédéric

PARLER/ÉCRIRE Frédéric has drawn his family tree. Study it and explain the relationships between the people below.

▶ Éric/Alice Vidal
   Éric est le fils d'Alice Vidal.

1. Léa/Frédéric
2. Martine Mallet/Léa
3. Albert et Julie Mallet/Éric
4. Alice Vidal/Frédéric
5. Jean Mallet/Martine Mallet
6. Alice Vidal/Maurice Vidal
7. Julie Mallet/Éric
8. Élodie/Maurice Vidal
9. Léa/Éric
10. Frédéric/Élodie

Albert Mallet   +   Julie Mallet

Maurice Vidal   +   Alice Vidal   Jean Mallet   +   Martine Mallet

Élodie Vidal   Éric Vidal   Léa Mallet   Frédéric Mallet

Whenever possible, **authentic French drawings, photos, and realia** are used to increase comprehension and success for all students, addressing a variety of learning styles.

Pair and group activities allow students to communicate and exchange information while practicing new structures in both guided and open-ended activities.

After students have become comfortable with material in context, **formal charts** help them analyze forms and structure.

Learning about language notes focus on strategies for authentic language production, explain terminology, and help students understand how language functions.

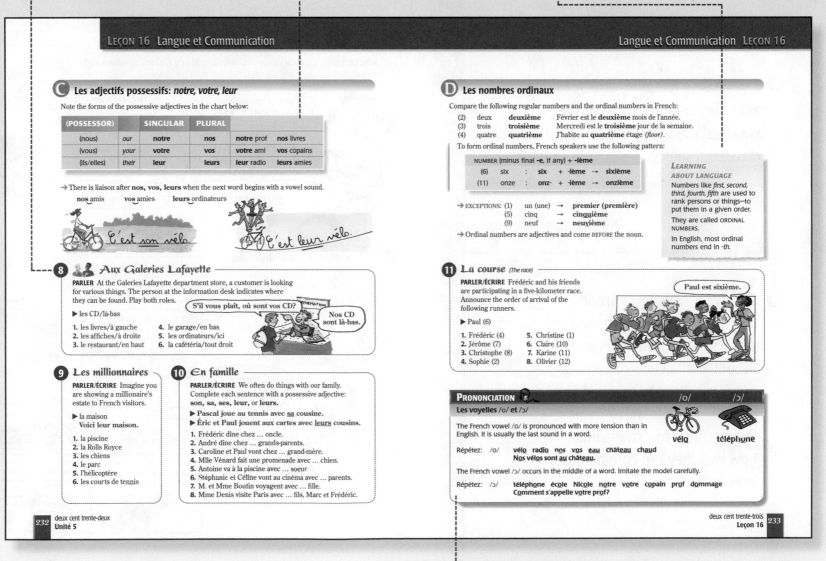

LEÇON 16 Langue et Communication

C Les adjectifs possessifs: *notre, votre, leur*

Note the forms of the possessive adjectives in the chart below:

(POSSESSOR)		SINGULAR	PLURAL		
(nous)	*our*	**notre**	**nos**	**notre** prof	**nos** livres
(vous)	*your*	**votre**	**vos**	**votre** ami	**vos** copains
(ils/elles)	*their*	**leur**	**leurs**	**leur** radio	**leurs** amies

→ There is liaison after **nos, vos, leurs** when the next word begins with a vowel sound.

nos amis   vos amies   **leurs** ordinateurs

C'est son vélo.   C'est leur vélo.

8 **Aux Galeries Lafayette**

PARLER At the Galeries Lafayette department store, a customer is looking for various things. The person at the information desk indicates where they can be found. Play both roles.

▶ les CD/là-bas

S'il vous plaît, où sont vos CD?

Nos CD sont là-bas.

1. les livres/à gauche
2. les affiches/à droite
3. le restaurant/en haut
4. le garage/en bas
5. les ordinateurs/ici
6. la cafétéria/tout droit

9 **Les millionnaires**

PARLER/ÉCRIRE Imagine you are showing a millionaire's estate to French visitors.

▶ la maison
Voici leur maison.

1. la piscine
2. la Rolls Royce
3. les chiens
4. le parc
5. l'hélicoptère
6. les courts de tennis

10 **En famille**

PARLER/ÉCRIRE We often do things with our family. Complete each sentence with a possessive adjective: **son, sa, ses, leur,** or **leurs.**

▶ Pascal joue au tennis avec sa cousine.
▶ Éric et Paul jouent aux cartes avec leurs cousins.

1. Frédéric dîne chez … oncle.
2. André dîne chez … grands-parents.
3. Caroline et Paul vont chez … grand-mère.
4. Mlle Vénard fait une promenade avec … chien.
5. Antoine va à la piscine avec … sœur.
6. Stéphanie et Céline vont au cinéma avec … parents.
7. M. et Mme Boutin voyagent avec … fille.
8. Mme Denis visite Paris avec … fils, Marc et Frédéric.

Langue et Communication LEÇON 16

D Les nombres ordinaux

Compare the following regular numbers and the ordinal numbers in French:

(2) deux **deuxième** Février est le **deuxième** mois de l'année.
(3) trois **troisième** Mercredi est le **troisième** jour de la semaine.
(4) quatre **quatrième** J'habite au **quatrième** étage *(floor)*.

To form ordinal numbers, French speakers use the following pattern:

NUMBER (minus final **-e**, if any) + **-ième**					
(6)	six	:	**six** + **-ième** →	**sixième**
(11)	onze	:	**onz-** + **-ième** →	**onzième**

LEARNING ABOUT LANGUAGE

Numbers like *first, second, third, fourth, fifth* are used to rank persons or things—to put them in a given order.
They are called ORDINAL NUMBERS.
In English, most ordinal numbers end in *-th*.

→ EXCEPTIONS:
(1) un (une) → **premier (première)**
(5) cinq → **cinquième**
(9) neuf → **neuvième**

→ Ordinal numbers are adjectives and come BEFORE the noun.

11 **La course** *(The race)*

PARLER/ÉCRIRE Frédéric and his friends are participating in a five-kilometer race. Announce the order of arrival of the following runners.

Paul est sixième.

▶ Paul (6)

1. Frédéric (4)
2. Jérôme (7)
3. Christophe (8)
4. Sophie (2)
5. Christine (1)
6. Claire (10)
7. Karine (11)
8. Olivier (12)

PRONONCIATION   /o/   /ɔ/

Les voyelles /o/ et /ɔ/

The French vowel /o/ is pronounced with more tension than in English. It is usually the last sound in a word.

vélo   téléphone

Répétez: /o/ vélo radio nos vos eau château chaud
Nos vélos sont au château.

The French vowel /ɔ/ occurs in the middle of a word. Imitate the model carefully.

Répétez: /ɔ/ téléphone école Nicole notre votre copain prof dommage
Comment s'appelle votre prof?

Prononciation features give students the opportunity to practice single "key" words and then to use them in context. All pronunciation sections, coded in purple, are available on the audio program.

Unit Walkthrough T39

Culminating the lesson, the *À votre tour* activities provide opportunities for self assessment in a variety of contextualized formats.

Culminating **listening and speaking activities** are ideal for expanding students' use of language beyond the classroom setting.

The *Créa-dialogue* provides models to guide but not limit students' creative language use. Recombination and re-entry of previously learned material provide students with opportunities to demonstrate how well they can communicate in French.

À votre tour!

OBJECTIFS

Now you can …
• talk about your family and your relatives
• identify things as belonging to you or to someone else
• talk about your pets

1 🎧 👥 Allô!

PARLER Émilie is on the phone with Bernard. Match Émilie's questions with Bernard's answers. Then act out the dialogue with a classmate.

1. Avec qui est-ce que tu vas au cinéma?
2. C'est le cousin de Monique?
3. Tu connais leurs parents?
4. Ils sont canadiens, n'est-ce pas?

a. Non, c'est son frère.
b. Bien sûr, ils sont très sympathiques.
c. Avec mon copain Marc.
d. Non, mais leurs voisins sont de Québec.

2 🎧 👥 Créa-dialogue

PARLER We often identify objects by their color. Create conversations with your classmates according to the model.

le vélo / Paul?

1. la guitare / Alice?
2. le scooter / Paul et Anne?
3. le chien / tes cousins?
4. la mobylette / Isabelle?
5. la maison / M. et Mme Lavoie?
6. la voiture / ton oncle?

▶ —C'est <u>le vélo de Paul</u>?
—Non, ce n'est pas <u>son vélo</u>.
—Tu es sûr?
—Mais oui. <u>Son vélo</u> est <u>bleu</u>.

234 deux cent trente-quatre
Unité 5

3 **Composition: un animal domestique**

ÉCRIRE Write a short composition about a pet: either your own pet, a pet belonging to a friend, or an imaginary pet. You may mention …

- the type of animal
- its name
- its age
- its colors
- its size
- its eating habits
- some physical and personality traits

4 **Composition: Ma famille**

ÉCRIRE Select five people in your family and write one to three sentences about each person.

Mon cousin s'appelle John. Il habite à San Francisco. Il a seize ans.

Writing activities encourage students to present their thoughts and ideas in written form and provide material for student portfolios.

5 **Arbre généalogique** *(Family tree)*

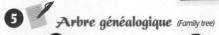

ÉCRIRE On a separate sheet of paper, draw your own (real or imaginary) family tree. Label the people and indicate their relationships to you.

LESSON REVIEW
CLASSZONE.COM

deux cent trente-cinq 235
Leçon 16

Follow up with Diagnostic Review

○ *Tests de contrôle* provide comprehensive review activities that students can use to check their comprehension.

○ The **"learning tabs"** in the side column help students self diagnose and review what they can do and where to go for help.

Tests de contrôle

By taking the following tests, you can check your progress in French and also prepare for the unit test. Write your answers on a separate sheet of paper.

① The right place

Complete each of the following sentences by filling in the blank with one of the places in the box. Be logical and do not use the same word more than once.

> bibliothèque chambre cuisine école église immeuble
> jardin magasin piscine plage salle de bains salle à manger

1. Le réfrigérateur est dans la —.
2. Quand il y a des invités *(guests)*, nous dînons dans la —.
3. Dans le —, il y a un lilas *(lilac tree)*.
4. Dans le complexe sportif où nous allons, il y a une — olympique.
5. Il y a beaucoup de livres à la — de la ville.
6. Dans ma —, il y a une table et un grand lit.
7. En été, nous allons en vacances sur une — de l'Atlantique.
8. Il y a une — catholique dans notre quartier.
9. Le samedi, les élèves américains ne vont pas à l'—.
10. Le shampooing *(shampoo)* est dans la —.
11. Mes cousins habitent dans un grand — moderne.
12. Je vais acheter un ordinateur dans un — d'équipement électronique.

Review...
• places and rooms of the house: pp. 197 and 200

② The right choice

Choose the word or expression in parentheses which logically completes each of the following sentences.

1. Marc dîne — restaurant. (à, au)
2. Thomas nage — piscine. (la, à la)
3. Le professeur parle — élèves. (aux, les)
4. Les élèves vont — école en bus. (à la, à l')
5. Nous faisons une promenade — pied. (à, au)
6. Pauline va — sa copine Isabelle. (à, chez)
7. Nous revenons — école à trois heures. (à l', de l')
8. Les touristes arrivent — musée. (du, de l')
9. J'aime jouer — football. (au, du)
10. Est-ce que tu joues — clarinette? (à la, de la)
11. Comment s'appelle la copine — Monique? (de, à)
12. Voici la maison — voisins. (des, de)

Review...
• use of à, de, and chez pp. 208, 210, 211, 219, 220, and 223

③ The right owner

Complete each of the following sentences with the possessive adjective that corresponds to the underlined subject.

▶ Jean-Paul regarde **ses** photos.

1. Tu téléphones à — copine.
2. Je vais souvent au cinéma avec — amis.
3. Marc dîne chez — tante.
4. Alice invite — voisins à la boum.
5. Isabelle n'a pas — appareil-photo avec elle.
6. Thomas et Charlotte sont en vacances chez — oncle.
7. Les élèves respectent — professeurs.
8. Vous parlez avec — amie Mélanie.
9. Nous allons visiter Paris avec — professeur de français.
10. Est-ce que vous écoutez toujours — parents?

Review...
• possessive adjectives: pp. 230 and 232

④ Aller and venir

Complete the following sentences with the appropriate forms of **aller** or **venir**.

1. Attendez-moi *(Wait for me)*! Je —.
2. Thomas et Céline — très souvent au cinéma.
3. Qu'est-ce que tu — faire samedi?
4. Nous — aller à une boum.
5. Le professeur est canadien. Il — de Montréal.
6. Je — souvent à la piscine parce que j'aime nager.
7. Nicolas n'a pas faim. Il — du restaurant.
8. D'où est-ce que vous —?

Review...
• aller and venir: pp. 206, 212, and 218

⑤ Composition: La maison idéale

Write a short paragraph of five or six sentences describing your ideal house and its rooms. Does it have a garden? Where is it located? What do you especially like about it?

STRATEGY Writing		
a	**b**	**c**
Sketch out a floor plan of your ideal house, labelling the rooms.	Organize your paragraph, concluding with why you like this house.	Reread your composition to be sure you have spelled all the names of the rooms correctly.

deux cent trente-sept
Tests de contrôle
237

○ **Pre-writing strategies** and **graphic organizers** help students become successful writers.

Thematic French-English vocabulary presentation brings together all unit vocabulary for easy review.

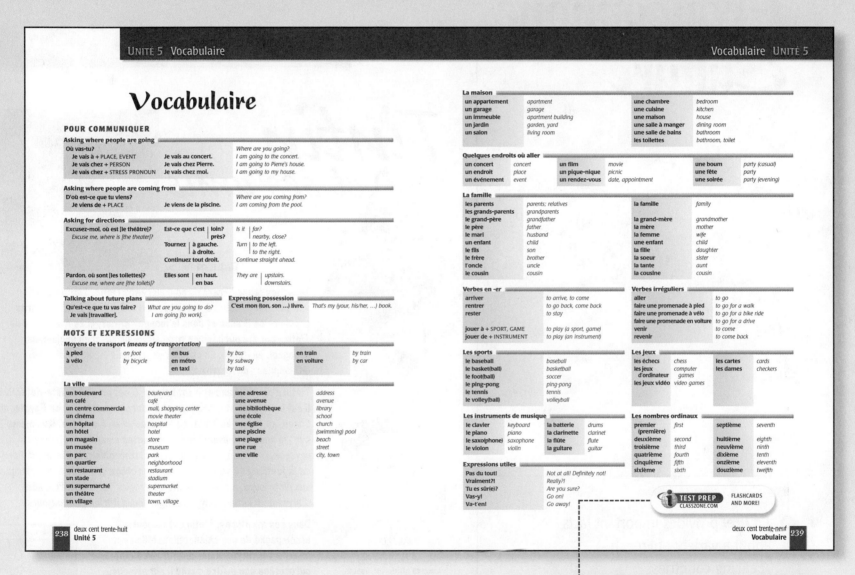

Vocabulaire

POUR COMMUNIQUER

Asking where people are going

Où vas-tu?			Where are you going?
Je vais à + PLACE, EVENT	Je vais au concert.		I am going to the concert.
Je vais chez + PERSON	Je vais chez Pierre.		I am going to Pierre's house.
Je vais chez + STRESS PRONOUN	Je vais chez moi.		I am going to my house.

Asking where people are coming from

D'où est-ce que tu viens?		Where are you coming from?
Je viens de + PLACE	Je viens de la piscine.	I am coming from the pool.

Asking for directions

Excusez-moi, où est [le théâtre]?	Est-ce que c'est	loin?	Is it | far?
Excuse me, where is [the theater]?		près?	*nearby, close?*
	Tournez	à gauche.	Turn | to the left.
		à droite.	to the right.
	Continuez tout droit.		Continue straight ahead.
Pardon, où sont [les toilettes]?	Elles sont	en haut.	They are | upstairs.
Excuse me, where are [the toilets]?		en bas.	*downstairs.*

Talking about future plans

Qu'est-ce que tu vas faire?	What are you going to do?
Je vais [travailler].	I am going [to work].

Expressing possession

C'est mon (ton, son ...) livre.	That's my (your, his/her, ...) book.

MOTS ET EXPRESSIONS

Moyens de transport *(means of transportation)*

à pied	on foot	en bus	by bus	en train	by train
à vélo	by bicycle	en métro	by subway	en voiture	by car
		en taxi	by taxi		

La ville

un boulevard	boulevard	une adresse	address
un café	café	une avenue	avenue
un centre commercial	mall, shopping center	une bibliothèque	library
un cinéma	movie theater	une école	school
un hôpital	hospital	une église	church
un hôtel	hotel	une piscine	(swimming) pool
un magasin	store	une plage	beach
un musée	museum	une rue	street
un parc	park	une ville	city, town
un quartier	neighborhood		
un restaurant	restaurant		
un stade	stadium		
un supermarché	supermarket		
un théâtre	theater		
un village	town, village		

La maison

un appartement	apartment	une chambre	bedroom
un garage	garage	une cuisine	kitchen
un immeuble	apartment building	une maison	house
un jardin	garden, yard	une salle à manger	dining room
un salon	living room	une salle de bains	bathroom
		les toilettes	bathroom, toilet

Quelques endroits où aller

un concert	concert	un film	movie	une boum	party (casual)
un endroit	place	un pique-nique	picnic	une fête	party
un événement	event	un rendez-vous	date, appointment	une soirée	party (evening)

La famille

les parents	parents; relatives	la famille	family
les grands-parents	grandparents		
le grand-père	grandfather	la grand-mère	grandmother
le père	father	la mère	mother
le mari	husband	la femme	wife
un enfant	child	une enfant	child
le fils	son	la fille	daughter
le frère	brother	la soeur	sister
l'oncle	uncle	la tante	aunt
le cousin	cousin	la cousine	cousin

Verbes en -er

arriver	to arrive, to come
rentrer	to go back, come back
rester	to stay
jouer à + SPORT, GAME	to play (a sport, game)
jouer de + INSTRUMENT	to play (an instrument)

Verbes irréguliers

aller	to go
faire une promenade à pied	to go for a walk
faire une promenade à vélo	to go for a bike ride
faire une promenade en voiture	to go for a drive
venir	to come
revenir	to come back

Les sports

le baseball	baseball
le basket(ball)	basketball
le foot(ball)	soccer
le ping-pong	ping-pong
le tennis	tennis
le volley(ball)	volleyball

Les jeux

les échecs	chess	les cartes	cards
les jeux d'ordinateur	computer games	les dames	checkers
les jeux vidéo	video games		

Les instruments de musique

le clavier	keyboard	la batterie	drums
le piano	piano	la clarinette	clarinet
le saxo(phone)	saxophone	la flûte	flute
le violon	violin	la guitare	guitar

Les nombres ordinaux

premier (première)	first	septième	seventh
deuxième	second	huitième	eighth
troisième	third	neuvième	ninth
quatrième	fourth	dixième	tenth
cinquième	fifth	onzième	eleventh
sixième	sixth	douzième	twelfth

Expressions utiles

Pas du tout!	Not at all! Definitely not!
Vraiment?!	Really?!
Tu es sûr(e)?	Are you sure?
Vas-y!	Go on!
Va-t'en!	Go away!

TEST PREP CLASSZONE.COM — FLASHCARDS AND MORE!

deux cent trente-huit	
Unité 5	238

deux cent trente-neuf	
Vocabulaire	239

● Online test prep at ClassZone.com prepares students to be successful test takers.

Develop Reading Skills and Experience French and Francophone Culture

Tintin *et ses amis*

Tintin et Milou

Tous° les jeunes Français connaissent° Tintin. Tintin n'est pas une personne réelle. C'est le héros d'une bande dessinée° très populaire en France et dans le monde° entier. «Les Aventures de Tintin» ont été publiées en français, mais aussi en anglais, en espagnol, en italien, en chinois, en japonais ... au total dans 40 langues° différentes.

Tintin a dix-sept ans et il est belge.° C'est un journaliste-détective. Il est intelligent et courageux et il adore voyager. Il va en Égypte, au Congo, en Chine, au Tibet, au Mexique et en Amérique. Il va même° sur° la lune, bien avant° les astronautes américains. Dans ses voyages, il connaît° des aventures extraordinaires. Tintin est l'ami de la justice et l'ennemi du mal.° Il protège ses amis et il s'attaque aux dictateurs, aux trafiquants de drogue° et aux marchands d'armes.° Il est souvent en danger, mais il triomphe toujours.

Dans ses aventures, Tintin est toujours accompagné de son chien, Milou. Milou est un petit fox terrier blanc intuitif et courageux qui protège son maître quand il est attaqué. Il accompagne Tintin dans toutes ses aventures. Quand il va avec lui sur la lune, il est équipé d'une combinaison spatiale° pour chiens.

Bruxelles
★
La Belgique

EN BREF: LA BELGIQUE

Capitale: Bruxelles
Population: 10 250 000
Langues officielles: français, flamand° et allemand°

La Belgique est une monarchie constitutionnelle avec un roi,° le roi Albert II. Sa capitale, Bruxelles, est le siège° de la Commission Européenne.

flamand *Flemish* **allemand** *German*
roi *king* **siège** *seat*

Voilà qui est fait.°

Tous *All* **connaissent** *know* **bande dessinée** *comic strip* **monde** *world* **langues** *languages* **belge** *Belgian* **même** *even* **sur** *on* **avant** *before* **connaît** *experiences* **mal** *evil* **trafiquants de drogue** *drug dealers* **armes** *weapons* **combinaison spatiale** *space suit* **Voilà qui est fait.** *There, you're all set.*

242 deux cent quarante-deux
Unité 5

○ **En bref** provides important facts about a variety of French-speaking countries.

● **Entracte: lecture et culture** supports the development of reading skills, cultural awareness, and vocabulary in context.

Lecture et Culture ENTRACTE UNITÉ 5

Tintin a d'autres compagnons d'aventures, très sympathiques, mais un peu bizarres.

le capitaine Haddock

Le capitaine Haddock habite au château° de Moulinsart en Belgique. C'est un ancien° officier de la marine marchande. Il est brave et courageux ... mais il est aussi très irritable.

Garnements! *Rascals!* **Iconoclastes!** *Iconoclasts! (people who attack and seek to overthrow traditional ideas)* **château** *castle* **ancien** *former*

Dupont et Dupond

Dupont et Dupond sont presque° identiques, mais ils ne sont pas frères. Ce sont des policiers méthodiques ... mais incompétents.

presque *almost*

le professeur Tournesol

Le professeur Tournesol est un génie scientifique. Il est modeste et réservé et comme° beaucoup de professeurs, il est très distrait.°

comme *like* **distrait** *absent-minded*

STRATEGY Reading

Recognizing Cognate Patterns Recognizing French-English cognate patterns will help you increase your reading vocabulary and improve your reading comprehension. Here are some common patterns:

FRENCH	ENGLISH	FRENCH	ENGLISH
-aire	*-ar, -ary*	extraordinaire	*extraordinary*
-eux, -euse	*-ous*	courageux	*courageous*
-ique	*-ic, -ical*	identique	*identical*
-iste	*-ist, istic*	journaliste	*journalist*
-é	*-ed*	réservé	*reserved*

●---- **Reading Strategies** emphasize different ways to approach a variety of readings and genres.

COMMUNAUTÉ

Organize a **fête Tintin** for the language classes in your school. You may display Tintin books in French and other languages and show a video or DVD of some of Tintin's adventures. Encourage your classmates to come dressed as Tintin characters.

Et vous?

Quelle est ta bande dessinée favorite? Qui sont les héros? Pourquoi est-ce que tu aimes cette bande dessinée?

deux cent quarante-trois
Lecture et Culture 243

Bonjour, Ousmane!

Bonjour! Je m'appelle Ousmane. J'adore la musique.
J'aime surtout le rap et le rock. Mon chanteur° préféré est
MC Solaar. Il chante très bien. J'ai beaucoup de CD
de lui. Ma soeur, elle, préfère le blues et le jazz.

Je suis un peu musicien. Je joue de la guitare.
Et je ne joue pas trop mal. J'ai organisé°
un petit orchestre° de rock avec des
copains. Nous répétons° le mercredi
après-midi. Nous ne répétons pas chez
moi, parce que ma mère déteste ça.°
Parfois,° le week-end, nous jouons
à des boums pour nos amis.

chanteur *singer* **ai organisé** *organized* **orchestre** *band*
répétons *rehearse* **ça** *that* **Parfois** *Sometimes*

Compréhension

1. Quelle est la musique préférée d'Ousmane?
2. De quel instrument est-ce qu'il joue?
3. Quand est-ce qu'il répète avec ses copains?
4. Pourquoi est-ce qu'il ne répète pas à
   la maison?

Activité écrite

Write a short note to Ousmane in which
you describe your musical preferences.
Use the following suggestions:

• J'aime … (quelles musiques?)
• Je déteste … (quelles musiques?)
• Mon groupe préféré est … (qui?)
• Ils/Elles chantent … (comment?)

MC Solaar
le «Monsieur Rap» français

MC Solaar est né° à Dakar au Sénégal. Il s'appelle
en réalité Claude M'Barali. Ses parents émigrent
en France quand il a six mois. Il fait
ses études dans la région parisienne.
Après° le bac, il s'intéresse à°
la musique. Il compose des chansons°
françaises sur des rythmes de rap américain.
Ses chansons ont beaucoup de succès. MC Solaar
donne° des concerts en France, mais aussi en
Angleterre,° en Allemagne,° en Russie et dans
les pays° d'Afrique.

Aujourd'hui, MC Solaar est le «Monsieur Rap»
français! Dans ses chansons, il exprime° des
messages positifs contre° la violence et pour
la paix.° Voilà pourquoi il est très populaire
en France et dans le monde° francophone.

est né *was born* **Après** *After* **s'intéresse à** *becomes interested in* **chansons** *songs* **donne** *gives*
Angleterre *England* **Allemagne** *Germany* **pays** *countries* **exprime** *expresses* **contre** *against*
la paix *peace* **monde** *world*

CONNEXIONS

With 2 or 3 classmates, select a French singer, such as MC Solaar. Go on the
Internet and obtain as much information as you can about the person you
have chosen. If possible, get samples of his or her music. Share your findings
with the rest of the class.

COMMUNAUTÉ

Prepare a short program about music from the French-speaking world. You
may want to include pictures of the performers, selections of their recordings,
and perhaps a world map showing their countries of origin. Present your
program to another class at school or at a local senior center.

● *Connexions* and *Communauté* help
students connect French to real-world
communities.

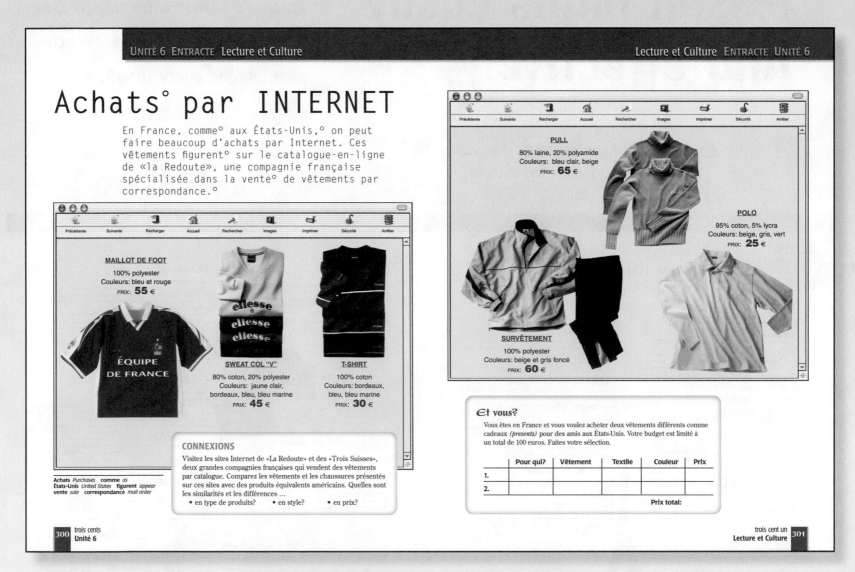

UNITÉ 6 ENTRACTE Lecture et Culture

Lecture et Culture ENTRACTE UNITÉ 6

Achats° par INTERNET

En France, comme° aux États-Unis,° on peut faire beaucoup d'achats par Internet. Ces vêtements figurent° sur le catalogue-en-ligne de «la Redoute», une compagnie française spécialisée dans la vente° de vêtements par correspondance.°

MAILLOT DE FOOT
100% polyester
Couleurs: bleu et rouge
PRIX: **55 €**

ÉQUIPE DE FRANCE

SWEAT COL "V"
80% coton, 20% polyester
Couleurs: jaune clair, bordeaux, bleu, bleu marine
PRIX: **45 €**

T-SHIRT
100% coton
Couleurs: bordeaux, bleu, bleu marine
PRIX: **30 €**

Achats *Purchases* **comme** *as*
États-Unis *United States* **figurent** *appear*
vente *sale* **correspondance** *mail order*

CONNEXIONS
Visitez les sites Internet de «La Redoute» et des «Trois Suisses», deux grandes compagnies françaises qui vendent des vêtements par catalogue. Comparez les vêtements et les chaussures présentés sur ces sites avec des produits équivalents américains. Quelles sont les similarités et les différences …
• en type de produits?   • en style?   • en prix?

PULL
80% laine, 20% polyamide
Couleurs: bleu clair, beige
PRIX: **65 €**

POLO
95% coton, 5% lycra
Couleurs: beige, gris, vert
PRIX: **25 €**

SURVÊTEMENT
100% polyester
Couleurs: beige et gris foncé
PRIX: **60 €**

Et vous?
Vous êtes en France et vous voulez acheter deux vêtements différents comme cadeaux *(presents)* pour des amis aux États-Unis. Votre budget est limité à un total de 100 euros. Faites votre sélection.

	Pour qui?	Vêtement	Textile	Couleur	Prix
1.					
2.					
				Prix total:	

Entracte: Development of Reading Skills
- Pre- and post-reading strategies and skill-building activities
- Reading comprehension hints
- Vocabulary enrichment techniques
- Advance organizers
- Authentic documents, letters, interviews, and surveys to encourage critical thinking and build rapid reading and information gathering skills
- Reading for pleasure and deriving meaning by word association build critical thinking skills

Implement ideas and lesson plans easily and effectively

The Expansion Activities, Planning Guide and Pacing Guide in the Teacher's Edition offer outstanding support to make teaching French adaptable to every situation.

● **Expansion Activities** spark students' excitement with new ways to learn language and culture.

UNITÉ 5 Expansion activities PLANNING AHEAD

Games

• Les directions
Give each student a copy of a simple city map in French from the Internet, or use an overhead projector to project an image of a map for the students. Divide the class into two teams. Have Team A give directions from a designated starting point and have Team B identify where the directions lead. As an alternative, you may want to give students a copy of a map of your school and the area around it, and have one team give directions while the other identifies specific locations.

Pacing Suggestion: Upon completion of Leçon 13.

• Le jeu de la mémoire
Before class, create pairs of cards for the vocabulary on page 220: the first card will be the French vocabulary word, and the second card will be an illustration or an English translation of the word. Tape the cards on the blackboard in random order so they form a 5 x 5 card grid. Create a second set of note cards numbered 1–25. Tape a numbered card over each of the vocabulary cards, so the words and illustrations are not visible. Divide the class into two teams. Have a player from the first team call out two numbers. Lift the numbered cards to reveal the vocabulary cards underneath. If they match and the team uses the word correctly in a sentence, they receive a point. Those cards are then removed from the board. If they don't match, the cards are covered again, and the turn passes to the other team.

Pacing Suggestion: Upon completion of Leçon 15.

Projects

• Où est-ce?
Have students work in pairs to write a dialogue in which one student asks for directions and the other gives directions. (You may want to specify the length of the exchange.) Have students exchange and proofread each other's work. Finally, have students act out their dialogues for the class.

Pacing Suggestion: Upon completion of Leçon 13.

Bulletin Boards

• À Paris
Divide the class into several small groups. Assign different tourist attractions in Paris and have each group create a bulletin board with the following information:

• a map that shows where the attraction is located
• the days and hours when the attraction is open
• what there is to see and do there
• illustrations or photos to show what the attraction looks like
• street signs for famous streets in the vicinity of the attraction, such as the **Champs-Élysées**

Pacing Suggestion: Upon completion of Leçon 14.

• Ma famille
Have each student use a poster board to create a real or imagined family tree. Have students include a picture for each family member and a paragraph explaining their relationship to the student. Imaginary family members can be cut out of magazines. You may wish to provide students with additional vocabulary for extended families.

Pacing Suggestion: Upon completion of Leçon 16.

Music

• Au clair de la lune
You may wish to teach students the traditional French song Au clair de la lune, which includes some of the possessive adjectives presented in Leçon 16. You can find the lyrics and music on the Internet.

«Au clair de la lune,
Mon ami, Pierrot,
Prête-moi ta plume
Pour écrire un mot!
Ma chandelle est morte,
Je n'ai plus de feu;
Ouvre-moi ta porte,
Je suis très peureux!»

Pacing Suggestion: Upon completion of Leçon 16.

• Les grands boulevards
Play Les grands boulevards from the Chansons CD for students. Give students a copy of the lyrics and have them listen first to get the gist of the song. Play it a second time and have students list all the words they hear that they recognize. Have the class discuss the general meaning of the song. As an alternative, you may wish to have students listen for and underline forms of the possessive adjectives they hear in the song.

Pacing Suggestion: Upon completion of Leçon 16.

Storytelling

• Une mini-histoire
Distribute a copy of a map of a French town, or if unavailable, use the map of Villeneuve on page 202. Model a short story about where one character goes and what he or she does while in the town. Add details to your story like date, time, and what the weather is like. When you are finished, hand out copies of your story with blanks for students to fill in. Have students fill in the blanks individually, with details they recall from your version, and review the story as a group.

Pacing Suggestion: Upon completion of Leçon 14.

Recipe

• Diabolo menthe
The diabolo menthe is a popular café beverage among French teenagers. The bright green drink is made using limonade, which is similar to a lemon-lime soda, and mint syrup. You may be able to find traditional French limonade at the grocery store. If necessary, substitute a sweetened lemon-lime–flavored soda. Variations on the diabolo menthe are made using different flavored syrups, such as strawberry, raspberry, and red or black currant.

Pacing Suggestion: Upon completion of Leçon 15.

Hands-on Crafts

• Les modèles
Allow students to choose a Parisian landmark (historical monument, cathedral, museum, or other well-known structure). Have students learn more about their landmark, through library or Internet research, and then construct a small model of it. Students may use whatever materials they deem appropriate to create their models. Once their reproductions are complete, have them add a brief paragraph about the landmark and a map showing where it is located. Have students present their models to the class. As a variation, you may expand the project to include landmarks from anywhere in the francophone world.

Pacing Suggestion: Upon completion of Leçon 14.

End of Unit

• Une maison
Students will create an audiovisual home tour. Students can use their own home, a friend's or a relative's home, or a home featured in a magazine. First, have students select three rooms they wish to present and write short paragraphs describing each room. Students should then proofread each other's work. Next, have students make audio recordings of their paragraphs and select appropriate photographs for them. Students may show slides, create a poster, or enlarge individual photographs to accompany their audio recordings. Finally, have students present their tours to the class. You may wish to give students the options of videotaping or creating computer audiovisuals of their presentations.

Rubric A = 13–15 pts. B = 10–12 pts. C = 7–9 pts. D = 4–6 pts. F = < 4 pts.

Criteria	Scale
Vocabulary Use	1 2 3 4 5
Grammar/Spelling Accuracy	1 2 3 4 5
Creativity	1 2 3 4 5

Diabolo menthe

Ingrédients
• 150 ml limonade
• 30 ml sirop de menthe

Ingredients
• approx. 5 oz. of limonade (lemon-lime soda)
• approx. 1 oz. of mint syrup

Préparation
1. Versez la limonade froide dans un verre.
2. Ajoutez le sirop de menthe et remuez.

Pour une personne.

Directions
1. Pour the chilled limonade into a glass.
2. Add the mint syrup and stir.

Serves one person.

● **Easy-to-prepare recipes** give students a delicious opportunity to experience cuisine from France and the French-speaking world.

At-a-glance overviews outline the objectives and program resources for at-a-glance support.

Listening scripts in the Teacher's Edition provide the practical information needed for easier lesson preparation.

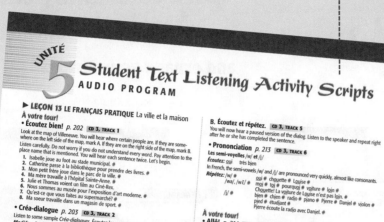

Time-saving lessons present sequenced teaching suggestions.

Suggests practical teaching ideas

The comprehensive Teacher's Edition and resource materials provide the support you need to introduce, explain, and expand your lessons.

Point-of-use references to program components help you integrate a variety of resources into your lessons with ease.

Practical suggestions for tailoring and enhancing your lessons help you meet the learning needs of all your students.

SECTION D

Communicative function
Describing one's home

Teaching Resource Options

PRINT
Workbook PE, pp. 117–121
Unit 5 Resource Book
 Communipak, pp. 140–163
 Video Activities, pp. 25–26
 Videoscript, p. 28
 Workbook TE, pp. 1–5

AUDIO & VISUAL
Overhead Transparencies
31 *La maison*

VIDEO PROGRAM

VIDÉO   DVD
MODULE 13

13.5 Vignette culturelle: La maison d'Olivier (6:03–7:02 min.)

Pronunciation Be sure students do NOT pronounce an "n" in **en haut:** /ã o/. The word **haut** begins with an *aspirate h*. There is never liaison or elision before an *aspirate h*.

Language notes
• **Les toilettes:** also **les WC** (called **double vécé** or simply **vécé**); or **les cabinets.** Tell students that **WC** stands for 'water closet.'
• **Une chambre** is a *room,* in the sense of *bedroom.*
• **Une pièce** is the more general word for *room of a house.*

Cultural notes
• Traditionally in a French home the toilet is in a small room separate from the bathroom.
• **Un salon** is a traditional formal living room. In modern, less formal homes, one may find **un séjour (une salle de séjour),** also referred to as **un living (un living-room).**
• In French homes, the shutters (**les volets**) are usually closed every night.

Supplementary vocabulary
une entrée
un escalier *staircase*
un ascenseur *elevator*
le toit *roof*
le grenier *attic*
le sous-sol *basement*
la cave *cellar*

200 • Vocabulaire et Communication
Unité 5 LEÇON 13

D VOCABULAIRE Ma maison

▶ *How to describe one's home:*

J'habite dans | une **maison** *(house).*
 un **appartement**
 un **immeuble** *(apartment building)*

Ma maison/mon appartement est | **moderne.**
 confortable

Ma chambre est | **en haut** *(upstairs).*
 en bas *(downstairs)*

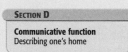

J'habite dans une maison.

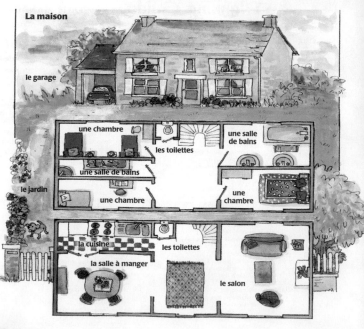

La maison

le garage
le jardin
une chambre
les toilettes
une salle de bains
une chambre
une salle de bains
une chambre
la cuisine
la salle à manger
les toilettes
le salon

200 deux cents
Unité 5

COMPREHENSION The house

PROPS: Transparency 31: *La maison;* magazine pictures of various rooms

Identify the new words on the transparency.
 Voici le salon. Voilà la cuisine. ...
 X, viens ici et montre-nous le jardin. ...

Place the magazine pictures on the desk. Have students pick up specific pictures and place themselves around the room.
 X, prends le salon et mets-toi près de la porte.
 Y, prends la salle à manger et mets-toi devant le tableau noir.

Vocabulaire et Communication LEÇON 13

6 Ma maison

PARLER/ÉCRIRE Describe your home by completing the following sentences.

1. J'habite dans … (une maison? un appartement?)
2. Mon appartement est … (grand? petit? confortable? joli?)
   Ma maison est … (grande? petite? confortable? jolie?)
3. La cuisine est … (grande? petite? moderne?)
4. La cuisine est peinte *(painted)* en … (jaune? vert? gris? blanc? ??)
5. Ma chambre est peinte en … (bleu? rose? ??)
6. Dans le salon, il y a … (une télé? un sofa? des plantes vertes? ??)
7. En général, nous dînons dans … (la cuisine? la salle à manger?)
8. Ma maison/mon appartement a … (un jardin? un garage? ??)

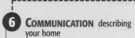

CHAMBRE 2
408 x 290

CHAMBRE 1
419 x 311

S. de B
300 x 170

SÉJOUR
467 x 436

ENTRÉE

W.C.

CUISINE
601 x 170

7 En haut ou en bas?

PARLER Imagine that you live in a two-story house. Indicate where the following rooms are located.

▶ ma chambre

Ma chambre est en haut.

Ma chambre est en bas.

1. la cuisine
2. la salle à manger
3. les toilettes
4. la salle de bains
5. la chambre de mes *(my)* parents
6. le salon

COMPARAISON CULTURELLE

In traditional French homes, the toilet **(WC)** is in a small room separate from the main bathroom.

8 Où sont-ils?

PARLER/ÉCRIRE From what the following people are doing, guess where they are — in or around the house.

▶ Madame Martin répare *(is repairing)* la voiture.
   Elle est dans le garage.

1. Nous dînons.
2. Tu regardes la télé.
3. Antoine et Juliette jouent au frisbee.
4. J'étudie le français.
5. Monsieur Martin prépare le dîner.
6. Henri se lave *(is washing up)*.
7. Ma soeur téléphone à son copain.

deux cent un 201
Leçon 13

---

6 COMMUNICATION describing your home

Answers will vary.
1. J'habite dans un appartement (une maison).
2. Mon appartement est (joli). Ma maison est (petite).
3. La cuisine est (grande).
4. La cuisine est peinte en (blanc et rouge).
5. Ma chambre est peinte en (bleu).
6. Dans le salon, il y a (un sofa et une télé).
7. En général, nous dînons dans (la salle à manger).
8. Mon appartement a (un garage).

7 DESCRIPTION indicating where rooms are located

Answers will vary.
1. La cuisine est en haut. (La cuisine est en bas.)
2. La salle à manger est en haut. (La salle à manger est en bas.)
3. Les toilettes sont en haut. (Les toilettes sont en bas.)
4. La salle de bains est en haut. (La salle de bains est en bas.)
5. La chambre de mes parents est en haut. (La chambre de mes parents est en bas.)
6. Le salon est en haut. (Le salon est en bas.)

Language note Be sure students use the plural in item 3: Les toilettes sont…

8 COMPREHENSION describing where people are

1. Vous êtes dans la salle à manger.
2. Je suis dans le salon.
3. Ils sont dans le jardin.
4. Tu es dans ta chambre. (Tu es dans le salon.)
5. Il est dans la cuisine.
6. Il est dans la salle de bains.
7. Elle est dans le salon.

Realia note Ask questions about the floor plan:

Trouvez l'entrée, le séjour, les deux chambres, la cuisine, la salle de bains, les toilettes (les WC).

Est-ce qu'il y a aussi des toilettes dans la salle de bains?

Combien de placards *(closets)* **y a-t-il?**

Once the layout of the house has been set, have other students go to various rooms.
Z, tu as faim. Va à la cuisine.
Qui est dans la cuisine? [Z]
W, tu veux regarder la télé. Va au salon.
V, tu dois te laver les mains [gesture].
Va dans la salle de bains. …

Answers for every activity are included in the wrap.

Cultural Reference Guide
Discovering French, *Nouveau!* BLEU Première partie

Note: *Page numbers in bold type refer to the Teacher's Edition.*

CULTURAL REFERENCES

Cultural Reference Guide

Discovering French, *Nouveau!* BLEU Deuxième partie

Note: *Page numbers in bold type refer to the Teacher's Edition.*

Universal Access in the Foreign Language Classroom

by Linda Carnine and Doug Carnine

Instructional Goal

The goal for all foreign language students in today's world is to learn to **speak** the language as well as to read and write it. Everyone can learn a foreign language as long as the instruction is explicit, direct, and systematic, and the learner is well placed. Forty years ago, foreign language instruction was mostly geared to the study of literature in the target language. More recently, due to more economical air travel, large waves of immigration, and more advanced technology, the emphasis has shifted to promoting spoken proficiency in the language studied. Students can advance to reading and writing according to their skill level, which is usually related to their skills in their native languages. Students who begin foreign language study in middle school or earlier (in immersion programs, for example) have an opportunity to study the culture, geography, history, and even dialects of the language. Nonetheless, the first expectation of instruction is that students will learn how to speak the language.

Adjusting Instruction for Diverse Learners

In this section we suggest strategies teachers can use to adjust instruction for diverse groups of students. Because research on teaching foreign language to diverse learners is quite limited, the suggestions are usually extrapolations from findings and practices in other areas. The student texts for *Discovering*

French, Nouveau! are designed for students near grade level. Instructional strategies provided in this section allow teachers to provide universal access to all students. Teachers may find it helpful to view students as members of four basic groups, namely, advanced learners, grade level learners, students with learning difficulties—including special education students—and Heritage learners. As a general guideline, the proficiency level students possess in their native language will determine how much differentiated instruction they need.

Three key strategies are recommended to meet the needs of students in all four groups:

1. **Frequent assessment** allows you to determine what each student does and does not know and provides the basis for instructional planning.
2. **Flexible grouping** strategies facilitate the management of a variety of achievement levels and learning needs (Learning Environments/ Teaching Strategies).
3. **Planned modifications in instruction** - planning ahead of time allows you to differentiate as the need arises during instruction.

Frequent Assessment

Assessment is an important way to create strong language students. Likewise, providing students with feedback via clear, well-articulated grading procedures also fosters strong language learners. Assessing foreign language

STRATEGIES BY STUDENT GROUP

STRATEGIES FOR ADVANCED GROUP Advanced students will be placed in accelerated classes in 9th grade and in Sophomore Honors, take the AP Language test (SAT-II) at the end of Junior year, and take the AP Literature test (SAT-II) at the end of Senior year. They will progress rapidly through the basics of the oral language and begin studying literature.	1. Involve students in a Pen Pal project to develop communication skills with peers in foreign countries. 2. Schedule meetings between Foreign Language and English teachers to develop common rubrics for literary analysis. 3. If taught in a heterogeneous class, substitute more challenging assignments for easier ones. 4. Make sure instruction is sufficiently complex and in-depth.
STRATEGIES FOR GRADE LEVEL GROUP Grade level students are usually college-oriented, have an adequate foreign language reading level, but need lots of visuals for instruction.	1. Assess what these students already know and adjust the rate of introduction of new material based on frequent assessments during instruction. 2. Provide cumulative review of sound/symbol relationships, vocabulary and grammatical forms taught; use flash cards for class and partner review. 3. Progress through *Discovering French, Nouveau!* at the recommended pace and sequence.
STRATEGIES FOR STUDENTS WITH LEARNING DIFFICULTIES GROUP Learners have the lowest functional vocabulary level, are very visual learners, and need more cumulative review.	1. Assess what these students already know and adjust rate of introduction of new material based on frequent assessments during instruction. 2. Focus primarily on oral language. 3. Explicitly teach sound/symbol relationships, separating difficult discriminations in introduction. 4. Introduce vocabulary through drawings and personalized vocabulary. 5. Provide daily oral practice through group responding, partner practice, and short presentations.
STRATEGIES FOR STUDENTS NEEDING INTENSIVE HELP (SPECIAL EDUCATION) Intensive needs students are those whose performance is two or more standard deviations below the mean on standardized measures. These students will probably be eligible for special education services. This is a very small percentage of the general population.	1. Determine reading level in English to guide the introduction of oral language content. 2. Follow the guidelines given for Students with Learning Difficulties. 3. Use a very visual approach and concentrate on oral language. 4. Directly teach sound/symbol relationships and vocabulary by clustering vocabulary words using sound/symbol relationship. 5. Place these students in lower grade level material if at all possible.

skills can be time consuming and demanding. *Discovering French, Nouveau!* offers multiple avenues for efficient assessment, including Lesson Quizzes, Unit Tests, and Proficiency Tests for Reading, Writing, Listening and Speaking. Complete guidelines for implementing Portfolio Assessment are also provided. Scoring criteria/rubrics accompany the Speaking and Writing Proficiency tests.

At the initial stages of language instruction, assessment can include simple tasks based on vocabulary students have learned, such as having students respond appropriately to greetings and simple classroom instructions. In addition to checking for listening comprehension, written comprehension tasks are also appropriate at the initial stages. For example, having students write a list of their 5 favorite foods (or 5 pieces of clothing) can serve as a quick writing assessment.

At the advanced levels, assessment of written work is structured by each classroom teacher. Grammatical structures and themes to be evaluated can be highlighted in the assessment directions and in the rubrics. If students are writing an essay based on a literary piece that they have read, allow the students to bring 3 x 5 cards to the test. These cards are prepared by the students to include quotes, verb forms, or special vocabulary they wish to include in their essay. No paragraphs should be allowed on the cards.

At a very formal level, national foreign language assessments provide schools with a summative evaluation of the advanced foreign language program. The SAT II is a traditional grammar and literature test. If your students take the SAT II in the fall, it will have a listening component. Advanced Placement tests in language and literature also provide program evaluation information. The Advanced Placement exams have a speaking component, whereas the SAT II does not.

Flexible Grouping Strategies

For large district implementations, flexible homogenous groupings are recommended.

Most districts organize foreign language students into three groups: the advanced/honors group, the grade level group, and the students with learning difficulties group. The emphasis for the scholarly, advanced group will be on literature and writing after the initial instruction in the spoken language. These students are usually expected to take both the SAT II language and literatures exams. The grade level, college-bound groups will progress at a less accelerated pace, taking the SAT II language test at the end of their senior year. The last group, students with learning difficulties, will have a primary emphasis on the spoken language during the high school program. Heritage learners may fit into any of the groups, but are more likely to be on or above grade level in their French class.

Planned Modification: Learning Environments and Teaching Strategies

For all types of students, one way to improve achievement is by providing high-quality, well-paced instruction. Depending on the learning activity, different seating arrangements may be desirable. Moveable chairs with an attached writing surface provide optimal flexibility. They allow for rearranging the room depending on the activity. For teacher-directed instruction in sound/symbol relationships, vocabulary, or grammar conventions, a large U shaped arrangement can work well. This allows you to observe all students, maximize active participation, and provide frequent feedback and quick pacing for familiar instructional routines.

Previous success in an area is a strong predictor of motivation. We also know that below-grade level students perform better when they are given the opportunity to have a higher rate of correct responses. Seating strategic learners closer to you may allow you to focus on their success rate and to give corrective feedback when confusions/errors occur.

Whenever possible, allow students to respond to a partner. The advantage of peer responses is that partnering fulfills students' desire to talk to each other. Besides having a social benefit, it provides a safe opportunity to respond as well as to receive feedback. The more opportunities students have to verbalize their answers and to receive feedback, the better they will be able to develop their oral language skills.

Planned Modifications for Vocabulary Development

Use visuals as much as possible, and have students bring in visuals to talk about. Anything from family photos to a video of their bedrooms will enhance and personalize oral communication, plus offer a supplement to the activities provided in the text. This emphasis on visuals is effective across all groups and levels, and will support the learning of all students, regardless of the diversity of their background knowledge.

The more personal the teacher can make vocabulary instruction, the more meaningful the response of the student. For example, in the classroom with students with learning difficulties, you may act out a dialog between friends eating at a sidewalk cafe. A quick discussion of the similarities and differences between eating at a sidewalk café and a food court in a shopping mall will personalize the vocabulary and the setting. In an advanced class, as students read a literary piece about a king who threatens capital punishment, the class can debate the pros and cons of capital punishment. Personalize your class activities and support them with visuals.

Students with learning difficulties, including special education students, will require the most frequent cumulative review. This can be done efficiently using flash cards. When initially introducing a new sound/symbol relationship or term, add the new item much more frequently among the review cards to provide massed practice. Once students are responding correctly 100% of the time, review the new items less frequently. Try to separate the introduction of difficult-to-discriminate symbols and words.

For grade level learners as well as strategic learners, set up all new vocabulary on cards, using either a picture, an English word or symbol, or a cue for an idiomatic expression. Students also benefit from having their own deck of cards, which can then be used in partner review in the classroom. For advanced learners, the cards can be extended to include lists of vocabulary and summarize grammatical structures and cultural notes. For all students, pictures can be drawn on large oak tag (8 x 10) to elicit stories.

GENERAL BACKGROUND: Questions and Answers

What are the Goals and Standards for Foreign Language Learning?

Over the past several years, the federal government has supported the development of Standards in many K-12 curriculum areas such as math, English, fine arts, and geography. These Standards are "content" standards and define what students should "know and are able to do" at the end of grades 4, 8 and 12. Moreover, the Standards are meant to be challenging, and their attainment should represent a strengthening of the American educational system.

In some subject matter areas, these Standards have formed the basis for building tests used in the National Assessment of Education Progress (NAEP). At that point, it was necessary to develop "performance" standards which define "how well" students must do on the assessment measure to demonstrate that they have met the content standards.

As far as states and local school districts are concerned, both implementation of the Standards and participation in the testing program are voluntary. However, the very existence of these standards is seen as a way of improving our educational system so as to make our young people more competitive on the global marketplace.

How are the Goals and Standards for Foreign Language Learning defined?

The Goals and Standards for Foreign Language Learning contain five general goals which focus on communication, culture, and the importance of second language competence in enhancing the students' ability to function more effectively in the global community of the 21st century. These five goals, each with their accompanying standards, are shown in the chart below. In the formal report, these standards are defined in greater detail with the addition of sample "benchmarks" or learning outcomes for grades 4, 8 and 12, and are illustrated with sample learning scenarios.

STANDARDS FOR THE LEARNING OF FRENCH

GOAL 1: Communication Communicate in French	**Standard 1.1 Interpersonal Communication** Students engage in conversations or correspondence in French to provide and obtain information, express feelings and emotions, and exchange opinions. **Standard 1.2 Interpretive Communication** Students understand and interpret spoken and written French on a variety of topics. **Standard 1.3 Presentational Communication** Students present information, concepts, and ideas in French to an audience of listeners or readers.
GOAL 2: Cultures Gain Knowledge and Understanding of the Cultures of the Francophone World	**Standard 2.1 Practices of Culture** Students demonstrate an understanding of the relationship between the practices and perspectives of the cultures of the francophone world. **Standard 2.2 Products of Culture** Students demonstrate an understanding of the relationship between the products and perspectives of the cultures of the francophone world.
GOAL 3: Connections Use French to Connect with Other Disciplines and Expand Knowledge	**Standard 3.1 Making Connections** Students reinforce and further their knowledge of other disciplines through French. **Standard 3.2 Acquiring Information** Students acquire information and recognize the distinctive viewpoints that are available through francophone cultures.
GOAL 4: Comparisons Develop Insight through French into the Nature of Language and Culture	**Standard 4.1 Language Comparisons** Students demonstrate understanding of the nature of language through comparisons of French and their native language. **Standard 4.2 Cultural Comparisons** Students demonstrate understanding of the concept of culture through comparisons of francophone cultures and their own.
GOAL 5: Communities Use French to Participate in Communities at Home and Around the World	**Standard 5.1 School and Community** Students use French both within and beyond the school setting. **Standard 5.2 Lifelong Learning** Students show evidence of becoming life-long learners by using French for personal enjoyment and enrichment.

Teaching to the Standards

The new Standards for Foreign Language Learning focus on the outcomes of long K-12 sequences of instruction. In most schools, however, French programs begin at the Middle School or Secondary level. With **Discovering French, *Nouveau!*** teachers can effectively teach toward these goals and standards while at the same time maintaining realistic expectations for their students.

> With **Discovering French, *Nouveau!*** teachers can effectively teach towards these goals and standards while at the same time maintaining realistic expectations for their students.

GOAL ONE: Communicate in French

From the outset, **Discovering French, *Nouveau!*** students learn to communicate in French. In the *Invitation au français* opening section of **DFN-Bleu**, the focus is on understanding what French young people are saying (on video, DVD, and audio) and on exchanging information in simple conversations. In units 3–6, the oral skills are supplemented by the written skills, and students learn to read and express themselves in writing.

As students progress through **DFN-Blanc** and **DFN-Rouge**, they learn to engage in longer conversations, read and interpret more challenging texts, and understand French-language films and videos. Teachers who incorporate portfolio assessment into their programs will have the opportunity to keep samples of both written and recorded student presentations.

GOAL TWO: Gain Knowledge and Understanding of the Cultures of the Francophone World

In **Discovering French, *Nouveau!*** students are introduced to the diversity of the French-speaking world. In **DFN-Bleu**, the emphasis is on contemporary culture — in France, of course, but also in Quebec, the Caribbean, and Africa. Students learn to observe and analyze cultural differences in photographs and on the video program.

GOAL THREE: Use French to Connect with Other Disciplines and Expand Knowledge

It is especially in **DFN-Rouge** that students have the opportunity to use the French language to learn about history, art, music, social concerns and civic responsibilities. Topics suggested in the student text can be coordinated with colleagues across the school curriculum.

GOAL FOUR: Develop Insight through French into the Nature of Language and Culture

From the outset, **Discovering French, *Nouveau!*** draws the students' attention to the way in which French speakers communicate with one another, and how some of these French patterns differ from American ones (for example, shaking hands or greeting friends with a *bise*). Notes in the Teacher's Edition provide suggestions for encouraging cross-cultural observation. English and French usage are also compared and contrasted, as appropriate.

GOAL FIVE: Use French to Participate in Communities at Home and Around the World

In **Discovering French, *Nouveau!*** beginning students are invited to exchange letters with French-speaking pen pals. In addition, students are encouraged to participate in international student exchanges. The Teacher's Edition has a listing of addresses of organizations that can provide these types of services. In addition, teachers are given information on where to obtain French-language publications for their classes, and where to find French-language material on the Internet. In **DFN-Rouge**, students are invited to discover French-language videos which in many parts of the country can be found in a local video store. As students experience the satisfaction of participating in authentic cultural situations, they become more confident in their ability to use their skills in the wider global community.

For more information on the National Standards project and its publications, contact: **National Standards in Foreign Language Education, 6 Executive Plaza, Yonkers, NY 10701-6801; phone: (914) 963-8830 or on the Internet go to: www.actfl.org**

Since young adolescents have their own specific learning needs, an effective foreign language program for the middle level must provide both age-appropriate and developmentally-appropriate materials and activities. Teaching French to middle school students presents a special challenge: many types of learners as well as varying developmental ability levels need to be addressed. With **Discovering French, Nouveau!** the middle school language classroom can become an exciting environment that provides opportunities for success for all students.

Teaching French at the Middle School level

What are the primary educational goals in Middle School?

The primary educational goals at the middle level are similar to those at any stage of early language introduction. Students should be given the opportunity to:

- learn successfully
- develop critical thinking skills
- become better global citizens

How are these goals best reached?

It is at the "how" level that teachers at the middle level need to establish age-appropriate learning environments and select developmentally appropriate learning experiences. In particular, effective Middle School programs...

- focus on process, rather than memorization of content
- use a full range of communication skills
- integrate technology into the subject area
- organize the curriculum around meaningful themes
- incorporate a variety of methodologies linked to differing learning styles
- encourage active participation of all students in the learning process
- provide opportunities for authentic assessment

In what way can these goals be realized in French classes?

In French classes, young adolescents learn to communicate with one another in a second language. They are introduced to the richness and variety of the multi-cultural French-speaking world, thus increasing their own global awareness. In **Discovering French, Nouveau!** the focus is precisely on interactive learning. The daily-life lesson themes encourage students to learn about one another and appreciate their classmates' similarities and differences. As they progress through the program in manageable steps, they experience success in using the French language for communication and can assess their progress in realistic contexts.

What is the role of the textbook in a Middle School French class?

With the emphasis on process, rather than content, many teachers at the middle level prefer to focus on non-textbook materials for much of the class work, using the textbook more as a reference tool and source of reading materials. An important role of the effective French textbook, however, is to present the new language in meaningful, yet manageable, increments, and allow for continuous recycling and regular reentry of new phrases and vocabulary. In this way, the textbook provides a carefully constructed framework around which each teacher can personalize his or her lesson plans.

What should be the place of technology in the Middle School French program?

For young adolescents, technology in the classroom should encourage interaction and collaboration, rather than having students work alone or be passive spectators. Moreover, media should be used to enhance students' learning and to encourage self-expression in purposeful contexts.

In **Discovering French, Nouveau!** the media support has been designed specifically to meet the above goals. The *Video Program* not only has interactive segments that elicit students' responses, but the *Video Activities* encourage multiple viewings and provide communicative practice. Similarly, the *Audio Program* lets students listen to authentic speech, and encourages them to work together in guided listening activities.

How do French classes interrelate with other Middle School subject matter areas?

Many of the themes and topics which are explored in the French class parallel and reinforce concepts students are learning in other areas of study: friendship, family life, the home, the local community, and, of course, the global community. Students build skills that can be equally well used in social studies, language arts, or math classes. Creative Middle School teachers have found that the opportunities for contact between French classes and other curriculum areas are numerous.

> Young adolescents need to discover that French is a living language.

Implementing Discovering French, *Nouveau!* at the Middle Level

French classes in Middle School differ somewhat from those at the secondary level because young adolescents perform best within an age-appropriate curriculum designed for their needs. Middle School teachers have found that there are many effective ways of implementing the **Discovering French, *Nouveau!*** materials in the classroom.

Here are a few specific suggestions:

Plan daily lessons so that they incorporate non-textbook materials and techniques which respond to the needs of different learners.

In Middle School classes, the textbook is used primarily as a reference and a source of specific readings and small group activities. With **Discovering French, *Nouveau!*** teachers have a variety of non-textbook means of presenting and practicing the new material.

- **Video** The *Video Program* is made up of 28 modules. Each include conversations, candid interviews, listening practice, speaking practice, and a cultural vignette. These videos are carefully integrated with each lesson of the student text, and they lend themselves exceptionally well to a Middle School program. Many segments were filmed in a *collège,* the French equivalent of a middle school.
- **Overhead Transparencies** Colorful overhead visuals allow the teacher to present the new vocabulary and speech patterns for visual learners. Many of these visuals also allow for student interaction.
- **Interpersonal Communication** The *Communipak* activities, especially the *Échanges* (information gathering) and *Tête à Tête* (information gap activities) encourage students to use French in meaningful conversation and interpersonal communication.
- **Middle School Copymasters** offer additional age-appropriate activities, games, and puzzles

Within the classroom, set up several different "learning stations."

At the middle level, the emphasis is on the language learning process: developing communication skills. Young adolescents learn more effectively in small groups where each person is actively involved in a given activity. There are many possibilities:

- **Video/DVD Station:** Place several desks around a monitor, and have students do the *Video Activities* in groups, checking comprehension together.
- **Listening Practice Station:** This station is furnished with CD players, preferably each with two headsets. Students, in pairs, do the *Listening activities,* replaying the audio as needed.

- **Conversation Station:** Copy the *Answer Key* pages which correspond to the *Communipak* activities for the lesson, especially those entitled *Interviews, Tu as la parole* and *Conversations.* In each triad, two students engage in the conversations while the third student acts as a coach.
- **Writing Practice Station:** Students work in pairs or small groups to check their Workbook writing activities. If they disagree as to the correct answer, they can consult the appropriate pages of the Workbook TE in the Unit Resource Book.
- **Assessment Station:** Students can be invited individually to take the brief teacher-administered *Speaking Proficiency Tests* or take make-up quizzes. (Since the *Lesson Quizzes* all have a listening portion, the Assessment Station would need a CD player and headset.) Students can also come to this station to work on material for their portfolios.

Encourage students to use French outside the classroom.

Young adolescents need to discover that French is a living language. They should be encouraged to use French in reaching out to their families, to others in the school community, and to those in the community at large.

- **At home:** Since each lesson of **Discovering French, *Nouveau!*–Bleu Première partie** focuses on common conversational themes, students can be encouraged (perhaps for extra credit) to teach a few of their newly-learned phrases to siblings and other family members.
- **Within the school:** As an assignment, have students take the *Communipak Interview* and *Échange* sheets and interview students in the school who are now in more advanced French classes. You might also be able to identify some colleagues and administrators who (with a bit of advanced warning, e.g., by giving them copies of the *Communipak* sheets) would be willing to be interviewed in French.
- **Within the community:** Students can be given the opportunity to be "teachers" at an elementary school and introduce the younger students to a bit of French (perhaps with the support of some **Discovering French, *Nouveau!*–Bleu** overhead transparencies). They can also be encouraged to identify adults who speak French and have brief conversations with them, perhaps by using modified forms of the *Communipak* sheets. (Some teachers have found that this is an excellent way of involving young adolescents with people across generations.)

Discovering French, *Nouveau!* provides tools for building the foundation for continued future success in the study of French. Students at the middle level are encouraged to develop positive attitudes toward linguistic and cultural diversity while expanding their own individual language skills.

Building Comprehension in the French Classroom

The Role of Listening Comprehension

Listening comprehension provides a very effective introduction to second-language learning. More specifically, listening activities in which students respond physically in some way (moving around, pointing, handling objects, etc.) are not only excellent ways of establishing comprehension of new phrases, but material learned in this manner is remembered longer. This explains why students learn the parts of the body more quickly by playing "Simon Says" than by repeating the same vocabulary words after the teacher.

How is an effective comprehension activity structured?

In a typical comprehension activity, the teacher gives commands to the students, either as a full class, a small group, or individually. The activity often consists of four steps:

STEP 1 Group performance with a teacher model

The teacher gives a command and then performs the action. The students listen, watch and imitate the teacher. Three to five new commands are presented in this way.

STEP 2 Group performance without a teacher model

When the teacher feels the students understand the new phrases, he or she gives the command without moving. It is the students who demonstrate their comprehension by performing the desired action. If the students seem unsure about what to do, the teacher will model the action again.

STEP 3 Individual performance without a teacher model

Once the group can perform the new commands easily, the teacher gives these commands to individual students. If an individual student does not remember a given command, the teacher calls on the group to perform the command. It is important to maintain a relaxing atmosphere where all students feel comfortable.

STEP 4 Individual performance of a series of commands

When the class is comfortable with the new commands, the teacher gives an individual student a series of two or more commands. This type of activity builds retention and encourages more careful listening.

These four steps are repeated each time new commands are introduced. As the activities progress, the new commands are intermingled with those learned previously.

How many new commands are introduced at any one time?

Generally three to five new commands are introduced and then practiced. It is important not to bring in new items until all the students are comfortable with the current material. Practice can be made more challenging by giving the commands more rapidly.

There are essentially two kinds of comprehension activities:

• **TEXT-RELATED ACTIVITIES** These activities introduce material which will be immediately activated in the corresponding lesson of the book. The comprehension activity helps students build their listening comprehension before being asked to produce this new material in speaking and writing. Then, when students are presented with this material formally, they can concentrate on details such as pronunciation and spelling because they will already know what all the new words mean.

• **COMPREHENSION-EXPANSION ACTIVITIES** These activities are designed to expand the students' listening proficiency and introduce vocabulary and structures which will not be formally presented until later in the program. Since this approach is fun, and since the material presented is not formally "tested," comprehension activities can be effectively used for vocabulary expansion and for introduction of new material.

Sample classroom commands

Here is a listing of some sample commands in both the "tu" and the "vous" forms. As a teacher, you have two options:

• You can use the formal "vous" form for both group and individual commands.
• You can address the class and small groups with the plural "vous" form and then address individual students as "tu."

Movements			
	Stand up.	**Lève-toi.**	**Levez-vous.**
		Debout.	**Debout.**
	Sit down.	**Assieds-toi.**	**Asseyez-vous.**
	Walk.	**Marche.**	**Marchez.**
	Jump.	**Saute.**	**Sautez.**
	Stop.	**Arrête.**	**Arrêtez.**
	Turn around.	**Tourne-toi.**	**Tournez-vous.**
	Turn right / left.	**Tourne à droite/à gauche.**	**Tournez à droite/à gauche.**
	Go …	**Va** (au tableau).	**Allez** (à la fenêtre).
	Come …	**Viens** (au bureau).	**Venez** (au tableau).
	Raise …	**Lève** (la main).	**Levez** (le bras).
	Lower …	**Baisse** (la tête).	**Baissez** (les yeux).
Pointing out and manipulating objects	Point out …	**Montre** (le cahier).	**Montrez** (le livre).
	Touch …	**Touche** (la porte).	**Touchez** (la fenêtre).
	Pick up / Take …	**Prends** (le crayon).	**Prenez** (le stylo).
	Put …	**Mets** (le livre sur la table).	**Mettez** (le cahier sous la chaise).
	Take away …	**Enlève** (le livre).	**Enlevez** (le cahier).
	Empty …	**Vide** (le sac).	**Videz** (la corbeille).
	Give …	**Donne** (la cassette à Anne).	**Donnez** (le CD à Paul).
	Give back …	**Rends** (la cassette à Marie).	**Rendez** (le CD à Michel).
	Pass …	**Passe** (le stylo à Denise).	**Passez** (le crayon à Marc).
	Keep …	**Garde** (la cassette).	**Gardez** (la cassette).
	Open …	**Ouvre** (la porte).	**Ouvrez** (le livre).
	Close …	**Ferme** (la fenêtre).	**Fermez** (le cahier).
	Throw …	**Lance** (la balle à Jean).	**Lancez** (le ballon à Claire).
	Bring me …	**Apporte-moi** (la balle).	**Apportez-moi** (le ballon).
Activities with pictures and visuals	Look at …	**Regarde** (la carte).	**Regardez** (le plan de Paris).
	Look for / Find …	**Cherche** (la Suisse).	**Cherchez** (la tour Eiffel).
	Show me …	**Montre-moi** (Genève).	**Montrez-moi** (Notre-Dame).
Paper or chalkboard activities	Draw …	**Dessine** (une maison).	**Dessinez** (un arbre).
	Write …	**Écris** (ton nom).	**Écrivez** (votre nom).
	Erase …	**Efface** (le dessin).	**Effacez** (la carte).
	Color …	**Colorie** (le chat en noir).	**Coloriez** (le chien en jaune).
	Put an "x" on …	**Mets un "x" sur** (le garçon).	**Mettez un "x" sur** (la fille).
	Circle …	**Trace un cercle autour de** (la chemise rouge).	**Tracez un cercle autour de** (la jupe blanche).
	Cut out …	**Découpe** (un coeur).	**Découpez** (un cercle).

Professional Language Organizations

American Association of Teachers of French (AATF)

Mailcode 4510
Southern Illinois University
Carbondale, IL 62901-4510

Phone: (618) 453-5731

www.frenchteachers.org

> *As an AATF member:*
>
> • you will receive subscriptions to the French Review and the AATF National Bulletin.
>
> • you will be able to attend local, regional, and national AATF meetings where you can share ideas and meet new colleagues.
>
> • you have the opportunity to apply for one of the many summer scholarships to France and Quebec offered to AATF members.
>
> • you may sponsor a chapter of the *Société Honoraire de Français* at your school so that your students will then be eligible to compete for study abroad travel grants and participate in the SHF creative writing contest.
>
> • you can have your students participate in the National French Contest and be considered for local, regional, and national awards.
>
> • you can obtain pen pals for your students through the *Bureau de Correspondance Scolaire.*

American Council on the Teaching of Foreign Languages (ACTFL)

6 Executive Plaza
Yonkers, NY 10701

Phone: (914) 963-8830

headquarters@actfl.org

www.actfl.org

Governmental Organizations

Alliance Française

The *Alliance Française* is a French organization dedicated to the promotion of French language and culture.

To obtain the address of the Alliance Française nearest you, write:

Délégation Générale de l'Alliance Française, Inc.
1900 L Street NW, Suite 314
Washington, DC 20036-5027

Phone: 800-6-FRANCE (800-637-2623)

federation@afusa.org

www.afusa.org

French Cultural Services

The French Cultural Services are very supportive of French teaching in the United States. For more information, contact the French Cultural Officer at the French Consulate nearest you or write the New York office.

To obtain information about available French cultural materials, write:

Services Culturels de France
934 Fifth Avenue
New York, NY 10021-2603

Phone: (212) 606-3688

www.consulfrance-newyork.org

info@consulfrance-newyork.org

Other Useful Addresses

Sister Cities International

If your town has a Sister City in a French-speaking country, you might want to explore the possibility of initiating a youth or education exchange program. If your town does not yet have a French-speaking Sister City, you might want to encourage your community to set up such an affiliation.

For information on both youth exchanges and the establishment of a sister-city association, contact:

Sister Cities International
120 South Payne St.
Alexandria, VA 22314-2939

Phone: (703) 836-3535

www.sister-cities.org

info@sister-cities.org

Nacel Open Door

Nacel Open Door is a nonprofit organization sponsoring cultural exchanges between American and foreign families and students. If you have students who would like to host a French-speaking student for a month during the summer, or who would themselves like to stay with a family in France or Senegal, have them contact the non-profit organization Nacel Open Door.

Nacel Open Door
3410 Federal Drive, Suite 101
St. Paul, MN 55122-1337

Phone: 800-NACELLE (800-622-3553)

info@nacelopendoor.org

www.nacelopendoor.org

BLEU
1b

Deuxième
partie

Discovering FRENCH
Nouveau!

Jean-Paul Valette
Rebecca M. Valette

McDougal Littell
A HOUGHTON MIFFLIN COMPANY
Evanston, Illinois • Boston • Dallas

i

Cover photography

Background: Place de la Concorde, Paris, France; Inset: Iles des Saintes, Guadeloupe; Credits appear on page R52

McDougal Littell wishes to express its heartfelt appreciation to **Gail Smith,** Supervising Editor for DISCOVERING FRENCH. Her creativity, organizational skills, determination, and sheer hard work have been invaluable in all aspects of the program.

REPRISE

Bonjour!

Thème Getting reacquainted

iii

En ville 192

Thème Visiting a French city

UNITÉ 6

Le shopping 254

Thème Buying clothes

Le temps libre 306

Thème Leisure time activities

UNITÉ 8

Les repas 360

Thème Food and meals

Reference Section

Teaching Resource Options

PRINT

Unit 1 Resource Book
  Videoscript, pp. 193–194

AUDIO & VISUAL

Overhead Transparencies
1 Map of France

VIDEO PROGRAM

VIDÉO · DVD **IMAGES**

A.2 La France
  (0:49–2:34 min.)

Cultural notes France

• **Les Alpes et Chamonix**
  Chamonix is located in a valley in
  the Alps at the foot of the **Massif
  du Mont Blanc. (Mont Blanc** is
  the highest mountain in Europe.)
  Chamonix is a famous ski resort. The
  first Winter Olympics were held there
  in 1924.

• **La Côte d'Azur**
  The French Riviera, or **la Côte
  d'Azur,** stretches about 100 miles
  along the Mediterranean, from the
  Toulon area to the Italian border. For
  the French, the Côte d'Azur is their
  favorite summer vacation place.

• **Les Pyrénées**
  The **Pyrénées** are a high mountain
  chain which separates France from
  Spain (**l'Espagne**).

• **Les Châteaux de la Loire**
  There are many castles located in
  the Loire Valley. **Les Châteaux de
  la Loire,** such as the Château de
  Chenonceau, were built by the
  French kings nearly 500 years ago.

Bonjour, la France!

CONNAISSEZ-VOUS LA FRANCE? *(Do you know France?)*

• In area, France is the second-largest country in Western Europe. It is smaller than
  Texas, but bigger than California.

• Geographically, France is a very diversified country, with the highest mountains in
  Europe (**les Alpes** and **les Pyrénées**) and an extensive coastline along the
  Atlantic (**l'océan Atlantique**) and the Mediterranean (**la Méditerranée**).

• France consists of many different regions which have maintained their traditions,
  their culture, and — in some cases — their own language. Some of the traditional
  provinces are Normandy and Brittany (**la Normandie** and **la Bretagne**) in the
  west, Alsace (**l'Alsace**) in the east, Touraine (**la Touraine**) in the center, and
  Provence (**la Provence**) in the south.

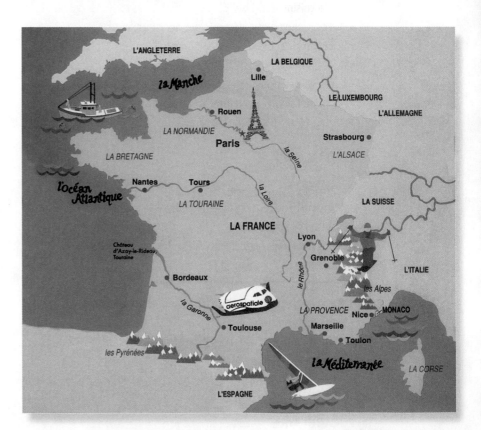

CLASSROOM PROJECT

You might have students prepare a bulletin board
display about France using maps, postcards, travel
brochures, etc.

Paris: Montmartre
Paris, the capital of France, is also its economic, intellectual, and artistic center. For many people, Paris is the most beautiful city in the world.

Snowboarding in the Alps
During winter vacation, many French young people enjoy snowboarding or skiing. The most popular destinations are the Alps and the Pyrenees.

Château de Chenonceau
The long history of France is evident in its many castles and monuments. This chateau, built in the 16th century, attracts nearly one million visitors a year.

Home in Provence
The French love flowers and take pride in making their homes beautiful. This house is built in the traditional style of Provence, a region in southern France.

Photo cultural notes

- The Paris neighborhood of **Montmartre** is well-known as a haven for artists. The white, domed Sacré-Coeur church sits atop the hill and can be seen from many parts of Paris.

- The **Château de Chenonceau** was completed in 1521. It is picturesque because part of the castle sits on a bridge over the river Cher. This addition was made by Catherine de Médicis in the late 1500s.

- This house is located in Moustier, Provence. Note the typically French shutters.

Bonjour, le monde francophone!

Teaching Resource Options

PRINT

Unit 1 Resource Book
    Videoscript, pp. 193–194

AUDIO & VISUAL

Overhead Transparencies
2b Map of the French-speaking world
(page R10)
2c Map of the French-speaking world
(page R11)

VIDEO PROGRAM

VIDÉO   DVD
 IMAGES

A.3 Le monde francophone
(2:35-4:42 min.)

**A.4 Des francophones aux
États-Unis** (4:43-6:42 min.)

Cultural note There are also two
small French islands in the Atlantic, off
the Canadian coast: Saint Pierre and
Miquelon. Since 1985, Saint-Pierre and
Miquelon (**Saint-Pierre-et-Miquelon**)
are considered as a "collectivité
territoriale" and not as a
"département".

CANADA
About one-third of the population speaks
French. These French speakers live mainly in
the province of Quebec (**le Québec**). They
are descendants of French settlers who came
to Canada in the 17th and 18th centuries.

HAÏTI
Haïti is the first Black Republic. Its
people speak Creole and French.

MARTINIQUE AND GUADELOUPE
These two Caribbean islands (**la Martinique**
and **la Guadeloupe**) are part of France.
Their inhabitants, primarily of African
ancestry, are French citizens.

LE CANADA

LE QUÉBEC

SAINT-PIERRE-
ET-MIQUELON

OCÉAN
PACIFIQUE

AMÉRIQUE
DU NORD

LES ÉTATS-UNIS

LA NOUVELLE-
ANGLETERRE

LA LOUISIANE

CUBA

OCÉAN
ATLANTIQUE

LE MEXIQUE

HAÏTI

PORTO RICO

AMÉRIQUE
CENTRALE

LE VENEZUELA

LA GUADELOUPE
LA MARTINIQUE

LE GUATEMALA

LA GUYANE
FRANÇAISE

LA COLOMBIE

équateur

AMÉRIQUE
DU SUD

LE PÉROU

TAHITI

LA POLYNÉSIE
FRANÇAISE

LE BRÉSIL

LA NOUVELLE-
CALÉDONIE

French is the
most important
language

L'ARGENTINE

Some French
is spoken

Cultural note Two African countries are named after the Congo river, one of the longest rivers in the world. In size, **la République démocratique du Congo** is the largest French-speaking country of Africa. It was known as **le Congo belge** before its independence in 1960, and as **le Zaïre** until 1997. Its eastern neighbor, **la République du Congo,** is a former French colony.

Cultural expansion

Names of African countries where French is an important language (capitals are given in parentheses):
   Algérie (Alger)
   Bénin (Porto-Novo)
   Burkina Faso (Ougadougou)
   Burundi (Bujumbura)
   Cameroun (Yaoundé)
   Côte d'Ivoire (Yamoussoukro)
   Djibouti (Djibouti)
   Gabon (Libreville)
   Guinée (Conakry)
   Madagascar (Antananarivo)
   Mali (Bamako)
   Maroc (Rabat)
   Mauritanie (Nouakchott)
   Niger (Niamey)
   République Centrafricaine (Bangui)
   République Démocratique du
      Congo (Kinshasa)
   République du Congo (Brazzaville)
   Ruanda [Rwanda] (Kigali)
   Sénégal (Dakar)
   Tchad (N'Djamena)
   Togo (Lomé)
   Tunisie (Tunis)

Middle School Copymasters

Class Starters

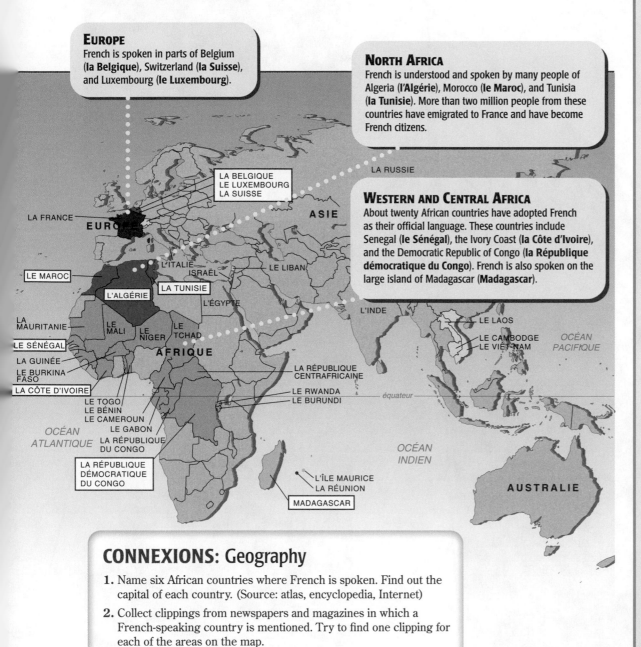

EUROPE
French is spoken in parts of Belgium (**la Belgique**), Switzerland (**la Suisse**), and Luxembourg (**le Luxembourg**).

NORTH AFRICA
French is understood and spoken by many people of Algeria (**l'Algérie**), Morocco (**le Maroc**), and Tunisia (**la Tunisie**). More than two million people from these countries have emigrated to France and have become French citizens.

WESTERN AND CENTRAL AFRICA
About twenty African countries have adopted French as their official language. These countries include Senegal (**le Sénégal**), the Ivory Coast (**la Côte d'Ivoire**), and the Democratic Republic of Congo (**la République démocratique du Congo**). French is also spoken on the large island of Madagascar (**Madagascar**).

CONNEXIONS: Geography

1. Name six African countries where French is spoken. Find out the capital of each country. (Source: atlas, encyclopedia, Internet)

2. Collect clippings from newspapers and magazines in which a French-speaking country is mentioned. Try to find one clipping for each of the areas on the map.

Bonjour!

We hope that you had a relaxing summer vacation and we would like to welcome you back to **Discovering French—Nouveau!** This year you will learn how to carry out longer conversations in French: talking about your family and discussing things you plan to do. You will learn how to go shopping for clothes and discuss fashions, how to go shopping for food and order in a restaurant. You will also learn how to talk about things you did yesterday or last week or last month.

First, however, you will probably want to review what you learned last year. The opening section, which we call *Reprise*, gives you the opportunity to get to know your classmates and refresh your French. You may also want to familiarize yourself with the review charts and summaries in Appendix A on pages R1-R8. Finally, the *Le savez-vous?* section lets you see how much you remember about French and francophone culture around the world.

Once you feel comfortable hearing and speaking French again, you will continue with the new lessons, each accompanied by video segments which introduce you to French young people and how they live their daily lives.

We trust that as the year progresses you will find it both fun and exciting to communicate more effectively in French and to learn more about the French-speaking world.

Bonne chance!

Jean-Paul Valette   Rebecca M. Valette

Planning Guide CLASSROOM MANAGEMENT

OBJECTIVES

Communication
- Describe yourself and others *pp. 8, 9, 10*
- Talk about your possessions and your room *pp. 12, 13, 14*
- Ask and answer questions about what people are doing *pp. 16, 17, 18*
- Express your preferences *p. 19*
- Extend and accept (or turn down) invitations *p. 19*
- Ordering food in a café *p. 23*
- Count *pp. 10, 22*
- Give the date and tell time *p. 22*
- Talk about the weather *p. 23*

Grammar
- Rappel *pp. 8, 9, 10, 12, 16, 17, 18*
- Révision *pp. 8, 9, 13, 16*
- Appendix A *pp. R1, R5*

Vocabulary
- Révision *pp. 8, 9, 10, 12, 22, 23*
- Vocabulaire *pp. 10, 13, 14, 18, 19, 23*
- Appendix A *pp. R2, R3, R4, R6, R7, R8*

Culture
- Note culturelle–La France multi-culturelle *p. 5*
- Note culturelle–La Guadeloupe *p. 5*
- Le savez-vous *pp. 24–25*

PROGRAM RESOURCES

 Print
- Workbook PE, *pp. R1–R11*
- Teacher to Teacher Copymasters
- Middle School Bridging Packet
  Reprise Resources
    Workbook TE
    Audioscript
    Middle School Copymasters

 Audiovisual
- Middle School Audio CD
- Video Program Modules 1–4
- Overhead Transparencies
  2a, 2b, 2c, 4, 7, 27, S3, S4,
  13, 15, 18, S3, S5,
  19, 26a, 26b, 53, 55,
  8, S6, S16,
  20, 21, 22, S12, S2,
  14a, 14b, 15, 18, S9, S10, S14,
  6, 9, 10, 12, 11, S7

 Technology

Optional Use: Units 1–4
- Online Workbook
- ClassZone.com
- eTest Plus Online/Test Generator CD-ROM
- EasyPlanner Plus Online/EasyPlanner CD-ROM
- Power Presentations on CD-ROM

 Assessment Program Options

Optional Use: Units 1–4
Lesson Quizzes
Portfolio Assessment
Unit Test Form A
Unit Test Form B
Unit Test Part III (Alternate)
  Cultural Awareness
Listening Comprehension
  Performance Test
Speaking Performance Test
Reading Comprehension
  Performance Test
Writing Performance Test
Multiple Choice Test Items
Test Scoring Tools
Answer Keys
eTest Plus Online/Test Generator
  CD-ROM

Pacing Guide SAMPLE LESSON PLAN

DAY 1	DAY 2	DAY 3	DAY 4	DAY 5
Reprise Opener **Rappel 1** • Les personnes	**Rappel 1** • How to ask someone's name and age • À votre tour!	**Rappel 2** • Les choses de la vie courante • How to ask or say where things are	**Rappel 2** • How to say where things are located • À votre tour!	**Rappel 3** • Les activités • How to express what you like, want, can, and must do

DAY 6	DAY 7	DAY 8	DAY 9	
Rappel 3 • How to ask for information • À votre tour!	**Rappel 4** • Expressions de tous les jours • To order in a café	**Révision** • Bonjour • Note culturelle— La France multi-culturelle • Note culturelle— La Guadeloupe	**Révision** • Et vous? • Le savez-vous?	

REPRISE Workbook Listening Activity Scripts
AUDIO PROGRAM

All *Reprise* audio can be found on the **Middle School Audio CD** in the **Middle School Bridging Packet**.

1. Amélie

• Compréhension orale

BONJOUR!

You will hear three French teenagers introduce themselves. As you listen to each one, indicate whether the information in your Workbook is true **(vrai)** or false **(faux)** by checking the appropriate column. You will hear each person twice.
First, listen to Amélie. Écoutez.

Bonjour! Je m'appelle Amélie Blanchard et j'ai quinze ans. J'habite avec ma famille à Orléans, une ville située à 100 kilomètres de Paris. J'ai un frère, mais je n'ai pas de soeur. Mon frère s'appelle Jean-Marc. Il a neuf ans et il est très pénible!

J'aime beaucoup les animaux. J'ai un canari, un chat et un chien. Mon chien s'appelle Attila, mais il est très gentil. Il est beaucoup plus gentil que mon petit frère!

J'aime beaucoup la musique, en particulier le rock et le rap. J'ai une chaine hi-fi et beaucoup de CD.

Je suis sportive. Mes sports préférés sont le snowboard et le tennis. Je joue bien – mais je ne suis pas une championne!

En classe, je suis une assez bonne élève, excepté en maths où ça ne va pas très bien. Mes matières préférées sont l'anglais et l'espagnol. Je parle assez bien ces deux langues. (Aujourd'hui, il est important de parler plusieurs langues si on veut avoir un bon travail.)

J'adore voyager. Un jour, je voudrais visiter les Etats-Unis et aussi le Mexique.

Let's listen again to Amélie.

Now let's check your answers.
1. Amélie a quinze ans.
   C'est vrai.
2. Elle habite à Paris.
   C'est faux. Elle habite à Orléans.
3. Elle a un frère.
   C'est vrai.
4. Son frère s'appelle Jean-Marc.
   C'est vrai.
5. Elle a une soeur.
   C'est faux. Elle n'a pas de soeur.
6. Elle a un chien et un chat.
   C'est vrai.
7. Elle a une chaîne hi-fi.
   C'est vrai.
8. Elle joue au tennis.
   C'est vrai.
9. Elle est bonne en maths.
   C'est faux. En maths, ça ne va pas très bien.
10. Elle étudie l'anglais et l'italien.
    C'est faux. Elle étudie l'anglais et l'espagnol.

2. Jean-Philippe

• Compréhension orale

Now you will hear Jean-Philippe. Again, as you listen to Jean-Philippe, indicate whether the information in your Workbook is true **(vrai)** or false **(faux)** by checking the appropriate column. You will hear his introduction twice.
Listen. Écoutez.

Salut! Je m'appelle Jean-Philippe Jamin. J'ai seize ans et j'habite à la Guadeloupe avec ma famille. J'ai une petite soeur et un grand frère. Ma petite soeur a six ans. Elle s'appelle Claudine et elle est très mignonne. Mon frère s'appelle Thomas. Il n'habite pas avec nous. Il habite à Paris où il est étudiant en médecine.

Moi, je suis élève au lycée Baimbridge à Pointe-à-Pitre. Mes matières préférées, sont les maths et l'informatique. Je voudrais être ingénieur.

J'aime les sports, en particulier le foot. Je joue dans un club amateur. J'aime aussi nager. Je nage très souvent parce qu'ici, à la Guadeloupe, il fait toujours beau.

Let's listen again to Jean-Philippe.

Now let's check your answers.
1. Jean-Philippe a treize ans.
   C'est faux. Il a seize ans.
2. Il habite à la Martinique.
   C'est faux. Il habite à la Guadeloupe.
3. Il a une petite soeur.
   C'est vrai.
4. Sa petite soeur s'appelle Claudine.
   C'est vrai.
5. Son frère est étudiant à Paris.
   C'est vrai.
6. Jean-Philippe va au collège.
   C'est faux. Il va au lycée.
7. Il aime les maths.
   C'est vrai.
8. Il aime jouer au foot.
   C'est vrai.
9. À la Guadeloupe, il fait mauvais.
   C'est faux. Il fait toujours beau.

3. Martine

• Compréhension orale

Finally you will hear Martine. Again, as you listen to her, indicate whether the information in your Workbook is true **(vrai)** or false **(faux)** by checking the appropriate column. You will hear her introduction twice. Listen. Écoutez.

Ça va? Je m'appelle Martine Nguyen et j'ai quinze ans. Ma famille est d'origine vietnamienne, mais maintenant nous habitons en France, dans la région de Lyon.

J'ai un grand frère. Il s'appelle Guillaume et il est très sympa. J'ai beaucoup d'amis. J'ai une bonne copine (c'est une voisine), mais je n'ai pas de copain.

J'aime la danse et la musique classique. J'aime aussi la nature. Le week-end, quand il fait beau, je fais des promenades en scooter dans la campagne avec ma copine. Parfois, je travaille dans le restaurant de mes parents. C'est un restaurant vietnamien, bien sûr! Et vous, qu'est-ce que vous faites le week-end?

Let's listen again to Martine.

Now let's check your answers.

1. Martine a quinze ans.
   C'est vrai.
2. Sa famille est d'origine vietnamienne.
   C'est vrai.
3. Elle a un grand frère.
   C'est vrai.
4. Son frère s'appelle Nicolas.
   C'est faux. Il s'appelle Guillaume.
5. Elle a un copain.
   C'est faux. Elle n'a pas de copain.
6. Elle aime danser.
   C'est vrai.
7. Elle a un scooter.
   C'est vrai.
8. Ses parents ont un café.
   C'est faux. Ils ont un restaurant.

REPRISE

Main Theme
• Getting reacquainted

COMMUNICATION
• Talking about oneself
• Describing other people
• Naming one's possessions
• Describing objects
• Describing daily and leisure activities
• Describing one's likes, dislikes, wishes and obligations
• Asking questions
• Inviting friends; accepting or refusing invitations
• Counting from 0 to 100
• Telling time and giving the date
• Talking about the weather
• Ordering in a café

CULTURES
• Learning about multi-cultural France
• Learning about Guadeloupe
• Learning about French culture
• Learning about Franco-American relations

CONNECTIONS
• Connecting to Math: Counting
• Connecting to Math: Calculating a restaurant check
• Connecting to Social Studies: Taking a cultural quiz

COMPARISONS
• Comparing yourself with some French teenagers

COMMUNITIES
• Using French to communicate with French-speakers in day-to-day situations
• Using French when you travel

REPRISE
Bonjour!

RAPPEL 1
Les personnes

RAPPEL 2
Les choses de la vie courante

RAPPEL 3
Les activités

RAPPEL 4
Expressions de tous les jours

LE SAVEZ-VOUS?

THÈME ET OBJECTIFS

Getting Reacquainted

In **Reprise**, you will become reacquainted with the French-speaking world: its people, its culture, its language.

In this opening unit, you will have the opportunity to brush up on your French skills. In particular, you will practice . . .

• describing yourself and others
• talking about your possessions and your room
• asking and answering questions about what people are doing
• expressing your preferences
• extending and accepting (or turning down) invitations
• ordering food in a café

In addition, you will review . . .

• how to count
• how to give the date and tell time
• how to talk about the weather

WEBQUEST
CLASSZONE.COM

2 deux
Reprise

OVERALL STRATEGY

Since the **Reprise** is a review unit, it should be considered optional. The unit can be presented in its entirety, covered partly, or completely omitted. The manner in which the unit is used will depend on the linguistic and communicative proficiency which the students have reached after having completed **Discovering French**, *Nouveau!–Bleu, Première partie.*

You may evaluate your students' proficiency by having them complete the activities presented in the first two sections of this unit: **Bonjour!** and **Et vous?** Depending on the ease or difficulty with which the students handle this material, an appropriate review can be designed by incorporating elements from the four **Rappel** sections of the **Reprise**.

Linguistic objectives

RAPPEL 1
- **être**
- the noun group (people): nouns, articles, adjectives

RAPPEL 2
- **avoir**
- the noun group (objects)

RAPPEL 3
- **faire**
- present tense of **-er** verbs
- negative and interrogative construction

Overview

The purpose of the *Reprise* unit is to review the basic material that students acquired in their beginning course of study.

The emphasis is on communication skills, especially . . .
- talking about oneself
- giving simple descriptions of people and things
- asking and answering simple questions

Teaching Note
Contents

The *Reprise* unit consists of four parts:

- **Bonjour!** and **Et vous?** (pp. 4–7) for diagnostic purposes
- Four **Rappel** sections (pp. 8–23) for more detailed review
- **Le savez-vous?** (pp. 24–25) for cultural discovery and enrichment
- **Appendix A** (pp. R1–R8) for grammar reference and vocabulary listings

trois
Reprise 3

This "bridge" may take one of the following forms:
- a complete review of the four **Rappel** sections
- a selective review of those elements which present problems
- a quick review using only the **Reprise** activities in the Student Workbook.

Bonjour!

Main Topic Meeting people

Teaching Resource Options

PRINT

Workbook PE, pp. R1–R2
Middle School Bridging Packet
   Audioscript, pp. R1–R2
   Workbook TE, pp. R12–R15

AUDIO & VISUAL

Audio Program
Middle School Audio CD Tracks 1–6
Overhead Transparencies
2a, 2b, 2c, 4, 7, 27, S3, S4

Amélie Blanchard

Questions sur le texte

1. Quel âge a Amélie? [quinze ans]
2. Où est-ce qu'elle habite? [à Orléans]
3. Comment s'appelle le frère d'Amélie? [Jean-Marc]
4. Est-ce qu'il est gentil? [Non, il est pénible.]
5. Quels animaux est-ce qu'elle a? [un canari, un chat et un chien]
6. Quelle sorte de musique est-ce qu'elle aime? [le rock et le rap]
7. Quelles langues est-ce qu'elle parle? [Elle parle français, anglais et espagnol.]
8. Quelle matière est-ce qu'elle n'aime pas? [les maths]

Questions personnelles

9. Quel âge as-tu? [J'ai ... ans.]
10. Où est-ce que tu habites? [J'habite à ...]
11. Est-ce que tu as un animal à la maison? Qu'est-ce que c'est? [Oui, j'ai (un chien). [Non, je n'ai pas d'animal.]
12. Quelle sorte de musique est-ce que tu aimes? [J'aime (le rap).]
13. Quelles langues est-ce que tu parles? [Je parle (anglais et français).]

Jean-Philippe Jamin

Questions sur le texte

1. Où habite Jean-Philippe? [à la Guadeloupe]
2. Quel âge a sa petite soeur? [six ans]
3. Qu'est-ce que son frère fait à Paris? [Il est étudiant en médecine.]
4. En classe, quelles sont les matières préférées de Jean-Philippe? [les maths et l'informatique]
5. Quel est son sport préféré? [le foot]

Questions personnelles

6. As-tu un frère ou une soeur? Comment s'appelle-t-il/elle? Quel âge a-t-il/elle? [J'ai (un frère). Il s'appelle (Robert). Il a (huit) ans.]
7. En classe, quelles sont tes matières préférées? [Mes matières préférées sont (le français et l'anglais).]

Bonjour

Bonjour!

Je m'appelle Amélie Blanchard et j'ai quinze ans. J'habite avec ma famille à Orléans, une ville° située à 100 (cent) kilomètres de Paris. J'ai un frère, mais je n'ai pas de soeur. Mon frère s'appelle Jean-Marc. Il a neuf ans et il est très pénible!

J'aime beaucoup les animaux. J'ai un canari, un chat et un chien. Mon chien s'appelle Attila, mais il est très gentil. (Il est beaucoup plus gentil que° mon petit frère.)

J'aime beaucoup la musique, en particulier le rock et le rap. J'ai une chaîne hi-fi et beaucoup de CD.

Je suis sportive. Mes sports préférés sont le snowboard et le tennis. Je joue bien (mais je ne suis pas une championne!).

En classe, je suis une assez bonne élève, excepté en maths où ça ne va pas très bien. Mes matières préférées sont l'anglais et l'espagnol. Je parle assez bien ces° deux langues. (Aujourd'hui, il est important de parler plusieurs° langues si on° veut avoir un bon travail.°)

J'adore voyager. Un jour, je voudrais visiter les États-Unis et aussi le Mexique.

Salut!

Je m'appelle Jean-Philippe Jamin. J'ai seize ans et j'habite à la Guadeloupe avec ma famille. J'ai une petite soeur et un grand frère. Ma petite soeur a six ans. Elle s'appelle Claudine et elle est très mignonne. Mon frère s'appelle Thomas. Il n'habite pas avec nous. Il habite à Paris où il est étudiant en médecine.

Moi, je suis élève au lycée Baimbridge à Pointe-à-Pitre. Mes matières préférées sont les maths et l'informatique. Je voudrais être ingénieur.

J'aime les sports, en particulier le foot. Je joue dans un club amateur. J'aime aussi nager. Je nage très souvent parce qu'ici, à la Guadeloupe, il fait toujours beau.

ville *city*   **plus gentil que** *nicer than*   **ces** *those*   **plusieurs** *several*   **on** *one*   **travail** *job*

TEACHING STRATEGY

- To help students prepare for this reading, you can review the key vocabulary by doing the **Et vous?** activity on pages 6–7.
- As an opening activity, play the corresponding audio. Have the students listen to Amélie, Jean-Philippe and Martine introducing themselves, while they read along in their books.
- As a listening comprehension check, have the students answer the true-false statements in the listening activities in their Workbooks.
- Once the students are comfortable with the reading, ask them the *Questions sur le texte/Questions personnelles* in the notes on the side of the pages.

Ça va?

Je m'appelle Martine Nguyen et j'ai quinze ans. Ma famille est d'origine vietnamienne, mais maintenant nous habitons en France, dans la région de Lyon.

J'ai un grand frère. Il s'appelle Guillaume et il est très sympa.° J'ai beaucoup d'amis. J'ai une bonne copine (c'est une voisine), mais je n'ai pas de copain.

J'aime la danse et la musique classique. J'aime aussi la nature. Le week-end, quand il fait beau, je fais des promenades en scooter dans la campagne° avec ma copine. Parfois,° je travaille dans le restaurant de mes parents. (C'est un restaurant vietnamien, bien sûr!) Et vous, qu'est-ce que vous faites le week-end?

sympa = sympathique   campagne *countryside*   **Parfois** *Sometimes*

À votre tour!

Of the three French teenagers who have introduced themselves, which one would you choose as a penpal? In a short paragraph, explain …

- what you have in common with that person
- why you find him/her interesting.

Je voudrais correspondre avec Amélie. Elle a un petit frère. Moi, aussi, j'ai un petit frère. Il a 9 ans et …

NOTE culturelle

1 La France multi-culturelle

Although of different origins, Amélie, Jean-Philippe and Martine are typical French teenagers. France, like many modern countries, has a very diverse population which includes people of a great variety of cultural and ethnic backgrounds. Since France is located in Western Europe, the great majority of its citizens are of European, but not necessarily of French, origin. As a matter of fact, many French people claim Spanish, Italian or Polish ancestry. Because of various historical circumstances, France also has an ever-growing non-European population. These new French immigrants come primarily from North Africa (Algeria, Morocco, Tunisia), West Africa (Senegal, Mali, Ivory Coast, Chad), and Southeast Asia (Vietnam and Cambodia). And we

should not forget the people of the Caribbean islands of Martinique and Guadeloupe, who are French citizens of African origin, and the people of Tahiti, also French citizens, who are Polynesian.

France is truly multi-ethnic and multi-cultural. The growing cultural diversity of its population makes it a richer and more interesting country. As the French people say: "Vive la différence!"

2 La Guadeloupe

Like Martinique, Guadeloupe is a Caribbean island which is part of the French national territory. Its inhabitants, who are mostly of African ancestry, are therefore French citizens.

Pierre - un jeune de la Guadeloupe

Martine Nguyen
Questions sur le texte
1. Où habite la famille de Martine? [En France, dans la région de Lyon]
2. Comment s'appelle le frère de Martine? [Guillaume]
3. Qu'est-ce que fait Martine le week-end quand il fait beau? [Elle fait des promenades en scooter dans la campagne avec sa copine.]
4. Où est-ce qu'elle travaille parfois? [dans le restaurant de ses parents]

Questions personnelles
5. Dans quelle région est-ce que tu habites? [J'habite ...]
6. Quel temps est-ce qu'il fait dans ta région? [Il fait (chaud).]
7. Qu'est-ce que tu fais le week-end quand il fait beau? [Je (nage).]
8. Est-ce que tu travailles? Où? [Oui, je travaille (au cinéma). (Non, je ne travaille pas.)]

Cultural Notes

- **Orléans** (pop. 100,000 +) is a city in north central France located on the Loire River. It is an important marketing center for the surrounding region. In addition to agricultural and electrical equipment, the city's major industries produce beverages, leather goods and textiles. **Jeanne d'Arc, la pucelle** *(maid)* **d'Orléans**, liberated the city from the English in 1429 during the Hundred Years' War.

- Many French students study two foreign languages: one for six years and the other for four years. They begin their first language in **sixième** *(sixth grade)* and their second in **quatrième** *(eighth grade)*. English is the most popular **langue vivante** (modern language).

- **Guadeloupe** is a French overseas department in the West Indies. It consists of two main islands, Basse-Terre and Grande-Terre, and several small islands. Pointe-à-Pitre on Grande-Terre is Guadeloupe's chief port and largest city.

PORTFOLIO ASSESSMENT

Students might wish to keep a sample of their work from early in the year to show how they've progressed.

USING THE VIDEO

You can use Modules 1–4 for additional review.

Et vous?

Maintenant, parlez de vous. Pour cela, complétez les phrases avec l'une des expressions suggérées ou une expression de votre choix.

1. Je suis …
   - américain(e)
   - canadien(ne)
   - français(e)
   - ?

2. J'ai …
   - 13 ans
   - 14 ans
   - 15 ans
   - ?

3. Ma famille est d'origine …
   - européenne
   - africaine
   - hispanique
   - asiatique
   - amérindienne (native American)
   - mixte
   - ?

4. J'ai …
   - un frère
   - une soeur
   - un frère, mais pas de soeur
   - ?

5. À la maison, j'ai …
   - un chien
   - un chat
   - un canari
   - un hamster
   - un poisson rouge (goldfish)
   - un lapin (rabbit)
   - ?

6. À l'école, ma matière préférée est …
   - l'histoire
   - l'anglais
   - le français
   - les maths
   - les sciences
   - ?

7. En général, les professeurs sont …
   - sympathiques
   - intéressants
   - stricts
   - justes (fair)
   - ?

8. À la maison, quand je n'étudie pas, je préfère …
   - regarder la télé
   - jouer aux jeux vidéo
   - téléphoner à mes copains
   - aider (help) mes parents
   - ?

9. Quand je suis dans ma chambre, je préfère …
   - étudier
   - écouter la radio
   - lire (read) un livre
   - lire un magazine
   - ?

10. Ma musique préférée est …
    - le rock
    - le rap
    - la musique classique
    - ?

11. En général, j'écoute mes CD préférés sur …
    - mon baladeur
    - une chaîne hi-fi
    - une radio-cassette
    - ?

12. Pour mon anniversaire, je voudrais avoir …
    - un vélo
    - un portable
    - des vêtements
    - 2 billets pour un concert
    - ?

TEACHING STRATEGIES Et vous?

▶ **Full class introduction**
First go over the 20 statements with the entire class, calling on individuals to give their responses.

▶ **Pair practice**
Have students share their responses with each other, taking notes on their partner's answers.

13. Le week-end, je préfère dîner …
- à la maison
- au restaurant avec ma famille
- au restaurant avec mes copains
- ?

14. Quand je suis au restaurant, je préfère manger …
- un hamburger
- une pizza
- une salade
- ?

15. Mon sport préféré est …
- le basket
- le baseball
- le foot
- le football américain
- ?

16. Ma saison préférée est …
- l'automne
- l'hiver
- le printemps
- l'été

17. Quand il fait beau, je préfère …
- nager
- faire une promenade à vélo
- faire du sport
- rester (stay) à la maison
- ?

18. En été, quand je suis en vacances, je préfère …
- travailler
- étudier
- rester (stay) à la maison
- voyager
- ?

19. Un jour (one day), je voudrais visiter …
- la France
- le Mexique
- le Canada
- l'Afrique
- ?

20. Pour moi, la chose la plus (most) importante dans la vie (life), est de (d')…
- avoir des amis sympathiques
- faire des choses intéressantes
- avoir un bon job
- voyager beaucoup
- ?

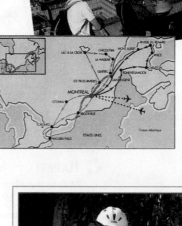

Assessment Options
If you are using *Bonjour* and *Et vous?* for diagnostic purposes, you may wish to broaden the scope of your assessment by using the following components.

Discovering French, Nouveau!–Bleu Test Generator CD-ROM/eTest Plus Online

Discovering French, Nouveau!–Bleu Video program (Modules 1–4)

If you have access to your students' portfolios from **Discovering French, Nouveau!–Première partie,** they are an invaluable tool for assessing students' previous level of performance.

Middle School Copymasters

Drill: Chain drill, pp. T2–T3; Conversations, pp. 2–4, 17, 49; Class Starter: Charades, p. 33; Game: 'Round the room, p. 27

EXPANSION

Call on students to find out their partner's preferences.

—[Marie], quelle est la matière préférée de [Pierre]?
—La matière préférée de [Pierre] est l'histoire.

Rappel 1

Communicative Functions
• Talking about oneself
• Describing other people

Teaching Resource Options

PRINT

Workbook PE, pp. R2–R4
Middle School Bridging Packet
    Workbook TE, pp. R2–R4

AUDIO & VISUAL

Overhead Transparencies
19, 26a, 26b, 53, 55

1 DESCRIPTION describing people

Answers will vary.
1. La mère de Véronique s'appelle Marthe. Elle a quarante et un ans.
2. Le père de Véronique s'appelle Jean-François. Il a quarante-trois ans.
3. Le grand-père de Véronique s'appelle Henri. Il a soixante-neuf ans.
4. La soeur de Véronique s'appelle Anne-Sophie. Elle a dix-neuf ans.
5. La grand-mère de Véronique s'appelle Joséphine. Elle a soixante-six ans.
6. Le frère de Véronique s'appelle Thomas. Il a dix ans.
7. Le chien de Véronique s'appelle César. Il est mignon.
8. Le chat de Véronique s'appelle Minette.

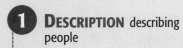 **Review** use of the definite article; names of family members

Note How to give one's age is formally reviewed on page 10.

Variation Véronique introduces her family: **Mon frère s'appelle . . .**

Les personnes

♻ **RAPPEL**

In French, all nouns are MASCULINE or FEMININE, SINGULAR or PLURAL.

un frère **une** soeur **des** copains

RÉVISION

If you need to review the forms of other words that introduce nouns, go to Appendix A, p. R1.

RÉVISION

If you need to review the names of family members and other people, go to Appendix A, p. R2.

1 La famille de Véronique

PARLER/ÉCRIRE This picture was taken at a gathering of Véronique's family. Choose a member of the family (or a pet) and give his/her name. If you wish, you may describe the person (approximate age, other characteristics).

▶ Le frère de Véronique s'appelle Thomas. Il a dix ans. Il est petit.

TEACHING NOTE Workbook

Have students do the writing activities in the Workbook. By analyzing how well they do, you can determine:

• which **Rappel** sections to emphasize
• which **Rappel** sections can be omitted

RÉVISION

If you need to review the forms of descriptive adjectives, go to Appendix A, p. R1.

RÉVISION

If you need to review adjectives describing common nationalities and physical traits, go to Appendix A, p. R2.

♻ **RAPPEL**

ADJECTIVES agree with the NOUNS they describe.

Philippe est **grand.**   Pauline est **grande.**

❷ Le congrès des jeunes

PARLER/ÉCRIRE The following young people are representing their countries at an international youth conference. Choose one of the delegates. Give his/her nationality and a brief physical description.

▶ **Bob est américain. Il est blond. Il n'est pas très grand.**

| Bob | Anita | Valérie | Martin | Michiko | Tatsuya | Brian | Danielle |

❸ Nationalités

PARLER/ÉCRIRE The following people live in the cities indicated in parentheses. Give each one's nationality.

▶ **(Acapulco) Teresa est mexicaine.**

1. (Rome) Mario et Silvia …
2. (Hong Kong) Madame Li …
3. (Genève) Nous …
4. (Madrid) Toi et José, vous …
5. (Zurich) Tu …
6. (Barcelona) Mes cousins …
7. (Liverpool) Ma tante …
8. (Beijing) Vous …

RÉVISION

If you need to review the forms of **être**, go to Appendix A, p. R5.

❷ DESCRIPTION describing people

♻ **Review** adjective agreement

Answers will vary.
- Anita est américaine. Elle est grande.
- Valérie est française. Elle est grande. Elle est blonde.
- Martin est français. Il n'est pas très grand. Il est de taille moyenne.
- Michiko est japonaise. Elle est petite. Elle a les cheveux noirs.
- Tatsuya est japonais. Il est grand. Il a les cheveux noirs.
- Brian est canadien. Il est blond. Il est grand.
- Danielle est canadienne. Elle est brune. Elle est petite.

❸ DESCRIPTION giving people's nationality

♻ **Review** present tense of **être**

1. Mario et Silvia sont italiens.
2. Madame Li est chinoise.
3. Nous sommes suisses.
4. Toi et José, vous êtes espagnols.
5. Tu es suisse.
6. Mes cousins sont espagnols.
7. Ma tante est anglaise.
8. Vous êtes chinois(e)(s).

Middle School Copymasters

Class Starters: Ten-second categories, p. T19, to practice descriptions; Game: Bingo, p. 9

PACING

The material of the **Rappel** sections is frequently re-entered in subsequent units. Try to move through these lessons as rapidly as possible.

Students may continue individualized review through homework assignments and pair/group work (peer teaching).

Teaching Resource Options

PRINT
Workbook PE, pp. R2–R4
Middle School Bridging Packet
Workbook TE, pp. R2–R4

AUDIO & VISUAL
Overhead Transparencies
8, S6, S16

4 **COMMUNICATION** expressing one's opinion about people

 Review position of adjectives

Answers will vary.
• Albert Einstein est un homme intelligent.
• Mon copain est un garçon timide.
• Le prof est une personne sympathique.
• Ma copine est une fille sportive.
• Matt Damon est un acteur sympathique.
• Oprah Winfrey est une femme intéressante.

Supplementary Vocabulary

la belle-mère *stepmother*
le beau-père *stepfather*
le demi-frère *stepbrother*
la demi-soeur *stepsister*
un poisson
un oiseau
une perruche
un perroquet
un lapin
un hamster
un cochon d'Inde

5 **DESCRIPTION** giving people's ages

 Review giving one's name and age

Answers will vary.
• —Comment s'appelle-t-il?
  —Il s'appelle Titi.
  —Quel âge a-t-il?
  —Il a dix mois.
• —Comment s'appelle-t-il?
  —Il s'appelle Monsieur Lecourbe.
  —Quel âge a-t-il?
  —Il a quatre-vingts ans.
• —Comment s'appelle-t-elle?
  —Elle s'appelle Zoé.
  —Quel âge a-t-elle?
  —Elle a dix ans.
• —Comment s'appelle-t-elle?
  —Elle s'appelle Madame Martin.
  —Quel âge a-t-elle?
  —Elle a trente-sept ans.
• —Comment s'appelle-t-il?
  —Il s'appelle Cédric.
  —Quel âge a-t-il?
  —Il a vingt-trois ans.

♻ **RAPPEL**
In French, adjectives usually come after the noun.
un garçon **sympathique**   une fille **sportive**

RÉVISION
If you want to review adjectives describing personality traits, go to Appendix A, p. R2.

4 *Opinion personnelle*

PARLER/ÉCRIRE Choose one of the following people and express your opinion about that person by using the suggested nouns and adjectives.

▶ **Whoopi Goldberg est une actrice amusante.**

mon copain	un garçon
ma copine	une fille
le/la prof	un homme
Matt Damon	une femme
Oprah Winfrey	une personne
Harrison Ford	un acteur
Whoopi Goldberg	une actrice
Britney Spears	
Albert Einstein	
Harry Potter	
??	

sportif?
timide?   mignon?
intelligent?
intéressant?
amusant?   sympathique?
bête?   gen-
méchant?

▶ *How to ask someone's name and age:*

Comment t'appelles-tu?	*What's your name?*	Je m'appelle Frédéric.
Je m'appelle ...	*My name is ...*	
Comment s'appelle ...?	*What's the name of ...*	**Comment s'appelle ta copine?**
[Comment s'appelle-t-il/elle?]	*What's his/her name?*	
Il/elle s'appelle ...	*His/her name is ...*	**Elle s'appelle Sophie.**
Quel âge as-tu?	*How old are you?*	
J'ai ... ans.	*I'm ... (years old).*	**J'ai seize ans.**
Quel âge a ...	*How old is ...?*	**Quel âge a ton frère?**
[Quel âge a-t-il/elle?]	*How old is he/she?*	
Il/elle a ... ans.	*He/she is ... (years old).*	**Il a quinze ans.**

5 *À votre avis* (In your opinion)

PARLER Point to the pictures and ask your partner the name and age of each person.

Titi   **Monsieur Lecourbe**   **Zoé**   **Madame Martin**   **Cédric**

RÉVISION
If you need to review numbers, go to Appendix A, p. R7.

TEACHING NOTE "Club d'anniversaires"

You may wish to set up a "Birthday Club" with the class singing to individual students on their birthdays. The French lyrics to the traditional melody are:

Joyeux anniversaire *(bis)*
Joyeux anniversaire *(tag on student's name)*
Joyeux anniversaire.

Quel âge as-tu? *(bis)*
Quel âge as-tu? *(tag on student's name)*
Quel âge as-tu?

Using this melody, the birthday students sings a response or answers verbally with **J'ai . . . ans.**
Note: Be sure to include students whose birthdays fall over vacation periods.

À votre tour!

1  **Auto-portrait**

ÉCRIRE Write a brief self-portrait in which you mention …

- your name
- your nationality
- your age
- 2 physical traits
- 2 personality traits that you have
- 1 personality trait that you do not have

2  **Les amis parfaits**

PARLER/ÉCRIRE Describe the perfect friends — one male and one female. List 5 traits for each friend, ranking them in order of importance. Compare your lists with those of your partner. Are you in agreement?

3 **Famille**

ÉCRIRE In a letter to your French penpal, describe your brothers and sisters (or cousins, if you prefer). You may also write about your pets.

- Say how many brothers and sisters (or cousins) you have.
- Write a short description of each one: age, physical and personality traits.
- Mention what pets you have (if any) and describe them.

4 **Situations**

PARLER Find a partner and imagine that the two of you are in the following situations Prepare and act out the conversations.

1. At a party organized by the International Students' Club, you meet a teenager who speaks French. Ask this new person …
- his/her name
- how old he/she is
- if he/she is French or Canadian

2. Your French friend is showing you photos of his/her family. You want to know more about his/her younger brother. Ask your friend …
- the name of his/her brother
- his/her age
- if he/she is nice

3. You are looking for people to form a basketball team. Your friend mentions his/her neighbor as a possible candidate. Ask your friend …
- how old his/her neighbor is
- if he/she is tall or short
- if he/she is athletic

4. During vacation, your cousin has met an interesting French teenager at the beach. Ask your cousin …
- the name of his/her friend
- if he/she is cute
- if he/she is an interesting boy/girl

LESSON REVIEW
CLASSZONE.COM

1 **COMMUNICATION** describing one's self

Answers will vary.
Je m'appelle (Claire). Je suis (américaine). J'ai (treize) ans. Je suis (brune) et (petite). Je suis (sportive) et (gentille). Je ne suis pas (timide).

2 **COMMUNICATION** expressing one's opinion

Answers will vary.
L'ami idéal est …
- gentil
- amusant
- intéressant
- sportif
- intelligent

L'amie idéal est …
- sympathique
- amusante
- intelligente
- intéressante
- sportive

3 **COMMUNICATION** describing one's family

Answers will vary.
Chère Anne,
   J'ai (un frère). Il s'appelle (Mark). Il a (dix) ans. Il est (petit) et (blond). Il est (timide) et (bête)!
   J'ai (une soeur). Elle s'appelle (Christine). Elle a (seize) ans. Elle est (grande) et (brune). Elle est (intelligente) et (sportive).
   Ton amie,
   Julie

4 **EXCHANGES** talking about people

Answers will vary.
1. • Comment t'appelles-tu?
   • Quel âge as-tu?
   • Tu es français(e) ou canadien(ne)?
2. • Comment s'appelle ton frère?
   • Quel âge a-t-il?
   • Est-ce qu'il est sympathique?
3. • Quel âge a ton voisin (ta voisine)?
   • Il (elle) est grand(e) ou petit(e)?
   • Est-ce qu'il (elle) est sportif (sportive)?
4. • Comment s'appelle ton copain (ta copine)?
   • Est-ce qu'il (elle) est mignon(ne)?
   • Est-ce que c'est un garçon intéressant (une fille intéressante)?

À VOTRE TOUR

The communicative activities in this section give students the opportunity to express themselves orally and in writing.

Select those activities which are most appropriate for your students. You may or may not wish to do them all.

Rappel 2

Communicative Functions
- Naming one's possessions
- Describing objects

Teaching Resource Options

PRINT
Workbook PE, pp. R4–R6
Middle School Bridging Packet
  Workbook TE, pp. R4–R6

AUDIO & VISUAL
Overhead Transparencies
20, 21, 22, S12, S2

1 **EXCHANGES** talking about one's possessions

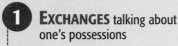 **Review** use of the indefinite article; names of objects, colors

Answers will vary.
- —Tu as une bicyclette?
  —Oui, j'ai une bicyclette. Elle est rouge. Elle marche bien. (Non, je n'ai pas de bicyclette.)
- —Tu as des affiches?
  —Oui, j'ai des affiches. Elles sont grandes. Elles sont jolies. (Non, je n'ai pas d'affiches.)
- —Tu as une montre?
  —Oui, j'ai une montre. Elle est italienne. Elle est verte et rouge. (Non, je n'ai pas de montre.)
- —Tu as des CD?
  —Oui, j'ai beaucoup de CD. (Non, je n'ai pas de CD.)
- —Tu as un sac?
  —Oui, j'ai un sac. Il est grand et vert. (Non, je n'ai pas de sac.)
- —Tu as une moto?
  —Oui, j'ai une moto. Elle est japonaise. Elle est verte. (Non, je n'ai pas de moto.)

RAPPEL 2

Les choses de la vie courante

NOUS N'AVONS PAS DE VOITURE....   ..MAIS NOUS AVONS UN VÉLO!

♻ RAPPEL

In French, objects are MASCULINE or FEMININE.
They are introduced by **un, une** in the singular, or **des** in the plural.
un vélo **une** voiture **des** livres

> **RÉVISION**
> If you need to review the names of common objects, go to Appendix A, p. R3.

♻ RAPPEL

In NEGATIVE sentences, **un, une, des** —> **de (d')**
J'ai **un** vélo. Je n'ai **pas de** moto. Je n'ai **pas d'**auto.

> **RÉVISION**
> If you need to review colors, go to Appendix A, p. R4.

1 👥 Mes possessions

PARLER Ask if your partner has the following objects. (If the answer is yes, your partner may want to describe the object: its color, size, or other characteristics.)

▶ — Tu as un appareil-photo?
  — Oui, j'ai un appareil-photo. Il est noir.
    Il est japonais. Il marche assez bien.
    (Non, je n'ai pas d'appareil-photo.)

▶

TEACHING NOTE

As a warm-up activity, review the names of the items pictured in Activity 1.

a) Listening comprehension: As you name items, have students point to the corresponding pictures in their books. **Montrez-moi un appareil-photo.**

b) Speaking practice: Have the students identify each object:

Qu'est-ce que c'est?	**Ce sont des CD.**
C'est un appareil-photo.	**C'est un sac.**
C'est un vélo.	**Ce sont des affiches.**
C'est une moto.	
C'est une montre.	

2 Qu'est-ce qu'ils ont?

LIRE Read what the people below are doing, and say which objects they have. Be logical!

▶ Pauline fait un problème de maths.
   Elle a une calculatrice.

1. Nous jouons au tennis.
2. Vous écoutez des CD.
3. Philippe écrit *(is writing)* une lettre à une copine.
4. Mes parents font un voyage au Canada.
5. J'étudie la leçon.
6. Tu regardes une comédie.

RÉVISION

If you need to review the forms of **avoir**, go to Appendix A, p. R6.

Quel objet?

▶ **How to ask or say where things are:**

Qu'est-ce qu'il y a …?	*What is there …?*	Qu'est-ce qu'il y a dans le garage?
Il y a …		Il y a une voiture.
Il n'y a pas …		Il n'y a pas de vélos.
Est-ce qu'il y a …?		Est-ce qu'il y a une mobylette?

3 Qu'est-ce qu'il y a …?

PARLER/ÉCRIRE Identify at least four objects in each of the following illustrations.

Sur le bureau, il y a …

Sur la table, …

Dans la chambre, …

Dans le sac, …

treize
Rappel 2   13

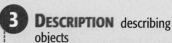

2 COMPREHENSION describing possessions

♻ **Review** present tense of **avoir**

1. Nous avons une raquette.
2. Vous avez une chaîne hi-fi.
3. Il a un stylo.
4. Ils ont une auto (voiture).
5. J'ai un livre.
6. Tu as une télé.

3 DESCRIPTION describing objects

♻ **Review** use of **il y a**

Answers will vary.
- Sur le bureau, il y a un ordinateur, un stylo, des crayons, des livres et un téléphone.
- Sur la table, il y a des CD, une radiocassette/CD, une montre, des crayons et une raquette.
- Dans la chambre, il y a un lit, un bureau, une table, des chaises, des affiches, une télé, une chaîne hi-fi et des CD.
- Dans le sac, il y a un baladeur, des livres, une calculatrice et un appareil-photo.

Variation Make statements about the pictures, which the students can confirm as being either true or false.

- —Sur le bureau, il y a un téléphone.
  —Oui, il y a un téléphone.
  —Sur le bureau, il y a un appareil-photo.
  —Non, il n'y a pas d'appareil-photo.

Teaching Resource Options

PRINT

Workbook PE, pp. R4–R6
Middle School Bridging Packet
Workbook TE, pp. R4–R6

 4 **EXCHANGES** talking about where things are located

♻ **Review** prepositions of place

- –Dis, Stéphanie, tu sais où est ma télé?
  –Ta télé? Elle est sous le bureau.
- –Dis, Stéphanie, tu sais où est ma guitare?
  –Ta guitare? Elle est derrière le lit.
- –Dis, Stéphanie, tu sais où est mon stylo?
  –Ton stylo? Il est sur le bureau.
- –Dis, Stéphanie, tu sais où est ma bicyclette?
  –Ta bicyclette? Elle est derrière la porte.
- –Dis, Stéphanie, tu sais où est ma radiocassette?
  –Ta radiocassette? Elle est devant le lit.
- –Dis, Stéphanie, tu sais où est ma raquette?
  –Ta raquette? Elle est dans le sac.
- –Dis, Stéphanie, tu sais où est mon appareil-photo?
  –Ton appareil-photo? Il est derrière la chaise.
- –Dis, Stéphanie, tu sais où est mon chien?
  –Ton chien? Il est sous la chaise.
- –Dis, Stéphanie, tu sais où est ma montre?
  –Ta montre? Elle est sur le bureau.
- –Dis, Stéphanie, tu sais où est mon chat?
  –Ton chat? Il est sur le lit.
- –Dis, Stéphanie, tu sais où est mon livre?
  –Ton livre? Il est sous le lit.

How to say where things are located:

dans — sur — devant — sous — derrière

4 **La chambre d'Éric**

PARLER Éric is not too orderly. Whenever he is looking for something, it is his sister Stéphanie who tells him where it is. With a partner, choose an object in the room and play the roles of Éric and Stéphanie.

ÉRIC: **Dis, Stéphanie, tu sais où est ma raquette?**
STÉPHANIE: **Ta raquette? Elle est dans le sac.**

À votre tour!

1 Joyeux anniversaire
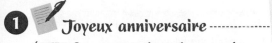

ÉCRIRE On a separate sheet of paper, make a wish list of six different things you would like to have for your birthday, ranking them in order of importance. Compare your list with that of a partner.

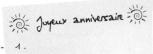

2 Ma chambre

ÉCRIRE Write a letter to a French penpal describing your room. You may want to mention …

- the size and color of your room
- the various items of furniture
- various objects that you have in your room and where they are located

3 Situations

PARLER Imagine that you and your partner are in the following situations. Prepare and act out the conversations.

1. You are spending two weeks in France with a host family. A classmate has invited you to play tennis, but you don't have a racket. Ask Pierre, your "French brother," …

- if he has a racket
- if it is a good racket
- where the racket is (in his room? on his bed?)

2. You are with a host family in France and would like to listen to some CDs you have just bought. Ask Sylvie, your "French sister," …

- if she has a boombox
- if it is French or Japanese
- if it works well

LESSON REVIEW
CLASSZONE.COM

quinze **15**
Rappel 2

À VOTRE TOUR

Main Topic
- Recapitulation and review

1 COMMUNICATION listing preferences

Answers will vary.
Je voudrais avoir…
1. un ordinateur
2. un vélo
3. une chaîne hi-fi
4. un appareil-photo
5. des affiches
6. des CD

Teaching note This activity can be used as the basis of a class survey.

---

2 COMMUNICATION describing one's room

Answers will vary.
Cher Marc,
    Ma chambre est petite et bleue. Dans ma chambre, il y a un lit, un bureau et deux chaises. Il y a des livres, des CD et un ordinateur sur mon bureau. Il y a une guitare et une raquette sous le lit.
    Ton ami,
        Christophe

 Review furniture

---

3 EXCHANGES talking about possessions

Answers will vary.
1. —Tu as une raquette?
   —Oui, j'ai une raquette.
   —C'est une bonne raquette?
   —Oui, c'est une bonne raquette.
   —Où est-ce qu'elle est?
   —Elle est dans ma chambre, sur mon lit.
2. —Est-ce que tu as une radiocassette?
   —Oui, j'ai une radiocassette.
   —Elle est française ou japonaise?
   —Elle est japonaise.
   —Est-ce qu'elle marche bien?
   —Oui, elle marche très bien.

Middle School Copymasters

Game: Play Ball, pp. T4–T5;
Worksheet 1: *Où?*, p.37

À VOTRE TOUR

Activities 2 and 3 may be used for student portfolios.

Activities 1 and 2 provide an opportunity for personalization.

Activity 3 is excellent for pair/group work.

French penpal exchanges should be set up early in the school year.

Use Activities 2 and 3 as the basis for cross-cultural discussion.

À votre tour! **• 15**
Reprise RAPPEL 2

Rappel 3

Communicative Functions

- Describing daily and leisure activities
- Describing likes, dislikes, wishes, and obligations
- Asking questions
- Inviting friends; accepting or refusing an invitation

Teaching Resource Options

PRINT

Workbook PE, pp. R6–R8
Middle School Bridging Packet
   Workbook TE, pp. R6–R8

AUDIO & VISUAL

Overhead Transparencies
14a, 14b, 15, 18, S9, S10, S14

---

1 **DESCRIPTION** describing what people are doing

 Review present tense of **-er** verbs

1. Ils habitent à Paris.
2. Ils dînent au restaurant.
3. Ils mangent un steak-frites.
4. Elle étudie l'anglais.
5. Elle n'écoute pas son baladeur. Elle écoute la radio.
6. Non, elle ne regarde pas la télé.
7. Ils ne font pas de match de volley. Ils font un match de tennis.
8. Elle joue bien.
9. Non, il ne fait pas attention.

RAPPEL

3 Les activités

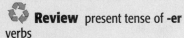 **RAPPEL**

To describe what people do, we use VERBS.

- Many French verbs end in **-er**.
- **Faire** *(to do, to make)* is an important verb to know.

RÉVISION

If you need to review …
- the common **-er** verbs and their forms, go to Appendix A, pp. R5-R6.
- the forms of **faire**, go to Appendix A, p. R5.

1 *Qu'est-ce qu'ils font?* PARLER

1. Est-ce qu'ils habitent à Paris ou à Québec?
2. Est-ce qu'ils dînent à la maison ou au restaurant?
3. Est-ce qu'ils mangent un steak-frites ou une omelette?

4. Est-ce que Catherine étudie l'anglais ou l'espagnol?
5. Est-ce qu'elle écoute la radio ou un baladeur?
6. Est-ce qu'elle regarde la télé?

7. Est-ce qu'ils font un match de volley ou un match de tennis?
8. Est-ce que la fille joue bien ou mal?
9. Est-ce que le garçon fait attention?

16 seize
Reprise

GAME Charades

Materials: 12 index cards for each group

Procedure: Divide the students into groups of three or four. Give each group 12 cards. Referring to **Quelques activités** on page R6, students write a different activity on each card (e.g., **jouer au basket**). Then they shuffle the cards and deal them out, face down. At a given signal, students take turns miming the activities as the other students guess (**Tu joues au basket/nages?** etc.). The first group to go through the stack of cards is the winner.

♻ RAPPEL

The most common way to ask a YES/NO QUESTION is to begin the sentence with **est-ce que.**

Est-ce que tu joues au foot?

♻ RAPPEL

To make a sentence NEGATIVE, use the following pattern:

ne + VERB + **pas**	Je **ne** parle **pas** chinois.	Vous **ne** travaillez **pas.**
↓ **n'** (+ VOWEL SOUND)	Je **n'**habite **pas** en France.	Nous **n'**étudions **pas.**

② 👥 Conversation

PARLER Ask your partner if he/she does the following activities. If your partner answers yes, ask a second question using the expression in parentheses.

▶ —**Est-ce que tu joues au tennis?**
—**Oui, je joue au tennis!**
—**Est-ce que tu joues bien?**
—**Non, je ne joue pas bien.**

(bien?)	(souvent?)	(bien?)	(beaucoup?)
(souvent?)	(très bien?)	(souvent?)	(beaucoup?)

③ Oui ou non?

PARLER Say whether or not the people below are engaged in the following activities.

1. À la maison, je ...
   • étudier beaucoup?
   • téléphoner souvent?
   • regarder la télé?

2. En classe, **nous ...**
   • parler toujours français?
   • écouter le prof?
   • faire attention?

3. Le week-end, mes copains et moi, **nous ...**
   • travailler?
   • faire des promenades en ville?
   • organiser des boums?

4. **Mon copain/ma copine ...**
   • parler français?
   • étudier l'espagnol?
   • jouer au basket?

5. Quand je suis en vacances, **je ...**
   • travailler?
   • nager souvent?
   • voyager?

6. En général, **les jeunes Américains ...**
   • étudier beaucoup?
   • aimer la musique classique?
   • faire beaucoup de sport?

Language Notes

• In conversational French, speakers often convert a statement to a question by omitting **est-ce que** and using rising intonation:
Tu joues au foot. Tu joues au foot?

• In casual speech, the **ne (n')** of the negative expression is often omitted:
Je parle pas chinois.

② EXCHANGES talking about one's activities

♻ **Review** asking and answering yes/no questions

Answers will vary.
• —Oui (non), je (ne) joue (pas) au foot./—Oui (non), je (ne) joue (pas) souvent.
• —Oui (non), je (ne) chante (pas)./—Oui (non), je (ne) chante (pas) bien.
• —Oui (non), je (ne) téléphone (pas)./—Oui (non), je (ne) téléphone (pas) beaucoup.
• —Oui (non), je (ne) voyage (pas) en avion.
• —Oui (non), je (ne) nage (pas).
—Oui (non), je (ne) nage (pas) très bien.
• —Oui (non), je (ne) dîne (pas) au restaurant./—Oui (non), je (ne) dîne (pas) souvent au restaurant.
• —Oui (non), je (ne) regarde (pas) la télé.
—Oui (non), je (ne) regarde (pas) beaucoup la télé.

③ COMMUNICATION describing one's actions and the actions of others

♻ **Review** affirmative and negative of **-er** verbs

Answers will vary.
1. À la maison, je (n')étudie (pas) beaucoup. Je (ne) téléphone (pas) souvent.
2. En classe, nous (ne) parlons (pas) français. Nous (n')écoutons (pas) le prof.
3. Le week-end, mes copains et moi nous (ne) travaillons (pas). Nous (ne) faisons (pas de) des promenades en ville.
4. Mon copain (ne) parle (pas) français. Il (n')étudie (pas) l'espagnol.
5. Quand je (ne) suis (pas) en vacances, je (ne) travaille (pas). Je (ne) nage (pas) souvent.
6. En général, les jeunes Américains (n')étudient (pas) beaucoup. Ils (n')aiment (pas) la musique classique. Ils (ne) font (pas) beaucoup de sport.

CHALLENGE ACTIVITY

Have students give original affirmative or negative completions to each item in Activity 3.

À la maison, j'écoute la radio. En classe, nous ne parlons pas anglais.

Teaching Resource Options

PRINT

Workbook PE, pp. R6–R8
Middle School Bridging Packet
  Workbook TE, pp. R6–R8

Language note In familiar language, French speakers often end with the question word:
Tu habites où?

In very casual speech, they may use the standard construction, omitting **est-ce que:**
Où tu habites?

---

4 **EXCHANGES** finding out information about classmates

 Review information questions

Teaching note If necessary, help students formulate their answers in French.

- Où est-ce que tu habites?
- À quelle heure est-ce que tu dînes?
- Quand est-ce que tu regardes la télé?
- À qui est-ce que tu téléphones souvent?
- Comment est-ce que tu chantes?
- Avec qui est-ce que tu parles français?
- Pourquoi est-ce que tu étudies le français?
- Avec qui est-ce que tu dînes au restaurant?
- Où est-ce que tu joues au basket?
- Où est-ce que tu nages en été?

♻ **RAPPEL**

To ask for SPECIFIC INFORMATION, you can use the following construction:

QUESTION WORD + **est-ce que** + rest of sentence
Où est-ce que tu habites? *Where do you live?*

▶ *How to ask for information:*

où?	*where?*	**Où est-ce que** ton copain habite?
quand?	*when?*	**Quand est-ce que** vous voyagez?
comment?	*how? how well?*	**Comment est-ce que** vous jouez au foot? bien ou mal?
pourquoi?	*why?*	**Pourquoi est-ce que** tu étudies le français?
à quelle heure?	*at what time?*	**À quelle heure est-ce que** nous dînons?
qui?	*whom?*	**Qui est-ce que** tu invites à la boum?
à qui?	*to whom?*	**À qui est-ce que** Pauline téléphone?
avec qui?	*with whom?*	**Avec qui est-ce que** vous jouez aux jeux vidéo?

➜ to ask WHAT people are doing, use the construction:

    qu'est-ce que + rest of sentence   **Qu'est-ce que** tu fais demain?

➜ To ask WHO is doing something, use the construction:

    qui + verb   **Qui** habite ici?

4 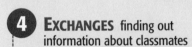 **Faisons connaissance** *(Let's get to know each other)*

PARLER Find out more about your classmates by asking them a few questions. Use the suggested cues.

- où? / habiter
- à quelle heure? / dîner
- quand? / regarder la télé
- à qui? / téléphoner souvent
- comment? / chanter

- avec qui? / parler français
- pourquoi? / étudier le français
- avec qui? / dîner au restaurant
- où? / jouer au basket
- où ? / nager en été

LANGUAGE NOTE Interrogative expressions

Remind students that, contrary to English, interrogative expressions in French can never be separated, even in casual speech.

Who(m) are you talking to? **À qui** est-ce que tu parles?

Tu parles **à qui?** *(casual speech)*

▶ *How to express what you like, want, can and must do:*

Est-ce que tu aimes ...?
   J'aime ...   *I like ...*
   Je n'aime pas ...
   Je préfère ...

Est-ce que tu peux ...?
   Je peux ...   *I can, I am able to ...*
   Je ne peux pas ...

Est-ce que tu veux ...?
   Je veux ...   *I want ...*
   Je ne veux pas ...
   Je voudrais ...   *I would like ...*

Est-ce que tu dois ...?
   Je dois ...   *I have to, I must ...*

   Je ne dois pas ...

→ Note the use of **je veux bien** to answer an invitation.

—Est-ce que tu veux faire une promenade avec moi?

—Oui, **je veux bien.**

---

5 **Et toi?**

PARLER/ÉCRIRE Create original sentences, completing them with an expression of your choice.

En général,	j'aime ...
À la maison,	je n'aime pas ...
En classe,	je préfère ...
Quand je suis avec mes amis,	je peux ...
Quand je suis en vacances,	je ne peux pas ...
	je dois ...

---

6  **Invitations**

PARLER Invite your partner to do one of the following activities with you. If your partner accepts, he/she may ask for more details (**où? quand? à quelle heure?**). If he/she does not accept, ask why and your partner will give you an excuse.

▶ —Est-ce que tu veux jouer au tennis avec moi?
   —Oui, je veux bien! Quand?
   —Samedi après-midi.

   [Non, je ne peux pas.
   —Pourquoi?
   —Je dois étudier.]

INVITATIONS
- jouer au foot
- jouer au basket
- dîner en ville
- faire une promenade
- regarder la télé
- écouter des CD
- organiser une boum
- ??

EXCUSES
- étudier
- travailler
- téléphoner à mon cousin
- aider *(to help)* ma mère
- aider mon petit frère
- ??

---

5 **COMMUNICATION** expressing one's preferences, abilities and obligations

 Review infinitive constructions

Answers will vary.
- En général, j'aime écouter des CD.
- À la maison, je peux regarder la télé.
- En classe, je dois faire attention.
- Quand je suis avec mes amis, je peux organiser des boums.
- Quand je suis en vacances, je préfère voyager.

6 **EXCHANGES** offering, accepting and declining invitations

Review yes/no questions and infinitive constructions

Answers will vary.
- —Est-ce que tu veux dîner en ville avec moi?
  —Oui, je veux bien! À quelle heure?
  —À huit heures.
- —Est-ce que tu veux faire une promenade avec moi?
  —Non, je ne peux pas.
  —Pourquoi?
  —Je dois aider ma mère.
- —Est-ce que tu veux regarder la télé avec moi?
  —Non, je ne peux pas.
  —Pourquoi?
  —Je dois étudier.
- —Est-ce que tu veux écouter des CD avec moi?
  —Oui, je veux bien! Où?
  —Dans ma chambre.
- —Est-ce que tu veux organiser une fête avec moi?
  —Oui, je veux bien! Quand?
  —Samedi soir.

À votre tour!

1  Vive la différence!

ÉCRIRE On a sheet of paper, write in order of preference the five activities you like best. (Mention only those you can name in French). Also write two activities that you do not like to do. Get together with a partner and compare your lists.

• What are the activities that you both like?
• What are the activities that neither of you like?

2  Correspondance

ÉCRIRE Write an e-mail to your new French penpal Véronique.

In your e-mail, mention ...

• your name
• where you live
• what language(s) you study
• if you speak them well
• what things you like to do at home
• what sports you play
• what other things you like to do

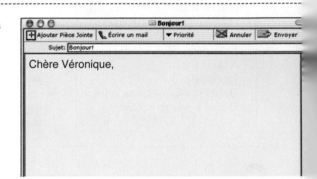

3  Week-end

ÉCRIRE Make a list of three activities that you would like to do this weekend, and ask your partner if he/she likes these activities.

When you have found an activity you both like, ask your partner if he/she would like to join you in that activity.

Determine the place **(où?),** the date **(quand?)** and the time **(à quelle heure?).**

 LESSON REVIEW
CLASSZONE.COM

MIDDLE SCHOOL COPYMASTERS

Use the suggested activities, puzzles, games, and projects to vary the review process. Pair and group work are particularly well-suited to the situational activities in **À votre tour!**

À votre tour!

4 **Situations** --

PARLER Imagine that you and your partner are in the following situations. Prepare and act out the conversations below.

You meet a Canadian teenager on the bus.

Ask him/her …
- where he/she lives
- if he/she prefers to speak English or French
- if he/she travels a lot

You meet a French teenager at the beach.

Ask your new friend …
- if he/she likes to swim
- if he/she wants to play soccer
- what he/she wants to do after that **(après)**

Your partner has invited two French friends, Philippe and Olivier, to a party. You are going to the same party.

Ask your partner …
- if Philippe and Olivier speak English
- if they like to dance
- what they like to do

Your friend has a cousin named Valérie who is French. You want to know more about Valérie.

Ask your friend …
- where his/her cousin lives
- if she studies English in class
- how well she speaks English

It is Saturday afternoon. You and your French friend have decided to have dinner downtown.

Ask your friend …
- at what time he/she wants to have dinner
- where he/she wants to have dinner
- what he/she wants to eat

You are at a summer tennis camp. There you have met a young Haitian who speaks French.

Ask your Haitian friend …
- if he/she has a tennis racket
- how well he/she plays tennis
- if he/she wants to play a game with you
- at what time?

You are in a café in Paris with a friend.

Ask your friend …
- what he/she wants to eat
- what he/she wants to drink **(boire)**
- if he/she wants to go for a walk afterwards **(après)**

LESSON REVIEW
CLASSZONE.COM

PORTFOLIO ASSESSMENT

À votre tour! activities may be used for student portfolios or as a class portfolio or video for presentation to parents.

---

3 **EXCHANGES** making arrangements for leisure activities

Answers will vary.
Activités
1. organiser une boum
2. jouer aux jeux vidéo
3. écouter des CD

– Est-ce que tu aimes jouer aux jeux vidéo?
– Oui, j'aime jouer aux jeux vidéo.
– Est-ce que tu veux jouer aux jeux vidéo avec moi?
– Oui, bien sûr! Où?
– Chez moi.
– Quand?
– Samedi après-midi.
– À quelle heure?
– À trois heures.

Teaching note Encourage student creativity by providing appropriate vocabulary and expressions.

---

4 **EXCHANGES** finding out about others and their preferences

Answers may vary. Sample questions and answers may include:
- –Où est-ce que tu habites?
  –J'habite à Québec.
  –Est-ce que tu préfères parler français ou anglais?
  –Je préfère parler français.
  –Est-ce que tu voyages beaucoup?
  –Non, je ne voyage pas beaucoup.

Questions may include:
- À quelle heure est-ce que tu veux dîner?
- Où est-ce que tu veux dîner?
- Qu'est-ce que tu veux manger?
- Est-ce que tu aimes nager?
- Est-ce que tu veux jouer au foot?
- Qu'est-ce que tu veux faire après?
- Est-ce que tu as une raquette?
- Est-ce que tu joues bien au tennis?
- Est-ce que tu veux faire un match avec moi?
- À quelle heure?
- Est-ce que Philippe et Olivier parlent anglais?
- Est-ce qu'ils aiment danser?
- Qu'est-ce qu'ils aiment faire?
- Qu'est-ce que tu veux manger?
- Qu'est-ce que tu veux boire?
- Est-ce que tu veux faire une promenade après?
- Où est-ce que ta cousine habite?
- Est-ce qu'elle étudie l'anglais?
- Est-ce qu'elle parle bien anglais?

Rappel 4

Communicative Functions

- Counting from 0 to 100
- Telling time
- Giving the date
- Talking about the weather
- Ordering in a café

Teaching Resource Options

PRINT

Workbook PE, pp. R8–R9
Middle School Bridging Packet
 Workbook TE, pp. R8–R9

Teaching note: Numbers

Students should be able to understand and use numbers orally. At this level, they do not need to write out and spell numbers beyond 20. The French, like the Americans, generally use digits to write the higher numbers.

1 **COUNTING**

 Review numbers from 0 to 100

Culture Note The Ariane rockets are launched from Kourou in French Guiana. Have students locate the approximate launch site on a map of South America.

2 **COMPREHENSION**
understanding spoken numbers

 Review numbers from 0 to 100

Teacher Script Read out the following numbers. Those marked with an asterisk [*] are on the Loto card in the student text.

3* 96 13 42* 84* 75 32 95*
11 56* 72 41 50* 78* 16* 99
53 75 7* 49* 68 12* 25 91
90* 18* 19 61* 37 89* 27*
15 97* 36* 65* 57 28* 71*

Expressions de tous les jours

1 **Ariane**

PARLER Ariane is the French rocket that launches European space satellites. With your partners, start the countdown for liftoff. You may start from 100, or any other number of your choice. You may stop the countdown when you wish.

quatre
trois
deux
un
zéro

RÉVISION

If you need to review numbers from 0 to 100, go to Appendix A, p. R7.

2 **Loto**

ÉCOUTER Your teacher will call out certain numbers. Raise your hand when you hear a number on your card.

3	12		36		50	61	71		90
7	16	27		42		65		84	95
	18	28		49	56		78	89	97

3 **Dis-moi ...** **PARLER**

1. Quelle heure est-il?
2. À quelle heure finit la classe de français?
3. À quelle heure est-ce que tu dînes en général?
4. Quelle heure est-il maintenant à Paris? et à Québec?
5. Quel jour est-ce aujourd'hui? et demain?
6. Quel est ton jour préféré?
7. Quel est ton mois préféré?
8. Quelle est la date d'aujourd'hui?
9. Quand est-ce, ton anniversaire?

RÉVISION

If you need to review time, dates and the days of the week, go to Appendix A, pp. R7-R8.

4 **Joyeux anniversaire!**

PARLER Ask 5 different classmates when their birthdays are and find out who has a birthday closest to your own.

CULTURE NOTE

Depending on your time zone, you can calculate the time in Paris and Quebec as follows:

	PACIFIC	MOUNTAIN	CENTRAL	EASTERN
PARIS	+ 9 hours	+ 8 hours	+ 7 hours	+ 6 hours
QUEBEC	+ 3 hours	+ 2 hours	+ 1 hour	(no change)

5 Quel temps fait-il?

PARLER/ÉCRIRE You are the weather reporter at a French TV station. Give the weather for each of the following French-speaking cities.

 Québec Genève Fort-de-France Paris Nice Tours

6 Les quatre saisons

ÉCRIRE Write a note to your French penpal describing the weather in your region for each season of the year.

RÉVISION
If you need to review weather and seasons, go to Appendix A, p. R8.

To order in a café:

— Vous désirez, monsieur, mademoiselle?
— Je voudrais un jus de pomme. une crêpe.

— Ça fait combien?
C'est combien?
— C'est 9 euros.

RÉVISION
If you need to review names of foods and beverages, go to Appendix A, p. R4.

7 Au Rallye

PARLER You are at a French café called **Le Rallye**. The server (your partner) is taking your order. Order something to drink and something to eat from the menu. Then ask the server for the bill.

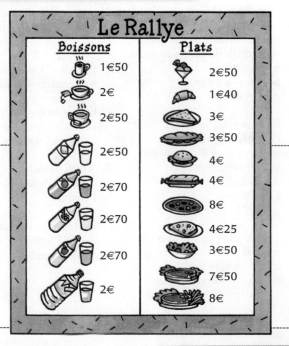

Le Rallye — Boissons / Plats

Boissons: 1€50, 2€, 2€50, 2€50, 2€70, 2€70, 2€70, 2€
Plats: 2€50, 1€40, 3€, 3€50, 4€, 4€, 8€, 4€25, 3€50, 7€50, 8€

vingt-trois **Rappel 4** 23

3 COMMUNICATION answering questions

Review time, days of the week, dates, seasons

Answers will vary.
1. Il est (onze) heures.
2. La classe de français finit à (midi).
3. En général, je dîne à (six) heures.
4. À Paris, il est (cinq) heures. À Québec, il est (onze) heures.
5. Aujourd'hui, c'est (vendredi). Demain, c'est (samedi).
6. Mon jour préféré est (samedi).
7. Mon mois préféré est (juillet).
8. C'est le (15 septembre).
9. Mon anniversaire est (le 15 juin).

4 EXCHANGES talking about birthdays

Review dates

Answers will vary.
– Quand est-ce, ton anniversaire?
– C'est le (31 juillet).

5 DESCRIPTION describing the weather

Review weather expressions

- À Québec, il neige.
- À Genève, il fait très froid.
- À Fort-de-France, il fait beau (du soleil).
- À Paris, il pleut.
- À Nice, il fait bon.
- À Tours, il fait mauvais. (Il fait du vent. Il y a du tonnerre. Il y a un orage).

6 COMMUNICATION describing weather conditions

Review weather expressions

Answers will vary.
Cher Pierre,
À Boston, en hiver il fait froid et il neige. Au printemps, il fait frais et il pleut. En été, il fait très chaud. En automne, il fait beau.
Ton ami,
Jason

7 EXCHANGES ordering in a café

Review names of foods and beverages

Answers will vary.
- —Vous désirez, monsieur?
—Je voudrais un steak-frites et une eau minérale, s'il vous plaît. Ça fait combien?
—Ça fait onze euros.
- —Vous désirez, mademoiselle?
—Je voudrais un hot dog et une limonade, s'il vous plaît. C'est combien?
—C'est six euros cinquante.

GAME Quel temps fait-il?

Materials: a colored marker (or another small object)
Procedure: One student (S1) leaves the room and the other students decide where to hide the marker (e.g., on the teacher's chair). S1 returns, stands firmly in one place and asks **Quel temps fait-il?** Depending upon his/her distance from the marker, students respond with **Il fait très froid/froid/frais/chaud/très chaud.** S1 continues changing places and asking the question until the class answers **Il fait très chaud!** Upon finding the hidden marker, S1 must say where it is located—**Le feutre est sur la chaise.** The game continues with another student leaving the room, and so on.

Teaching Resource Options

PRINT

Workbook PE, pp. R10–R11
Middle School Bridging Packet
  Workbook TE, pp. R10–R11

Cross-Cultural Understanding

Awareness and discovery of:

• aspects of French daily life (items 1–9)

• the French-speaking world (items 10–15)

• French-American relations (items 16–25)

Teaching notes

• Most of the information presented in this section will be expanded upon throughout *Discovering French, Nouveau!–Bleu, Blanc, Rouge.* Depending on the course syllabus and student interest, this section can be covered or omitted.

• Personalization of cultural and linguistic information is particularly effective for motivating students at the middle level. Interviews with local French speakers in the community, individual research into local "French-American connections," personal family histories or travel, even a visit to a French restaurant or renting a French film can bring the concept of the close ties between France and the United States alive.

Language Learning Benchmarks

FUNCTION

• Engage in conversations p. 17
• Express likes and dislikes p. 19
• Obtain information pp. 11, 18
• Begin to provide information p. 12

CONTEXT

• Converse in face-to-face social interactions pp. 12, 17, 19
• Listen to audio and video texts pp. 4–5
• Use authentic materials when reading: menus p. 23
• Write lists p. 11
• Write short letters p. 5

Le savez-vous?

What do you know about France and the French-speaking world? Maybe more than you think! Read the following questions and try to answer them, guessing when necessary. How many questions did you answer correctly? (The answers are at the end of the self-test.)

1. If you were in France, where would you go to buy **croissants?**
   a. a bakery
   b. a dairy shop
   c. a vegetable stand

2. Which of the following popular cheeses is *not* of French origin?
   a. brie
   b. camembert
   c. parmesan

3. In an American supermarket you can often find bottles labeled **Évian** and **Perrier.** What do these bottles contain?
   a. fruit juice
   b. mineral water
   c. soft drinks

4. If you wanted to rent a French car while visiting Europe, which of the following would you choose?
   a. an Audi
   b. a Renault
   c. an Alfa-Roméo

5. For the Parisians, what is the **métro?**
   a. an art museum
   b. a large soccer stadium
   c. the local subway system

6. The **Tour de France** is the most-watched sporting event in France. What is it?
   a. a soccer championship
   b. a tennis tournament
   c. a bicycle race

7. France is considered a pioneer in transportation technology. What is **le Concorde?**
   a. a high-speed train
   b. a supersonic passenger plane
   c. an automated subway system

8. The **Eurotunnel** is a 30-mile tunnel beneath the sea. Which countries does it connect?
   a. France and Spain
   b. France and England
   c. France and Germany

9. What is a "francophone"?
   a. a person who enjoys French cuisine
   b. a person who likes France
   c. a person who speaks French natively

10. Which French-speaking region is known as **la Belle Province?**
    a. Normandy (in France)
    b. Touraine (in France)
    c. the Province of Quebec (in Canada)

11. If you were going to Africa, in which of the following countries would you be able to use your French?
    a. Senegal
    b. Kenya
    c. South Africa

12. Which of the following Caribbean islands are part of France?
    a. Jamaica and Bermuda
    b. Martinique and Guadeloupe
    c. Aruba and Bonaire

13. Jacques-Yves Cousteau was a famous French scientist. If you were to become a member of the **Société Cousteau**, which cause would you promote?
    a. the anti-smoking campaign
    b. the protection of the oceans
    c. the anti-nuclear movement

14. Claude Monet (1840-1926) is one of the best-known French painters. With which artistic movement is he associated?
    a. Cubism
    b. Impressionism
    c. Surrealism

15. Since its inception, the Nobel Prize has been awarded to many French citizens. In which of the following categories do the French have the highest percentage of winners?
    a. physics
    b. literature
    c. medicine

CLASSROOM MANAGEMENT Groups

Have students work in pairs or groups of three to select answers to the above questions. Then have the groups exchange papers. Go over the responses to all the items. Which group had the most correct answers?

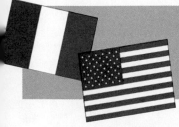

Les relations franco-américaines

Ever since the French came to help the American patriots during the American Revolution (1775-1783), France and the United States have maintained a strong friendship. What do you know about this "French-American connection"?

16. Which of the following American cities is named after a French king?
a. Saint Louis
b. Georgetown
c. Williamsburg

17. Which American state was formerly a French territory?
a. Virginia
b. Florida
c. Louisiana

18. LaFayette is a hero to both the French and the Americans. In which aspect of United States history did he play an important role?
a. the American Revolution
b. the Civil War
c. the exploration of the West

19. Which famous American statesman was ambassador to France?
a. Benjamin Franklin
b. George Washington
c. Andrew Jackson

20. Which American city was designed by the French architect Pierre L'Enfant?
a. Boston
b. Chicago
c. Washington, DC

21. Which large American company was founded by a French industrialist?
a. Exxon
b. DuPont
c. General Motors

22. Which famous monument is a gift of the people of France to the people of the United States?
a. the Statue of Liberty
b. the Lincoln Memorial
c. the Liberty Bell

23. Which future American president commanded the Allied forces which liberated France in 1944?
a. Harry Truman
b. Dwight Eisenhower
c. John F. Kennedy

24. Approximately how many Americans are of French origin?
a. 100,000
b. 1,000,000
c. 3,500,000

25. Which state in the United States has the highest proportion of native speakers of French?
a. Nevada
b. New Hampshire
c. New Mexico

Correct answers.
1-a, 2-c, 3-b, 4-b, 5-c, 6-c, 7-b, 8-b, 9-c, 10-c, 11-a, 12-b, 13-b, 14-b, 15-b, 16-a, 17-c, 18-a, 19-a, 20-c, 21-b, 22-a, 23-b, 24-c, 25-b

vingt-cinq **25**
Le savez-vous?

MIDDLE SCHOOL COPYMASTERS

Teaching tips to help in creating a range of activities responding to the needs of varied learning styles, as well as encouraging success for all students are included in the *Middle School Copymasters*.

TEXT TYPE
- Use short sentences when speaking pp. 6–7
- Use short sentences when writing p. 8
- Use learned words and phrases when speaking p. 9
- Use learned words and phrases when writing p. 13
- Use simple questions when speaking pp. 10, 14
- Understand short texts enhanced by visual clues when reading pp. 13, 16

CONTENT
- Understand and convey information about:
  - family p. 8
  - friends p. 9
  - home p. 14
  - leisure activities pp. 17–19
  - likes and dislikes pp. 6–7
  - prices p. 23
  - pets and animals p. 8
  - geography pp. 9, 25
  - directions p. 14
  - buildings and monuments p. 25
  - weather and seasons p. 23
  - cultural and historical figures pp. 24–25
  - places and events pp. 24–25
  - numbers p. 22
  - days p. 22
  - dates p. 22
  - months p. 22
  - time p. 22
  - food and customs p. 23

ASSESSMENT
- Communicate effectively with some hesitation and errors, which do not hinder comprehension pp. 15, 21
- Demonstrate culturally acceptable behavior for:
  - engaging in conversations p. 11
  - expressing likes and dislikes p. 20
  - obtaining information pp. 15, 21
  - understanding some ideas and familiar details p. 20
  - providing information pp. 11, 15

Games

• Les directions

Give each student a copy of a simple city map in French from the Internet, or use an overhead projector to project an image of a map for the students. Divide the class into two teams. Have Team A give directions from a designated starting point and have Team B identify where the directions lead. As an alternative, you may want to give students a copy of a map of your school and the area around it, and have one team give directions while the other identifies specific locations.

Pacing Suggestion: Upon completion of Leçon 13.

• Le jeu de la mémoire

Before class, create pairs of cards for the vocabulary on page 220: the first card will be the French vocabulary word, and the second card will be an illustration or an English translation of the word. Tape the cards on the blackboard in random order so they form a 5 x 5 card grid. Create a second set of note cards numbered 1–25. Tape a numbered card over each of the vocabulary cards, so the words and illustrations are not visible. Divide the class into two teams. Have a player from the first team call out two numbers. Lift the numbered cards to reveal the vocabulary cards underneath. If they match and the team uses the word correctly in a sentence, they receive a point. Those cards are then removed from the board. If they don't match, the cards are covered again, and the turn passes to the other team.

Pacing Suggestion: Upon completion of Leçon 15.

Projects

• Où est-ce?

Have students work in pairs to write a dialogue in which one student asks for directions and the other gives directions. (You may want to specify the length of the exchange.) Have students exchange and proofread each other's work. Finally, have students act out their dialogues for the class.

Pacing Suggestion: Upon completion of Leçon 13.

Bulletin Boards

• À Paris

Divide the class into several small groups. Assign different tourist attractions in Paris and have each group create a bulletin board with the following information:

- a map that shows where the attraction is located
- the days and hours when the attraction is open
- what there is to see and do there
- illustrations or photos to show what the attraction looks like
- street signs for famous streets in the vicinity of the attraction, such as the **Champs-Élysées**

Pacing Suggestion: Upon completion of Leçon 14.

• Ma famille

Have each student use a poster board to create a real or imagined family tree. Have students include a picture for each family member and a paragraph explaining their relationship to the student. Imaginary family members can be cut out of magazines. You may wish to provide students with additional vocabulary for extended families.

Pacing Suggestion: Upon completion of Leçon 16.

Music

• *Au clair de la lune*

You may wish to teach students the traditional French song *Au clair de la lune,* which includes some of the possessive adjectives presented in Leçon 16. You can find the lyrics and music on the Internet.

> «Au clair de la lune,
> Mon ami, Pierrot,
> Prête-moi ta plume
> Pour écrire un mot!
> Ma chandelle est morte,
> Je n'ai plus de feu;
> Ouvre-moi ta porte,
> Je suis très peureux!»

Pacing Suggestion: Upon completion of Leçon 16.

• Les grands boulevards

Play *Les grands boulevards* from the *Chansons* CD for students. Give students a copy of the lyrics and have them listen first to get the gist of the song. Play it a second time and have students list all the words they hear that they recognize. Have the class discuss the general meaning of the song. As an alternative, you may wish to have students listen for and underline forms of the possessive adjectives they hear in the song.

Pacing Suggestion: Upon completion of Leçon 16.

Storytelling

• Une mini-histoire

Distribute a copy of a map of a French town, or if unavailable, use the map of *Villeneuve* on page 202. Model a short story about where one character goes and what he or she does while in the town. Add details to your story like date, time, and what the weather is like. When you are finished, hand out copies of your story with blanks for students to fill in. Have students fill in the blanks individually, with details they recall from your version, and review the story as a group.

Pacing Suggestion: Upon completion of Leçon 14.

Recipe

• Diabolo menthe

The *diabolo menthe* is a popular café beverage among French teenagers. The bright green drink is made using *limonade,* which is similar to a lemon-lime soda, and mint syrup. You may be able to find traditional French *limonade* at the grocery store. If necessary, substitute a sweetened lemon-lime–flavored soda. Variations on the *diabolo menthe* are made using different flavored syrups, such as strawberry, raspberry, and red or black currant.

Pacing Suggestion: Upon completion of Leçon 15.

Hands-on Crafts

• Les modèles

Allow students to choose a Parisian landmark (historical monument, cathedral, museum, or other well-known structure). Have students learn more about their landmark, through library or Internet research, and then construct a small model of it. Students may use whatever materials they deem appropriate to create their models. Once their reproductions are complete, have them add a brief paragraph about the landmark and a map showing where it is located. Have students present their models to the class. As a variation, you may expand the project to include landmarks from anywhere in the francophone world.

Pacing Suggestion: Upon completion of Leçon 14.

End of Unit

• Une maison

Students will create an audiovisual home tour. Students can use their own home, a friend's or a relative's home, or a home featured in a magazine. First, have students select three rooms they wish to present and write short paragraphs describing each room. Students should then proofread each other's work. Next, have students make audio recordings of their paragraphs and select appropriate photographs for them. Students may show slides, create a poster, or enlarge individual photographs to accompany their audio recordings. Finally, have students present their tours to the class. You may wish to give students the options of videotaping or creating computer audiovisuals of their presentations.

Rubric   **A** = 13–15 pts. **B** = 10–12 pts. **C** = 7–9 pts. **D** = 4–6 pts. **F** = < 4 pts.

Criteria	Scale				
Vocabulary Use	1	2	3	4	5
Grammar/Spelling Accuracy	1	2	3	4	5
Creativity	1	2	3	4	5

Diabolo menthe

Ingrédients
- 150 ml limonade
- 30 ml sirop de menthe

Préparation
1. Versez la limonade froide dans un verre.
2. Ajoutez le sirop de menthe et remuez.

Pour une personne.

Ingredients
- approx. 5 oz. of limonade (lemon-lime soda)
- approx. 1 oz. of mint syrup

Directions
1. Pour the chilled limonade into a glass.
2. Add the mint syrup and stir.

Serves one person.

UNITÉ 5

Planning Guide CLASSROOM MANAGEMENT

Communication
- Describe your city, its public buildings, and places of interest *pp. 196, 197*
- Ask and give directions *p. 199*
- Talk about the various places you go to during the week and on weekends *pp. 197, 210*
- Describe your house or apartment *p. 200*
- Discuss your future plans and say what you are going to do *p. 212*
- Talk about your friends and their families *p. 229*

Grammar
- Le verbe *aller p. 206*
- La préposition *à; à* + l'article défini *p. 208*
- La préposition *chez p. 211*
- La construction *aller* + l'infinitif *p. 212*
- Le verbe *venir p. 218*
- La préposition *de; de* + l'article défini *p. 219*
- Les pronoms accentués *p. 221*
- La construction: nom + *de* + nom *p. 223*
- La possession avec *de p. 228*
- Les adjectifs possessifs: *mon, ton, son p. 230*
- Les adjectifs possessifs: *notre, votre, leur p. 232*
- Les nombres ordinaux *p. 233*

Vocabulary
- Où habites-tu? *p. 196*
- Ma ville *p. 197*
- Pour demander un renseignement *p. 199*
- Ma maison *p. 200*
- En ville *p. 210*
- Les sports, les jeux et la musique *p. 220*
- Expressions pour la conversation *pp. 222, 231*
- La famille *p. 229*

Pronunciation
- Les semi-voyelles /w/ et /j/ *p. 213*
- Les voyelles /ø/ et /œ/ *p. 223*
- Les voyelles /o/ et /ɔ/ *p. 233*

Culture
- Le nom des rues *p. 196*
- À Paris *p. 205*
- Au café *p. 217*
- Les animaux domestiques en France *p. 227*

 Print
- Workbook PE, *pp. 117–148*
- *Activités pour tous* PE, *pp. 71–89*
- Block Scheduling Copymasters, *pp. 97–128*
- Teacher to Teacher Copymasters
- Unit 5 Resource Book
  Lessons 13–16 Resources
    Workbook TE
    Activités pour tous TE
    Lesson Plans
    Block Scheduling Lesson Plans
    Family Letter
    Absent Student Copymasters
    Family Involvement
    Video Activities
    Videoscripts
    Audioscripts
    Assessment Program
  Unit 5 Resources
    Communipak
    Activités pour tous TE Reading
    Workbook TE Reading and
      Culture Activities
    Assessment Program
    Answer Keys

 Audiovisual
- Audio Program PE CD 3
  Tracks 1–19
- Audio Program Workbook CD 9
  Tracks 1–32
- *Chansons* Audio CD
- Video Program Modules 13, 14, 15, 16, *Images À Paris*
- Overhead Transparencies
  30a, 30b *Ma ville;*
  31 *La maison;*
  32 Map of Villeneuve;
  33 Means of transportation;
  16 Subject pronouns;
  34 Apartment building;
  8 Family tree

 Technology
- Online Workbook
- ClassZone.com
- eTest Plus Online/Test Generator CD-ROM
- EasyPlanner Plus Online/EasyPlanner CD-ROM
- Power Presentations on CD-ROM

Assessment Program Options

Lesson Quizzes
Portfolio Assessment
Unit Test Form A
Unit Test Form B
Unit Test Part III (Alternate)
  Cultural Awareness
Listening Comprehension
  Performance Test
Speaking Performance Test
Reading Comprehension
  Performance Test
Writing Performance Test
Multiple Choice Test Items
Test Scoring Tools
Audio Program CD 15 Tracks 1–8
Answer Keys
eTest Plus Online/Test Generator
  CD-ROM

Pacing Guide SAMPLE LESSON PLAN

DAY	DAY	DAY	DAY	DAY
1 Unité 5 Opener Leçon 13 • Vocabulaire et Culture– La ville et la maison • Vocabulaire et Culture– Ici à Tours • Vocabulaire–Où habites-tu?	**2** Leçon 13 • Note culturelle– Le nom des rues • Vocabulaire–Ma ville	**3** Leçon 13 • Vocabulaire– Pour demander un renseignement • Vocabulaire–Ma maison	**4** Leçon 13 • À votre tour!	**5** Leçon 14 • Conversation et Culture– Week-end à Paris • Note culturelle–À Paris • Le verbe *aller*
6 Leçon 14 • La préposition *à;* *à* + l'article défini	**7** Leçon 14 • Vocabulaire–En ville • La préposition *chez*	**8** Leçon 14 • La construction *aller* + l'infinitif • Prononciation– Les semi-voyelles /w/ et /j/	**9** Leçon 14 • À votre tour!	**10** Leçon 15 • Conversation et Culture– Au Café de l'Univers • Note culturelle–Au café
11 Leçon 15 • Le verbe *venir* • La préposition *de;* *de* + l'article défini	**12** Leçon 15 • Vocabulaire–Les sports, les jeux et la musique • Les pronoms accentués	**13** Leçon 15 • Vocabulaire–Expressions pour la conversation • La construction: nom + *de* + nom • Prononciation– Les voyelles /ø/ et /œ/	**14** Leçon 15 • À votre tour!	**15** Leçon 16 • Conversation et Culture– Mes voisins • Note culturelle– Les animaux domestiques en France • La possession avec *de*
16 Leçon 16 • La possession avec *de* (continued) • Vocabulaire–La famille • Les adjectifs possessifs: *mon, ton, son*	**17** Leçon 16 • Les adjectifs possessifs: *mon, ton, son* (continued) • Vocabulaire–Expressions pour la conversation • Les adjectifs possessifs: *notre, votre, leur*	**18** Leçon 16 • Les adjectifs possessifs: *notre, votre, leur* (continued) • Les nombres ordinaux • Prononciation– Les voyelles /o/ et /ɔ/	**19** Leçon 16 • À votre tour!	**20** • Tests de contrôle
21 • Unit 5 Test	**22** • Entracte–Lecture et culture			

Student Text Listening Activity Scripts
AUDIO PROGRAM

▶ **LEÇON 13 LE FRANÇAIS PRATIQUE** La ville et la maison
À votre tour!
• **Écoutez bien!** *p. 202*　CD 3, TRACK 1

Look at the map of Villeneuve. You will hear where certain people are. If they are somewhere on the left side of the map, mark A. If they are on the right side of the map, mark B.

Listen carefully. Do not worry if you do not understand every word. Pay attention to the place name that is mentioned. You will hear each sentence twice. Let's begin.

1. Isabelle joue au foot au stade municipal. #
2. Catherine passe à la bibliothèque pour prendre des livres. #
3. Mon petit frère joue dans le parc de la ville. #
4. Ma mère travaille à l'hôpital Sainte-Anne. #
5. Julie et Thomas voient un film au Ciné-Rex.
6. Nous sommes au musée pour l'exposition d'art moderne. #
7. Qu'est-ce que vous faites au supermarché? #
8. Ma soeur travaille dans un magasin de sport. #

• **Créa-dialogue** *p. 203*　CD 3, TRACK 2

Listen to some sample *Créa-dialogues*. Écoutez les conversations.
Modèle: —Pardon, monsieur. Où est-ce qu'il y a un hôtel?
　　　　—Il y a un hôtel avenue de Bordeaux.
　　　　—Est-ce que c'est loin?
　　　　—Non, c'est près.
　　　　—Merci beaucoup!

Maintenant, écoutez le dialogue numéro 1.

—Pardon, madame. Où est-ce qu'il y a un café?
—Il y a un café avenue de Bordeaux.
—Est-ce que c'est loin?
—Non, c'est près.
—Merci beaucoup!

• **Où est-ce?** *p. 203*　CD 3, TRACK 3

Listen to the conversation with the tourist. Écoutez la conversation avec le touriste.
Modèle: —Pardon, monsieur. Où est l'hôpital Sainte-Anne?
　　　　—C'est tout droit, mademoiselle.
　　　　—Merci bien, monsieur.

Voici une autre conversation:
—Pardon, mademoiselle. Où est le musée La Salle?
—Tournez à gauche, rue Danton, monsieur.

▶ **LEÇON 14** Week-end à Paris
• **Week-end à Paris** *p. 204*

A. Compréhension orale　CD 3, TRACK 4

Aujourd'hui c'est samedi. Les élèves ne vont pas en classe. Où est-ce qu'ils vont alors? Ça dépend!

Thomas va au café. Il a un rendez-vous avec une copine.

Florence et Karine vont aux Champs-Élysées. Elles vont regarder les vêtements dans les magasins. Après, elles vont aller au cinéma.

Daniel va chez son copain Laurent. Les garçons vont jouer aux jeux vidéo. Après, ils vont aller au musée des sciences de la Villette. Ils vont jouer avec les machines électroniques.

Béatrice a un grand sac et des lunettes de soleil. Est-ce qu'elle va à un rendez-vous secret? Non! Elle va au Centre Pompidou. Elle va regarder les acrobates. Et après, elle va aller à un concert.

Et Jean-François? Qu'est-ce qu'il va faire aujourd'hui? Est-ce qu'il va visiter le Centre Pompidou? Est-ce qu'il va regarder les acrobates? Est-ce qu'il va aller à un concert? Hélas, non! Il va rester à la maison. Pourquoi? Parce qu'il est malade. Pauvre Jean-François! Il fait si beau dehors!

B. Écoutez et répétez.　CD 3, TRACK 5

You will now hear a paused version of the dialog. Listen to the speaker and repeat right after he or she has completed the sentence.

• **Prononciation** *p. 213*　CD 3, TRACK 6

Les semi-voyelles /w/ **et** /j/

Écoutez: oui　　très bien

In French, the semi-vowels /w/ and /j/ are pronounced very quickly, almost like consonants.

Répétez: /w/ #　　　　oui # chouette # Louise #
　　　/wa/, /wɛ̃/ #　moi # toi # pourquoi # voiture # loin #
　　　　　　　　　　Chouette! La voiture de Louise n'est pas loin. #
　　　/j/ #　　　　　bien # chien # radio # piano # Pierre # Daniel # violon #
　　　　　　　　　　pied # étudiant #
　　　　　　　　　　Pierre écoute la radio avec Daniel. #

À votre tour!
• **Allô!** *p. 214*　CD 3, TRACK 7

Listen to the phone conversation. Écoutez la conversation entre Anne et Jérôme.

　Anne: Tu restes chez toi samedi?
Jérôme: Non, j'ai un rendez-vous avec Christine.
　Anne: Qu'est-ce que vous allez faire?
Jérôme: Nous allons faire une promenade en ville.
　Anne: Est-ce que vous allez aller au cinéma?
Jérôme: Peut-être! Il y a un très bon film au Rex.
　Anne: À quelle heure est-ce que tu vas rentrer?
Jérôme: À dix heures.

• **Créa-dialogue** *p. 214*　CD 3, TRACK 8

Listen to some sample *Créa-dialogues*. Écoutez les conversations.
Modèle: —Salut, Alison. Ça va?
　　　　—Oui, ça va!
　　　　—Où vas-tu?
　　　　—Je vais au restaurant.
　　　　—Ah bon? Qu'est-ce que tu vas faire là-bas?
　　　　—Je vais dîner avec un copain.
　　　　—Avec qui?
　　　　—Avec Chris.

Maintenant, écoutez le dialogue numéro 1.

—Salut, Tom.
—Ça va?
—Oui, ça va!
—Où vas-tu?
—Je vais au café.
—Ah bon? Qu'est-ce que tu vas faire là-bas?
—Je vais manger une pizza.
—Avec qui?
—Avec Sally.

▶ **LEÇON 15** Au Café de l'Univers
• **Au Café de l'Univers** *p. 216*

A. Compréhension orale　CD 3, TRACK 9

Où vas-tu après les cours? Est-ce que tu vas directement chez toi? Valérie, elle, ne va pas directement chez elle. Elle va au Café de l'Univers avec ses copines Fatima et Zaïna. Elle vient souvent ici avec elles.

À la table de Valérie, la conversation est toujours très animée. De quoi parlent les filles aujourd'hui?

Est-ce qu'elles parlent de l'examen d'histoire? du problème de maths? de la classe de sciences?

Non!

Est-ce qu'elles parlent du week-end prochain? des vacances?

Non plus!

Est-ce qu'elles parlent du nouveau copain de Marie-Claire? de la cousine de Pauline? des amis de Véronique?

Pas du tout!

Aujourd'hui, les filles parlent d'un sujet beaucoup plus important! Elles parlent du nouveau prof d'anglais! (C'est un jeune professeur américain. Il est très intéressant, très amusant, très sympathique . . . et surtout il est très mignon!)

B. Écoutez et répétez. CD 3, TRACK 10

You will now hear a paused version of the dialog. Listen to the speaker and repeat right after he or she has completed the sentence.

• Prononciation p. 223 CD 3, TRACK 11

Les voyelles /ø/ et /œ/

Écoutez: deux   neuf

The letters "eu" and "oeu" represent vowel sounds that do not exist in English but that are not very hard to pronounce.

Répétez: /ø/ #   deux # eux # je veux # un peu # jeux #
il pleut # un euro #
Tu peux aller chez eux. #

/œ/ #   neuf # soeur # heure # professeur # jeune #
Ma soeur arrive à neuf heures. #

À votre tour!

• Conversation p. 224 CD 3, TRACK 12

Listen to the conversation. Écoutez la conversation entre Henri et Stéphanie.

Henri: Salut, Stéphanie! D'où viens-tu?
Stéphanie: Du supermarché.
Henri: Et où vas-tu maintenant?
Stéphanie: Je rentre chez moi.
Henri: Tu ne veux pas venir au cinéma avec moi?
Stéphanie: Je ne peux pas. Je dois étudier.
Henri: Ah bon? Pourquoi?
Stéphanie: J'ai un examen d'anglais lundi.

• Créa-dialogue p. 224 CD 3, TRACK 13

Listen to the sample *Créa-dialogues.* Écoutez les conversations.

Modèle: —Où vas-tu?
—Je vais chez Jean-Claude. Tu viens?
—Ça dépend! Qu'est-ce que tu vas faire chez lui?
—Nous allons jouer au ping-pong.
—D'accord, je viens!

Maintenant, écoutez le dialogue numéro 1.

—Où vas-tu?
—Je vais chez Françoise. Tu viens?
—Ça dépend! Qu'est-ce que tu vas faire chez elle?
—Nous allons regarder la télé.
—D'accord, je viens!

▶ LEÇON 16 Mes voisins

• Mes voisins p. 226

A. Compréhension orale CD 3, TRACK 14

Bonjour! Je m'appelle Frédéric Mallet. J'habite à Paris avec ma famille. Nous habitons dans un immeuble de six étages. Voici mon immeuble et voici mes voisins.

Monsieur Lacroche habite au sixième étage avec sa femme. Ils sont musiciens. Lui, il joue du piano et elle, elle chante. Oh là là, quelle musique!

Mademoiselle Jolivet habite au cinquième étage avec son oncle et sa tante. Paul, mon meilleur ami, habite au quatrième étage avec sa soeur et ses parents.

Mademoiselle Ménard habite au troisième étage avec son chien Pomme, ses deux chats Fritz et Arthur, son perroquet Coco et son canari Froufrou. (Je pense que c'est une personne très intéressante, mais mon père pense qu'elle est un peu bizarre.)

Monsieur et Madame Boutin habitent au deuxième étage avec leur fils et leurs deux filles.

Et qui habite au premier étage? C'est un garçon super-intelligent, super-cool et très sympathique! Et ce garçon . . . c'est moi!

B. Écoutez et répétez. CD 3, TRACK 15

You will now hear a paused version of the dialog. Listen to the speaker and repeat right after he or she has completed the sentence.

• Vocabulaire p. 229 CD 3, TRACK 16

La famille

Écoutez et répétez. Repeat the names of the family members after the speaker.

la famille #
les grands-parents #   le grand-père # la grand-mère #
les parents #   le père # la mère # le mari # la femme
les enfants #   un enfant # une enfant # le frère # la soeur # le fils # la fille #
les parents #   l'oncle # la tante # le cousin # la cousine

• Prononciation p. 233 CD 3, TRACK 17

Les voyelles /o/ et /ɔ/

Écoutez: vélo   téléphone

The French vowel /o/ is pronounced with more tension than in English. It is usually the last sound in a word.

Répétez: /o/ #   vélo # radio # nos # vos # eau # château # chaud #
Nos vélos sont au château. #

The French vowel /ɔ/ occurs in the middle of a word. Imitate the model carefully.

Répétez: /ɔ/ #   téléphone # école # Nicole # notre # votre # copain #
prof # dommage #
Comment s'appelle votre prof? #

À votre tour!

• Allô! p. 234 CD 3, TRACK 18

Listen to the phone conversation. Écoutez la conversation entre Émilie et Bernard.

Émilie: Avec qui est-ce que tu vas au cinéma?
Bernard: Avec mon copain Marc.
Émilie: C'est le cousin de Monique?
Bernard: Non, c'est son frère.
Émilie: Tu connais leurs parents?
Bernard: Bien sûr, ils sont très sympathiques.
Émilie: Ils sont canadiens, n'est-ce pas?
Bernard: Non, mais leurs voisins sont de Québec.

• Créa-dialogue p. 234 CD 3, TRACK 19

Listen to some sample *Créa-dialogues.* Écoutez les conversations.

Modèle: —C'est le vélo de Paul?
—Non, ce n'est pas son vélo.
—Tu es sûr?
—Mais oui. Son vélo est bleu.

Maintenant, écoutez le dialogue numéro 1.

—C'est la guitare d'Alice?
—Non, ce n'est pas sa guitare.
—Tu es sûr?
—Mais oui. Sa guitare est brune.

> Complete videoscripts, plus Workbook and Assessment audioscripts, are available in the Unit Resource Books.

UNITÉ 5

Main Theme
• City Life

COMMUNICATION
• Describing a city, public buildings, and places of interest
• Asking for and giving directions
• Talking about the places you go
• Describing a house or apartment
• Discussing future plans and saying what you're going to do
• Talking about friends and their families

CULTURES
• Learning about French cities in general
• Learning about Tours
• Learning about Paris and its monuments
• Learning about street names
• Learning about cafés
• Learning about pets in France
• Learning about French movie-going habits
• Learning about *Tintin*
• Learning about Belgium
• Learning about francophone music

CONNECTIONS
• Connecting to Geography: Reading and creating maps
• Connecting to English: Making language comparisons between French and English
• Connecting to Math: Using ordinal numbers
• Connecting to Music: Creating a project on franchophone music

UNITÉ 5

En ville

LEÇON 13 LE FRANÇAIS PRATIQUE: La ville et la maison

LEÇON 14 Week-end à Paris

LEÇON 15 Au Café de l'Univers

LEÇON 16 Mes voisins

THÈME ET OBJECTIFS

Visiting a French city

There are many things to do in a city: places to visit, concerts to attend, sports to play.

In this unit, you will learn ...

• to describe your city, its public buildings, and places of interest

• to ask for and give directions

• to talk about the various places you go to during the week and on weekends

• to describe your house or apartment

You will also be able ...

• to discuss your future plans and say what you are going to do

• to talk about your friends and their families

 WEBQUEST
CLASSZONE.COM

192 cent quatre-vingt-douze
Unité 5

UNIT OVERVIEW

► **Communication Goals:** Students will be able to ask and give directions, and to describe their city and their home. They will also learn to talk about future plans.

► **Linguistic Goals:** Students will learn to use the verbs **aller** and **venir,** and the possessive adjectives.

► **Critical Thinking Goals:** Students will observe both linguistic similarities (use of **aller** to express future time) and differences (use of possessive adjectives) between French and English.

► **Cultural Goals:** This unit introduces students to two French cities: Paris (in the student text) and Tours (in the video).

cent quatre-vingt-treize
Unité 5 193

COMPARISONS
- Comparing houses in France and the U.S.
- Comparing building floors in France and the U.S.
- Comparing movie-going preferences of teens in France and the U.S.

COMMUNITIES
- Using French to prepare a map for French-speaking visitors to your city
- Using French to host a **fête Tintin** at your school
- Using francophone music to entertain other classes or local senior citizens

Teaching Resource Options

PRINT
Unit 5 Resource Book
    Family Letter

AUDIO & VISUAL
Audio Program
Chansons CD

TECHNOLOGY
EasyPlanner CD-ROM/EasyPlanner Plus Online

Photo cultural note

The teens are at **La Place des Vosges** in Paris. The buildings of stone and faux brick were home to many famous people, such as Richelieu and Victor Hugo.

People can visit the museum at **Maison de Victor Hugo** 6, place des Vosges, where he lived from 1832–1848.

Middle School Copymasters

Unité 5: City Planner and Tour Guide projects, *La maison* crossword, conversations, drills, paired game, worksheets, pp. T25–T29

Leçon 13

Main Topic Getting around in a French city

Teaching Resource Options

PRINT

Workbook PE, pp. 117–121
Activités pour tous PE, pp. 71–73
Block Scheduling Copymasters, pp. 97–104
Unit 5 Resource Book
  Activités pour tous TE, pp. 7–9
  Audioscript, pp. 30–31
  Communipak, pp. 140–163
  Lesson Plans, pp. 10–11
  Block Scheduling Lesson Plans, pp. 12–13
  Absent Student Copymasters, pp. 15–18
  Video Activities, pp. 21–26
  Videoscript, pp. 27–28
  Workbook TE, pp. 1–5

AUDIO & VISUAL

Audio Program
CD 9 Tracks 1–7

TECHNOLOGY

Online Workbook

VIDEO PROGRAM

VIDÉO DVD

MODULE 13
Le français pratique
La ville et la maison

TOTAL TIME: 7:02 min.
  DVD Disk 2
  Videotape 3 (COUNTER: 00:00 min.)

13.1 Introduction: Listening
  – Les villes de France
  (0:10–1:09 min.)

13.2 Dialogue: La ville de Tours
  (1:10–4:06 min.)

13.3 Mini-scenes: Speaking
  – Qu'est-ce que c'est?
  (4:07–5:10 min.)

13.4 Mini-scenes: Listening
  – Pardon! Excusez-moi!
  (5:11–6:02 min.)

13.5 Vignette culturelle:
  La maison d'Olivier
  (6:03–7:02 min.)

LEÇON 13

La ville et la maison

LE FRANÇAIS PRATIQUE
VIDÉO DVD AUDIO

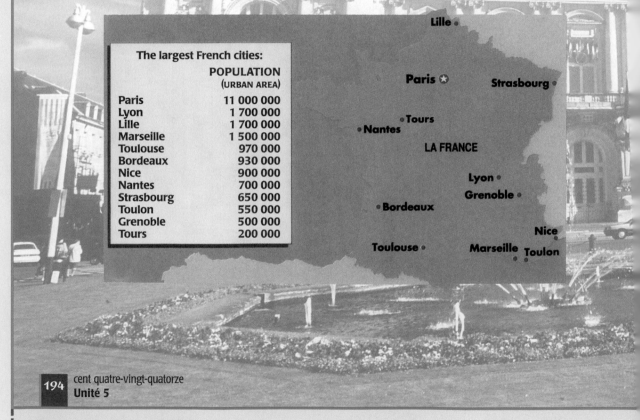

Accent sur … les villes françaises

• Today 80% of the French population lives in cities and their surrounding suburbs.

• French cities have a long history. Paris, Lyon, Marseille, and Nice were founded well over two thousand years ago!

• Cities in France differ in urban design from cities in the United States.

  –The downtown area **(le centre-ville)** is the historical district with buildings and monuments dating back several centuries. Usually no buildings are taller than six stories. With the many cafés, restaurants, stores, and movie houses, it is a very animated area that attracts many young people.

  –The suburbs **(la banlieue)** is where the tall apartment buildings and office buildings are located. Young people who live in the Parisian suburbs often get together in the local shopping mall **(le centre commercial)** which offers shops, cafés, and cinemas.

The largest French cities:

	POPULATION (URBAN AREA)
Paris	11 000 000
Lyon	1 700 000
Lille	1 700 000
Marseille	1 500 000
Toulouse	970 000
Bordeaux	930 000
Nice	900 000
Nantes	700 000
Strasbourg	650 000
Toulon	550 000
Grenoble	500 000
Tours	200 000

LA FRANCE

Lille · Paris ⚝ Strasbourg · Tours · Nantes · Lyon · Grenoble · Bordeaux · Toulouse · Marseille · Toulon · Nice

194 cent quatre-vingt-quatorze
Unité 5

SETTING THE SCENE

PROPS: Worksheets with a map of France and 11 dots representing the above cities. Names of the 11 cities are listed at bottom.

Have students keep their books closed. Divide the class into teams of 4 or 5. Have the teams try to locate the cities on the map.

Have the teams open their books to correct their maps.

  • How many cities did they find correctly?
  • Have they heard about any of these cities?

Tell students that in the video they will visit the city of Tours, in the Loire valley.

Ici, à Tours

Tours est une ville de 200 000 (deux cent mille) habitants située à 200 kilomètres au sud-ouest de Paris. C'est une ville française typique.

L'Hôtel de Ville

Au centre, il y a l'hôtel de ville qui est le <u>bâtiment</u> administratif principal. C'est ici que les gens <u>viennent</u> <u>se marier</u>.

building
come
to get married

La place Plumereau

La place Plumereau est située dans un <u>quartier</u> très ancien. Il y a beaucoup de maisons historiques, et aussi beaucoup de cafés où viennent les jeunes de Tours. C'est un <u>endroit</u> très animé.

district

place

Le Château de Tours

Comme beaucoup de villes françaises, Tours a un château historique. Ce château est une <u>ancienne</u> forteresse royale. Aujourd'hui, c'est un bâtiment administratif.

former

Une maison près de Tours

Les Français qui n'habitent pas dans le centre-ville préfèrent habiter dans une maison individuelle. Cette maison de la région de Tours a deux <u>étages</u>.

floors

cent quatre-vingt-quinze
Leçon 13 195

TALKING ABOUT PAST EVENTS

Let's talk about what time you did certain things. (Review times, if needed.)

▶ **À quelle heure est-ce que tu as dîné hier?**
  J'ai dîné à sept heures et quart.
  • X, à quelle heure est-ce que tu as étudié?
  • À quelle heure est-ce que tu as téléphoné à des amis?

• **Y et Z, à quelle heure est-ce que vous avez dîné samedi soir?**
• **À quelle heure est-ce que vous avez regardé la télé?**

Comprehension practice Play the entire module through as an introduction to the lesson.

Cultural note Marseille was founded by the Phoenicians in 600 B.C. Paris and Lyon were founded by the Romans at the time of Julius Caesar around 43 B.C.

Photo culture note
• L'Hôtel de Ville is located at Place Jean-Jaurès.

SECTION A

Communicative function
Talking about where one lives

Teaching Resource Options

PRINT

Workbook PE, pp. 117–121
Unit 5 Resource Book
  Communipak, pp. 140–163
  Video Activities, p. 123
  Videoscript, pp. 27–28
  Workbook TE, pp. 1–5

AUDIO & VISUAL

Overhead Transparencies
30a, 30b *Ma ville*

VIDEO PROGRAM

VIDÉO   DVD

MODULE 13

**13.3 Mini-scenes: Qu'est-ce que
c'est?** (4:07–5:10 min.)

Vocabulary note Point out that
adresse is feminine.

Supplementary vocabulary
au centre-ville *downtown*
dans la banlieue *in the suburbs*
à la campagne *in the country*
dans un immeuble *in an apartment
  house*

1 COMMUNICATION describing
where you live

Language note In item 4, help
students with numbers.
  In France, P.O. Box =
  B.P. (Boîte postale).
  In Canada, P.O. Box =
  C.P. (Case postale).

Answers will vary.
1. J'habite à (Boston).
2. Ma ville est (grande).
   (Ma ville [n'est pas moderne].)
   Mon village est (joli).
   (Mon village [n'est pas grand].)
3. Mon quartier est (moderne).
   (Mon quartier n'est pas [joli].)
4. Mon adresse est (150 Willow Avenue).
5. Ma ville favorite est (Chicago).
6. Un jour, je voudrais visiter (Paris).

A VOCABULAIRE Où habites-tu?

J'habite à Tours.

▶ *How to talk about where one lives:*

Où habites-tu?
J'habite | à Tours.
         | à Villeneuve
         | dans **une grande ville** (*city, town*)
         | dans **un petit village**
         | dans **un joli quartier** (*neighborhood*)
         | dans **une rue** (*street*) intéressante

Quelle est **ton adresse?**
J'habite | 32, **avenue** Victor Hugo.
         | 14, **rue** La Fayette
         | 50, **boulevard** Wilson

NOTE *culturelle*

Le nom des rues

En France, les rues ont très souvent le nom de
personnes célèbres,° en particulier écrivains,°
artistes et personnalités politiques.

- **Victor Hugo** (1802-1885) est un très grand
  poète. Il a aussi écrit° *Les Misérables* qui° a inspiré
  une comédie musicale moderne.

- **La Fayette** (1757-1834) est un aristocrate français.
  Ami de Georges Washington, il a joué un rôle important
  pendant la Révolution américaine.

célèbres *famous* **écrivains** *writers* **a écrit** *wrote* **qui** *which*

---

1 *Expression personnelle*

PARLER/ÉCRIRE Describe where you live by
completing the following sentences.

1. J'habite à …
2. Ma ville est (n'est pas) …
   (grande? petite? moderne? jolie?)
   Mon village est (n'est pas) …
   (grand? petit? joli?)
3. Mon quartier est (n'est pas) …
   (intéressant? joli? moderne?)
4. Mon adresse est …
5. Ma ville favorite est …
6. Un jour, je voudrais visiter … (*name of city*)

2 **Interview**

PARLER/ÉCRIRE You are a French
journalist writing an article about
living conditions in the United States.
Interview a classmate and find out
the following information.

1. Where does he/she live?
2. Is his/her city large or small?
3. Is his/her city pretty?
4. What is his/her address?

196
cent quatre-vingt-seize
Unité 5

COMPREHENSION Places

PROPS: Vocabulary cards of the places on p. 197:
blue borders on masculine nouns, red
borders on feminine nouns.
Model nouns as you place them on chalktray.
  Voici un théâtre. Voici une église. …

Hold up a picture. [museum card]
  Est-ce un café? [non]
  Est-ce un musée? [oui]

Ask students to pass cards to classmates.
  **X, prends le parc et donne-le à Y. …
  Qui a le parc?** [Y] …

Have all students with cards hold them up.
  Montrez-nous vos cartes.

B VOCABULAIRE Ma ville

▶ *How to talk about one's hometown:*

Dans ma rue, il y a …

un hôtel   **un café**   **un restaurant**   **un supermarché**   **un magasin**

Dans mon quartier, il y a …

un cinéma   **une école**   **une église**   **un centre commercial**

Dans ma ville, il y a …

une bibliothèque   **un théâtre**   **un musée**   **un hôpital**

Il y a aussi …

une piscine   **un parc**   **un stade**   **une plage**

cent quatre-vingt-dix-sept
Leçon 13 197

Photo cultural note

Le "Vieux Tours" In the background you see the **Place Plumereau** with its houses dating back to the 16th and 17th centuries. The exposed wooden beams and the steep slate roofs are typical of the period. Since its renovation in the 1960s, this area of Tours with its cafés and outdoor concerts has become very popular with young people.

2 ROLE PLAY asking where people live

Answers will vary.
1. Elle habite à Cambridge.
2. Sa ville n'est pas grande.
3. Sa ville est jolie.
4. Son adresse est 1020 Massachusetts Avenue.

Expansion Ask students questions about the person they were interviewing.

   X, où est-ce que Y habite?

SECTION B

Communicative function
Identifying places in one's hometown

Supplementary vocabulary

un aéroport *airport*
un collège *junior high school*
un fast-food *fast-food restaurant*
un lycée *senior high school*
un terrain de sport *athletic field*
une banque *bank*
une boutique *shop*
un centre sportif *sport center*
une gare *(train) station*
une grande surface *combination giant supermarket/discount store*
un hypermarché *giant supermarket*
un jardin public *public garden*
une mairie *city hall*
une Maison des jeunes *youth center*
une pharmacie *drugstore*
la poste *post office*
une station-service *gas station*
une université *university*
une mosquée *mosque*
un temple *Protestant church*
une synagogue *Jewish temple or synagogue*

Middle School Copymasters

Worksheet 2: *Lieux et activités,* pp. 71–72

Note two cards on either side of the room.
   Qui a l'hôtel? [X] **Qui a la piscine?** [Z]
   Oh là là! L'hôtel est loin de la piscine!
   [gesture distance]

Note two cards that are close together.
   Où est le stade? Où est le parc?
   Est-ce que le stade est loin du parc? [non]
   Non, le stade est près du parc. ...

If time allows, have students pass around the cards. For example, have X give the hotel card to a student who is near Z.
   X, lève-toi et donne l'hôtel à Y.
   Et maintenant, est-ce que l'hôtel est loin de la piscine? [non]
   L'hôtel est près de la piscine.

3 COMMUNICATION describing your town

Answers will vary.
1. Il y a un restaurant. Il s'appelle Chez Bob. (Il n'y a pas de restaurant.)
2. Il y a un cinéma. Il s'appelle The Capitol. (Il n'y a pas de cinéma.)
3. Il y a une église. Elle s'appelle St. Paul's. (Il n'y a pas d'église.)
4. Il y a un centre commercial. Il s'appelle Chestnut Hill Mall. (Il n'y a pas de centre commercial.)
5. Il y a une bibliothèque. Elle s'appelle The Wilson Memorial Library. (Il n'y a pas de bibliothèque.)
6. Il y a un café. Il s'appelle Cappuccino's. (Il n'y a pas de café.)
7. Il y a une plage. Elle s'appelle Ellis Beach. (Il n'y a pas de plage.)
8. Il y a un supermarché. Il s'appelle Shop Till You Drop. (Il n'y a pas de supermarché.)
9. Il y a un hôpital. Il s'appelle Boston Medical Center. (Il n'y a pas d'hôpital.)
10. Il y a un parc. Il s'appelle Boston Common. (Il n'y a pas de parc.)
11. Il y a un stade. Il s'appelle Veterans' Memorial Stadium. (Il n'y a pas de stade.)
12. Il y a un musée. Il s'appelle The Museum of Contemporary Art. (Il n'y a pas de musée.)
13. Il y a un hôtel. Il s'appelle The Traveller's Repose. (Il n'y a pas d'hôtel.)
14. Il y a une piscine. Elle s'appelle The Local Dip. (Il n'y a pas de piscine.)
15. Il y a un théâtre. Il s'appelle Center Stage. (Il n'y a pas de théâtre.)

4 ROLE PLAY asking about various places in a city

–Pauline, est-ce qu'il y a ... dans ton quartier?

1. un café	6. un théâtre
2. un cinéma	7. un supermarché
3. une piscine	8. un musée
4. un stade	9. un parc
5. une bibliothèque	10. un hôpital

Teaching strategy Be sure students use expressions they have learned in the lesson.

---

3 **Mon quartier**

PARLER Say whether the following places are located in the area where you live. If so, you may want to give the name of the place.

▶ école   **Il y a une école. Elle s'appelle «Washington School». (Il n'y a pas d'école.)**

1. restaurant	6. café	11. stade
2. cinéma	7. plage	12. musée
3. église	8. supermarché	13. hôtel
4. centre commercial	9. hôpital	14. piscine
5. bibliothèque	10. parc	15. théâtre

HÔTEL CHÂTEAU BELLEVUE
16, rue de La Porte, Vieux-Québec,
Qc Canada G1R 4M9
Tél. : 418.692.2573
Téléc. : 418.692.4876
bellevue@vieuxquebec.com

4 **À Montréal**

PARLER You are visiting your friend Pauline in Montreal. For each of the situations below, decide where you would like to go. Ask Pauline if there is such a place in her neighborhood.

▶ You are hungry.

Pauline, est-ce qu'il y a un restaurant dans ton quartier?

1. You want to have a soft drink.
2. You want to see a movie.
3. You want to swim a few laps.
4. You want to run on a track.
5. You want to read a book about Canada.
6. You want to see a French play.
7. You want to buy some fruit and crackers.
8. You want to see an art exhibit.
9. You want to play frisbee on the grass.
10. You slipped and you're afraid you sprained your ankle.

COMMUNAUTÉS

Do French-speaking visitors sometimes come to your community? As a class project, prepare a map of your city on which you label key places and buildings in French. Maybe your local chamber of commerce would like to make such a map available for tourists.

TEACHING NOTE Sounding French

An aim of Act. 3 is to get students to sound French as they use the new words.

Warm-up: First, have students imagine that they live in a large city. Ask the class:
   Est-ce qu'il y a une école?
   Oui, il y a une école. ...

Be sure to correct pronunciation problems. Then ask them to imagine they live in the desert, and have them answer negatively.
   Est-ce qu'il y a une école?
   Non, il n'y a pas d'école. ...

When they can handle the place names fluently, have students describe the area where they actually live.

C VOCABULAIRE Pour demander un renseignement (information)

▶ **How to ask for directions:**

| Pardon,
Excusez-moi, | monsieur.
madame
mademoiselle | Où est l'hôtel Normandie? |

Il est dans la rue Jean Moulin.

Pardon, monsieur, Où est l'hôtel Normandie?

Il est dans la rue Jean Moulin.

Où est-ce qu'il y a un café?

| Il y a un café | **rue** Saint Paul.
boulevard Masséna
avenue de Lyon | **une rue**
un boulevard
une avenue |

Où est-ce? *(Where is it?)*
Est-ce que c'est **loin** *(far)*?

Non, ce n'est pas loin.
C'est **près** *(nearby)*.

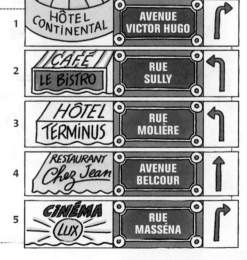

Où est-ce? Est-ce que c'est loin?

Non, ce n'est pas loin. C'est près.

| C'est | **à gauche** *(to the left)*.
à droite *(to the right)*
tout droit *(straight ahead)* | **Tournez** | à gauche.
à droite
Continuez tout droit. |

Merci beaucoup!

5 *En ville*

PARLER A tourist who is visiting a French city asks a local resident how to get to the following places. Act out the dialogues.

▶ —Pardon, mademoiselle (monsieur).
  Où est le Café de la Poste?
—Le Café de la Poste? Il est dans la rue Pascal.
—Où est-ce?
—Continuez tout droit!
—Merci, mademoiselle (monsieur).

▶

1	HÔTEL CONTINENTAL	AVENUE VICTOR HUGO	↱
2	CAFÉ LE BISTRO	RUE SULLY	↰
3	HÔTEL TERMINUS	RUE MOLIÈRE	↖
4	RESTAURANT Chez Jean	AVENUE BELCOUR	↑
5	CINÉMA LUX	RUE MASSÉNA	↱

cent quatre-vingt-dix-neuf
Leçon 13 199

EXPANSION Communautés

Have students use the maps they created for the **Communautés** activity (p. 198) for role-play activities in which they show visitors how to get around.

SECTION C

Communicative function
Asking for directions

Cultural notes
• Jean Moulin (1899–1943) was a hero of the French resistance against the Nazi occupation in World War II.
• Masséna (1758–1817) was one of Napoleon's marshals.

Supplementary vocabulary
C'est près d'ici.   **C'est à côté.**
C'est tout près.   **C'est en face.**
C'est loin d'ici.

5 ROLE PLAY asking and giving directions

1. – Pardon, mademoiselle (monsieur). Où est l'hôtel Continental?
   – L'hôtel Continental? Il est dans l'avenue Victor Hugo.
   – Où est-ce?
   – Tournez à droite!
   – Merci, mademoiselle (monsieur).
2. – Pardon, mademoiselle (monsieur). Où est le café «Le Bistro»?
   – Le café «Le Bistro»? Il est dans la rue Sully.
   – Où est-ce?
   – Tournez à gauche!
   – Merci, mademoiselle (monsieur).
3. – Pardon, mademoiselle (monsieur). Où est l'hôtel Terminus?
   – L'hôtel Terminus? Il est dans la rue Molière.
   – Où est-ce?
   – Tournez à gauche!
   – Merci, mademoiselle (monsieur).
4. – Pardon, mademoiselle (monsieur). Où est le restaurant «Chez Jean»?
   – Le restaurant «Chez Jean»? Il est dans l'avenue Belcour.
   – Où est-ce?
   – Continuez tout droit!
   – Merci, mademoiselle (monsieur).
5. – Pardon, mademoiselle (monsieur). Où est le cinéma Lux?
   – Le cinéma Lux? Il est dans la rue Masséna.
   – Où est-ce?
   – Tournez à droite!
   – Merci, mademoiselle (monsieur).

Cultural notes
• Blaise Pascal (1623–1662), mathematician and philosopher.
• Duc de Sully (1559–1641), finance minister of Henri IV.
• Molière (1622–1673), classical author, writer of comedies.

Teaching Resource Options

PRINT

Workbook PE, pp. 117–121
Unit 5 Resource Book
    Communipak, pp. 140–163
    Video Activities, pp. 25–26
    Videoscript, p. 28
    Workbook TE, pp. 1–5

AUDIO & VISUAL

Overhead Transparencies
31 *La maison*

VIDEO PROGRAM

VIDÉO   DVD

MODULE 13

13.5 Vignette culturelle: La maison d'Olivier (6:03–7:02 min.)

Pronunciation Be sure students do NOT pronounce an "n" in **en haut**: /ã o/. The word **haut** begins with an *aspirate h*. There is never liaison or elision before an *aspirate h*.

Language notes
- **Les toilettes:** also **les WC** (called **double vécé** or simply **vécé**); or **les cabinets**. Tell students that **WC** stands for 'water closet.'
- **Une chambre** is a *room,* in the sense of *bedroom.*
- **Une pièce** is the more general word for *room of a house.*

Cultural notes
- Traditionally in a French home the toilet is in a small room separate from the bathroom.
- **Un salon** is a traditional formal living room. In modern, less formal homes, one may find **un séjour (une salle de séjour),** also referred to as **un living (un living-room).**
- In French homes, the shutters (**les volets**) are usually closed every night.

Supplementary vocabulary
une entrée
un escalier *staircase*
un ascenseur *elevator*
le toit *roof*
le grenier *attic*
le sous-sol *basement*
la cave *cellar*

D VOCABULAIRE Ma maison

J'habite dans une maison.

▶ *How to describe one's home:*

J'habite dans	**une maison** *(house).*
	un appartement
	un immeuble *(apartment building)*
Ma maison/mon appartement est	**moderne.**
	confortable
Ma chambre est	**en haut** *(upstairs).*
	en bas *(downstairs)*

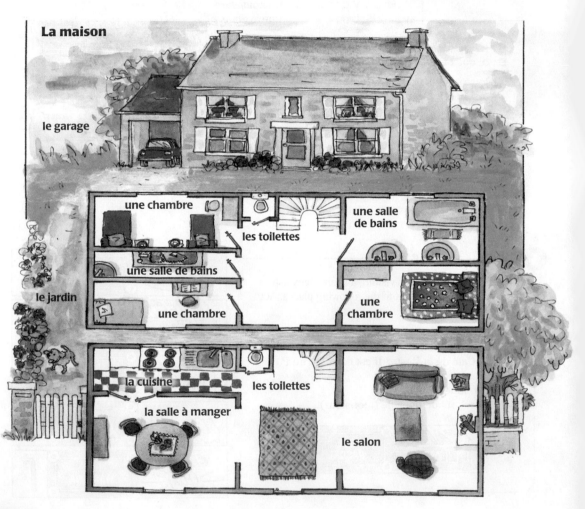

La maison

le garage

une chambre

les toilettes

une salle de bains

une salle de bains

le jardin

une chambre

une chambre

la cuisine

les toilettes

la salle à manger

le salon

COMPREHENSION The house

PROPS: Transparency 31: *La maison*; magazine pictures of various rooms

Identify the new words on the transparency.
    Voici le salon. Voilà la cuisine. ...
    X, viens ici et montre-nous le jardin. ...

Place the magazine pictures on the desk. Have students pick up specific pictures and place themselves around the room.
    X, prends le salon et mets-toi près de la porte.
    Y, prends la salle à manger et mets-toi devant le tableau noir.

6 Ma maison

PARLER/ÉCRIRE Describe your home by completing the following sentences.

1. J'habite dans … (une maison? un appartement?)
2. Mon appartement est … (grand? petit? confortable? joli?)
   Ma maison est … (grande? petite? confortable? jolie?)
3. La cuisine est … (grande? petite? moderne?)
4. La cuisine est peinte *(painted)* en … (jaune? vert? gris? blanc?   ??)
5. Ma chambre est peinte en … (bleu? rose?   ??)
6. Dans le salon, il y a … (une télé? un sofa? des plantes vertes?   ??)
7. En général, nous dînons dans … (la cuisine? la salle à manger?)
8. Ma maison/mon appartement a … (un jardin? un garage?   ??)

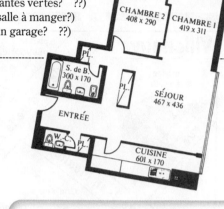

7 En haut ou en bas?

PARLER Imagine that you live in a two-story house. Indicate where the following rooms are located.

▶ ma chambre

Ma chambre est en haut.

Ma chambre est en bas.

1. la cuisine
2. la salle à manger
3. les toilettes
4. la salle de bains
5. la chambre de mes *(my)* parents
6. le salon

COMPARAISON CULTURELLE

In traditional French homes, the toilet **(WC)** is in a small room separate from the main bathroom.

8 Où sont-ils?

PARLER/ÉCRIRE From what the following people are doing, guess where they are — in or around the house.

▶ Madame Martin répare *(is repairing)* la voiture.
Elle est dans le garage.

1. Nous dînons.
2. Tu regardes la télé.
3. Antoine et Juliette jouent au frisbee.
4. J'étudie le français.
5. Monsieur Martin prépare le dîner.
6. Henri se lave *(is washing up)*.
7. Ma sœur téléphone à son copain.

---

6 COMMUNICATION describing your home

Answers will vary.
1. J'habite dans un appartement (une maison).
2. Mon appartement est (joli). Ma maison est (petite).
3. La cuisine est (grande).
4. La cuisine est peinte en (blanc et rouge).
5. Ma chambre est peinte en (bleu).
6. Dans le salon, il y a (un sofa et une télé).
7. En général, nous dînons dans (la salle à manger).
8. Mon appartement a (un garage).

7 DESCRIPTION indicating where rooms are located

Answers will vary.
1. La cuisine est en haut. (La cuisine est en bas.)
2. La salle à manger est en haut. (La salle à manger est en bas.)
3. Les toilettes sont en haut. (Les toilettes sont en bas.)
4. La salle de bains est en haut. (La salle de bains est en bas.)
5. La chambre de mes parents est en haut. (La chambre de mes parents est en bas.)
6. Le salon est en haut. (Le salon est en bas.)

Language note Be sure students use the plural in item 3: Les toilettes sont …

8 COMPREHENSION describing where people are

1. Vous êtes dans la salle à manger.
2. Je suis dans le salon.
3. Ils sont dans le jardin.
4. Tu es dans ta chambre. (Tu es dans le salon.)
5. Il est dans la cuisine.
6. Il est dans la salle de bains.
7. Elle est dans le salon.

Middle School Copymasters

Puzzle: *La maison*, pp. 66–67

Realia note Ask questions about the floor plan:

Trouvez l'entrée, le séjour, les deux chambres, la cuisine, la salle de bains, les toilettes (les WC).

Est-ce qu'il y a aussi des toilettes dans la salle de bains?

Combien de placards *(closets)* **y a-t-il?**

Once the layout of the house has been set, have other students go to various rooms.
Z, tu as faim. Va à la cuisine.
Qui est dans la cuisine? [Z]
W, tu veux regarder la télé. Va au salon.
V, tu dois te laver les mains [gesture].
Va dans la salle de bains. …

À VOTRE TOUR

Main Topic
• Recapitulation and review

Teaching Resource Options

PRINT

Workbook PE, pp. 117–121
Unit 5 Resource Book
   Audioscript, p. 29
   Communipak, pp. 140–163
   Family Involvement, pp. 19–20
   Workbook TE, pp. 1–5

Assessment
Lesson 13 Quiz, pp. 33–34
Portfolio Assessment, Unit 1 URB
  pp. 155–164
Audioscript for Quiz 13, p. 32
Answer Keys, pp. 210–213

AUDIO & VISUAL

Audio Program
CD 3 Tracks 1–3
CD 15 Track 1

Overhead Transparencies
32 Map of Villeneuve

TECHNOLOGY

Test Generator CD-ROM/eTest Plus
Online

① LISTENING COMPREHENSION

1. B   2. A   3. B   4. B   5. A
6. A   7. B   8. B

Middle School Copymasters

Worksheet 1: *Ville et campagne,*
pp. 69–70

---

② WRITTEN SELF-EXPRESSION

Answers will vary.
Dans mon quartier, il y a un parc. C'est le parc
Menotomy Rocks.
Il y a une église. C'est l'église Holy Trinity.
Il y a une bibliothèque. C'est la bibliothèque
d'Arlington.
Il y a un cinéma. C'est le cinéma Orson Wells.
Il y a un centre commercial. Il s'appelle The
Burlington Mall.

À votre tour!

OBJECTIFS
Now you can …
• describe your town and your neighborhood
• ask and give directions

① Écoutez bien!

ÉCOUTER Look at the map of Villeneuve. You will hear where certain people are. If they are somewhere on the left side of the map, mark A. If they are on the right side of the map, mark B.

	1	2	3	4	5	6	7	8
A								
B								

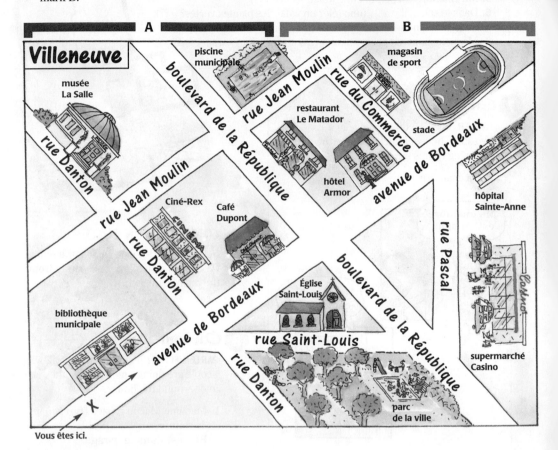

② Mon quartier

ÉCRIRE Describe your neighborhood, listing five places and giving their names.

▶ **Dans mon quartier, il y a un supermarché. C'est le supermarché Casino.**

202   deux cent deux
Unité 5

À VOTRE TOUR

Select those activities which are most appropriate for your students.

GROUP PRACTICE

In Act. 3 and 4, you may want to have students work in trios, with two performing and one acting as monitor.

PORTFOLIO ASSESSMENT

You will probably select only one speaking activity and one writing activity to go into the students' portfolios for Unit 5.

In this lesson, Act. 5 offers an excellent writing portfolio topic.

3  Créa-dialogue

PARLER You have just arrived in Villeneuve, where you will spend the summer. Ask a pedestrian where you can find the places represented by the symbols. He (She) will give you the location of each place, according to the map.

▶ —Pardon, monsieur (madame). Où est-ce qu'il y a un hôtel?
—Il y a un hôtel avenue de Bordeaux.
—Est-ce que c'est loin?
—Non, c'est près.
—Merci beaucoup!

4 Où est-ce?

PARLER Now you have been in Villeneuve for several weeks and are familiar with the city. You meet a tourist on the **avenue de Bordeaux** at the place indicated by an X on the map. The tourist asks you where certain places are and you indicate how to get there.

▶ l'hôpital Sainte-Anne

1. le musée La Salle
2. le supermarché Casino
3. l'hôtel Armor
4. le restaurant Le Matador
5. l'église Saint-Louis

Pardon, monsieur. Où est l'hôpital Sainte-Anne?

C'est tout droit, mademoiselle.

Merci bien, monsieur.

5 Composition: La maison idéale

ÉCRIRE Briefly describe your dream house. You may use the following adjectives to describe the various rooms: **grand, petit, moderne, confortable, joli,** as well as colors. If you wish, sketch and label a floor plan.

La maison idéale est grande et moderne. Le salon est ...

 LESSON REVIEW
CLASSZONE.COM

—Pardon, monsieur (madame). Où est-ce qu'il y a ...?
—Il y a ...
—Est-ce que c'est loin?
— ...
—Merci beaucoup!

1. un café/avenue de Bordeaux/Non, c'est près.
2. un restaurant/boulevard de la République/ Non, c'est près. (Oui, c'est loin.)
3. une église/rue Saint-Louis/Non, c'est près.
4. un supermarché/rue Pascal/Oui, c'est loin.
5. une bibliothèque/avenue de Bordeaux/Non, c'est près.
6. un stade/avenue de Bordeaux/Oui, c'est loin.
7. une piscine/rue Jean Moulin/Oui, c'est [très] loin.
8. un cinéma/rue Danton/Non, c'est près.
9. un hôpital/avenue de Bordeaux/Oui, c'est loin.

4 GUIDED ORAL EXPRESSION

1. —Pardon, monsieur (mademoiselle). Où est le musée La Salle?
—Tournez à gauche (rue Danton), monsieur (mademoiselle).
—Merci bien, monsieur.
2. —Pardon, monsieur (mademoiselle). Où est le supermarché Casino?
—Continuez tout droit et tournez à droite (rue Pascal), monsieur (mademoiselle).
—Merci bien, monsieur.
3. —Pardon, monsieur (mademoiselle). Où est l'hôtel Armor?
—C'est tout droit, monsieur (mademoiselle).
—Merci bien, monsieur.
4. —Pardon, monsieur (mademoiselle). Où est le restaurant le Matador?
—Continuez tout droit et tournez à gauche, monsieur (mademoiselle).
—Merci bien, monsieur.
5. —Pardon, monsieur (mademoiselle). Où est l'église Saint-Louis?
—Tournez à droite (rue Saint-Louis), monsieur (mademoiselle).
—Merci bien, monsieur.

5 WRITTEN SELF-EXPRESSION

Answers will vary.
Ma maison idéale est confortable et jolie. Elle a deux chambres, une salle de bains, des toilettes, un salon, une salle à manger et un jardin. Le garage n'est pas grand. Les chambres sont grandes mais la salle à manger est petite. Le salon est très confortable. Le jardin est joli.

CHALLENGE ACTIVITIES Villeneuve

If appropriate, you can introduce additional challenge activities using the map of Villeneuve.

Have students give more complex directions, using **continuez tout droit, tournez à gauche dans la rue Pascal, ...**

Getting around: Have students give directions from one place to the next, e.g., from **l'hôtel Armor** to **le musée La Salle**, from **le musée** to **le supermarché,** etc.

Mystery destination: Tell students that they are at place "x" on the map. Give them instructions in French to get to a new location. **Maintenant, où êtes-vous?**

Leçon 14

Main Topics Going to places, Talking about future plans

Teaching Resource Options

PRINT

Workbook PE, pp. 123–130
Activités pour tous PE, pp. 75–77
Block Scheduling Copymasters,
 pp. 105–112
Unit 5 Resource Book
 Activités pour tous TE, pp. 43–45
 Audioscript, pp. 64–67
 Communipak, pp. 140–163
 Lesson Plans, pp. 46–47
 Block Scheduling Lesson Plans,
  pp. 48–49
 Absent Student Copymasters,
  pp. 50–53
 Video Activities, pp. 56–61
 Videoscript, pp. 62–63
 Workbook TE, pp. 35–42

AUDIO & VISUAL

Audio Program
CD 3 Tracks 4, 5
CD 9 Tracks 8–16

TECHNOLOGY

Online Workbook

VIDEO PROGRAM

  MODULE 14
Une promenade en ville

TOTAL TIME: 6:55 min.
 DVD Disk 2
 Videotape 3 (COUNTER: 7:14 min.)

14.1 Mini-scenes: Listening
 — Où allez-vous? (7:47–8:20 min.)

14.2 Mini-scenes: Listening
 — Où est-ce que tu vas?
 (8:21–8:46 min.)

14.3 Mini-scenes: Speaking
 — Où vont-ils? (8:47–9:41 min.)

14.4 Mini-scenes: Listening
 — Qu'est-ce que vous allez faire?
 (9:42–11:00 min.)

14.5 Mini-scenes: Speaking
 — Tu vas nager? (11:01–11:49 min.)

14.6 Dialogue: Julien travaille
 (11:50–12:40 min.)

14.7 Vignette culturelle: Le métro
 (12:41–14:09 min.)

LEÇON 14 Conversation et Culture

Week-end à Paris AUDIO

Aujourd'hui c'est samedi.
Les élèves <u>ne vont pas</u> en classe.   *are not going*
Où est-ce qu'ils vont alors?
Ça dépend!

Thomas <u>va</u> au café.   *is going*
Il a un <u>rendez-vous</u> avec une copine.   *date*

Florence et Karine vont aux Champs-Élysées.
Elles vont regarder les <u>vêtements</u> dans les magasins.   *clothes*
<u>Après</u>, elles vont <u>aller</u> au cinéma.   *Afterward / to go*

Daniel va <u>chez son</u> copain Laurent.   *to the house of / his*
Les garçons vont jouer aux jeux vidéo.
Après, ils vont aller au musée des sciences de la Villette.
Ils vont jouer avec les machines électroniques.

Béatrice a un grand sac et des <u>lunettes de soleil</u>.   *sunglasses*
Est-ce qu'elle va à un rendez-vous secret?
Non! Elle va au Centre Pompidou.
Elle va regarder les acrobates.
Et après, elle va aller à un concert.

Et Jean-François? Qu'est-ce qu'il va faire aujourd'hui?
Est-ce qu'il va visiter le Centre Pompidou?
Est-ce qu'il va regarder les acrobates?
Est-ce qu'il va aller à un concert?
<u>Hélas</u>, non!   *Alas (Unfortunately)*
Il va <u>rester</u> à la maison.   *to stay*
Pourquoi? Parce qu'il est <u>malade</u>.   *sick*
<u>Pauvre</u> Jean-François!   *Poor*
Il fait <u>si</u> beau <u>dehors</u>!   *so / outside*

TALKING ABOUT PAST EVENTS

Let's talk about where you have been recently. Note that the past participle of **être** is **été**.

▶ **Est-ce que tu as été en ville le week-end dernier?**

Oui, j'ai été en ville.
(Non, je n'ai pas été en ville.)
 • **Est-ce que tu as été à la piscine samedi?**
 • **Est-ce que tu as été à la bibliothèque?**

 • **Est-ce que tu as été au centre commercial? au musée? au parc?**
 • **Est-ce que tu as été au théâtre samedi soir?**
 • **Est-ce que tu as été à l'hôpital?**
 • **Où est-ce que tu as été dimanche dernier?**

Compréhension

1. Quel jour est-ce aujourd'hui?
2. Pourquoi est-ce que Thomas va au café?
3. Avec qui est-ce que Florence va au cinéma?
4. Où va Daniel? Qu'est-ce qu'il fait avec Laurent?
5. Où va Béatrice?
6. Pourquoi est-ce que Jean-François ne va pas en ville?
7. Quel temps fait-il aujourd'hui?

NOTE culturelle

À Paris

Paris offre beaucoup d'attractions diverses pour les jeunes.

Les Champs-Élysées

Les Champs-Élysées sont une très longue et très large° avenue avec beaucoup de cafés, de restaurants, de cinémas et de boutiques élégantes.

Le Centre Pompidou

Le Centre Pompidou est un grand musée d'art moderne. C'est aussi un centre culturel avec un grand nombre de salles° multimédia pour les jeunes. Devant le musée, il y a une place où les acrobates, les mimes, les jongleurs° et les musiciens démontrent leurs° talents. Ici, le spectacle est permanent.

Le Parc de la Villette

Le Parc de la Villette est un musée scientifique pour les jeunes. À la Géode, ils peuvent° voir° des films sur un grand écran panoramique Omni. Au Zénith, ils peuvent assister à° des concerts de rock et de musique techno.

large *wide*   salles *large rooms*   jongleurs *jugglers*   leurs *their*   peuvent *can*   voir *see*   assister à *attend*

deux cent cinq **205**
Leçon 14

COMPREHENSION Visiting Paris

PROPS: 3 signs that read
"Le Parc de la Villette"
"Le Centre Pompidou"
"Les Champs-Élysées"

Place the signs around the classroom.
Voici le Parc de la Villette., etc.
(Pronunciation: Villette /vilɛt/)

Have students go to these places.
X, lève-toi et va aux Champs-Élysées.
Où va X? Il va aux Champs-Élysées.
Y et Z, allez au Centre Pompidou.
Où vont Y et Z? aux Champs-Élysées?
[non] Ils vont au Centre Pompidou. ...

Follow-up questions:
Où est X? Qu'est-ce qu'il va visiter?

Compréhension
Answers will vary.
1. Aujourd'hui, c'est samedi.
2. Il a un rendez-vous avec une copine.
3. Elle va au cinéma avec Karine.
4. Daniel va chez son copain Laurent. Ils jouent aux jeux vidéo.
5. Béatrice va au Centre Pompidou.
6. Il est malade.
7. Il fait (très) beau.

Note culturelle Paris
- **La Seine** flows through Paris. As you face downstream, the part of the city on your left is called the Left Bank (**la rive gauche**), while the part on your right, is called the Right Bank (**la rive droite**).
- **Les Champs-Élysées** is the most famous avenue of Paris and a favorite place for strolling with friends. The avenue runs from the **Arc de Triomphe** to the **Place de la Concorde**. The **Champs-Élysées** is also the scene of the **Défilé** (parade) **du Quatorze Juillet** and the **Arrivée** (finish) **du Tour de France** bicycle race.
- **Le Centre Pompidou,** was named in honor of Georges Pompidou who was President of France (1969–1974).
- In the photo of **le Parc de la Villette,** on p. 204, you see a large steel sphere, **La Géode,** which houses the Omni theater and its circular panoramic screen.

Critical thinking activity
Write on the chalkboard:
Elles vont aux Champs-Élysées.
Elles vont regarder les magasins.
Ask: How would you express these sentences in English?
- In which sentence does **vont** mean that the girls are actually going to *a place*? Is the place mentioned?
- In which sentence does **vont** mean that the girls are going to *do something*? Is the activity mentioned?
Read the opening text and look for examples of **va** and **vont**.
- Which ones refer to movement?
- Which ones refer to future activities?

Teaching strategy
- Have students read the cultural notes and look at the photos.
- Play the audio of the opening text (books closed).
- On the board, write words and phrases students remembered.

SECTION A

Communicative function
Talking about where one is going

Teaching Resource Options

PRINT

Workbook PE, pp. 123–130
Unit 5 Resource Book
  Communipak, pp. 140–163
  Workbook TE, pp. 35–42

TECHNOLOGY

Power Presentations

Language note Remind students of the elision (with **ne**) in the negative forms:
nous n'allons pas, vous n'allez pas

Language usage The verb **aller** is usually accompanied by a word or phrase indicating a place. (After the verb *to go* in English, the place is often left out.) Compare:

Quand est-ce que tu vas à Paris?
When are you going to Paris?

Je vais à Paris en mai.
I am going (to Paris) in May.

Pronunciation Be sure that students use liaison in **vas-y** and **allons-y.**

Vocabulary expansion

When speaking to several people:

Allez-y!
Allez-vous-en!

Note also:
On y va! *Let's go!*

Middle School Copymasters

Conversation 1: Travel plans, p. 63

A Le verbe *aller*

Aller *(to go)* is the only IRREGULAR verb that ends in **-er.** Note the forms of **aller** in the present tense.

aller	to go	J'aime **aller** au cinéma.
je **vais**	*I go, I am going*	Je **vais** à un concert.
tu **vas**	*you go, you are going*	**Vas**-tu à la boum?
il/elle **va**	*he/she goes, he/she is going*	Paul **va** à l'école.
nous **allons**	*we go, we are going*	Nous **allons** au café.
vous **allez**	*you go, you are going*	Est-ce que vous **allez** là-bas?
ils/elles **vont**	*they go, they are going*	Ils ne **vont** pas en classe.

→ Remember that **aller** is used in asking people how they feel.

Ça **va?**	Oui, ça **va.**
Comment **vas**-tu?	Je **vais** bien, merci.
Comment **allez**-vous?	Très bien.

→ **Aller** is used in many common expressions.

- To encourage someone to do something:
  Vas-y! *Come on! Go ahead! Do it!*

- To tell someone to go away:
  Va-t'en! *Go away!*

- To tell friends to start doing something:
  Allons-y! *Let's go!*

TEACHING NOTE Listening activities

A. Review gestures for the subject pronouns (see Lesson 7, Comprehension activity, p. 96).
Make statements about where people are going; have students identify the subject.
  Il va au stade.
  [signal **il/elle**]
  Elles vont au cinéma.
  [signal **ils/elles**] ...

B. On the board, write **aller/avoir/être/faire.**
Make statements using the four verbs. Students say which one they heard.
  Mes amis sont à Tours. [être]
  Ils ont des vélos. [avoir]
  Ils font une promenade. [faire]
  Ils vont à la piscine. [aller]
  Ils vont nager. [aller] ...

1 Les vacances

PARLER/ÉCRIRE The following students at a boarding school in Nice are going home for vacation. Indicate to which of the cities they are going, according to the luggage tags shown below.

▶ Jean-Michel est canadien.

Jean-Michel va à Québec.

1. Je suis suisse.
2. Charlotte est américaine.
3. Nous sommes italiens.
4. Tu es français.
5. Vous êtes espagnols.
6. Michiko est japonaise.
7. Mike et Shelley sont anglais.
8. Ana et Carlos sont mexicains.

QUÉBEC · ACAPULCO · Lyon · Madrid · TOKYO · Londres (London) · ROME · Genève · CHICAGO

2 Jamais le dimanche! *(Never on Sunday!)*

PARLER/ÉCRIRE On Sundays, French students do not go to class. They all go somewhere else. Express this according to the model.

▶ nous / en ville
**Le dimanche, nous n'allons pas en classe.
Nous allons en ville.**

1. Philippe / au café
2. vous / au cinéma
3. Céline et Michèle / à un concert
4. Jérôme / au restaurant
5. je / à un match de foot
6. tu / à la piscine
7. Éric et Léa / à la plage
8. Mes copains / au stade
9. Hélène / au centre commercial
10. Vous / dans les magasins

deux cent sept
Leçon 14 **207**

---

1 COMPREHENSION telling people what cities to go to

1. Je vais à Genève.
2. Charlotte va à Chicago.
3. Nous allons à Rome.
4. Tu vas à Lyon.
5. Vous allez à Madrid.
6. Michiko va à Tokyo.
7. Mike et Shelley vont à Londres.
8. Ana et Carlos vont à Acapulco.

♻ **Re-entry and review**
Adjectives of nationality (from Lesson 11).

Challenge Let students name another city in the appropriate country.
Jean-Michel va à Montréal.

2 PRACTICE describing where people are going/not going

1. Le dimanche, Philippe ne va pas en classe. Il va au café.
2. Le dimanche, vous n'allez pas en classe. Vous allez au cinéma.
3. Le dimanche, Céline et Michèle ne vont pas en classe. Elles vont à un concert.
4. Le dimanche, Jérôme ne va pas en classe. Il va au restaurant.
5. Le dimanche, je ne vais pas en classe. Je vais à un match de foot.
6. Le dimanche, tu ne vas pas en classe. Tu vas à la piscine.
7. Le dimanche, Éric et Léa ne vont pas en classe. Ils vont à la plage.
8. Le dimanche, mes copains ne vont pas en classe. Ils vont au stade.
9. Le dimanche, Hélène ne va pas en classe. Elle va au centre commercial.
10. Le dimanche, vous n'allez pas en classe. Vous allez dans les magasins.

WARM-UP Cities and nationalities

Review nationalities, with books closed.

Indicate where people live, and have students give their nationalities. First use masculine singular subjects.
Henri habite à Paris. [Il est français.]
Bill habite à Boston. [Il est américain.]

Practice with the cities of Act. 1.

Then continue with feminine singular subjects.
Marie habite à Genève. [Elle est suisse.]

Finally practice with plural subjects.
Tatsuo et Michiko habitent à Kyoto.
[Ils sont japonais.]
Sally et Susie habitent à Liverpool.
[Elles sont anglaises.]

Teaching Resource Options

VIDEO PROGRAM

MODULE 14

14.1 Mini-scenes: Où allez-vous?
(7:47–8:20 min.)

14.2 Mini-scenes: Où est-ce que tu vas? (8:21–8:46 min.)

14.3 Mini-scenes: Où vont-ils?
(8:47–9:41 min.)

  EXCHANGES asking where people are going

1. –Tu vas au stade?
   –Non, je vais à la piscine.
2. –Tu vas au cinéma?
   –Non, je vais au théâtre.
3. –Tu vas à l'hôtel?
   –Non, je vais au supermarché.
4. –Tu vas à la bibliothèque?
   –Non, je vais au musée.
5. –Tu vas à l'école?
   –Non, je vais au parc.

Teaching note: Be sure students realize that the words in heavy print in the green chart correspond to *at the* and *to the*.

Teaching note: You may want to point out the use of **à** with certain verbs.
téléphoner à:
   Je téléphone à Pierre.
   Je téléphone au professeur.
jouer à:
   Je joue au tennis.
   Nous jouons à la balle.

B La préposition *à*; *à* + l'article défini

The preposition **à** has several meanings:

in	Patrick habite **à** Paris.	*Patrick lives **in** Paris.*
at	Nous sommes **à** la piscine.	*We are **at** the pool.*
to	Est-ce que tu vas **à** Toulouse?	*Are you going **to** Toulouse?*

CONTRACTIONS

Note the forms of **à** + DEFINITE ARTICLE in the sentences below.

Voici **le** café.	Marc est **au** café.	Corinne va **au** café.
Voici **les** Champs-Élysées.	Tu es **aux** Champs-Élysées.	Je vais **aux** Champs-Élysées.
Voici **la** piscine.	Anne est **à la** piscine.	Éric va **à la** piscine.
Voici **l'**hôtel.	Je suis **à l'**hôtel.	Vous allez **à l'**hôtel.

The preposition **à** contracts with **le** and **les,** but not with **la** and **l'**.

CONTRACTION	NO CONTRACTION			
à + le → **au**	à + la = **à la**	**au** cinéma	**à la** piscine
à + les → **aux**	à + l' = **à l'**	**aux** Champs-Élysées	**à l'**école

→ There is liaison after **aux** when the next word begins with a vowel sound.
   Le professeur parle **aux élèves.**   Je téléphone **aux amis** de Claire.

3 **Dans la rue**

PARLER Two friends meet in the street and talk about where they are going.

TEACHING NOTE Additional practice

Although contractions are not hard to learn, students often fail to use them in conversation. Sometimes extra drill practice helps them internalize the patterns.

Je suis au café.

(le cinéma)	Je suis au cinéma.
(la piscine)	Je suis à la piscine.
(l'hôpital)	Je suis à l'hôpital.
(le stade)	Je suis au stade.
(l'appartement)	Je suis à l'appartement.
(le musée)	Je suis au musée.
(la maison)	Je suis à la maison.
(le restaurant)	Je suis au restaurant.

4 Préférences

PARLER Ask your classmates about their preferences. Be sure to use contractions when needed.

▶ aller à (le concert ou le théâtre?)

1. dîner à (la maison ou le restaurant)?
2. étudier à (la bibliothèque ou la maison)?
3. nager à (la piscine ou la plage)?
4. regarder un match de foot à (la télé ou le stade)?
5. aller à (le cinéma ou le musée)?

> Tu préfères aller au concert ou au théâtre?

> Je préfère aller au concert.
> (Je préfère aller au théâtre.)

5 À Paris

PARLER You are living in Paris. A friend asks you where you are going and why. Act out the dialogues with a classmate.

▶ —Où vas-tu?
—Je vais à l'Opéra.
—Pourquoi?
—Parce que j'aime la danse classique.

OÙ?	POURQUOI?
▶ l'Opéra	J'aime la danse classique.
1. l'Alliance Française	J'ai une classe de français.
2. le Centre Pompidou	J'aime l'art moderne.
3. le musée d'Orsay	C'est un musée intéressant.
4. les Champs-Élysées	J'ai un rendez-vous là-bas.
5. la tour Eiffel	Il y a une belle vue *(view)* sur Paris.
6. le Zénith	Il y a un concert de rock.
7. la Villette	Il y a une exposition *(exhibit)* intéressante.
8. le stade de France	Il y a un match de foot.

6 Où vont-ils?

PARLER/ÉCRIRE Say where the following people are going, according to what they like to do.

▶ Daniel aime danser.
Il va à la discothèque.

1. Corinne aime l'art moderne.
2. Jean-François aime manger.
3. Delphine aime les westerns.
4. Marina aime nager.
5. Éric aime regarder les magazines.
6. Denise aime faire des promenades.
7. Philippe aime la musique.
8. Alice aime le football.
9. Cécile aime le shopping.
10. Léa aime surfer sur l'Internet.

le stade
la bibliothèque
le cinéma
le centre commercial
la discothèque
le musée
le cybercafé
le parc
le restaurant
la piscine
le concert

PISCINE SERVICE — Didier Souchoy • Camaruche • Saint-Barthélemy • Tel: 0590 27 81

4 COMMUNICATION expressing preferences

1. —Tu préfères dîner à la maison ou au restaurant?
   —Je préfère dîner à la maison (dîner au restaurant).
2. —Tu préfères étudier à la bibliothèque ou à la maison?
   —Je préfère étudier à la bibliothèque (à la maison).
3. —Tu préfères nager à la piscine ou à la plage?
   —Je préfère nager à la piscine (à la plage).
4. —Tu préfères regarder un match de foot à la télé ou au stade?
   —Je préfère regarder un match de foot à la télé (au stade).
5. —Tu préfères aller au cinéma ou au musée?
   —Je préfère aller au cinéma (au musée).

Expansion Additional cues:
aller à (le musée ou la bibliothèque)?
aller à (le café ou le restaurant)?
aller à (l'école ou le parc)?

5 EXCHANGES explaining why one goes somewhere

—Où vas-tu?
—Je vais ...
—Pourquoi?
—Parce que (qu') ...

1. —à l'Alliance Française/j'ai une classe de français.
2. —au Centre Pompidou/j'aime l'art moderne.
3. —au musée d'Orsay/c'est un musée intéressant.
4. —aux Champs Élysées/j'ai un rendez-vous là-bas.
5. —à la tour Eiffel/une belle vue sur Paris.
6. —au Zénith/il y a un concert de rock.
7. —à la Villette/il y a une exposition intéressante.
8. —au stade de France/il y a un match de foot.

Teaching note Have students find as many of these places as possible on the map of Paris in the photo essay on p. 250.

Cultural background L'Opéra
There are two opera buildings in Paris:
• **L'Opéra Garnier,** the old opera house, now home of the Paris ballet.
• **L'Opéra de la Bastille,** concert hall built in 1989, home of the Paris opera.

6 COMPREHENSION concluding where people are going

1. Corinne va au musée.
2. Jean-François va au restaurant.
3. Delphine va au cinéma.
4. Marina va à la piscine.
5. Éric va à la bibliothèque.
6. Denise va au parc.
7. Philippe va au concert.
8. Alice va au stade.
9. Cécile va au centre commercial.
10. Léa va au cybercafé.

Langue et Communication • 209
Unité 5 LEÇON 14

Teaching Resource Options

PRINT

Workbook PE, pp. 123–130
Unit 5 Resource Book
Communipak, pp. 140–163
Video Activities, pp. 56–61
Videoscript, pp. 62–63
Workbook TE, pp. 35–42

AUDIO & VISUAL

Overhead Transparencies
33 Means of transportation

TECHNOLOGY

Power Presentations

VIDEO PROGRAM

 MODULE 14

14.7 Vignette culturelle: Le métro
(12:41–14:09 min.)

Supplementary vocabulary
une exposition *exhibit*

Language notes
- **Un bus (un autobus)** is a city bus that follows a regular route.
- An intercity or tour bus is **un car** or **un autocar.**
- A school bus is **un car scolaire.**

7 COMMUNICATION answering personal questions

Answers will vary.
1. En général, j'arrive à l'école à (huit heures et demie).
2. Je rentre à la maison à (cinq heures). Quand je rentre à la maison, je (joue au football et j'étudie).
3. Je vais à l'école (à pied / en vélo / en bus / en métro).
4. Le week-end, je reste à la maison. (Le week-end, je ne reste pas à la maison. Je vais [à la plage / au cinéma].)
5. Je vais à la piscine (à pied). Je vais à la plage (en voiture). Je vais au cinéma (à vélo).
6. Oui, j'aime faire des promenades à pied. Je vais (au parc) avec (un[e] ami[e] / ma sœur / des copains, etc.). (Non, je n'aime pas faire de promenades à pied.)
7. Oui j'aime faire des promenades à vélo. Je vais (au parc / en ville / au stade, etc.). (Non, je n'aime pas faire de promenades à vélo.)
8. Oui, j'aime regarder des films à la télé. Je préfère (les comédies). (Non, je n'aime pas regarder de films à la télé.)
9. Quand j'ai un rendez-vous avec une copine (un copain), je vais (au café).
10. J'aime aller (aux concerts / aux matchs de football, etc.)

VOCABULAIRE En ville

▶ *Quelques endroits et quelques événements où aller*

un endroit	*place*	un match	*game*	une boum	*party*
un événement	*event*	un pique-nique	*picnic*	une fête	*party*
un concert	*concert*	un rendez-vous	*appointment, date*	une soirée	*evening party*
un film	*movie*				

Verbes

arriver	*to arrive, come*	J'arrive à l'école à 9 heures.
rentrer	*to go back, come back*	À quelle heure rentres-tu à la maison?
rester	*to stay*	Les touristes restent à l'hôtel.

Expressions

à pied	*on foot*	en voiture	*by car*	en métro	*by subway*
à vélo	*by bicycle*	en bus	*by bus*	en taxi	*by taxi*
		en train	*by train*		

faire une promenade à pied	*to go for a walk*
faire une promenade à vélo	*to go for a ride (by bike)*
faire une promenade en voiture	*to go for a drive*

7 Questions personnelles PARLER/ÉCRIRE

1. En général, à quelle heure est-ce que tu arrives à l'école?
2. À quelle heure est-ce que tu rentres à la maison? Qu'est-ce que tu fais quand tu rentres à la maison?
3. Comment vas-tu à l'école? à pied, à vélo, en voiture ou en bus?
4. Le week-end, est-ce que tu restes à la maison? Où vas-tu?
5. Comment vas-tu à la piscine? à la plage? au cinéma?
6. Est-ce que tu aimes faire des promenades à pied? Où vas-tu? avec qui?
7. Est-ce que tu aimes faire des promenades à vélo? Où vas-tu?
8. En général, est-ce que tu aimes regarder les films à la télé? Quels films est-ce que tu préfères? (les films d'action? les films de science-fiction? les comédies?)
9. Quand tu as un rendez-vous avec un copain ou une copine, où allez-vous?
10. À quels événements aimes-tu aller? Pourquoi?

TALKING ABOUT PAST EVENTS

Let's talk about where you went yesterday. We will use the passé composé of **aller:**

present of **être + allé(e)**

(Note: since the focus is on spoken French, there is no need to introduce the agreement of the past participle at this time.)

▶ **Est-ce que tu es allé(e) en ville hier?**
Oui, je suis allé(e) en ville.
(Non, je ne suis pas allé(e) en ville.)

- **X, est-ce que tu es allé(e) au cinéma hier? à l'école? au supermarché?**

C La préposition *chez*

Note the use of **chez** in the following sentences.

Paul est **chez Céline.**   *Paul is **at Céline's** (house).*
Je dîne **chez un copain.**   *I am having dinner **at a friend's** (home).*

Nathalie va **chez Juliette.**   *Nathalie is going **to Juliette's** (apartment).*
Tu vas **chez ta cousine.**   *You are going **to your cousin's** (place).*

The French equivalent of *to* or *at someone's (house, home)* is the construction:

| **chez** + PERSON | **chez** Béatrice | **chez** ma cousine |

→ Note the interrogative expression: **chez qui?**
     Chez qui vas-tu?   *To whose house are you going?*

8 En vacances

PARLER/ÉCRIRE When we are on vacation, we often like to visit friends and relatives. Say where the following people are going.

▶ Claire / Marc
Claire va chez Marc.

1. Hélène / Jérôme
2. Jean-Paul / Lucie
3. tu / un copain
4. Corinne / une cousine
5. vous / des copines à Québec
6. nous / un cousin à Paris

Chez Antoine
3, rue Clemenceau
13100 Aix-en-Provence
Tél. 04 42 38 27 10

9 Week-end

PARLER On weekends, we often like to visit friends and do things together. Say how the following people are spending Sunday afternoon.

▶ Cécile / jouer au ping-pong / Robert

1. Julie / aller / Béatrice
2. Claire / dîner / des cousins
3. Antoine / jouer au croquet / Sylvie
4. Marc / écouter des CD / un copain
5. Mathieu / regarder la télé / une copine
6. Élodie / jouer aux jeux vidéo / Thomas
7. Nous / manger une pizza / Léa
8. Vous / regarder un DVD / Éric
9. Tu / jouer au basket / Alice

Cécile joue au ping-pong chez Robert.

deux cent onze
Leçon 14 211

Language note The word **rendez-vous** includes all types of appointments with friends, teachers, as well as professional appointments with doctors, dentists, etc. The term means that people have arranged to meet somewhere.

SECTION C

Communicative function
Talking about going to someone's house

Language notes

- **Chez** also means at *the office of*: **Je vais chez le docteur.**
- Be sure students see that the word **chez** means *to* or *at someone's place.* The preposition **à** is NEVER used with **chez.**

Looking ahead **Chez** + stress pronouns is presented in Lesson 15.

Pronunciation There is no liaison between **chez** and the name of a person:
    chez Alice, chez Éric

However there is liaison with **un/une:**
    chez un(e) ami(e)

8 PRACTICE saying whom people are visiting

1. Hélène va chez Jérôme.
2. Jean-Paul va chez Lucie.
3. Tu vas chez un copain.
4. Corinne va chez une cousine.
5. Vous allez chez des copines à Québec.
6. Nous allons chez un cousin à Paris.

9 DESCRIPTION stating at whose home people do certain activities

1. Julie va chez Béatrice.
2. Claire dîne chez des cousins.
3. Antoine joue au croquet chez Sylvie.
4. Marc écoute des CD chez un copain.
5. Mathieu regarde la télé chez une copine.
6. Élodie joue aux jeux vidéo chez Thomas.
7. Nous mangeons une pizza chez Léa.
8. Vous regardez un DVD chez Éric.
9. Tu joues au basket chez Alice.

- **Y, est-ce que tu es allé(e) chez des amis? chez des cousins?**
- **Est-ce que tu es allé(e) à un pique-nique? à la bibliothèque?**
- **Z, où est-ce que tu es allé(e) hier matin? hier après-midi? hier soir?**

Follow-up: Ask students what others did.
- **Est-ce que X est allé(e) au cinéma hier?**
- **Est-ce que Y est allé(e) chez des amis hier?**
- **Où est-ce que Z est allé(e) hier matin?**

Middle School Copymasters
Game: *Chez les Clément,* pp. 75–76

SECTION D

Communicative function
Talking about future plans

Teaching Resource Options

PRINT

Workbook PE, pp. 123–130
Unit 5 Resource Book
    Audioscript, p. 64
    Communipak, pp. 140–163
    Video Activities, pp. 58–60
    Videoscript, pp. 62–63
    Workbook TE, pp. 35–42

AUDIO & VISUAL

Audio Program
CD 3 Track 6

TECHNOLOGY

Power Presentations

VIDEO PROGRAM

VIDÉO   DVD

MODULE 14

14.4 Mini-scenes: Qu'est-ce que vous allez faire?
(9:42–11:00 min.)

14.5 Mini-scenes: Tu vas nager?
(11:01–11:49 min.)

14.6 Dialogue: Julien travaille
(11:50–12:40 min.)

Casual speech One can also say:
Vous allez rentrer quand?

Note that **Tu vas faire quoi?** is less common than **Qu'est-ce que tu vas faire?**

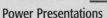

10 DESCRIPTION describing destinations and plans

1. Alice va à New York. Elle va visiter la statue de la Liberté.
2. Nous allons en Égypte. Nous allons visiter les pyramides.
3. Vous allez à Rome. Vous allez visiter le Colisée.
4. Tu vas à la Nouvelle Orléans. Tu vas visiter le Vieux Carré.
5. Je vais à San Francisco. Je vais visiter Chinatown.
6. Les élèves vont à San Antonio. Ils vont visiter l'Alamo.
7. Madame Lambert va à Beijing. Elle va visiter la Cité interdite.
8. Les touristes vont à Kyoto. Ils vont visiter les temples.

D La construction *aller* + l'infinitif

The following sentences describe what people are *going to do*.
Note how the verb **aller** is used to describe these FUTURE events.

Nathalie **va nager.**	*Nathalie is going to swim.*
Paul et Marc **vont jouer** au tennis.	*Paul and Marc are going to play tennis.*
Nous **allons rester** à la maison.	*We are going to stay home.*
Je **vais aller** en ville.	*I am going to go downtown.*

To express the NEAR FUTURE, the French use the construction:

> PRESENT of **aller** + INFINITIVE

➙ In negative sentences, the construction is:

> SUBJECT + **ne** + PRESENT of **aller** + **pas** + INFINITIVE …
>
> Sylvie **ne** va **pas** écouter le concert avec nous.

➙ Note the interrogative forms:

Qu'est-ce que tu vas faire?	*What are you going to do?*
Quand est-ce que vous allez rentrer?	*When are you going to come back?*

LANGUAGE COMPARISON
To talk about FUTURE plans and intentions, French and English frequently use similar verbs: **aller** *(to be going to)*.

10 Tourisme

PARLER/ÉCRIRE Say where the following people are going this summer and what they are going to visit.

▶ Monique (à Paris / le Louvre)
Monique va à Paris. Elle va visiter le Louvre.

1. Alice (à New York / la statue de la Liberté)
2. nous (en Égypte / les pyramides)
3. vous (à Rome / le Colisée)
4. tu (à La Nouvelle Orléans / le Vieux Carré)
5. je (à San Francisco / Chinatown)
6. les élèves (à San Antonio / l'Alamo)
7. Madame Lambert (à Beijing / la Cité interdite [*Forbidden City*])
8. les touristes (à Kyoto / les temples)

carte musées **3** jours
+ monuments

CULTURAL NOTES

• The coliseum (**le Colisée**) is a large stadium built by the Romans.
• The **Vieux Carré** is the part of the French Quarter known for its jazz clubs and its picturesque old buildings with wrought iron balconies.
• Historically, Kyoto was the capital of Japan; one can still visit the many Buddhist temples there as well as the Emperor's palace.

11 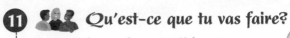 *Qu'est-ce que tu vas faire?*

PARLER Ask your classmates if they are
going to do the following things
this weekend.

▶ étudier

> Est-ce que tu
> vas étudier?

> Oui, je vais étudier.
> (Non, je ne vais pas étudier.)

1. travailler
2. surfer sur le Net
3. regarder la télé
4. aller au cinéma
5. inviter des amis
6. aller à une boum
7. jouer aux jeux vidéo
8. rester à la maison
9. faire une promenade
   à vélo

12 *Un jeu:* **Descriptions**

PARLER/ÉCRIRE Choose a person from Column A and say where the person is,
what he or she has, and what he or she is going to do. Use the verbs **être, avoir,**
and **aller** with the phrases in columns B, C, and D. How many logical descriptions
can you make?

▶ Monique est en ville. Elle a un vélo. Elle va faire une promenade.

A	B (être)	C (avoir)	D (aller)
tu	sur le court	des livres	aller dans les magasins
Monique	à la bibliothèque	un vélo	étudier
je	au salon	20 euros	faire une promenade
les amis	en ville	une télé	regarder un film
nous	à la maison	une chaîne hi-fi	faire un match
vous	au café	une raquette	écouter des CD

PRONONCIATION

Les semi-voyelles /w/ et /j/

In French, the semi-vowels /w/ and /j/ are
pronounced very quickly, almost like
consonants.

Répétez:

/w/   **oui chouette Louise**

/wa/, /wɛ̃/ **moi toi pourquoi voiture loin**
             Chouette! La voiture de Louise n'est pas loin.

/j/   **bien chien radio piano Pierre Daniel violon pied étudiant**
             Pierre écoute la radio avec Daniel.

/w/

/j/

oui   **très bien**

GAME Un jeu

Act. 12 can be done as a team game. Divide the class
into groups of 3 or 4 students. Have each group take
out a sheet of paper and choose a recorder (**un/une
secrétaire**). As the group creates a description, the
recorder will write it down.

Give a signal for the groups to start. At the end of the
time limit, stop the groups. Have them exchange

papers (Group 1 passes its paper to Group 2, Group 2
to Group 3, etc.).

Each group checks the paper it received for accuracy
and records the number of correct and logical
descriptions. The group with the highest score wins.

Realia note See if the students can
guess that it is the Mona Lisa's eye
that appears in the **Carte musées et
monuments**. Then ask if they remember
the name of the museum where the
Mona Lisa is located (**le Louvre**). The
Carte musée et monuments allows the
bearer to visit 70 museums and
monuments for 1, 3, or 5 days.

11 **EXCHANGES** talking about
weekend plans

—Est-ce que tu vas ... ?
—Oui, je vais ... (Non, je ne vais pas ...)

1. travailler
2. surfer sur le Net
3. regarder la télé
4. aller au cinéma
5. inviter des amis
6. aller à une boum
7. jouer aux jeux vidéo
8. rester à la maison
9. faire une
   promenade à vélo

Variation (with **vous** and **nous**)
  – Est-ce que vous allez étudier?
  – Oui, nous allons étudier. (Non, nous
    n'allons pas étudier.)

Teaching strategy: Act. 11 may be
conducted as a classroom survey. See
Game: Getting acquainted on p. 108.

12 **DESCRIPTION** describing
people and their plans

Answers will vary.

- Tu es (au salon). Tu as (une télé). Tu vas
  (regarder un film).
- Je suis (en ville). J'ai (20 euros). Je vais (aller
  dans les magasins).
- Les amis sont (à la maison). Ils ont (une
  chaîne hi-fi). Ils vont (écouter des CD).
- Nous sommes (à la bibliothèque). Nous
  avons (des livres). Nous allons (étudier).
- Vous êtes (sur le court). Vous avez (une
  raquette). Vous allez (faire un match).

♻ **Re-entry and review**
This activity reviews the forms of **être,
avoir,** and **aller**.

PRONUNCIATION

- Be sure students pronounce the
  /j/ very quickly. The following
  words should sound like two
  (and not three) syllables:
  pia-no   **Da-niel**
  ra-dio   **vio-lon**

  These words are pronounced in
  one syllable:
  Pierre /ɛer/   **pied** /ɛe/
- You may want to present the
  other French semi vowel /ɥ/,
  which is not formally introduced
  at this level: It is spelled **u** +
  vowel, as in **lui, suis, juillet** and
  aujourd'hui.

Teaching Resource Options

PRINT

Workbook PE, pp. 123–130
Unit 5 Resource Book
   Audioscript, pp. 64–65
   Communipak, pp. 140–163
   Family Involvement, pp. 54–55
   Workbook TE, pp. 35–42
   Assessment
   Lesson 14 Quiz, pp. 69–70
   Portfolio Assessment, Unit 1 URB
     pp. 155–164
   Audioscript for Quiz 14, p. 68
   Answer Keys, p. 210–213

AUDIO & VISUAL

Audio Program
CD 3 Tracks 7, 8
CD 15 Track 2

TECHNOLOGY

Test Generator CD-ROM/eTest Plus
Online

① COMPREHENSION

1. Tu restes chez toi samedi?
   (d) Non, j'ai un rendez-vous avec Christine.
2. Qu'est-ce que vous allez faire?
   (c) Nous allons faire une promenade en ville.
3. Est-ce que vous allez aller au cinéma?
   (b) Peut-être! Il y a un très bon film au Rex.
4. À quelle heure est-ce que tu vas rentrer?
   (a) À dix heures.

Middle School Copymasters

Conversations 2: Shopping in Paris,
p.64; Conversation 3: *Qui vient?*,
p. 65; Project 1: Map Work: *Pour
prendre le métro*, pp. 78–85;
Project 2: Tour Guide, p. 86

À votre tour!

OBJECTIFS

Now you can …
• talk about places you go to
• discuss what you are going to do in the future

① 🎧 👥 Allô!

PARLER Anne is calling Jérôme. Match Jérôme's answers with Anne's questions. Then act out the dialogue with a friend.

1. Tu restes chez toi samedi?
2. Qu'est-ce que vous allez faire?
3. Est-ce que vous allez aller au cinéma?
4. À quelle heure est-ce que tu vas rentrer?

a. À dix heures.
b. Peut-être! Il y a un très bon film au Rex.
c. Nous allons faire une promenade en ville.
d. Non, j'ai un rendez-vous avec Christine.

② 🎧 👥 Créa-dialogue

PARLER As you are going for a walk in town, you meet several friends. Ask them where they are going and what they are going to do there.

OÙ?	ACTIVITÉ
	dîner avec un copain

▶ —Salut, <u>Alison</u>. Ça va?
  —Oui, ça va!
  —Où vas-tu?
  —Je vais au <u>restaurant</u>.
  —Ah bon? Qu'est-ce que tu vas faire là-bas?
  —Je vais <u>dîner avec un copain</u>.
  —Avec qui?
  —Avec <u>Chris</u>.

OÙ?	ACTIVITÉ
1 CAFÉ	manger une pizza
2	faire une promenade
3	jouer au foot
4	nager
5	jouer au volley
6	travailler
7	??

À VOTRE TOUR

Select those activities which are most appropriate for your students.

PAIR PRACTICE

Act 1–3 lend themselves well to pair practice. For preparation, have the class listen to the corresponding audio recordings.

PORTFOLIO ASSESSMENT

You will probably select only one speaking activity and one writing activity to go into the students' portfolios for Unit 5.

In this lesson, Act. 2 can be the basis for an oral portfolio dialogue. Act. 5 can be used as a writing portfolio topic.

3 👥 Conversation libre

PARLER Have a conversation with a classmate. Ask your classmate questions about what he/she plans to do on the weekend. Try to find out as much as possible, using yes/no questions.

Est-ce que tu vas rester à la maison?

Non, je ne vais pas rester à la maison.

Est-ce que tu vas aller en ville?

Oui, je vais aller en ville.

Est-ce que tu vas aller au cinéma?

Oui, je vais aller au cinéma.
(Non, je ne vais pas aller au cinéma.)

4 ✏️ Qu'est-ce que vous allez faire?

ÉCRIRE Leave a note for your friend Jean-Marc, telling him three things that you and your friends are going to do tonight and three things that you are going to do this weekend.

Jean-Marc
Ce soir (Tonight)
1. Nous allons ...
2.
3.

5 ✏️ Bonnes résolutions

ÉCRIRE Imagine that it is January 1 and you are making up New Year's resolutions. On a separate sheet of paper, describe six of your resolutions by saying what you are going to do and what you are not going to do in the coming year.

1ᵉʳ JANVIER
1. Je vais toujours parler français en classe.
2. Je ne vais pas être pénible avec mes copains...

 **LESSON REVIEW**
CLASSZONE.COM

deux cent quinze
Leçon 14 215

CLASSROOM MANAGEMENT Group reading and writing practice

Have all students prepare Act. 5 as homework. Then, divide the class into groups of 4.

Ask students to share their lists of resolutions with those in their group. Then have each group compare the 4 lists and vote on the 6 best resolutions.

The recorder (**le/la secrétaire**) rewrites the 6 resolutions in the **nous**-form.

1. **Nous allons toujours parler français en classe.**
2. **Nous n'allons pas être pénibles avec nos copains.**, etc.

The reporter (**le reporter**) will read the group's list to the rest of the class.

---

2 GUIDED ORAL EXPRESSION

—Salut, (X). Ça va?
—Oui, ça va!
—Où vas-tu?
—Je vais ...
—Ah bon, qu'est-ce que tu vas faire là-bas?
—Je vais ...
—Avec qui?
—Avec (X).

1. Thomas/au café/manger une pizza/Sandrine
2. Jean-Paul/au parc/faire une promenade/Karine
3. Robert/au stade/jouer au foot/mes copains
4. Nancy/à la piscine/nager/Caroline
5. Sylvie/à la plage/jouer au volley/mes amis
6. Patrick/au supermarché/travailler/Julien
7. Claire/au centre commercial/(regarder des vêtements / aller dans les magasins)/Julie

Teaching strategy If students have difficulty with item 7, you may wish to suggest possible activities: **retrouver des amis, aller dans les magasins, manger un hot-dog,** etc.

(The verb **acheter** is introduced in Lesson 17.)

3 CONVERSATION

Answers will vary.
- —Est-ce que tu vas aller à la plage?
  —Oui, je vais aller à la plage. (Non, je ne vais pas aller à la plage.)
- —Est-ce que tu vas aller au restaurant?
  —Oui, je vais aller au restaurant. (Non, je ne vais pas aller au restaurant.)
- —Est-ce que tu vas aller au centre commercial?
  —Oui, je vais aller au centre commercial. (Non, je ne vais pas aller au centre commercial.)
- —Est-ce que tu vas aller au match de foot?
  —Oui, je vais aller au match de foot. (Non, je ne vais pas aller au match de foot.)

4 WRITTEN SELF-EXPRESSION

Answers will vary.
Jean-Marc

Ce soir
1. Nous allons dîner chez Paul.
2. Nous allons faire une promenade en ville.
3. Nous allons étudier.

Ce week-end
1. Nous allons organiser une boum.
2. Nous allons danser.
3. Nous allons regarder un film.

5 WRITTEN SELF-EXPRESSION

Answers will vary.
1. Je vais travailler à la maison.
2. Je ne vais pas regarder la télé.
3. Je vais écouter le professeur en classe.
4. Je vais étudier.
5. Je ne vais pas être pénible avec mon frère.
6. Je vais jouer au tennis avec ma soeur.

Leçon 15

Main Topic Finding out what people are talking about

Teaching Resource Options

PRINT

Workbook PE, pp. 131–136
Activités pour tous PE, pp. 79–81
Block Scheduling Copymasters, pp. 113–120
Unit 5 Resource Book
  Activités pour tous TE, pp. 77–79
  Audioscript, pp. 97–99
  Communipak, pp. 140–163
  Lesson Plans, p. 80–81
  Block Scheduling Lesson Plans, pp. 82–83
  Absent Student Copymasters, pp. 84–88
  Video Activities, pp. 91–94
  Videoscript, pp. 95–96
  Workbook TE, pp. 71–76

AUDIO & VISUAL

Audio Program
CD 3 Tracks 9, 10
CD 9 Tracks 17–24

TECHNOLOGY
Online Workbook

VIDEO PROGRAM

 MODULE 15
Sports et musique

TOTAL TIME: 6:03 min.
DVD Disk 2
Videotape 3 (COUNTER: 14:20 min.)

15.1 Mini-scenes: Listening
–Quels sports est-ce que vous pratiquez? (15:43–16:11 min.)

15.2 Mini-scenes: Listening
–Tu veux jouer au volley?
(16:12–16:32 min.)

15.3 Mini-scenes: Speaking
–Est-ce que Paul joue au tennis?
(16:33–17:21 min.)

15.4 Mini-scenes: Listening
–De quel instrument est-ce que tu joues? (17:22–18:20 min.)

15.5 Dialogue: Interview avec Éric
(18:21–18:55 min.)

15.6 Vignette culturelle: À la Maison des jeunes
(18:56–20:23 min.)

Comprehension practice Play the entire module through as an introduction to the lesson.

216 • **Conversation et Culture**
Unité 5 LEÇON 15

 **Conversation et Culture**

LEÇON 15

Au Café de l'Univers
AUDIO

Où vas-tu <u>après les cours</u>?	*after school*
Est-ce que tu vas <u>directement</u> <u>chez toi?</u>	*straight/home*
Valérie, elle, ne va pas directement <u>chez elle</u>.	*to her house*
Elle va au Café de l'Univers avec ses copines Fatima et Zaïna.	
Elle <u>vient</u> souvent ici avec elles.	*comes*
À la table de Valérie, la conversation est toujours très <u>animée</u>.	*lively*
<u>De quoi</u> parlent les filles aujourd'hui?	*About what*

Est-ce qu'elles parlent	de l'<u>examen d'histoire?</u>	*history test*
	du problème de maths?	
	de la classe de sciences?	

Non!

| Est-ce qu'elles parlent | du week-end <u>prochain?</u> | *next* |
| | des vacances? | |

<u>Non plus!</u>   *Not that either!*

Est-ce qu'elles parlent	du <u>nouveau</u> copain de Marie-Claire?	*new*
	de la cousine de Pauline?	
	des amis de Véronique?	

<u>Pas du tout!</u>   *Not at all!*

Aujourd'hui, les filles parlent d'un <u>sujet</u> beaucoup <u>plus</u> important! Elles parlent du nouveau prof d'anglais! (C'est un jeune professeur américain. Il est très intéressant, très amusant, très sympathique … et <u>surtout</u> il est très mignon!)	*subject/more* *above all*

SETTING THE STAGE

With books closed, ask students what they talk about when they get together. List the topics (in English) on the board.

Then play the audio recording of the above text. Have students listen to see what topics of conversation are mentioned in the text.

Which of the topics on the students' list are the same as those mentioned by the speaker? Which are new?

Play the audio again, and ask them to try to get additional information.

Finally have them open their books and follow along as you play the audio once more.

Compréhension

1. Où va Valérie après les cours?
2. Avec qui est-ce qu'elle va au café?
3. Qu'est-ce que les filles font au café?
4. Est-ce qu'elles parlent de l'école?
5. Est-ce qu'elles parlent des activités du week-end?
6. De quelle *(which)* personne parlent-elles aujourd'hui?
7. De quelle nationalité est le professeur d'anglais?
8. Comment est-il?

Et toi?

Describe what you do by completing the following sentences.

1. En général, après les cours,
   je vais …
   je ne vais pas …

   • à la bibliothèque   • au café
   • chez mes *(my)* copains • directement chez moi

2. Avec mes copains,
   je parle …
   je ne parle pas …

   • de la classe de français   • des examens
   • du prof de français   • du week-end

3. Avec mes parents,
   je parle …
   je ne parle pas …

   • de l'école   • de mes notes *(grades)*
   • de la classe de français   • de mes copains

4. Avec mon frère ou ma soeur,
   je parle …
   je ne parle pas …

   • de mes copains   • de mes problèmes
   • du week-end   • des vacances

NOTE culturelle

Au café

On peut° faire beaucoup de choses différentes dans un café français. On peut manger un sandwich. On peut commander° un jus de fruits. On peut étudier. On peut jouer aux jeux électroniques. Dans les cybercafés, on peut aussi surfer sur l'Internet. Les jeunes Français vont au café principalement pour retrouver° leurs° copains et passer° un bon moment avec eux.°

Un café français est divisé en deux parties: l'intérieur et la terrasse.° Au printemps et en été, les Français préfèrent s'asseoir à la terrasse. Là, ils peuvent° profiter du soleil° et regarder les gens qui passent dans la rue.

On peut *One can* **commander** *order* **retrouver** *meet* **leurs** *their* **passer** *spend* **eux** *them*
la terrasse *terrace (outdoor section of a café)* **s'asseoir** *to sit* **peuvent** *can* **profiter du soleil** *enjoy the sun*

TALKING ABOUT PAST EVENTS

Let's talk about where you went Saturday.

X et Y, est-ce que vous êtes allé(e)s au cinéma samedi soir?

Oui, nous sommes allé(e)s au cinéma.

(Non, nous ne sommes pas allé(e)s au cinéma.)

• **Est-ce que vous êtes allé(e)s en ville? chez des amis? à un concert?**

• **Où êtes-vous allé(e)s samedi matin? samedi après-midi?**

Let's say where others went last weekend.

Est-ce que X et Y sont allé(e)s au cinéma samedi soir?

Oui, ils/elles sont allé(e)s au cinéma.

(Non, ils/elles ne sont pas allé(e)s au cinéma.)

Compréhension
Answers
1. Valérie va au Café de l'Univers.
2. Elle va au café avec Fatima et Zaïna.
3. Elles parlent.
4. non
5. non
6. Elles parlent du nouveau prof d'anglais.
7. Il est américain.
8. Il est intéressant, amusant, sympathique et... mignon.

Et toi?
Answers will vary.
1. En général, après les cours, je vais (chez mes copains).
   Je ne vais pas (directement chez moi).
2. Avec mes copains, je parle (du week-end).
   Je ne parle pas (de la classe de français).
3. Avec mes parents, je parle (de l'école).
   Je ne parle pas (de mes notes).
4. Avec mon frère et ma soeur, je parle (de mes problèmes).
   Je ne parle pas (des vacances).

Teaching strategy Have students raise their hands as you read through the items in **Et toi?**

(Note: Read only the affirmative sentences.)

En général, après les classes, qui va à la bibliothèque?

Qui va chez ses copains?, etc.

Critical thinking activity Have students give the English equivalents of the following phrases in the dialogue on p. 216.

le nouveau copain de Marie-Claire
[Marie-Claire's new boyfriend]

la cousine de Pauline
[Pauline's cousin]

Ask: Is the word order the same in French and English?

Does French use an apostrophe to express relationship?

What is a word-for-word translation of the French construction?

Looking ahead Possession with **de** is formally introduced in Lesson 16.

Pronunciation note Be sure that students pronounce the third person plural form correctly: **viennent** /vjɛn/.

Language note If someone is waiting for you and calls out: **Tu viens?** the usual French response is: **J'arrive** (which means *I'm just about ready and I'm coming*). However, if the person is simply asking if you are planning to join them, the French response is: **Oui, je viens** (which means, *Yes I'm coming along with you*).

1 EXCHANGES inviting friends to come along

1. –Je vais au café. Tu viens avec moi?
   –D'accord, je viens. (Non, je ne viens pas.)
2. –Je vais à la bibliothèque. Tu viens avec moi?
   –D'accord, je viens. (Non, je ne viens pas.)
3. –Je vais à la piscine. Tu viens avec moi?
   –D'accord, je viens. (Non, je ne viens pas.)
4. –Je vais au cybercafé. Tu viens avec moi?
   –D'accord, je viens. (Non, je ne viens pas.)
5. –Je vais au centre commercial. Tu viens avec moi?
   –D'accord, je viens. (Non, je ne viens pas.)
6. –Je vais au magasin de CD. Tu viens avec moi?
   –D'accord, je viens. (Non, je ne viens pas.)
7. –Je vais au stade. Tu viens avec moi?
   –D'accord, je viens. (Non, je ne viens pas.)
8. –Je vais en classe. Tu viens avec moi?
   –D'accord, je viens. (Non, je ne viens pas.)

Challenge For negative answers, explain why you cannot come.
Non, je ne viens pas.
Je dois dîner avec Michelle.

2 PRACTICE saying who is coming to an event

1. Alice vient.
2. Jean-Pierre ne vient pas.
3. Paul et Caroline viennent.
4. Vous ne venez pas.
5. Je viens.
6. Nous ne venons pas.
7. Tu ne viens pas.
8. Le prof de français vient.
9. Le prof d'anglais vient.

A Le verbe *venir*

The verb **venir** *(to come)* is irregular. Note the forms of **venir** in the present tense.

venir	Nous allons **venir** avec des amis.
je **viens**	Je **viens** avec toi.
tu **viens**	Est-ce que tu **viens** au cinéma?
il/elle **vient**	Monique ne **vient** pas avec nous.
nous **venons**	Nous **venons** à cinq heures.
vous **venez**	À quelle heure **venez**-vous à la boum?
ils/elles **viennent**	Ils **viennent** de Paris, n'est-ce pas?

→ **Revenir** *(to come back)* is conjugated like **venir.**
   —À quelle heure **revenez**-vous?
   —Nous **revenons** à dix heures.
→ Note the interrogative expression: **d'où?** *(from where?)*
   D'où viens-tu?   ***Where** do you come **from**?*

1 **Tu viens?**

PARLER Tell a friend where you are going and ask him or her to come along.

▶ à la pizzeria

1. au café
2. à la bibliothèque
3. à la piscine
4. au cybercafé
5. au centre commercial
6. au magasin de CD
7. au stade
8. en classe

Je vais à la pizzeria. Tu viens avec moi?

D'accord, je viens. (Non, je ne viens pas.)

2 Le pique-nique du Club français

PARLER/ÉCRIRE The French Club has organized a picnic. Say who is coming and who is not.

▶ Philippe (non)
   Philippe ne vient pas.

1. Alice (oui)
2. Jean-Pierre (non)
3. Paul et Caroline (oui)
4. vous (non)
5. je (oui)
6. nous (non)
7. tu (non)
8. le prof de français (oui)
9. le prof d'anglais (oui)

218 deux cent dix-huit
Unité 5

B La préposition *de; de* + l'article défini

The preposition **de** has several meanings:

from	Nous venons **de** la bibliothèque.	*We are coming **from** the library.*
of	Quelle est l'adresse **de** l'école?	*What is the address **of** the school?*
about	Je parle **de** mon copain.	*I am talking **about** my friend.*

CONTRACTIONS

Note the forms of **de** + DEFINITE ARTICLE in the sentences below.

Voici **le** café.	Marc vient **du** café.
Voici **les** Champs-Élysées.	Nous venons **des** Champs-Élysées.
Voici **la** piscine.	Tu reviens **de la** piscine.
Voici **l'**hôtel.	Les touristes arrivent **de l'**hôtel.

The preposition **de** contracts with **le** and **les,** but not with **la** and **l'.**

CONTRACTION	NO CONTRACTION			
de + le → **du**	de + la = **de la**	**du** café	**de la** plage
de + les → **des**	de + l' = **de l'**	**des** magasins	**de l'**école

→ There is liaison after **des** when the next word begins with a vowel sound.
   Où sont les livres **des étudiants?**

3 Rendez-vous

PARLER The following students live in Paris. On a Saturday afternoon they are meeting in a café. Say where each one is coming from.

▶ Jacques: le musée d'Orsay

1. Sylvie: le Louvre
2. Isabelle: le parc de la Villette
3. Jean-Paul: le Centre Pompidou
4. François: le Quartier latin
5. Cécile: l'avenue de l'Opéra
6. Nicole: la tour Eiffel
7. Marc: le jardin du Luxembourg
8. André: les Champs-Élysées
9. Pierre: les Galeries Lafayette
10. Corinne: la rue Bonaparte

Jacques vient du musée d'Orsay.

Review **aller** and contractions with **à.**

Ask each group where they are going.

Qui va au Louvre?
[Nous, nous allons au Louvre.]
Vous allez à l'Arc de Triomphe?
[Non, nous allons au Louvre!]...

On the board write: **au Louvre, aux Champs-Élysées, à la tour Eiffel, à l'Arc de Triomphe.**

Practice **venir** and contractions with **de.**

Qui vient des Champs-Élysées?
[Moi, je viens des Champs-Élysées.]
Et X, est-ce qu'il vient des Champs-Élysées?
[Non, il vient de la tour Eiffel.] ...

On the board write: **du Louvre, des Champs-Élysées, de la tour Eiffel, de l'Arc de Triomphe.**

SECTION B

Communicative function
Talking about where people are coming from

Teaching strategy Be sure students realize that the words in heavy print in the sentences on the left correspond to *the* and that those in the sentences on the right correspond to *from the.*

3 PRACTICE saying where people are coming from

1. Sylvie vient du Louvre.
2. Isabelle vient du parc de la Villette.
3. Jean-Paul vient du Centre Pompidou.
4. François vient du Quartier latin.
5. Cécile vient de l'avenue de l'Opéra.
6. Nicole vient de la tour Eiffel.
7. Marc vient du jardin de Luxembourg.
8. André vient des Champs-Élysées.
9. Pierre vient des Galeries Lafayette.
10. Corinne vient de la rue Bonaparte.

Cultural background
The **Quartier latin** is the historical students' quarter on the Left Bank. One of the streets is **la rue Bonaparte,** named in honor of Napoleon.

Le jardin du Luxembourg is also in that part of Paris.

Les Galeries Lafayette is a well-known Paris department store.

Teaching strategy This exercise should be done quickly with the rhythm of a practice drill. Be sure to read the cues aloud, carefully modeling the pronunciation of the new place names.

Variation Repeat the drill, changing the subjects orally.

nous: le musée d'Orsay
Nous venons du musée d'Orsay.

♻ Re-entry and review Say that the people are going to these places.

Jacques va au musée d'Orsay.

Teaching Resource Options

PRINT

Workbook PE, pp. 131–136
Unit 5 Resource Book
   Communipak, pp. 140–163
   Video Activities, pp. 91–94
   Videoscript, pp. 95–96
   Workbook TE, pp. 71–76

AUDIO & VISUAL

Overhead Transparencies
16 Subject pronouns

TECHNOLOGY
Power Presentations

VIDEO PROGRAM

VIDÉO   DVD

MODULE 15
Sports et musique
(14:20–20:23 min.)

4 ROLE PLAY finding out where people are coming from

–D'où viens-tu?
–Je viens ...
1. du restaurant
2. de la bibliothèque
3. du concert de rock
4. de la boum de Christine
5. du pique-nique de Monique
6. de l'opéra

Language notes
• **Le foot (le football)** is soccer; American football is **le football américain.**
• In the expressions **jouer du piano** and **jouer de la flûte, du** and **de la** represent the preposition **de** plus a definite article. Therefore, in the negative one does not use **de.** Compare:
Je n'ai pas de clarinette.
Je ne joue pas de la clarinette.

Supplementary vocabulary
SPORTS
le croquet   le golf
le frisbee   le rugby
le hockey sur glace, sur gazon
INSTRUMENTS
le cor anglais *French horn*
le synthé, synthétiseur
le trombone
le tuba
la flûte à bec *recorder*
la guitare électrique
la trompette
le violoncelle *cello*

---

4 **D'où viens-tu?**

PARLER During vacation, Olivier goes out every day. When he gets home, his sister Sophie asks him where he is coming from.

▶ mardi

1. lundi
2. mercredi
3. vendredi
4. dimanche
5. samedi
6. jeudi

LUNDI	le restaurant
MARDI	le cybercafé
MERCREDI	la bibliothèque
JEUDI	l'opéra
VENDREDI	le concert de rock
SAMEDI	le pique-nique de Monique
DIMANCHE	la boum de Christine

VOCABULAIRE Les sports, les jeux et la musique

▶ *Les sports*

le foot(ball)	**le volley(ball)**
le basket(ball)	**le tennis**
le ping-pong	**le baseball**

▶ *Les jeux* (games)

les échecs (chess)	**les dames** (checkers)
les jeux vidéo	**les cartes** (cards)
les jeux d'ordinateur	

▶ *Les instruments de musique*

le piano	**le saxo(phone)**	**la flûte**	**la clarinette**
le violon	**le clavier** (keyboard)	**la guitare**	**la batterie** (drums)

jouer à + le, la, les + SPORT or GAME	*to play*	Nous **jouons au** tennis.
jouer de + le, la, les + INSTRUMENT	*to play*	Alice **joue du** piano.

5 **Activités**

PARLER Ask your classmates if they play the following instruments and games.

▶ —Est-ce que tu joues au ping-pong?
  —Oui, je joue au ping-pong.
   (Non, je ne joue pas au ping-pong.)

▶ —Est-ce que tu joues du piano?
  —Oui, je joue du piano.
   (Non, je ne joue pas du piano.)

USING THE VIDEO

The entire video module for this lesson develops the themes of sports and music, and utilizes the expressions **jouer à** and **jouer de.**

If you do not want to present the whole module at once, you can show some of the segments at the end of the lesson for review.

Les pronoms accentués

In the answers to the questions below, the nouns in heavy print are replaced by pronouns. These pronouns are called STRESS PRONOUNS. Note their forms.

—François dîne avec **Florence?**   *Is François having dinner with* ***Florence?***
—Oui, il dîne avec **elle.**   *Yes, he is having dinner with* ***her.***

—Tu parles de **Jean-Paul?**   *Are you talking about* ***Jean-Paul?***
—Non, je ne parle pas de **lui.**   *No, I'm not talking about* ***him.***

FORMS

(SUBJECT PRONOUNS)	STRESS PRONOUNS	(SUBJECT PRONOUNS)	STRESS PRONOUNS
(je)	**moi**	(nous)	**nous**
(tu)	**toi**	(vous)	**vous**
(il)	**lui**	(ils)	**eux**
(elle)	**elle**	(elles)	**elles**

USES

Stress pronouns are used:

- to reinforce a subject pronoun
  Moi, je parle français.
  Vous, vous parlez anglais.

  I speak French.
  You speak English.

- after **c'est** and **ce n'est pas**
  —C'est Paul là-bas?
  —Non, ce n'est pas **lui.**

  No, it's not ***him.***

- in short sentences where there is no verb
  —Qui parle français ici?
  —**Moi!**

  I do!

- before and after **et** and **ou**
  Lui et moi, nous sommes copains.

  He and I, (we) are friends.

- After prepositions such as **de, avec, pour, chez**
  Voici Marc et Paul. Je parle souvent **d'eux.**
  Voici Isabelle. Je vais au cinéma **avec elle.**
  Voici M. Mercier. Nous travaillons **pour lui.**

  I often talk ***about them.***
  I go to the movies ***with her.***
  We work ***for him.***

  → Note the meaning of **chez** + STRESS PRONOUN:
  Je vais **chez moi.**
  Paul étudie **chez lui.**

  I am going ***home.***
  Paul is studying ***at home.***

  Tu viens **chez nous?**
  Je suis chez Alice. Je dîne **chez elle.**

  Are you coming ***to our house?***
  I am having dinner ***at her place.***

deux cent vingt et un
Leçon 15 221

TALKING ABOUT PAST EVENTS

Let's talk about what sports and games you and your friends played last weekend.

X et Y, est-ce que vous avez joué au tennis le week-end dernier?

Oui, nous avons joué au tennis.

(Non, nous n'avons pas joué au tennis.)

- **Est-ce que vous avez joué au football? au baseball? au ping-pong? au volley? aux échecs? aux cartes? aux dames? au Monopoly?**

Additional challenge questions
- **Où est-ce que vous avez joué?**
- **Avec qui est-ce que vous avez joué?**
- **Qui a gagné?** (Who won?)

Teaching Resource Options

PRINT

Workbook PE, pp. 131–136
Unit 5 Resource Book
   Audioscript, p. 97
   Communipak, pp. 140–163
   Workbook TE, pp. 71–76

AUDIO & VISUAL

Audio Program
CD 3 Track 11

TECHNOLOGY
Power Presentations

---

6 **COMPREHENSION** stating who is home and who isn't

1. Il est chez lui. (Il n'est pas chez lui.)
2. Elle n'est pas chez elle.
3. Ils ne sont pas chez eux.
4. Elles sont chez elles. (Elles ne sont pas chez elles.)
5. Ils ne sont pas chez eux.
6. Je suis chez moi. (Je ne suis pas chez moi.)
7. Tu n'es pas chez toi.
8. Nous ne sommes pas chez nous.
9. Tu es chez toi. (Tu n'est pas chez toi.)

Expansion The first model and items 1, 4, 6, 9 could be either: the people could be at home or at another person's home. If students give a negative response, ask them to clarify.

Alice étudie.

Elle n'est pas chez elle.

Elle étudie (chez Sophie, à la bibliothèque, etc.**).**

---

7 **COMMUNICATION** answering personal questions

1. Oui, j'étudie souvent avec eux. (Non, je n'étudie pas souvent avec eux.)
2. Oui, je vais souvent chez elle. (Non, je ne vais pas souvent chez elle.)
3. Oui, je travaille pour eux. (Non, je ne travaille pas pour eux.)
4. Oui, je parle français avec lui. (Non, je ne parle pas français avec lui.)
5. Oui, je vais souvent au cinéma avec elles. (Non, je ne vais pas souvent au cinéma avec elles.)
6. Oui, je reste chez moi le week-end. (Non, je ne reste pas chez moi le week-end.)
7. Oui, je reste chez moi pendant les vacances. (Non, je ne reste pas chez moi pendant les vacances.)
8. Oui, je voyage avec mes parents. (Non, je ne voyage pas avec mes parents.)
9. Oui, je joue aux jeux vidéo avec lui. (Non, je ne joue pas aux jeux vidéo avec lui.)
10. Oui, je vais souvent chez eux. (Non, je ne vais pas souvent chez eux.)

---

6 **Samedi soir** *(Saturday night)*

PARLER/ÉCRIRE On Saturday night, some people stay home and others do not. Read what the following people are doing and say whether or not they are at home.

▶ Alice étudie.
  Elle est chez elle.

▶ Paul va au cinéma.
  Il n'est pas chez lui.

1. François regarde la télé.
2. Mélanie va au cinéma.
3. Marc et Pierre dînent en ville.
4. Léa et Pauline écoutent des CD.
5. Les voisins font une promenade.
6. Je travaille avec mon père.
7. Tu vas au théâtre.
8. Nous allons à la bibliothèque.
9. Tu prépares le dîner.

7 **Questions personnelles**

PARLER/ÉCRIRE Use stress pronouns in your answers.

1. Tu étudies souvent avec tes *(your)* copains?
2. Tu vas souvent chez ta cousine?
3. Tu travailles pour les voisins?
4. Tu parles français avec ton père?
5. Tu vas souvent au cinéma avec tes copines?
6. Tu restes chez toi le week-end?
7. Tu restes chez toi pendant *(during)* les vacances?
8. Tu voyages avec tes parents?
9. Tu joues aux jeux vidéo avec ton copain?
10. Tu vas souvent chez tes voisins?

VOCABULAIRE Expressions pour la conversation

▶ *How to express surprise:*

Vraiment?!   *Really?!*
  —Je parle chinois.
  —Vraiment?!

▶ *How to contradict someone:*

Pas du tout!   *Not at all! Definitely not!*
  —Tu es anglais?
  —Pas du tout! Je suis français!

---

8 **Commérage** *(Gossip)*

PARLER Élodie likes to gossip. Act out the dialogues between her and her friend Thomas.

▶ Marina dîne avec Jean-Pierre.

1. Éric dîne avec Alice.
2. Thérèse va chez Paul.
3. Jérôme est au cinéma avec Delphine.
4. Monsieur Mercier travaille pour Mademoiselle Duval.
5. Philippe travaille pour le voisin.
6. Marc et Vincent dansent avec Mélanie et Juliette.

Marina dîne avec Jean-Pierre.

Vraiment?

Mais oui! Elle dîne avec lui!

D La construction: nom + *de* + nom

Compare the word order in French and English.

J'ai une raquette.　　　C'est une **raquette de tennis.**　　*It's a **tennis racket.***
Paul a une voiture.　　C'est une **voiture de sport.**　　*It's a **sports car.***

When one noun is used to modify another noun, the French construction is:

MAIN NOUN + **de** + MODIFYING NOUN	une classe de français.
↓ **d'** (+ VOWEL SOUND)	une classe d'espagnol.

→ There is no article after **de.**

LANGUAGE COMPARISON

In French, when one noun modifies another, the main noun comes FIRST.

In English, the main noun comes SECOND.

un **jeu** d'ordinateur　　　*a computer **game***

9 Précisions

PARLER/ÉCRIRE Complete the following sentences with an expression consisting of **de** + underlined noun.

▶ J'aime le <u>sport</u>. J'ai une voiture …

J'ai une voiture de sport!

1. Claire aime le <u>ping-pong</u>. Elle a une raquette …
2. Nous adorons le <u>rock</u>. Nous écoutons un concert …
3. Jacques aime le <u>jazz</u>. Il écoute un programme …
4. Vous étudiez l'<u>anglais</u>. Vous avez un livre …
5. Tu étudies le <u>piano</u>. Aujourd'hui, tu as une leçon …
6. Léa étudie l'<u>espagnol</u>. Elle a un bon prof …
7. Je regarde mes <u>photos</u>. J'ai un album …
8. Pierre joue au <u>baseball</u>. Il a une batte …
9. J'aime la <u>musique africaine</u>. J'ai des CD …
10. Paul est bon en <u>maths</u>. Il fait un problème …

PRONONCIATION

Les voyelles /ø/ et /œ/

The letters "**eu**" and "**oeu**" represent vowel sounds that do not exist in English but that are not very hard to pronounce.

/ø/　　/œ/
2　**9**
d<u>eu</u>x　n<u>eu</u>f

Répétez:

/ø/　d<u>eu</u>x　<u>eu</u>x　je v<u>eu</u>x　je p<u>eu</u>x　un p<u>eu</u>　j<u>eu</u>x　il pl<u>eu</u>t　un <u>eu</u>ro
　　Tu p<u>eu</u>x aller chez <u>eu</u>x.

/œ/　n<u>eu</u>f　s<u>oeu</u>r　h<u>eu</u>re　profess<u>eu</u>r　j<u>eu</u>ne
　　Ma s<u>oeu</u>r arrive à n<u>eu</u>f h<u>eu</u>res.

8 ROLE PLAY talking about others

1. –Éric dîne avec Alice.
   –Vraiment?
   –Mais oui! Il dîne avec elle!
2. –Thérèse va chez Paul.
   –Vraiment?
   –Mais oui! Elle va chez lui!
3. –Jérôme est au cinéma avec Delphine.
   –Vraiment?
   –Mais oui! Il est au cinéma avec elle!
4. –M. Mercier travaille pour Mlle Duval.
   –Vraiment?
   –Mais oui! Il travaille pour elle!
5. –Philippe travaille pour le voisin.
   –Vraiment?
   –Mais oui! Il travaille pour lui!
6. –Marc et Vincent dansent avec Mélanie et Juliette.
   –Vraiment?
   –Mais oui! Ils dansent avec elles!

SECTION D

Communicative function
Describing objects and people

Critical thinking Point out that in English, the main noun comes second: *tennis <u>racket</u>, sports <u>car</u>.*

In French, the main noun comes first: **une <u>raquette</u> de tennis, une <u>voiture</u> de sport.**

How do the French say:
orange juice **[un jus d'orange]**
tomato salad **[une salade de tomates]**
bathroom **[une salle de bains]**

9 PRACTICE describing objects using **de** + noun

1. Elle a une raquette de ping-pong.
2. Nous écoutons un concert de rock.
3. Jacques écoute un programme de jazz.
4. Vous avez un livre d'anglais.
5. Aujourd'hui, tu as une leçon de piano.
6. Elle a un bon prof d'espagnol.
7. J'ai un album de photos.
8. Il a une batte de baseball.
9. J'ai des CD de musique africaine.
10. Il fait un problème de maths.

Pronunciation Item 7: album /albɔm/

Teaching Resource Options

PRINT

Workbook PE, pp. 131–136
Unit 5 Resource Book
   Audioscript, pp. 97–98
   Communipak, pp. 140–163
   Family Involvement, pp. 89–90
   Workbook TE, pp. 71–76

   Assessment
   Lesson 15 Quiz, pp. 101–102
   Portfolio Assessment, Unit 1 URB
     pp. 155–164
   Audioscript for Quiz 15, p. 100
   Answer Keys, pp. 210–213

AUDIO & VISUAL
Audio Program
CD 3 Tracks 12, 13
CD 15 Track 3

TECHNOLOGY
Test Generator CD-ROM/eTest Plus
Online

1 COMPREHENSION

1. Salut, Stéphanie! D'où viens-tu?
   (b) Du supermarché.
2. Et où vas-tu maintenant?
   (c) Je rentre chez moi.
3. Tu ne veux pas venir au cinéma avec moi?
   (d) Je ne peux pas. Je dois étudier.
4. Ah bon? Pourquoi?
   (a) J'ai un examen d'anglais lundi.

2 GUIDED ORAL EXPRESSION

—Où vas-tu?
—Je vais ... Tu viens?
—Ça dépend! Qu'est-ce que tu vas faire chez ... ?
—Nous allons ...
—D'accord, je viens! (Non, je ne viens pas.)

1. chez Françoise / elle / regarder la télé.
2. chez Corinne et Claire / elles / dîner.
3. chez Nicolas et Patrick / eux / jouer aux cartes.
4. chez mon cousin / lui / jouer aux échecs.
5. chez ma cousine / elle / jouer du piano.
6. chez des copains / eux / écouter la radio.

À votre tour!

OBJECTIFS

Now you can ...
• let people know if you are coming with them or not
• talk about the musical instruments, sports, and games that you play

1 🎧 Conversation

PARLER Saturday afternoon, Henri meets Stéphanie downtown. Match Henri's questions with Stéphanie's answers. Then act out the conversation with a classmate.

1 Salut, Stéphanie! D'où viens-tu?
2 Et où vas-tu maintenant?
3 Tu ne veux pas venir au cinéma avec moi?
4 Ah bon? Pourquoi?

a J'ai un examen d'anglais lundi.
b Du supermarché.
c Je rentre chez moi.
d Je ne peux pas. Je dois étudier.

2 🎧 Créa-dialogue

PARLER Ask your classmates whom they are going to visit and what they are going to do. Then decide if you are going to come along.

▶ —Où vas-tu?
—Je vais chez <u>Jean-Claude</u>. Tu viens?
—Ça dépend! Qu'est-ce que tu vas faire chez <u>lui</u>?
—Nous allons <u>jouer au ping-pong</u>.
—D'accord, je viens!
  (Non, je ne viens pas.)

CHEZ QUI?	1. Françoise	2. Corinne et Claire	3. Nicolas et Patrick	4. mon cousin	5. ma cousine	6. des copains
ACTIVITÉ						

▶ Jean-Claude

3 Retour à la maison

PARLER This afternoon, the following people went downtown. Say which places they are coming from.

▶ Nous venons de l'école.

1 tu
2 vous
3 Madame Simon
4 Monsieur Dupont
5 Claire et Diane
6 Daniel et Philippe

▶ nous

À VOTRE TOUR

Depending on your goals and objectives, you may or may not wish to assign all of the activities in the **À votre tour** section.

PAIR PRACTICE

Act. 1–4 lend themselves to pair practice.

For Act. 2 and 4, you may have students work in trios, with two performing while the other holds the Answer Key and acts as monitor.

4 Message illustré

ÉCRIRE Frédéric likes to use illustrations in his diary. Transcribe what he has written about himself and others, replacing the pictures with the corresponding missing words.

Je joue 🏐
J'aime aussi aller 🏊
Ma sœur Catherine joue très bien 🎾
Elle est musicienne aussi. Elle joue 🎶 et 🎻

Mon frère Marc préfère jouer 🃏.
Tiens, voilà ma copine Stéphanie.
Elle vient 🏟
Elle joue très bien ⚽

5 Un mail à Sandrine

ÉCRIRE In a recent e-mail, Sandrine, your French pen pal, mentioned various hobbies she enjoys. In a short e-mail, tell her …

- which sports you play
- which musical instruments you play
- which games you play

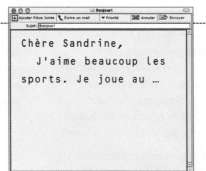

Chère Sandrine,
    J'aime beaucoup les
    sports. Je joue au …

parc supermarché stade
école bibliothèque piscine

LESSON REVIEW
CLASSZONE.COM

---

3 COMPREHENSION

1. Tu viens de l'école.
2. Vous venez de la bibliothèque.
3. Madame Simon vient du parc.
4. Monsieur Dupont vient du supermarché.
5. Claire et Diane viennent du stade (du parc).
6. Daniel et Philippe viennent de la piscine (du parc).

4 READING COMPREHENSION

Je joue <u>au volleyball</u>.
J'aime aussi aller <u>à la piscine</u>.
Ma sœur Catherine joue très bien <u>au tennis</u>.
Elle est musicienne aussi. Elle joue <u>de la clarinette</u> et <u>du violon</u>.
Mon frère Marc préfère jouer <u>aux cartes</u>.
Tiens, voilà ma copine Stéphanie. Elle vient <u>du stade</u>.
Elle joue très bien <u>au foot[ball]</u>.

Challenge You may wish to have the students prepare their own **"messages illustrés."** (See *Challenge De nouveaux messages,* p. 103.)

Middle School Copymasters

Drill: *Vacances d'été,* p. 68

---

5 WRITTEN SELF-EXPRESSION

Answers will vary.
Chère Sandrine,
J'aime beaucoup les sports. Je joue au tennis et au volley. J'aime nager. Je joue du piano. J'aime jouer aux cartes et aux échecs avec mes copines. Et toi?

Amitiés,

Anne

PORTFOLIO ASSESSMENT

You will probably select only one speaking activity and one writing activity to go into the students' portfolios for Unit 5.

In this lesson, Act. 2 lends itself well to an oral portfolio recording.

Act. 5 offers an excellent writing portfolio topic.

Leçon 16

Main Topic Talking about one's family

Teaching Resource Options

PRINT

Workbook PE, pp. 137–143
Activités pour tous PE, pp. 83–85
Block Scheduling Copymasters, pp. 121–128
Unit 5 Resource Book
  Activités pour tous TE, pp. 111–113
  Audioscript, pp. 132–135
  Communipak, pp. 140–163
  Lesson Plans, pp. 114–115
  Block Scheduling Lesson Plans, pp. 116–118
  Absent Student Copymasters, pp. 119–122
  Video Activities, pp. 125–128
  Videoscript, pp. 129–131
  Workbook TE, pp. 103–109

AUDIO & VISUAL

Audio Program
CD 3 Tracks 14, 15
CD 9 Tracks 25–32

Overhead Transparencies
34 Apartment building

TECHNOLOGY
Online Workbook

VIDEO PROGRAM

VIDÉO   DVD

MODULE 16
Où habitez-vous?

TOTAL TIME: 5:12 min.
  DVD Disk 2
  Videotape 3 (COUNTER: 20:35 min.)

16.1 Presentation: Listening
– C'est ma maison
(21:28–22:29 min.)

16.2 Mini-scenes: Listening
– C'est ta voiture?
(22:30–23:27 min.)

16.3 Dialogue: C'est ta famille?
(23:28–24:27 min.)

16.4 Vignette culturelle:
Un immeuble à Paris
(24:28–25:47 min.)

Comprehension practice Play the entire module through as an introduction to the lesson.

LEÇON **16** **Mes voisins** AUDIO

Bonjour!
Je m'appelle Frédéric Mallet.
J'habite à Paris avec ma famille.
Nous habitons dans un <u>immeuble</u> de   *building*
six <u>étages</u>.   *floors*
Voici mon immeuble et voici <u>mes</u> voisins.   *my*

Monsieur Lacroche habite au <u>sixième</u>   *sixth*
étage avec sa femme. Ils sont
musiciens. Lui, il joue du piano et elle,
elle chante. Oh là là, <u>quelle</u> musique!   *what*

Mademoiselle Jolivet habite au
<u>cinquième</u> étage avec <u>son</u> oncle et   *fifth / her*
<u>sa</u> tante.   *her*
Paul, mon <u>meilleur</u> ami, habite au   *best*
<u>quatrième</u> étage avec <u>sa</u> soeur et   *fourth / his*
<u>ses</u> parents.   *his*

Mademoiselle Ménard habite au
<u>troisième</u> étage avec son chien   *third*
Pomme, ses deux chats Fritz et Arthur,
son <u>perroquet</u> Coco et son canari   *parrot*
Froufrou. (Je <u>pense que</u> c'est une   *think / that*
personne très intéressante, mais mon
père pense qu'elle est un peu bizarre.)

Monsieur et Madame Boutin habitent
au <u>deuxième</u> étage avec <u>leur</u>   *second / their*
<u>fils</u> et leurs deux <u>filles</u>.   *son / daughters*

Et qui habite au premier étage?
C'est un garçon super-intelligent,
super-cool et très sympathique!
Et ce garçon … c'est moi!

SETTING THE STAGE

PROPS: Transparency 34: Apartment building
(Have students keep their books closed.)

Describe the building on the transparency.
  Voici un immeuble.
  Voici le rez-de-chaussée.
  Voici le premier étage, le deuxième étage, …

On the chalkboard, write the following list:
  Paul
  Frédéric Mallet
  Mademoiselle Jolivet
  Mademoiselle Ménard
  Monsieur et Madame Boutin
  Monsieur et Madame Lacroche

Compréhension

1. Où habite Frédéric Mallet?
2. Combien *(How many)* d'étages a son immeuble?
3. Qui habite à chaque *(each)* étage?
4. Quelle est la profession des Lacroche?
5. Selon toi *(In your opinion)*, est-ce que Mademoiselle Ménard est une personne bizarre ou intéressante? Pourquoi?

COMPARAISONS CULTURELLES

The floors of buildings are numbered differently in France and in the United States. Compare:

- **rez-de-chaussée**   *ground floor or first floor*
- **premier étage (1ᵉʳ étage)**   *second floor*
- **deuxième étage (2ᵉᵐᵉ étage)**   *third floor*

NOTE: In the older downtown areas of French cities, apartment houses have a maximum of six stories. This is because until the twentieth century there were no elevators and people had to use the stairs.

NOTE culturelle

Les animaux domestiques en France

La France a une population de 60 millions d'habitants et de 42 millions d'animaux domestiques.° Les Français adorent les animaux. Une famille sur deux° a un animal domestique. Par ordre de préférence, les principaux animaux domestiques sont les chiens (39%: trente-neuf pour cent), les chats (35%), les poissons (12%), les oiseaux (5%) et les hamsters (4%). Il y a aussi un certain nombre de serpents, de tortues et de lapins.

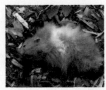
un hamster

un lapin

une tortue

un oiseau

un poisson

un poisson rouge

animaux domestiques *pets*   une ... sur deux *one out of two*

Compréhension
Answers
1. Il habite à Paris.
2. Son immeuble a six étages.
3. Les Lacroche habitent au 6ᵉ étage. Mlle Jolivet, son oncle et sa tante habitent au 5ᵉ étage. Paul et sa famille habitent au 4ᵉ étage. Mlle Ménard et ses animaux habitent au 3ᵉ étage. Les Boutin habitent au 2ᵉ étage. Frédéric Mallet habite au premier étage.
4. Ils sont musiciens.
5. Mlle Ménard est bizarre (intéressante) parce qu'elle a un chien, deux chats et deux oiseaux.

Language note You may want to point out the irregular plural forms:

un animal   des animaux
un oiseau   des oiseaux

Prononciation note Un hamster is pronounced almost as in English, but with a silent "h" and no liaison: /amstɛr/

Teaching suggestion Take a class poll of pet ownership. **Qui a un chat? Qui a un chien?** Tabulate your results in percentages and compare them with the percentages in France.

Tell students to listen carefully to determine who lives on which floor. You may want to play the audio recording more than once.

Then have students open their books and follow along as you play the recording once more.

Answers:
Paul (4e)
Frédéric Mallet (1er)
Mademoiselle Jolivet (5e)
Mademoiselle Ménard (3e)
Monsieur et Madame Boutin (2e)
Monsieur et Madame Lacroche (6e)

SECTION A

Communicative function
Talking about possessions

Teaching Resource Options

PRINT

Workbook PE, pp. 137–143
Unit 5 Resource Book
   Audioscript, p. 132
   Communipak, pp. 140–163
   Workbook TE, pp. 103–109

AUDIO & VISUAL

Audio Program
CD 3 Track 16

Overhead Transparencies
8 Family tree

TECHNOLOGY

Power Presentations

Teaching strategy To help students remember the word order, have them think of **de** as meaning *of* or *which belongs to.*

1 **PRACTICE** expressing relationships

1. Carole est la cousine de Jacques.
2. Michel est le copain de Caroline.
3. Philippe est le camarade de Charles.
4. Robert est le frère de Guillaume.
5. Marina est la copine de Paul.
6. Pauline est l'amie d'Éric.
7. Alice est la soeur de Karine.

2 **DESCRIPTION** describing ownership

- Marc a la guitare d'Alice et la radio d'Éric.
- Alice a le vélo de Laure et le baladeur de Marc.
- Éric a la raquette de Marc et l'appareil-photo de Laure.
- Laure a le scooter d'Alice et les CD d'Éric.

A La possession avec *de*

Note the words in heavy print:

Voici une moto.   C'est la moto **de Frédéric.**   *It's **Frédéric's** motorcycle.*
Voici un vélo.   C'est le vélo **de Sophie.**   *It's **Sophie's** bike.*

To express POSSESSION, French speakers use the construction:

le/la/les + NOUN + **de** + OWNER	la radio **de** Thomas
↓	les livres **de** Claire
d'(+ VOWEL SOUND)	la maison **d'**Émilie

→ The same construction is used to express RELATIONSHIP:
   C'est **le copain de Daniel.**   *That's **Daniel's** friend.*
   C'est **la mère de Paul.**   *That's **Paul's** mother.*

→ Remember that **de** contracts with **le** and **les:**
   Où est le chat **du voisin?**   *Where is the **neighbor's** cat?*
   C'est la chambre **des enfants.**   *This is the **children's** room.*

→ While English often indicates possession with **'s,** French always uses **de.**
   la copine **de Monique**   ***Monique's** friend (the friend **of Monique**)*

THEATRE
DÉJAZET
CRÉATIONS D'YVES LE GUILLOCHET
41, boulevard du Temple · métro République · Paris 3ème
Les aventures de
PinocchiO
du 27 octobre au 25 avril

1 **Présentations** *(Introductions)*

PARLER Imagine that you are hosting a party in France. Introduce the following people.

▶ Jean-Marc (cousin/Sylvie)

Jean-Marc est le cousin de Sylvie.

1. Carole (cousine/Jacques)
2. Michel (copain/Caroline)
3. Philippe (camarade/Charles)
4. Robert (frère/Guillaume)
5. Marina (copine/Paul)
6. Pauline (amie/Éric)
7. Alice (soeur/Karine)

2 **Échanges**

PARLER/ÉCRIRE The following friends have decided to trade a few of their possessions. On a separate sheet of paper, write out what each person has, once the exchange has been completed.

Marc   Alice   Éric   Laure

TALKING ABOUT PAST EVENTS

Let's talk about what you and your friends did last weekend.

(Reminder: If the question contains **tu as...,** students should answer with **j'ai...** or **je n'ai pas...** If it contains **tu es...,** they should answer with **je suis...** or **je ne suis pas...**)

Est-ce que tu es allé(e) à la plage?
Oui, je suis allé(e) à la plage.
(Non, je ne suis pas allé(e) à la plage.)
Est-ce que tu as nagé?
Oui, j'ai nagé.
(Non, je n'ai pas nagé.)

VOCABULAIRE La famille

la famille (family)

les grands-parents
  le grand-père   **la grand-mère**

les parents (parents)   **les parents** (relatives)
  le père   **la mère**   **l'oncle**   **la tante** (aunt)
  le mari (husband) **la femme** (wife)

les enfants (children)
  un enfant   **une enfant**
  le frère   **la soeur**   **le cousin**   **la cousine**
  le fils (son)   **la fille** (daughter)

Re-entry and review

The following words were taught in Lesson 2C: **père, mère, frère, soeur, cousin, cousine.**

Pronunciation Make sure that students pronounce the following nouns correctly:
femme /fam/
fils /fis/
cousin /kuzɛ̃/ and **cousine** /kuzin/

Supplementary vocabulary

les petits-enfants *grandchildren*
le petit-fils / la petite-fille, *grandson / granddaughter*
les jumeaux *twins*
un jumeau / une jumelle *male twin / female twin*
un frère aîné / une soeur aînée *older brother / sister*
un frère cadet / une soeur cadette *younger brother / sister*
un(e) enfant unique *only child*
le neveu / la nièce *nephew / niece*
le beau-père / la belle-mère *stepfather, father-in-law / stepmother, mother-in-law*
le beau-frère / la belle-soeur *stepbrother, brother-in-law / stepsister, sister-in-law*
le demi-frère / la demi-soeur *half-brother / half-sister*
le parrain / la marraine *godfather / godmother*

③ La famille de Frédéric

PARLER/ÉCRIRE Frédéric has drawn his family tree. Study it and explain the relationships between the people below.

▶ Éric/Alice Vidal
  Éric est le fils d'Alice Vidal.

1. Léa/Frédéric
2. Martine Mallet/Léa
3. Albert et Julie Mallet/Éric
4. Alice Vidal/Frédéric
5. Jean Mallet/Martine Mallet
6. Alice Vidal/Maurice Vidal
7. Julie Mallet/Éric
8. Élodie/Maurice Vidal
9. Léa/Éric
10. Frédéric/Élodie

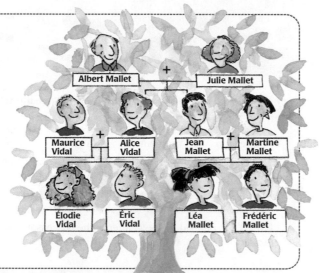

▶ Marc a la guitare d'Alice et …

Marc   Alice   Éric   Laure

③ **COMPREHENSION** describing family relationships

1. Léa est la soeur de Frédéric.
2. Martine Mallet est la mère de Léa.
3. Albert et Julie Mallet sont les grands-parents d'Éric.
4. Alice Vidal est la tante de Frédéric.
5. Jean Mallet est le mari de Martine Mallet.
6. Alice Vidal est la femme de Maurice Vidal.
7. Julie Mallet est la grand-mère d'Éric.
8. Élodie est la fille de Maurice Vidal.
9. Léa est la cousine d'Éric.
10. Frédéric est le cousin d'Élodie.

- Est-ce que tu es allé(e) à la plage?
- Est-ce que tu as nagé?
- Est-ce que tu es allé(e) au restaurant?
- Est-ce que tu as mangé une pizza?
- Est-ce que tu es allé(e) en ville?

- Est-ce que tu as acheté des vêtements?
- Est-ce que tu es allé(e) au parc?
- Est-ce que tu as joué au frisbee?
- Où est-ce que tu es allé(e)?
- Qu'est-ce que tu as fait?

B Les adjectifs possessifs: *mon, ton, son*

LEARNING ABOUT LANGUAGE
French, like English, shows possession and relationship with POSSESSIVE ADJECTIVES:
ma voiture (*my car*), **mon** père (*my father*)
In French, possessive adjectives AGREE with the nouns they introduce.

Note the forms of the possessive adjectives in the chart below:

(POSSESSOR)		SINGULAR		PLURAL			
		MASCULINE	FEMININE				
(je)	my	mon	ma	mes	mon frère	ma soeur	mes copains
(tu)	your	ton	ta	tes	ton oncle	ta tante	tes cousins
(il)	his	son	sa	ses	son père	sa mère	ses parents
(elle)	her	son	sa	ses	son père	sa mère	ses parents

→ The feminine singular forms **ma, ta, sa** become **mon, ton, son** before a vowel sound.

| une amie | mon amie | ton amie | son amie |
| une auto | mon auto | ton auto | son auto |

→ There is liaison after **mon, ton, son, mes, tes, ses** before a vowel sound.
   mon oncle   **mes** amis

→ The choice between **son, sa,** and **ses** depends on the gender (masculine or feminine) and the number (singular or plural) of the noun that *follows*.

It does NOT depend on the gender of the possessor (that is, whether the owner is male or female). Compare:

PERSONNALISE TON PORTABLE

COMPREHENSION Possessions

PROPS: Books, watches, etc.

Hold up your own textbook, saying:
   Voici un livre de français.
   C'est mon livre.
   X, montre-nous ton livre de français.

Continue with **ma/ta** montre.

Walk around holding up students' items.
   C'est le livre de X [boy]?
   Oui, c'est son livre.
   C'est le livre de Y [girl]?
   Oui, c'est son livre.
   C'est la montre de Z?
   Oui, c'est sa montre.

Follow-up (pointing out items):
   Comment dit-on: *his book? her book?*

4 Marc et Hélène

PARLER Marc never knows where his things are, but Hélène does. Play both roles.

▶ le vélo/dans le garage
—Où est mon vélo?
—Ton vélo? Il est dans le garage.

1. les CD/ici
2. la raquette/là-bas
3. la montre/sur toi
4. les livres/dans le sac
5. le portable/sur le bureau
6. le chat/derrière la porte
7. l'appareil-photo/dans la chambre
8. le baladeur/sur la table

5 Invitations

PARLER/ÉCRIRE Say whom each person is inviting to the school party, using the appropriate possessive adjectives.

▶ Michel/la copine
Michel invite sa copine.

1. André/la cousine
2. Jean-Claude/la soeur
3. Marie-Noëlle/les frères
4. Pascal/l'amie Sophie
5. Monique/les cousins
6. Nathalie/l'ami Marc
7. Georges/l'amie Cécile
8. Paul/l'amie Thérèse

6 Chez Marie et Christophe Boutin

PARLER/ÉCRIRE Items 1 to 8 belong to Marie. Items 9 to 16 belong to Christophe. Point these things out.

Marie		Christophe	
▶ le vélo C'est son vélo.		▶ les CD Ce sont ses CD.	
1. le baladeur	5. l'ordinateur	9. la guitare	13. les livres
2. le sac	6. la guitare	10. la chaîne hi-fi	14. la montre
3. le chien	7. les CD	11. le chat	15. les photos
4. l'album	8. les cassettes	12. le scooter	16. les skis

VOCABULAIRE Expression pour la conversation

▶ **How to question a statement or express a doubt:**

Tu es sûr(e)? *Are you sure?*

—C'est mon pantalon (*pants*)!
—**Tu es sûr?**

7   Après la soirée

PARLER Last night Frédéric and Paul gave a party. They realize that their friends left certain things behind. Frédéric thinks he knows what belongs to whom.

▶ le sac/Claire   FRÉDÉRIC: **Voici le sac de Claire.**
   PAUL: **Tu es sûr?**
   FRÉDÉRIC: **Mais oui, c'est son sac!**

1. le sac/Jean-Pierre
2. la guitare/Antoine
3. l'appareil-photo/Cécile
4. le baladeur/Stéphanie
5. les CD/Léa
6. le portable/Thomas

TALKING ABOUT PAST EVENTS

Let's talk about a recent party.

Imaginez que vous avez organisé une boum le week-end dernier avec des amis.

Est-ce que tu as organisé une boum le week-end dernier?
Oui, j'ai organisé une boum.

• **Avec qui est-ce que tu as organisé la boum?**
• **À qui est-ce que vous avez téléphoné?**
• **Qui est-ce que vous avez invité?**
• **Est-ce que vous avez dansé?**
• **Est-ce que vous avez chanté?**
• **Qu'est-ce que vous avez mangé?**

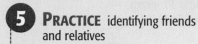

4 ROLE PLAY finding one's things

1. —Où sont mes CD?
   —Tes CD? Ils sont ici.
2. —Où est ma raquette?
   —Ta raquette? Elle est là-bas.
3. —Où est ma montre?
   —Ta montre? Elle est sur toi.
4. —Où sont mes livres?
   —Tes livres? Ils sont dans le sac.
5. —Où est mon portable?
   —Ton portable? Il est sur le bureau.
6. —Où est mon chat?
   —Ton chat? Il est derrière la porte.
7. —Où est mon appareil-photo?
   —Ton appareil-photo? Il est dans la chambre.
8. —Où est mon baladeur?
   —Ton baladeur? Il est sur la table.

Language note Be sure students use plural forms in items 1 and 4.

5 PRACTICE identifying friends and relatives

1. André invite sa cousine.
2. Jean-Claude invite sa soeur.
3. Marie-Noëlle invite ses frères.
4. Pascal invite son amie Sophie.
5. Monique invite ses cousins.
6. Nathalie invite son ami Marc.
7. Georges invite son amie Cécile.
8. Paul invite son amie Thérèse.

6 PRACTICE identifying possessions

1. C'est son baladeur.
2. C'est son sac.
3. C'est son chien.
4. C'est son album.
5. C'est son ordinateur.
6. C'est sa guitare.
7. Ce sont ses CD.
8. Ce sont ses cassettes.
9. C'est sa guitare.
10. C'est sa chaîne hi-fi.
11. C'est son chat.
12. C'est son scooter.
13. Ce sont ses livres.
14. C'est sa montre.
15. Ce sont ses photos.
16. Ce sont ses skis.

7 ROLE PLAY identifying ownership

1. Frédéric: Voici le sac de Jean-Pierre.
   Paul: Tu es sûr?
   Frédéric: Mais oui, c'est son sac!
2. Frédéric: Voici la guitare d'Antoine.
   Paul: Tu es sûr?
   Frédéric: Mais oui, c'est sa guitare!
3. Frédéric: Voici l'appareil-photo de Cécile.
   Paul: Tu es sûr?
   Frédéric: Mais oui, c'est son appareil-photo!
4. Frédéric: Voici le baladeur de Stéphanie.
   Paul: Tu es sûr?
   Frédéric: Mais oui, c'est son baladeur!
5. Frédéric: Voici les CD de Léa.
   Paul: Tu es sûr?
   Frédéric: Mais oui, ce sont ses CD!
6. Frédéric: Voici le portable de Thomas.
   Paul: Tu es sûr?
   Frédéric: Mais oui, c'est son portable!

Language note Be sure students use the plural **Ce sont** in item 5.

C Les adjectifs possessifs: *notre, votre, leur*

Note the forms of the possessive adjectives in the chart below:

(POSSESSOR)		SINGULAR	PLURAL		
(nous)	*our*	**notre**	**nos**	**notre** prof	**nos** livres
(vous)	*your*	**votre**	**vos**	**votre** ami	**vos** copains
(ils/elles)	*their*	**leur**	**leurs**	**leur** radio	**leurs** amies

→ There is liaison after **nos, vos, leurs** when the next word begins with a vowel sound.

  nos amis   **vos** amies   **leurs** ordinateurs

8 Aux Galeries Lafayette

PARLER At the Galeries Lafayette department store, a customer is looking for various things. The person at the information desk indicates where they can be found. Play both roles.

▶ les CD/là-bas

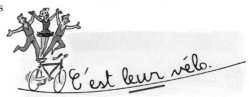

1. les livres/à gauche
2. les affiches/à droite
3. le restaurant/en haut
4. le garage/en bas
5. les ordinateurs/ici
6. la cafétéria/tout droit

9 Les millionnaires

PARLER/ÉCRIRE Imagine you are showing a millionaire's estate to French visitors.

▶ la maison
  Voici leur maison.

1. la piscine
2. la Rolls Royce
3. les chiens
4. le parc
5. l'hélicoptère
6. les courts de tennis

10 En famille

PARLER/ÉCRIRE We often do things with our family. Complete each sentence with a possessive adjective: **son, sa, ses, leur,** or **leurs.**

▶ Pascal joue au tennis avec **sa** cousine.
▶ Éric et Paul jouent aux cartes avec <u>leurs</u> cousins.

1. Frédéric dîne chez … oncle.
2. André dîne chez … grands-parents.
3. Caroline et Paul vont chez … grand-mère.
4. Mlle Vénard fait une promenade avec … chien.
5. Antoine va à la piscine avec … soeur.
6. Stéphanie et Céline vont au cinéma avec … parents.
7. M. et Mme Boutin voyagent avec … fille.
8. Mme Denis visite Paris avec … fils, Marc et Frédéric.

GAME Possessions

PREPARATION: Prepare 2 bags.
Bag A contains 12 sentence cards.
  • (6 cards with names of single people)
    Voici Pierre. Voici Michelle. Voici...
  • (6 cards with names of two people)
    Voici Anne et Paul. Voici Éric et Sylvie. ...

Bag B contains 12 sentence cards.
  • (6 cards with singular nouns)
    Voici son crayon, ...son stylo, sa montre.
    Voici leur crayon, ...leur stylo, leur montre.
  • (6 cards with plural nouns)
    Voici ses crayons, ...ses stylos, ses montres.
    Voici leurs crayons, ...leurs stylos,
    leurs montres.

D Les nombres ordinaux

Compare the following regular numbers and the ordinal numbers in French:

(2)	deux	**deuxième**	Février est le **deuxième** mois de l'année.
(3)	trois	**troisième**	Mercredi est le **troisième** jour de la semaine.
(4)	quatre	**quatrième**	J'habite au **quatrième** étage *(floor)*.

To form ordinal numbers, French speakers use the following pattern:

> NUMBER (minus final **-e**, if any) + **-ième**
>
> (6) six : **six** + **-ième** → **sixième**
>
> (11) onze : **onz-** + **-ième** → **onzième**

→ EXCEPTIONS: (1) un (une) → **premier (première)**
(5) cinq → **cinquième**
(9) neuf → **neuvième**

→ Ordinal numbers are adjectives and come BEFORE the noun.

LEARNING ABOUT LANGUAGE

Numbers like *first, second, third, fourth, fifth* are used to rank persons or things—to put them in a given order.

They are called ORDINAL NUMBERS.

In English, most ordinal numbers end in *-th*.

11 La course *(The race)*

PARLER/ÉCRIRE Frédéric and his friends are participating in a five-kilometer race. Announce the order of arrival of the following runners.

▶ Paul (6)

1. Frédéric (4)
2. Jérôme (7)
3. Christophe (8)
4. Sophie (2)
5. Christine (1)
6. Claire (10)
7. Karine (11)
8. Olivier (12)

Paul est sixième.

PRONONCIATION

Les voyelles /o/ et /ɔ/

/o/   /ɔ/

The French vowel /o/ is pronounced with more tension than in English. It is usually the last sound in a word.

vélo   téléphone

Répétez: /o/ **vél<u>o</u> rad<u>io</u> n<u>o</u>s v<u>o</u>s <u>eau</u> chât<u>eau</u> cha<u>ud</u>**
N<u>o</u>s vél<u>o</u>s sont <u>au</u> chât<u>eau</u>.

The French vowel /ɔ/ occurs in the middle of a word. Imitate the model carefully.

Répétez: /ɔ/ **téléph<u>o</u>ne éc<u>o</u>le Nic<u>o</u>le n<u>o</u>tre v<u>o</u>tre c<u>o</u>pain pr<u>o</u>f d<u>o</u>mmage**
C<u>o</u>mment s'appelle v<u>o</u>tre pr<u>o</u>f?

---

9 PRACTICE pointing out possessions

1. Voici leur piscine.
2. Voici leur Rolls-Royce.
3. Voici leurs chiens.
4. Voici leur parc.
5. Voici leur hélicoptère.
6. Voici leurs courts de tennis.

Challenge To practice adjectives, have students make a comment on each thing they are pointing out.
Voici leur maison.
Elle est belle (grande, super, extra, etc.), n'est-ce pas?

10 COMPREHENSION indicating family relationships

1. son
2. ses
3. leur
4. son
5. sa
6. leurs
7. leur
8. ses

Language notes
- For **deuxième,** one can also say **second(e),** pronounced /səgɔ̃(d)/
- 21st = **vingt et unième**
  31st = **trente et unième,** etc.
  Note that the "u" of **unième** is pronounced /y/.

Extra practice Write the numbers 1 to 20 on the board. Point to a number and have students give the corresponding ordinal number. For example: 15 **[quinzième]**, etc.

SECTION D

Communicative function
Indicating sequence

11 PRACTICE ranking people

1. Frédéric est quatrième.
2. Jérôme est septième.
3. Christophe est huitième.
4. Sophie est deuxième.
5. Christine est première.
6. Claire est dixième.
7. Karine est onzième.
8. Olivier est douzième.

PRONUNCIATION

- Have students pronounce the /o/ with tension and clip off the ending before the glide /oᵘ/ of the English *go.*

- Be sure students do not pronounce these words with the vowel /o/. The French /ɔ/ is close to the "o" sound of the English *orange.*

PROCEDURE: Divide the class into two teams: **logique** and **illogique.** Each team names a scorekeeper.

Two players (one from each team) come to the front. One reads a card from Bag A, the other reads a card from Bag B.

If the sentences fit logically, the **logique** team earns a point. If not, a point goes to the **illogique** team. For example:
Voici Marc. Voici leur stylo. = illogique

Have students at their seats decide if the sentences are logical or not.

À VOTRE TOUR

Main Topic
• Recapitulation and review

Teaching Resource Options

PRINT

Workbook PE, pp. 137–143
Unit 5 Resource Book
  Audioscript, p 133
  Communipak, pp. 140–163
  Family Involvement, pp. 123–124
  Workbook TE, pp. 103–109

Assessment
Lesson 16 Quiz, pp. 137–138
Portfolio Assessment, Unit 1 URB
  pp. 155–164
Audioscript for Quiz 16, p. 136
Answer Keys, pp. 210–213

AUDIO & VISUAL

Audio Program
CD 3 Tracks 18, 19
CD 15 Track 4

TECHNOLOGY

Test Generator CD-ROM/eTest
  Plus Online

1 **COMPREHENSION**

1. Avec qui est-ce que tu vas au cinéma?
  (c) Avec mon copain Marc.
2. C'est le cousin de Monique?
  (a) Non, c'est son frère.
3. Tu connais leurs parents?
  (b) Bien sûr, ils sont très sympathiques.
4. Ils sont canadiens, n'est-ce pas?
  (d) Non, mais leurs voisins sont de Québec.

2 **GUIDED ORAL EXPRESSION**

1. —C'est la guitare d'Alice?
  —Non, ce n'est pas sa guitare.
  —Tu es sûr?
  —Mais oui. Sa guitare est orange.
2. —C'est le scooter de Paul et Anne?
  —Non, ce n'est pas leur scooter.
  —Tu es sûr?
  —Mais oui. Leur scooter est vert.
3. —C'est le chien de tes cousins?
  —Non, ce n'est pas leur chien.
  —Tu es sûr?
  —Mais oui. Leur chien est noir.
4. —C'est la mobylette d'Isabelle?
  —Non, ce n'est pas sa mobylette.
  —Tu es sûr?
  —Mais oui. Sa mobylette est rouge.
5. —C'est la maison de M. et Mme Lavoie?
  —Non, ce n'est pas leur maison.
  —Tu es sûr?
  —Mais oui. Leur maison est blanche.
6. —C'est la voiture de ton oncle?
  —Non, ce n'est pas sa voiture.
  —Tu es sûr?
  —Mais oui. Sa voiture est jaune.

234 • À votre tour!
Unité 5 LEÇON 16

À votre tour!

1 **Allô!**

PARLER Émilie is on the phone with Bernard. Match Émilie's questions with Bernard's answers. Then act out the dialogue with a classmate.

1. Avec qui est-ce que tu vas au cinéma?
2. C'est le cousin de Monique?
3. Tu connais leurs parents?
4. Ils sont canadiens, n'est-ce pas?

a. Non, c'est son frère.
b. Bien sûr, ils sont très sympathiques.
c. Avec mon copain Marc.
d. Non, mais leurs voisins sont de Québec.

2 **Créa-dialogue**

PARLER We often identify objects by their color. Create conversations with your classmates according to the model.

le vélo / Paul?

1. la guitare / Alice?
2. le scooter / Paul et Anne?
3. le chien / tes cousins?
4. la mobylette / Isabelle?
5. la maison / M. et Mme Lavoie?
6. la voiture / ton oncle?

▶ —C'est le vélo de Paul?
  —Non, ce n'est pas son vélo.
  —Tu es sûr?
  —Mais oui. Son vélo est bleu.

234   deux cent trente-quatre
Unité 5

À VOTRE TOUR

Depending on your goals and objectives, you may or may not wish to assign all of the activities in the **À votre tour** section.

③ Composition: un animal domestique

ÉCRIRE Write a short composition about a pet: either your own pet, a pet belonging to a friend, or an imaginary pet. You may mention …

- the type of animal
- its name
- its age
- its colors
- its size
- its eating habits
- some physical and personality traits

④ Composition: Ma famille

ÉCRIRE Select five people in your family and write one to three sentences about each person.

Mon cousin s'appelle
John. Il habite
à San Francisco.
Il a seize ans.

⑤ Arbre généalogique *(Family tree)*

ÉCRIRE On a separate sheet of paper, draw your own (real or imaginary) family tree. Label the people and indicate their relationships to you.

LESSON REVIEW
CLASSZONE.COM

deux cent trente-cinq **235**
Leçon 16

---

③ WRITTEN SELF-EXPRESSION

Answers will vary.
J'ai un chat. Mon chat s'appelle Trotter. Il a trois ans. Mon chat est petit et blanc. Il mange trop. Trotter est gentil. J'aime mon chat!

④ WRITTEN SELF-EXPRESSION

Answers will vary.
- Mon frère s'appelle Jay. Il a quinze ans. Il aime beaucoup les sports.
- Ma mère n'aime pas faire la cuisine. Elle a beaucoup de soeurs. J'ai beaucoup de tantes!
- Mon grand-père a quatre-vingt-cinq ans. Il aime beaucoup la musique. Il a un baladeur!
- Ma cousine Jen a treize ans. Elle habite à Cincinnati. J'aime parler avec elle.
- Mon père s'appelle Paul. Il a quarante-deux ans. Il voyage souvent.

⑤ WRITTEN SELF-EXPRESSION

Answers will vary.

Marc Dubois (mon grand-père)		Alice Dubois (ma grand-mère)	
Laure Dubois (ma mère)	Bernard Dubois (mon père)	Sylvie Trocmé (ma tante)	Daniel Trocmé (mon oncle)
Catherine (moi)	Georges (mon frère)	Alice (ma cousine)	Jean (mon cousin)	Marc (mon cousin)

Teaching strategy Some students may prefer preparing the family tree of a TV family or a family in the public eye.

Photo culture note French people of African ancestry come principally from the French Carribean islands of **Martinique** and **Guadeloupe,** and from countries of western Africa, especially **Mali, Sénégal, Cameroun, Congo,** and **Côte d'Ivoire.**

PORTFOLIO ASSESSMENT

You will probably select only one speaking activity and one writing activity to go into the students' portfolios for Unit 5.

In this lesson, Act. 2 lends itself well to an oral portfolio recording. Act. 3, 4, and 5 are appropriate writing portfolio topics.

Middle School Copymasters

Class Starters 1–3, p. T25;
Drills 1&2, pp. T26–T27;
Worksheet 3: *Cadeaux d'anniversaire,* p. 73;
Project 3: City Planner, p. 87

À votre tour! **· 235**
Unité 5 Leçon 16

UNITÉ 5

TESTS DE CONTRÔLE

Teaching Resource Options

PRINT

Unit 5 Resource Book
   Communipak, pp. 140–163
   Assessment
   Unit 5 Test, pp. 177–185
   Portfolio Assessment, Unit 1 URB
     pp. 155–164
   Multiple Choice Test Items, pp. 198–206
   Listening Comprehension
     Performance Test, pp. 186–187
   Reading Performance Test, pp. 192–194
   Speaking Performance Test, pp. 188–191
   Writing Performance Test, pp. 195–197
   Test Scoring Tools, p. 207
   Audioscript for Tests, pp. 208–209
   Answer Keys, pp. 210–213

AUDIO & VISUAL

Audio Program
CD 15 Tracks 5–8

TECHNOLOGY

Test Generator CD-ROM/eTest Plus
   Online

① COMPREHENSION

1. Le réfrigérateur est dans la <u>cuisine</u>.
2. Quand il y a des invités, nous dînons dans la <u>salle à manger</u>.
3. Dans le <u>jardin</u>, il y a un lilas.
4. Dans le complexe sportif où nous allons, il y a une <u>piscine</u> olympique.
5. Il y a beaucoup de livres à la <u>bibliothèque</u> de la ville.
6. Dans ma <u>chambre</u>, il y a une table et un grand lit.
7. En été, nous allons en vacances sur une <u>plage</u> de l'Atlantique.
8. Il y a une <u>église</u> catholique dans notre quartier.
9. Le samedi, les élèves américains ne vont pas à l'<u>école</u>.
10. Le shampooing est dans la <u>salle de bains</u>.
11. Mes cousins habitent dans un grand <u>immeuble</u> moderne.
12. Je vais acheter un ordinateur dan un <u>magasin</u> d'équipement électronique.

UNITÉ 5 Tests de contrôle

Tests de contrôle

By taking the following tests, you can check your progress in French and also prepare for the unit test. Write your answers on a separate sheet of paper.

① The right place

Review...
• places and rooms of the house: pp. 197 and 200

Complete each of the following sentences by filling in the blank with one of the places in the box. Be logical and do not use the same word more than once.

> bibliothèque   chambre   cuisine   école   église   immeuble
> jardin   magasin   piscine   plage   salle de bains   salle à manger

1. Le réfrigérateur est dans la —.
2. Quand il y a des invités *(guests)*, nous dînons dans la —.
3. Dans le —, il y a un lilas *(lilac tree)*.
4. Dans le complexe sportif où nous allons, il y a une — olympique.
5. Il y a beaucoup de livres à la — de la ville.
6. Dans ma —, il y a une table et un grand lit.
7. En été, nous allons en vacances sur une — de l'Atlantique.
8. Il y a une — catholique dans notre quartier.
9. Le samedi, les élèves américains ne vont pas à l'—.
10. Le shampooing *(shampoo)* est dans la —.
11. Mes cousins habitent dans un grand — moderne.
12. Je vais acheter un ordinateur dans un — d'équipement électronique.

② The right choice

Review...
• use of à, de, and chez pp. 208, 210, 211, 219, 220, and 223

Choose the word or expression in parentheses which logically completes each of the following sentences.

1. Marc dîne — restaurant. **(à, au)**
2. Thomas nage — piscine. **(la, à la)**
3. Le professeur parle — élèves. **(aux, les)**
4. Les élèves vont — école en bus. **(à la, à l')**
5. Nous faisons une promenade — pied. **(à, au)**
6. Pauline va — sa copine Isabelle. **(à, chez)**
7. Nous revenons — école à trois heures. **(à l', de l')**
8. Les touristes arrivent — musée. **(du, de l')**
9. J'aime jouer — football. **(au, du)**
10. Est-ce que tu joues — clarinette? **(à la, de la)**
11. Comment s'appelle la copine — Monique? **(de, à)**
12. Voici la maison — voisins. **(des, de)**

3 The right owner

Complete each of the following sentences with the possessive adjective that corresponds to the underlined subject.

▶ <u>Jean-Paul</u> regarde **ses** photos.

1. <u>Tu</u> téléphones à — copine.
2. <u>Je</u> vais souvent au cinéma avec — amis.
3. <u>Marc</u> dîne chez — tante.
4. <u>Alice</u> invite — voisins à la boum.
5. <u>Isabelle</u> n'a pas — appareil-photo avec elle.
6. <u>Thomas et Charlotte</u> sont en vacances chez — oncle.
7. <u>Les élèves</u> respectent — professeurs.
8. <u>Vous</u> parlez avec — amie Mélanie.
9. <u>Nous</u> allons visiter Paris avec — professeur de français.
10. Est-ce que <u>vous</u> écoutez toujours — parents?

Review...
- possessive adjectives: pp. 230 and 232

4 Aller and venir

Complete the following sentences with the appropriate forms of **aller** or **venir**.

1. Attendez-moi *(Wait for me)*! Je —.
2. Thomas et Céline — très souvent au cinéma.
3. Qu'est-ce que tu — faire samedi?
4. Nous — aller à une boum.
5. Le professeur est canadien. Il — de Montréal.
6. Je — souvent à la piscine parce que j'aime nager.
7. Nicolas n'a pas faim. Il — du restaurant.
8. D'où est-ce que vous —?

Review...
- aller and venir: pp. 206, 212, and 218

5 Composition: La maison idéale

Write a short paragraph of five or six sentences describing your ideal house and its rooms. Does it have a garden? Where is it located? What do you especially like about it?

STRATEGY Writing

a	b	c
Sketch out a floor plan of your ideal house, labelling the rooms.	Organize your paragraph, concluding with why you like this house.	Reread your composition to be sure you have spelled all the names of the rooms correctly.

---

2 COMPREHENSION

1. Marc dîne <u>au</u> restaurant.
2. Thomas nage <u>à la</u> piscine.
3. Le professeur parle <u>aux</u> élèves.
4. Les élèves vont <u>à</u> l'école en bus.
5. Nous faisons une promenade <u>à</u> pied.
6. Pauline va <u>chez</u> sa copine Isabelle.
7. Nous revenons <u>de</u> l'école à trois heures.
8. Le touristes arrivent <u>du</u> musée.
9. J'aime jouer <u>au</u> football.
10. Est-ce que tu joues <u>de la</u> clarinette?
11. Comment s'appelle la copine <u>de</u> Monique?
12. Voici la maison <u>des</u> voisins.

3 COMPREHENSION

1. Tu téléphones à <u>ta</u> copine.
2. Je vais souvent au cinéma avec <u>mes</u> amis.
3. Marc dîne chez <u>sa</u> tante.
4. Alice invite <u>ses</u> voisins à la boum.
5. Isabelle n'a pas <u>son</u> appareil-photo avec elle.
6. Thomas et Charlotte sont en vacances chez <u>leur</u> oncle.
7. Les élèves respectent <u>leurs</u> professeurs.
8. Vous parlez avec <u>votre</u> amie Mélanie.
9. Nous allons visiter Paris avec <u>notre</u> professeur de français.
10. Est-ce que vous écoutez toujours <u>vos</u> parents?

4 COMPREHENSION

1. Je <u>viens</u>!
2. Thomas et Céline <u>vont</u> très souvent au cinéma.
3. Qu'est-ce que tu <u>vas</u> faire samedi?
4. Nous <u>allons</u> aller à une boum.
5. Il <u>vient</u> de Montréal.
6. Je <u>vais</u> souvent à la piscine parce que j'aime nager.
7. Il <u>vient</u> du restaurant.
8. D'où est-ce que vous <u>venez</u>?

5 WRITTEN SELF-EXPRESSION

Answers will vary.
Ma maison idéale est à Paris. Elle est très grande et moderne. Il y a un salon, une salle à manger, une cuisine, quatre chambres, deux salles de bain, deux toilettes et un garage. Ma chambre est confortable. Il y a une piscine et beaucoup de fleurs dans le jardin. J'aime ma maison parce qu'elle est à Paris!

VOCABULAIRE

Language Learning Benchmarks

FUNCTION
- Introduce and respond to introductions p. 228
- Engage in conversations p. 199, 213
- Make requests pp. 218, 232
- Obtain information pp. 196, 199
- Understand some ideas and familiar details pp 205, 217
- Begin to provide information p. 199, 201, 210, 222

CONTEXT
- Converse in face-to-face social interactions pp. 199, 209, 213, 220, 222
- Listen during social interactions p. 196
- Listen to audio and video texts pp. 194-195, 216, 226
- Use authentic materials when reading: posters p. 211
- Use authentic materials when reading: charts p. 201
- Use authentic materials when reading: signs pp. 196, 198, 247
- Use authentic materials when reading: short narratives pp. 243, 244
- Write notes pp. 215, 235
- Write lists p. 215
- Write short letters p. 225

TEXT TYPE
- Use short sentences when speaking pp. 198, 229, 232
- Use short sentences when writing pp. 198. 207, 231
- Use learned words and phrases when speaking pp. 196, 220, 222, 231
- Use learned words and phrases when writing pp. 196, 223
- Use simple questions when speaking pp. 198, 209, 213, 231

Vocabulaire

POUR COMMUNIQUER

Asking where people are going

Où vas-tu?		Where are you going?
Je vais à + PLACE, EVENT	Je vais au concert.	I am going to the concert.
Je vais chez + PERSON	Je vais chez Pierre.	I am going to Pierre's house.
Je vais chez + STRESS PRONOUN	Je vais chez moi.	I am going to my house.

Asking where people are coming from

D'où est-ce que tu viens?		Where are you coming from?
Je viens de + PLACE	Je viens de la piscine.	I am coming from the pool.

Asking for directions

Excusez-moi, où est [le théâtre]? *Excuse me, where is [the theater]?*	Est-ce que c'est	loin? près?	Is it	far? nearby, close?
	Tournez	à gauche. à droite.	Turn	to the left. to the right.
	Continuez tout droit.		Continue straight ahead.	
Pardon, où sont [les toilettes]? *Excuse me, where are [the toilets]?*	Elles sont	en haut. en bas	They are	upstairs. downstairs.

Talking about future plans

Qu'est-ce que tu vas faire?	What are you going to do?
Je vais [travailler].	I am going [to work].

Expressing possession

C'est mon (ton, son …) livre.	That's my (your, his/her, …) book.

MOTS ET EXPRESSIONS

Moyens de transport *(means of transportation)*

à pied	on foot	en bus	by bus	en train	by train
à vélo	by bicycle	en métro	by subway	en voiture	by car
		en taxi	by taxi		

La ville

un boulevard	boulevard	une adresse	address
un café	café	une avenue	avenue
un centre commercial	mall, shopping center	une bibliothèque	library
un cinéma	movie theater	une école	school
un hôpital	hospital	une église	church
un hôtel	hotel	une piscine	(swimming) pool
un magasin	store	une plage	beach
un musée	museum	une rue	street
un parc	park	une ville	city, town
un quartier	neighborhood		
un restaurant	restaurant		
un stade	stadium		
un supermarché	supermarket		
un théâtre	theater		
un village	town, village		

Vocabulaire UNITÉ 5

La maison

un appartement	apartment	une chambre	bedroom
un garage	garage	une cuisine	kitchen
un immeuble	apartment building	une maison	house
un jardin	garden, yard	une salle à manger	dining room
un salon	living room	une salle de bains	bathroom
		les toilettes	bathroom, toilet

Quelques endroits où aller

un concert	concert	un film	movie	une boum	party (casual)
un endroit	place	un pique-nique	picnic	une fête	party
un événement	event	un rendez-vous	date, appointment	une soirée	party (evening)

La famille

les parents	parents; relatives	la famille	family
les grands-parents	grandparents	la grand-mère	grandmother
le grand-père	grandfather	la mère	mother
le père	father	la femme	wife
le mari	husband	une enfant	child
un enfant	child	la fille	daughter
le fils	son	la soeur	sister
le frère	brother	la tante	aunt
l'oncle	uncle	la cousine	cousin
le cousin	cousin		

Verbes en -er

arriver	to arrive, to come
rentrer	to go back, come back
rester	to stay
jouer à + SPORT, GAME	to play (a sport, game)
jouer de + INSTRUMENT	to play (an instrument)

Verbes irréguliers

aller	to go
faire une promenade à pied	to go for a walk
faire une promenade à vélo	to go for a bike ride
faire une promenade en voiture	to go for a drive
venir	to come
revenir	to come back

Les sports

le baseball	baseball
le basket(ball)	basketball
le foot(ball)	soccer
le ping-pong	ping-pong
le tennis	tennis
le volley(ball)	volleyball

Les jeux

les échecs	chess	les cartes	cards
les jeux d'ordinateur	computer games	les dames	checkers
les jeux vidéo	video games		

Les instruments de musique

le clavier	keyboard	la batterie	drums
le piano	piano	la clarinette	clarinet
le saxo(phone)	saxophone	la flûte	flute
le violon	violin	la guitare	guitar

Les nombres ordinaux

premier (première)	first	septième	seventh
deuxième	second	huitième	eighth
troisième	third	neuvième	ninth
quatrième	fourth	dixième	tenth
cinquième	fifth	onzième	eleventh
sixième	sixth	douzième	twelfth

Expressions utiles

Pas du tout!	Not at all! Definitely not!
Vraiment?!	Really?!
Tu es sûr(e)?	Are you sure?
Vas-y!	Go on!
Va-t'en!	Go away!

TEST PREP — CLASSZONE.COM — FLASHCARDS AND MORE!

deux cent trente-neuf
Vocabulaire 239

- Understand some ideas and familiar details presented in clear, uncomplicated speech when listening pp. 204, 217, 226
- Understand short texts enhanced by visual clues when reading pp. 205, 226, 242-243, 248-251

CONTENT
- Understand and convey information about home p. 201
- Understand and convey information about rooms p. 201
- Understand and convey information about directions p. 199
- Understand and convey information about buildings and monuments p. 198
- Understand and convey information about cultural and historical figures p. 245
- Understand and convey information about places and events p. 251
- Understand and convey information about travel pp. 249, 251, 253

ASSESSMENT
- Communicate effectively with some hesitation and errors, which do not hinder comprehension pp. 203, 214, 224
- Demonstrate culturally acceptable behavior for engaging in conversations pp. 203, 215, 225, 234
- Demonstrate culturally acceptable behavior for obtaining information pp. 203, 215
- Demonstrate culturally acceptable behavior for understanding some ideas and familiar details p. 203
- Demonstrate culturally acceptable behavior for providing information pp. 203, 225
- Understand most important information pp. 202, 214, 225, 235

UNITÉ 5

ENTRACTE

Objectives
- Reading skills development
- Re-entry of material in the unit
- Development of cultural awarenesss

Teaching Resource Options

PRINT

Workbook PE, pp. 145–148
Activités pour tous PE, pp. 87–89
Unit 5 Resource Book
   Activités pour tous TE, pp. 165–167
   Workbook TE, 169–172

Le cinéma

Objectives
- Reading at the paragraph level
- Reading for cultural information about the cinema

Comparaisons culturelles

Answers will vary.

Les préférences	Les jeunes Français	Moi	Différence ou similarité
jour	samedi	(vendredi)	(différence)
sorte de cinéma	les multiplexes	(les multiplexes)	(similarité)
films	les films d'action, les comédies	(les comédies)	(similarité)

LES JEUNES FRANÇAIS ET *le cinéma*

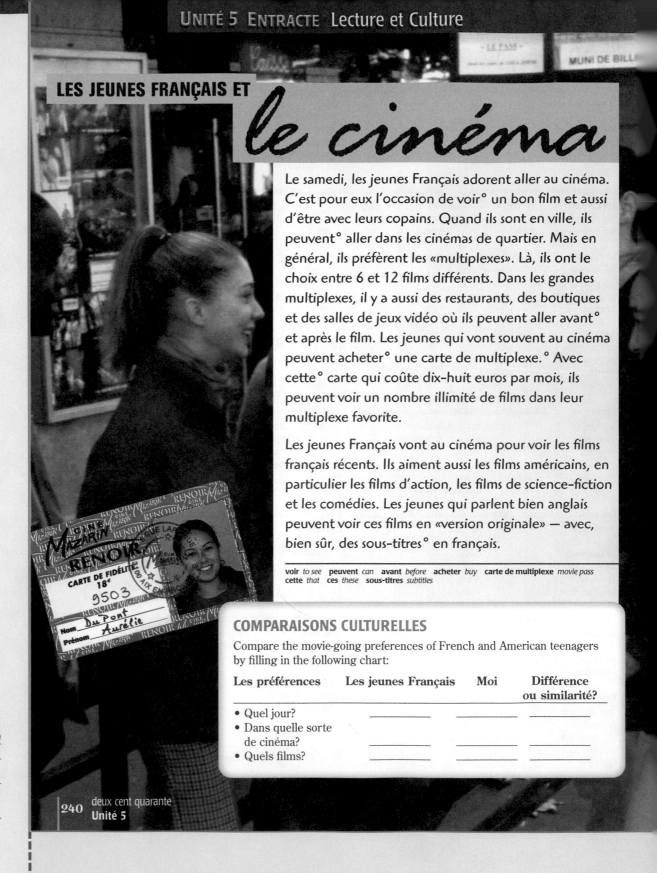

Le samedi, les jeunes Français adorent aller au cinéma. C'est pour eux l'occasion de voir° un bon film et aussi d'être avec leurs copains. Quand ils sont en ville, ils peuvent° aller dans les cinémas de quartier. Mais en général, ils préfèrent les «multiplexes». Là, ils ont le choix entre 6 et 12 films différents. Dans les grandes multiplexes, il y a aussi des restaurants, des boutiques et des salles de jeux vidéo où ils peuvent aller avant° et après le film. Les jeunes qui vont souvent au cinéma peuvent acheter° une carte de multiplexe.° Avec cette° carte qui coûte dix-huit euros par mois, ils peuvent voir un nombre illimité de films dans leur multiplexe favorite.

Les jeunes Français vont au cinéma pour voir les films français récents. Ils aiment aussi les films américains, en particulier les films d'action, les films de science-fiction et les comédies. Les jeunes qui parlent bien anglais peuvent voir ces films en «version originale» — avec, bien sûr, des sous-titres° en français.

---

voir *to see* **peuvent** *can* **avant** *before* **acheter** *buy* **carte de multiplexe** *movie pass* **cette** *that* **ces** *these* **sous-titres** *subtitles*

COMPARAISONS CULTURELLES

Compare the movie-going preferences of French and American teenagers by filling in the following chart:

Les préférences	Les jeunes Français	Moi	Différence ou similarité?
• Quel jour?	_____	_____	_____
• Dans quelle sorte de cinéma?	_____	_____	_____
• Quels films?	_____	_____	_____

240   deux cent quarante
Unité 5

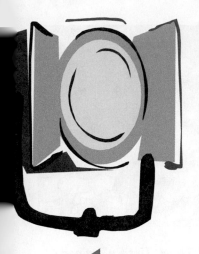

Films américains, public français

Voici une liste de films américains qui ont eu° beaucoup de succès en France. Est-ce que vous pouvez° identifier ces films? Lisez° le titre° français de chaque° film. Faites correspondre° le titre de ce film avec le titre américain.

ont eu *have had* **pouvez** *can* **Lisez** *Read* **titre** *title* **chaque** *each*
Faites correspondre *Match*

TITRES FRANÇAIS
1. Blanche-Neige et les sept nains (1937)
2. Le Magicien d'Oz (1939)
3. La mélodie du bonheur (1965)
4. Devine qui vient dîner? (1967)
5. Le Parrain (1972)
6. Les aventuriers de l'arche perdue (1981)
7. E.T. l'extra-terrestre (1982)
8. Le roi Lion (1994)
9. Il faut sauver le soldat Ryan (1998)
10. En pleine tempête (2000)

TITRES AMÉRICAINS
A. E.T. the Extra-Terrestrial
B. The Lion King
C. The Godfather
D. Snow White and the Seven Dwarves
E. Guess Who's Coming to Dinner?
F. The Perfect Storm
G. Raiders of the Lost Ark
H. Saving Private Ryan
I. The Sound of Music
J. The Wizard of Oz

CONNEXIONS

Use the Internet to find out which American films are currently playing in Paris. As you read the French titles, can you guess the original English titles?

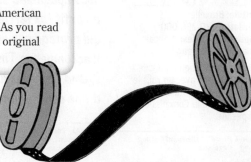

Films américains, public français
Objectives
• Reading for fun
• Deriving meaning by word association

Films américains, public français
1. d
2. j
3. i
4. e
5. c
6. g
7. a
8. b
9. h
10. f

Variation (books closed)

Write only the French film titles on the chalkboard or on a transparency.

Divide the class into groups and see how many English titles each group can discover.

PRE-READING

Ask students to look at the illustrations and the title at the top of the page.
• What do they think is the topic of this reading?

Ask pairs of students to name their favorite movies.
Quel est votre film favori?
Notre film favori est [Lord of the Rings].

POST-READING

Ask students which of these movies they have seen.
• Which ones did they like best?

OPTIONAL: Prepare a movie poster in French.

Teaching Resource Options

PRINT

Workbook PE, pp. 145–148
Activités pour tous PE, pp. 87–89
Unit 5 Resource Book
  Activités pour tous TE, pp. 165–167
  Workbook TE, pp. 169–172

Tintin et ses amis
Objectives
• Reading a longer text
• Building reading skills

Questions sur le texte

1. Quel âge a Tintin? (17 ans)
2. Est-ce que Tintin est français? (Non, il est belge.)
3. Comment est Tintin? (Il est intelligent et courageux.)
4. Comment s'appelle le chien de Tintin? (Milou)
5. Est-ce que la capitaine Haddock habite dans une maison? (Non, il habite au château de Moulinsart.)
6. Est-ce que Dupont et Dupond sont frères? (Non, mais ils sont presque identiques.)
7. Qui est un génie scientifique? (Le professeur Tournesol)

Teaching tip Students may be interested in getting their own Tintin books. Direct them to an appropriate online store or to a local bookstore that sells foreign books.

Tintin et ses amis

Tintin et Milou

Tous° les jeunes Français connaissent° Tintin. Tintin n'est pas une personne réelle. C'est le héros d'une bande dessinée° très populaire en France et dans le monde° entier. «Les Aventures de Tintin» ont été publiées en français, mais aussi en anglais, en espagnol, en italien, en chinois, en japonais … au total dans 40 langues° différentes.

Tintin a dix-sept ans et il est belge.° C'est un journaliste-détective. Il est intelligent et courageux et il adore voyager. Il va en Égypte, au Congo, en Chine, au Tibet, au Mexique et en Amérique. Il va même° sur° la lune, bien avant° les astronautes américains. Dans ses voyages, il connaît° des aventures extraordinaires. Tintin est l'ami de la justice et l'ennemi du mal.° Il protège ses amis et il s'attaque aux dictateurs, aux trafiquants de drogue° et aux marchands d'armes.° Il est souvent en danger, mais il triomphe toujours.

Dans ses aventures, Tintin est toujours accompagné de son chien, Milou. Milou est un petit fox terrier blanc intuitif et courageux qui protège son maître quand il est attaqué. Il accompagne Tintin dans toutes ses aventures. Quand il va avec lui sur la lune, il est équipé d'une combinaison spatiale° pour chiens.

EN BREF: LA BELGIQUE
Capitale: Bruxelles
Population: 10 250 000
Langues officielles: français, flamand° et allemand°

La Belgique est une monarchie constitutionnelle avec un roi,° le roi Albert II. Sa capitale, Bruxelles, est le siège° de la Commission Européenne.

flamand *Flemish* **allemand** *German* **roi** *king* **siège** *seat*

Tous *All* **connaissent** *know* **bande dessinée** *comic strip* **monde** *world* **langues** *languages* **belge** *Belgian* **même** *even* **sur** *on* **avant** *before* **connaît** *experiences* **mal** *evil* **trafiquants de drogue** *drug dealers* **armes** *weapons* **combinaison spatiale** *space suit* **Voila qui est fait.** *There, you're all set.*

 deux cent quarante-deux
Unité 5

PRE-READING

Ask if any students have heard of Tintin. **Est-ce que vous connaissez Tintin?** If yes, ask if they have their own copies of any of the Tintin books. **Est-ce que vous avez des livres de Tintin?**

Tintin a d'autres compagnons d'aventures, très sympathiques, mais un peu bizarres.

le capitaine Haddock

Le capitaine Haddock habite au château° de Moulinsart en Belgique. C'est un ancien° officier de la marine marchande. Il est brave et courageux … mais il est aussi très irritable.

Garnements! Rascals!
Iconoclastes! Iconoclasts! (people who attack and seek to overthrow traditional ideas) **château** castle **ancien** former

Dupont et Dupond

Dupont et Dupond sont presque° identiques, mais ils ne sont pas frères. Ce sont des policiers méthodiques … mais incompétents.

presque almost

le professeur Tournesol

Le professeur Tournesol est un génie scientifique. Il est modeste et réservé et comme° beaucoup de professeurs, il est très distrait.°

comme like **distrait** absent-minded

STRATEGY Reading

Recognizing Cognate Patterns Recognizing French-English cognate patterns will help you increase your reading vocabulary and improve your reading comprehension. Here are some common patterns:

FRENCH	ENGLISH	FRENCH	ENGLISH
-aire	-ar, -ary	**extraordinaire**	extraordinary
-eux, -euse	-ous	**courageux**	courageous
-ique	-ic, -ical	**identique**	identical
-iste	-ist, istic	**journaliste**	journalist
-é	-ed	**réservé**	reserved

COMMUNAUTÉ

Organize a **fête Tintin** for the language classes in your school. You may display Tintin books in French and other languages and show a video or DVD of some of Tintin's adventures. Encourage your classmates to come dressed as Tintin characters.

Et vous?

Quelle est ta bande dessinée favorite? Qui sont les héros? Pourquoi est-ce que tu aimes cette bande dessinée?

Et vous?
Answers will vary.
Ma bande dessinée favorite est (Garfield).

Le héros est (Garfield).

J'aime cette bande dessinée parce que (j'aime les chats).

Bonjour, Ousmane!

Objectives
• Reading at the paragraph level
• Developing logical thinking

Teaching Resource Options

PRINT

Workbook PE, pp. 145–148
Activités pour tous PE, pp. 87–89
Unit 5 Resource Book
    Activités pour tous TE, pp. 165–169
    Workbook TE, pp. 169–172

Compréhension
Answers
1. le rap et le rock
2. de la guitare
3. le mercredi après-midi
4. parce que sa mère déteste ça

Activité écrite
Answers will vary.
J'aime le rock. Je déteste la musique classique. Mon groupe préféré est U2. Ils chantent bien.

Bonjour, Ousmane!

Bonjour! Je m'appelle Ousmane. J'adore la musique. J'aime surtout le rap et le rock. Mon chanteur préféré est MC Solaar. Il chante très bien. J'ai beaucoup de CD de lui. Ma sœur, elle, préfère le blues et le jazz.

Je suis un peu musicien. Je joue de la guitare. Et je ne joue pas trop mal. J'ai organisé un petit orchestre de rock avec des copains. Nous répétons le mercredi après-midi. Nous ne répétons pas chez moi, parce que ma mère déteste ça. Parfois, le week-end, nous jouons à des boums pour nos amis.

chanteur *singer* **ai organisé** *organized* **orchestre** *band*
répétons *rehearse* **ça** *that* **Parfois** *Sometimes*

Compréhension
1. Quelle est la musique préférée d'Ousmane?
2. De quel instrument est-ce qu'il joue?
3. Quand est-ce qu'il répète avec ses copains?
4. Pourquoi est-ce qu'il ne répète pas à la maison?

Activité écrite
Write a short note to Ousmane in which you describe your musical preferences. Use the following suggestions:

• J'aime … (quelles musiques?)
• Je déteste … (quelles musiques?)
• Mon groupe préféré est … (qui?)
• Ils/Elles chantent … (comment?)

MC Solaar
le «Monsieur Rap» français

MC Solaar est né° à Dakar au Sénégal. Il s'appelle en réalité Claude M'Barali. Ses parents émigrent en France quand il a six mois. Il fait ses études dans la région parisienne. Après° le bac, il s'intéresse à° la musique. Il compose des chansons° françaises sur des rythmes de rap américain. Ses chansons ont beaucoup de succès. MC Solaar donne° des concerts en France, mais aussi en Angleterre,° en Allemagne,° en Russie et dans les pays° d'Afrique.

Aujourd'hui, MC Solaar est le «Monsieur Rap» français! Dans ses chansons, il exprime° des messages positifs contre° la violence et pour la paix.° Voilà pourquoi il est très populaire en France et dans le monde° francophone.

---

est né *was born* **Après** *After* **s'intéresse à** *becomes interested in* **chansons** *songs* **donne** *gives* **Angleterre** *England* **Allemagne** *Germany* **pays** *countries* **exprime** *expresses* **contre** *against* **la paix** *peace* **monde** *world*

CONNEXIONS

With 2 or 3 classmates, select a French singer, such as MC Solaar. Go on the Internet and obtain as much information as you can about the person you have chosen. If possible, get samples of his or her music. Share your findings with the rest of the class.

COMMUNAUTÉ

Prepare a short program about music from the French-speaking world. You may want to include pictures of the performers, selections of their recordings, and perhaps a world map showing their countries of origin. Present your program to another class at school or at a local senior center.

IMAGES

Cultural Theme
• Paris

À Paris

Objectives
• Reading a complete text
• Building reading skills

Teaching Resource Options

PRINT

Workbook PE, pp. 145–148
Activités pour tous PE, pp. 87–89
Unit 5 Resource Book
  Activités pour tous TE, pp. 165–167
  Lesson Plans, pp. 173–174
  Block Scheduling Lesson Plans,
   pp. 175–176
  Videoscript, pp. 130–131
  Workbook TE, pp. 169–172

VIDEO PROGRAM

VIDÉO   DVD
 IMAGES
À Paris

TOTAL TIME: 7:18 min.
  DVD Disk 2
  Videotape 3 (COUNTER: 26:01 min.)

C.1 Introduction à Paris
  (26:10–27:23 min.)

C.2 Interview avec Jean-Marc Lacoste
  (27:24–28:15 min.)

C.3 Visite de Paris
  (28:16–32:22 min.)

C.4 Promenade en bateau-mouche
  (32:23–34:19 min.)

IMAGES
À Paris
Bonjour, Paris!

Quelques faits

• Paris est la capitale de la France.

• Paris est une très grande ville. La ville de Paris a deux millions d'habitants. La région parisienne a onze millions d'habitants. Vingt pour cent (20%) des Français habitent dans la région parisienne.

• Paris est situé° sur la Seine. Ce fleuve° divise° la ville en deux parties: la rive° droite (au nord) et la rive gauche (au sud).

• Administrativement, Paris est divisé en vingt arrondissements.°

• Paris est une ville très ancienne.° Elle a plus de° deux mille° ans.

• Paris est aussi une ville moderne et dynamique. C'est le centre économique, industriel et commercial de la France.

• Avec ses musées, ses théâtres, ses bibliothèques et ses écoles d'art, Paris est un centre culturel et artistique très important.

• Avec ses nombreux° monuments et ses larges avenues, Paris est une très belle ville. Pour beaucoup de gens, c'est la plus° belle ville du monde.° Chaque année,° des millions de touristes visitent Paris.

---

situé *located* **fleuve** *river* **divise** *divides*
rive *(river)bank* **arrondissements** *districts*
ancienne *old* **plus de** *more than* **mille** *thousand*
nombreux *many* **la plus** *the most* **monde** *world*
Chaque année *Each year*

246 deux cent quarante-six
Images

IMAGES

- The **Place de la Concorde,** at the end of the Champs-Élysées, is one of the largest squares in the world. At the center stands **l'obélisque,** a gift to the king of France (Charles X) from the viceroy of Egypt.

- **Les Invalides** is a former French military hospital (hence its name). Tourists come to **Les Invalides** to see Napoleon's tomb and visit the military museum.

- **Le jardin des Tuileries** is a large public park which extends from the **Place de la Concorde** to the **Louvre.**

- The French legislature has two houses, **l'Assemblée nationale** (similar to the U.S. House of Representatives) and **le Sénat.**

Photo cultural notes

- Top left: **artistes à Montmartre**

- Bottom left: **Les Champs-Élysées** with **L'arc de Triomphe** in the background

- Bottom right: **un arrêt du Métro**

deux cent quarante-sept
Lecture et Culture 247

USING THE VIDEO

In this Essay, **À Paris,** Jean-Marc Lacoste (see p. 252) takes the students around Paris. Play the entire module as an introduction to the IMAGES.

Teaching Resource Options

PRINT

Workbook PE, pp. 145–148
Activités pour tous PE, pp. 87–89
Unit 5 Resource Book
  Activités pour tous TE, pp. 165–167
  Workbook TE, pp. 169–172

Cultural background

• The Eiffel Tower was built to commemorate the 100th anniversary of the French Revolution which began July 14, 1789 and lasted ten years.

IMAGES

Le Paris TRADITIONNEL

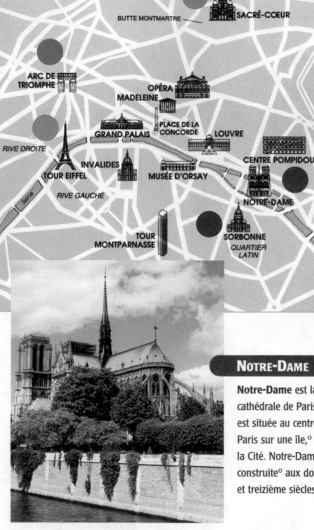

LA TOUR EIFFEL

Pour beaucoup de gens, **la tour Eiffel** est le symbole de Paris. Cette° immense tour de fer° a trois cent mètres de haut.° Elle a été inaugurée en 1889 (dix-huit cent quatre-vingt-neuf) par l'ingénieur Gustave Eiffel. Du sommet de la tour Eiffel, on° a une très belle vue sur Paris.

NOTRE-DAME

Notre-Dame est la cathédrale de Paris. Elle est située au centre de Paris sur une île,° l'île de la Cité. Notre-Dame a été construite° aux douzième et treizième siècles.°

Cette *This* **fer** *iron* **a trois cent mètres de haut** *is 300 meters high* **on** *one*
île *island* **a été construite** *was built* **siècles** *centuries*

LE SACRÉ-COEUR

Le Sacré-Coeur est une église de pierre° blanche qui domine Paris. Cette église est située sur la butte° Montmartre. Montmartre est un quartier pittoresque. Les artistes viennent ici pour peindre° et les touristes viennent pour regarder les artistes. Si vous voulez° avoir un souvenir personnel de Paris, allez à Montmartre et demandez à° un artiste de faire votre portrait.

LE QUARTIER LATIN

Le Quartier latin est le quartier des étudiants. C'est un quartier très animé avec des cafés, des cinémas, des librairies° et des restaurants exotiques et bon marché.° Pourquoi est-ce que ce quartier s'appelle «Quartier latin»? Parce qu'autrefois° les étudiants parlaient° latin ici.

L'ARC DE TRIOMPHE ET LES CHAMPS-ÉLYSÉES

L'Arc de Triomphe est un monument qui° commémore les victoires de Napoléon (1769–1821). Ce monument est situé en haut° des Champs-Élysées.

Les Champs-Élysées sont une très grande et très belle avenue. Pour les Parisiens, c'est la plus° belle avenue du monde.

Activité Culturelle

Imaginez que vous passez une journée° à Paris. Où allez-vous aller le matin? Où allez-vous aller l'après-midi? Choisissez deux endroits à visiter et expliquez° votre choix.°

---

pierre *stone* **butte** *hill* **peindre** *to paint* **voulez** *want* **demandez à** *ask* **librairies** *bookstores*
bon marché *inexpensive* **autrefois** *in the past* **parlaient** *used to speak* **qui** *which* **en haut** *at the top*
la plus *the most* **passez une journée** *are spending a day* **expliquez** *explain* **choix** *choice*

Teaching Resource Options

PRINT

Workbook PE, pp. 145–148
Activités pour tous PE, pp. 87–89
Unit 5 Resource Book
  Activités pour tous TE, pp. 165–167
  Workbook TE, pp. 169–172

Cultural background

- Mona Lisa (also known as "la Joconde") was painted by Leonardo da Vinci (1452–1519).

- Le Centre Pompidou was named after Georges Pompidou (1911–1974), President of France (1969–1974).

- Claude Monet (1840–1926) and Auguste Renoir (1841–1919), Impressionist painters; Henri de Toulouse-Lautrec (1864–1901).

IMAGES Le nouveau Paris

● LE LOUVRE ET LA PYRAMIDE DU LOUVRE

Le Louvre est une ancienne° résidence royale transformée en musée. C'est dans ce° musée que se trouve° la fameuse «Mona Lisa». On entre dans le Louvre par° une pyramide de verre.° Cette pyramide moderne a été construite° par l'architecte américain I.M. Pei. Avec sa pyramide, le Louvre est le symbole du nouveau° Paris, à la fois° moderne et traditionnel.

● LE CENTRE POMPIDOU

Le Centre Pompidou est le monument le plus° visité de Paris. C'est un musée d'art moderne. C'est aussi une bibliothèque, une cinémathèque et un centre audio-visuel. À l'extérieur,° sur l'esplanade, il y a des musiciens, des mimes, des acrobates, des jongleurs° … Un peu plus loin,° il y a une place° avec des fontaines, un bassin° et des sculptures mobiles.

● LE MUSÉE D'ORSAY

Autrefois,° c'était° une gare.° Aujourd'hui, c'est un musée. On vient ici admirer les chefs-d'oeuvre° des grands peintres° et sculpteurs français du dix-neuvième siècle.° On peut,° par exemple, admirer les oeuvres° de Monet, de Renoir et de Toulouse-Lautrec. À l'extérieur, il y a des sculptures qui représentent les cinq continents.

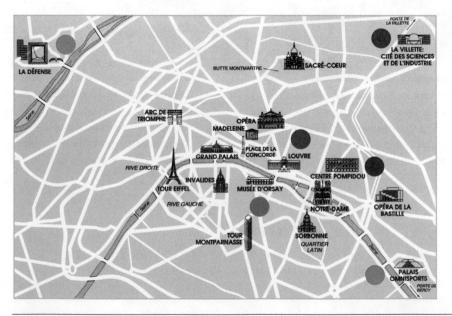

ancienne *former* **ce** *this* **se trouve** *is located* **par** *by* **verre** *glass* **a été construite** *was built* **nouveau** *new* **à la fois** *at the same time* **le plus** *the most* **À l'extérieur** *Outside* **jongleurs** *jugglers* **plus loin** *farther away* **place** *square* **bassin** *ornamental pool* **Autrefois** *Formerly* **c'était** *it used to be* **gare** *train station* **chefs-d'oeuvre** *masterpieces* **peintres** *painters* **siècle** *century* **peut** *can* **oeuvres** *works*

IMAGES

● LE PALAIS OMNISPORTS DE BERCY

Sport ou musique? **Bercy** est un stade couvert° pour tous les sports. C'est aussi une immense salle° de concert. On vient ici écouter et applaudir les vedettes° de la chanson° française … et de la chanson américaine.

● LE PARC DE LA VILLETTE

Le parc de la Villette est un lieu° de récréation pour les jeunes de tout âge.° On trouve ici des parcs pour enfants,° des terrains de jeu° et différentes° constructions ultra-modernes.

- Le Zénith est une salle de concert où viennent les vedettes du monde° entier.
- La Géode est un cinéma omnimax avec un écran° circulaire géant.
- La Cité des sciences et de l'industrie est un grand musée scientifique où les jeunes peuvent° faire leurs propres° expériences° et jouer avec toutes sortes de gadgets électroniques.

● LA DÉFENSE ET SON ARCHE

La Défense est le nouveau centre d'affaires° situé à l'ouest de Paris. Chaque° jour, des milliers° de Parisiens viennent travailler dans ses gratte-ciel° de verre. Il y a aussi des magasins, des cinémas, des restaurants et une patinoire.° La Grande Arche a été construite pour commémorer le deux centième anniversaire de la Révolution française.

sidebar

Activité Culturelle

Vous êtes à Paris pour une semaine. Pendant votre séjour, vous voulez faire les choses suivantes. Dites où vous allez pour cela.

▶ **Lundi, je veux voir une exposition d'art moderne. Je vais au Centre Pompidou.**

Quand?	Pourquoi?	Où?
▶ lundi	voir *(to see)* une exposition d'art moderne	??
mardi	voir une exposition sur les lasers	??
mercredi	voir la «Mona Lisa»	??
jeudi	voir un match de basket	??
vendredi	voir une exposition sur Toulouse-Lautrec	??
samedi	aller dans les magasins et faire du shopping	??

---

couvert *covered* **salle** *hall* **vedettes** *stars* **chanson** *song* **lieu** *place* **de tout âge** *of all ages* **parcs pour enfants** *playgrounds*
terrains de jeu *playing fields* **différentes** *several* **monde** *world* **écran** *screen* **peuvent** *can* **propres** *own*
expériences *experiments* **affaires** *business* **Chaque** *Each* **des milliers** *thousands* **gratte-ciel** *skyscrapers*
patinoire *skating rink*

deux cent cinquante et un
Lecture et Culture 251

If students ask: Un **gratte-ciel** is a "sky-scratcher." Which term do they find more appropriate: the French word or the English word?

Activité culturelle
Answers
- Mardi, je veux voir une exposition sur les lasers. Je vais au parc de la Villette.
- Mercredi, je veux voir la «Mona Lisa». Je vais au Louvre.
- Jeudi, je veux voir un match de basket. Je vais au palais Omnisports de Bercy.
- Vendredi, je veux voir une exposition sur Toulouse-Lautrec. Je vais au musée d'Orsay.
- Samedi, je veux aller dans les magasins et faire du shopping. Je vais à la Défense.

IMAGES • **251**
Unité 5

Salut, les amis!

Teaching Resource Options

PRINT

Workbook PE, pp. 145–148
Activités pour tous PE, pp. 87–89
Unit 5 Resource Book
   Activités pour tous TE, pp. 165–167
   Videoscript, pp. 130–131
   Workbook TE, pp. 169–172

VIDEO PROGRAM

VIDÉO   DVD

  IMAGES

C.1 Introduction à Paris
(26:10–27:23 min.)

C.2 Interview avec Jean-Marc Lacoste
(27:24–28:15 min.)

C.3 Visite de Paris
(28:16–32:22 min.)

C.4 Promenade en bateau-mouche
(32:23–34:19 min.)

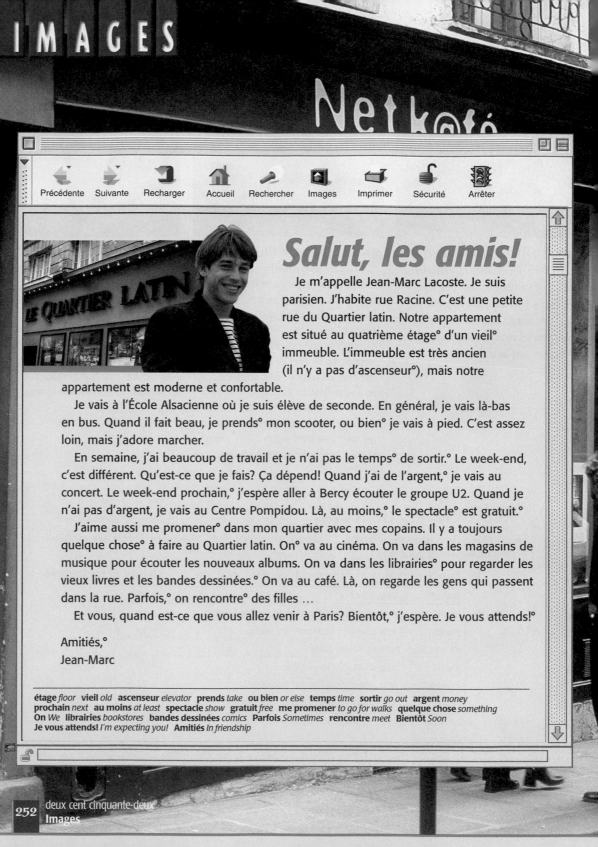

IMAGES

Salut, les amis!

Je m'appelle Jean-Marc Lacoste. Je suis parisien. J'habite rue Racine. C'est une petite rue du Quartier latin. Notre appartement est situé au quatrième étage° d'un vieil° immeuble. L'immeuble est très ancien (il n'y a pas d'ascenseur°), mais notre appartement est moderne et confortable.

Je vais à l'École Alsacienne où je suis élève de seconde. En général, je vais là-bas en bus. Quand il fait beau, je prends° mon scooter, ou bien° je vais à pied. C'est assez loin, mais j'adore marcher.

En semaine, j'ai beaucoup de travail et je n'ai pas le temps° de sortir.° Le week-end, c'est différent. Qu'est-ce que je fais? Ça dépend! Quand j'ai de l'argent,° je vais au concert. Le week-end prochain,° j'espère aller à Bercy écouter le groupe U2. Quand je n'ai pas d'argent, je vais au Centre Pompidou. Là, au moins,° le spectacle° est gratuit.°

J'aime aussi me promener° dans mon quartier avec mes copains. Il y a toujours quelque chose° à faire au Quartier latin. On° va au cinéma. On va dans les magasins de musique pour écouter les nouveaux albums. On va dans les librairies° pour regarder les vieux livres et les bandes dessinées.° On va au café. Là, on regarde les gens qui passent dans la rue. Parfois,° on rencontre° des filles …

Et vous, quand est-ce que vous allez venir à Paris? Bientôt,° j'espère. Je vous attends!°

Amitiés,°
Jean-Marc

étage *floor* **vieil** *old* **ascenseur** *elevator* **prends** *take* **ou bien** *or else* **temps** *time* **sortir** *go out* **argent** *money* **prochain** *next* **au moins** *at least* **spectacle** *show* **gratuit** *free* **me promener** *to go for walks* **quelque chose** *something* **On** *We* **librairies** *bookstores* **bandes dessinées** *comics* **Parfois** *Sometimes* **rencontre** *meet* **Bientôt** *Soon* **Je vous attends!** *I'm expecting you!* **Amitiés** *In friendship*

252 deux cent cinquante-deux
Images

PRE-READING ACTIVITY

Replay parts 2 and 3 of the video, so that students get to know Jean-Marc.

Then have them read his letter.

POST-READING ACTIVITY

Have students make a list of the places that Jean-Marc mentions in his e-mail and then locate them on the map of Paris.

Which place or places they would like to visit with him?

252 · **IMAGES**
Unité 5

PARIS en BATEAU-MOUCHE

CIRCUIT TOURISTIQUE
EN HIVER VEDETTES CHAUFFÉES
IN WINTER WARMED
PARKING PONT N
BUS Nº

DÉPART
et
RETOUR
DURÉE 1 HEURE

089798
VEDETTES DU PONT-NEUF
PLEIN TARIF
PARIS 1er

089790
VEDETTES DU
PONT-NEUF
PARIS 1er
PLEIN TARIF
15 €
089798

VEDETTES
PONT-NF
PARI
PLEIN TARI
15 €
089790

Comment visiter Paris? On peut° visiter Paris en taxi, mais c'est cher.° On peut prendre° le bus. C'est amusant, mais la circulation° à Paris est souvent difficile. On peut prendre le métro. C'est pratique, rapide et bon marché,° mais on ne voit rien.°

Pourquoi ne pas faire une promenade° en bateau-mouche?° Les bateaux-mouches sont des bateaux modernes et confortables qui circulent sur la Seine. Pendant° la promenade, on peut prendre des photos et admirer les monuments le long de° la Seine. Le soir, on peut voir les monuments illuminés!

Activité Culturelle

Vous faites une promenade en bateau-mouche.
• Combien coûte le billet?
• Quels° monuments est-ce que vous pouvez° voir?

On peut *One can* **cher** *expensive* **prendre** *take* **circulation** *traffic* **bon marché** *inexpensive* **ne voit rien** *sees nothing*
Pourquoi ne pas faire une promenade *Why not take a ride* **bateau-mouche** *sight-seeing boat* **Pendant** *During* **le long de** *along*
Quels *Which* **pouvez** *can*

Paris en bateau-mouche
-------------------------------253

Activité culturelle Answers

• 15 euros
• la tour Eiffel
 les Invalides
 l'Assemblé Nationale
 le musée d'Orsay
 l'École Nationale des Beaux Arts
 l'Institut de France
 le Palais de Justice
 Notre Dame
 St-Louis-en-l'Île
 l'Hôtel de Ville
 le Louvre
 le jardin des Tuileries
 le Grand Palais.

USING THE VIDEO

Play Part 4 of the video, in which students are taken on a bateau-mouche ride. Students may look for **Notre Dame, la tour Eiffel,** and the many beautiful bridges and **quais** along the Seine.

Expansion activities PLANNING AHEAD

Games

• Je fais un voyage et j'apporte . . .
Divide the class into two teams. The first person on Team A begins «**Je fais un voyage et j'apporte...**» plus one article of clothing. The first person on Team B continues «**Je fais un voyage et j'apporte...**», repeats the first article of clothing the person from Team A mentioned, and adds a second article of clothing. Teams will take turns adding items to the list. When someone forgets an item, or gets the items out of order, the turn passes to the other team. The other team gets a point if they list all the items in the correct order. Otherwise, no one gets a point and the game starts over with the person who made the original error. Students could make the game more difficult by adding colors and sizes to the articles of clothing they name.

Pacing Suggestion: Upon completion of Leçon 17.

• L'espionnage
Divide students into three or four groups. Have one student in each group begin by describing what they see someone else in the group is wearing. Students should begin with the phrase, «**Je vois...**» The first person to guess the name of the chosen person correctly will do the next description.

Pacing Suggestion: Upon completion of Leçon 18.

Projects

• Mon magasin
Have students create a catalog page for their own department store. Each student will select the items for his or her catalog page and include a description and price for each item. They will also include photographs or illustrations to accompany each item. Have students lay out the images and descriptions to create an appealing catalog page. As an alternative, you could give students the names of French department stores, such as **Les Galeries Lafayette** and **Le Bon Marché,** and have them do research online in order to create a catalog page for one of these stores.

Pacing Suggestion: Upon completion of Leçon 17.

• Fashion Review
Students will work in small groups to create magazine-style fashion reviews. Members of each group will choose a celebrity or model, bring in photos of the chosen celebrity or model, and agree on an outfit to critique. Groups will then write a short fashion review (For example, «**Nous trouvons cette chemise jolie, mais la jupe est démodée.**») One student from each group should then present their group's review to the class.

Pacing Suggestion: Upon completion of Leçon 19.

Bulletin Boards

• L'Algérie
Divide the class into small groups. Have each group research some aspect of Algeria. Groups may:

- create a map that shows where Algeria is located
- find or create illustrations to show what Algeria looks like
- find information about the cuisine of Algeria
- find information about activities that are common among Algerian young people
- learn about Algerian immigrants in France

Have the groups create a bulletin board and each group present their information to the rest of the class.

Pacing Suggestion: Upon completion of Unité 6.

Music

• Le Pont d'Avignon
Teach students the words to the traditional French song «*Le Pont d'Avignon*». The music is available on the Internet and the lyrics are provided below.

«Sur le pont d'Avignon,
L'on y danse, l'on y danse;
Sur le pont d'Avignon,
L'on y danse tout en rond

Les beaux messieurs font comme ça,
Et puis encore comme ça.»
(Repeat first stanza)

Storytelling

• Mini-histoire

Model a brief conversation in which you shop for clothes. In the conversation, get help from a salesperson, compare two similar garments, and discuss the fit of a garment. Act out the conversation using gestures to help convey meaning. Pass out copies of your scripted conversation to students. Repeat the conversation with pauses, allowing students to either repeat after you or fill in the words. Then have them work in pairs to expand on the conversation. Ask students to write out their expanded conversations, practice them aloud for intonation, and perform them for the class.

Pacing Suggestion: Upon completion of Leçon 19.

Recipe

• Omelette au fromage

Omelets, a staple of French cuisine, make a simple but elegant dinner. This recipe is for a plain cheese omelet, but you may want to allow students to try fillings such as ham, green onions, and tomatoes.

Pacing Suggestion: Upon completion of Leçon 20.

Hands-on Crafts

• Flipbook à la mode

Ask students to bring in old magazines to cut figures from. Then, have them cut out separately three heads, three torsos, and three pairs of legs. Next, students will randomly line up the heads, torsos, and pairs of legs and glue them to a rectangular piece of construction paper. Finally, keeping the heads exposed, students should cut out three or four more layers of construction paper and glue three new torsos and pairs of legs to each one in alignment with the three visible heads to create a "fashion" flipbook.

Pacing Suggestion: Upon completion of Leçon 18.

End of Unit

• À la mode

Have students work in pairs to create entries for a fashion show. Students will select one of their own outfits to wear for the fashion show and write a detailed description of it. You may wish to give students vocabulary for additional colors, fabrics, styles, etc. Then partners will trade, read and edit each other's descriptions. Once the final descriptions are written, have students read aloud the description of their partner's outfit to practice intonation. On the day of the fashion show, each student will model for the class while their partner describes the outfit. You may wish to have students vote on the most elegant, bizarre, or trendy outfits. Students may also videotape their fashion show with music as background.

Rubric **A** = 13–15 pts. **B** = 10–12 pts. **C** = 7–9 pts. **D** = 4–6 pts. **F** = < 4 pts.

Criteria	Scale
Vocabulary Use	1 2 3 4 5
Grammar/Spelling Accuracy	1 2 3 4 5
Creativity	1 2 3 4 5

Omelette au fromage

Ingrédients
• 2 oeufs
• 15 grammes de beurre
• 1 cuillère à soupe de lait
• sel et poivre
• 85 grammes de fromage râpé

Préparation
1. Cassez les oeufs dans un saladier.
2. Avec une fourchette, battez les oeufs.
3. Ajoutez le lait, le sel et le poivre.
4. Faites chauffer une poêle et ajoutez le beurre.
5. Versez les oeufs dans la poêle.
6. Inclinez la poêle pour bien étendre les oeufs.
7. Quand les oeufs commencent à devenir solides, levez le bord et laissez couler le liquide au-dessous.
8. Faites cuire jusqu'à ce que les oeufs soient fermes.
9. Ajoutez le fromage au milieu de l'omelette.
10. Pliez l'omelette en deux et servez-la.

Ingredients
• 2 eggs
• approx. 2 teaspoons butter
• 1 tablespoon milk
• salt and pepper
• approx. 3 oz. grated cheese

Directions
1. Crack eggs into a mixing bowl.
2. Beat eggs with a fork.
3. Add milk, salt, and pepper.
4. Heat an 8-inch frying pan over high heat and add butter.
5. Pour egg mixture into pan.
6. Tilt pan to spread egg mixture evenly.
7. As eggs begin to firm, lift the edge of the omelet and allow the liquid to flow underneath.
8. Continue to cook until eggs are mostly firm.
9. Add cheese along the middle of the omelet.
10. Fold the omelet in half or in thirds and tip onto a plate.

UNITÉ 6

Planning Guide CLASSROOM MANAGEMENT

OBJECTIVES

Communication
- Name and describe the clothes you wear pp. 258–259, 260, 272
- Discuss style p. 262
- Shop for clothes and other items pp. 262, 268
- Talk about money p. 286
- Make comparisons p. 280
- Point out certain people or objects to your friends p. 270

Grammar
- Les verbes *acheter* et *préférer* p. 268
- L'adjectif démonstratif *ce* p. 270
- L'adjectif interrogatif *quel?* p. 271
- Le verbe *mettre* p. 272
- Les verbes réguliers en *-ir* p. 278
- Les adjectifs *beau, nouveau* et *vieux* p. 279
- La comparaison avec les adjectifs p. 280
- Le pronom *on* p. 288
- Les verbes réguliers en *-re* p. 290
- L'impératif p. 291

Vocabulary
- Les vêtements pp. 258–259
- D'autres vêtements et accessoires p. 260
- Dans un magasin p. 262
- Les nombres de 100 à 1000 p. 263
- Verbes comme *acheter* et *préférer* p. 269
- Verbes réguliers en *-ir* p. 278
- Expressions pour la conversation pp. 281, 289
- L'argent p. 286
- Verbes réguliers en *-re* p. 290

Pronunciation
- Les lettres «e» et «è» p. 273
- Les lettres «ill» p. 281
- Les lettres «an» et «en» p. 293

Culture
- Le grand magasin p. 266
- Les jeunes et la mode p. 276
- L'argent des jeunes p. 285
- Les soldes p. 303
- Prénoms arabes p. 304
- L'Algérie p. 305

PROGRAM RESOURCES

 Print
- Workbook PE, pp. 149–179
- *Activités pour tous* PE, pp. 91–109
- Block Scheduling Copymasters, pp. 129–159
- Teacher to Teacher Copymasters
- Unit 6 Resource Book
  - Lessons 17–20 Resources
    - Workbook TE
    - *Activités pour tous* TE
    - Lesson Plans
    - Block Scheduling Lesson Plans
    - Family Letter
    - Absent Student Copymasters
    - Family Involvement
    - Video Activities
    - Videoscripts
    - Audioscripts
    - Assessment Program
  - Unit 6 Resources
    - Communipak
    - *Activités pour tous* TE Reading
    - Workbook TE Reading and Culture Activities
    - Assessment Program
    - Answer Keys

 Audiovisual
- Audio Program PE CD 3 Tracks 20–43
- Audio Program Workbook CD 10 Tracks 1–27
- *Chansons* Audio CD
- Video Program Modules 17, 18, 19, 20
- Overhead Transparencies
  - 35 *Les vêtements*;
  - 36 *Vêtements et accessoires*;
  - 12 Menu from *Le Select*
  - 37 Comparing clothing;
  - 38 *Au grand magasin*;
  - 39 *-ir* Verbs;
  - 6 Clock face *Quelle heure est-il?*
  - 40 Adjectives *beau, nouveau, vieux*;

20 Objects (a) *Quelques objets (a)*; 41 *-re* Verbs

 Technology
- Online Workbook
- ClassZone.com
- eTest Plus Online/Test Generator CD-ROM
- EasyPlanner Plus Online/EasyPlanner CD-ROM
- Power Presentations on CD-ROM

 Assessment Program Options

Lesson Quizzes
Portfolio Assessment
Unit Test Form A
Unit Test Form B
Unit Test Part III (Alternate) Cultural Awareness
Listening Comprehension Performance Test
Speaking Performance Test
Reading Comprehension Performance Test
Writing Performance Test
Multiple Choice Test Items
Test Scoring Tools
Audio Program CD 15 Tracks 9–22
Answer Keys
eTest Plus Online/Test Generator CD-ROM

Pacing Guide SAMPLE LESSON PLAN

DAY	DAY	DAY	DAY	DAY
1 **Unité 6 Opener** **Leçon 17** • Vocabulaire et Culture–L'achat des vêtements • Vocabulaire–Les vêtements	**2** **Leçon 17** • Vocabulaire–D'autres vêtements et accessoires • Vocabulaire–Dans un magasin	**3** **Leçon 17** • Vocabulaire–Dans un magasin (continued) • Les nombres de 100 à 1000	**4** **Leçon 17** • À votre tour!	**5** **Leçon 18** • Conversation et Culture–Rien n'est parfait! • Note culturelle–Le grand magasin • Les verbes acheter et préférer
6 **Leçon 18** • Vocabulaire–Verbes comme acheter et préférer • L'adjectif démonstratif ce	**7** **Leçon 18** • L'adjectif démonstratif ce (continued) • L'adjectif interrogatif quel?	**8** **Leçon 18** • Le verbe mettre • Prononciation–Les lettres «e» et «è»	**9** **Leçon 18** • À votre tour!	**10** **Leçon 19** • Conversation et Culture–Un choix difficile • Note culturelle–Les jeunes et la mode • Les verbes réguliers en -ir
11 **Leçon 19** • Vocabulaire–Verbes réguliers en -ir • Les adjectifs beau, nouveau et vieux	**12** **Leçon 19** • La comparaison avec les adjectifs	**13** **Leçon 19** • Vocabulaire–Expressions pour la conversation • Prononciation–Les lettres «ill»	**14** **Leçon 19** • À votre tour!	**15** **Leçon 20** • Conversation et Culture–Alice a un job • Note culturelle–L'argent des jeunes • Vocabulaire–L'argent
16 **Leçon 20** • Vocabulaire–L'argent (continued) • Le pronom on • Vocabulaire–Expressions pour la conversation	**17** **Leçon 20** • Les verbes réguliers en -re • Vocabulaire–Verbes réguliers en -re	**18** **Leçon 20** • L'impératif • Prononciation–Les lettres «an» et «en»	**19** **Leçon 20** • À votre tour!	**20** • Tests de contrôle
21 • Unit 6 Test	**22** • Entracte–Lecture et culture	**23** • Entracte–Lecture et culture (continued)		

Pacing Guide • **253D**
Unité 6

Student Text Listening Activity Scripts
AUDIO PROGRAM

▶ **LEÇON 17 LE FRANÇAIS PRATIQUE** L'achat des vêtements

• Vocabulaire *p. 263* `CD 3, TRACK 20`

Les nombres de 100 à 1 000

Repeat the numbers after the speaker. Écoutez et répétez.

100 # 101 # 102 # 200 # 300 # 400 #
500 # 600 # 700 # 800 # 900 # 1 000 #

À votre tour!
• Écoutez bien! *p. 264* `CD 3, TRACK 21`

Thomas and Frédéric are both getting ready to leave on vacation. Listen to the following sentences which mention items that they are packing. If the item belongs to Thomas, mark A. If the item belongs to Frédéric, mark B. You will hear each sentence twice.

Let's begin. Commençons.

1. Il a une casquette. #
2. Où est sa ceinture? #
3. Quand il pleut, il porte un imperméable. #
4. Il a un blouson noir. #
5. Ses chaussures sont marron. #
6. Le pull est sur le lit. #
7. Il porte souvent des sandales. #
8. Oui, c'est sa cravate. #
9. Ce survêtement est très cher. #
10. J'aime bien la veste. #
11. Il a des chaussettes blanches. #
12. Tiens, voilà ses lunettes de soleil. #
13. Quand il fait chaud, il porte un tee-shirt. #
14. Le pantalon est dans la valise. #

• Créa-dialogue *p. 264* `CD 3, TRACK 22`

Listen to the sample *Créa-dialogues.* Écoutez les conversations.

Modèle: —Vous désirez, mademoiselle?
—Je cherche un pantalon.
—Comment trouvez-vous le pantalon gris?
—Il est joli. Combien est-ce qu'il coûte?
—Soixante dollars.
—Oh là là, il est cher!

Maintenant, écoutez le dialogue numéro 1.

—Vous désirez, monsieur?
—Je cherche un pull.
—Comment trouvez-vous le pull rouge?
—Il est élégant. Combien est-ce qu'il coûte?
—Trente dollars.
—Il est bon marché.

• Conversation dirigée *p. 265* `CD 3, TRACK 23`

Listen to the conversation. Écoutez la conversation entre Sophie et Christophe.

Sophie: Qu'est-ce que tu cherches, Christophe?
Christophe: Je cherche une casquette.
Sophie: Comment trouves-tu la casquette jaune?
Christophe: Elle est géniale, mais je vais acheter la casquette bleu.
Sophie: Combien est-ce qu'elle coûte?
Christophe: Elle coûte 5 euros.
Sophie: Elle est bon marché, mais elle est trop petite.

▶ **LEÇON 18** Rien n'est parfait!

• Rien n'est parfait! *p. 266*

A. Compréhension orale `CD 3, TRACK 24`

Please turn to page 266 for complete *Compréhension orale* text.

B. Écoutez et répétez. `CD 3, TRACK 25`

You will now hear a paused version of the dialog. Listen to the speaker and repeat right after he or she has completed the sentence.

• Grammaire *p. 268* `CD 3, TRACK 26`

Les verbes *acheter* et *préférer*

Écoutez et répétez. Repeat the sentences after the speaker.

J'**achète** une veste. #	Je **préfère** la veste bleue. #
Tu **achètes** une cravate. #	Tu **préfères** la cravate jaune. #
Il **achète** un imper. #	Il **préfère** l'imper gris. #
Nous **achetons** un jean. #	Nous **préférons** le jean noir. #
Vous **achetez** un short. #	Vous **préférez** le short blanc. #
Elles **achètent** un pull. #	Elles **préfèrent** le pull rouge. #

• Prononciation *p. 273* `CD 3, TRACK 27`

Les lettres «e» et «è»

Écoutez: ch_e_mise   chauss_e_tte   ch_è_re

Practice pronouncing "**e**" within a word:

• /ə/ (as in **je**)   [. . . "**e**" + _one_ CONSONANT + VOWEL]
  Répétez: ch_e_mise # r_e_garder # D_e_nise # R_e_née # p_e_tit # v_e_nir #
  Note that in the middle of a word the /ə/ is sometimes silent.
  Répétez: ach_e_ter # ach_e_tons # am_e_ner # sam_e_di # rar_e_ment # av_e_nue #

• /ɛ/ (as in **elle**)   [. . . "**e**" + _two_ CONSONANTS + VOWEL]
  Répétez: chauss_e_tte # v_e_ste # qu_e_lle # c_e_tte # r_e_ster # prof_e_sseur # raqu_e_tte #

Now practice pronouncing "**è**" within a word:

• /ɛ/ (as in **elle**)   [. . . "**e**" + _one_ CONSONANT + VOWEL]
  Répétez: ch_è_re # p_è_re # m_è_re # ach_è_te # am_è_nent # esp_è_re # deuxi_è_me #

À votre tour!
• La bonne réponse *p. 274* `CD 3, TRACK 28`

Listen to the conversation. Écoutez la conversation entre Alice et Jérôme.

Alice: Je vais à la soirée de Delphine. Et toi?
Jérôme: Moi aussi.
Alice: Tu amènes une copine?
Jérôme: Oui, Christine.
Alice: Qu'est-ce que vous allez apporter?
Jérôme: Nous allons acheter des pizzas.
Alice: Qu'est-ce que tu vas mettre?
Jérôme: Mon pull jaune et mon blouson marron.

• Créa-dialogue *p. 274* `CD 3, TRACK 29`

Listen to some sample *Créa-dialogues.* Écoutez les conversations.

Modèle: —Comment trouves-tu cette fille?   —Quelle fille?
—Cette fille-là!   —Eh bien, je pense qu'elle est jolie.

Maintenant, écoutez le dialogue numéro 1.

—Comment trouves-tu ces livres?   —Quels livres?
—Ces livres-là!   —Eh bien, je pense qu'ils sont intéressants.

▶ **LEÇON 19** Un choix difficile

• **Un choix difficile** *p. 276*

A. Compréhension orale `CD 3, TRACK 30`

Please turn to page 276 for complete *Compréhension orale* text.

B. Écoutez et répétez. `CD 3, TRACK 31`

You will now hear a paused version of the dialog. Listen to the speaker and repeat right after he or she has completed the sentence.

• **Grammaire** *p. 278* `CD 3, TRACK 32`

Les verbes réguliers en *-ir*

Repeat the sentences after the speaker. Écoutez et répétez.

Je finis à deux heures. #   Tu finis à une heure. #
Elle finit à cinq heures. #   Nous finissons à midi. #
Vous finissez à une heure. #   Ils finissent à minuit. #

• **Vocabulaire** *p. 278* `CD 3, TRACK 33`

Verbes réguliers en *-ir*

choisir #   Quelle veste **choisis**-tu? #
finir #   Les classes **finissent** à midi. #
grossir #   Marc **grossit** parce qu'il mange beaucoup. #
maigrir #   Je **maigris** parce que je mange peu. #
réussir #   Tu vas **réussir** parce que tu travailles! #
réussir à un examen #   Nous **réussissons à nos examens.** #

• **Prononciation** *p. 281* `CD 3, TRACK 34`

Les lettres «ill»

Écoutez: ma<u>ill</u>ot

In the middle of a word, the letters **"ill"** usually represent the sound /j/ like the **"y"** of <u>yes</u>.

Répétez: ma<u>ill</u>ot # trava<u>ill</u>ez # ore<u>ill</u>e # vie<u>ill</u>e # f<u>ill</u>e # fam<u>ill</u>e # ju<u>ill</u>et #
En ju<u>ill</u>et, Mire<u>ill</u>e va trava<u>ill</u>er pour sa vie<u>ill</u>e tante. #

At the end of a word, the sound /j/ is sometimes spelled **il**.

Répétez: appare<u>il</u>-photo # vie<u>il</u> # trava<u>il</u> #
Mon oncle a un vie<u>il</u> appare<u>il</u>-photo. #

EXCEPTION: The letters **ill** are pronounced /il/ in the following words:

Répétez: v<u>ill</u>e # v<u>ill</u>age # m<u>ill</u>e # L<u>ill</u>e #

À votre tour!

• **La bonne réponse** *p. 282* `CD 3, TRACK 35`

Listen to the conversation. Écoutez la conversation entre François et Stéphanie.

François: Tu aimes cette veste verte?
Stéphanie: Oui, mais elle est très chère.
François: Combien est-ce qu'elle coûte?
Stéphanie: 300 euros.
François: Et qu'est-ce que tu penses de cette veste rouge?
Stéphanie: À mon avis, elle est moins jolie.
François: Alors, qu'est-ce que tu vas choisir?
Stéphanie: La veste bleue. Elle est meilleur marché et elle est aussi élégante.

• **Créa-dialogue** *p. 282* `CD 3, TRACK 36`

Listen to the sample *Créa-dialogues*. Écoutez les conversations.

Modèle: –Tu choisis la voiture rouge ou la voiture noire?
          –Je choisis la voiture rouge.
          –Pourquoi?
          –Parce qu'elle est plus petite et moins chère.

Maintenant, écoutez le dialogue numéro 1.

–Tu achètes la chaîne hi-fi ou le baladeur?
–J'achète la chaîne hi-fi.
–Pourquoi?
–Parce qu'elle est meilleure et plus grande.

▶ **LEÇON 20** Alice a un job

• **Alice a un job** *p. 284*

A. Compréhension orale `CD 3, TRACK 37`

Please turn to page 284 for complete *Compréhension orale* text.

B. Écoutez et répétez. `CD 3, TRACK 38`

You will now hear a paused version of the dialog. Listen to the speaker and repeat right after he or she has completed the sentence.

• **Grammaire** *p. 290* `CD 3, TRACK 39`

Les verbes réguliers en *-re*

Repeat the sentences with *vendre.* Écoutez et répétez.

Je **vends** ma raquette. #   Tu **vends** ton scooter. #
Il **vend** son ordinateur. #   Nous **vendons** nos livres. #
Vous **vendez** vos CD. #   Elles **vendent** leur voiture. #

• **Vocabulaire** *p. 290* `CD 3, TRACK 40`

Verbes réguliers en *-re*

Repeat these sentences containing *-re* verbs.

attendre #   Pierre **attend** Michèle au café. #
entendre #   Est-ce que tu **entends** la radio? #
perdre #   Jean-Claude **perd** le match. #
rendre visite à #   Je **rends** visite à mon oncle. #
répondre à #   Nous **répondons** à la question du prof. #
vendre #   À qui **vends**-tu ton vélo? #

• **Prononciation** *p. 293* `CD 3, TRACK 41`

Les lettres «an» et «en»

Écoutez: <u>en</u>f<u>an</u>t

The letters **"an"** and **"en"** represent the nasal vowel /ã/. Be sure not to pronounce the sound **"n"** after the vowel.

Répétez: /ã/ #   <u>en</u>f<u>an</u>t # <u>an</u> # m<u>an</u>teau # coll<u>an</u>ts # gr<u>an</u>d # élég<u>an</u>t #
                 André m<u>an</u>ge un gr<u>an</u>d s<u>an</u>dwich.
           /ã/ #   <u>en</u>f<u>an</u>t # <u>en</u> # arg<u>en</u>t # dép<u>en</u>ser # att<u>en</u>ds # <u>en</u>t<u>en</u>d #
                 v<u>en</u>d # <u>en</u>vie #
                 Vincent dép<u>en</u>se rarem<u>en</u>t son arg<u>en</u>t. #

À votre tour!

• **La bonne réponse** *p. 294* `CD 3, TRACK 42`

Listen to the conversation. Écoutez la conversation entre Anne et Jean-François.

Anne: Est-ce que tu rends visite à tes cousins ce week-end?
Jean-François: Non, je reste ici.
Anne: Tu veux aller dans les boutiques avec moi?
Jean-François: Écoute! Je n'ai pas besoin de vêtements.
Anne: Est-ce que tu as envie d'aller au cinéma?
Jean-François: Bonne idée! Il y a un nouveau film au «Majestic».
Anne: Et après, qu'est-ce qu'on fait?
Jean-François: Eh bien, allons au restaurant!

• **Créa-dialogue** *p. 294* `CD 3, TRACK 43`

Listen to some sample *Créa-dialogues*. Écoutez les conversations.

Modèle: –Qu'est-ce qu'on fait samedi?
          –Allons au cinéma.
          –Je n'ai pas envie d'aller au cinéma.
          –Eh bien, rendons visite à nos amis. D'accord?
          –Oui, c'est une bonne idée!

Maintenant, écoutez le dialogue numéro 1.

–Qu'est-ce qu'on fait ce soir?
–Étudions.
–Je n'ai pas envie d'étudier.
–Eh bien, regardons la télé. D'accord?
–Oui, c'est une bonne idée!

Complete videoscripts, plus Workbook and Assessment audioscripts, are available in the Unit Resource Books.

Main Theme
• Buying clothes

COMMUNICATION
• Naming and describing clothes
• Discussing style
• Shopping for clothes and other items
• Talking about money
• Making comparisons
• Pointing out certain people and objects

CULTURES
• Learning about French stores, including *le grand magasin*
• Learning about French shopping habits and *les soldes*
• Learning about how French teens buy clothing
• Learning how French teenagers get their spending money
• Learning about North Africa and Algeria

CONNECTIONS
• Connecting to Math: Deciding on purchases within a budget
• Connecting to Computer Science: Using the Internet to do research

COMPARISONS
• Comparing French and American department stores
• Comparing how teens in France and the U.S. obtain their spending money

COMMUNITIES
• Surveying people in the community
• Using the Internet to learn about other cultures

UNITÉ 6

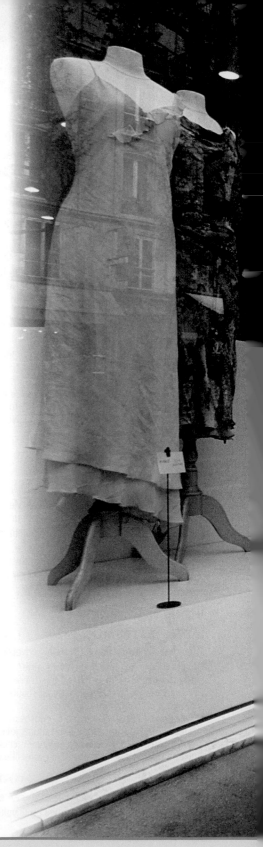

Le shopping

LEÇON 17 LE FRANÇAIS PRATIQUE: L'achat des vêtements

LEÇON 18 Rien n'est parfait!

LEÇON 19 Un choix difficile

LEÇON 20 Alice a un job

THÈME ET OBJECTIFS

Buying clothes

Are you interested in clothes? When you visit France, you will enjoy going window shopping. In fact, you will probably want to try on a few items and buy something special to bring home.

In this unit, you will learn …
• to name and describe the clothes you wear
• to discuss style
• to shop for clothes and other items
• to talk about money

You will also be able …
• to make comparisons
• to point out certain people or objects to your friends

 WEBQUEST CLASSZONE.COM

254   deux cent cinquante-quatre
Unité 6

UNIT OVERVIEW

• **Communication Goals:** Students will be able to shop for clothing, describe what people are wearing, and make comparisons.

• **Linguistic Goals:** Students will learn the present tense of **-ir** and **-re** verbs, the imperative, and comparative forms of adjectives.

• **Critical Thinking Goals:** Students will observe similarities and differences in the ways French and English make commands and express comparisons.

• **Cultural Goals:** Students will become aware of the French concept of style and the ways in which young people earn and spend their money.

Teaching Resource Options

PRINT
Unit 6 Resource Book
  Family Letter

AUDIO & VISUAL
Audio Program
Chansons CD

TECHNOLOGY
EasyPlanner CD-ROM/EasyPlanner
  Plus Online

Middle School Copymasters

Unité 6: *La valise* and *Qui est-ce?*
games, conversations, puzzles, drill,
worksheets, wardrobe and Mardi
Gras mask projects, pp. T31–T34

Leçon 17

Main Topic Shopping for clothing

Teaching Resource Options

PRINT

Workbook PE, pp. 149–155
Activités pour tous PE, pp. 91–93
Block Scheduling Copymasters,
   pp. 129–135
Unit 6 Resource Book
   Activités pour tous TE, pp. 9–11
   Audioscript, pp. 32–34
   Communipak, pp. 140–158
   Lesson Plans, pp. 12–13
   Block Scheduling Lesson Plans, pp. 14–15
   Absent Student Copymasters, pp. 17–20
   Video Activities, pp. 23–28
   Videoscript, pp. 29–30
   Workbook TE, pp. 1–7

AUDIO & VISUAL

Audio Program
CD 10 Tracks 1–8

TECHNOLOGY

Online Workbook

VIDEO PROGRAM

MODULE 17
Le français pratique
L'achat des vêtements

TOTAL TIME: 7:33 min.
   DVD Disk 2
   Videotape 3 (COUNTER: 34:31 min.)

17.1 Introduction: Listening
   – Le shopping (34:40–35:55 min.)

17.2 Dialogue: Aux Galeries Lafayette
   (35:56–37:11 min.)

17.3 Mini-scenes: Listening
   – Qu'est-ce que vous cherchez?
   (37:12–38:08 min.)

17.4 Mini-scenes: Speaking
   – Vous désirez? (38:09–39:08 min.)

17.5 Mini-scenes: Speaking
   – Combien coûte la veste?
   (39:09–39:52 min.)

17.6 Mini-scenes: Listening
   – Comment trouves-tu ma robe?
   (39:53–40:28 min.)

**17.7 Vignette culturelle: Où acheter
   les vêtements?** (40:29–42:04 min.)

Comprehension practice Play
the entire module through as an
introduction to the lesson.

LE FRANÇAIS
PRATIQUE
VIDÉO   DVD   AUDIO

L'achat des vêtements

Accent sur ... l'élégance française

France is a leader in high fashion. French fashion design houses, such as Dior, Chanel, Yves Saint Laurent and Pierre Cardin, are known all over the world for the style and quality of their creations.

French young people like to be in style, even if their clothes are casual and not too expensive. Depending on their budgets, they buy their clothes at …

• **une grande surface** (*low-cost chain store*)
• **un grand magasin** (*department store*)
• **une boutique de vêtements** (*clothing store*)
• **une boutique de soldes** (*discount clothing shop*)
• **le marché aux puces** (*flea market*)

Mélanie cherche une robe pour aller au mariage de sa cousine. Quelle robe est-ce qu'elle va acheter?

SETTING THE STAGE

Ask your students if they like to shop for clothes and where they go.

> **Est-ce que vous aimez faire du shopping?**
>   **Où allez-vous?**
> **Allez-vous dans un grand magasin?**
>   **Comment s'appelle-t-il?**
> **Allez-vous dans une boutique de vêtements?**
>   **Comment s'appelle-t-elle?**
> **Allez-vous dans une boutique de soldes?**
>   **Comment s'appelle-t-elle?**
> **Est-ce qu'il y a une marché aux puces dans
>   notre ville?**

Tell students that in the video they will observe French young people shopping for clothes. In the **Vignette culturelle,** they will see various types of clothing stores.

Fatima est dans une boutique de vêtements. Ici les vêtements sont très élégants …
et très chers aussi.

Patrick et Béatrice achètent leurs vêtements dans
une grande surface. Ici les vêtements sont de
bonne qualité et ils ne sont pas trop chers.

Michel est dans un magasin de chaussures. Quelles chaussures
est-ce qu'il va acheter? Des baskets ou des chaussures de sport?

deux cent cinquante-sept
Leçon 17 257

CRITICAL THINKING SKILLS

English has borrowed many words pertaining to
clothing and fashion: **boutique, eau de cologne,
haute couture.**

Ask students to list other borrowed French words
relating to fashion and clothes.

For example:
chemise	**crêpe**
culottes	**maillot**
chic	

Communicative function
Talking about clothing

Teaching Resource Options

PRINT

Workbook PE, pp. 149–155
Unit 6 Resource Book
    Communipak, pp. 140–158
    Video Activities, p. 25
    Videoscript, p. 29
    Workbook TE, pp. 1–7

AUDIO & VISUAL

Overhead Transparencies
35 *Les vêtements*

VIDEO PROGRAM

VIDÉO   DVD

MODULE 17

17.3 Mini-scenes: Qu'est-ce que vous cherchez? (37:12–38:08 min.)

Looking ahead Students will learn the forms of **acheter** in Lesson 18.

Extra activity To review **euros**, ask the prices of each item.
Combien coûte le blouson?

Language notes

- **Un pull** is a shortened form of **un pull-over**, which is a borrowed word from English. It is used for any sweater which is pulled over the head. French has also borrowed the word **un sweater** /swɛTɛr/.

- In Quebec, **un chandail** /ʃãdaj/ is used for **un pull**.

Pronunciation Be sure students say **pull** /pyl/ with the /y/ of **tu.**

Supplementary vocabulary

faire les magasins *to go shopping (browsing from store to store)*
un anorak *ski jacket*
un costume *man's suit*
un tailleur *woman's suit*

A VOCABULAIRE **Les vêtements**

Je vais dans un magasin.

▶ *How to talk about shopping for clothes:*

Où vas-tu?
  Je vais | dans **une boutique** *(shop)*.
               dans **un magasin** *(store)*
               dans **un grand magasin** *(department store)*
Qu'est-ce que tu vas **acheter** *(to buy)*?
  Je vais acheter **des vêtements** *(clothes)*.

Les vêtements

→ Nouns that end in **-eau** in the singular end in **-eaux** in the plural.
    un chap**eau**   des chap**eaux**   un mant**eau**   des mant**eaux**

COMPREHENSION Clothes

PROPS: A bag of old clothes in large sizes

Give students various items of clothing.
    X, montre-nous le pull.
    Y, montre-nous la cravate. ...
    Qui a le pull? [X]...

If appropriate, have students try items on.
    Z, mets le chapeau. Ah, c'est très joli!
    Qui porte le chapeau? [Z]

Have students move the clothing around.
    X, mets le pull sur la chaise de Z.
    Où est le pull? [sur la chaise de Z]
    Z, donne le pull à W.
    Qui a le pull maintenant? [W]

Middle School Copymasters

Class Starter: *Qui est-ce?*, p. T31

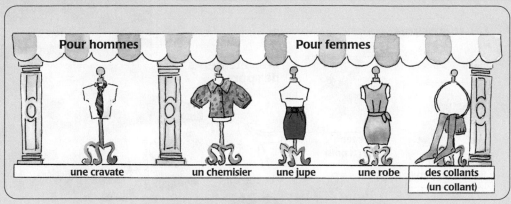

Pour hommes   Pour femmes

une cravate   un chemisier   une jupe   une robe   des collants (un collant)

acheter	to buy	Je vais **acheter** une cravate.
porter	to wear	Qu'est-ce que tu vas **porter** demain?
mettre	to put on, wear	Oh là là, il fait froid. Je vais **mettre** un pull.

→ **Mettre** is irregular. (Its forms are presented in Leçon 18.)

❶ 👥 Shopping

PARLER Below are the names of several Paris stores. Using the illustrations as a guide, talk to a classmate about where you are going shopping and what you plan to buy.

▶ —Où vas-tu?
—Je vais au Monoprix.
—Qu'est-ce que tu vas acheter?
—Je vais acheter une chemise.

▼

(au) MONOPRIX
1. (au) PRINTEMPS
2. (au) BON MARCHÉ
3. (chez) KOOKAÏ
4. (chez) CÉLINE
5. (aux) GALERIES LAFAYETTE
6. (chez) LECLERC
7. (chez) DIOR
8. (à) LA SAMARITAINE

❷ Quels vêtements?

PARLER/ÉCRIRE What we wear often depends on the circumstances: where we are, what we will be doing, what the weather is like. Complete the following sentences with the appropriate items of clothing.

1. Aujourd'hui, je porte …
2. Le professeur porte …
3. L'élève à ma gauche porte …
4. L'élève à ma droite porte …
5. Quand je vais à une boum, je porte …
6. Quand je vais dans un restaurant élégant, je porte …
7. S'il pleut *(If it rains)* demain, je vais mettre …
8. S'il fait chaud demain, je vais mettre …
9. Si *(If)* je vais en ville samedi, je vais mettre …
10. Si je vais à un concert dimanche, je vais mettre …

deux cent cinquante-neuf
Leçon 17 259

❶ EXCHANGES talking about shopping plans

1. —Où vas-tu?
 —Je vais au Printemps.
 —Qu'est-ce que tu vas acheter?
 —Je vais acheter un pantalon.
2. —Où vas-tu?
 —Je vais au Bon Marché.
 —Qu'est-ce que tu vas acheter?
 —Je vais acheter une robe.
3. —Où vas-tu?
 —Je vais chez Kookaï.
 —Qu'est-ce que tu vas acheter?
 —Je vais acheter des chaussettes.
4. —Où vas-tu?
 —Je vais chez Céline.
 —Qu'est-ce que tu vas acheter?
 —Je vais acheter une jupe.
5. —Où vas-tu?
 —Je vais aux Galeries Lafayette.
 —Qu'est-ce que tu vas acheter?
 —Je vais acheter un blouson.
6. —Où vas-tu?
 —Je vais chez Leclerc.
 —Qu'est-ce que tu vas acheter?
 —Je vais acheter un imper[méable].
7. —Où vas-tu?
 —Je vais chez Dior.
 —Qu'est-ce que tu vas acheter?
 —Je vais acheter un chemisier.
8. —Où vas-tu?
 —Je vais à la Samaritaine.
 —Qu'est-ce que tu vas acheter?
 —Je vais acheter un manteau.

❷ COMMUNICATION talking about clothes

Answers will vary.
1. Aujourd'hui, je porte (un pantalon).
2. Le professeur porte (une veste).
3. L'élève à ma gauche porte (un jean).
4. L'élève à ma droite porte (un pull).
5. Quand je vais à une boum, je porte (une jupe / une veste).
6. Quand je vais dans un restaurant élégant, je porte (une cravate / une robe).
7. S'il pleut demain, je vais mettre (un imperméable).
8. S'il fait chaud demain, je vais mettre (un polo).
9. Si je vais en ville samedi, je vais mettre (une chemise et un pantalon élégant).
10. Si je vais à un concert dimanche, je vais mettre (une veste).

Expansion
Quand il neige, je porte…
Quand je vais en ville, je porte…
Quand je vais à un match de football américain, je porte…
Quand je vais au cinéma avec mes copains, je porte…

SUPPLEMENTARY LISTENING PRACTICE

You can build listening comprehension skills by talking about the clothing that students are wearing. Students respond with gestures or one-word answers. Repeat each item of clothing in several different questions and responses.

For example:
Qui porte un polo aujourd'hui?
W et X portent un polo.
Y ne porte pas de polo.
Et toi, Z, tu portes un polo? [oui]
De quelle couleur est le polo de Z? [bleu]
Mais oui, il est bleu…

SECTION B

Communicative function
Talking about clothing and accessories

Teaching Resource Options

PRINT

Workbook PE, pp. 149–155
Unit 6 Resource Book
  Communipak, pp. 140–158
  Video Activities, p. 25
  Videoscript, pp. 29–30
  Workbook TE, pp. 1–7

AUDIO & VISUAL

Overhead Transparencies
36 *Vêtements et accessoires*

VIDEO PROGRAM

VIDÉO   DVD
 MODULE 17

17.4 Mini-scenes: Vous désirez?
(38:08–39:08 min.)

Pronunciation **Un sweat** is pronounced /swit/.

Casual speech **Un maillot de bain** is often referred to as **un maillot.**

Language note Point out that **des lunettes (de soleil)** is feminine.

 3

DESCRIPTION indicating what people are wearing

1. Anne porte des lunettes de soleil, un polo, un short et des sandales.
2. Sophie porte un maillot de bain et des tennis.
3. Michel porte un survêtement (un jogging) et des baskets.
4. Catherine porte un sweat, un short et des lunettes de soleil.
5. Je porte (un tee-shirt, des sandales, et des lunettes de soleil).

Challenge Students say what each person is NOT wearing, using **pas de.**

Paul ne porte pas de tee-shirt.

B VOCABULAIRE D'autres vêtements et accessoires

Je vais mettre des lunettes de soleil.

Les chaussures
des chaussures (une chaussure)
des tennis (un tennis)
des bottes (une botte)
des sandales (une sandale)
des baskets (un basket)
Les vêtements de sport
un tee-shirt
un short
un sweat
un survêtement (un jogging)
un maillot de bain
Les accessoires
une ceinture
des lunettes (f.)
des lunettes de soleil

3 À la plage de Deauville

PARLER/ÉCRIRE You are spending the summer vacation in Deauville, a popular seaside resort in Normandy. Describe what you and your friends are wearing.

▶ **Paul porte un maillot de bain …**

▶ Paul   1. Anne   2. Sophie   3. Michel   4. Catherine   5. moi

TALKING ABOUT PAST EVENTS

Let's talk about what you wore yesterday. Remember to use **pas de** in negative answers.
    Est-ce que tu as porté un manteau hier?
    Oui, j'ai porté un manteau.
    (Non, je n'ai pas porté de manteau.)

- **Est-ce que tu as porté un chapeau hier?**
- **Est-ce que tu as porté un survêtement?**
- **Est-ce que tu as porté des lunettes de soleil?**
- **Est-ce que tu as porté des tennis?**
- **Est-ce que tu as porté une cravate?**
- **Est-ce que tu as porté une robe?**

4 👥👤 *Qu'est-ce que tu portes?*

PARLER Ask your classmates what they wear in the following circumstances. Let them use their imagination.

▶ jouer au tennis

1. aller à la piscine
2. aller à la plage
3. jouer au basket
4. travailler dans le jardin
5. aller au gymnase *(gym)*
6. faire une promenade dans la forêt *(forest)*
7. faire une promenade dans la neige *(snow)*

Qu'est-ce que tu portes quand tu joues au tennis?

Je porte un tee-shirt, un short et des tennis.

5 *Un jeu*

PARLER/ÉCRIRE When you see what people are wearing, you can often tell what they are going to do. How many different logical sentences can you make in five minutes using the elements of A, B, and C? Follow the model below.

A	B	C
André	un maillot de bain	nager
Sylvie	des lunettes de soleil	aller à la plage
Paul et Éric	un short	aller à un concert
Michèle et Anne	des chaussettes blanches	jouer au tennis
	un sweat	jouer au volley
	un pantalon très chic	jouer au foot
	des chaussures noires	aller à la campagne *(country)*
	des bottes	faire du jogging *(to jog)*
	un costume *(suit)*	dîner en ville
	une robe	
	une casquette	

Sylvie porte un short. Elle va jouer au foot.

6 *Joyeux anniversaire!*

PARLER/ÉCRIRE The following people are celebrating their birthdays. Find a present for each person by choosing an item of clothing from pages 258, 259, or 260.

1. Pour mon père (ma mère), je vais acheter …
2. Pour ma grand-mère (mon grand-père), …
3. Pour ma petite cousine Élodie (10 ans), …
4. Pour mon grand frère Guillaume (18 ans), …
5. Pour le professeur, …
6. Pour mon meilleur *(best)* ami, …
7. Pour ma meilleure amie, …

• **Qu'est-ce que tu as porté hier?**
• **Qu'est-ce que tu as porté vendredi soir? samedi après-midi? dimanche matin?**

Follow-up:
• **Qu'est-ce que X a porté hier?**
• **Qu'est-ce que Y a porté vendredi soir?**
• **Qu'est-ce que Z a porté dimanche matin?**

4 COMMUNICATION talking about what one wears when

Answers will vary.
—Qu'est-ce que tu portes quand tu … ?
—Je porte …
1. vas à la piscine/(un maillot de bain)
2. vas à la plage/(un short, un tee-shirt, des sandales, et des lunettes de soleil)
3. joues au basket/(un survêtement et des baskets)
4. travailles dans le jardin/(un tee-shirt et un jean)
5. vas au gymnase/(un survêtement et des tennis)
6. fais une promenade dans la forêt/(des baskets, un jean, un sweat et un blouson)
7. fais une promenade dans la neige/(des bottes, un pantalon, un pull, un chapeau et un manteau)

5 COMPREHENSION describing clothes and related activities

Answers will vary.
André porte un maillot de bain. Il va nager.
Sylvie porte des lunettes de soleil et une casquette. Elle va aller à la plage.
Paul et Éric portent un short. Ils vont jouer au volley.
Michèle et Anne portent des chaussettes blanches. Elles vont jouer au tennis.
André porte un sweat. Il va faire du jogging.

Variation (conversation format)
Student 1 states what someone is wearing. Student 2 asks why. Student 3 gives the reason.
– Sylvie porte un short.
– Pourquoi?
– Elle va jouer au football.

Variation
Have students reverse columns B and C, using **mettre**.
André va nager.
Il va mettre un maillot de bain.

6 COMMUNICATION selecting gifts

Answers will vary.
1. une ceinture
2. un chapeau
3. un tee-shirt
4. un survêtement
5. un polo
6. un sweat
7. un chemisier

Supplementary vocabulary

LES ACCESSOIRES
des gants *(m.)* gloves
un foulard *(silk)* scarf
un mouchoir handkerchief
des verres *(m.)* **de contact** contact lenses
une écharpe *(winter)* scarf

LES BIJOUX
un bijou piece of jewelry
un collier necklace
un bracelet
une bague ring
une chaîne chain
des boucles *(f.)* **d'oreille** earrings

SECTION C

Communicative function
Buying clothing in a store

Teaching Resource Options

PRINT

Workbook PE, pp. 149–155
Unit 6 Resource Book
   Audioscript, p. 31
   Communipak, pp. 140–158
   Video Activities, pp. 23–24, 26
   Videoscript, pp. 29–30
   Workbook TE, pp. 1–7

AUDIO & VISUAL

Audio Program
CD 3 Track 20

Overhead Transparencies
37 Comparing clothing
12 Menu from *Le Select*

VIDEO PROGRAM

VIDÉO   DVD
 MODULE 17

17.1 Introduction: Le shopping
(34:40–35:55 min.)

17.2 Dialogue: Aux Galeries Lafayette
(35:56–37:11 min.)

17.5 Mini-scenes: Combien coûte la veste? (39:09–39:52 min.)

17.6 Mini-scenes: Comment trouves-tu ma robe? (39:53–40:28 min.)

Supplementary vocabulary

trop serré *(too tight)*

Vocabulary note

The masculine plural of **génial** is **géniaux**.

Note: In the text, students will only be using this adjective in the singular.

C VOCABULAIRE Dans un magasin

Vous désirez, mademoiselle?
Pardon, madame.
Je cherche un pantalon.

▶ *How to get help from a salesperson:*

Pardon, monsieur (madame).
Vous désirez *(May I help you),* | monsieur?
| madame
| mademoiselle

Je cherche *(I'm looking for)* …
   un pantalon.
Quel est le prix *(What is the price)* du pantalon?
Combien *(How much)* **coûte** le pantalon?
Combien est-ce qu'il coûte?
   Il coûte 40 euros.

Je cherche …
   une veste.
Quel est le prix de la veste?
Combien coûte la veste?
Combien est-ce qu'elle coûte?
   Elle coûte 65 euros.

▶ *How to discuss clothes with a friend:*

Qu'est-ce que tu penses du pantalon vert?
   (What do you think of …?)
Comment trouves-tu le pantalon vert?
   (What do you think of …?)

Qu'est-ce que tu penses de
   la veste verte?
Comment trouves-tu
   la veste verte?

Comment trouves-tu le pantalon vert?
Il est trop petit.

Il est	joli.		Elle est	jolie.
	élégant			élégante
	génial *(terrific)*			géniale
	chouette *(neat)*			chouette
	à la mode *(in style)*			à la mode
Il est	moche *(plain, ugly).*		Elle est	moche.
	démodé *(out of style)*			démodée
Il est **trop** *(too)*	petit.		Elle est **trop**	petite.
	grand *(big)*			grande
	court *(short)*			courte
	long *(long)*			longue
Il est	cher *(expensive).*		Elle est	chère.
	bon marché *(cheap)*			bon marché

→ The expression **bon marché** is INVARIABLE. It does not take adjective endings.
   Les chaussures blanches sont **bon marché.**

VERBES

chercher	*to look for*	Je **cherche** un jean.
coûter	*to cost*	Les chaussures **coûtent** 60 euros.
penser	*to think*	Qu'est-ce que tu **penses** de cette *(this)* robe?
penser que	*to think (that)*	Je **pense qu'**elle est géniale!
trouver	*to find*	Je ne **trouve** pas ma veste.
	to think of	Comment **trouves**-tu mes lunettes de soleil?

→ The verb **penser** is often used alone.
   Tu **penses?** *Do you think so?*   Je **ne pense pas.** *I don't think so.*

GAME Prices

PROPS: Transparency 12: Menu from *Le Select*
Using the menu on the transparency, have each student write an addition problem with an answer that is under 40 euros. For example:
   Combien coûtent 2 steak-frites et 2 thés? [22 euros]

Place the problems into a hat. Divide the class into two teams. Draw a problem from the hat and read it aloud. Player A-1 plays against player B-1. The first player from either team to stand and answer correctly wins a point. If the response is incorrect, the other player tries to answer. Continue with players A-2 and B-2, etc.

Les nombres de 100 à 1000

100	cent	200	deux cents	500	cinq cents	800	huit cents
101	cent un	300	trois cents	600	six cents	900	neuf cents
102	cent deux	400	quatre cents	700	sept cents	1000	mille

7 *Au marché aux puces*

PARLER You are at the Paris flea market looking for clothes with a French friend. Explain why you are not buying the following items. Use your imagination … and expressions from the **Vocabulaire**.

▶ —Tu vas acheter le blouson?
—Non, je ne pense pas.
—Pourquoi pas?
—Il est trop grand.

▶

8 *C'est combien?*

PARLER Ask your friends how much the following items cost.

▶ —Combien coûte la veste?
—Elle coûte cent vingt euros.

▶

deux cent soixante-trois
Leçon 17 263

Les nombres de 100 à 1000
Language notes
• The word **mille** never takes an "s": **deux mille, trois mille,** etc.
• Note: at this level, students are not expected to spell the numbers.

7 **EXCHANGES** explaining why one is not buying certain items

Answers will vary.

1. —Tu vas acheter la cravate?
—Non, je ne pense pas.
—Pourquoi pas?
—Elle est trop (moche).
2. —Tu vas acheter le pull?
—Non, je ne pense pas.
—Pourquoi pas?
—Il est trop grand.
3. —Tu vas acheter le jean?
—Non, je ne pense pas.
—Pourquoi pas?
—Il est trop court.
4. —Tu vas acheter le chapeau?
—Non, je ne pense pas.
—Pourquoi pas?
—Il est trop (démodé).
5. —Tu vas acheter la veste?
—Non, je ne pense pas.
—Pourquoi pas?
—Elle est trop petite.
6. —Tu vas acheter l'imper[méable]?
—Non, je ne pense pas.
—Pourquoi pas?
—Il est trop (long / grand).
7. —Tu vas acheter les bottes?
—Non, je ne pense pas.
—Pourquoi pas?
—Elles sont (démodées).

8 **ROLE PLAY** asking about prices

1. — Combien coûte le blouson?
— Il coûte 150 (cent cinquante) euros.
2. — Combien coûte le manteau?
— Il coûte 200 (deux cents) euros.
3. — Combien coûte l'impérmeable?
— Il coûte 250 (deux cent cinquante) euros.
4. — Combien coûte l'appareil-photo?
— Il coûte 180 (cent quatre-vingts) euros.
5. — Combien coûte la mini-chaîne?
— Elle coûte 350 (trois cent cinquante) euros.
6. — Combien coûte l'ordinateur?
— Il coûte 1 400 (mille quatre cents) euros.
7. — Combien coûte le vélo?
— Il coûte 275 (deux cent soixante-quinze) euros.
8. — Combien coûte le téléviseur?
— Il coûte 725 (sept cent vingt-cinq) euros.
9. — Combien coûte le scooter?
— Il coûte 890 (huit cent quatre-vingt-dix) euros.

CHALLENGE ACTIVITY Une idole

Une idole is a music superstar. Have students bring in a picture of an American **idole** and describe what he/she is wearing. They can give the approximate prices and comment on the style. For example:
Mon idole est Will Smith. Ici il porte un blouson qui *(which)* **coûte $150 et un pantalon qui coûte $75. Le blouson est trop grand mais le pantalon est très élégant. Il porte aussi des lunettes de soleil. Elles sont chouettes mais chères: elles coûtent $200!**

À VOTRE TOUR

Main Topic
• Recapitulation and review

Teaching Resource Options

PRINT

Workbook PE, pp. 149–155
Unit 6 Resource Book
  Audioscript, p. 31
  Communipak, pp. 140–158
  Family Involvement, pp. 21–22
  Workbook TE, pp. 1–7

Assessment
Lesson 17 Quiz, pp. 35–36
Portfolio Assessment, Unit 1 URB
  pp. 155–164
Audioscript for Quiz 17, p. 34
Answer Keys, pp. 230–234

AUDIO & VISUAL

Audio Program
CD 3 Tracks 21–23
CD 15 Track 9

TECHNOLOGY

Test Generator CD-ROM/eTest Plus
Online

❶ COMPREHENSION

1. B	4. A	7. B	10. A
2. A	5. A	8. A	11. A
3. A	6. B	9. B	12. B

❷ GUIDED ORAL EXPRESSION

1. – Vous désirez, monsieur (mademoiselle)?
   – Je cherche un pull.
   – Comment trouvez-vous le pull rouge?
   – Il est élégant. Combien est-ce qu'il coûte?
   – Trente dollars.
   – Oh là là, il est cher! (Il est bon marché.)
2. – Vous désirez, monsieur (mademoiselle)?
   – Je cherche un imperméable.
   – Comment trouvez-vous l'imperméable bleu?
   – Il est joli. Combien est-ce qu'il coûte?
   – Trois cent cinquante dollars.
   – Oh là là, il est cher!
3. – Vous désirez, monsieur (mademoiselle)?
   – Je cherche une veste.
   – Comment trouvez-vous la veste jaune?
   – Elle est à la mode. Combien est-ce qu'elle coûte?
   – Deux cent cinquante dollars.
   – Oh là là, elle est chère!
4. – Vous désirez, monsieur (mademoiselle)?
   – Je cherche un tee-shirt.
   – Comment trouvez-vous le tee-shirt blanc?
   – Il est génial. Combien est-ce qu'il coûte?
   – Quinze dollars.
   – Il est bon marché.

À votre tour!

❶ Écoutez bien!

ÉCOUTER Thomas and Frédéric are both getting ready to leave on vacation. Listen to the following sentences which mention items that they are packing. If the item belongs to Thomas, mark A. If the item belongs to Frédéric, mark B.

	1	2	3	4	5	6
A: Thomas						
B: Frédéric						

A. Thomas

B. Frédéric

❷ Créa-dialogue

PARLER You are at Place Bonaventure in Montreal looking at clothes in various shops. You like what the salesperson shows you and ask how much each item costs. React to the price.

joli / $60

 1. élégant / $30

 2. joli / $350

3. à la mode / $250

 4. génial / $15

▶ —Vous désirez, monsieur (mademoiselle)?
—Je cherche un pantalon.
—Comment trouvez-vous le pantalon gris?
—Il est joli. Combien est-ce qu'il coûte?
—Soixante dollars.
—Oh là là, il est cher! (Il est bon marché.)

À VOTRE TOUR

Depending on your goals and objectives, you may or may not wish to assign all of the activities in the **À votre tour** section.

3 🎧 👥 Conversation dirigée

PARLER Sophie and Christophe are shopping in a department store. Act out their conversation in French.

Sophie

asks Christophe what he is looking for	→ ↙	answers that he is looking for a baseball cap	
asks him what he thinks of the yellow cap	→ ↙	says that it is terrific but adds that he is going to buy the blue cap	
asks how much it costs	⇄	answers 5 euros	
says that it is inexpensive but adds that it is too small			

Christophe

4 Qu'est-ce qui ne va pas? *(What's wrong?)*

PARLER Explain what is wrong with the clothes that these people just bought at a sale.

▶ **Le chapeau de Monsieur Dupont est trop grand.**

Monsieur Dupont   **Édouard**

5 ✏️ Les valises

ÉCRIRE You are an exchange student in Paris. Your host family has invited you to spend:

- one weekend in Nice to go sailing
- one weekend in Chamonix to go skiing

Make a list of the different clothes you will take on each trip.

6 ✏️ À l'aéroport

ÉCRIRE You are flying to Paris tomorrow on an exchange program. Your hosts plan to meet you at the airport, but don't have your picture. Write them an e-mail explaining what you look like and what you will be wearing.

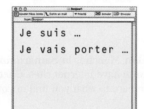

Je suis …
Je vais porter …

LESSON REVIEW
CLASSZONE.COM

deux cent soixante-cinq
Leçon 17 265

---

3 GUIDED ORAL EXPRESSION

S: Qu'est-ce que tu cherches, Christophe?
C: Je cherche une casquette.
S: Comment trouves-tu la casquette jaune?
C: Elle est géniale, mais je vais acheter la casquette bleue.
S: Combien est-ce qu'elle coûte?
C: Elle coûte cinq euros.
S: Elle est bon marché (elle n'est pas chère), mais elle est trop petite.

4 COMPREHENSION

M. Dupont: La veste de M. Dupont est trop grande. Le pantalon de M. Dupont est trop court.
Édouard: La chemise d'Édouard est trop petite. La cravate d'Édouard est trop longue (grande). Le pantalon d'Édouard est trop long (grand).

5 WRITTEN SELF-EXPRESSION ✏️

Answers will vary.

Ma liste de vêtements pour Nice (pour aller à Nice)	Ma liste de vêtements pour Chamonix (pour aller à Chamonix)
un maillot de bain	un jean
deux shorts	un pull
des lunettes de soleil	deux pantalons
un chapeau	des bottes
une casquette	un manteau
trois tee-shirts	deux collants
des tennis	un chapeau
des sandales	
un sweat	

6 WRITTEN SELF-EXPRESSION ✏️

Answers will vary.
Je suis petit(e) et brun(e). (Je suis grand[e] et blond[e].)
Je vais porter un pantalon vert, un pull marron, des chaussures marron et un blouson noir. (Je vais porter un jean bleu, un sweat jaune, une veste grise et des tennis blanches. / Je vais porter une robe rouge et un manteau bleu.)

Cultural note

Place Bonaventure is part of Montreal's unique underground city. Various underground neighborhoods are linked by metro and climate-controlled corridors, a feature which Montrealers greatly appreciate in the wintertime. Between **Place Bonaventure** and **Place du Canada** one can find supermarkets, banks, boutiques, beauty salons, cinemas, theaters, hotels, and two railway stations.

Middle School Copymasters

Games: *La valise*, pp. T33–T34;
Conversation: Shopping, p. 89;
Puzzle 1: *Au Bon Marché*, p. 90;
Puzzle 2: *Ça me va bien?*, p. 91

À votre tour! • **265**
Unité 6 Leçon 17

Leçon 18

Main Topics Shopping and talking about clothes

Teaching Resource Options

PRINT

Workbook PE, pp. 157–162
Activités pour tous PE, pp. 95–97
Block Scheduling Copymasters,
  pp. 137–143
Unit 6 Resource Book
  Activités pour tous TE, pp. 43–45
  Audioscript, pp. 62, 63–65
  Communipak, pp. 140–158
  Lesson Plans, pp. 46–47
  Block Scheduling Lesson Plans,
    pp. 48–49
  Absent Student Copymasters,
    pp. 50–53
  Video Activities, pp. 56–59
  Videoscript, pp. 60–61
  Workbook TE, pp. 37–42

AUDIO & VISUAL

Audio Program
CD 3 Tracks 24, 25
CD 10 Tracks 9–14

Overhead Transparencies
38 *Au grand magasin*

TECHNOLOGY

Online Workbook

VIDEO PROGRAM

VIDÉO   DVD

MODULE 18
Rien n'est parfait!

TOTAL TIME: 5:19 min.
  DVD Disk 2
  Videotape 3 (COUNTER: 42:15 min.)

18.1 Dialogue: Rien n'est parfait!
(42:45–43:44 min.)

18.2 Mini-scenes: Listening
– Comment trouves-tu ce pull?
(43:45–44:58 min.)

18.3 Mini-scenes: Listening
– Quel café? (44:59–45:25 min.)

18.4 Mini-scenes: Speaking
– Quelle veste désirez-vous?
(45:26–46:09 min.)

18.5 Vignette culturelle: Un grand magasin (46:10–47:34 min.)

Comprehension practice Play the entire module through as an introduction to the lesson.

266 • **Conversation et Culture**
  Unité 6 LEÇON 18

LEÇON 18

Rien n'est parfait!

VIDÉO DVD AUDIO

<u>Cet</u> après-midi, Frédéric et Jean-Claude vont acheter des vêtements. Ils vont acheter <u>ces</u> vêtements dans un grand magasin. <u>Ce</u> magasin s'appelle le Bon Marché.

This

these/This

SCÈNE 1.
Frédéric et Jean-Claude regardent les pulls.

Frédéric:	Regarde! Comment trouves-tu ce pull?	
Jean-Claude:	<u>Quel</u> pull?	*Which*
Frédéric:	Ce pull bleu.	
Jean-Claude:	Il est chouette.	
Frédéric:	C'est vrai, il est très chouette.	
Jean-Claude:	*(qui regarde le prix)* Il est aussi très cher.	
Frédéric:	Combien est-ce qu'il coûte?	
Jean-Claude:	Deux cents euros.	
Frédéric:	Deux cents euros! <u>Quelle horreur!</u>	*What a scandal!*

NOTE culturelle

Le grand magasin

Le grand magasin est un magasin de 4 ou 5 étages où on peut° acheter toutes° sortes de produits différents: vêtements, parfums, meubles,° alimentation° générale, etc. … Le grand magasin est une idée française. Le premier grand magasin a été créé° en 1852 par Aristide Boucicaut (1810-1877). Ce magasin existe toujours° et s'appelle «le Bon Marché». L'idée de Monsieur Boucicaut était° d'offrir à sa clientèle une marchandise de bonne qualité à des prix bon marché … d'où° le nom «Bon Marché». Son idée a été vite° copiée dans toutes les villes.

on peut *one can*   **toutes** *all*   **meubles** *furniture*   **alimentation** *food*
a été créé *was created*   **toujours** *still*   **était** *was*   **d'où** *hence*   **vite** *quickly*

COMPARAISONS CULTURELLES

French department stores, such as **le Bon Marché, la Samaritaine, le Printemps,** and **les Galeries Lafayette** have Internet sites. Check out one of these stores. How do its products compare to what you find in your local department stores?

 266   deux cent soixante-six
Unité 6

WARM-UP AND REVIEW

PROPS: Transparency 38: *Au grand magasin*
Using a transparency marker, fill in prices up to 300 euros in the price tags on the transparency. Then ask questions about the items of clothing and their prices.
  Qu'est-ce que c'est?
  C'est un pantalon noir.

Combien coûte le pantalon?
Il coûte [cent trente] euros.
C'est cher?
Mais oui, c'est très cher.

Scène 2.

Maintenant Frédéric et Jean-Claude regardent les vestes.

Frédéric: Quelle veste est-ce que tu préfères?

Jean-Claude: Je préfère cette veste jaune. Elle est très élégante et elle n'est pas très chère.

Frédéric: Oui, mais elle est trop grande pour toi!

Jean-Claude: Dommage!

Scène 3.

Frédéric est au <u>rayon</u> des chaussures.   *department*
Quelles chaussures est-ce qu'il va acheter?

Jean-Claude: Alors, quelles chaussures est-ce que tu achètes?

Frédéric: J'achète ces chaussures noires. Elles sont très confortables … et elles ne sont pas chères. Regarde, elles sont <u>en solde</u>.   *on sale*

Jean-Claude: C'est vrai, elles sont en solde … mais elles <u>ne sont plus</u> à la mode.   *are no longer*

Frédéric: <u>Hélas</u>, <u>rien n'est parfait</u>!   *Too bad/nothing is perfect*

Compréhension Answers

1. Cet après-midi, Frédéric et Jean-Claude vont dans un grand magasin (au Bon Marché).
2. Ils vont acheter des vêtements.
3. Ils regardent d'abord les pulls.
4. Le pull bleu coûte deux cents euros.
5. Frédéric pense que le pull est trop cher. (Il ne va pas acheter le pull.)
6. Jean-Claude pense que la veste jaune est élégante. Elle n'est pas chère.
7. Il n'achète pas la veste parce qu'elle est trop grande.
8. Frédéric pense que les chaussures noires sont confortables (ne sont pas chères).
9. Il n'achète pas les chaussures parce qu'elles ne sont pas à la mode.

Note culturelle

In 1989, **Au Bon Marché** changed its name to **Le Bon Marché.**

Compréhension

1. Où vont Frédéric et Jean-Claude cet après-midi?
2. Qu'est-ce qu'ils vont faire?
3. Qu'est-ce qu'ils regardent d'abord *(first)*?
4. Combien coûte le pull bleu?
5. Quelle est la réaction de Frédéric?
6. Qu'est-ce que Jean-Claude pense de la veste jaune?
7. Pourquoi est-ce qu'il n'achète pas la veste?
8. Qu'est-ce que Frédéric pense des chaussures noires?
9. Pourquoi est-ce qu'il n'achète pas les chaussures?

SECTION A

Communicative function
Indicating what people prefer and what people are buying

Teaching Resource Options

PRINT

Workbook PE, pp. 157–162
Unit 6 Resource Book
   Audioscript, p. 62
   Communipak, pp. 140–158
   Workbook TE, pp. 37–42

AUDIO & VISUAL

Audio Program
CD 3 Track 26

TECHNOLOGY

Power Presentations

Teaching strategies

• Point out that the stem changes occur only in those forms of the verb where the ending is not pronounced. There is no stem change before **-ons** and **-ez.**

• For your visually-minded students you can present stem-changing verbs as "boot verbs." Within the "boot" the verb endings are not pronounced and there is the same change in the stem. Outside the boot, the endings are pronounced, and there is no stem change.

j'achète	nous achetons
tu achètes	vous achetez
il achète	ils achètent

1 COMPREHENSION describing purchases

Answers will vary.
1. Avec dix dollars, tu achètes (un CD / des lunettes de soleil).
2. Avec quinze dollars, j'achète (des lunettes de soleil / une cravate).
3. Avec trente dollars, nous achetons (un jean / un polo).
4. Avec cinquante dollars, Jean-Claude achète (une veste / un survêtement).
5. Avec cent dollars, vous achetez (un survêtement et une cravate).
6. Avec quinze mille dollars, mes parents achètent (une voiture).
7. Avec vingt-cinq dollars, mon cousin achète (un polo).
8. Avec (soixante dollars), j'achète (des chaussures).

A Les verbes *acheter* et *préférer*

Verbs like **acheter** *(to buy)* end in: **e** + CONSONANT + **-er.**
Verbs like **préférer** *(to prefer)* end in: **é** + CONSONANT + **-er.**

Note the forms of these two verbs in the chart, paying attention to:
• the **e** of the stem of ach**e**ter
• the **é** of the stem of pr**é**férer

INFINITIVE	acheter	préférer
PRESENT	J' ach**è**te une veste. Tu ach**è**tes une cravate. Il/Elle ach**è**te un imper.	Je préf**è**re la veste bleue. Tu préf**è**res la cravate jaune. Il/Elle préf**è**re l'imper gris.
	Nous **achetons** un jean. Vous **achetez** un short. Ils/Elles ach**è**tent un pull.	Nous **préférons** le jean noir. Vous **préférez** le short blanc. Ils/Elles préf**è**rent le pull rouge.

→ Verbs like **acheter** and **préférer** take regular endings and have the following changes in the stem:

ach**e**ter	e → è	in the **je**, **tu**, **il**, and **ils**
préf**é**rer	é → è	forms of the present

1 Achats (Purchases) - - - - - - - - - - - - - - - -

PARLER/ÉCRIRE What we buy depends on how much money we have. Complete the sentences below with **acheter** and one or more of the items from the list.

1. Avec dix dollars, tu …
2. Avec quinze dollars, j' …
3. Avec trente dollars, nous …
4. Avec cinquante dollars, Jean-Claude …
5. Avec cent dollars, vous …
6. Avec quinze mille dollars, mes parents …
7. Avec ?? dollars, mon cousin …
8. Avec ?? dollars, j' …

une voiture

des chaussures

une cravate

un survêtement

??

des lunettes de soleil

un polo

une veste

un CD

un jean

TALKING ABOUT PAST EVENTS Introducing the past tense

Let's talk about what clothes you bought last summer.
Est-ce que tu as acheté un jean l'été dernier?
Oui, j'ai acheté un jean.
   (Non, je n'ai pas acheté de jean.)

• **Est-ce que tu as acheté un polo?**
• **Est-ce que tu as acheté des sandales?**

• **Est-ce que tu as acheté un maillot de bain?**
• **Est-ce que tu as acheté une veste?**
• **Qu'est-ce que tu as acheté?**

Follow-up:
   Est-ce que X a acheté un jean?

VOCABULAIRE Verbes comme *(like)* acheter et préférer

acheter	to buy	Qu'est-ce que tu **achètes**?
amener	to bring (a person)	François **amène** sa copine à la boum.
préférer	to prefer	**Préfères**-tu le manteau ou l'imper?
espérer	to hope	J'**espère** visiter Paris en été.

➔ In French, there are two verbs that correspond to the English *to bring*:

amener + PEOPLE   J'**amène** une copine au pique-nique.
apporter + THINGS   J'**apporte** des sandwichs au pique-nique.

2 Pique-nique

PARLER/ÉCRIRE Everyone is bringing someone or something to the picnic. Complete the sentences below with the appropriate forms of **amener** or **apporter**.

▶ **Nous** <u>amenons</u> un copain.   **Marc** <u>apporte</u> des sandwichs.

1. Tu … ta guitare.
2. Philippe … sa soeur.
3. Nous … nos voisins.
4. Vous … un dessert.
5. Michèle … des sodas.

6. Antoine et Vincent … leur cousine.
7. Raphaël … ses CD.
8. Mon cousin … sa copine.
9. J' … ma radiocassette.
10. Léa et Émilie … leurs portables.

3 Expression personnelle

PARLER/ÉCRIRE Complete the sentences below with one of the suggested options or an expression of your choice. Note: You may wish to make some of the sentences negative.

Quand je vais à une fête, j'apporte mon portable.

Et moi, j'apporte ma guitare.

1. Quand je vais à une fête, j'amène … (des copains, une copine, ma grand-mère, ??)
   J'apporte … (des sandwichs, ma guitare, mes CD, mon portable, ??)
2. Quand je vais à un pique-nique, j'amène … (ma soeur, une copine, mon chien, ??)
   J'apporte … (mon baladeur, mon livre de français, des sandwichs, ??)
3. Le week-end, je préfère … (étudier, aller au cinéma, rester à la maison, ??)
   Ce *(This)* week-end, j'espère … (avoir un rendez-vous avec un copain ou une copine, travailler, jouer au volley, ??)

4. Pendant *(During)* les vacances, j'espère … (rester à la maison, trouver un job, voyager, ??)
5. Un jour, j'espère … (visiter la France, parler français, aller à l'université, être millionnaire, ??)

deux cent soixante-neuf
Leçon 18 269

TALKING ABOUT PAST EVENTS

Let's talk about what things you brought to a recent party.
Tu es allé(e) à une boum récemment.
  Est-ce que tu as apporté des CD?
  Oui, j'ai apporté des CD.
  (Non, je n'ai pas apporté de CD.)

- **Est-ce que tu as apporté des DVD?**
- **Est-ce que tu as apporté une guitare?**
- **Est-ce que tu as apporté des pizzas?**
- **Est-ce que tu as apporté des sodas?**
- **Qu'est-ce que tu as apporté?**

Teaching strategy Using subject pronoun cue cards, have students conjugate **amener** and **espérer** orally and in writing.

Middle School Copymasters
Worksheet 2: *En solde*, p. 93

2 COMPREHENSION describing what and whom people are bringing to a picnic

1. apportes
2. amène
3. amenons
4. apportez
5. apporte
6. amènent
7. apporte
8. amène
9. apporte
10. apportent

3 COMMUNICATION describing what one does and hopes to do

Answers will vary.
1. Quand je vais à une fête, j'amène (une copine).
   J'apporte (mes CD).
2. Quand je vais à un pique-nique, j'amène (ma soeur).
   J'apporte (des sandwichs).
3. Le week-end, je préfère (aller au cinéma).
   Ce week-end, j'espère (jouer au volley).
4. Pendant les vacances, j'espère (voyager).
5. Un jour, j'espère (visiter la France).

Expansion In trios, have students discuss and vote on the choices. The recorder **(secrétaire)** then writes the sentences in the **nous**-form.
1. Quand nous allons à une fête, nous amenons (des copains). Nous apportons (nos portables).
2. Quand nous allons à un pique-nique, nous amenons (des copines). Nous apportons (des sandwichs).
3. Le week-end, nous préférons (aller au cinéma).
   Ce week-end, nous espérons (jouer au volley).
4. Pendant les vacances, nous espérons (voyager).
5. Un jour, nous espérons (visiter la France).

Variation (with **amener**)

Est-ce que tu as amené
- **un copain?**
- **une copine?**
- **des amis français?**
- **des cousins?**

SECTION B

Communicative function
Pointing out people and things

Teaching Resource Options

PRINT

Workbook PE, pp. 157–162
Unit 6 Resource Book
 Communipak, pp. 140–158
 Video Activities, pp. 57–58
 Videoscript, pp. 60–61
 Workbook TE, pp. 37–42

TECHNOLOGY

Power Presentations

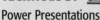
VIDEO PROGRAM

  MODULE 18

18.2 Mini-scenes: Comment trouves-tu ce pull? (43:45–44:58 min.)

18.3 Mini-scenes: Quel café?
(44:59–45:25 min.)

18.4 Mini-scenes: Quelle veste désirez-vous? (45:26–46:09 min.)

4 ROLE PLAY commenting on
items in a store

1. **N:** Regarde cet imper!
 M: Il est élégant!
2. **N:** Regarde ces bottes!
 M: Elles sont à la mode!
3. **N:** Regarde cette casquette!
 M: Elle est géniale!
4. **N:** Regarde ce survêtement!
 M: Il est chouette!
5. **N:** Regarde ces livres!
 M: Ils sont amusants!
6. **N:** Regarde cet ordinateur!
 M: Il est génial!
7. **N:** Regarde cette télé!
 M: Elle est moderne!
8. **N:** Regarde cette ceinture!
 M: Elle est jolie!
9. **N:** Regarde ces sandales!
 M: Elles sont jolies!

5 ROLE PLAY discussing
preferences

—J'aime ...
—Eh bien, moi, je préfère ...
1. cette chemise-ci/cette chemise-là
2. ce blouson-ci/ce blouson-là
3. ces chaussures-ci/ces chaussures-là
4. ces lunettes-ci/ces lunettes-là
5. cette casquette-ci/cette casquette-là
6. cette affiche-ci/cette affiche-là
7. ce stylo-ci/ce stylo-là
8. cet ordinateur-ci/cet ordinateur-là
Point out to students that the French often use
"Eh bien" to emphasize a question or remark.
– **Eh bien, est-ce que tu viens en ville avec
 nous?**
– **Eh bien, non!**

270 • Langue et Communication
Unité 6 LEÇON 18

B L'adjectif démonstratif *ce*

> **LEARNING ABOUT LANGUAGE**
>
> DEMONSTRATIVE ADJECTIVES *(this, that)* are
> used to point out specific people or things.
>
> In French, the demonstrative adjective **ce**
> always agrees with the noun it introduces.

Note the forms of the demonstrative
adjective **ce** in the chart below.

	SINGULAR *(this, that)*	PLURAL *(these, those)*		
MASCULINE	**ce** / **cet** (+ VOWEL SOUND)	**ces**	**ce** blouson / **cet** homme	**ces** blousons / **ces** hommes
FEMININE	**cette**	**ces**	**cette** veste / **cette** amie	**ces** vestes / **ces** amies

→ There is liaison after **cet** and **ces** when the next word begins with a vowel sound.

→ To distinguish between a person or an object that is close by and one that is further
away, the French sometimes use **-ci** or **-là** after the noun.

 Philippe achète **cette chemise-ci**. *Philippe is buying **this shirt** (over here).*
 François achète **cette chemise-là**. *François is buying **that shirt** (over there).*

4   **À la Samaritaine**

PARLER Marc and Nathalie are at the Samaritaine department store.
Marc likes everything that Nathalie shows him. Play both roles.

▶ une robe (jolie) NATHALIE: **Regarde cette robe!**
       MARC: **Elle est jolie!**

1. un imper (élégant) 4. un survêtement (chouette) 7. une télé (moderne)
2. des bottes (à la mode) 5. des livres (amusants) 8. une ceinture (jolie)
3. une casquette (géniale) 6. un ordinateur (génial) 9. des sandales (jolies)

5   **Différences d'opinion**

PARLER Whenever they go shopping
together, Éric and Brigitte cannot agree
on what they like. Play both roles.

▶ un short

1. une chemise 5. une casquette
2. un blouson 6. une affiche
3. des chaussures 7. un stylo
4. des lunettes 8. un ordinateur

J'aime ce short-ci.

Eh bien, moi, je
préfère ce short-là.

270 deux cent soixante-dix
Unité 6

TEACHING STRATEGIES

• Point out that **ces** (like **les, des, mes**) is used with
both masculine and feminine plural nouns. (There is
no **cettes**.)

• Tell students that the masculine singular form **cet** is
derived from the feminine singular form **cette** minus
-te: **cette → cet**.

LANGUAGE NOTE

The tag **-ci** is related to **ici** *(here)* and **-là** means
there. The expression **voici** has evolved from **vois ici**
(see here) and **voilà** from **vois là** *(see there)*.

C L'adjectif interrogatif *quel?*

The interrogative adjective **quel** *(what? which?)* is used in questions. It agrees with
the noun it introduces and has the following forms:

	SINGULAR	PLURAL		
MASCULINE	quel	quels	**Quel** garçon?	**Quels** cousins?
FEMININE	quelle	quelles	**Quelle** fille?	**Quelles** copines?

→ Note the liaison after **quels** and **quelles** when the next word begins with a vowel sound.
Quelles affiches est-ce que tu préfères?

 6  *Vêtements d'été*

PARLER You are shopping for the
following items before going on a
summer trip to France. A friend is
asking you which ones you are
buying. Identify each item by color.

Quel pantalon est-ce que tu achètes?

J'achète un pantalon.

Ce pantalon noir.

▶ **un pantalon/noir**

1. un maillot de bain/bleu

2. des chaussettes/vertes

3. une jupe/jaune

4. une veste/bleue

5. des chaussures/blanches

6. des sandales/marron

7. un sweat/gris

8. une chemise/orange

9. un pull/rouge

7 *Questions personnelles* **PARLER/ÉCRIRE**

1. À quelle école vas-tu?
2. Dans quel magasin achètes-tu tes vêtements?
3. Dans quel magasin achètes-tu tes chaussures?
4. Quels CD aimes-tu écouter?
5. Quels programmes aimes-tu regarder à la télé?
6. Quel est ton restaurant préféré?
7. Quelle est ta classe préférée?

LISTENING ACTIVITY Préférences

PROPS: One red and one blue index card for each
student
On the board, write **quel(s)** in blue chalk and
quelle(s) in red chalk. Then read aloud questions
containing forms of **quel.** If the form is spelled
quel(s), students hold up the blue card. If it is spelled
quelle(s), they hold up the red card.

1. **Quel sweat préfères-tu?** [B]
2. **Quels appareils...?** [B]
3. **Quelle jupe...?** [R]
4. **Quel blouson...?** [B]
5. **Quelles affiches...?** [R]
6. **Quelles chaussettes...?** [R]
7. **Quel pull...?** [B]
8. **Quelle école...?** [R]

Communicative function
Asking for clarification

Language notes
• Point out that all four forms of **quel**
sound the same.
• **Quel** may be separated from its
noun by **être.**
Quelle est la date?

Teaching strategy Ask students if
they can remember any questions
they learned that use **quel.**

Quelle est la date?
Quelle heure est-il?
Quel temps fait-il?
Quel jour est-ce?
De quelle couleur est...?

6 **ROLE PLAY** discussing
purchases

1. – J'achète un maillot de bain.
   – Quel maillot de bain est-ce que tu achètes?
   – Ce maillot de bain bleu.
2. – J'achète des chaussettes.
   – Quelles chaussettes est-ce que tu achètes?
   – Ces chaussettes vertes.
3. – J'achète une jupe.
   – Quelle jupe est-ce que tu achètes?
   – Cette jupe jaune.
4. – J'achète une veste.
   – Quelle veste est-ce que tu achètes?
   – Cette veste bleue.
5. – J'achète des chaussures.
   – Quelles chaussures est-ce que tu achètes?
   – Ces chaussures blanches.
6. – J'achète des sandales.
   – Quelles sandales est-ce que tu achètes?
   – Ces sandales marron.
7. – J'achète un sweat.
   – Quel sweat est-ce que tu achètes?
   – Ce sweat gris.
8. – J'achète une chemise.
   – Quelle chemise est-ce que tu achètes?
   – Cette chemise orange.
9. – J'achète un pull.
   – Quel pull est-ce que tu achètes?
   – Ce pull rouge.

 Re-entry and review

This activity reviews colors from
Lesson 20.

---

7 **COMMUNICATION** answering
personal questions

Answers will vary.
1. Je vais à (North Quincy High School).
2. J'achète mes vêtements à (La Boutique Chic).
3. J'achète mes chaussures chez (Bata).
4. J'aime écouter les CD de (MC Solaar).
5. À la télé, je regarde (les comédies).
6. Mon restaurant préféré est (Chez Antoine).
7. Ma classe préféré est (le français).

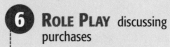

SECTION D

Communicative function
Saying where to put things

Teaching Resource Options

PRINT

Workbook PE, pp. 157–162
Unit 6 Resource Book
  Audioscript, pp. 62–63
  Communipak, pp. 140–158
  Workbook TE, pp. 37–42

AUDIO & VISUAL

Audio Program
CD 3 Track 27

TECHNOLOGY

Power Presentations

Supplementary vocabulary

VERBS LIKE **METTRE**
mettre la table *to set the table*
  (introduced in Lesson 25)
permettre *to permit, allow, let*
promettre *to promise*

8 **COMPREHENSION** describing
where people put things

Answers will vary.
Je mets la glace dans le réfrigérateur.
Nous mettons la voiture dans le garage.
Tu mets les livres sur le bureau (sur la table /
  dans le salon).
Vous mettez le téléphone sur la table (dans le
  salon / sur le bureau).
Christine met les vêtements dans le placard.
Le professeur met les plantes vertes dans le
  salon (sur la table / sur le bureau).
Madame Arnaud met une pellicule dans
  l'appareil-photo.
Marc et Philippe mettent les cartes sur la table
  (sur le bureau).

Variation Have students give
illogical answers.

**Mme Arnaud met la voiture dans le
salon.**

D Le verbe *mettre*

The verb **mettre** *(to put, place)* is irregular. Note its forms in the chart below.

INFINITIVE	mettre	
PRESENT	je **mets**	nous **mettons**
	tu **mets**	vous **mettez**
	il/elle **met**	ils/elles **mettent**

→ In the singular forms, the "**t**" of the stem is silent. The "**t**" is pronounced in the plural forms.

→ The verb **mettre** has several English equivalents:

to put, place	Je **mets** mes livres sur la table.
to put on, wear	Caroline **met** une robe rouge.
to turn on	Nous **mettons** la télé.

8 *Où?*

PARLER/ÉCRIRE Say where the people of
Column A put the objects of Column B,
by choosing a place from Column C. Be logical!

> Madame Arnaud met
> la voiture dans le garage.

A	B	C
moi	la glace	dans le salon
nous	la voiture	dans l'appareil-photo
toi	les livres	sur la table
vous	le téléphone	dans le placard *(closet)*
Christine	les vêtements	dans le garage
le professeur	des plantes vertes	sur le bureau
Madame Arnaud	une pellicule *(film)*	dans le réfrigérateur
Marc et Philippe	les cartes	sous le lit

TEACHING NOTE Un jeu

Divide the students into pairs. Have each student take
a sheet of paper. At a given signal, students write a
phrase using elements from columns A and B (e.g., **Je
mets la glace...**). As soon as they finish, they
exchange papers and complete their partner's
sentence using an element from column C (**...dans le
réfrigérateur**).

Then, they write another phrase using columns A
and B, exchange papers, and again complete their
partner's sentence using column C.

After you have called time, have the pairs
exchange papers for peer correction. The winner is
the pair with the most correct sentences.

9 *Questions personnelles* PARLER/ÉCRIRE

1. Est-ce que tu mets la radio quand tu étudies?
2. Chez vous, est-ce que vous mettez la télé quand vous dînez?
3. Est-ce que tu mets des lunettes de soleil quand tu vas à la plage?
4. Où est-ce que tes parents mettent leur voiture? (dans le garage? dans la rue?)
5. Quels programmes de télé est-ce que tu mets le dimanche? le samedi?
6. Quels CD est-ce que tu mets quand tu vas à une boum?
7. Quels vêtements est-ce que tu mets quand il fait froid?
8. Quels vêtements est-ce que tu mets quand tu joues au basket?

PRONONCIATION

Les lettres «e» et «è»

e = /ə/   e = /ɛ/   è = /ɛ/

chemise   chaussette   chère

Practice pronouncing "**e**" within a word:

- /ə/ (as in **je**)   [… "e" + *one* CONSONANT + VOWEL]

  Répétez: chemise regarder Denise Renée petit venir

  Note that in the middle of a word the /ə/ is sometimes silent.

  Répétez: acheter achetons amener samedi rarement avenue

- /ɛ/ (as in **elle**)   [… "e" + *two* CONSONANTS + VOWEL]

  Répétez: chaussette veste quelle cette rester professeur raquette

Now practice pronouncing "**è**" within a word:

- /ɛ/ (as in **elle**)   [… "è" + *one* CONSONANT + VOWEL]

  Répétez: chère père mère achète amènent espère deuxième

NOS CHEMISES

deux cent soixante-treize
Leçon 18 273

9 COMMUNICATION answering personal questions

Answers will vary.
1. Oui, je mets la radio quand j'étudie. (Non, je ne mets pas la radio quand j'étudie.)
2. Oui, chez nous, nous mettons la télé quand nous dînons. (Non, chez nous, nous ne mettons pas la télé quand nous dînons.)
3. Oui, je mets des lunettes de soleil quand je vais à la plage. (Non, je ne mets pas de lunettes de soleil quand je vais à la plage.)
4. Mes parents mettent leur voiture dans le garage (dans la rue).
5. Le dimanche je mets (le match de football américain). Le samedi, je mets (un film).
6. Quand je vais à une boum, je mets des CD (de MC Solaar et [de] Pascal Obispo).
7. Quand il fait froid, je mets (un manteau, des bottes, et des gants).
8. Quand je joue au basket, je mets (un short, un tee-shirt, des chaussettes et des baskets).

PRONUNCIATION

- The sound /ə/ is called a *mute e* because it is sometimes mute or silent.
- The sound /ɛ/ is called an *open e* because when you say it your mouth is more open than when you say /e/ as in **café**.

Realia note
Monoprix
Les Trois Suisses is a moderately priced chain store that sells clothing, cosmetics, stationery supplies, toys, and housewares. Many of the stores also have a supermarket section.

Teaching Resource Options

PRINT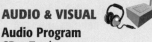

Workbook PE, pp. 157–162
Unit 6 Resource Book
   Audioscript, p. 63
   Communipak, pp. 140–158
   Family Involvement, pp. 54–55
   Workbook TE, pp. 37–42

Assessment
Lesson 18 Quiz, pp. 66–67
Portfolio Assessment, Unit 1 URB
  pp. 155–164
Audioscript for Quiz 18, p. 65
Answer Keys, pp. 230–234

AUDIO & VISUAL

Audio Program
CD 3 Tracks 28, 29
CD 15 Track 10

TECHNOLOGY

Test Generator CD-ROM/eTest Plus
Online

① COMPREHENSION

1. d   **3.** c
2. a   **4.** b

② GUIDED ORAL EXPRESSION

– Comment trouves-tu ... ?
– ... ?
– ... -là!
– Eh bien, je pense qu'...
1. ces livres/Quels livres/Ces livres/ils sont intéressants. (Ils ne sont pas intéressants.)
2. ce monsieur (cet homme)/Quel homme/Cet homme/il n'est pas sympathique. (Il est sympathique.)
3. cette jupe/Quelle jupe/Cette jupe/elle est courte. (Elle n'est pas courte.)
4. cette cravate/Quelle cravate/Cette cravate/elle est moche. (Elle n'est pas moche.)
5. ces chaussures/Quelles chaussures/Ces chaussures/elles ne sont pas bon marché (Elles sont bon marché.)
6. ces lunettes de soleil/Quelles lunettes de soleil/Ces lunettes de soleil/elles sont (super) (Elles sont moches.)
7. ce manteau/Quel manteau/Ce manteau/il est (cher) (Il n'est pas cher.)

Middle School Copymasters

Worksheet 1: *Où va t-on?*, p. 92;
Project 1: Costumes, pp. 99–100;
Project 2: *Mes vêtements*, pp. 101–103

À votre tour!

OBJECTIFS

Now you can …
• talk about what you plan to buy
• discuss your preferences
• point out certain people or objects

① La bonne réponse

PARLER Alice is talking to her cousin Jérôme. Match Alice's questions with Jérôme's answers. Act out the dialogue with a classmate.

Alice

1. Je vais à la soirée de Delphine. Et toi?
2. Tu amènes une copine?
3. Qu'est-ce que vous allez apporter?
4. Qu'est-ce que tu vas mettre?

a. Oui, Christine.
b. Mon pull jaune et mon blouson marron.
c. Nous allons acheter des pizzas.
d. Moi aussi.

Jérôme

② Créa-dialogue

PARLER Ask your classmates what they think about the following. They will answer affirmatively or negatively.

▶ —Comment trouves-tu <u>cette fille</u>?
  —<u>Quelle fille</u>?
  —<u>Cette fille-là</u>!
  —Eh bien, je pense qu'<u>elle</u> est <u>jolie</u>.
  (<u>Elle</u> n'est pas <u>jolie</u>.)

▶ jolie?

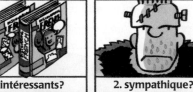

1. intéressants?

2. sympathique?

3. courte?

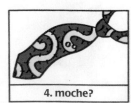

4. moche?

5. bon marché?

6. ??

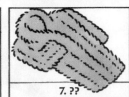

7. ??

À VOTRE TOUR

Depending on your goals and objectives, you may or may not wish to assign all of the activities in the **À votre tour** section.

PAIR PRACTICE

Act. 1–3 lend themselves to pair practice.

3 Shopping

PARLER You and a friend are shopping by catalog. Choose an object and tell your friend what you are buying. Identify it by color and explain why you like it.

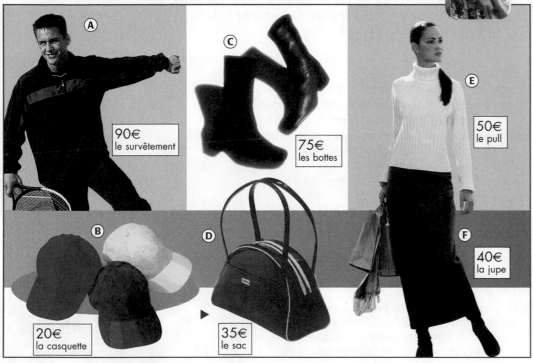

A
90€
le survêtement

C
75€
les bottes

E
50€
le pull

B
20€
la casquette

D
35€
le sac

F
40€
la jupe

▶ —Je vais acheter un sac.
—Quel sac?
—Ce sac rouge.
—Pourquoi?
—Parce qu'il est joli.

4 Composition: La soirée

ÉCRIRE You have been invited to a party by a French friend. In a short paragraph, describe …

- what clothes you are going to wear
- whom you are going to bring along
- what things you are going to bring (food? CDs? boombox? camera?)

LESSON REVIEW
CLASSZONE.COM

---

3 CONVERSATION

Answers will vary.

A. —Je vais acheter un survêtement.
—Quel survêtement?
—Ce survêtement bleu et rouge.
—Pourquoi?
—Parce qu'il est (chouette).
B. —Je vais acheter une casquette.
—Quelle casquette?
—Cette casquette rouge.
—Pourquoi?
—Parce qu'elle est (bon marché).
C. —Je vais acheter des bottes.
—Quelles bottes?
—Ces bottes noires.
—Pourquoi?
—Parce qu'elles sont (chouettes).
D. —Je vais acheter un sac.
—Quel sac?
—Ce sac rouge.
—Pourquoi?
—Parce qu'il est (super).
E. —Je vais acheter un pull.
—Quel pull?
—Ce pull blanc.
—Pourquoi?
—Parce qu'il est (chic).
F. —Je vais acheter une jupe.
—Quelle jupe?
—Cette jupe grise.
—Pourquoi?
—Parce qu'elle (n'est pas chère).

Language note
depuis 20€ = *prices begin at 20€*

4 WRITTEN SELF-EXPRESSION

Answers will vary.
Vendredi, je vais aller à la boum de Nicole. Je vais porter mon nouveau pantalon (ma nouvelle jupe), une jolie chemise et des chaussures noires. Je vais aussi porter mon blouson. Je vais amener mes cousins Brigitte et Paul. Je vais apporter des sandwichs et une salade.
Je vais aussi apporter mes CD de chansons françaises.

PORTFOLIO ASSESSMENT

You will probably select only one speaking activity and one writing activity to go into the students' portfolios for Unit 6.

Act. 4 offers a good writing portfolio topic.

Leçon 19

Main Topics Talking about clothes, Making comparisons

Teaching Resource Options

PRINT

Workbook PE, pp. 163–168
Activités pour tous PE, pp. 99–101
Block Scheduling Copymasters,
   pp. 145–151
Unit 6 Resource Book
   Activités pour tous TE, pp. 75–77
   Audioscript, pp. 94, 95–97
   Communipak, pp. 140–158
   Lesson Plans, pp. 78–79
   Block Scheduling Lesson Plans,
      pp. 80–81
   Absent Student Copymasters,
      pp. 82–85
   Video Activities, pp. 88–91
   Videoscript, pp. 92–93
   Workbook TE, pp. 69–74

AUDIO & VISUAL

Audio Program
CD 3 Tracks 30, 31
CD 10 Tracks 15–20

TECHNOLOGY

Online Workbook

VIDEO PROGRAM

 MODULE 19
Un choix difficile

TOTAL TIME: 5:32 min.
   DVD Disk 2
   Videotape 3 (COUNTER: 47:47 min.)

19.1 Dialogue: Un choix difficile
   (48:25–49:35 min.)

19.2 Mini-scenes: Listening
   – Comparaisons (49:36–51:10 min.)

19.3 Mini-scenes: Speaking
   – Comparaisons (51:11–51:55 min.)

**19.4 Vignette culturelle: Dans un
   centre commercial**
   (51:56–53:19 min.)

Comprehension practice Play
the entire module through as an
introduction to the lesson.

LEÇON 19 | Conversation et Culture

Un choix difficile

VIDÉO DVD AUDIO

Dans un mois, Delphine va aller au mariage de sa cousine. Elle va acheter une <u>nouvelle</u> robe pour cette occasion. Pour cela, elle va dans un magasin de vêtements avec sa copine Véronique. Il y a beaucoup de jolies robes dans ce magasin.

new

Delphine <u>hésite</u> <u>entre</u> une robe jaune et une robe rouge. Quelle robe est-ce que Delphine va <u>choisir</u>? Ah là là, le <u>choix</u> n'est pas facile.

is hesitating/between
to choose
choice

SCÈNE 1.

Véronique: Alors, quelle robe est-ce que tu choisis?

Delphine: Eh bien, <u>finalement</u> je choisis la robe rouge. Elle est <u>plus jolie que</u> la robe jaune.

finally
prettier than

Véronique: C'est vrai, elle est plus jolie … mais la robe jaune est <u>moins</u> chère et elle est <u>plus grande</u>. Regarde. La robe rouge est trop petite pour toi.

less/larger

Delphine: Mais non, elle n'est pas trop petite.

Véronique: Bon, écoute, <u>essaie-la!</u>

try it!

NOTE culturelle

Les jeunes et la mode

Les jeunes Français aiment être à la mode. Ils dépensent° trente pour cent (30%) de leur budget pour les vêtements. Parce que ce budget est limité, ils font très attention quand ils choisissent leurs vêtements. Heureusement,° il y a des boutiques spécialisées dans la mode des jeunes, comme Zara, Mango et Etam, où les vêtements ne sont pas trop° chers.

Certains jeunes préfèrent la «mode rétro». Ils achètent leurs vêtements au marché aux puces.°

dépensent *spend*   **Heureusement** *Fortunately*   **trop** *too*
marché aux puces *flea market*

SETTING THE SCENE

Have the class imagine they have all been invited to a wedding. What will they wear?
   **Imaginez que nous sommes invités à un
   mariage ce week-end.
   Moi, je vais mettre ...** [describe the outfit you
   would plan to wear]

Have various students describe what they are going to wear.
   **Et toi, X, qu'est-ce que tu vas mettre?
   Y, est-ce que tu vas mettre [...] aussi?**
Introduce Section 19.1 of the video:
   **Ce week-end Delphine va à un mariage.
   Qu'est-ce qu'elle va mettre?**

1. Elles vont dans un magasin de vêtements.
2. Delphine va acheter une nouvelle robe.
3. Elle va acheter une robe parce qu'elle va aller au mariage de sa cousine.
4. Une robe est jaune et l'autre est rouge.
5. Elle choisit la robe rouge.
6. Elle préfère la robe rouge parce qu'elle est plus jolie que la robe jaune.
7. Elle est trop petite.
8. Elle doit maigrir.

Note culturelle

Cultural note In France, window displays almost always include the prices of the items shown. Only the most expensive designer boutiques do not indicate prices.

SCÈNE 2.

Delphine <u>sort</u> de la <u>cabine d'essayage</u>.   *comes out/fitting room*

Delphine: C'est vrai, la robe rouge est <u>plus petite</u> mais ce n'est pas   *smaller*
un problème.

Véronique: Pourquoi?

Delphine: Parce que j'ai un mois pour <u>maigrir</u>.   *to lose weight*

Véronique: Et <u>si</u> tu <u>grossis</u>?   *if/gain weight*

Delphine: Toi, <u>tais-toi</u>!   *be quiet*

Compréhension

1. Où vont Delphine et Véronique?
2. Qu'est-ce que Delphine va acheter?
3. Pourquoi?
4. Delphine hésite entre deux robes. De quelle couleur sont-elles?
5. Quelle robe est-ce qu'elle choisit?
6. Pourquoi est-ce qu'elle préfère la robe rouge?
7. Selon *(According to)* Véronique, quel est le problème avec la robe rouge?
8. Qu'est-ce que Delphine doit *(must)* faire pour porter la robe?

TALKING ABOUT PAST EVENTS

Let's talk about where you went yesterday and what you wore. Note that the past participle of **mettre** is **mis**.

Imagine que tu es allé(e) à la plage hier. Qu'est-ce que tu as mis?

J'ai mis un maillot de bain et des sandales.

- **Imagine que tu es allé(e) à une boum hier. Qu'est-ce que tu as mis?**
- **Imagine que tu es allé(e) en ville hier. Qu'est-ce que tu as mis?**
- **Imagine que tu es allé(e) au stade hier. Qu'est-ce que tu as mis?**
- **Imagine que tu es allé(e) à un pique-nique hier. Qu'est-ce que tu as mis?**

Teaching Resource Options

PRINT

Workbook PE, pp. 163–168
Unit 6 Resource Book
    Audioscript, p. 94
    Communipak, pp. 140–158
    Workbook TE, pp. 69–74

AUDIO & VISUAL

Audio Program
CD 3 Tracks 32, 33

Overhead Transparencies
39 -**ir** Verbs
40 Adjectives *beau, nouveau, vieux*
6 Clock face *Quelle heure est-il?*

TECHNOLOGY

Power Presentations

Teaching strategy Using subject
pronoun cue cards, have students
conjugate other -**ir** verbs orally and in
writing (e.g., **choisir, réussir**).
Remind students that in the present
tense of -**ir** verbs, all final consonants
are silent.

 1 **PRACTICE** saying who finishes
a race

1. Je finis.
2. Tu ne finis pas.
3. Nous finissons.
4. Vous ne finissez pas.
5. Éric finit.
6. Stéphanie ne finit pas.
7. Frédéric et Marc ne finissent pas.
8. Anne et Cécile finissent.

Supplementary vocabulary

a) Some -**ir** verbs correspond to
English verbs in -**ish**
    finir *to finish*
    établir *to establish*
    abolir *to abolish*
b) Verbs derived from adjectives often
end in -**ir**
COLORS:
    (rouge) rougir *to blush, to turn red*
    (blanc, blanche) blanchir *to blanche, to turn white*
    (jaune) jaunir *to turn yellow*
    (brun) brunir *to turn brown, to tan*
SIZE:
    (grand) grandir *to grow tall*
Note:
    (gros, grosse–fat) **grossir**
    (maigre–thin) **maigrir**

A Les verbes réguliers en -*ir*

Many French verbs end in -**ir.** Most of these verbs are conjugated like **finir** *(to finish).*
Note the forms of this verb in the present tense, paying special attention to the endings.

INFINITIVE	finir	STEM (infinitive minus -**ir**)	ENDINGS
PRESENT	Je **finis** à deux heures.	fin-	-is
	Tu **finis** à une heure.		-is
	Il/Elle **finit** à cinq heures.		-it
	Nous **finissons** à midi.		-issons
	Vous **finissez** à une heure.		-issez
	Ils/Elles **finissent** à minuit.		-issent

1 Le marathon de Paris

PARLER/ÉCRIRE Not all runners finish the Paris marathon. Say who does and who does not.

▶ Philippe (non)   **Philippe ne finit pas.**

1. moi (oui)   3. nous (oui)   5. Éric (oui)   7. Frédéric et Marc (non)
2. toi (non)   4. vous (non)   6. Stéphanie (non)   8. Anne et Cécile (oui)

VOCABULAIRE Verbes réguliers en -*ir*

choisir	to choose	Quelle veste **choisis**-tu?
finir	to finish	Les classes **finissent** à midi.
grossir	to gain weight, get fat	Marc **grossit** parce qu'il mange beaucoup.
maigrir	to lose weight, get thin	Je **maigris** parce que je mange peu.
réussir	to succeed	Tu vas **réussir** parce que tu travailles!
réussir à un examen	to pass an exam	Nous **réussissons à nos examens.**

2 Le régime *(Diet)*

PARLER/ÉCRIRE Read about the following people. Say if they are gaining or losing weight.

▶ Philippe mange beaucoup de pizzas.
    Il grossit. Il ne maigrit pas.

1. Vous faites des exercices.
2. Nous allons souvent au gymnase.
3. Vous êtes inactifs.
4. Je mange des carottes.
5. Monsieur Moreau adore la bonne cuisine.
6. Vous n'êtes pas très sportifs.
7. Ces personnes mangent trop *(too much)*.
8. Je nage, je joue au volley et je fais des promenades.

WARM-UP AND REVIEW Telling time

PROPS: Clock with movable hands or Transparency 6:
Clock face *Quelle heure est-il?*
Review times by changing the hands on the clock.
    Quelle heure est-il?
    Il est deux heures vingt-cinq. ...

Have students practice forms of the verb **finir**
together with clock times.
    [moi: 1h30] **Je finis à une heure et demie.**
    [vous: 8h45] **Vous finissez à neuf heures moins le quart.**
    [X: 3h10] **X finit à trois heures dix.**

3 ***Questions personnelles*** PARLER/ÉCRIRE

1. À quelle heure finissent les classes?
2. À quelle heure finit la classe de français?
3. Quand finit l'école cette année *(year)*?
4. Tu es invité(e) au restaurant ou au cinéma. Où choisis-tu d'aller?
5. Quand tu vas au cinéma avec ta famille, qui choisit le film?
6. En général, est-ce que tu réussis à tes examens? Est-ce que tu vas réussir à l'examen de français? Et tes copains?

B Les adjectifs *beau, nouveau* et *vieux*

The adjectives **beau** *(beautiful, good-looking)*, **nouveau** *(new)*, and **vieux** *(old)* are irregular.

		beau	nouveau	vieux
SINGULAR	**MASC.**	le **beau** manteau (le **bel** imper)	le **nouveau** manteau (le **nouvel** imper)	le **vieux** manteau (le **vieil** imper)
	FEM.	la **belle** veste	la **nouvelle** veste	la **vieille** veste
PLURAL	**MASC.**	les **beaux** manteaux	les **nouveaux** manteaux	les **vieux** manteaux
	FEM.	les **belles** vestes	les **nouvelles** vestes	les **vieilles** vestes

→ The adjectives **beau, nouveau,** and **vieux** usually come BEFORE the noun. If the noun begins with a vowel sound, there is liaison between the adjective and the noun.

    les **nouveaux** ordinateurs   les **belles** affiches   les **vieux** impers

→ In the masculine singular, the liaison forms **bel, nouvel,** and **vieil** are used before a vowel sound. Note that **vieil** is pronounced like **vieille:**

    un **vieil** imper   une **vieille** robe

4 ***La collection de printemps***

PARLER Mod Boutique is presenting its spring collection. Point out all the items you like to a French friend, using the appropriate forms of **beau.**

▶ une chemise
   Regarde la belle chemise!

1. une robe
2. un pantalon
3. des jeans
4. des blousons
5. une veste
6. un imper
7. des sandales
8. un manteau
9. un chapeau
10. des tee-shirts

5 ***Différences d'opinion***

PARLER François is showing the new things he bought to his sister Valérie. She prefers his old things.

▶ des chaussures

1. un polo
2. des lunettes de soleil
3. un imper
4. des affiches
5. une casquette
6. une montre
7. un ordinateur
8. des baskets
9. un survêtement

Tu aimes mes nouvelles chaussures?

En bien, non, je préfère tes vieilles chaussures.

TALKING ABOUT PAST EVENTS

Let's talk about what you ordered when you ate out the last time. Note that the past participle of -**ir** verbs ends in -**i.**

Est-ce que tu as choisi une pizza?
Oui, j'ai choisi une pizza.
(Non, je n'ai pas choisi de pizza.)

• **Est-ce que tu as choisi une salade?**
• **Est-ce que tu as choisi un steak?**
• **Est-ce que tu as choisi une glace?**
• **Est-ce que tu as choisi un soda?**
• **Est-ce que tu as choisi un café?**
• **Qu'est-ce que tu as choisi?**

Follow-up:
• **Est-ce que X a choisi une pizza? ...**

---

2 **COMPREHENSION** indicating who is gaining or losing weight

1. Vous maigrissez. Vous ne grossissez pas.
2. Nous maigrissons. Nous ne grossissons pas.
3. Vous grossissez. Vous ne maigrissez pas.
4. Je maigris. Je ne grossis pas.
5. M. Moreau grossit. Il ne maigrit pas.
6. Vous grossissez. Vous ne maigrissez pas.
7. Ces personnes grossissent. Elles ne maigrissent pas.
8. Je maigris. Je ne grossis pas.

3 **COMMUNICATION** answering personal questions

Answers will vary.
1. Les classes finissent à (trois heures).
2. La classe de français finit à (onze heures et demie).
3. L'école finit cette année le (quinze juin).
4. Je choisis d'aller (au restaurant).
5. Quand je vais au cinéma avec ma famille, (ma petite soeur) choisit le film.
6. En général, je réussis à mes examens. (Je ne réussis pas à mes examens.) Oui, je vais réussir à l'examen de français. (Non, je ne vais pas réussir à l'examen de français.) Mes copains vont réussir à l'examen de français. (Ils ne vont pas réussir à l'examen de français.)

SECTION B

Communicative function
Describing people and things (beautiful, new, old)

Pronunciation notes
• Remind students that in liaison "x" is pronounced /z/; the "il" of **vieil** is pronounced /j/.
• Point out that all three masculine singular liaison forms sound like the corresponding feminine singular forms.

4 **PRACTICE** saying things are beautiful

Regarde ...
1. la belle robe
2. le beau pantalon
3. les beaux jeans
4. les beaux blousons
5. la belle veste
6. le bel imper
7. les belles sandales
8. le beau manteau
9. le beau chapeau
10. les beaux tee-shirts

5 **ROLE PLAY** discussing preferences between old and new items

—Tu aimes ...
—Eh bien, non, je préfère ...
1. mon nouveau polo/ton vieux polo
2. mes nouvelles lunettes de soleil/tes vieilles lunettes de soleil
3. mon nouvel imper/ton vieil imper
4. mes nouvelles affiches/tes vieilles affiches
5. ma nouvelle casquette/ta vieille casquette
6. ma nouvelle montre/ta vieille montre
7. mon nouvel ordinateur/ton vieil ordinateur
8. mes nouveaux baskets/tes vieux baskets
9. mon nouveau survêtement/ton vieux survêtement

SECTION C

Communicative function
Expressing comparisons

Teaching Resource Options

PRINT

Workbook PE, pp. 163–168
Unit 6 Resource Book
   Audioscript, p. 95
   Communipak, pp. 140–158
   Video Activities, p. 89
   Videoscript, pp. 92–93
   Workbook TE, pp. 69–74

AUDIO & VISUAL

Audio Program
CD 3 Track 34

TECHNOLOGY

Power Presentations

VIDEO PROGRAM

VIDÉO   DVD

 MODULE 19

19.2 Mini-scenes: Comparaisons
   (49:36–51:10 min.)

19.3 Mini-scenes: Comparaisons
   (51:11–51:55 min.)

Language notes
- In French as in English, the second part of the comparison may be left out: **Cette robe est plus chère.**
- The comparative form of **bon marché** is **meilleur marché.** This form is not actively presented at this time.
- Remind students that the other comparative forms of **bon** follow the regular pattern:
Cette cassette est **moins bonne que** ce CD.
Est-ce que les Red Sox sont **aussi bons que** les Yankees?

Middle School Copymasters

Worksheet 4: *Dans un grand magasin,* p. 95

C La comparaison avec les adjectifs

Note how COMPARISONS are expressed in French.

Cet imper est **plus cher que** ce manteau.	*… more expensive than …*
Cette jupe est **plus jolie que** cette robe.	*… prettier than …*
Paul est **moins sportif que** Patrick.	*… less athletic than …*
Il est **moins amusant que** lui.	*… less amusing than …*
Je suis **aussi grand que** toi.	*… as tall as …*
Tu **n'es pas aussi timide que** moi.	*… not as timid as …*

To make comparisons with adjectives, French speakers use the following constructions:

+ **plus**		**plus cher (que)**	*more expensive (than)*
− **moins**	+ ADJECTIVE (+ **que** …)	**moins cher (que)**	*less expensive (than)*
= **aussi**		**aussi cher (que)**	*as expensive (as)*

→ Note the irregular **plus**-form of **bon** *(good):*

> **plus + bon(ne) → meilleur(e)** *(better)*

Ta pizza est **bonne**, mais mon sandwich est **meilleur**.

→ There is liaison after **plus** and **moins** when the next word begins with a vowel sound.

   Cette robe-ci est **plus ͜ élégante**.   Ce livre-là est **moins ͜ intéressant**.

→ In comparisons, the adjective always agrees with the noun (or pronoun) it describes.

> **La jupe** est plus **chère** que le chemisier.

> **Les vestes** sont moins **chères** que les manteaux.

→ In comparisons with people, STRESS PRONOUNS are used after **que**.

   Paul est plus petit **que moi**.   Je suis plus grand **que lui**.

6 *Comparaisons* ————————————————

PARLER/ÉCRIRE How much do you think the following pairs of items cost? Give your opinion, saying whether the first one is more expensive, less expensive, or as expensive as the second one.

▶ une guitare/une raquette   **Une guitare est plus (moins, aussi) chère qu'une raquette.**

1. un vélo/un scooter
2. une mobylette/une moto
3. une pizza/un sandwich
4. une télé/un ordinateur
5. des chaussures/des sandales
6. une casquette/des lunettes de soleil
7. des bottes/des tennis
8. un short/un maillot de bain
9. un baladeur/une montre
10. un portable/une mini-chaîne

COMPREHENSION Comparisons

PROPS: Plastic bag with 30 "money cards" (labeled with amounts from $50–$1000)
Have students come up and draw a "prize."
   Vous êtes tous riches.
   Vous avez gagné à la loterie hier.
   Venez chercher vos prix!
Review numbers by asking what they drew.

X, montre-nous ton prix. [holds up $100]
Combien d'argent as-tu? [cent dollars]
Est-ce que X est riche aujourd'hui? [oui!]
Y, montre-nous ton prix. ...

Call up two students with different "prizes."
   X et Y, venez ici.
   Combien d'argent a X? [$100] **Et Y?** [$500]

VOCABULAIRE Expression pour la conversation

▶ **How to introduce a personal opinion:**

à mon avis …   *in my opinion …*   **À mon avis**, le français est facile.

7 *Expression personnelle*

PARLER/ÉCRIRE Compare the following by using the adjectives suggested. Give your personal opinion.

▶ le tennis/intéressant/le ping-pong

À mon avis, le tennis est plus (moins, aussi) intéressant que le ping-pong.

1. le basket/intéressant/le foot
2. l'anglais/facile/le français
3. la classe de français/amusant/la classe d'anglais
4. la Floride/beau/la Californie
5. les Yankees/bon/les Red Sox
6. la cuisine américaine/bon/la cuisine française
7. les filles/intelligent/les garçons
8. l'argent *(money)*/important/l'amitié *(friendship)*

8 *Et toi?*

PARLER Use the appropriate stress pronouns in answering the questions below.

▶ —Es-tu plus grand(e) que ton copain?   (Non, je suis moins grand(e) que lui.)
  —Oui, je suis plus grand(e) que lui.   (Je suis aussi grand(e) que lui.)

1. Es-tu plus grand(e) que ta mère?
2. Es-tu aussi riche que Bill Gates?
3. Es-tu plus sportif (sportive) que tes copains?
4. Es-tu plus intelligent(e) qu'Einstein?

PRONONCIATION   ill /j/

Les lettres «ill»

In the middle of a word, the letters "**ill**" usually represent the sound /**j**/ like the "**y**" of *yes*.

Répétez: **maillot travaillez oreille vieille fille famille juillet**
         En juillet, Mireille va travailler pour sa vieille tante.

At the end of a word, the sound /j/ is sometimes spelled **il**.

Répétez: **appareil-photo vieil travail** *(job)*
         Mon oncle a un vieil appareil-photo.

EXCEPTION: The letters **ill** are pronounced /il/ in the following words:

Répétez: **ville village mille Lille**

maillot

deux cent quatre-vingt-un **281**
Leçon 19

Place Y next to the chalkboard to the left, and place X to the right.
   Mais Y est plus riche que X.

Between the two, write: **plus riche que.**

Call on other students to demonstrate the other comparisons, also writing them.
   Z est moins riche que B. [$300 < $650]
   A est aussi riche que C. [$400 = $400]

Ask all students to hold up their cards.
   Montrez-nous vos prix. Qui a $200? [M]
   Qui est plus riche que M? Qui est moins riche que lui/elle? Qui est aussi riche?

Have students hand around their "prizes."
   En ce moment, Z est moins riche que M.
   S'il te plaît, D, va donner tes $1000 à Z.
   Maintenant Z est plus riche que B., etc.

---

6 **COMMUNICATION** expressing one's opinion about relative prices

Answers will vary.
1. Un vélo est moins cher qu'un scooter.
2. Une mobylette est moins chère qu'une moto.
3. Une pizza est plus (aussi / moins) chère qu'un sandwich.
4. Une télé est moins chère qu'un ordinateur.
5. Des chaussures sont aussi (plus / moins) chères que des sandales.
6. Une casquette est moins (aussi / moins) chère que des lunettes de soleil.
7. Des bottes sont aussi (plus / moins) chères que des tennis.
8. Un short est moins (aussi / plus) cher qu'un maillot de bain.
9. Un baladeur est plus cher qu'une montre.
10. Un portable est moins cher qu'une mini-chaîne.

7 **COMMUNICATION** comparing people and things

Answers will vary.
1. À mon avis, le basket est moins (plus / aussi) intéressant que le foot.
2. À mon avis, l'anglais est plus (moins / aussi) facile que le français.
3. À mon avis, la classe de français est plus (moins / aussi) amusante que la classe d'anglais.
4. À mon avis, la Floride est aussi (moins / plus) beau que la Californie.
5. À mon avis, les Yankees sont moins bons (meilleurs / aussi bons) que les Red Sox.
6. À mon avis, la cuisine américaine est moins bonne (aussi bonne / meilleure) que la cuisine française.
7. À mon avis, les filles sont aussi (plus / moins) intelligentes que les garçons.
8. À mon avis, l'argent est moins (aussi / plus) important que l'amitié.

Teaching strategies
• Remind students that the adjective must agree with the subject.
• For items 5 and 6, remind students that **plus + bon(ne) → meilleur(e);** as in English, there is no change for **moins bon(ne)** and **aussi bon(ne).**

8 **COMMUNICATION** comparing oneself to others

1. Oui, je suis plus grand(e) qu'elle. (Non, je suis moins grand[e] qu'elle./ Je suis aussi grand[e] qu'elle.)
2. Non, je suis moins riche que lui. (Oui, je suis plus riche que lui. / Je suis aussi riche que lui.)
3. Oui, je suis plus sportif (sportive) qu'eux. (Non, je suis moins sportif [sportive] qu'eux. / Je suis aussi sportif [sportive] qu'eux.)
4. Je suis aussi intelligent(e) que lui. (Oui, je suis plus intelligent[e] que lui. / Non, je suis moins intelligent[e] que lui.)

PRONUNCIATION

Note that **tranquille** *(quiet)* also contains the sound /il/: /tränkil/

Teaching Resource Options

PRINT

Workbook PE, pp. 163–168
Unit 6 Resource Book
   Audioscript, p. 95
   Communipak, pp. 140–158
   Family Involvement, pp. 86–87
   Workbook TE, pp. 69–74

Assessment
Lesson 19 Quiz, pp. 98–99
Portfolio Assessment, Unit 1 URB
   pp. 155–164
Audioscript for Quiz 19, p. 97
Answer Keys, pp. 230–234

AUDIO & VISUAL

Audio Program
CD 3 Tracks 35, 36
CD 15 Track 11

TECHNOLOGY

Test Generator CD-ROM/eTest Plus
Online

❶ COMPREHENSION

1. d   3. b
2. a   4. c

❷ GUIDED ORAL EXPRESSION

Answers will vary.

1. – Tu achètes la chaîne hi-fi ou le baladeur?
   – J'achète le baladeur (la chaîne hi-fi).
   – Pourquoi?
   – Parce qu'il est plus petit et moins cher. (Je préfère la chaîne hi-fi parce qu'elle est meilleure et plus grande.)
2. – Tu préfères les bottes ou les chaussures?
   – Je préfères les chaussures (les bottes).
   – Pourquoi?
   – Parce qu'elles sont plus jolies et plus confortables. (Je préfère les bottes parce qu'elles sont meilleures et moins chères.)
3. – Tu choisis le chien jaune ou le chien blanc?
   – Je choisis le chien jaune (le chien blanc).
   – Pourquoi?
   – Parce qu'il est plus petit et plus mignon. (Je choisis le chien blanc parce qu'il est plus grand et plus joli.)
4. – Tu amènes Alice ou Anne?
   – J'amène Alice (Anne).
   – Pourquoi?
   – Parce qu'elle est plus intéressante (sympathique, mignonne).
5. – Tu invites Paul ou Philippe?
   – J'invite Philippe (Paul).
   – Pourquoi?
   – Parce qu'il est plus amusant (intelligent, beau).

À votre tour!

OBJECTIFS

Now you can …
• make comparisons
• discuss your choices

❶ 🎧 👥 La bonne réponse

PARLER François and Stéphanie are shopping. Match François's questions with Stéphanie's answers. You may act out the dialogue with a friend.

François

1 Tu aimes cette veste verte?

2 Combien est-ce qu'elle coûte?

3 Et qu'est-ce que tu penses de cette veste rouge?

4 Alors, qu'est-ce que tu vas choisir?

Stéphanie

a 300 euros.

b À mon avis, elle est moins jolie.

c La veste bleue. Elle est meilleur marché et elle est aussi élégante.

d Oui, mais elle est très chère.

❷ 🎧 👥 Créa-dialogue

PARLER With a classmate, prepare a dialogue comparing the items in one of the following pictures. Use the suggested verb and some of the suggested adjectives.

▶ —Tu <u>choisis</u> <u>la voiture rouge</u> ou <u>la voiture noire</u>?
—Je <u>choisis</u> <u>la voiture rouge</u>.
—Pourquoi?
—Parce qu'<u>elle</u> est <u>plus petite</u> et <u>moins chère</u>.

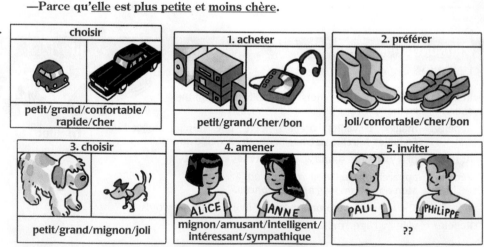

| choisir |
| petit/grand/confortable/rapide/cher |

| 1. acheter |
| petit/grand/cher/bon |

| 2. préférer |
| joli/confortable/cher/bon |

| 3. choisir |
| petit/grand/mignon/joli |

| 4. amener |
| mignon/amusant/intelligent/intéressant/sympathique |

| 5. inviter |
| ?? |

À VOTRE TOUR

Depending on your goals and objectives, you may or may not wish to assign all of the activities in the **À votre tour** section.

3 *Choix personnels* --

PARLER Select two people or two items in each of the following categories and ask a classmate to indicate which one he/she prefers. You may ask your classmate to explain why.

▶ 2 actors

Tu préfères Tom Hanks ou Brad Pitt?

Je préfère Brad Pitt.

Pourquoi?

Parce que Brad Pitt est plus mignon que Tom Hanks.
(plus beau, plus jeune ...)

CATEGORIES:

▶ 2 actors
• 2 actresses
• 2 singers (male)
• 2 singers (female)
• 2 baseball teams
• 2 cities
• 2 restaurants in your town
• 2 stores in your town

4 *Composition: Portrait comparatif* ------------------------

ÉCRIRE Write a description of yourself, comparing yourself to six other people (your friends, your family, well-known personalities, etc.) You may use some of the following adjectives:

> grand petit jeune vieux amusant intelligent bête
> sportif sympathique timide gentil génial optimiste

▶

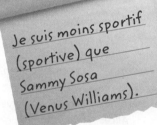

Je suis moins sportif (sportive) que Sammy Sosa (Venus Williams).

5 *Composition: Comparaisons personnelles* -------------------

Mon cousin s'appelle Patrick. Il a quinze ans. Je suis plus jeune que lui, mais il est moins grand que moi ...

▶

ÉCRIRE Choose a friend or relative about your age. Give this person's name and age. Then, in a short paragraph, compare yourself to that person in terms of physical appearance and personality traits.

 LESSON REVIEW
CLASSZONE.COM

deux cent quatre-vingt-trois **283**
Leçon 19

---

3 **GUIDED ORAL EXPRESSION**

Answers will vary.
—Tu préfères ... ou ...?
—Je préfère ...
—Pourquoi?
—Parce qu' ...
• Cameron Diaz/Julia Roberts/Cameron Diaz/elle est plus intéressante que Julia Roberts.
• Will Smith/Rob Thomas/Rob Thomas/il chante mieux que Will Smith.
• Sheryl Crow/Jewel/Jewel/elle est plus sympathique que Sheryl Crow.
• les Red Sox/les White Sox/les Red Sox/ils sont plus sportifs que les White Sox.
• Boston/Pittsburgh/Boston/Boston est plus belle que Pittsburgh.
• Chez Joseph/Maison Albert/Maison Albert/Maison Albert est moins cher que Chez Joseph.
• Le Bon Marché/Le Printemps/Le Printemps/Le Printemps est moins cher que Le Bon Marché.

4 **WRITTEN SELF-EXPRESSION**

Answers will vary.
• Je suis moins sportif (sportive) que Sammy Sosa (Venus Williams).
• Je suis plus sportif (sportive) que mon frère.
• Je suis plus grand(e) que ma soeur.
• Je suis plus petit(e) que Ben Affleck.
• Je suis moins jeune que mon frère.
• Je suis plus vieux (vieille) que ma petite soeur.
• Je suis moins amusant(e) que ma meilleure amie.
• Je suis plus intelligent(e) que mon meilleur ami.
• Je suis aussi timide que ma petite soeur.
• Je suis moins élégant(e) que ma meilleure amie.
• Je suis aussi mignon(ne) que ma cousine.

5 **WRITTEN SELF-EXPRESSION**

Answers will vary.
Mon amie s'appelle Louise. Elle a treize ans. Elle est plus jeune que moi. Elle est aussi plus jolie. Mais moi, je suis plus intélligent(e) et plus drôle qu'elle. Elle est aussi grande que moi. On joue au basket ensemble, mais elle est plus sportive que moi. Elle est aussi plus timide.

Middle School Copymasters
Worksheet 3: *Et après?*, p. 94

PORTFOLIO ASSESSMENT

You will probably select only one speaking activity and one writing activity to go into the students' portfolios for Unit 6.

In this lesson, Act. 2 lends itself well to an oral portfolio recording.

Act. 4 and 5 are good writing portfolio topics.

Leçon 20

Main Topics Discovering what stores are selling, Giving suggestions and commands

Teaching Resource Options

PRINT

Workbook PE, pp. 169–175
Activités pour tous PE, pp. 103–105
Block Scheduling Copymasters,
  pp. 153–159
Unit 6 Resource Book
  Activités pour tous TE, pp. 109–111
  Audioscript, pp. 132, 133–135
  Communipak, pp. 140–158
  Lesson Plans, pp. 112–113
  Block Scheduling Lesson Plans,
    pp. 114–116
  Absent Student Copymasters,
    pp. 117–121
  Video Activities, pp. 124–129
  Videoscript, pp. 130–131
  Workbook TE, pp. 101–107

AUDIO & VISUAL

Audio Program
CD 3 Tracks 37, 38
CD 10 Tracks 21–27

Overhead Transparencies
20 Objects (a) *Quelques objets* (a)

TECHNOLOGY

Online Workbook

VIDEO PROGRAM

 MODULE 20
Alice a un job

TOTAL TIME: 6:39 min.
  DVD Disk 2
  Videotape 3 (COUNTER: 53:31 min.)

20.1 Dialogue: Alice a un job
  (54:15–55:10 min.)

20.2 Mini-scenes: Listening
  – Qu'est-ce qu'on vend?
  (55:11–55:59 min.)

20.3 Mini-scenes: Speaking
  – Qu'est-ce qu'on vend ici?
  (56:00–56:43 min.)

20.4 Mini-scenes: Listening
  – On dîne? (56:44–57:19 min.)

20.5 Mini-scenes: Speaking
  – On joue au tennis?
  (57:20–58:13 min.)

20.6 Vignette culturelle: Au magasin hi-fi
  (58:14–1:00:00 min.)

Comprehension practice Play the entire module through as an introduction to the lesson.

LEÇON 20

Alice a un job

Alice a un nouveau job. Elle travaille dans un magasin de matériel audio-visuel. Dans ce magasin, <u>on</u> <u>vend</u> <u>toutes</u> sortes de choses: des baladeurs, des chaînes hi-fi, des radiocassettes/CD, des lecteurs de DVD …   *one, they / sell(s) / all*

Un jour, son cousin Jérôme <u>lui rend visite</u>.   *comes to visit her*

Jérôme: Salut, ça va?
Alice: Oui, ça va.
Jérôme: Et ce nouveau job?
Alice: C'est super.
Jérôme: Qu'est-ce qu'on vend dans ton magasin?
Alice: Eh bien, tu <u>vois</u>, on vend toutes sortes de matériel audio-visuel …   *see*
    Moi, je vends des mini-chaînes.
Jérôme: Tu es bien <u>payée</u>?   *paid*
Alice: Non, on n'est pas très bien payé, mais on a des réductions
    sur l'équipement stéréo et sur les CD et les DVD.
Jérôme: Qu'est-ce que tu vas faire avec ton <u>argent</u>?   *money*
Alice: Je ne sais pas … J'<u>ai envie de</u> voyager cet été.   *feel like*
Jérôme: Tu <u>as de la chance</u>. Moi aussi, j'ai envie de voyager,   *are lucky*
    mais je n'ai pas d'argent.
Alice: Écoute, Jérôme, si tu as <u>besoin</u> d'argent, <u>fais comme moi</u>.   *need / do as I do*
Jérôme: <u>Comment</u>?   *What?*
Alice: <u>Cherche</u> un job!   *Find*

WARM-UP AND REVIEW

PROP: Transparency 20: Objects (a) *Quelques objets* (a)
Review the names of the objects.
  Qu'est-ce que c'est? C'est une radio.
  X, est-ce que tu as une radio?
  Oui, j'ai une radio. (Je n'ai pas de radio.)

Ask where one can buy these objects locally.
Introduce the phrase **on achète.**

Ici, à [name of town], **où est-ce qu'on achète des radios?**
On achète des radios à [name of local store].

Tell students that in the opening scene of the video they will visit a hi-fi store.

Compréhension

1. Où travaille Alice?
2. Qu'est-ce qu'elle vend?
3. Qu'est-ce qu'elle espère faire cet été?
4. Pourquoi est-ce que Jérôme ne va pas voyager?
5. Qu'est-ce que Jérôme doit *(must)* faire pour avoir de l'argent?

NOTE *culturelle*

L'argent° des jeunes

Contrairement à beaucoup de jeunes Américains, les jeunes Français n'ont pas de travail° régulier. Par exemple, ils ne travaillent pas dans les supermarchés, les boutiques ou les stations-service. Occasionnellement, ils font des petits jobs pour leurs voisins: baby-sitting, promenade de chiens,° lavage° de voitures, etc.

En général, ils dépendent de la générosité de leurs parents pour leur argent. Le montant° qu'ils reçoivent varie avec l'âge, les résultats scolaires,° et la situation économique de la famille. Ils reçoivent aussi de l'argent de leur famille et de leurs parrains° et marraines° pour des occasions spéciales: Noël, jour de l'An° et anniversaire.

Voici combien d'argent les jeunes Français ont en moyenne: °

ÂGE	MONTANT PAR MOIS
2-7 ans	5 euros
8-14 ans	15 euros
15-17 ans	100 euros

argent *money*   **travail** *work*
promenade de chiens *dog walking*   **lavage** *washing*
montant *amount*   **résultats scolaires** *report cards*
parrains *godfathers*   **marraines** *godmothers*
jour de l'An *New Year's Day*   **en moyenne** *on the average*

COMPARAISONS CULTURELLES

- Compare how teenagers in France and in the United States get their spending money.
- Why do you think French teenagers do not have regular jobs?

deux cent quatre-vingt-cinq 285
Leçon 20

Compréhension
Answers

1. Alice travaille dans un magasin de matériel audio-visuel.
2. Elle vend des mini-chaînes.
3. Elle espère voyager.
4. Il n'a pas d'argent.
5. Il doit chercher un job.

Cultural note for **Comparaisons culturelles**

Some reasons why French teenagers do not have regular jobs:

(1) They have to spend a lot of time on their schoolwork.

(2) French laws discourage teenage work.

TALKING ABOUT PAST EVENTS

Let's talk about what you and your family did during a recent vacation.

Toi et ta famille, est-ce que vous avez voyagé pendant les vacances?
Oui, nous avons voyagé.
(Non, nous n'avons pas voyagé.)
- **Où êtes-vous allés?**

- **Est-ce que vous êtes allés à la Maison Blanche?**
- **Est-ce que vous avez trouvé un bon hôtel?**
- **Est-ce que vous avez dîné au restaurant?**
- **Qu'est-ce que vous avez visité?**

Language notes
- Point out that **payer** is also a "boot" verb (see p. 268).
- Some students may understand the **avoir** idioms better if they think of them as *I have need of...* and *I have desire of...*

Casual speech One can also say:
Ce CD coûte combien?
Tu as combien d'argent?
Tu as combien de CD?

Supplementary vocabulary
un euro
un centime
un eurocentime
l'argent de poche *allowance, pocket money*
la monnaie *change*
un job *(part-time) job*
économiser *to save money*
par jour *per day, a day*
par semaine *per week, a week*
par heure *per hour, an hour*

① EXCHANGES asking how many things people have

Answers will vary.
—Combien de (d') ... as tu?
—J'ai (...) ... (Je n'ai pas de [d'] ...)
1. frères/(deux) frères/frères
2. soeurs/(deux) soeurs/soeurs
3. casquettes/(trois) casquettes/casquettes
4. affiches/(dix) affiches/affiches
5. tee-shirts/(cinq) tee-shirts/tee-shirts
6. jeans/(deux) jeans/jeans
7. billets d'un dollar/(quatre) billets d'un dollar/billets d'un dollar
8. pièces de dix cents/(trois) pièces de dix cents/pièces de dix cents

Pronunciation Be sure students pronounce the **de** of **combien de** correctly with a mute "e" so that it does not sound like **des.**

Language note There is no elision before **un** when it represents the number *one:*

un billet <u>de un</u> dollar. (cf. item 7)

Variation (using casual speech) **Tu as combien de CD?**

VOCABULAIRE L'argent

NOMS

l'argent *(m.)*	money	une pièce	coin
un billet	bill, paper money		

ADJECTIFS

riche ≠ pauvre *rich ≠ poor*

VERBES

dépenser	to spend	Je n'aime pas **dépenser** mon argent.
gagner	to earn, to win	Je **gagne** 10 dollars par *(per)* jour. Tu joues bien. Tu vas **gagner** le match.
payer	to pay, pay for	Qui va **payer** aujourd'hui?

EXPRESSIONS

combien + VERB	how much	**Combien** coûte cette chaîne hi-fi?
combien de + NOUN	how much / how many	**Combien** d'argent as-tu? / **Combien** de CD as-tu?
avoir besoin de + NOUN	to need	J'ai **besoin de** 5 dollars.
+ INFINITIVE	to need to, have to	J'ai **besoin de** travailler.
avoir envie de + NOUN	to want	J'ai **envie d'**une pizza.
+ INFINITIVE	to feel like, want to	J'ai **envie de** manger.

→ Verbs like **payer** that end in **-yer**, have the following stem change:

y → i in the **je, tu, il, ils** forms of the verb
  je **paie**   tu **paies**   il/elle **paie**   ils/elles **paient**
but: nous **payons** vous **payez**

L'ARGENT NE FAIT PAS LE BONHEUR

Money does not buy happiness.

① Combien?

PARLER Ask your classmates how many of the following they have.

▶ des CD —Combien de CD as-tu?
      —J'ai vingt CD.
      (Je n'ai pas de CD.)

1. des frères
2. des soeurs
3. des casquettes
4. des affiches
5. des tee-shirts
6. des jeans
7. des billets d'un dollar
8. des pièces de dix cents

2 Qu'est-ce que tu as envie de faire?

PARLER Ask your classmates if they feel like doing the following things.

▶ aller au cinéma

1. aller au restaurant
2. manger une pizza
3. aller à la piscine
4. parler français
5. écouter un CD
6. visiter Paris
7. jouer au Frisbee
8. acheter une moto
9. faire une promenade
10. surfer sur l'Internet

Est-ce que tu as envie d'aller au cinéma?

Et toi?

Oui, j'ai envie d'aller au cinéma.

Non, je n'ai pas envie d'aller au cinéma.

3 Au restaurant

PARLER/ÉCRIRE The following students are in a restaurant in Quebec. Say what they feel like buying and estimate how much money they need.

▶ Hélène/une pizza
Hélène a envie d'une pizza. Elle a besoin de cinq dollars.

1. Marc/un sandwich
2. nous/une glace
3. moi/un soda
4. toi/un jus d'orange
5. vous/une salade
6. mes copains/un steak

4 Questions personnelles PARLER/ÉCRIRE

1. Est-ce que tu as un job? Où est-ce que tu travailles? Combien est-ce que tu gagnes par *(per)* heure? par semaine?
2. Quand tu vas au cinéma, qui paie? toi ou ton copain (ta copine)?
3. Combien est-ce que tu paies quand tu achètes un hamburger? une pizza? une glace?
4. Est-ce que tu as des pièces dans ta poche *(pocket)*? quelles pièces?
5. Qui est représenté sur le billet d'un dollar? sur le billet de cinq dollars? sur le billet de dix dollars?
6. Est-ce que tu préfères dépenser ou économiser *(to save)* ton argent? Pourquoi?
7. Est-ce que tu espères être riche un jour? Pourquoi?

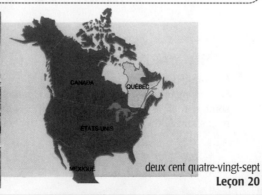

Le Vendôme
36, Côte de la Montagne
Québec
tél 692.0557

LE VENDOME

CANADA

QUÉBEC

ÉTATS-UNIS

MEXIQUE

deux cent quatre-vingt-sept 287
Leçon 20

---

2 EXCHANGES discussing what one feels like doing

—Est-ce que tu as envie de (d') ...
—Oui, j'ai envie de (d') ...
—Et toi?
—Non, je n'ai pas envie de (d') ...
1. aller au restaurant
2. manger une pizza
3. aller à la piscine
4. parler français
5. écouter un CD
6. visiter Paris
7. jouer au Frisbee
8. acheter une moto
9. faire une promenade
10. surfer sur l'Internet

3 COMPREHENSION describing what people in a restaurant want and what it costs

Answers will vary.
1. Marc a envie d'un sandwich. Il a besoin de (quatre) dollars.
2. Nous avons envie d'une glace. Nous avons besoin de (deux) dollars.
3. J'ai envie d'un soda. J'ai besoin de (deux) dollars.
4. Tu as envie d'un jus d'orange. Tu as besoin de (deux) dollars.
5. Vous avez envie d'une salade. Vous avez besoin de (sept) dollars.
6. Mes copains ont envie d'un steak. Ils ont besoin de (dix) dollars.

Expansion Have students discuss their wants and needs by completing the following open-ended sentences.
J'ai envie de (d')... (réussir en français.)
J'ai besoin de (d')... (étudier souvent.)

4 COMMUNICATION answering personal questions

Answers will vary.
1. Oui, j'ai un job. Je travaille dans un magasin. Je gagne sept dollars par heure et soixante-dix dollars par semaine. (Non, je n'ai pas de job.)
2. Quand je vais au cinéma, je (mon copain / ma copine) paie.
3. Je paie quatre dollars et demi quand j'achète un hamburger. Je paie six dollars quand j'achète une pizza. Je paie un dollar et demi quand j'achète une glace.
4. Oui, j'ai des pièces dans ma poche. J'ai deux «quarters», trois «dimes» et un «nickle». (Non, je n'ai pas de pièces dans ma poche.)
5. George Washington est représenté sur le billet d'un dollar, Abraham Lincoln sur le billet de cinq dollars et Alexander Hamilton sur le billet de dix dollars.
6. Je préfère dépenser mon argent. Je travaille pour avoir de l'argent et pour acheter des choses. (Je préfère économiser mon argent. Je veux être riche un jour.)
7. Oui, j'espère être riche un jour. Avec beaucoup d'argent, je peux beaucoup dépenser et beaucoup économiser! (Non, je n'espère pas être riche un jour. L'argent n'est pas important.)

REALIA NOTE

Ask students:
Comment s'appelle ce restaurant? [Le Vendôme]
Quelle est l'adresse du restaurant? [36, Côte de la Montagne]
Quel est son numéro de téléphone? [692.0557]

NOTE: Remind students that in Quebec telephone numbers are given digit by digit.

CULTURE NOTE

The Château Frontenac (a four-star hotel) is located in upper town (**la Haute Ville**) and **Le Vendôme** restaurant is located in lower town (**la Basse Ville**). The oldest part of Quebec City is located around the **Place Royale** in lower town. Here one finds historic houses, restaurants, boutiques, antique stores, and art galleries. A **funiculaire** and the Breakneck Stairs (**l'Escalier Casse-Cou**) connect lower town with upper town.

LEÇON 20 Langue et Communication

Left column

SECTION A

Communicative function
Talking about people in general

Teaching Resource Options

PRINT

Workbook PE, pp. 169–175
Unit 6 Resource Book
  Communipak, pp. 140–158
  Video Activities, pp. 125–127
  Videoscript, pp. 130–131
  Workbook TE, pp. 101–107

TECHNOLOGY
Power Presentations

VIDEO PROGRAM

VIDÉO DVD
  MODULE 20

20.2 Mini-scenes: Qu'est-ce qu'on vend? (55:11–55:59 min.)

20.3 Mini-scenes: Qu'est-ce qu'on vend ici? (56:00–56:43 min.)

20.4 Mini-scenes: On dîne? (56:44–57:19 min.)

20.5 Mini-scenes: On joue au tennis? (57:20–58:13 min.)

Looking ahead The forms of **vendre** are presented in section B of this lesson.

5 COMPREHENSION discussing what languages are spoken in certain cities

1. À Québec, on parle français (ou anglais).
2. À Boston, on parle anglais.
3. À Madrid, on parle espagnol.
4. À Bruxelles, on parle français.
5. À Genève, on parle français.
6. À Tokyo, on parle japonais.
7. À Buenos Aires, on parle espagnol.
8. À Londres, on parle anglais.
9. À Rome, on parle italien.
10. À Beijing, on parle chinois.

Variation (using the negative in many responses)
– Est-ce qu'on parle français à Acapulco?
– Non, on ne parle pas français.

Challenge Have students turn to the world map on pp. R2–R3. They can ask additional questions: **Est-ce qu'on parle français à Dakar?**, etc.

Right column

A **Le pronom *on***

Note the use of the subject pronoun **on** in the sentences below.

Qu'est-ce qu'**on** vend ici? — *What do **they** (do **you**) sell here?*
Où est-ce qu'**on** achète ce CD? — *Where does **one** (do **people**) buy that CD?*
En France, **on** parle français. — *In France, **people** (you, they) speak French.*

The pronoun **on** is used in GENERAL statements, according to the construction:

on + il/elle - form of verb	**On** travaille beaucoup.	**One** works a lot. **They** work a lot. **You** work a lot. **People** work a lot.

▶ There is liaison after **on** when the next word begins with a vowel sound.
  Est-ce qu'**on** invite Stéphanie à la boum?

▶ In conversation, **on** is often used instead of **nous:**
  —Est-ce qu'**on** dîne à la maison? — *Are **we** having dinner at home?*
  —Non, **on** va au restaurant. — *No, **we** are going to the restaurant.*

5 Ici on parle …

PARLER/ÉCRIRE Imagine that you have won a grand prize of a world tour. Say which of the following languages is spoken in each of the cities that you will be visiting.

▶ Acapulco

À Acapulco, on parle espagnol.

1. Québec
2. Boston
3. Madrid
4. Bruxelles
5. Genève
6. Tokyo
7. Buenos Aires
8. Londres (*London*)
9. Rome
10. Beijing

anglais espagnol français
japonais italien chinois

COMMUNAUTÉS

In a multi-cultural society, people speak different languages and have different customs. How many different languages are spoken at home by classmates in your school? What are some of their different customs and different celebrations? As a class project, put up a wall map showing their countries of origin. Do some come from French-speaking areas?

VOCABULAIRE Expression pour la conversation

▶ *How to indicate approval:*

C'est une bonne idée! *That's a good idea!*

6 Projets de week-end

PARLER Suggest possible weekend activities to your classmates. They will let you know whether they think each idea is a good one or not.

▶ aller au café

1. jouer aux jeux vidéo?
2. aller à la bibliothèque?
3. aller à la plage?
4. téléphoner au professeur?
5. faire une promenade à vélo?
6. aller dans les magasins?
7. acheter des vêtements?
8. écouter des CD?

On va au café?

Oui, c'est une bonne idée!

Non, ce n'est pas une bonne idée.

7 En Amérique et en France

PARLER An American student and a French student are comparing certain aspects of life in their own countries. Play both roles.

▶ jouer au baseball (au foot)

En Amérique, on joue au baseball.

En France, on joue au foot.

1. parler anglais (français)
2. étudier le français (l'anglais)
3. dîner à six heures (à huit heures)
4. manger des hamburgers (des omelettes)
5. voyager souvent en avion *(by plane)* (en train)
6. skier dans le Colorado (dans les Alpes)
7. aller à l'école le mercredi après-midi (le samedi matin)
8. chanter «la Bannière étoilée» *("The Star-Spangled Banner")* («la Marseillaise»)

8 Expression personnelle

PARLER/ÉCRIRE Describe what you, your friends, and your relatives generally do. Complete the following sentences according to your personal routine.

1. À la maison, on dîne … (à quelle heure?)
2. À la télé, on regarde … (quel programme?)
3. À la cafétéria de l'école, on mange … (quoi?)
4. En été, on va … (où?)
5. Le week-end, avec mes copains, on va … (où?)
6. Avec mes copains, on joue … (à quel sport? à quel jeu?)
7. On a une classe de français … (quels jours?)
8. On a un examen de français … (quel jour?)

deux cent quatre-vingt-neuf
Leçon 20 289

Supplementary vocabulary

C'est une mauvaise idée.

6 EXCHANGES suggesting weekend activities and indicating one's approval

1. –On joue aux jeux vidéo?
   –Oui, c'est une bonne idée! (Non, ce n'est pas une bonne idée.)
2. –On va à la bibliothèque?
   –Oui, c'est une bonne idée! (Non, ce n'est pas une bonne idée.)
3. –On va à la plage?
   –Oui, c'est une bonne idée! (Non, ce n'est pas une bonne idée.)
4. –On téléphone au professeur?
   –Oui, c'est une bonne idée! (Non, ce n'est pas une bonne idée.)
5. –On fait une promenade à vélo?
   –Oui, c'est une bonne idée! (Non, ce n'est pas une bonne idée.)
6. –On va dans les magasins?
   –Oui, c'est une bonne idée! (Non, ce n'est pas une bonne idée.)
7. –On achète des vêtements?
   –Oui, c'est une bonne idée! (Non, ce n'est pas une bonne idée.)
8. –On écoute des CD?
   –Oui, c'est une bonne idée! (Non, ce n'est pas une bonne idée.)

7 ROLE PLAY describing cultural differences

1. –En Amérique, on parle anglais.
   –En France, on parle français.
2. –En Amérique, on étudie le français.
   –En France, on étudie l'anglais.
3. –En Amérique, on dîne à six heures.
   –En France, on dîne à huit heures.
4. –En Amérique, on mange des hamburgers.
   –En France, on mange des omelettes.
5. –En Amérique, on voyage en avion.
   –En France, on voyage en train.
6. –En Amérique, on skie dans le Colorado.
   –En France, on skie dans les Alpes.
7. –En Amérique, on va à l'école le mercredi après-midi.
   –En France, on va à l'école le samedi matin.
8. –En Amérique, on chante «la Bannière étoilée».
   –En France, on chante «la Marseillaise».

8 COMMUNICATION describing one's usual activities

Answers will vary.
1. À la maison, on dîne (à six heures et demie).
2. À la télé, on regarde (des films).
3. À la cafétéria de l'école, on mange (des sandwichs).
4. En été, on va (à la plage).
5. Le week-end, avec mes copains, on va (au cinéma).
6. Avec mes copains, on joue (au basket).
7. On a une classe de français (le lundi et le mercredi).
8. On a un examen de français (jeudi).

Language note Be sure that students realize that in this activity **on** means *we*.

SECTION B

Communicative function
Describing actions

Teaching Resource Options

PRINT

Workbook PE, pp. 169–175
Unit 6 Resource Book
    Audioscript, p. 132
    Communipak, pp. 140–158
    Workbook TE, pp. 101–107

AUDIO & VISUAL

Audio Program
CD 3 Tracks 39, 40
Overhead Transparencies
4 -re Verbs

TECHNOLOGY

Power Presentations

Teaching strategy Point out that the plural endings of -re verbs are the same as those of -er verbs: **nous vendons, vous vendez,** and **ils vendent.**

Language note You may indicate that **vendre** is a REGULAR verb since many verbs follow the same pattern. However, **mettre** is IRREGULAR since the pattern applies only to verbs that have **mettre** as a root: **permettre, promettre,** etc.

 Re-entry and review

The verb chart reviews possessive adjectives (Lesson 16).

9 **PRACTICE** describing who's waiting for whom

1. Nous attendons nos copains.
2. Vous attendez vos cousines.
3. J'attends Antoine.
4. Tu attends Julie.
5. Olivier et Éric attendent Élodie et Sophie.
6. Les étudiants attendent les étudiantes.
7. Julien et moi, nous attendons Pauline et Mélanie.
8. Annette et toi, vous attendez Jean-Marc.
9. On attend notre copine.
10. Stéphanie attend Léa.

B Les verbes réguliers en -re

Many French verbs end in **-re.** Most of these are conjugated like **vendre** *(to sell).* Note the forms of this verb in the present tense, paying special attention to the endings.

INFINITIVE	vendre	STEM (infinitive minus -re)	ENDINGS
PRESENT	Je **vends** ma raquette.		-s
	Tu **vends** ton scooter.		-s
	Il/Elle/On **vend** son ordinateur.	vend-	—
	Nous **vendons** nos livres.		-ons
	Vous **vendez** vos CD.		-ez
	Ils/Elles **vendent** leur voiture.		-ent

→ The "**d**" of the stem is silent in the singular forms, but it is pronounced in the plural forms.

VOCABULAIRE Verbes réguliers en -re

attendre	*to wait, wait for*	Pierre **attend** Michèle au café.
entendre	*to hear*	Est-ce que tu **entends** la radio?
perdre	*to lose, waste*	Jean-Claude **perd** le match.
rendre visite à	*to visit (a person)*	Je **rends visite à** mon oncle.
répondre à	*to answer*	Nous **répondons à** la question du prof.
vendre	*to sell*	À qui **vends**-tu ton vélo?

→ There are two French verbs that correspond to the English verb *to visit.*

visiter (+ PLACES)   Nous **visitons** Québec.
rendre visite à (+ PEOPLE)   Nous **rendons visite à** nos cousins canadiens.

---

9 Rendez-vous

PARLER/ÉCRIRE The following people have been shopping and are now waiting for their friends at a café. Express this, using the appropriate forms of the verb **attendre.**

▶ Jérôme (Michèle)   **Jérôme attend Michèle.**

1. nous (nos copains)
2. vous (vos cousines)
3. moi (Antoine)
4. toi (Julie)
5. Olivier et Éric (Élodie et Sophie)
6. les étudiants (les étudiantes)
7. Julien et moi, nous (Pauline et Mélanie)
8. Annette et toi, vous (Jean-Marc)
9. on (notre copine)
10. Stéphanie (Léa)

TALKING ABOUT PAST EVENTS

Let's talk about whom you visited last summer. (Note that the past participle of -re verbs ends in -**u**.)

Est-ce que tu as rendu visite à ta tante l'été dernier?
Oui, j'ai rendu visite à ma tante.
(Je n'ai pas rendu visite à ma tante.)

- **Est-ce que tu as rendu visite à ton oncle l'été dernier?**
- **As-tu rendu visite à tes cousins?**
- **As-tu rendu visite à tes grands-parents?**
- **Et le week-end dernier, à qui est-ce que tu as rendu visite?**

Qui?

PARLER/ÉCRIRE Who is doing what? Answer the following questions, using the suggested subjects.

1. Qui perd le match?
   (toi, vous, Alice)
2. Qui rend visite à Pierre?
   (Paul, Léa et Hélène, toi)
3. Qui entend l'avion *(plane)?*
   (moi, vous, les voisins)
4. Qui vend des CD?
   (on, ce magasin, ces boutiques)
5. Qui attend le bus?
   (les élèves, le professeur, on, vous)
6. Qui répond au professeur?
   (toi, nous, les élèves)

11 Qu'est-ce qu'ils font?

PARLER/ÉCRIRE Say what the following people do by completing each sentence with the appropriate form of one of the verbs from the list. Be logical!

1. Guillaume est patient. Il … ses amis.
2. Vous êtes à Paris. Vous … à vos cousins français.
3. Tu joues mal. Tu … le match.
4. Je suis chez moi. J' … un bruit *(noise)* curieux.
5. Nous sommes en classe. Nous … aux questions du professeur.
6. Julie travaille dans une boutique. Elle … des robes.
7. On est au café. On … nos copains.

attendre	entendre	rendre visite
vendre	perdre	répondre

C L'impératif

Compare the French and English forms of the imperative.

Écoute ce CD!   ***Listen*** to this CD!
Ne vendez pas votre voiture!   ***Don't sell*** your car!
Allons au cinéma!   ***Let's go*** to the movies!

Note the forms of the imperative in the chart below.

INFINITIVE	parler	finir	vendre	aller
IMPERATIVE				
(tu)	parle	finis	vends	va
(vous)	parlez	finissez	vendez	allez
(nous)	parlons	finissons	vendons	allons

For regular verbs and most irregular verbs, the forms of the imperative are the same as the corresponding forms of the present tense.

→ NOTE: For all **-er** verbs, including **aller,** the **-s** of the **tu** form is dropped. Compare:
   Tu **parles** anglais.   **Parle** français, s'il te plaît!
   Tu **vas** au café.   **Va** à la bibliothèque!

→ The negative imperative is formed as follows:

ne + VERB + pas …	**Ne choisis pas** ce blouson.

---

10 PRACTICE describing what people are doing

1. Tu perds le match. (Vous perdez le match. Alice perd le match.)
2. Paul rend visite à Pierre. (Léa et Hélène rendent visite à Pierre. Tu rends visite à Pierre.)
3. J'entends l'avion. (Vous entendez l'avion. Les voisins entendent l'avion.)
4. On vend des CD. (Ce magasin vend des CD. Ces boutiques vendent des CD.)
5. Les élèves attendent le bus. (Le professeur attend le bus. On attend le bus. Vous attendez le bus.)
6. Tu réponds au professeur. (Nous répondons au professeur. Les élèves répondent au professeur.)

11 COMPREHENSION describing people and activities

1. attend
2. rendez visite à
3. perds
4. entends
5. répondons
6. vend
7. attend

SECTION C

Communicative function
Giving commands

Extra practice Have students give the **tu, vous,** and **nous** command forms of the following irregular verbs.

faire une promenade:
    fais une promenade
    faites une promenade
    faisons une promenade
revenir demain:
    reviens demain
    revenez demain
    revenons demain

Language note The irregular imperative forms of **avoir** and **être** are not presented at this level because they are used in only a few phrases. If students ask, you can mention them:

avoir: aie, ayez, ayons
    N'aie pas peur.
    Don't be afraid.

être: sois, soyez, soyons
    Ne sois pas bête.
    Don't be silly.

Follow-up:
• **Est-ce que X a rendu visite à son oncle l'été dernier?**
• **Est-ce que Y a rendu visite à ses cousins?**
• **À qui est-ce que Z a rendu visite le week-end dernier?**

Teaching Resource Options

PRINT

Workbook PE, pp. 169–175
Unit 6 Resource Book
 Audioscript, pp. 132–133
 Communipak, pp. 140–158
 Workbook TE, pp. 101–107

AUDIO & VISUAL

Audio Program
CD 3 Track 41

TECHNOLOGY

Power Presentations

12 **ROLE PLAY** offering and accepting assistance

1. —Je fais une salade?
   —Mais oui, fais une salade!
2. —J'invite nos copains?
   —Mais oui, invite nos copains!
3. —J'achète des sodas?
   —Mais oui, achète des sodas!
4. —J'apporte des CD?
   —Mais oui, apporte des CD!
5. —Je choisis la musique de danse?
   —Mais oui, choisis la musique de danse!
6. —Je viens à huit heures?
   —Mais oui, viens à huit heures!
7. —Je téléphone aux voisins?
   —Mais oui, téléphone aux voisins!
8. —J'apporte une mini-chaîne?
   —Mais oui, apporte une mini-chaîne!
9. —Je fais des sandwichs?
   —Mais oui, fais des sandwichs!

13 **ROLE PLAY** giving good and bad advice

1. —Téléphone à ta tante.
   —Ne téléphone pas à ta tante.
2. —Attends tes copains.
   —N'attends pas tes copains.
3. —Fais attention en classe.
   —Ne fais pas attention en classe.
4. —Va à l'école.
   —Ne va pas à l'école.
5. —Finis la leçon.
   —Ne finis pas la leçon.
6. —Écoute tes professeurs.
   —N'écoute pas tes professeurs.
7. —Mets la table.
   —Ne mets pas la table.
8. —Aide tes amis.
   —N'aide pas tes amis.
9. —Rends visite à ta grand-mère.
   —Ne rends pas visite à ta grand-mère.
10. —Choisis des copains sympathiques.
    —Ne choisis pas des copains sympathiques.
11. —Fais tes devoirs.
    —Ne fais pas tes devoirs.
12. —Réussis à l'examen.
    —Ne réussis pas à l'examen.

---

12 **Mais oui!**

J'apporte une pizza?

Mais oui, apporte une pizza!

PARLER You have organized a party at your home. Valérie offers to do the following. You accept.

▶ apporter une pizza?

1. faire une salade?
2. inviter nos copains?
3. acheter des sodas?
4. apporter des CD?
5. choisir la musique de danse?
6. venir à huit heures?
7. téléphoner aux voisins?
8. apporter une mini-chaîne?
9. faire des sandwichs?

13 **L'ange et le démon** *(The angel and the devil)*

PARLER Véronique is wondering whether she should do certain things. The angel gives her good advice. The devil gives her bad advice. Play both roles.

▶ étudier les verbes
 Étudie les verbes.
 N'étudie pas les verbes.

1. téléphoner à ta tante
2. attendre tes copains
3. faire attention en classe
4. aller à l'école
5. finir la leçon
6. écouter tes professeurs
7. mettre *(set)* la table
8. aider tes amis
9. rendre visite à ta grand-mère
10. choisir des copains sympathiques
11. faire tes devoirs *(homework)*
12. réussir à l'examen

14 **Oui ou non?**

PARLER For each of the following situations, give your classmates advice as to what to do and what not to do. Be logical.

▶ Nous sommes en vacances. (étudier? voyager?)
 N'étudiez pas! Voyagez!

1. Nous sommes à Paris. (parler anglais? parler français?)
2. C'est dimanche. (aller à la bibliothèque? aller au cinéma?)
3. Il fait beau. (rester à la maison? faire une promenade?)
4. Il fait froid. (mettre un pull? mettre un tee-shirt?)
5. Il est onze heures du soir. (rester au café? rentrer à la maison?)
6. Il fait très chaud. (aller à la piscine? regarder la télé?)

292 deux cent quatre-vingt-douze
Unité 6

GAME Drilling with dice

PROPS: Dice (one for every pair of students). Create a transparency with the verb list at right.

INSTRUCTIONS: (students play in pairs):
Student A rolls the die. For example, 5 spots = **vous.** Student B writes the corresponding form of the first verb: **vous cherchez.**

Then Student B rolls the die and Student A writes the corresponding form of the next verb: 2 spots + **gagner → tu gagnes.**

Keep track of pairs as they finish. Then have teams exchange their papers for peer correction. The first pair with the most correct answers is the winning team.

15 👥 L'esprit de contradiction (Disagreement)

PARLER Make suggestions to your friends about things to do. Your friends will not agree and will suggest something else.

▶ aller au cinéma (à la plage)

Allons au cinéma!

Non, n'allons pas au cinéma! Allons à la plage!

1. jouer au tennis (aux jeux vidéo)
2. écouter la radio (des CD)
3. regarder la télé (un film vidéo)
4. dîner au restaurant (à la maison)
5. inviter Michèle (Sophie)
6. organiser un barbecue (une boum)
7. faire des sandwichs (une pizza)
8. aller au musée (à la bibliothèque)
9. faire une promenade à pied (en voiture)
10. rendre visite à nos voisins (à nos copains)

PRONONCIATION 🎧   an, en /ɑ̃/

Les lettres «an» et «en»

The letters "**an**" and "**en**" represent the nasal vowel /ɑ̃/. Be sure not to pronounce the sound "**n**" after the vowel.

enfant

Répétez:

/ɑ̃/ **enf<u>an</u>t <u>an</u> m<u>an</u>teau coll<u>an</u>ts gr<u>an</u>d élég<u>an</u>t**
     <u>An</u>dré m<u>an</u>ge un gr<u>an</u>d s<u>an</u>dwich.

/ɑ̃/ **<u>en</u>fant <u>en</u> arg<u>en</u>t dép<u>en</u>ser att<u>en</u>ds <u>en</u>t<u>en</u>d v<u>en</u>d <u>en</u>vie**
     Vinc<u>en</u>t dép<u>en</u>se rarem<u>en</u>t son arg<u>en</u>t.

---

14 COMPREHENSION giving logical advice

1. Ne parlez pas anglais! Parlez français!
2. N'allez pas à la bibliothèque! Allez au cinéma!
3. Ne restez pas à la maison! Faites une promenade!
4. Mettez un pull! Ne mettez pas de tee-shirt!
5. Ne restez pas au café! Rentrez à la maison!
6. Allez à la piscine! Ne regardez pas la télé!

Variation (using the **nous** form)
N'étudions pas! Voyageons!

Challenge For each situation, have students invent additional advice. Encourage them to be creative.

Visitez Québec!
Faites «la route des baleines».
Dînez au Vendôme!

---

15 EXCHANGES making plans

1. —Jouons au tennis!
   —Non, ne jouons pas au tennis! Jouons aux jeux vidéo!
2. —Écoutons la radio!
   —Non, n'écoutons pas la radio! Écoutons des CD!
3. —Regardons la télé!
   —Non, ne regardons pas la télé! Regardons un film vidéo!
4. —Dînons au restaurant!
   —Non, ne dînons pas au restaurant! Dînons à la maison!
5. —Invitons Michèle!
   —Non, n'invitons pas Michèle! Invitons Sophie!
6. —Organisons un barbecue!
   —Non, n'organisons pas de barbecue! Organisons une boum!
7. —Faisons des sandwichs!
   —Non, ne faisons pas de sandwichs! Faisons une pizza!
8. —Allons au musée!
   —Non, n'allons pas au musée! Allons à la bibliothèque!
9. —Faisons une promenade à pied!
   —Non, ne faisons pas de promenade à pied! Faisons une promenade en voiture!
10. —Rendons visite à nos voisins!
   —Non, ne rendons pas visite à nos voisins! Rendons visite à nos copains!

Note the word 'barbecue' in item 6. Barbecue is pronounced as in English /barbəkju/

Challenge Expand the conversation to include three people. The third one does not like the second suggestion and has another idea.

– **Allons au cinéma!**
– **Non, n'allons pas au cinéma! Allons à la plage.**
– **Mais non, n'allons pas à la plage. Restons à la maison!**

PRONUNCIATION 🎧

• Exception: the "**en**" in **examen** represents the sound /ɛ̃/ as in **p<u>ain</u>: examen** /egzamɛ̃/

• In the combination **ien**, the letters "**en**" also represent the sound /ɛ̃/: **italien** /italjɛ̃/

Drilling with dice

1. chercher	9. attendre	18. permettre (permit)
2. gagner	10. entendre	19. revenir
3. acheter	11. perdre	20. venir
4. amener	12. répondre	
5. finir	13. aller	1 = je
6. grossir	14. avoir	2 = tu
7. maigrir	15. être	3 = elle
8. réussir	16. faire	4 = nous
	17. mettre	5 = vous
		6 = ils

1 COMPREHENSION

1. Est-ce que tu rends visite à tes cousins ce week-end?
   (d) Non, je reste ici.
2. Tu veux aller dans les boutiques avec moi?
   (c) Écoute! Je n'ai pas besoin de vêtements.
3. Est-ce que tu as envie d'aller au cinéma?
   (b) Bonne idée! Il y a un nouveau film au «Majestic».
4. Et après qu'est-ce qu'on fait?
   (a) Eh bien, allons au restaurant!

2 GUIDED ORAL EXPRESSION

Answers will vary.
—Qu'est-ce qu'on fait ... ?
—(X)
—Je n'ai pas envie de (d') ...
—Eh bien, (X). D'accord?
—Oui, c'est une bonne idée!
1. ce soir/(Étudions)/étudier/(regardons la télé)
2. dimanche/(Allons en ville)/aller en ville/(dînons au restaurant)
3. après les classes/(Jouons au basket)/jouer au basket/(faisons une promenade)
4. cet été/(Cherchons un job)/chercher un job/(voyageons)
5. ce week-end/(Faisons un pique-nique)/faire un pique-nique/(organisons une boum)
6. demain/(Allons à la bibliothèque)/aller à la bibliothèque/(allons à la piscine)

À votre tour!

1 🎧 👥 La bonne réponse

PARLER Anne is talking to Jean-François. Match Anne's questions with Jean-François's answers. You may act out the conversation with a classmate.

Anne

1 Est-ce que tu rends visite à tes cousins ce week-end?

2 Tu veux aller dans les boutiques avec moi?

3 Est-ce que tu as envie d'aller au cinéma?

4 Et après *(afterwards)* qu'est-ce qu'on fait?

Jean-François

a Eh bien, allons au restaurant!

b Bonne idée! Il y a un nouveau film au «Majestic».

c Écoute! Je n'ai pas besoin de vêtements.

d Non, je reste ici.

2 🎧 👥 Créa-dialogue

PARLER When we are with our friends, it is not always easy to agree on what to do. With your classmates, discuss the following possibilities.

Qu'est-ce qu'on fait **samedi**?

Allons au cinéma.

Je n'ai pas envie d'**aller au cinéma**.

Eh bien, **rendons visite à nos amis. D'accord?**

Oui, c'est une bonne idée!

Quand?	Première suggestion	Deuxième suggestion
▶ samedi	aller au cinéma	rendre visite à nos amis
1. ce soir *(tonight)*	étudier	regarder la télé
2. dimanche	aller en ville	dîner au restaurant
3. après *(after)* les classes	jouer au basket	faire une promenade
4. cet été	chercher un job	voyager
5. ce week-end	faire un pique-nique	??
6. demain	aller à la bibliothèque	??

294 deux cent quatre-vingt-quatorze
Unité 6

À VOTRE TOUR

Depending upon your goals and objectives, you may or may not wish to assign all of the activities in the **À votre tour** section.

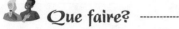

③ **Conseils** ----------------------------

PARLER Your friends tell you what they would like to do. Give them appropriate advice, either positive or negative. Use your imagination.

▶ Je voudrais maigrir. **Alors, mange moins.**
(Alors, ne mange pas de pizza.)

1. Je voudrais avoir un «A» en français.
2. Je voudrais gagner beaucoup d'argent.
3. Je voudrais organiser une boum.
4. Je voudrais préparer un barbecue.

④  **Que faire?** ----------------------------

PARLER Give a classmate advice about what to do or not to do in the following circumstances.

Pendant *(During)* la classe	Ce soir	Ce week-end	Pendant les vacances
écouter le prof	étudier	rester à la maison	voyager
parler à tes copains	aller au cinéma	aller en ville	travailler
regarder les bandes dessinées *(comics)*	préparer tes leçons	dépenser ton argent	grossir
manger un sandwich	aider *(help)* ta mère	organiser une boum	oublier *(forget)* ton français
répondre en français	surfer sur l'Internet	faire une promenade à pied	??
??	??	??	

▶ 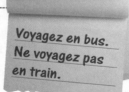 Pendant la classe, écoute le prof. Ne parle pas à tes copains.

⑤ **Bon voyage!** ----------------------------

ÉCRIRE Your French friend Ariane is going to visit the United States next summer with her cousin. They are traveling on a low budget and are asking you for advice as to how to save money. Make a list of suggestions, including five things they could do and five things they should not do. You may want to use some of the following ideas:

▶  Voyagez en bus. Ne voyagez pas en train.

- voyager *(comment?)*
- rester *(dans quels hôtels?)*
- dîner *(dans quels restaurants?)*
- visiter *(quelles villes?)*
- aller *(où?)*
- acheter *(quelles choses?)*
- apporter *(quelles choses?)*

 LESSON REVIEW CLASSZONE.COM

deux cent quatre-vingt-quinze **Leçon 20** 295

PORTFOLIO ASSESSMENT

You will probably select only one speaking activity and one writing activity to go into the students' portfolios for Unit 6.

In this lesson, Act. 2 lends itself well to an oral portfolio recording.

Act. 5 offers a good writing portfolio topic.

Middle School Copymasters

Drills: *Qu'est-ce que je fais?*, pp. T31–T32; Worksheet 5: *La baby-sitter*, p. 96; Worksheet 6: *Témoin*, p. 97; Project 3: Mardi Gras mask, pp. 104–107

③ **GUIDED ORAL EXPRESSION**

Answers will vary.
1. Alors, parle français en classe. (Alors, étudie bien.)
2. Alors, travaille beaucoup.
3. Alors, invite tes copains.
4. Alors, va au supermarché. (Alors, téléphone à tes amis.)

④ **COMPREHENSION**

Answers will vary.
- Pendant la classe, ne regarde pas les bandes dessinées. Écoute le prof.
  Pendant la classe, ne mange pas de sandwich. Réponds aux questions en français.
- Ce soir, étudie. Ne va pas au cinéma.
  Ce soir aide ta mère. Ne surfe pas sur l'Internet.
  Prépare tes leçons.
- Ce week-end, ne reste pas à la maison. Va à la campagne.
  Ce week-end, ne va pas en ville. Organise une boum.
  Ce week-end, ne dépense pas ton argent. Fais une promenade à pied.
- Pendant les vacances, n'oublie pas ton français. Voyage.
  Pendant les vacances, travaille à la plage. Ne reste pas à la maison.
  Pendant les vacances, ne grossis pas. Fais du sport.

⑤ **WRITTEN SELF-EXPRESSION**

Answers will vary.
Restez dans les hôtels bon marché, ne restez pas dans les hôtels chers.
Dînez dans les restaurants américains. Ne dînez pas dans les restaurants français.
Visitez Québec et Montréal. Ne visitez pas New York.
Allez à la plage et à la montagne. N'allez pas en ville.
Apportez un imper. N'apportez pas de manteau.
Voyagez en train. Ne voyagez pas en avion.
Regardez la télé. N'allez pas au cinéma.
Mangez des hamburgers. Ne mangez pas de steaks.
Allez à la bibliothèque. N'achetez pas de livres.

TESTS DE CONTRÔLE

Teaching Resource Options

PRINT

Unit 6 Resource Book
  Communipak, pp. 140–158
  Assessment
  Unit 6 Test, pp. 166–174
  Portfolio Assessment, Unit 1 URB
    pp. 155–164
  Multiple Choice Test Items, pp. 187–195
  Listening Comprehension
    Performance Test, pp. 175–176
  Reading Performance Test, pp. 181–183
  Speaking Performance Test, pp. 177–180
  Writing Performance Test, pp. 184–186
  Comprehensive Test 2, Unit 4–6,
    pp. 197–220
  Test Scoring Tools, p. 221–223
  Audioscript for Tests, pp. 224–229
  Answer Keys, pp. 230–234

AUDIO & VISUAL

Audio Program
CD 15 Tracks 13–22

TECHNOLOGY

Test Generator CD-ROM/eTest Plus
Online

① COMPREHENSION

1. un blouson	6. un chapeau
2. une jupe	7. un maillot de bain
3. une cravate	8. des chaussures
4. une veste	9. des chaussettes
5. une robe	10. une ceinture

② COMPREHENSION

1. Philippe <u>apporte</u> ses CD à la boum.
2. Caroline <u>porte</u> sa nouvelle robe.
3. Thomas <u>grossit</u> parce qu'il mange trop.
4. Léa <u>amène</u> un copain au pique-nique.
5. Céline <u>réussit</u> aux examens parce qu'elle étudie beaucoup.
6. Mélanie ne <u>trouve</u> pas son stylo.
7. Elle <u>rend visite</u> à son oncle.
8. Pierre <u>répond</u> à un mail.
9. Je <u>n'entends</u> pas bien.
10. Elle <u>attend</u> un copain.

③ COMPREHENSION

1. Dans ce quartier moderne, il y a beaucoup de <u>nouveaux</u> immeubles.
2. Elle est <u>vieille</u>.
3. C'est une <u>belle</u> fille, n'est-ce pas?
4. J'ai besoin d'un <u>nouvel</u> ordinateur.
5. Il met ses <u>vieux</u> vêtements.

296 · Tests de contrôle
Unité 6

Tests de contrôle

By taking the following tests, you can check your progress in French and also prepare for the unit test. Write your answers on a separate sheet of paper.

Review...
- items of clothing: pp. 258, 259, and 260

① The right item

Give the names of the following items of clothing, using the appropriate article: **un, une,** or **des.**

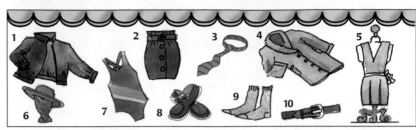

Dans ce magasin, il y a ...

1. —	3. —	5. —	7. —	9. —
2. —	4. —	6. —	8. —	10. —

Review...
- new verbs: pp. 259, 262, 269, 278, and 290

② The right activity

Complete each of the following sentences with the appropriate forms of the verbs in the box. Be logical in your choice of verbs and do not use the same word more than once.

1. Philippe — ses CD à la boum.
2. Caroline — sa nouvelle robe.
3. Thomas — parce qu'il mange trop *(too much)*.
4. Léa — un copain au pique-nique.
5. Céline — aux examens parce qu'elle étudie beaucoup.
6. Mélanie ne — pas son stylo. Où est-il?
7. Charlotte est en vacances. Elle — à son oncle.
8. Pierre — à un mail.
9. Je n' — pas bien. Répète, s'il te plaît.
10. Cécile regarde sa montre. Elle — un copain.

> amener
> apporter
> attendre
> entendre
> grossir
> porter
> rendre visite
> répondre
> réussir
> trouver

Review...
- beau, nouveau, and vieux: p. 279

③ The right form

Complete the following sentences with the appropriate forms of **beau, nouveau,** and **vieux.** Be logical in your choices.

1. Dans ce quartier moderne, il y a beaucoup de — immeubles.
2. Ma grand-mère a 82 ans. Elle est —.
3. Catherine est très jolie. C'est une — fille, n'est-ce pas?
4. Mon ordinateur ne marche pas. J'ai besoin d'un — ordinateur.
5. Nicolas va nettoyer *(to clean)* le garage. Il met ses — vêtements.

296 deux cent quatre-vingt-seize
Unité 6

4 The right comparison

Make logical comparisons using the adjectives in parentheses.

(grand) 1. La France est — les États-Unis *(United States)*.
(élégant) 2. Une belle chemise est — un vieux tee-shirt.
(rapide) 3. Les voitures de sport sont — les limousines.
(bon) 4. À l'examen, un «A» est — un «C».

Review...
• comparisons:
p. 280

5 Ce or quel?

Complete the following sentences with the appropriate forms of **ce** or **quel**.

1. — blouson préfères-tu?
2. J'aime — lunettes!
3. — veste est chère!
4. — casquette achetez-vous?
5. — copains invites-tu?
6. — chaussures mets-tu?
7. Comment s'appelle — garçon?
8. Qui est — homme?

Review...
• ce and quel
pp. 270 and 271

6 The right verb

Complete the following sentences with the appropriate forms of the verbs in parentheses.

1. **(acheter)**
   J'— une chemise.   Nous — des CD.   Qu'est-ce que tu —?
2. **(mettre)**
   Marc — un tee-shirt.   Je — un short.   Qu'est-ce que vous —?
3. **(choisir)**
   Vous — des vêtements.   Ils — des CD.   Éric — un polo.
4. **(finir)**
   Nous — les devoirs.   Je — un livre.   Pauline — la pizza.
5. **(vendre)**
   Ils — leur maison.   Je — mon vélo.   Claire — sa voiture.
6. **(attendre)**
   Les touristes — le train.   J'— le bus.   Nous — un copain.

Review...
• verb forms:
pp. 268, 272, 278
and 290

7 Composition: Un mariage

Imagine that you are a reporter for the society column of your local newspaper. You are attending an elegant wedding. Describe what the following people are wearing: **la mariée** *(the bride)*, **le marié** *(the groom)*, and **les demoiselles d'honneur** *(the bridesmaids)*. Be imaginative but use only vocabulary and expressions that you know in French.

STRATEGY Writing

a For each of the following, list the clothes and their colors.

la mariée	le marié	les demoiselles d'honneur
_____	_____	_____
_____	_____	_____

b Write three short paragraphs describing what each person is wearing.

c Reread your composition and be sure you have spelled all the items of clothing correctly and have used the correct forms of the color adjectives.

---

4 COMPREHENSION

1. La France est <u>moins grande</u> que les États-Unis.
2. Une belle chemise est <u>plus élégante</u> qu'un vieux tee-shirt.
3. Les voitures de sport sont <u>plus rapides</u> que les limousines.
4. À l'examen, un «A» est meilleur qu'un «C».

5 COMPREHENSION

1. <u>Quel</u> blouson préfères-tu?
2. J'aime <u>ces</u> lunettes!
3. <u>Cette</u> veste est chère!
4. <u>Quelle</u> casquette achetez-vous?
5. <u>Quels</u> copains invites-tu?
6. <u>Quelles</u> chaussures mets-tu?
7. Comment s'appelle <u>ce</u> garçon?
8. Qui est <u>cet</u> homme?

6 COMPREHENSION

1. J'<u>achète</u> une chemise. Nous <u>achetons</u> des CD. Qu'est-ce que tu <u>achètes</u>?
2. Marc <u>met</u> un tee-shirt. Je <u>mets</u> un short. Qu'est-ce que vous <u>mettez</u>?
3. Vous <u>choisissez</u> des vêtements. Ils <u>choisissent</u> des CD. Éric <u>choisit</u> un polo.
4. Nous <u>finissons</u> les devoirs. Je <u>finis</u> un livre. Pauline <u>finit</u> la pizza.
5. Ils <u>vendent</u> leur maison. Je <u>vends</u> mon vélo. Claire <u>vend</u> sa voiture.
6. Les touristes <u>attendent</u> le train. J'<u>attends</u> le bus. Nous <u>attendons</u> un copain.

7 WRITTEN SELF-EXPRESSION

Answers will vary.
La mariée, Claire Lapointe, porte une belle robe blanche. La robe est très élégante. Mademoiselle Lapointe porte aussi des belles chaussures blanches.

Le marié, Jean-Pierre Letourneau, porte une veste noire et un pantalon noir. Il porte aussi des nouvelles chaussures noires et des belles lunettes.

Les demoiselles d'honneur portent des belles robes bleues. Elles portent des chaussures bleues aussi.

Vocabulaire

Vocabulaire

Language Learning Benchmarks

FUNCTION
- Engage in conversations pp. 263, 287
- Express likes and dislikes p. 270
- Obtain information p. 263
- Understand some ideas and familiar details p. 305
- Begin to provide information pp. 261, 271, 273

CONTEXT
- Converse in face-to-face social interactions pp. 270, 271
- Listen to audio and video texts pp. 257-258, 266-267, 276-277, 284
- Use authentic materials when reading: posters p. 287
- Write notes p. 283
- Write lists p. 265
- Write short letters p. 265

TEXT TYPE
- Use short sentences when speaking pp. 272, 278, 289
- Use short sentences when writing pp. 278, 281, 288
- Use learned words and phrases when speaking pp. 259, 260, 269
- Use learned words and phrases when writing pp. 259, 260, 269
- Use simple questions when speaking pp. 279, 281, 289
- Use commands when speaking pp. 279, 292, 293
- Understand some ideas and familiar details presented in clear, uncomplicated speech when listening p. 264
- Understand short texts enhanced by visual clues when reading pp. 256-257

POUR COMMUNIQUER

Shopping for clothes

Pardon...	Excuse me ...	Quel est le prix de ...?	What is the price of ...?
Vous désirez, (monsieur)?	May I help you, (Sir)?	Combien coûte ...	How much does ... cost?
Je cherche ...	I'm looking for ...		

Expressing opinions and making comparisons

Qu'est-ce que tu penses de [la robe rose]? — What do you think of [the pink dress]?
Comment tu trouves [la robe noire]? — What do you think of [the black dress]?

La robe rose est	plus belle que / moins belle que / aussi belle que	la robe noire.	The pink dress is	more beautiful than / less beautiful than / as beautiful as	the black dress.

MOTS ET EXPRESSIONS

Les magasins

un magasin	store	une boutique	shop
un grand magasin	department store		

L'argent

l'argent	money	une pièce	coin
un billet	bill, paper money		

Les vêtements et les accessoires

des baskets	(hightop) sneakers	des bottes	boots
un blouson	jacket	une casquette	baseball cap
un chapeau	hat	une ceinture	belt
un chemisier	blouse	des chaussettes	socks
des collants	tights	des chaussures	shoes
un imper(méable)	raincoat	une chemise	shirt
un jean	jeans	une cravate	tie
un jogging	jogging suit	une jupe	skirt
un maillot de bain	bathing suit	des lunettes	glasses
un manteau	overcoat	des lunettes de soleil	sunglasses
un pantalon	pants	une robe	dress
un polo	polo shirt	des sandales	sandals
un pull	sweater	une veste	jacket
un short	shorts		
un survêtement	track suit		
un sweat	sweatshirt		
un tee-shirt	t-shirt		
des tennis	sneakers		

La description

à la mode	in style	joli(e)	pretty
beau (belle)	beautiful	long(ue)	long
bon marché	cheap	meilleur(e)	better
cher (chère)	expensive	moche	ugly
chouette	neat	nouveau (nouvelle)	new
court(e)	short	pauvre	poor
démodé(e)	out of style	petit(e)	small
élégant(e)	elegant	riche	rich
génial(e)	terrific	vieux (vieille)	old
grand(e)	big		

Verbes réguliers en -er

		Verbes avec changements orthographiques	
chercher	to look for	acheter	to buy
coûter	to cost	amener	to bring (a person)
dépenser	to spend		
gagner	to earn; to win	espérer	to hope
penser (que)	to think (that)	préférer	to prefer
porter	to wear		
trouver	to find; to think of	payer	to pay, to pay for

Verbes réguliers en -ir

		Verbes réguliers en -re	
choisir	to choose	attendre	to wait, to wait for
finir	to finish	entendre	to hear
grossir	to gain weight	perdre	to lose, to waste
maigrir	to lose weight	rendre visite à	to visit (a person)
réussir	to succeed	répondre à	to answer
réussir à un examen	to pass an exam	vendre	to sell

Verbes irréguliers

avoir besoin de + noun	to need	avoir envie de + noun	to want
avoir besoin de + infinitive	to need to, to have to	avoir envie de + infinitive	to feel like, to want to
		mettre	to put, to put on

Les nombres de 100 à 1000

100	cent	200	deux cents	500	cinq cents	800	huit cents
101	cent un	300	trois cents	600	six cents	900	neuf cents
102	cent deux	400	quatre cents	700	sept cents	1000	mille

Expressions utiles

à mon avis	in my opinion	combien + verb	how much
Eh bien!	Well!	combien de + noun	how much, how many
C'est une bonne idée!	That's a good idea!	trop + adjective	too
ce, cet, cette, ces	this, that, these, those		
quel, quelle, quels, quelles	what, which		

TEST PREP
CLASSZONE.COM
FLASHCARDS AND MORE!

CONTENT
• Understand and convey information about shopping p. 259
• Understand and convey information about clothes pp. 259, 260, 261, 268
• Understand and convey information about prices pp. 263, 268, 301
• Understand and convey information about colors pp. 271, 301

ASSESSMENT
• Communicate effectively with some hesitation and errors, which do not hinder comprehension pp. 265, 295
• Demonstrate culturally acceptable behavior for engaging in conversations pp. 265, 275, 282, 294
• Demonstrate culturally acceptable behavior for obtaining information pp. 264, 274, 283
• Demonstrate culturally acceptable behavior for understanding some ideas and familiar details p. 265
• Demonstrate culturally acceptable behavior for providing information pp. 265, 275, 283
• Understand most important information pp. 264, 274, 294

ENTRACTE 6

Objectives
- Reading skill development
- Re-entry of material in the unit
- Development of cultural awareness

Achats par Internet
Objectives
- Reading for information about clothes and fashion

Teaching Resource Options

PRINT

Workbook PE, pp. 177–179
Activités pour tous PE, pp. 107–109
Unit 6 Resource Book
    Activités pour tous TE, pp. 159–161
    Workbook TE, pp. 163–165

Achats° par INTERNET

En France, comme° aux États-Unis,° on peut faire beaucoup d'achats par Internet. Ces vêtements figurent° sur le catalogue-en-ligne de «la Redoute», une compagnie française spécialisée dans la vente° de vêtements par correspondance.°

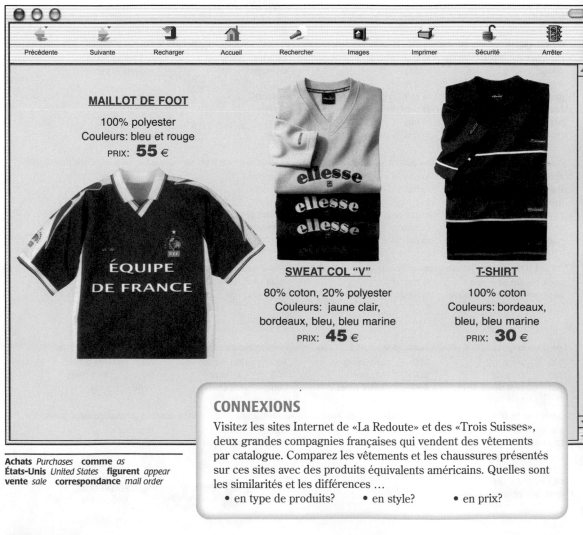

MAILLOT DE FOOT

100% polyester
Couleurs: bleu et rouge
PRIX: **55** €

ÉQUIPE DE FRANCE

SWEAT COL "V"

80% coton, 20% polyester
Couleurs: jaune clair, bordeaux, bleu, bleu marine
PRIX: **45** €

T-SHIRT

100% coton
Couleurs: bordeaux, bleu, bleu marine
PRIX: **30** €

CONNEXIONS

Visitez les sites Internet de «La Redoute» et des «Trois Suisses», deux grandes compagnies françaises qui vendent des vêtements par catalogue. Comparez les vêtements et les chaussures présentés sur ces sites avec des produits équivalents américains. Quelles sont les similarités et les différences …
- en type de produits?
- en style?
- en prix?

Achats *Purchases* **comme** *as* **États-Unis** *United States* **figurent** *appear* **vente** *sale* **correspondance** *mail order*

300 trois cents
Unité 6

PRE-READING

Ask students if they sometimes order clothes from the Internet.

Which websites do they like best?

POST-READING

Have students each select an item they plan to buy (for themselves or as a gift for a friend). In pairs, have students describe their intended purchases to one another.

– Moi, je vais acheter un sweat.
– Ah bon? Pour qui? …

Précédente   Suivante   Recharger   Accueil   Rechercher   Images   Imprimer   Sécurité   Arrêter

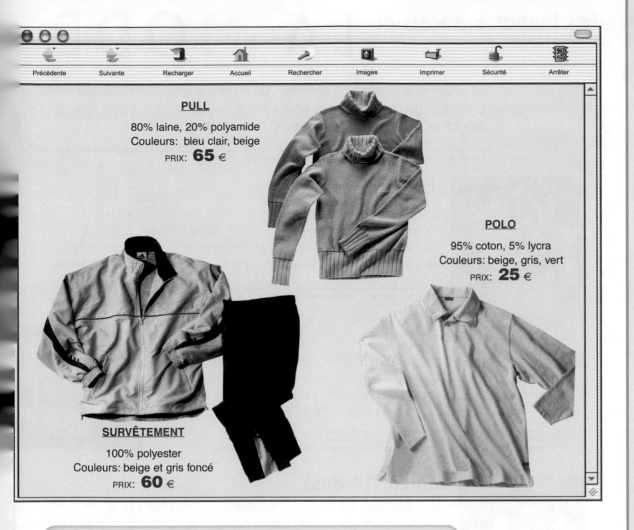

PULL

80% laine, 20% polyamide
Couleurs: bleu clair, beige
PRIX: **65** €

POLO

95% coton, 5% lycra
Couleurs: beige, gris, vert
PRIX: **25** €

SURVÊTEMENT

100% polyester
Couleurs: beige et gris foncé
PRIX: **60** €

Et vous?

Vous êtes en France et vous voulez acheter deux vêtements différents comme cadeaux *(presents)* pour des amis aux États-Unis. Votre budget est limité à un total de 100 euros. Faites votre sélection.

	Pour qui?	Vêtement	Textile	Couleur	Prix
1.					
2.					
				Prix total:	

PAIR PRACTICE

Using the book or the websites for **La Redoute** or **Trois Suisses,** have students do the **Et vous?** activity in pairs. You can increase the spending limit to allow them to "purchase" more items.

Vocabulary notes

jaune clair *light yellow*
bleu marine *navy blue*
bordeaux *maroon*
laine *wool*
gris foncé *dark grey*

Et vous?

Answers will vary.

1. Mon frère
   un polo
   coton et lycra
   gris
   25 euros
2. Ma soeur
   un tee-shirt
   coton
   bleu marine
   30 euros

Les jeunes Français et la mode

Objectives
- Reading at the paragraph level
- Building reading skills

Teaching Resource Options

PRINT

Workbook PE, pp. 177–179
Activités pour tous PE, pp. 107–109
Unit 6 Resource Book
    Activités pour tous TE, pp. 159–161
    Workbook TE, pp. 163–165

Pronunciation Chloé /kloe/

Questions sur le texte

1. Comment est-ce que Florence gagne son argent?
   [Elle travaille dans une boutique de mode.]
2. Où est-ce qu'elle achète ses vêtements?
   [Elle achète ses vêtements à la boutique où elle travaille.]
3. Est-ce que Chloé achète beaucoup de vêtements?
   [Non, elle n'achète pas beaucoup de vêtements.]
4. Qu'est-ce qu'elle fait pour être à la mode?
   [Elle coud (met) des rubans et des patchs sur ses vêtements.]
5. Est-ce que Julien aime être à la mode?
   [Non, Julien n'aime pas être à la mode.]
6. Qu'est-ce qu'il fait avec son argent?
   [Il achète des CD.]
7. Est-ce que Robert aime être bien habillé?
   [Oui, il aime être bien habillé.]
8. Est-ce qu'il achète beaucoup de vêtements?
   [Non, il achète peu de vêtements mais il fait attention à la qualité.]
9. Qui achète les vêtements d'Éric?
   [Sa mère achète ses vêtements.]
10. Où est-ce que la mère d'Éric achète les vêtements de son fils?
    [Elle achète ses vêtements sur catalogue.]

Les jeunes Français et LA MODE

Est-ce que vous aimez être à la mode? Où est-ce que vous achetez vos vêtements? Et qu'est-ce qui compte le plus pour vous? le style? la qualité? le prix? Nous avons posé ces questions à cinq jeunes Français. Voilà leurs réponses.

à la mode *in style* **compte** *counts* **le plus** *the most* **avons posé** *asked*

Florence (16 ans)

J'aime être à la mode. Malheureusement,° mon budget est limité. La solution? Le samedi après-midi je travaille dans une boutique de mode. Là, je peux acheter mes jupes et mes pulls à des prix très avantageux.° Pour le reste, je compte sur la générosité de mes parents.

Malheureusement *Unfortunately* **avantageux** *reasonable*

Chloé (15 ans)

Pour moi, le style, c'est tout.° Hélas, la mode n'est pas bon marché. Heureusement,° j'ai une cousine qui a une machine à coudre° et qui est très adroite.° Alors, nous cousons° des rubans° et des patchs sur nos vêtements. De cette façon,° nous créons notre propre° style. C'est génial, non?

tout *everything* **Heureusement** *Fortunately* **machine à coudre** *sewing machine*
adroite *skillful* **cousons** *sew* **rubans** *ribbons* **façon** *manner, way* **propre** *own*

Julien (14 ans)

Vous connaissez° le proverbe: «L'habit ne fait pas le moine*.» Eh bien, pour moi, les vêtements n'ont pas d'importance. Avec mon argent, je préfère acheter des CD. Quand j'ai besoin de jeans ou de tee-shirts, je vais aux puces.° C'est pas cher et c'est marrant!°

connaissez *know* **[marché] aux puces** *flea market* **marrant** *fun*
*Clothes don't make the man. (The habit doesn't make the monk.)

Robert (15 ans)

Aujourd'hui la présentation extérieure est très importante. Mais il n'est pas nécessaire d'être à la mode pour être bien habillé.° Pour moi, la qualité des vêtements est aussi importante que leur style. En général, j'attends les soldes. J'achète peu de vêtements mais je fais attention à la qualité.

habillé *dressed*

 trois cent deux
Unité 6

PRE-READING

Have students glance over the reading quickly. What are the questions that were asked in the interview?

POST-READING

Ask each student to decide which of the four people he/she would most want to be introduced to and why.

**Imaginez que vous pouvez faire la connaissance d'un de ces jeunes Français.
Qui voulez-vous rencontrer?
Pourquoi?**

Éric (12 ans)

Moi, je n'ai pas le choix!° C'est ma mère qui choisit mes vêtements. En ce qui concerne° la mode, elle n'est pas dans le coup.° Elle achète tout sur catalogue et elle choisit ce qui est le moins cher.° C'est pas drôle.

---

choix *choice*   **En ce qui concerne** *As for*   **dans le coup** *with it*
le moins cher *the cheapest (the least expensive)*

STRATEGY Reading

Understanding casual French speech
The interviews you read were conducted orally. Notice how casual French speech is different from standard written language.

• Spoken language often contains slang expressions.
   Elle n'est pas dans le coup!   C'est marrant!   C'est génial!

• Spoken French sometimes drops the **ne** in **ne … pas.**
   C'est pas cher. = Ce n'est pas cher.

NOTE *culturelle*

Les soldes

En France, les boutiques de vêtements ont des soldes deux fois par an.° Les dates de ces soldes sont déterminées par le gouvernement et sont les mêmes° dans tout le pays.° Au moment des soldes, on peut acheter des vêtements de bonne qualité à des prix avantageux.

---

deux fois par an *twice a year*   **mêmes** *same*
tout le pays *the entire country*

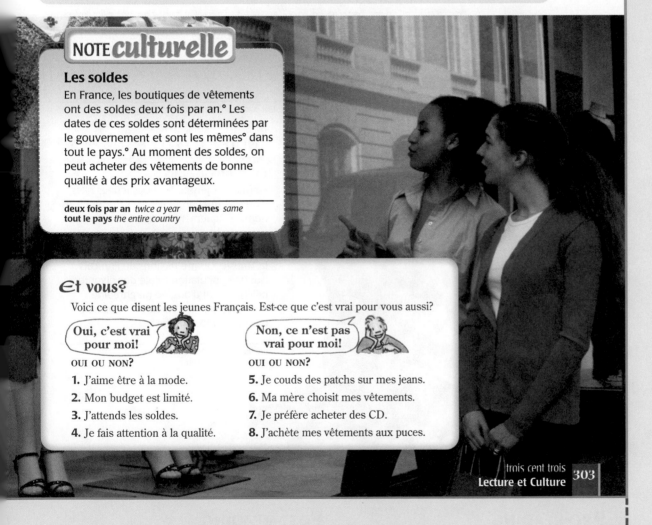

Et vous?

Voici ce que disent les jeunes Français. Est-ce que c'est vrai pour vous aussi?

Oui, c'est vrai pour moi!

OUI OU NON?

1. J'aime être à la mode.
2. Mon budget est limité.
3. J'attends les soldes.
4. Je fais attention à la qualité.

Non, ce n'est pas vrai pour moi!

OUI OU NON?

5. Je couds des patchs sur mes jeans.
6. Ma mère choisit mes vêtements.
7. Je préfère acheter des CD.
8. J'achète mes vêtements aux puces.

trois cent trois
Lecture et Culture 303

Questions personnelles

Answers will vary.
1. Comment est-ce que tu gagnes ton argent?
   (Je fais du baby-sitting.)
2. Est-ce que tu travailles? Où?
   (Oui, je travaille dans une boutique.)
3. Où est-ce que tu achètes tes vêtements?
   (J'achète mes vêtements au centre commercial.)
4. Est-ce que tu attends les soldes pour acheter tes vêtements?
   (Oui, j'attends les soldes pour acheter mes vêtements.)
5. Qu'est-ce que tu achètes sur catalogue/sur Internet?
   (J'achète des CD.)
6. Robert dit: «La présentation extérieure est très importante.» Est-ce que tu es d'accord avec cette opinion?
   (Oui, je suis d'accord.)
7. Julien dit: «L'habit ne fait pas le moine.» Est-ce que tu es d'accord avec ce proverbe?
   (Non, je ne suis pas d'accord.)

Et vous?

Answers will vary.
1. Oui, c'est vrai pour moi.
   (Non, ce n'est pas vrai pour moi.)
2. Oui, c'est vrai pour moi.
   (Non, ce n'est pas vrai pour moi.)
3. Oui, c'est vrai pour moi.
   (Non, ce n'est pas vrai pour moi.)
4. Oui, c'est vrai pour moi.
   (Non, ce n'est pas vrai pour moi.)
5. Non, ce n'est pas vrai pour moi.
   (Oui, c'est vrai pour moi.)
6. Non, ce n'est pas vrai pour moi.
   (Oui, c'est vrai pour moi.)
7. Oui, c'est vrai pour moi.
   (Non, ce n'est pas vrai pour moi.)
8. Non, ce n'est pas vrai pour moi.
   (Oui, c'est vrai pour moi.)

Bonjour, Fatima!

Objectives
- Reading a complete text
- Building reading skills

Teaching Resource Options

PRINT

Workbook PE, pp. 177–179
Activités pour tous PE, pp. 107–109
Unit 6 Resource Book
   Activités pour tous TE, pp. 159–161
   Workbook TE, pp. 163–165

Bonjour, Fatima!

Je m'appelle Fatima et j'ai quinze ans. J'habite dans la banlieue° de Paris. Mes parents sont généreux mais ils ne sont pas très riches. Alors, je n'ai pas beaucoup d'argent de poche: cinquante euros par mois. Ce n'est pas une fortune! Heureusement,° je fais du baby-sitting pour les voisins quand ils vont au cinéma le week-end. Je gagne cinq euros par heure.

J'adore les vêtements. Avec ma copine Djemila, on achète des magazines de mode et on va dans les magasins. Quand on entre dans une boutique, c'est généralement plus pour regarder que pour acheter. J'achète mes nouveaux pulls pendant la période des soldes. Par contre,° j'achète assez souvent des bracelets et des boucles d'oreille.° On trouve des choses géniales dans les petites boutiques de mon quartier. Quand je veux changer de «look», je change de boucles d'oreille et je change de vernis à ongles° et de rouge à lèvres.° C'est facile et ça ne coûte pas cher!

banlieue *suburbs* **Heureusement** *Fortunately* **Par contre** *On the other hand* **boucles d'oreille** *earrings*
vernis à ongles *nail polish* **rouge à lèvres** *lipstick*

NOTE culturelle

Prénoms arabes

Fatima et **Djemila** sont des jeunes filles d'origine «maghrébine». Elles portent° des noms typiquement arabes.

Le Maghreb est une région géographique constituée par **le Maroc,°** l'**Algérie** et **la Tunisie**. Quatre millions de Français (sur une population totale de soixante millions) sont d'origine maghrébine. Beaucoup parlent arabe et pratiquent la religion musulmane.°

---

portent = ont **Maroc** *Morocco*
musulmane *Moslem*

304   trois cent quatre
Unité 6

PRE-READING

Ask students to look at this page and decide what type of reading it is. [a letter]

POST-READING

Have students use their answers to the **Et vous?** activity as the basis for writing a letter to Fatima, explaining how similar or different their lives are from hers.

Compréhension

1. Comment est-ce que Fatima gagne son argent?
2. Qu'est-ce qu'elle fait avec sa copine?
3. Qu'est-ce qu'elle achète avec son argent?
4. Qu'est-ce qu'elle fait pour changer de look?

Et vous?

Quelles ressemblances *(similarities)* et quelles différences est-ce que vous trouvez entre Fatima et vous? Faites une liste de ces ressemblances et de ces différences.

- âge
- parents
- argent de poche
- achats de vêtements
- achats d'accessoires
- comment changer de look

★ Alger
L'Algérie

EN BREF: L'ALGÉRIE

Population: 32 millions
Capitale: Alger
Langues: arabe, berbère, français

L'Algérie est un pays° d'Afrique du Nord. Colonie française pendant plus de 100 ans, l'Algérie est devenue indépendante en 1962. La majorité des Algériens sont arabes et pratiquent la religion musulmane. Des millions d'Algériens ont immigré en France et sont devenus Français. Pour cette raison,° la France est maintenant le pays avec la plus grande population musulmane d'Europe.

La présence algérienne influence la vie° ordinaire des Français. Par exemple, les Français mangent du couscous* qui est une spécialité d'Afrique du Nord, et beaucoup de jeunes écoutent le raï qui est une musique d'origine algérienne.

---

pays *country*   **raison** *reason*   **vie** *life*

* **Couscous** *is a type of semolina (white gritty wheat) which is usually cooked with meat and vegetables as a main dish, but which can also be steamed and served cold in salads.*

COMMUNAUTÉS

Explore Internet sources to find out more about the Muslim religion. Or perhaps there is a Muslim person in your school or in your community whom you could invite to talk to your class. Use the information you gather to make a bulletin board display explaining the basic tenets of the Muslim faith.

Expansion activities PLANNING AHEAD

Games

• Dessinez, c'est gagné

After reviewing the vocabulary from pages 310–313, divide the class into two or three teams. Tell one member from each team, the artist, the word for that round. Have the artists draw pictures for their teams until one team guesses the word. The first team to guess the correct word gets one point and a new member of each team becomes the artist. Set a two-minute time limit for each round and let the artists know that they should not use any words to help their teammates guess. The team with the most points wins.

Pacing Suggestion: Upon completion of Leçon 21.

• Attrapez et répondez!

Have students stand in a circle. Announce a subject and a verb (for example, **je** and **choisir**) and toss a ball to one player. That player must conjugate the verb in **passé composé** for that subject pronoun (**j'ai choisi**), pass the ball to another player, and change either the subject pronoun or verb for that player (**nous** and **choisir** or **je** and **parler,** for example). Any player who answers incorrectly is out and must stand outside the circle. For larger classes, you may want to divide the class into two circles. You may want to impose a time limit of five seconds for the student with the ball to respond. As an added challenge, allow students the option of alternating between **passé composé** and present tense.

Pacing Suggestion: Upon completion of Leçon 23.

Projects

• Les fêtes

Have students work in small groups to learn more about holidays and celebrations in France. Students may wish to investigate *Mardi Gras, Premier Avril, 14 Juillet, Chandeleur,* and *Saint Nicolas.* Each group will present a holiday to the class. They will tell when the holiday is celebrated and what traditions and foods are associated with the holiday. The presentations should include a visual component, such as photographs of people celebrating the holiday. Students may also wish to include some of the foods or music associated with the holiday as part of their presentations. Expand the project by having students investigate holidays in other French-speaking areas of the world.

Pacing Suggestion: Upon completion of Leçon 21.

© Robert Fried

Bulletin Boards

• Les cartes postales

Each student will design a postcard. First, have each student choose a French-speaking country that he or she might like to visit and locate pictures, or create an image, for the front of the card. Have students then use the vocabulary in the lesson to create a message for the back of the card and ask a classmate to proofread their message. Students may also research and recreate French or francophone stamps to put on their cards. You may wish to compile the cards and display them on a bulletin board.

Pacing Suggestion: Upon completion of Leçon 21.

• Le Maroc

Divide the class into small groups. Have each group research a piece of information about Morocco. Groups can:

• create a colorful map that shows where Morocco is located
• find or create illustrations of what Morocco looks like
• learn about activities that are common in Morocco
• find information about the weather, people, politics, industry, crafts, music, etc. of Morocco
• learn how Morocco gained its independence from France

Each group will create a colorful poster they can use to present the information they obtained to the rest of the class.

Pacing Suggestion: Upon completion of Leçon 24.

Music

• Le dernier qui a parlé

Play *Le dernier qui a parlé* for students. (The song is on the *Chansons* CD.) Give students a copy of the lyrics and have them listen to the song. Play it a second time and have students list all the words that they recognize. Have the class discuss the general meaning of the song. As alternatives, you may wish to have students listen for, and underline, verbs in the **passé composé** or hand out a version of the song with blanks that the students have to fill in as they listen.

Pacing Suggestion: Upon completion of Leçon 22.

Storytelling

• Les expressions avec *avoir*

Have each student write a story based on the vocabulary on page 320 using expressions with *avoir*. You may wish to choose several of the better stories to have students read aloud in class. The class can then vote on the best story and best use of each expression with *avoir*.

Pacing Suggestion: Upon completion of Leçon 22.

Recipe

• Soupe à l'oignon

Easy to make and delicious, **soupe à l'oignon** is a French classic. This soup is best served with salad and French bread.

Pacing Suggestion: Upon completion of Leçon 22.

Hands-on Crafts

• Vacation Scrapbook

Have students create a scrapbook from a favorite or an "ideal" vacation. Ask students to bring in photos or illustrations of a favorite place that they have visited or would like to visit. Then using construction paper, have them build up a scrapbook of images and text. Encourage students to write a brief paragraph describing the scene or the activities shown in each photo or illustration. Have students use thick cardboard or book backing to cover their scrapbooks. Finally, they should decorate the front cover of their books with collages made from stamps, postcards, and other objects, either picked up en route or that relate to their vacation.

Pacing Suggestion: Upon completion of Leçon 22.

End of Unit

• Les infos

Students will work in pairs or in small groups to create a segment for a news broadcast in French. Assign each pair the type of segment they will need to create: a news story, a commercial, a segment on the weather, a sports story, or an interview. You may want to give students vocabulary lists to use for their specific segments. Also, make sure that all the segments contain enough parts so that each student has the opportunity to speak. Students will write a first draft of their segment, and ask another pair or group to proofread it. Have students read their segments out loud to practice intonation. Encourage students to use props to make their news segments more realistic. Finally, have students perform their news segments for the rest of the class. You may wish to videotape the segments to create an entire news program.

Soupe à l'oignon

Ingrédients
- 4 oignons coupés en tranches
- 8 gousses d'ail écrasées
- 1 cuillère à soupe de farine
- 1 litre de bouillon (de légumes ou de boeuf)
- 6 tranches de pain
- 1/2 tasse de Gruyère râpé

Préparation
1. Cuisez les oignons avec un peu de beurre à petit feu. Remuez doucement pendant 20 minutes.
2. Quand les oignons commencent à faire une pâte, ajoutez l'ail et cuisez jusqu'à ce que la préparation commence à dorer.
3. Ajoutez la farine et cuisez 2 minutes, puis ajoutez le bouillon. Faites bouillir.
4. Réduisez le feu et cuire, couvert, à petit feu pendant 20 minutes.
5. Mettez les tranches de pain à dorer au four. Retournez-les une fois. Mettez un peu de fromage râpé sur les tranches de pain grillé et faites-les griller jusqu'à ce que le fromage fonde.
6. Servez la soupe avec le pain grillé au-dessus. Saupoudrez avec le reste du fromage râpé.

Ingredients
- 4 onions, sliced
- 8 cloves garlic, chopped
- 1 tbsp. flour
- approx. 4 cups of broth (vegetable or beef)
- 6 slices of bread
- 1/2 cup of grated Gruyère (Swiss cheese)

Directions
1. Cook onions in a little bit of butter over low heat for 20 minutes. Stir occasionally.
2. When the onions begin to form a paste, add the garlic and cook until the mix begins to brown.
3. Add the flour and cook for 2 minutes, then add the broth and bring to a boil.
4. Reduce the heat and cook, covered, on low heat for 20 minutes.
5. Toast bread in oven. Turn once. Cover with grated cheese. Grill until the cheese begins to melt.
6. Top the soup with the toasted bread slices and more grated cheese.

Rubric
A = 13–15 pts. **B** = 10–12 pts. **C** = 7–9 pts. **D** = 4–6 pts. **F** = < 4 pts.

Criteria	Scale				
Vocabulary Use	1	2	3	4	5
Grammar/Spelling Accuracy	1	2	3	4	5
Creativity	1	2	3	4	5

VIVE LES VACANCES

viva

RÉSEAU DE VILLAGES
VACANCES ANIMÉS

UNITÉ 7

Planning Guide CLASSROOM MANAGEMENT

OBJECTIVES

Communication
- Discuss your weekend activities *p. 310*
- Talk about individual summer and winter sports *p. 313*
- Describe your vacation and travel plans *p. 312*
- Describe what you did and where you went yesterday, last week, or last summer *pp. 321, 333, 335, 336, 342*
- Narrate what occurred at any time in the past *pp. 321, 333, 335, 336, 342*

Grammar
- Les expressions avec *avoir p. 320*
- Le passé composé des verbes en -*er p. 321*
- Le passé composé: forme négative *p. 324*
- Les questions au passé composé *p. 326*
- Le verbe *voir p. 332*
- Le passé composé des verbes réguliers en -*ir* et -*re p. 333*
- Le passé composé des verbes *être, avoir, faire, mettre* et *voir p. 335*
- Le passé composé avec *être p. 342*
- La construction négative ne . . . *jamais p. 346*
- Les expressions *quelqu'un, quelque chose* et leurs contraires *p. 347*

Vocabulary
- Le week-end *p. 310*
- Les vacances *p. 312*
- Activités sportives *p. 313*
- Expressions avec *avoir p. 320*
- Expressions pour la conversation *p. 323*
- *Quand? p. 336*
- Quelques verbes conjugués avec *être* au passé composé *p. 344*

Pronunciation
- Les lettres «ain» et «in» *p. 327*
- Les lettres «gn» *p. 337*
- Les lettres «qu» *p. 347*

Culture
- Les sports d'hiver *p. 313*
- Le week-end *p. 319*
- Les jeunes Français et la télé *p. 331*
- Les jeunes Français et la musique *p. 341*
- Le Maroc *p. 357*

PROGRAM RESOURCES

 Print
- Workbook PE, *pp. 181–212*
- *Activités pour tous* PE, *pp. 111–129*
- Block Scheduling Copymasters *pp. 161–191*
- Teacher to Teacher Copymasters
- Unit 7 Resource Book
  - Lesson 21–24 Resources
    - Workbook TE
    - *Activités pour tous* TE
    - Lesson Plans
    - Block Scheduling Lesson Plans
    - Family Letter
    - Absent Student Copymasters
    - Family Involvement
    - Video Activities
    - Videoscripts
    - Audioscripts
    - Assessment Program
  - Unit 7 Resources
    - Communipak
    - *Activités pour tous* TE Reading
    - Workbook TE Reading and Culture Activities
    - Assessment Program
    - Answer Keys

 Audiovisual
- Audio Program PE CD 4 Tracks 1–20
- Audio Program Workbook CD 11 Tracks 1–25
- *Chansons* Audio CD
- Video Program Modules 21, 22, 23, 24
- Overhead Transparencies
  42 Weekend Activities;
  43 Les *activités sportives*;
  44 Expressions with *avoir*;
  16 Subject Pronouns

 Technology
- Online Workbook
- ClassZone.com
- eTest Plus Online/Test Generator CD-ROM
- EasyPlannerPlus Online/ Easy Planner CD-ROM
- Power Presentations on CD-ROM

✓ **Assessment Program Options**

Lesson Quizzes
Portfolio Assessment
Unit Test Form A
Unit Test Form B
Unit Test Part III (Alternate) Cultural Awareness
Listening Comprehension Performance Test
Speaking Performance Test
Reading Comprehension Performance Test
Writing Performance Test
Multiple Choice Test Items
Test Scoring Tools
Audio Program CD 16 Tracks 1–8
Answer Keys
eTest Plus Online/Test Generator CD-ROM

Pacing Guide SAMPLE LESSON PLAN

DAY	DAY	DAY	DAY	DAY
1 Unité 7 Opener **Leçon 21** • Vocabulaire et Culture–Le week-end et les vacances • Vocabulaire–Le week-end	**2** **Leçon 21** • Vocabulaire–Les vacances • Vocabulaire–Activités sportives	**3** **Leçon 21** • Vocabulaire–Activités sportives *(continued)* • Note culturelle–Les sports d'hiver	**4** **Leçon 21** • À votre tour!	**5** **Leçon 22** • Conversation et Culture–Vive le week-end! • Note culturelle–Le week-end
6 **Leçon 22** • Les expressions avec *avoir* • Vocabulaire–Expressions avec *avoir*	**7** **Leçon 22** • Le passé composé des verbes en *-er*	**8** **Leçon 22** • Vocabulaire–Expressions pour la conversation • Le passé composé: forme négative	**9** **Leçon 22** • Les questions au passé composé • Prononciation–Les lettres «ain» et «in»	**10** **Leçon 22** • À votre tour!
11 **Leçon 23** • Conversation et Culture–L'alibi • Note culturelle–Les jeunes Français et la télé	**12** **Leçon 23** • Le verbe *voir* • Le passé composé des verbes réguliers en *-ir* et *-re*	**13** **Leçon 23** • Le passé composé des verbes réguliers en *-ir* et *-re (continued)* • Le passé composé des verbes *être, avoir, faire, mettre* et *voir*	**14** **Leçon 23** • Vocabulaire–Quand? • Prononciation–Les lettres «gn»	**15** **Leçon 23** • À votre tour!
16 **Leçon 24** • Conversation et Culture–Qui a de la chance? • Note culturelle–Les jeunes Français et la musique	**17** **Leçon 24** • Le passé composé avec *être*	**18** **Leçon 24** • Le passé composé avec *être (continued)* • Vocabulaire–Quelques verbes conjugués avec *être* au passé composé	**19** **Leçon 24** • La construction négative *ne . . . jamais* • Les expressions *quelqu'un, quelque chose* et leurs contraires • Prononciation–Les lettres «qu»	**20** **Leçon 24** • À votre tour!
21 • Tests de contrôle	**22** • Unit 7 Test	**23** • Entracte–Lecture et culture		

Pacing Guide · 305D
Unité 7

UNITÉ 7 Student Text Listening Activity Scripts
AUDIO PROGRAM

▶ **LEÇON 21 LE FRANÇAIS PRATIQUE** Le week-end et les vacances
À votre tour!
• Écoutez bien! *p. 316* CD 4, TRACK 1

On weekends, you can stay in and take care of things at home, or you can go out and have fun. Listen carefully to what the people are saying. If they refer to an indoor activity, mark A. If they refer to an outdoor activity, mark B. You will hear each sentence twice. Commençons. Let's begin.

1. Est-ce que tu vas faire du roller? #
2. Je dois aider ma mère. #
3. Pauline lave son pantalon. #
4. Nous allons faire de la natation. #
5. J'aime bien faire du skate. #
6. Guillaume va ranger sa chambre. #
7. Léa va faire du VTT à la campagne. #
8. Alice aime beaucoup faire de la planche à voile. #
9. Monsieur Martin va nettoyer le garage. #
10. Sophie fait ses devoirs. #
11. Où est-ce que vous allez faire de l'escalade? #
12. Thomas va réparer la chaîne hi-fi de son cousin. #

• Créa-dialogue *p. 317* CD 4, TRACK 2

Listen to the sample *Créa-dialogues*. Écoutez les conversations.

Modèle: —Où vas-tu vendredi? —Je vais en ville.
　　　　 —Qu'est-ce que tu vas faire là-bas? —Je vais faire des achats.

Maintenant, écoutez le dialogue numéro 1.

—Où vas-tu samedi matin? —Je vais à la campagne.
—Qu'est-ce que tu vas faire là-bas? —Je vais faire une promenade à vélo.

• Conversation dirigée *p. 317* CD 4, TRACK 3

Listen to the conversation. Écoutez la conversation entre Thomas et Hélène.

Thomas: Où vas-tu cet été?
Hélène: Je vais à la mer avec des amis.
Thomas: Est-ce que vous allez voyager en voiture?
Hélène: Non, on va voyager en train parce qu'on n'a pas de voiture.
Thomas: Est-ce que tu vas faire de la voile?
Hélène: Oui, et je vais aussi faire de la planche à voile.
Thomas: Au revoir, Hélène, et bonnes vacances!
Hélène: Au revoir!

▶ **LEÇON 22** Vive le week-end!
• Vive le week-end! *p. 318*
A. Compréhension orale CD 4, TRACK 4

Le week-end, nous avons nos occupations préférées. Certaines personnes aiment aller en ville et rencontrer leurs amis.

D'autres préfèrent rester à la maison et bricoler. Qu'est-ce que les personnes suivantes ont fait le week-end dernier?

J'aime acheter des vêtements. — J'ai acheté des vêtements.
Tu aimes réparer ton vélo. — Tu as réparé ton vélo.
M. Lambert aime travailler dans le jardin. — Il a travaillé dans le jardin.
Nous aimons organiser des boums. — Nous avons organisé une boum.
Vous aimez jouer au foot. — Vous avez joué au foot.
Pluton et Philibert aiment rencontrer leurs amis. — Ils ont rencontré leurs amis.

B. Écoutez et répétez. CD 4, TRACK 5

You will now hear a paused version of the dialog. Listen to the speaker and repeat right after he or she has completed the sentence.

• Vocabulaire *p. 320* CD 4, TRACK 6

Expressions avec *avoir*

Repeat the sentences after the speaker.

avoir chaud # Quand j'**ai chaud** en été, je vais à la plage. #
avoir froid # Est-ce que tu **as froid**? Voici ton pull. #
avoir faim # Tu **as faim?** Est-ce que tu veux une pizza? #
avoir soif # J'**ai soif.** Je voudrais une limonade. #
avoir raison # Est-ce que les profs **ont** toujours **raison?** #
avoir tort # Marc ne fait pas ses devoirs. Il **a tort!** #
avoir de la chance # J'**ai de la chance.** J'ai des amis sympathiques. #

• Prononciation *p. 327* CD 4, TRACK 7

Les lettres «ain» et «in»

Écoutez: sa m<u>ain</u>　　sem<u>ain</u>e　　magas<u>in</u>　　maga<u>zin</u>e

When the letters "**ain**," "**aim**," "**in**," and "**im**" are at the end of a word or are followed by a *consonant*, they represent the nasal vowel /ɛ̃/.

REMEMBER: Do not pronounce an /n/ after the nasal vowel /ɛ̃/.

Répétez: /ɛ̃/ # dem<u>ain</u> # f<u>aim</u> # tr<u>ain</u> # m<u>ain</u> # vois<u>in</u> # cous<u>in</u> # jard<u>in</u> #
magas<u>in</u> # m<u>ain</u>tenant # <u>in</u>telligent # <u>in</u>téressant # <u>im</u>portant #

When the letters "**ain**," "**aim**," "**in(n)**," and "**im**" are followed by a *vowel,* they do NOT represent a nasal sound.

Répétez: /ɛn/ # sem<u>ain</u>e # améric<u>ain</u>e #
/ɛm/ # j'<u>aim</u>e #
/in/ # vois<u>in</u>e # cous<u>in</u>e # cuis<u>in</u>e # maga<u>zin</u>e # c<u>in</u>éma # Cor<u>inn</u>e # f<u>in</u>ir #
/im/ # t<u>im</u>ide # d<u>im</u>anche # M<u>im</u>i # cent<u>im</u>e #
Al<u>ain</u> M<u>in</u>ime a un rendez-vous <u>im</u>portant dem<u>ain</u> mat<u>in</u>, avenue du M<u>ain</u>e. #

À votre tour!
• Allô! *p. 328* CD 4, TRACK 8

Listen to the conversation. Écoutez la conversation entre Alain et Christine.

Alain: À quelle heure est-ce que tu as dîné hier soir?
Christine: À sept heures et demie.
Alain: Et après, tu as regardé la télé?
Christine: Oui, mais d'abord j'ai aidé ma mère.
Alain: Qu'est-ce que tu as regardé après?
Christine: Le match Marseille-Nice.
Alain: Qui a gagné?
Christine: Nice. Par un score de trois à un.
Alain: Dis, tu a préparé la leçon pour demain?
Christine: Mais oui! J'ai étudié avant le dîner!

• Créa-dialogue *p. 328* CD 4, TRACK 9

Listen to some sample *Créa-dialogues.* Écoutez les conversations.

Modèle: —Est-ce que tu as dîné au restaurant?
　　　　 —Oui, j'ai dîné au restaurant.
　　　　 —Avec qui?
　　　　 —Avec mes cousins.
　　　　 —Où est-ce que vous avez dîné?
　　　　 —Nous avons dîné Chez Tante Lucie

Maintenant, écoutez le dialogue numéro 1.

—Est-ce que tu as joué au tennis?
—Oui, j'ai joué au tennis.
—Avec qui?
—Avec Tom, Lucie et Karen.
—Quand est-ce que vous avez joué au tennis?
—Nous avons joué au tennis dimanche après-midi.

▶ LEÇON 23 L'alibi

• L'alibi p. 330 CD 4, TRACK 10

A. Compréhension orale

Êtes-vous bon détective? Pouvez-vous trouver la solution du mystère suivant?

Samedi dernier à deux heures de l'après-midi, il y a eu une panne d'électricité dans la petite ville de Marcillac-le-Château. La panne a duré une heure. Pendant la panne, un cambrioleur a pénétré dans la Banque Populaire de Marcillac-le-Château. Bien sûr, l'alarme n'a pas fonctionné et c'est seulement lundi matin que le directeur de la banque a remarqué le cambriolage: un million d'euros.

Lundi après-midi, l'inspecteur Leflic a interrogé quatre suspects, mais chacun a un alibi.

Sophie Filou: Euh . . . excusez-moi, Monsieur l'Inspecteur. Ma mémoire n'est pas très bonne. Voyons, qu'est-ce que j'ai fait samedi après-midi? Ah oui, j'ai fini un livre. Le titre du livre? *Le crime ne paie pas!*

Marc Laroulette: Qu'est-ce que j'ai fait samedi? J'ai rendu visite à mes copains. Nous avons joué aux cartes. C'est moi qui ai gagné!

Patrick Lescrot: Voyons, samedi dernier . . . Ah oui . . . cet après-midi-là, j'ai invité des amis chez moi. Nous avons regardé la télé. Nous avons vu le match de foot France-Allemagne. Quel match! Malheureusement, c'est la France qui a perdu! Dommage!

Pauline Malin: Ce n'est pas moi, Monsieur l'Inspecteur! Samedi j'ai fait un pique-nique à la campagne avec une copine. Nous avons choisi un coin près d'une rivière. Ensuite, nous avons fait une promenade à vélo. Nous avons eu de la chance! Il a fait un temps extraordinaire!

Lisez attentivement les quatre déclarations. À votre avis, qui est le cambrioleur ou la cambrioleuse? Pourquoi? (Vous pouvez comparer votre réponse avec la réponse de l'inspecteur à la page 337.)

B. Écoutez et répétez. CD 4, TRACK 11

You will now hear a paused version of the dialog. Listen to the speaker and repeat right after he or she has completed the sentence.

• Grammaire p. 332 CD 4, TRACK 12

Le verbe *voir*

Repeat the sentences after the speaker.

Je **vois** Marc. #   Tu **vois** ton copain. #
Il **voit** un accident. #   Nous **voyons** un film. #
Vous **voyez** un match de baseball. #   Elles **voient** le professeur. #

• Prononciation p. 337 CD 4, TRACK 13

Les lettres «gn»

Écoutez: espagnol

The letters "**gn**" represent a sound similar to the "**ny**" in *canyon*. First, practice with words you know.

Répétez: espa**gn**ol # ga**gn**er # mi**gn**on # la monta**gn**e # la campa**gn**e

Now try saying some new words. Make them sound French!

Répétez: Champa**gn**e # Espa**gn**e # un si**gn**e # la vi**gn**e # la li**gn**e # un si**gn**al # la di**gn**ité # i**gn**orer # ma**gn**étique # ma**gn**ifique # A**gn**ès # A**gn**ès Mi**gn**ard a gagné son match. C'est ma**gn**ifique! #

À votre tour!

• Allô! p. 338 CD 4, TRACK 14

Listen to the conversation. Écoutez la conversation entre Robert et Julien.

Robert: Tu as fini tes devoirs de français?
Julien: Non, je n'ai pas étudié cet après-midi.
Robert: Qu'est-ce que tu as fait alors?
Julien: J'ai joué au tennis avec Caroline.
Robert: Tu as gagné?
Julien: Non, j'ai perdu!
Robert: Mais d'habitude tu joues bien?
Julien: C'est vrai, mais aujourd'hui, je n'ai pas eu de chance . . .
Robert: Peut-être que Caroline a joué mieux que toi?
Julien: Tu as raison. Elle a joué comme une championne.

• Créa-dialogue p. 338 CD 4, TRACK 15

Listen to the sample *Créa-dialogues*. Écoutez les conversations.

Modèle: —Qu'est-ce que tu as fait dimanche après-midi?
　　　　 —J'ai joué au tennis avec ma soeur.
　　　　 —Est-ce que tu as gagné?
　　　　 —Non, j'ai perdu!
　　　　 —Dommage!

Maintenant écoutez un autre dialogue.

—Qu'est-ce que tu as fait hier soir?
—J'ai eu un rendez-vous.
—Avec qui est-ce que tu as eu un rendez-vous?
—Avec Thomas, mon meilleur ami.
—C'est chouette!

▶ LEÇON 24 Qui a de la chance?

• Qui a de la chance? p. 340

A. Compréhension orale CD 4, TRACK 16

Please turn to page 340 for complete *Compréhension orale* text.

B. Écoutez et répétez. CD 4, TRACK 17

You will now hear a paused version of the dialog. Listen to the speaker and repeat right after he or she has completed the sentence.

• Prononciation p. 347 CD 4, TRACK 18

Les lettres «qu»

Écoutez: un bou**qu**et

The letters "**qu**" represent the sound /k/.

Répétez: **qu**i # **qu**and # **qu**el**qu**e chose # **qu**el**qu**'un # **qu**atre # **qu**atorze # **Qu**ébec # Moni**qu**e # Véroni**qu**e # sympathi**qu**e # un pi**qu**e-ni**qu**e # le ski nauti**qu**e # Véroni**qu**e pense **qu**e Moni**qu**e aime la musi**qu**e classi**qu**e. #

À votre tour!

• Allô! p. 348 CD 4, TRACK 19

Listen to the conversation. Écoutez la conversation entre Sophie et Charlotte.

Sophie: Tu es restée chez toi samedi soir?
Charlotte: Non! J'ai téléphoné à une copine et nous sommes allées au cinéma.
Sophie: Qu'est-ce que vous avez vu?
Charlotte: Un vieux western avec Gary Cooper.
Sophie: Qu'est-ce que vous avez fait ensuite?
Charlotte: Nous sommes allées dans un café sur le boulevard Saint Michel.
Sophie: Vous avez mangé quelque chose?
Charlotte: Oui, des sandwichs.
Sophie: À quelle heure es-tu rentrée chez toi?
Charlotte: À onze heures et demie.

• Créa-dialogue p. 348 CD 4, TRACK 20

Listen to some sample *Créa-dialogues.* Écoutez les conversations.

Modèle: —Tu es resté chez toi hier matin?　　—Oui, je suis resté chez moi.
　　　　 —Qu'est-ce que tu as fait?　　　　—J'ai rangé ma chambre.

　　　　 —Tu es resté chez toi hier matin?　　—Non, je ne suis pas resté(e) chez moi.
　　　　 —Qu'est-ce que tu as fait?　　　　—Je suis allé à l'école.

Maintenant, écoutez le dialogue numéro 1.

—Tu es allé en ville samedi après-midi?　　—Oui, je suis allé en ville samedi après-midi.
—Qu'est-ce que tu as fait?　　　　—J'ai fait des achats.

—Tu es allée en ville samedi après-midi?　　—Non, je ne suis pas allée en ville.
—Qu'est-ce que tu as fait?　　　　—Je suis allée à la plage!

> Complete videoscripts, plus Workbook and
> Assessment audioscripts, are available in the
> Unit Resource Books.

UNITÉ 7

Main Theme
• Leisure-time activities

COMMUNICATION
• Discussing weekend activities
• Talking about individual summer and winter sports
• Describing vacation and travel plans
• What you did and where you went yesterday, last week, or last summer
• Narrating what happened at any time in the past

CULTURES
• Learning how the French spend their leisure time
• Learning about the sports the French enjoy
• Learning what the French do on weekends
• Learning about the variety of music French teens enjoy
• Learning about the **Fête de la Musique**
• Learning about Morocco

CONNECTIONS
• Connecting to Social Studies: Learning about the history and culture of Morocco
• Connecting to Gym: Learning about the benefits and safety equipment of in-line skating

COMPARISONS
• Comparing television watching habits of teens in France and the U.S.
• Comparing French and American teenagers' attitude toward and taste in music

COMMUNITIES
• Using French to do volunteer work in a French-speaking region
• Using French for personal enjoyment

Le temps libre

LEÇON 21 LE FRANÇAIS PRATIQUE:
Le week-end et les vacances

LEÇON 22 Vive le week-end!

LEÇON 23 L'alibi

LEÇON 24 Qui a de la chance?

THÈME ET OBJECTIFS

Leisure-time activities

We work hard during the week, but we also need time to relax.

In this unit, you will learn …

• to discuss your weekend activities
• to talk about individual summer and winter sports
• to describe your vacation and travel plans

You will also be able …

• to describe what you did and where you went yesterday, last week, or last summer
• more generally, to narrate what happened at any time in the past

WEBQUEST
CLASSZONE.COM

UNIT OVERVIEW

▶ **Communication Goals:** Students will be able to talk about individual sports, helping out at home, and what they did over the weekend or during vacation.

▶ **Linguistic Goals:** Students will learn to describe and narrate past events using the passé composé.

▶ **Critical Thinking Goals:** Students will observe the similarities and differences between the passé composé in French and the past tense in English.

▶ **Cultural Goals:** Students will learn about weekend and sports activities popular in France and the importance of leisure time to the French people.

trois cent sept
Unité 7 307

Teaching Resource Options

PRINT

Unit 7 Resource Book
  Family Letter, p. 15

AUDIO & VISUAL

Audio Program
Chansons CD

TECHNOLOGY

EasyPlanner CD-ROM/EasyPlanner
  Plus Online

Middle School Copymasters

Unité 7: Conversations, *Allons au cinéma* and *Qu'est-ce que tu as fait ce week-end?* games, *C'est bon!* class starter, worksheets, *Vacances idéales* project, pp. T35–T37

Pacing

Your pacing of Units 7 and 8 depends on what point in the academic year you begin these units.

Since this material is reintroduced in ***Discovering French, Nouveau! – Blanc,*** you may wish to present the material of Units 7 and 8 primarily for student recognition. Or you may wish to focus on Unit 7 so that the students have a solid introduction to the **passé composé**.

For further suggestions on pacing, see page 305D.

Leçon 21

Main Topic Talking about vacations, sports, and weekend activities

Teaching Resource Options

PRINT

Workbook PE, pp. 181–186
Activités pour tous PE, pp. 111–113
Block Scheduling Copymasters, pp. 161–168
Unit 7 Resource Book
  Activités pour tous TE, pp. 7–9
  Audioscript, pp. 30–31
  Communipak, pp. 148–170
  Lesson Plans, pp. 10–11
  Block Scheduling Lesson Plans, pp. 12–14
  Absent Student Copymasters, pp. 16–18
  Video Activities, pp. 21–26
  Videoscript, pp. 27–28
  Workbook TE, pp. 1–6

AUDIO & VISUAL

Audio Program
CD 11 Tracks 1–6

TECHNOLOGY

Online Workbook

VIDEO PROGRAM

VIDÉO   DVD

MODULE 21
Le français pratique: Le week-end et les vacances

TOTAL TIME: 6:21 min.
  DVD Disk 2
  Videotape 4 (COUNTER: 00:00 min.)

21.1 Introduction: Listening
  – Le week-end (0:10–0:35 min.)

21.2 Mini-scenes: Listening
  – Que faites-vous le week-end?
  (0:36–1:42 min.)

21.3 Dialogue: Le week-end
  (1:43–2:07 min.)

21.4 Mini-scenes: Speaking
  – Samedi (2:08–3:11 min.)

21.5 Introduction: Listening
  – Les vacances (3:12–3:45 min.)

21.6 Dialogue: Les vacances
  (3:46–4:17 min.)

21.7 Mini-scenes: Speaking
  – Qu'est-ce qu'il fait?
  (4:18–4:59 min.)

21.8 Vignette culturelle: La planche à voile (5:00–6:21 min.)

Comprehension practice Play the entire module through as an introduction to the lesson.

308 · **Vocabulaire et Culture**
Unité 7 LEÇON 21

Vocabulaire et Culture

LEÇON 21

LE FRANÇAIS PRATIQUE
VIDÉO · DVD · AUDIO

Le week-end et les vacances

Accent sur ... les loisirs

When given the choice, French people would rather have more free time than more money. For them, leisure time is an essential component of what they call **la qualité de la vie** (*quality of life*). By law, they work only thirty-five hours per week and they have a minimum of five weeks of vacation per year.

Like their parents, French teenagers value their leisure time and try to make the most of it. What are their favorite activities? Here is what they do when they have a free evening.

Qu'est-ce que tu aimes faire le soir?	GARÇONS	FILLES
Je regarde la télé.	24%	18%
Je sors° avec mes copains.	20%	18%
Je vais au cinéma.	16%	14%
Je lis.°	14%	20%
Je vais au concert ou au théâtre.	10%	12%
Je vais danser.	8%	12%
Je fais du sport.	6%	4%
Je bricole.°	2%	2%

sors *go out*   **lis** *read*   **bricole** *do things around the house*

Michèle est très sportive. Elle fait souvent du jogging dans le parc de la ville.

Thomas adore faire du skate. Le samedi, il va au skatepark avec ses copains.

308 trois cent huit
Unité 7

USING THE VIDEO

The main focus of Video Module 21 is on what French people do in their leisure time, both on weekends and on vacation. As students watch, have them look for similarities and differences in the ways the French and Americans spend their leisure time.

The **Vignette culturelle** introduces students to the sport of windsurfing **(la planche à voile),** which is very popular throughout metropolitan France, as well as in the overseas departments of Martinique and Guadeloupe.

Les vacances
You may want to point out that for French people from all walks of life, vacation time is sacred. Often they enjoy a week of winter sports or travel, plus a longer vacation in July or August.

Les examens
French students are concerned about doing well on their final **baccalauréat** exams in the last two years at the **lycée**. Younger students work hard to score well on the **entrée en sixième** (to enter the right secondary school sequence) and the **entrée en seconde** (to enter the right **lycée** sequence). See chart on p. 128.)

À la Martinique il fait beau tout le temps.
À la plage, on fait du surfing ou de la planche
à voile.

En hiver, beaucoup de jeunes Français vont à la montagne avec leur famille ou leur école. Le snowboard — ou le surf — est un sport très populaire.

trois cent neuf
Leçon 21 309

CROSS-CULTURAL COMPARISONS

Ask your students what they like to do when they have a free evening, using the suggestions in the **sondage** on p. 308. Then analyze your results and compare them to those in the reading.

You can review numbers by tallying the results in French, using a calculator.

Dans la classe, il y a [12] garçons et [16] filles.
[4] garçons regardent la télé.
Ça fait [25% – vingt-cinq pour cent].
[4] filles regardent la télé.
Ça fait [33 % – trente-trois pour cent].

SECTION A

Communicative function
Discussing weekend activities

Teaching Resource Options

PRINT

Workbook PE, pp. 181–186
Unit 7 Resource Book
    Communipak, pp. 148–170
    Video Activities, pp. 21–23
    Videoscript, pp. 27–28
    Workbook TE, pp. 1–6

AUDIO & VISUAL

Overhead Transparencies
42 Weekend activities

VIDEO PROGRAM

VIDÉO   DVD

MODULE 21

21.1 Introduction: Le week-end
(0:10–0:35 min.)

**21.2 Mini-scenes: Que faites-vous
le week-end?** (0:36–1:42 min.)

21.3 Dialogue: Le week-end
(1:43–2:07 min.)

21.4 Mini-scenes: Samedi
(2:08–3:11 min.)

Supplementary vocabulary
ranger (sa chambre) to clean (one's
room)
Compare:
ranger to straighten up, to pick up
nettoyer to dust and vacuum

Like **manger**, which the students
already know, the verb **ranger** has
a spelling change in the **nous** form:
nous rangeons.

retrouver (des amis) to meet (friends)
Compare:
retrouver to meet as arranged
rencontrer to run into (by chance)

Teaching strategy Like **payer**,
nettoyer is also a "boot" verb. Have
students draw a boot and write the
appropriate forms of **nettoyer** inside
and outside their drawing.

A **VOCABULAIRE Le week-end**

▶ *How to plan your weekend activities:*

> Qu'est-ce que tu
> vas faire samedi?

> Je vais rester
> chez moi pour
> réparer mon vélo.

Qu'est-ce que tu vas faire | samedi?
samedi **matin**   **le matin** *morning*
dimanche **après-midi**   **l'après-midi** *(m.) afternoon*
demain **soir**   **le soir** *evening*
ce **week-end**
le week-end **prochain** *(next)*

Je vais rester chez moi **pour** *(in order to)* | faire mes **devoirs** *(homework)*.
réparer *(to fix)* mon vélo
préparer le dîner
aider *(to help)* mes parents
laver *(to wash)* la voiture
nettoyer *(to clean)* le garage
ranger *(to pick up)* ma chambre

Je vais aller … | pour …
  en ville   **faire des achats**
  dans les magasins   *(to go shopping)*.
  au centre commercial   **louer** *(to rent)* un film

  au cinéma   **voir** *(to see)* un film
  au café   **rencontrer** *(to meet)* des copains
  au stade   **assister à** *(to go to, attend)*
       un match de foot

  à la campagne *(countryside)*   **faire un pique-nique**
       (to have a picnic)

> Moi, je vais aller
> en ville pour faire
> des achats.

Je vais aller à une boum.
Avant *(Before)* la boum, je vais faire des achats.
Pendant *(During)* la boum, je vais écouter des CD.
Après *(After)* la boum, je vais faire mes devoirs.

→ The verb **nettoyer** is conjugated like **payer**:

je **nettoie**   tu **nettoies**   il/elle/on **nettoie**   ils/elles **nettoient**
but: nous **nettoyons**   vous **nettoyez**

WARM-UP AND REVIEW

Review the gestures for the subject pronouns (page
96). Have students identify the forms of **faire**.

    C'est le week-end.
    Je fais une promenade. [gesture **je**]
    Vous faites une promenade. [**vous**]
    Ils font une promenade aussi., etc.

Review times and possessive adjectives, asking when
students do their homework.

    X, à quelle heure est-ce que tu fais tes devoirs?
    [Je fais mes devoirs à sept heures et demie.]
    Y, à quelle heure est-ce que X fait ses devoirs?
    [Il fait ses devoirs à sept heures et demie.]

1 Et toi?

PARLER/ÉCRIRE Décris tes activités.
Pour cela, complète les phrases suivantes.

1. En général,
   je vais au cinéma …
   - le vendredi soir
   - le samedi soir
   - le dimanche après-midi
   - … ?

2. En général,
   je fais mes devoirs …
   - avant le dîner
   - après le dîner
   - pendant la classe
   - … ?

3. Je préfère assister à …
   - un match de foot
   - un match de baseball
   - un concert de rock
   - … ?

4. En général, quand je rentre
   chez moi après les classes, …
   - je fais mes devoirs
   - je regarde la télé
   - j'aide ma mère ou mon père
   - … ?

5. J'aime aller en ville pour …
   - voir un film
   - rencontrer mes copains
   - faire des achats
   - … ?

6. En général, je préfère faire
   mes achats …
   - seul(e) (by myself)
   - avec mes copains
   - avec mes frères et mes soeurs
   - … ?

7. En été, je préfère faire
   un pique-nique …
   - dans mon jardin
   - à la campagne
   - à la plage
   - … ?

8. Pour aider mes parents à
   la maison, je préfère …
   - ranger le salon
   - laver la voiture
   - nettoyer le garage
   - … ?

2 Qu'est-ce qu'ils font?

PARLER/ÉCRIRE Informez-vous sur les personnes
suivantes. Décrivez ce qu'elles font ou ce qu'elles
vont faire. Pour cela, complétez les phrases avec
une expression du **Vocabulaire** à la page 310.

▶ Sandrine est au garage.
   Elle <u>répare son vélo</u> (sa mobylette).

1. Mme Jolivet est dans la cuisine. Elle …
2. Vincent Jolivet est aussi dans la cuisine. Il …
3. Anne et Sylvie sont au Bon Marché. Elles …
4. Je suis dans ma chambre et je regarde mon
   livre de français. Je …
5. Olivier et ses copains achètent des billets
   (tickets) de cinéma. Ils vont …
6. Mes amis vont à Yankee Stadium. Ils vont …
7. Tu vas au café. Tu vas …
8. Vous faites des sandwichs. Vous allez … à
   la campagne.

3 Mon calendrier personnel

PARLER/ÉCRIRE Décrivez ce que
vous allez faire.

MERCREDI
1. Après la classe, je vais …
2. Avant le dîner, …
3. Après le dîner, …
4. Demain soir, …
5. Vendredi soir, …
6. Samedi après-midi, …
7. Samedi soir, …
8. Dimanche après-midi, …
9. Pendant les vacances, …

TEACHING NOTE Directions to activities

From now on, direction lines for the activities are
given in French. You may want to present the key
verbs listed here. Encourage your students to guess
the meanings of other new words and expressions
from context.

With more challenging activities, you may wish to
have a volunteer paraphrase the instructions in English.

Key verbs for direction lines:

décrire *to describe*	**lire** *to read*
demander *to ask*	**poser une question** *to*
dire *to say*	*ask a question*
expliquer *to explain*	**utiliser** *to use*
indiquer *to indicate*	

Language notes
- Expressions used in Quebec:
  un centre d'achats *(a shopping center)*
  un mail /maj/ *(a mall)*
  magasiner/faire du magasinage *(to go shopping)*
- The French also say: **louer une cassette vidéo, louer un DVD**

Looking ahead The present tense forms of **voir** are presented in Lesson 23.

1 COMMUNICATION describing leisure activities

Answers will vary.
1. En général, je vais au cinéma (le samedi soir).
2. En général, je fais mes devoirs (après le dîner).
3. Je préfère assister à (un concert de rock).
4. En général, quand je rentre chez moi après les classes, (je regarde la télé).
5. J'aime aller en ville pour (faire des achats).
6. En général, je préfère faire mes achats (avec mes copains).
7. En été, je préfère faire un pique-nique (à la plage).
8. Pour aider mes parents à la maison, je préfère (ranger le salon).

Variations
- In pairs: Have students work in pairs, sharing their answers.
- In small groups: (See suggested activity on p. 75.)

Middle School Copymasters

Game: *Allons au cinéma*, pp. T36–T37

2 COMPREHENSION describing what people are doing

1. Elle prépare le dîner.
2. Il (aide sa mère / fait ses devoirs).
3. Elles (font des achats / rencontrent leurs copains).
4. Je fais mes devoirs.
5. Ils vont voir un film.
6. Ils vont assister à un match de baseball.
7. Tu vas rencontrer des copains.
8. Vous allez faire un pique-nique à la campagne.

3 COMMUNICATION describing future plans

Answers will vary.
1. Après la classe, je vais (rencontrer des copains).
2. Avant le dîner, je vais (nettoyer ma chambre).
3. Après le dîner, je vais (faire mes devoirs).
4. Demain soir, je vais (aller au café).
5. Vendredi soir, je vais (assister à un concert).
6. Samedi après-midi, je vais (faire des achats).
7. Samedi soir, je vais (voir un film).
8. Dimanche après-midi, je vais (réparer ma mobylette).
9. Pendant les vacances, je vais (aller à la campagne).

SECTION B

SECTION B

Communicative function
Discussing vacations

Teaching Resource Options

PRINT

Workbook PE, pp. 181–186
Unit 7 Resource Book
   Communipak, pp. 148–170
   Video Activities, pp. 24–25
   Videoscript, p. 28
   Workbook TE, pp. 1–6

AUDIO & VISUAL

Overhead Transparencies
43 *Les activités sportives*

VIDEO PROGRAM

  MODULE 21

21.5 Introduction: Les vacances
(3:12–3:45 min.)

21.6 Dialogues: Les vacances
(3:46–4:17 min.)

21.7 Mini-scenes: Qu'est-ce qu'il fait? (4:18–4:59 min.)

Supplementary vocabulary
HOLIDAYS
la Hanoukka
la Pâque *(Passover)*
SPORTS AND ACTIVITIES
faire du ballet
faire du bateau
faire du deltaplane *(hang gliding)*
faire du motocross
faire du ski alpin
faire du ski de fond *(cross-country)*
faire du vélo
faire de la danse moderne
faire de la gymnastique
faire de la marche *(fast walking)*
faire de la moto
faire de la natation *(swimming)*
faire du skate *(skateboarding)*

Looking ahead The negative construction (**Je ne fais pas de ski**) will be presented in Unit 8 when students learn the partitive.

B **VOCABULAIRE** Les vacances

Qu'est-ce que tu vas faire cet été?

Je vais aller à la mer.

▶ *How to plan your vacation activities:*

Qu'est-ce que tu vas faire	à **Noël?**	**Noël** *Christmas*
	à **Pâques**	**Pâques** *Easter*
	pendant *(during)* **les vacances** de printemps	**les vacances** *vacation*
	pendant **les grandes vacances**	**les grandes vacances** *summer vacation*
	cet été	

| Je vais aller | à **la mer** *(ocean, shore)*. |
| | à **la montagne** *(mountains)* |

Je vais voyager	en avion.	**un avion** *plane*
	en train	**un train** *train*
	en autocar	**un autocar, un car** *touring bus*
	en bateau	**un bateau** *boat, ship*
	en voiture	

Je vais voyager en avion.

| Je vais voyager | **seul(e)** *(alone)*. |
| | avec ma famille |

Je vais **passer** *(to spend)*	dix jours	là-bas.	**un jour** *day*
	six semaines		**une semaine** *week*
	deux mois		**un mois** *month*

J'aime le ski!

| J'aime | **le ski** *(skiing)*. | En hiver, je vais à la montagne pour **faire du ski** *(to ski)*. |
| | **le ski nautique** *(water-skiing)* | En été, je vais à la mer pour **faire du ski nautique** *(to water-ski)*. |

Mont Ste-Anne
Le Ski

312 trois cent douze
Unité 7

COMPREHENSION Sports

PROPS: Blue cards with logos for jogging, skiing, waterskiing, mountain climbing; red cards with logos for sailing, swimming, and windsurfing.

Identify the cards: **Ces cartes représentent des sports différents. Voici l'escalade.**
Hand out the sports cards.

Moi, j'aime le ski. Qui aime le ski ici?
X et Y, vous aimez le ski? [Oui.]
Give them "skiing" card.
Talk about who does what sport.
X et Y, vous faites du ski en hiver? [Oui]
Ils font du ski.

VOCABULAIRE Activités sportives

le sport	sport(s)	Je **fais du sport.**	I practice sports.
le jogging	jogging	Nous **faisons du jogging.**	We jog.
la natation	swimming	Tu **fais de la natation?**	Do you go swimming?
l'escalade (f.)	rock climbing	J'aime **faire de l'escalade.**	I like to go rock climbing.
le ski	skiing	Tu **fais du ski?**	Do you ski?
le ski nautique	water-skiing	Anne **fait du ski nautique.**	Anne water-skis.
la voile	sailing	Paul **fait de la voile.**	Paul sails.
la planche à voile	windsurfing	Vous **faites de la planche à voile?**	Do you windsurf?

le roller	in-line skating	**des rollers**	in-line skates
le skate	skateboarding	**un skate**	skateboard
le snowboard	snowboarding	**un snowboard**	snowboard
le VTT	mountain biking	**un VTT**	mountain bike

→ To describe participation in individual sports or other activities, the French use the construction:

faire	du / de la / de l'	+	SPORT or ACTIVITY	le roller → **faire du roller**
				la voile → **faire de la voile**
				l'escalade → **faire de l'escalade**

NOTE *culturelle*

Les sports d'hiver

À Noël et pendant les vacances de février, beaucoup de jeunes Français vont à la montagne avec leur famille pour faire des sports d'hiver. Certaines écoles organisent des «classes de neige». Les élèves étudient le matin et font du sport l'après-midi.

Le ski est un sport très populaire. Mais beaucoup de jeunes préfèrent faire du snowboard, une spécialité dans laquelle° plusieurs° Françaises ont été° championnes olympiques.

laquelle which   **plusieurs** several   **ont été** have been

trois cent treize
Leçon 21 313

Realia note
Mont Ste-Anne is a popular ski and snowboard resort in Beaupré, Quebec. It is about 400 miles from Boston, MA and 575 miles from New York, NY. There are more than 55 trails covering 40+ miles of terrain. The mountain's highest elevation is 2, 625 feet. Mont-Ste-Anne has an average season of over 160 days. The mountain is also a popular summer destination that offers golf **(le golf)**, mountain biking **(le vélo de montagne)**, hiking **(la randonnée pedestre)**, and paragliding **(le parapente)** to its visitors.

Language note
le snowboard: the French also may say: **le surf des neiges**
Also:
le surf (ocean surfboarding)
un surf (surfboard)
VTT = vélo tout terrain

Note culturelle
Culture notes
• Mardi Gras is the last Tuesday before Lent **(le Carême)**, which begins on Ash Wednesday **(le mercredi des cendres)**. Traditionally, Lent (the 40 days before Easter) was a period of penance and fasting, and so Mardi gras – or fat Tuesday – was the last day to eat and be merry. In France (and areas with historic ties to France: **le Québec, Haïti, la Nouvelle Orléans,** etc.), this day is known as **Carnaval** and is celebrated with parades, floats, and masked balls.

• **Le 14 juillet** commemorates the beginning of the French Revolution (1789–1799). The holiday is celebrated with fireworks **(des feux d'artifice)** and dancing in the streets **(des bals populaires)**.

• **Le onze novembre** commemorates the 1918 signing of the Armistice ending World War I. It is the day on which the French remember their veterans and those who died for their country.

GAME Activités

PROPS: Transparency 43: *Les activités sportives*
With the overhead projector turned off, have one student come to the front and write an "X" by one of the activities on the transparency. Students at their desks try to guess which activity the student has chosen.
Tu fais de la natation? [Non, je ne fais pas de natation.]

Tu fais du ski? [Oui, je fais du ski.]
The student at the front verifies the correct guess by turning on the overhead projector. The student who guesses then comes forward, turns off the projector, erases the "X," chooses another activity, and the game continues.

Teaching Resource Options

PRINT

Workbook PE, pp. 181–186
Unit 7 Resource Book
   Communipak, pp. 148–170
   Video Activities, pp. 25–26
   Videoscript, p. 28
   Workbook TE, pp. 1–6

VIDEO PROGRAM

  MODULE 21

21.8 Vignette culturelle: La planche à voile (5:00–6:21 min.)

4 **COMMUNICATION** describing one's vacation preferences

1. Mes vacances préférés sont (les grands vacances).
2. Pendant les grands vacances, je préfère (aller à la mer).
3. En été, je vais à la plage spécialement pour (nager).
4. Je voudrais aller dans le Colorado pour (faire du ski).
5. Je voudrais aller à la Martinique principalement pour (faire de la plongée).
6. Mon sport préféré est (le snowboard).
7. Pour mon anniversaire, je préfère avoir (un VTT).
8. Avec mes copains, je préfère (faire du skate).
9. Quand je voyage pendant les vacances, je préfère voyager (avec ma famille).
10. Je voudrais aller à Paris et rester là-bas pendant (dix jours).

Cultural note Remind students that Martinique is a French island in the Caribbean.

Variation See variation for Act. 1, p. 311.

Challenge Have students give an original completion for each sentence. For example:

1. Mes vacances préférées sont [les vacances de "Thanksgiving".]

5 **COMPREHENSION** describing people's activities

1. Il fait du sport (du jogging).
2. Tu fais de la planche à voile (du ski nautique).
3. Nous faisons de l'escalade (du camping).
4. Tu fais du ski.
5. Ils font du camping (de la voile).
6. Elles font de la gymnastique.
7. Vous faites de la voile (du ski nautique, de la planche à voile).
8. Nous faisons de la planche à voile (de la voile, du ski nautique).
9. Nous faisons du jogging (du sport).
10. Je fais du ski nautique (de la voile, de la planche à voile).

---

4 **Et toi?**

PARLER/ÉCRIRE Indique tes préférences personnelles en complétant les phrases suivantes.

1. Mes vacances préférées sont …
   - les vacances de Noël
   - les vacances de printemps
   - les grandes vacances
   - … ?

2. Pendant les grandes vacances, je préfère …
   - aller à la mer
   - aller à la montagne
   - aller à la campagne
   - … ?

3. En été, je vais à la plage spécialement (*especially*) pour …
   - nager
   - faire du ski nautique
   - bronzer (*to get a tan*)
   - … ?

4. Je voudrais aller dans le Colorado pour …
   - faire du ski
   - faire de l'escalade
   - faire du VTT
   - … ?

5. Je voudrais aller à la Martinique principalement (*mainly*) pour …
   - parler français
   - faire de la planche à voile
   - faire de la plongée (*scuba diving*)
   - … ?

5 **Leurs activités favorites**

PARLER/ÉCRIRE Les personnes suivantes ont certaines activités favorites. Lisez où elles sont et dites ce qu'elles font. Pour cela choisissez une activité appropriée de la liste à droite.

▶ Anne est dans un studio de danse.
  Elle fait de la danse moderne.

1. Jean-Pierre est au stade.
2. Je suis à la plage.
3. En juillet, nous allons dans le Colorado.
4. Tu passes les vacances de Noël en Suisse.
5. Mes copains passent les vacances à la campagne.
6. Pauline et Marie sont à la salle (*room*) de gymnastique.
7. Vous êtes à la mer.
8. Nous sommes à Tahiti.
9. Avant le dîner, nous allons au parc municipal.
10. Je suis à la Martinique.

- la gymnastique
- la danse moderne
- le sport
- le jogging
- le camping
- la voile
- la planche à voile
- le ski
- le ski nautique
- l'escalade

CLASSROOM MANAGEMENT Group practice

For Act. 4, divide the class into groups of 4 or 5 students. Name one person as recorder (**secrétaire**).

For each question, members of the group each state their preferences, by selecting one of the completions.

The **secrétaires** tally the responses of their groups and report back to the entire class or hand results to the teacher.

**La majorité préfère les grandes vacances.
Pendant les grands vacances, la majorité préfère rester avec leur famille. …**

6. Mon sport préféré est ...

- la natation
- le snowboard
- le roller
- ... ?

7. Pour mon anniversaire, je préfère avoir ...

- un skate
- des rollers
- un VTT
- ... ?

8. Avec mes copains, je préfère ...

- faire du roller
- faire du skate
- faire du jogging
- ... ?

9. Quand je voyage pendant les vacances, je préfère voyager ...

- seul(e)
- avec mes copains
- avec ma famille
- ... ?

10. Je voudrais aller à Paris et rester là-bas pendant *(for)* ...

- dix jours
- trois semaines
- six mois
- ... ?

6 ✐ *Questions personnelles* **PARLER/ÉCRIRE**

1. En général, qu'est-ce que tu fais pendant les vacances de Noël?
2. Est-ce que tu vas voyager pendant les grandes vacances? Où vas-tu aller? Combien de temps *(How long)* est-ce que tu vas rester là-bas?
3. Qu'est-ce que tu aimes faire quand tu es à la plage?
4. Est-ce que tu voyages souvent? Comment voyages-tu?

6 **COMMUNICATION** answering personal questions

Answers will vary.
1. En général, pendant les vacances de Noël je reste avec ma famille et je rends visite à ma grand-mère.
2. Oui, je vais voyager pendant les grandes vacances. Je vais aller au Canada. Je vais passer trois semaines là-bas. (Non, je ne vais pas voyager pendant les grandes vacances.)
3. Quand je suis à la plage, j'aime nager et parler avec mes amis. J'aime aussi faire de la voile et du ski nautique.
4. Oui, je voyage souvent. Je voyage en avion. (Non, je ne voyage pas souvent.)

COMMUNAUTÉS

During summer vacation, some American teenagers spend a month in a French-speaking region doing community service. At the same time they have the opportunity to meet other young people and to use their French skills.

You can go on the Internet to research some of the non-profit organizations that sponsor such exchanges. It is not too early to begin planning ahead.

trois cent quinze
Leçon 21 315

À VOTRE TOUR

Main Topic
• Recapitulation and review

Teaching Resource Options

PRINT

Workbook PE, pp. 181–186
Unit 7 Resource Book
    Audioscript, p. 29
    Communipak, pp. 148–170
    Family Involvement, pp. 19–20
    Workbook TE, pp. 1–6
    Assessment
    Lesson 21 Quiz, pp. 33–34
    Portfolio Assessment, Unit 1 URB
        pp. 155–164
    Audioscript for Quiz 21, pp. 31–32
    Answer Keys, pp. 213–216

AUDIO & VISUAL
Audio Program
CD 4 Tracks 1, 2, 3
CD 16 Track 1

TECHNOLOGY
Test Generator CD-ROM/eTest Plus
    Online

① ORAL COMPREHENSION

1. B	2. A	3. A	4. B
5. B	6. A	7. B	8. B
9. A	10. A	11. B	12. A

② WRITTEN SELF-EXPRESSION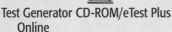

Answers will vary.
  • Le week-end prochain, je vais …
  –nettoyer ma chambre
  –regarder la télé
  –faire mes devoirs
  –aider mes parents

  • Je vais …
  –faire du jogging
  –jouer au basket
  –passer samedi après-midi avec mes amis
    au café
  –laver la voiture

Follow-up activity Have students compare compositions. How many similar activities did they choose?

Middle School Copymasters

Puzzle: *Qu'est-ce que tu fais ce week-end?*, pp. 113–115

À votre tour!

① 🎧 Écoutez bien!

ÉCOUTER On weekends, you can stay in and take care of things at home, or you can go out and have fun. Listen carefully to what the people are saying. If they refer to an indoor activity, mark A. If they refer to an outdoor activity, mark B.

	1	2	3	4	5	6
A: À l'intérieur						
B: À l'extérieur						

A. À l'intérieur

B. À l'extérieur

② ✏️ Composition: Le week-end prochain

ÉCRIRE Make plans for next weekend. Prepare a list of activities describing …

  • four things that you are going to do at home
  • four things that you are going to do outside

Samedi, je vais ranger ma chambre. Après, je …

③ ✏️ Composition: Mes sports préférés

ÉCRIRE Describe two sports that you engage in during each of the following times of year.

  • Pendant les vacances d'été
  • En hiver
  • En toute (any) saison

À VOTRE TOUR

Depending on your goals and objectives, you may or may not wish to assign all of the activities in the **À votre tour** section.

GROUP PRACTICE

In Act. 4 and 5, you may want to have students work in trios, with two performing and one consulting the Answer Key and acting as monitor.

Créa-dialogue

PARLER Des amis parlent de leurs projets. Avec un(e) camarade de classe, choisissez une scène et composez le dialogue correspondant.

▸ —Où vas-tu <u>vendredi</u>?
—Je vais <u>en ville</u>.
—Qu'est-ce que tu vas faire là-bas?
—Je vais <u>faire des achats</u>.

▸

| vendredi | en ville | |

1. samedi matin		2. samedi après-midi		3. à Noël	à Aspen	
4. pendant les vacances de printemps	en Floride		5. en juillet		6. en août	
7. demain matin		8. dimanche après-midi		9. cet été	

 Conversation dirigée

PARLER Avec un(e) camarade, composez un dialogue basé sur les instructions suivantes. Thomas demande à Hélène si elle a des projets de vacances.

Thomas 	asks Hélène where she is going this summer	→ ←	says that she is going to the ocean with friends	**Hélène** 
	asks her if they are going to travel by car	→ ←	answers that they are going to travel by train because they do not have a car	
	asks her if she is going to go sailing	→ ←	answers yes and says that she is also going to windsurf	
	says good-bye to Hélène and wishes her a good vacation **(Bonnes vacances!)**	→	answers good-bye	

 **LESSON REVIEW**
CLASSZONE.COM

PORTFOLIO ASSESSMENT

You will probably select only one speaking activity and one writing activity to go into the students' portfolios for Unit 7.

In this lesson, you might suggest that students do their own variations of Act. 5 as an oral portfolio recording.

---

3 **WRITTEN SELF-EXPRESSION**

Answers will vary.
Pendant les vacances d'été, je nage et je fais de la planche à voile).

En hiver, je (fais du ski et du snowboard).

En toute saison, je (fais du jogging et je fais du roller).

---

4 **COMPREHENSION**

Answers will vary.
1. —Où vas-tu samedi matin?
—Je vais à la campagne.
—Qu'est-ce que tu vas faire là-bas?
—Je vais faire une promenade à vélo.
2. —Où vas-tu samedi après-midi?
—Je vais à la campagne.
—Qu'est-ce que tu vas faire là-bas?
—Je vais faire un pique-nique.
3. —Où vas-tu à Noël?
—Je vais à Aspen.
—Qu'est-ce que tu vas faire là-bas?
—Je vais faire du ski.
4. —Où vas-tu pendant les vacances de printemps?
—Je vais en Floride.
—Qu'est-ce que tu vas faire là-bas?
—Je vais faire du ski nautique.
5. —Où vas-tu en juillet?
—Je vais à la mer (plage).
—Qu'est-ce que tu vas faire là-bas?
—Je vais faire de la voile.
6. —Où vas-tu en août?
—Je vais à la montagne.
—Qu'est-ce que tu vas faire là-bas?
—Je vais faire de l'escalade.
7. —Où vas-tu demain matin?
—Je vais (au parc).
—Qu'est-ce que tu vas faire là-bas?
—Je vais faire du jogging.
8. —Où vas-tu dimanche après-midi?
—Je vais (à la piscine).
—Qu'est-ce que tu vas faire là-bas?
—Je vais (nager).
9. —Où vas-tu cet été?
—Je vais (à la campagne).
—Qu'est-ce que tu vas faire là-bas?
—Je vais (faire du camping).

---

5 **GUIDED ORAL EXPRESSION**

JP: Où vas-tu cet été?
H: Je vais à la mer avec des amis.
JP: Est-ce que vous allez voyager en voiture?
H: (Non,) nous allons voyager en train parce que nous n'avons pas de voiture.
JP: Est-ce que tu vas faire de la voile?
H: Oui, et je vais faire de la planche à voile aussi.
JP: Au revoir, Hélène. Bonnes vacances!
H: Au revoir!

Leçon 22

Main Topic Describing what happened last weekend

Teaching Resource Options

PRINT

Workbook PE, pp. 187–194
Activités pour tous PE, pp. 115–117
Block Scheduling Copymasters, pp. 169–175
Unit 7 Resource Book
  Activités pour tous TE, pp. 43–45
  Audioscript, pp. 67, 68–70
  Communipak, pp. 148–170
  Lesson Plans, pp. 46–47
  Block Scheduling Lesson Plans, pp. 48–50
  Absent Student Copymasters, pp. 51–56
  Video Activities, pp. 59–64
  Videoscript, pp. 65–66
  Workbook TE, pp. 35–42

AUDIO & VISUAL

Audio Program
CD 4 Tracks 4, 5
CD 11 Tracks 7–12

TECHNOLOGY

Online Workbook

VIDEO PROGRAM

 MODULE 22
Mercredi après-midi

TOTAL TIME: 6:13 min.
  DVD Disk 2
  Videotape 4 (COUNTER: 6:35 min.)

22.1 Introduction: Listening
  – Mercredi après-midi
  (6:46–7:57 min.)

22.2 Dialogue: L'examen de maths
  (7:58–8:28 min.)

22.3 Mini-scenes: Listening
  – Qu'est-ce que vous avez fait hier?
  (8:29–9:53 min.)

22.4 Mini-scenes: Listening
  – Est-ce que tu as joué au tennis?
  (9:54–10:45 min.)

22.5 Mini-scenes: Speaking
  – Est-ce que tu as joué au tennis?
  (10:46–11:45 min.)

22.6 Vignette culturelle: Le cinéma
  (11:46–12:48 min.)

Comprehension practice Play the entire module through as an introduction to the lesson.

318 · Conversation et Culture
Unité 7 LEÇON 22

LEÇON 22

Vive le week-end!

Le week-end, nous avons nos occupations préférées. Certaines personnes aiment aller en ville et rencontrer leurs amis.

D'autres préfèrent rester à la maison et bricoler. Qu'est-ce que les personnes suivantes ont fait le week-end dernier?

Others / do things around the house
did … do
last

Le week-end	Le week-end dernier

J'aime acheter des vêtements.	J'ai acheté des vêtements. *bought*

Tu aimes réparer ton vélo.	Tu as réparé ton vélo. *fixed*

M. Lambert aime travailler dans le jardin.	Il a travaillé dans le jardin. *worked*

Nous aimons organiser des boums.	Nous avons organisé une boum. *organized*

318 trois cent dix-huit
Unité 7

SETTING THE SCENE

In this lesson, the video module is independent of the opening text. However, the opening scenes are narrated in Section 1 of the audio program.

The video first shows how Jean-Claude and Nathalie spent the day on Wednesday. Then it shows them talking on Thursday morning when Jean-Claude realizes that he has forgotten about his math test.

To set the scene, ask students if they have ever forgotten about a test (**oublier la date d'un examen**). If so, how did they perform on the exam?

Le week-end

Vous aimez jouer au foot.

Pluton et Philibert aiment rencontrer leurs amis.

Le week-end dernier

Vous <u>avez joué</u> au foot. *played*

Ils <u>ont rencontré</u> leurs amis. *met*

Et toi?

Indique si oui ou non tu as fait les choses suivantes le week-end dernier.
Pour cela complète les phrases suivantes.

1. (J'ai/Je n'ai pas) … acheté des vêtements.
2. (J'ai/Je n'ai pas) … réparé mon vélo.
3. (J'ai/Je n'ai pas) … travaillé dans le jardin.
4. (J'ai/Je n'ai pas) … organisé une boum.
5. (J'ai/Je n'ai pas) … joué au foot.
6. (J'ai/Je n'ai pas) … rencontré mes amis.

NOTE culturelle

Le week-end

Le week-end ne commence pas° le vendredi soir pour tout le monde.° Dans beaucoup d'écoles françaises, les élèves ont classe le samedi matin. Pour eux, le week-end commence seulement° le samedi à midi.

Que font les jeunes Français le samedi? Ça dépend. Beaucoup° vont en ville. Ils vont dans des magasins pour écouter les nouveaux CD ou pour regarder, essayer° et parfois° acheter des vêtements. Ils vont au café ou au cinéma avec leurs copains. Certains° préfèrent louer un film et rester chez eux ou aller chez des copains. Parfois

ils vont à une soirée. Là on écoute de la musique, on mange des sandwichs et on danse …

En général, le dimanche est réservé aux activités familiales.° Un week-end, on invite des cousins. Un autre° week-end, on rend visite aux grands-parents … Le dimanche, on déjeune° et on dîne en famille.° Le soir, on regarde la télé et souvent on fait ses devoirs pour les classes du lundi matin.

ne commence pas *does not begin* **tout le monde** *everyone* **seulement** *only* **Beaucoup** *Many* **essayer** *try on*
parfois *sometimes* **Certains** *Some of them* **activités familiales** *family activities* **Un autre** *Another* **déjeune** *has lunch*
en famille *at home (with the family)*

CROSS-CULTURAL OBSERVATION

The **Vignette culturelle** of the video presents one of the favorite pastimes of French young people: going to the movies.

Have students watch to see whether they have the same taste in films as the students who were interviewed in Paris.

The **Vignette** shows two short interviews, the first with two young boys and the second with a girl. The boys like going to see "L'Ours." The first boy likes **les films d'adventures**; his friend's favorite actress is Kim Basinger in "Batman." The girl's favorite actress is Marilyn Monroe.

Communication describing what one did last weekend

Answers will vary.
1. J'ai acheté des vêtements. (Je n'ai pas acheté de vêtements.)
2. J'ai réparé mon vélo. (Je n'ai pas réparé mon vélo.)
3. J'ai travaillé dans le jardin. (Je n'ai pas travaillé dans le jardin.)
4. J'ai organisé une boum. (Je n'ai pas organisé de boum.)
5. J'ai joué au foot. (Je n'ai pas joué au foot.)
6. J'ai rencontré mes amis. (Je n'ai pas rencontré mes amis.)

Expansion Ask for more information. Have students give only short answers unless they have been practicing the **passé composé**.
1. Où? Quels vêtements?
2. Quand?
3. Quel jour? Avec qui?
4. Quand? Où?
5. Où?
6. Où?

SECTION A

Communicative function
Expressing thirst, hunger, and other feelings

Teaching Resource Options

PRINT
Workbook PE, pp. 187–194
Unit 7 Resource Book
    Audioscript, p. 67
    Communipak, pp. 148–170
    Workbook TE, pp. 35–42

AUDIO & VISUAL
Audio Program
CD 4 Track 6

Overhead Transparencies
44 Expressions with *avoir*

TECHNOLOGY
Power Presentations

 Re-entry and review

The purpose of this section is to have students review **avoir** before practicing the passé composé. Students have already learned **avoir faim/soif** (Lesson 10).

Teaching strategy Introduce the **avoir** expressions using appropriate gestures. For example:
avoir faim *(pointing to stomach)*
avoir soif *(pointing to throat)*
avoir tort *(wagging index finger)*
avoir de la chance *(extending arms in a "youpie!" manner)*
See **Comprehension** activity, p. 74.

Supplementary vocabulary
avoir sommeil *to be (feel) sleepy*
avoir peur *to be scared, afraid*

 COMPREHENSION evaluating actions of others

1. Elle a raison!   6. Il a tort!
2. Nous avons raison! 7. Il a tort!
3. Tu as raison!   8. Ils ont tort!
4. Vous avez tort!   9. Vous avez raison!
5. Ils ont raison!   10. Elle a raison!

A Les expressions avec *avoir*

Note the use of **avoir** in the following sentences:

J'ai **faim**.   *I am **hungry.***
Brigitte **a soif**.   *Brigitte **is thirsty.***

French speakers use **avoir** in many expressions where English speakers use the verb *to be*.

VOCABULAIRE Expressions avec *avoir*

avoir chaud	*to be (feel) warm*	Quand j'**ai chaud** en été, je vais à la plage.
avoir froid	*to be (feel) cold*	Est-ce que tu **as froid?** Voici ton pull.
avoir faim	*to be hungry*	Tu **as faim?** Est-ce que tu veux une pizza?
avoir soif	*to be thirsty*	J'**ai soif.** Je voudrais une limonade.
avoir raison	*to be right*	Est-ce que les profs **ont** toujours **raison?**
avoir tort	*to be wrong*	Marc ne fait pas ses devoirs. Il **a tort!**
avoir de la chance	*to be lucky*	J'**ai de la chance.** J'ai des amis sympathiques.

1 Tort ou raison?

PARLER/ÉCRIRE Informez-vous sur les personnes suivantes et dites si, à votre avis, elles ont tort ou raison.

▶ Les élèves ne font pas leurs devoirs.
  Ils ont tort!

▶ Tu écoutes le prof.
  Tu as raison!

1. Catherine est généreuse avec ses copines.
2. Nous aidons nos parents.
3. Tu fais tes devoirs.
4. Vous êtes très impatients avec vos amis.
5. Mes copains étudient le français.
6. Jean-François dépense son argent inutilement *(uselessly)*.
7. M. Legros mange trop *(too much)*.
8. Alain et Nicolas sont impolis *(impolite)*.
9. Vous rangez votre chambre.
10. Léa est polie *(polite)* avec les voisins.

2 De bonnes questions

PARLER/ÉCRIRE Étudiez ce que font les personnes suivantes. Ensuite, posez une question logique sur chaque personne. Pour cela, utilisez l'une des expressions suivantes:

avoir faim	avoir soif	avoir chaud
avoir froid		avoir de la chance

▶ Philippe va au restaurant.
  Est-ce que Philippe a faim?

1. Tu veux un soda.
2. Jean-Pierre mange une pizza.
3. Cécile porte un manteau.
4. Vous gagnez à la loterie.
5. Vous faites des sandwichs.
6. Tu mets ton blouson.
7. Mes copains vont aller à la piscine.
8. Ces élèves n'étudient pas beaucoup, mais ils réussissent toujours à leurs examens.
9. Tu as des grands-parents très généreux.

WARM-UP Quel âge as-tu?

Quickly review the forms of **avoir** by asking students how old they are.
Quel âge as-tu, X? [J'ai [treize] ans.]
Dis, Y, quel âge a X? [X a treize ans.]
Et Z, quel âge as-tu? [J'ai treize ans.]
Comme X! Alors, Z et X, quel âge avez-vous? [Nous avons treize ans.]

Eh bien, tout le monde, quel âge ont X et Z? [Ils ont treize ans.]

Expansion: Hold up magazine ads and have the class estimate the people's ages.

B Le passé composé des verbes en *-er*

The sentences below describe past events. In the French sentences, the verbs are in the PASSÉ COMPOSÉ. Note the forms of the passé composé and its English equivalents.

Hier j'**ai réparé** mon vélo.
Le week-end dernier, Marc **a organisé** une boum.
Pendant les vacances, nous **avons visité** Paris.

*Yesterday I **fixed** my bicycle.*
*Last weekend, Marc **organized** a party.*
*During vacation, we **visited** Paris.*

FORMS

The PASSÉ COMPOSÉ is composed of two words. For most verbs, it is formed as follows:

> PRESENT of **avoir** + PAST PARTICIPLE

Note the forms of the passé composé for **visiter.**

PASSÉ COMPOSÉ		PRESENT OF avoir + PAST PARTICIPLE	
J'**ai visité** Québec.		j' **ai**	
Tu **as visité** Paris.		tu **as**	
Il/Elle/On **a visité** Montréal.		il/elle/on **a**	**visité**
Nous **avons visité** Genève.		nous **avons**	
Vous **avez visité** Strasbourg.		vous **avez**	
Ils/Elles **ont visité** Fort-de-France.		ils/elles **ont**	

→ For all **-er** verbs, the past participle is formed by replacing the **-er** of the infinitive by **-é** .

jou`er`	→	jou`é`	Nous **avons joué** au tennis.
parl`er`	→	parl`é`	Éric **a parlé** à Nathalie.
téléphon`er`	→	téléphon`é`	Vous **avez téléphoné** à Cécile.

LEARNING ABOUT LANGUAGE

The PASSÉ COMPOSÉ, as its name indicates, is a "past" tense "composed" of two parts. It is formed like the present perfect tense in English.

AUXILIARY VERB + PAST PARTICIPLE of the main verb

Nous **avons** **travaillé**.
We have   worked.

USES

The passé composé is used to describe past actions and events. It has several English equivalents.

J'**ai visité** Montréal. ⎰ *I visited Montreal.*
⎱ *I have visited Montreal.*
⎱ *I did visit Montreal.*

trois cent vingt et un
Leçon 22 321

COMPREHENSION Past activities

Review the gestures your class developed for the verbs on pp. 94-95.

Tout le monde: dansez.
Chantez. Téléphonez. Nagez.

Have an individual act out an activity.

X, joue au tennis. C'est bien. Merci.

Then describe what the student did.

Qu'est-ce que X a fait?
Il a joué au tennis.

Then have two students act out an activity.

Y et Z, dansez. Voilà, c'est très bien.

Describe what the students did.

Qu'est-ce que Y et Z ont fait?
Ils ont dansé.

---

2 COMPREHENSION asking logical questions

1. Est-ce que tu as soif?
2. Est-ce qu'il a faim?
3. Est-ce qu'elle a froid?
4. Est-ce que vous avez de la chance?
5. Est-ce que vous avez faim?
6. Est-ce que tu as froid?
7. Est-ce qu'ils ont chaud (ont de la chance)?
8. Est-ce qu'ils ont de la chance?
9. Est-ce que tu as de la chance?

SECTION B

Communicative function
Talking about what happened in the past

Language note/Looking ahead
In English, the auxiliary verb is always *to have.* In French, the auxiliary verb is usually, but not always, **avoir.** The passé composé with **être** is presented in Lesson 24.

Teaching strategy If you have been practicing the passé composé orally, this material will be familiar to the students. You will want to focus particularly on the written forms.

Realia notes

- With a population of over two million people, **Montréal** is a bustling commercial and industrial center as well as the artistic and intellectual capital of Quebec. Its inland port, located on an island in the St. Lawrence river, ranks among the busiest in North America. Below the skyscrapers of downtown Montreal is a honeycomb of shopping malls connected to one another and to the various subway stations by underground pedestrian tunnels. This way, in the ice and cold of the Canadian winter, shoppers have easy access to their favorite stores.

- **La Ronde,** an amusement park in Montreal (the largest one in Quebec), is located on a man-made island (**Ile Ste-Hélène**) on the St. Lawrence River. La Ronde is part of the **Parc Jean-Drapeau,** a park which includes other attractions such as the Biosphere. The Parc Jean-Drapeau resides on two islands: **Ile Ste-Hélène** and **Ile Notre-Dame.** There are over 30 rides for thrill-seekers visiting the La Ronde. Also hosted here is the annual Montreal International Fireworks Competition in the summer. The exciting displays can be seen from the nearby Jacques Cartier Bridge which is closed to traffic for this purpose.

Teaching Resource Options

PRINT

Workbook PE, pp. 187–194
Unit 7 Resource Book
    Communipak, pp. 148–170
    Workbook TE, pp. 35–42

3 DESCRIPTION saying what people bought

1. Pauline a acheté un jean.
2. J'ai acheté une montre.
3. Tu as acheté une guitare.
4. Vous avez acheté des chemises.
5. Nous avons acheté une chaîne stéréo.
6. Stéphanie et Isabelle on acheté des chaussures.
7. Patrick et Jean-Paul ont acheté des livres.
8. M. et Mme Dupont ont acheté une voiture.

4 ROLE PLAY talking about past activities

1. —J'ai acheté des CD.
   —Eh bien, moi, j'ai acheté des magazines.
2. —J'ai dîné au restaurant.
   —Eh bien, moi, j'ai dîné chez moi.
3. —J'ai invité mon cousin.
   —Eh bien, moi, j'ai invité un ami.
4. —J'ai téléphoné à ma tante.
   —Eh bien, moi, j'ai téléphoné à mon grand-père.
5. —J'ai aidé ma mère.
   —Eh bien, moi, j'ai aidé mon père.
6. —J'ai nettoyé la cuisine.
   —Eh bien, moi, j'ai nettoyé le garage.
7. —J'ai réparé ma mobylette.
   —Eh bien, moi, j'ai réparé mon vélo.
8. —J'ai assisté à un match de foot.
   —Eh bien, moi, j'ai assisté à un concert.
9. —J'ai lavé mes tee-shirts.
   —Eh bien, moi, j'ai lavé mes jeans.
10. —J'ai regardé un film.
    —Eh bien, moi, j'ai regardé une comédie.
11. —J'ai rangé ma chambre.
    —Eh bien, moi, j'ai rangé le salon.
12. —J'ai loué un DVD.
    —Eh bien, moi, j'ai loué une cassette vidéo.

5 ROLE PLAY asking about past actions

—Tu as … ?
—Mais oui, j'ai …

1. préparé les sandwichs
2. rangé le salon
3. réparé la chaîne hi-fi
4. apporté un DVD
5. invité nos copains
6. téléphoné aux voisins

Variation Have students ask and answer questions in the plural.
– **Vous avez acheté des sodas?**
– **Mais oui, nous avons acheté des sodas.**

---

3 Achats

PARLER/ÉCRIRE Samedi dernier *(Last Saturday)*, les personnes suivantes ont fait des achats. Dites ce que chaque personne a acheté.

▶ Philippe (des CD)
Philippe a acheté des CD.

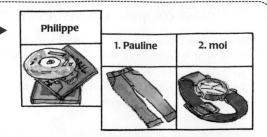

| | Philippe | 1. Pauline | 2. moi |

3. toi	4. vous	5. nous	6. Stéphanie et Isabelle	7. Patrick et Jean-Paul	8. M. et Mme Dupont

4 Vive la différence!

PARLER Caroline et Jean-Pierre sont des copains, mais ils aiment faire des choses différentes. Ils parlent de ce qu'ils ont fait ce week-end.

▶ jouer au volley (au tennis)

1. acheter des CD (des magazines)
2. dîner au restaurant (chez moi)
3. inviter mon cousin (un ami)
4. téléphoner à ma tante (à mon grand-père)
5. aider ma mère (mon père)
6. nettoyer la cuisine (le garage)
7. réparer ma mobylette (mon vélo)
8. assister à un match de foot (à un concert)
9. laver mes tee-shirts (mes jeans)
10. regarder un film (une comédie)
11. ranger ma chambre (le salon)
12. louer un DVD (une cassette vidéo)

J'ai joué au volley.

Eh bien, moi, j'ai joué au tennis.

5 La boum

PARLER Anne et Éric organisent une boum ce week-end. Anne demande à Éric s'il a fait les choses suivantes. Il répond oui.

▶ acheter des sodas? —**Tu as acheté des sodas?**
—**Mais oui, j'ai acheté des sodas.**

1. préparer les sandwichs?
2. ranger le salon?
3. réparer la chaîne hi-fi?
4. apporter un DVD?
5. inviter nos copains?
6. téléphoner aux voisins?

GAME Samedi dernier

You can treat Act. 6 as a team game. Divide the class into teams of three. Each team picks a person from column A and decides what that subject did last Saturday. All three team members must then write the same sentence down correctly.

Then the team formulates another sentence using elements of columns A, B, and C, and again all three members write it down.

The game is played against the clock. The team whose three members have written the greatest number of correct sentences in five minutes is the winner.

6 Un jeu

PARLER/ÉCRIRE Décrivez ce que certaines personnes ont fait samedi dernier. Pour cela, faites des phrases logiques en utilisant les éléments des Colonnes A, B et C.

▶ **Vous avez assisté à un concert de jazz.**

A	B	C
nous	acheter	une boum
vous	assister	un musée
Marc	dîner	des vêtements
Hélène et Juliette	jouer	un film
Éric et Stéphanie	organiser	aux jeux vidéo
mes copains	louer	dans le jardin
les voisins	travailler	dans un restaurant vietnamien
	visiter	à un concert de jazz

VOCABULAIRE Expressions pour la conversation

▶ *How to indicate the order in which actions take place:*

d'abord	*first*	**D'abord,** nous avons invité nos copains à la boum.
après	*after, afterwards*	**Après,** tu as préparé des sandwichs.
ensuite	*then, after that*	**Ensuite,** Jacques a acheté des jus de fruit.
enfin	*at last*	**Enfin,** vous avez décoré le salon.
finalement	*finally*	**Finalement,** j'ai apporté ma radiocassette.

7 Dans quel ordre?

PARLER/ÉCRIRE Décrivez ce que les personnes suivantes ont fait dans l'ordre logique.

▶ nous (manger / préparer la salade / acheter des pizzas)
D'abord, nous avons acheté des pizzas.
Après, nous avons préparé la salade.
Ensuite, nous avons mangé.

1. Alice (travailler / trouver un job / acheter une moto)
2. les touristes canadiens (voyager en avion / visiter Paris / réserver les billets [*tickets*])
3. tu (assister au concert / acheter un billet / acheter le programme)
4. vous (danser / apporter des CD / inviter des copains)
5. nous (payer l'addition [*check*]/dîner / trouver un restaurant)

trois cent vingt-trois
Leçon 22 323

---

6 COMPREHENSION making logical statements about past events

Answers will vary.
Nous avons (acheté des vêtements).
Vous avez (assisté à un concert de jazz).
Marc a (dîné dans un restaurant vietnamien).
Hélène et Juliette ont (joué aux jeux vidéo).
Éric et Stéphanie ont (organisé une boum).
Mes copains ont (loué un film).
Les voisins ont (travaillé dans le jardin).

Realia note
Le Jazz en France
The poster reads **"Nice, l'arène du jazz"** *(Nice, the arena of jazz)*. When said aloud, it could be interpreted as **"Nice, la reine du jazz"** *(Nice, the queen of jazz)*.
Jazz has always been popular in France, especially after the creation of the **Hot Club de France** in 1932. Festivals are regularly organized in many cities, attracting both French and American musicians.

7 COMPREHENSION narrating past events in logical sequence

Answers will vary.
1. D'abord, Alice a trouvé un job.
   Après, elle a travaillé.
   Ensuite, elle a acheté une moto.
2. D'abord, les touristes canadiens ont réservé les billets.
   Après, ils ont voyagé en avion.
   Ensuite, ils ont visité Paris.
3. D'abord, tu as acheté un billet.
   Après, tu as acheté le programme.
   Ensuite, tu as assisté au concert.
4. D'abord, vous avez invité des copains.
   Après, vous avez apporté des CD.
   Ensuite, vous avez dansé.
5. D'abord, nous avons trouvé un restaurant.
   Après, nous avons dîné.
   Ensuite, nous avons payé l'addition.

Teaching strategy Note that several logical sequences are sometimes possible.

Middle School Copymasters
Worksheet 2: *Qu'est-ce qu'ils ont?*, p. 117

Teaching Resource Options

PRINT

Workbook PE, pp. 187–194
Unit 7 Resource Book
    Communipak, pp. 148–170
    Video Activities, pp. 59–60
    Videoscript, p. 65
    Workbook TE, pp. 35–42

TECHNOLOGY

Power Presentations

VIDEO PROGRAM

VIDÉO   DVD
 MODULE 22

22.1 Introduction: Mercredi après-midi (6:46–7:57 min.)

22.2 Dialogue: L'examen de maths (7:58–8:28 min.)

Teaching strategy Point out to students that if the English sentence contains *did not* or *didn't,* the equivalent French sentence will use the negative passé composé.

8 **ROLE PLAY** talking about what one did not do

1. –Tu as réparé ta chaîne hi-fi?
   –Euh, non … Je n'ai pas réparé ma chaîne hi-fi.
2. –Tu as apporté tes livres?
   –Euh, non … Je n'ai pas apporté mes livres.
3. –Tu as étudié?
   –Euh, non … Je n'ai pas étudié.
4. –Tu as téléphoné à ta tante?
   –Euh, non … Je n'ai pas téléphoné à ma tante.
5. –Tu as invité tes copains?
   –Euh, non … Je n'ai pas invité mes copains.
6. –Tu as rangé ta chambre?
   –Euh, non … Je n'ai pas rangé ma chambre.
7. –Tu as lavé tes chemises?
   –Euh, non … Je n'ai pas lavé mes chemises.
8. –Tu as loué un film?
   –Euh, non … Je n'ai pas loué de film.
9. –Tu as aidé ta mère?
   –Euh, non … Je n'ai pas aidé ma mère.
10. –Tu as nettoyé le garage?
    –Euh, non … Je n'ai pas nettoyé le garage.
11. –Tu as cherché le programme de télé?
    –Euh, non … Je n'ai pas cherché le programme de télé.
12. –Tu as trouvé ton livre?
    –Euh, non … Je n'ai pas trouvé mon livre.

C Le passé composé: forme négative

Compare the affirmative and negative forms of the passé composé in the sentences below.

AFFIRMATIVE	NEGATIVE	
Alice **a travaillé.**	Éric **n'a pas travaillé.**	*Éric **has not worked.*** *Éric **did not work.***
Nous **avons visité** Paris.	Nous **n'avons pas visité** Lyon.	*We **have not visited** Lyon.* *We **did not visit** Lyon.*

In the negative, the passé composé follows the pattern:

> negative form of **avoir** + PAST PARTICIPLE

Note the negative forms of the passé composé of **travailler.**

PASSÉ COMPOSÉ (NEGATIVE)	PRESENT of **avoir** (NEGATIVE) + PAST PARTICIPLE	
Je **n'ai pas travaillé.** Tu **n'as pas travaillé.** Il/Elle/On **n'a pas travaillé.**	je **n'ai pas** tu **n'as pas** il/elle/on **n'a pas**	
Nous **n'avons pas travaillé.** Vous **n'avez pas travaillé.** Ils/Elles **n'ont pas travaillé.**	nous **n'avons pas** vous **n'avez pas** ils/elles **n'ont pas**	**travaillé**

8 *Oublis (Things forgotten)* - - - - - - - - -

PARLER Nicole demande à Jean-Marc s'il a fait *(did)* les choses suivantes. Jean-Marc a oublié *(forgot)*.

▶ acheter *Paris-Match?*

1. réparer ta chaîne hi-fi?
2. apporter tes livres?
3. étudier?
4. téléphoner à ta tante?
5. inviter tes copains?
6. ranger ta chambre?
7. laver tes chemises?
8. louer un film?
9. aider ta mère?
10. nettoyer le garage?
11. chercher le programme de télé?
12. trouver ton livre?

> Tu as acheté *Paris Match?*
>
> Euh, non …
> Je n'ai pas acheté *Paris Match.*

9 Quel mauvais temps!

PARLER/ÉCRIRE Ce week-end, il a fait mauvais et les personnes suivantes sont restées *(stayed)* chez elles. Dites qu'elles n'ont pas fait les choses suivantes.

▶ nous/nager
Nous n'avons pas nagé.

1. vous/jouer au tennis
2. Philippe/rencontrer ses copains à la plage
3. Nathalie/dîner en ville
4. les voisins/travailler dans le jardin
5. Mlle Lacaze/laver sa voiture
6. mes copains/organiser un pique-nique
7. nous/assister au match de foot
8. toi/visiter le musée

10 Une question d'argent

PARLER/ÉCRIRE Les personnes suivantes n'ont pas beaucoup d'argent. Décrivez leur choix. Pour cela, dites ce qu'elles ont fait et ce qu'elles n'ont pas fait.

▶ nous/dîner au restaurant ou chez nous?
Nous avons dîné chez nous.
Nous n'avons pas dîné au restaurant.

1. Philippe/acheter un tee-shirt ou une chemise?
2. vous/manger un steak ou un sandwich?
3. nous/assister au concert ou au match de foot?
4. les touristes/voyager en car ou en avion?
5. mes voisins/louer une petite maison ou un grand appartement?
6. Marc/passer dix jours ou trois semaines à Paris?

11 Impossibilités

PARLER/ÉCRIRE Sans *(Without)* certaines choses il n'est pas possible de faire certaines activités. Expliquez cela logiquement en choisissant une personne de la Colonne A, un objet de la Colonne B et une activité de la Colonne C.

▶ **Je n'ai pas d'aspirateur. Je n'ai pas nettoyé le salon.**

A	B	C
je	une raquette	surfer sur l'Internet
vous	un billet *(ticket)*	voyager en Europe
nous	un passeport	nettoyer le salon
Frédéric	un ordinateur	regarder la comédie
Éric et Olivier	une télé	assister au concert
Claire et Caroline	un aspirateur *(vacuum cleaner)*	jouer au tennis

---

9 PRACTICE describing what people didn't do

1. Vous n'avez pas joué au tennis.
2. Philippe n'a pas rencontré ses copains à la plage.
3. Nathalie n'a pas dîné en ville.
4. Les voisins n'ont pas travaillé dans le jardin.
5. Mlle Lacaze n'a pas lavé sa voiture.
6. Mes copains n'ont pas organisé de pique-nique.
7. Nous n'avons pas assisté au match de foot.
8. Tu n'as pas visité le musée.

Teaching note Be sure students use **pas de** in item 6.

Realia note
La météo (short for **météorologie**) is the French word for weather report.

10 COMPREHENSION describing what did and did not happen

1. Philippe a acheté un tee-shirt. Il n'a pas acheté de chemise.
2. Vous avez mangé un sandwich. Vous n'avez pas mangé de steak.
3. Nous avons assisté au match de foot. Nous n'avons pas assisté au concert.
4. Les touristes ont voyagé en car. Ils n'ont pas voyagé en avion.
5. Mes voisins ont loué une petite maison. Ils n'ont pas loué un grand appartement.
6. Marc a passé dix jours à Paris. Il n'a pas passé trois semaines à Paris.

Teaching note Be sure students use **pas de** in items 1, 2, and 5.

11 COMPREHENSION drawing conclusions about what did not happen

Answers will vary.
1. Je n'ai pas (de raquette. Je n'ai pas joué au tennis.)
2. Vous n'avez pas (de billets. Vous n'avez pas assisté au concert.)
3. Nous n'avons pas (de passeport. Nous n'avons pas voyagé en Europe.)
4. Frédéric n'a pas (d'ordinateur. Il n'a pas surfé sur l'Internet.)
5. Éric et Olivier n'ont pas (de télé. Ils n'ont pas regardé la comédie.)
6. Claire et Caroline n'ont pas (d'aspirateur. Elles n'ont pas nettoyé le salon.)

Teaching note Remind students to use **pas de** with the items in Column B.

Variation (game format) See how many logical sentences teams of students can construct within a given time limit.

See **Game: Samedi dernier** on p. 322.

SECTION D

Communicative function
Asking questions about the past

Teaching Resource Options

PRINT

Workbook PE, pp. 187–194
Unit 7 Resource Book
    Audioscript, p. 67
    Communipak, pp. 148–170
    Workbook TE, pp. 35–42

AUDIO & VISUAL

Audio Program
CD 4 Track 7

TECHNOLOGY

Power Presentations

Teaching strategy Remind students that in French, unlike English, interrogative expressions cannot be separated. Compare:
Pour qui as-tu travaillé?
For whom did you work?
Who(m) did you work *for*?

Expansion You may want to present inversion with **il/elle/on** for recognition.
A-t-il téléphoné?
A-t-elle téléphoné?
A-t-on téléphoné?

12 **EXCHANGES** discussing past activities

–Est-ce que tu as ... ?
–Oui, j'ai ... (Non, je n'ai pas ...)
1. visité le Tibet
2. voyagé en Alaska
3. piloté un (d')avion
4. dîné dans un restaurant vietnamien
5. mangé des (d')escargots
6. gagné à la loterie
7. assisté à un match de catch
8. rencontré un (de) fantôme

Teaching note Remind students to use **pas de** in items 3, 5, and 8.

Variation Have students ask and answer the questions in the plural.
– Est-ce que vous avez visité Paris?
– Oui, nous avons visité Paris. (Non, nous n'avons pas visité Paris.)

13 **PRACTICE** asking questions about past events

1. Quand est-ce qu'il a visité Québec?
2. À quelle heure est-ce qu'elle a téléphoné?
3. Comment est-ce qu'elle a voyagé en Italie?
4. Où est-ce qu'elle a acheté une (sa) robe?
5. Où est-ce qu'elle a rencontré sa copine?
6. Avec qui est-ce qu'elle a visité Genève?
7. Où est-ce qu'il a trouvé un job?
8. Dans quel restaurant est-ce qu'ils on dîné?
9. Quand est-ce qu'ils ont téléphoné?

D Les questions au passé composé

Compare the statements and questions in the passé composé.

STATEMENT	QUESTION	
Tu as travaillé.	Tu as travaillé?	*Did you work?*
	Est-ce que tu as travaillé?	
Philippe a voyagé cet été.	**Quand est-ce que** Philippe a voyagé?	*When did Philippe travel?*
	Où est-ce qu'il a voyagé?	*Where did he travel?*

For most verbs, questions in the passé composé are formed as follows:

interrogative form of **avoir** + PAST PARTICIPLE

	YES/NO QUESTIONS	INFORMATION QUESTIONS
WITH INTONATION	Tu as voyagé? Paul a téléphoné?	– –
WITH est-ce que	**Est-ce que** tu as voyagé? **Est-ce qu'**Alice a téléphoné?	**Avec qui est-ce que** tu as voyagé? **À qui est-ce qu'**Alice a téléphoné?

→ When the subject is a pronoun, questions in the passé composé can also be formed by inversion.

As-tu assisté au match de foot? *Did you go to the soccer game?*
Avec qui **avez-vous joué** au foot? *With whom did you play soccer?*
Who(m) did you play soccer with?

12  Expériences personnelles

PARLER Demandez à vos camarades s'ils ont déjà *(already)* fait les choses suivantes.

▶ visiter Paris?

Est-ce que tu as visité Paris?

Oui, j'ai visité Paris.
(Non, je n'ai pas visité Paris.)

1. visiter le Tibet?
2. voyager en Alaska?
3. piloter un avion?
4. dîner dans un restaurant vietnamien?
5. manger des escargots *(snails)*?
6. gagner à la loterie?
7. assister à un match de catch *(wrestling)*?
8. rencontrer un fantôme *(ghost)*?

13 Curiosité

PARLER Lisez ce que les personnes suivantes ont fait et posez des questions sur leurs activités.

▶ Paul a joué au tennis. (avec qui?)
Avec qui est-ce qu'il a joué au tennis?

1. Thomas a visité Québec. (quand?)
2. Corinne a téléphoné. (à quelle heure?)
3. Nathalie a voyagé en Italie. (comment?)
4. Marthe a acheté une robe. (où?)
5. Léa a rencontré sa copine. (où?)
6. Michèle a visité Genève. (avec qui?)
7. Philippe a trouvé un job. (où?)
8. Éric et Véronique ont dîné en ville. (dans quel restaurant?)
9. Les voisins ont téléphoné. (quand?)

CASUAL FRENCH

Information questions using intonation may be formed by placing the interrogative expression in the same position in the sentence as the corresponding answer. Usually, but not always, this is at the end.

Paul a voyagé <u>avec qui</u>?
    Paul a voyagé <u>avec ses parents.</u>

Vous avez téléphoné <u>quand</u>?
    J'ai téléphoné <u>à cinq heures.</u>

Claire a amené <u>qui</u> à la boum?
    Elle a amené <u>Bruno</u> à la boum.

14 Jérôme et Valérie

PARLER Jérôme est très curieux. Il veut toujours savoir ce que Valérie a fait. Valérie répond à ses questions.

▶ où / dîner? (dans un restaurant italien)
JÉRÔME: **Où est-ce que tu as dîné?**
VALÉRIE: **J'ai dîné dans un restaurant italien.**

1. avec qui / jouer au tennis? (avec Marc)
2. quand / assister au concert? (samedi après-midi)
3. qui / inviter au café? (ma copine Nathalie)
4. où / rencontrer Pierre? (dans la rue)

5. où / acheter ta veste? (au Bon Marché)
6. combien / payer ce CD? (10 euros)
7. à qui / téléphoner? (à ma grand-mère)
8. chez qui / passer le week-end? (chez une amie)

15 Conversation

PARLER Demandez à vos camarades ce qu'ils ont fait hier.

▶ à quelle heure / dîner?

1. avec qui / dîner?
2. à qui / téléphoner?
3. quel programme / regarder à la télé?
4. quel programme / écouter à la radio?
5. qui / rencontrer après les classes?
6. quand / étudier?

Dis, Hélène, à quelle heure est-ce que tu as dîné?

J'ai dîné à six heures.

PRONONCIATION

ain = /ɛ̃/   aine = /ɛn/   in = /ɛ̃/   ine = /in/

Les lettres «ain» et «in»

sa m**ain**   sem**aine**   maga**sin**   magaz**ine**

When the letters "**ain**," "**aim**," "**in**," "**im**" are at the end of a word or are followed by a *consonant*, they represent the nasal vowel /ɛ̃/.

REMEMBER: Do not pronounce an /n/ after the nasal vowel /ɛ̃/.

Répétez: /ɛ̃/ dem**ain** f**aim** tr**ain** m**ain** vois**in** cous**in** jard**in** magas**in**
m**ain**tenant **in**telligent **in**téressant **im**portant

When the letters "**ain**," "**aim**," "**in(n)**," "**im**" are followed by a *vowel*, they do NOT represent a nasal sound.

Répétez: /ɛn/ sem**aine** amér**icaine**
/ɛm/ j'**aime**

/in/ vois**ine** cous**ine** cu**isine** magaz**ine** c**iné**ma Cor**inne** f**inir**
/im/ t**imide** d**imanche** M**imi** cent**ime**

Alain M**inime** a un rendez-vous **im**portant dem**ain** mat**in**, avenue du M**aine**.

---

14 ROLE PLAY asking and answering questions about past events

1. J: Avec qui est-ce qu tu as joué au tennis?
   V: J'ai joué au tennis avec Marc.
2. J: Quand est-ce que tu as assisté au concert?
   V: J'ai assisté au concert samedi après-midi.
3. J: Qui est-ce que tu as invité au café?
   V: J'ai invité ma copine Nathalie au café.
4. J: Où est-ce que tu as rencontré Pierre?
   V: J'ai rencontré Pierre dans la rue.
5. J: Où est-ce que tu as acheté ta veste?
   V: J'ai acheté ma veste au Bon Marché.
6. J: Combien est-ce que tu as payé ce CD?
   V: J'ai payé ce CD dix euros.
7. J: À qui est-ce que tu as téléphoné?
   V: J'ai téléphoné à ma grand-mère.
8. J: Chez qui est-ce que tu as passé le week-end?
   V: J'ai passé le week-end chez une amie.

Variation (inversion) **Où as-tu dîné?**

---

15 EXCHANGES talking about yesterday

Answers will vary.
1. –Dis, (Léa), avec qui est-ce qu tu as dîné?
   –J'ai dîné avec (mes parents, mes amis).
2. –Dis, (Jean-Paul), à qui est-ce que tu as téléphoné?
   –J'ai téléphoné à (ma copine, à Roger).
3. –Dis, (Anne), quel programme est-ce que tu as regardé à la télé?
   –J'ai regardé (un film, une comédie).
4. –Dis, (Julie), quel programme est-ce que tu as écouté à la radio?
   –J'ai écouté (un concert de jazz).
5. –Dis, (Nancy), qui est-ce que tu as rencontré après les classes?
   –J'ai rencontré (Luc et Léa, un copain).
6. –Dis, (Luc), quand est-ce que tu as étudié?
   –J'ai étudié à (6 heures, après le dîner).

Teaching strategy Encourage students to give only affirmative answers, since they have not yet learned the negative forms **ne...rien, ne...personne.** These forms will be introduced in Lesson 24.

PRONUNCIATION

Teaching strategy Before doing the **prononciation** section, have students practice minimal pairs containing /ɛ̃/ /ɛn/ and /ɛ̃/, /in/.

/ɛ̃/	/ɛn/
certain	**certaine**
américain	**américaine**
musicien	**musicienne**

/ɛ̃/	/in/
cousin	**cousine**
voisin	**voisine**
Martin	**Martine**

Point out that **maintenant, intelligent,** etc. all end in the sound /ã/. Be sure students do not pronounce the final "n" or "t."

À votre tour!

OBJECTIFS
Now you can …
- talk with friends about what you did and did not do last weekend
- talk about past events in general

❶ Allô!

PARLER Reconstituez la conversation entre Alain et Christine. Pour cela, faites correspondre les réponses de Christine avec les questions d'Alain.

1. À quelle heure est-ce que tu as dîné hier soir?
2. Et après, tu as regardé la télé?
3. Qu'est-ce que tu as regardé après?
4. Qui a gagné?
5. Dis, tu as préparé la leçon pour demain?

a. Le match Marseille-Nice.
b. Nice. Par un score de trois à un.
c. Mais oui! J'ai étudié avant le dîner.
d. Oui, mais d'abord j'ai aidé ma mère.
e. À sept heures et demie.

❷ Dis-moi …

PARLER *I will tell you a few things that I did yesterday after school and a few things that I did not do, then you will tell me what you did and did not do.*

- J'ai étudié.
- J'ai dîné avec mes parents.
- J'ai téléphoné à une copine.
- Je n'ai pas rangé ma chambre.
- Je n'ai pas rencontré mes copains.
- Je n'ai pas regardé la télé.

Et maintenant, dis-moi …

❸ Créa-dialogue

PARLER Demandez à vos camarades s'ils ont fait les choses suivantes le week-end dernier. En cas de réponse affirmative, continuez la conversation.

▶ —Est-ce que tu as <u>dîné au restaurant</u>?
—Oui, j'ai <u>dîné au restaurant</u>.
—<u>Avec qui</u>?
—<u>Avec mes cousins</u>.
—<u>Où</u> est-ce que <u>vous avez dîné</u>?
—<u>Nous avons dîné Chez Tante Lucie</u> (à l'Hippopotamus, etc.).

▶ avec qui? / où?
1. avec qui? / quand?
2. quand? / où?
3. quand? / pourquoi?
4. quand? / où?
5. quand? / avec qui?

328 trois cent vingt-huit
Unité 7

4 Composition: Hier soir *(Last night)*

ÉCRIRE In one or two paragraphs describe what you did yesterday evening. You may wish to use the following suggestions:

- étudier (quoi?)
- dîner (à quelle heure?)
- manger (quoi?)
- téléphoner (à qui?)
- parler (de quoi?)
- écouter (quel type de musique?)
- regarder (quel programme à la télé?)
- aider (qui? comment?)
- ranger (quoi?)

STRATEGY Writing

Narrating the past When you write about past events, it is helpful to indicate the order in which these events occurred. In your composition, you can indicate the sequence in which you did certain things last night by using expressions such as **d'abord, après, ensuite, enfin**, and **finalement**.

COMMENT DIT-ON ...?

How to wish somebody a nice time:

Bon week-end! *(Have a nice weekend!)*

Bonnes vacances! *(Have a good vacation!)*

Bonne journée! *(Have a nice day!)*

Bon voyage! *(Have a good trip!)*

LESSON REVIEW
CLASSZONE.COM

PORTFOLIO ASSESSMENT

You will probably select only one speaking activity and one writing activity to go into the students' portfolios for Unit 7.

---

3 GUIDED ORAL EXPRESSION

Answers will vary.
1. —Est-ce que tu as joué au tennis?
   —Oui, j'ai joué au tennis.
   —Avec qui?
   —Avec (Jean, Luc et Karine).
   —Quand est-ce que tu as joué au tennis?
   —(Dimanche après-midi.) (Non, je n'ai pas joué au tennis.)
2. —Est-ce que tu as joué au volley?
   —Oui, j'ai joué au volley.
   —Quand?
   —(Samedi matin.)
   —Où est-ce que tu as joué au volley?
   —(Au stade.)
3. —Est-ce que tu as nettoyé ta chambre?
   —Oui, j'ai nettoyé ma chambre.
   —Quand est-ce que tu as nettoyé ta chambre?
   —(Vendredi après-midi.)
   —Pourquoi?
   —(Parce que je vais inviter mes copains.) (Non, je n'ai pas nettoyé ma chambre.)
4. —Est-ce que tu as rencontré tes (des) amis?
   —Oui, j'ai rencontré mes (des) amis.
   —Quand?
   —(Samedi après-midi.)
   —Où est-ce que tu as rencontré tes (des) amis?
   —(Au café.)
     (Non, je n'ai pas rencontré mes amis.)
5. —Est-ce que tu as dansé?
   —Oui, j'ai dansé.
   —Quand est-ce que tu as dansé?
   —(Samedi soir.)
   —Avec qui est-ce que tu as dansé?
   —Avec (Dominique).
     (Non, je n'ai pas dansé.)

Teaching strategy Have pairs of students each choose and prepare one of the dialogues and present it to the class.

4 WRITTEN SELF-EXPRESSION

Answers will vary.
Hier soir, j'ai étudié avant le dîner. Après le dîner, j'ai aidé mon père dans la cuisine. Après, j'ai téléphoné à ma copine. Nous avons parlé des devoirs. Ensuite, j'ai écouté du rock et j'ai regardé un film à la télé.

Supplementary vocabulary
Amuse-toi bien! *Have a good time*
Amusez-vous bien!

Language note In Quebec, the traditional term for *weekend* is **fin de semaine**: **Bonne fin de semaine!** *(Have a nice weekend!)*

Middle School Copymasters
Class starters 1&2, pp. T35, 109–111

Leçon 23

Main Topic Describing past events

Teaching Resource Options

PRINT

Workbook PE, pp. 195–200
Activités pour tous PE, pp. 119–121
Block Scheduling Copymasters, pp. 177–184
Unit 7 Resource Book
  Activités pour tous TE, pp. 81–83
  Audioscript, pp. 102, 103–105
  Communipak, pp. 148–170
  Lesson Plans, pp. 84–85
  Block Scheduling Lesson Plans, pp. 86–87
  Absent Student Copymasters, pp. 88–91
  Video Activities, pp. 94–99
  Videoscript, pp. 100–101
  Workbook TE, pp. 75–80

AUDIO & VISUAL

Audio Program
CD 4 Tracks 10, 11
CD 11 Tracks 13–18

TECHNOLOGY

Online Workbook

VIDEO PROGRAM

VIDÉO   DVD

MODULE 23
Pas de chance!

TOTAL TIME: 5:08 min.
  DVD Disk 2
  Videotape 4 (COUNTER: 13:06 min.)

23.1 Dialogue: Pas de chance!
  (13:24–14:40 min.)

23.2 Mini-scenes: Listening
  – Qu'est-ce que vous avez fait?
  (14:41–15:19 min.)

23.3 Mini-scenes: Speaking
  – Est-ce qu'ils ont perdu?
  (15:20–16:28 min.)

23.4 Vignette culturelle: La télé
  (16:29–18:14 min.)

Comprehension practice Play the entire module through as an introduction to the lesson.

Challenge activity Have students consult a French-English dictionary and try to find out the meanings of the suspects' last names.
filou *(dishonest person, thief)*
la roulette *(roulette wheel)*
l'escroc *(crook)*
malin *(shrewd, cunning)*

330 • Conversation et Culture
  Unité 7 LEÇON 23

LEÇON 23

L'alibi

l'inspecteur Leflic

Êtes-vous bon (bonne) détective? <u>Pouvez</u>-vous trouver la solution du mystère <u>suivant</u>? — *Can* / *following*

Samedi dernier à deux heures de l'après-midi, <u>il y a eu</u> une <u>panne d'électricité</u> dans la petite ville de Marcillac-le-Château. La panne <u>a duré</u> une heure. Pendant la panne, un <u>cambrioleur</u> <u>a pénétré</u> dans la Banque Populaire de Marcillac-le-Château. Bien sûr, l'alarme n'a pas fonctionné et c'est <u>seulement</u> lundi matin que le directeur de la banque <u>a remarqué</u> le <u>cambriolage</u>: un million d'euros. — *there was / power failure / lasted* / *burglar / entered* / *only* / *noticed / burglary*

Lundi après-midi, l'<u>inspecteur</u> Leflic a interrogé quatre suspects, mais <u>chacun</u> a un alibi. — *police detective* / *each one*

Sophie Filou
Euh, … excusez-moi, Monsieur l'Inspecteur.
Ma mémoire n'est pas très bonne.
<u>Voyons</u>, qu'est-ce que <u>j'ai fait</u> samedi après-midi? — *Let's see / did I do*
Ah oui, j'<u>ai fini</u> un livre. — *finished*
Le <u>titre</u> du livre? *Le crime ne paie pas!* — *title*

Marc Laroulette
Qu'est-ce que j'ai fait samedi?
J'<u>ai rendu visite à</u> mes copains. — *visited*
Nous avons joué aux cartes.
C'est moi qui ai gagné!

Patrick Lescrot
Voyons, samedi dernier …
Ah oui … cet après-midi-là, j'ai invité des amis chez moi.
Nous avons regardé la télé.
Nous <u>avons vu</u> le match de foot France-<u>Allemagne</u>. — *saw / Germany*
Quel match! <u>Malheureusement</u>, c'est la France qui <u>a perdu</u>! — *Unfortunately / lost*
Dommage!

Pauline Malin
Ce n'est pas moi, Monsieur l'Inspecteur!
Samedi j'ai fait un pique-nique à la campagne avec une copine.
Nous <u>avons choisi</u> un <u>coin</u> près d'une rivière. — *chose / spot*
Ensuite, nous avons fait une promenade à vélo.
Nous <u>avons eu de la chance</u>! — *were lucky*
<u>Il a fait un temps extraordinaire</u>! — *The weather was great!*

Lisez <u>attentivement</u> les quatre déclarations. À votre avis, qui est le cambrioleur ou la cambrioleuse? Pourquoi? (Vous pouvez comparer votre réponse avec la réponse de l'inspecteur à la page 337.) — *carefully*

330 trois cent trente
Unité 7

CLASSROOM MANAGEMENT Group reading

Since this is a longer story, you may want to use it as a recapitulation at the end of the lesson.

Divide the class into groups of three or four. Have each group read the story, without turning to p. 337 to see the solution.

The recorder (**secrétaire**) of each group writes down the solution: who is the guilty one and why. **Qui est le coupable et pourquoi?**

After all the recorders have given their reports to the class, the students may read the solution in the text.

Compréhension

Certains événements ont eu lieu *(took place)* samedi dernier. Indiquez si oui ou non les événements suivants ont eu lieu.

1. Le directeur de la banque a vu *(saw)* le cambrioleur.
2. Un cambriolage a eu lieu *(took place)* à Marcillac-le-Château.
3. L'inspecteur Leflic a arrêté *(arrested)* quatre personnes.
4. Sophie Filou a vu le film *Le crime ne paie pas* à la télé.
5. Marc Laroulette a perdu un million d'euros.
6. L'Allemagne a gagné un match de foot.
7. Pauline Malin a fait une promenade à vélo à la campagne.
8. Il a fait beau.

Et toi?

Dis si oui ou non tu as fait les choses suivantes le week-end dernier.

1. (J'ai/Je n'ai pas) … rendu visite à mes copains.
2. (J'ai/Je n'ai pas) … vu un match de foot à la télé.
3. (J'ai/Je n'ai pas) … fini un livre.
4. (J'ai/Je n'ai pas) … fait une promenade à vélo.
5. (J'ai/Je n'ai pas) … fait un pique-nique.

MARDI 20.35
FOOTBALL - COUPE DE FRANCE:
SEIZIÈME DE FINALE

NOTE *culturelle*

Les jeunes Français et la télé

Combien d'heures par° jour est-ce que tu regardes la télé? Une heure? deux heures? trois heures? plus? moins? En général, les jeunes Français regardent la télé moins souvent et moins longtemps° que les jeunes Américains: en moyenne° 1 heure 15 les jours d'école et 2 heures 15 les autres° jours (mercredi, samedi et dimanche). Dans beaucoup de familles, les parents contrôlent l'usage° de la télé. Souvent ils exigent° que leurs enfants finissent leurs devoirs avant de regarder la télé. Ainsi,° beaucoup de jeunes regardent la télé seulement° après le dîner.

Quels sont leurs programmes favoris? Les jeunes Français aiment surtout° les films, les programmes de sport, les variétés et les jeux télévisés,° comme «Qui veut gagner° des millions?». Les séries américaines sont aussi très populaires.

par *per* **moins longtemps** *for a shorter time* **en moyenne** *on an average of* **autres** *other* **usage** *use* **exigent** *insist* **Ainsi** *Thus* **seulement** *only* **surtout** *especially* **jeux télévisés** *game shows* **gagner** *to win*

Compréhension
Answers

1. Non, le directeur de la banque n'a pas vu le cambrioleur.
2. Oui, le cambriolage a eu lieu à Marcillac-le-Château.
3. Non, l'inspecteur n'a pas arrêté quatre personnes. Il a interrogé quatre personnes.
4. Non, Sophie Filou n'a pas vu le film *Le crime ne paie pas* à la télé. Elle a lu le livre.
5. Non, Marc Laroulette n'a pas perdu un million d'euros. Il a gagné à un jeu de cartes.
6. Oui, l'Allemagne a gagné le match de foot.
7. Oui, Pauline Malin a fait une promenade à vélo à la campagne.
8. Oui, il a fait beau.

Et toi? describing what one did last weekend

Answers will vary.
1. J'ai rendu visite à mes copains. (Je n'ai pas rendu visite à mes copains.
2. J'ai vu un match de foot à la télé. (Je n'ai pas vu de match de foot à la télé.)
3. J'ai fini un livre. (Je n'ai pas fini de livre.)
4. J'ai fait une promenade à vélo. (Je n'ai pas fait de promenade à vélo.)
5. J'ai fait un pique-nique. (Je n'ai pas fait de pique-nique.)

Realia note

La Coupe de France

The French national soccer tournament is called **La Coupe de France.**

This TV ad is for a game early in the playoffs where 32 teams are in competition and playing in 16 games around the country (**les seizièmes de finale).**

Note culturelle

Teaching strategy For more information on French TV channels, see p. 118.

SETTING THE SCENE

Video Module 23 opens with **Pas de chance!** *(out of luck),* a humorous series of dialogues. Philippe has had a bad day, and in these conversations he explains what happened.

The **Vignette culturelle** focuses on French television and expands on the cultural note in the student text.

SECTION A

Communicative function
Talking about what one sees

Teaching Resource Options

PRINT

Workbook PE, pp. 195–200
Unit 7 Resource Book
   Audioscript, p. 102
   Communipak. pp. 148–170
   Workbook TE, pp. 75–80

AUDIO & VISUAL

Audio Program
CD 4 Track 12

TECHNOLOGY

Power Presentations

Pronunciation Be sure students maintain the sound /vwa/ in all forms of the verb, especially in:
nous voyons /vwajɔ̃/
vous voyez /vwaje/

① PRACTICE seeing sights in Paris

1. Nous voyons le musée d'Orsay.
2. Tu vois l'Arc de Triomphe.
3. Je vois le Centre Pompidou.
4. Sophie voit le Quartier latin.
5. Vous voyez la pyramide du Louvre.
6. Les touristes japonais voient le musée Picasso.

Teaching strategy Tell students that **voir** is another "boot" verb.

je vois	nous voyons
tu vois	vous voyez
il voit	ils voient

② COMMUNICATION answering personal questions

Answers will vary.
1. Oui, je vois bien. Non, je ne porte pas de lunettes.
(Non, je ne vois pas bien. Oui, je porte des lunettes.)
2. Oui, je vois mes amis pendant les vacances.
(Non, je ne vois pas mes amis pendant les vacances.)
Oui, je vois mes professeurs. (Non, je ne vois pas mes professeurs.)
3. Oui, je vois souvent mes cousins. (Non, je ne vois pas souvent mes cousins.)
Oui, je vois mes cousins pendant les vacances. (Non, je ne vois pas mes cousins pendant les vacances.)
Oui, je vois mes cousins à Noël. (Non, je ne vois pas mes cousins à Noël.)
4. Je préfère voir un match de football à la télé.
(Je préfère voir un match de baseball à la télé.)
5. Quand je vais au cinéma, j'aime voir (les comédies).

A Le verbe *voir*

The verb **voir** *(to see)* is irregular. Note the forms of **voir** in the present tense.

INFINITIVE	voir	
PRESENT	Je **vois** Marc.	Nous **voyons** un film.
	Tu **vois** ton copain.	Vous **voyez** un match de baseball.
	Il/Elle/On **voit** un accident.	Ils/Elles **voient** le professeur.

1 Week-end à Paris

PARLER/ÉCRIRE Les personnes suivantes passent le week-end à Paris. Décrivez ce que chacun voit.

▶ Olivier   **Olivier voit Notre-Dame.** ▶

Notre-Dame

1. le musée d'Orsay   2. l'Arc de Triomphe   3. le Centre Pompidou

4. le Quartier latin   5. la pyramide du Louvre   6. le musée Picasso

1. nous	3. moi	5. vous
2. toi	4. Sophie	6. les touristes japonais

2 Questions personnelles   PARLER/ÉCRIRE

1. Est-ce que tu vois bien? Est-ce que tu portes des lunettes?
2. Est-ce que tu vois tes amis pendant les vacances? Est-ce que tu vois tes professeurs?
3. Est-ce que tu vois souvent tes cousins? Est-ce que tu vois tes cousins pendant les vacances? à Noël?
4. Qu'est-ce que tu préfères voir à la télé? un match de football ou un match de baseball?
5. Quand tu vas au cinéma, quels films aimes-tu voir? les comédies? les films d'aventures? les films policiers *(detective movies)*?

B Le passé composé des verbes réguliers en -ir et -re

Note the passé composé of the verbs below, paying special attention to the ending of the past participle.

choisir	J'ai choisi cette casquette.	Je n'ai pas choisi cette chemise.
finir	Nous avons fini le magazine.	Nous n'avons pas fini le livre.
vendre	Tu as vendu ton vélo.	Tu n'as pas vendu ta moto.
attendre	Jacques a attendu Paul.	Il n'a pas attendu François.
répondre	J'ai répondu au professeur.	Tu n'as pas répondu à la question.

The past participle of regular -ir and -re verbs is formed as follows:

-ir → -i	-re → -u
chois|ir| → chois|i|	vend|re| → vend|u|
fin|ir| → fin|i|	attend|re| → attend|u|

3 Besoins d'argent *(Money needs)*

PARLER/ÉCRIRE Parce qu'elles ont besoin d'argent, les personnes suivantes ont vendu certains objets. Dites ce que chaque personne a vendu.

▶ Philippe/sa guitare **Philippe a vendu sa guitare.**

1. M. Roche/sa voiture
2. mes copains/leur chaîne hi-fi
3. moi/mon appareil-photo
4. toi/ton skate
5. les voisins/leur piano
6. nous/nos livres
7. vous/votre ordinateur
8. François et Vincent/ leurs CD

À vendre
INSTRUMENTS
DE MUSIQUE

4 Bravo!

PARLER/ÉCRIRE Les personnes suivantes méritent *(deserve)* des félicitations *(congratulations)*. Expliquez pourquoi.

▶ les élèves/réussir à l'examen **Les élèves ont réussi à l'examen.**

1. M. Bedon/maigrir
2. Mlle Legros/perdre dix kilos
3. Florence/gagner le match de tennis
4. les élèves/finir la leçon
5. moi/ranger ma chambre
6. nous/choisir une classe difficile
7. toi/finir les exercices
8. Marc/rendre visite à un copain à l'hôpital
9. vous/attendre vos copains
10. les élèves/répondre en français

SECTION B

Communicative function
Talking about the past

Teaching strategy Point out that like -er verbs, most -ir and -re verbs form the passé composé with avoir. Note the endings of the past participle.

3 PRACTICE describing what people sold

1. M. Roche a vendu sa voiture.
2. Mes copains ont vendu leur chaîne hi-fi.
3. J'ai vendu mon appareil-photo.
4. Tu as vendu ton skate.
5. Les voisins ont vendu leur piano.
6. Nous avons vendu nos livres.
7. Vous avez vendu votre ordinateur.
8. François et Victor ont vendu leurs CD.

Variation (in the negative) **Philippe n'a pas vendu sa guitare.**

4 PRACTICE describing people's accomplishments

1. M. Bedon a maigri.
2. Mlle Legros a perdu dix kilos.
3. Florence a gagné le match de tennis.
4. Les élèves ont fini la leçon.
5. J'ai rangé ma chambre.
6. Nous avons choisi une classe difficile.
7. Tu as fini les exercises.
8. Marc a rendu visite à un copain à l'hôpital.
9. Vous avez attendu vos copains.
10. Les élèves ont répondu en français.

Variation (in the negative) **Les élèves n'ont pas réussi à l'examen.**

Realia note
à vendre *for sale*

Teaching Resource Options

PRINT

Workbook PE, pp. 195–200
Unit 7 Resource Book
  Communipak, pp. 148–170
  Video Activities, pp. 95–96
  Videoscript, pp. 100–101
  Workbook TE, pp. 75–80

TECHNOLOGY

Power Presentations

VIDEO PROGRAM

 MODULE 23

23.2 Mini-scenes: Qu'est-ce que vous avez fait? (14:41–15:19 min.)

23.3 Mini-scenes: Est-ce qu'ils ont perdu? (15:20–16:28 min.)

5 ROLE PLAY talking about past events

1. –Tu as étudié ce week-end?
 –Non! J'ai rendu visite à un copain.
2. –Tu as acheté un DVD?
 –Non! J'ai choisi un CD.
3. –Tu as fini ce livre?
 –Non! J'ai regardé la télé.
4. –Tu as vendu ta guitare?
 –Non! J'ai vendu mon appareil-photo.
5. –Tu as téléphoné à Marc?
 –Non! J'ai rendu visite à son cousin.
6. –Tu as maigri?
 –Non! J'ai grossi.
7. –Tu as répondu à la lettre?
 –Non! J'ai téléphoné.

6 DESCRIPTION contrasting present and past events

1. téléphone/j'ai téléphoné
2. finis/as fini
3. mangeons/avons mangé
4. choisit/a choisi
5. réussissent/ont réussi
6. vend/a vendu
7. rendent/ont rendu
8. attendent/ont attendu

7 ROLE PLAY explaining why one did not do certain things

–Tu as ... ?
–Non, je n'ai pas ...
–Pourquoi est-ce que tu n'as pas ... ?
–Parce que ...

1. travaillé/j'ai joué au foot
2. répondu/je n'ai pas entendu la question
3. joué au tennis/j'ai perdu ma raquette
4. acheté une veste/acheté de veste/j'ai choisi un blouson
5. fini le livre/j'ai regardé la télé
6. rendu visite à Marc/j'ai étudié
7. réussi à l'examen/j'ai perdu mes notes
8. écouté tes CD/écouté mes CD/écouté tes CD/j'ai vendu mon baladeur

---

5 **Non!**

PARLER Jean-Louis répond négativement aux questions de Béatrice. Jouez les deux rôles.

> gagner le match/perdre

> **Tu as gagné le match?** **Non! J'ai perdu!**

1. étudier ce week-end/rendre visite à un copain
2. acheter un DVD/choisir un CD
3. finir ce livre/regarder la télé
4. vendre ta guitare/vendre mon appareil-photo
5. téléphoner à Marc/rendre visite à son cousin
6. maigrir/grossir
7. répondre à la lettre/téléphoner

6 **Aujourd'hui et hier**

PARLER/ÉCRIRE Dites ce que les personnes suivantes font aujourd'hui et ce qu'elles ont fait hier.

> Paul/acheter un blouson/un pantalon
> **Aujourd'hui, Paul achète un blouson.**
> **Hier, il a acheté un pantalon.**

1. moi/téléphoner à mon cousin/à mes copains
2. toi/finir ce livre/ce magazine
3. nous/manger des sandwichs/une pizza
4. Mélanie/choisir une jupe/un chemisier
5. les élèves/réussir à l'examen de français/à l'examen d'anglais
6. Philippe/vendre sa chaîne hi-fi/ses vieilles cassettes
7. Philippe et Jean-Pierre/rendre visite à leurs cousins/à leur grand-mère
8. les touristes/attendre le train/le car

7 **Excuses**

PARLER Quand Michel ne fait pas une chose, il a toujours une excuse. Jouez le dialogue entre Michel et sa soeur Laure.

> **Tu as étudié?**
> **Non, je n'ai pas étudié.**
> **Pourquoi est-ce que tu n'as pas étudié?**
> **Parce que j'ai perdu mon livre.**

> étudier/perdre mon livre

1. travailler/jouer au foot
2. répondre/entendre la question
3. jouer au tennis/perdre ma raquette
4. acheter une veste/choisir un blouson
5. finir le livre/regarder la télé
6. rendre visite à Marc/étudier
7. réussir à l'examen/perdre mes notes
8. écouter tes CD/vendre mon baladeur

COMPREHENSION Past and present

Teach students gestures for present and past.

Montrez-moi le présent. [index finger pointing to floor]

Montrez-moi le passé. [thumb pointing back over shoulder]

Now read sentences aloud containing the present or the passé composé and have students identify the tense by using the appropriate gesture.

Est-ce que c'est le présent ou le passé?

- **Tu finis la leçon de natation.** [P]
- **J'ai fini la leçon de ski nautique.** [PC]
- **Paul a eu un accident de ski.** [PC]

C Le passé composé des verbes *être*, *avoir*, *faire*, *mettre* et *voir*

The verbs **être**, **avoir**, **faire**, **mettre**, and **voir** have irregular past participles.

être	→	été	Nous **avons été** à Paris.
avoir	→	eu	M. Lambert **a eu** un accident.
faire	→	fait	Qu'est-ce que tu **as fait** hier?
mettre	→	mis	Nous **avons mis** des jeans.
voir	→	vu	J'**ai vu** un bon film.

→ In the passé composé, the verb **être** has two different meanings:

Mme Lebrun **a été** malade. *Mme Lebrun **has been** sick.*
Elle **a été** à l'hôpital. *She **was** in the hospital.*

8 Dialogue

PARLER Demandez à vos camarades s'ils ont fait les choses suivantes récemment *(recently)*.

▶ faire une promenade?
—**Est-ce que tu as fait une promenade récemment?**
—**Oui, j'ai fait une promenade. (Non, je n'ai pas fait de promenade.)**

1. faire un pique-nique?
2. faire une promenade en voiture?
3. être malade *(sick)*?
4. avoir la grippe *(flu)*?
5. avoir une dispute *(fight)* avec ton copain?
6. avoir une bonne surprise?
7. avoir un «A» en français?
8. voir un film?
9. voir tes cousins?
10. mettre des affiches dans ta chambre?

9 Pourquoi?

PARLER Avec vos camarades de classe, parlez des personnes suivantes.

▶ Fabrice est content.
(avoir un «A» à l'examen)

1. Mes copains sont furieux. (avoir un «F» à l'examen)
2. Pauline est très contente. (voir son copain)
3. Mon père n'est pas content. (avoir une dispute avec son chef [*boss*])
4. Philippe est pâle. (voir un accident)
5. Juliette est fatiguée *(tired)*. (faire du jogging)
6. Alice et Laure sont bronzées *(tanned)*. (être à la mer)
7. Mon frère est fatigué. (faire de la gymnastique [*to work out*])
8. Patrick et Marc sont contents. (voir un bon film)
9. Isabelle est très élégante. (mettre une jolie robe)

Fabrice est content.

Il a eu un «A» à l'examen.

Ah bon? Pourquoi?

trois cent trente-cinq **335**
Leçon 23

- **Nous sommes à la mer.** [P]
- **Sophie fait de l'escalade.** [P]
- **Marc a fait de la planche à voile.** [PC]
- **Vous avez acheté un vélo.** [PC]
- **J'ai grossi cet été.** [PC]
- **Nous passons les vacances à la mer.** [P]
- **Mes cousins ont vu un match de tennis.** [PC]
- **Stéphanie met son maillot de bain.** [P]

SECTION C

Communicative function
Talking about the past

Language note Point out that the passé composé of most irregular verbs is formed with **avoir**.

Pronunciation Be sure students pronounce the past participle **eu** /y/, as in **tu**.

8 COMMUNICATION asking about past activities

Answers will vary.
—Est-ce que tu as ... récemment?
—Oui, j'ai ... (Non, je n'ai pas ...)

1. fait un pique-nique/je n'ai pas fait de pique-nique
2. fait une promenade en voiture/je n'ai pas fait de promenade
3. été malade
4. eu la grippe
5. eu une dispute avec ton copain/j'ai eu une (je n'ai pas eu de) dispute avec mon copain
6. eu une bonne surprise/je n'ai pas eu de bonne surprise
7. eu un «A» en français/je n'ai pas eu de «A» en français
8. vu un film/je n'ai pas vu de film
9. vu tes cousins/vu mes cousins
10. mis des affiches dans ta chambre/je n'ai pas mis d'affiches dans ma chambre

Pronunciation récemment /resamã/

Teaching note Remind students to use **pas de** in items 1, 2, 5, 6, 7, and 8 if they choose to answer in the negative.

9 EXCHANGES explaining people's looks and moods

1. —Mes copains sont furieux.
—Ah bon? Pourquoi?
—Ils ont eu un «F» à l'examen.
2. —Pauline est très contente.
—Ah bon? Pourquoi?
—Elle a vu son copain.
3. —Mon père n'est pas content.
—Ah bon? Pourquoi?
—Il a eu une dispute avec son chef.
4. —Philippe est pâle.
—Ah bon? Pourquoi?
—Il a vu un accident.
5. —Juliette est fatiguée.
—Ah bon? Pourquoi?
—Elle a fait du jogging.
6. —Alice et Laure sont bronzées.
—Ah bon? Pourquoi?
—Elles ont été à la mer.
7. —Mon frère est fatigué.
—Ah bon? Pourquoi?
—Il a fait de la gymnastique.
8. —Patrick et Marc sont contents.
—Ah bon? Pourquoi?
—Ils ont vu un bon film.
9. —Isabelle est très élégante.
—Ah bon? Pourquoi?
—Elle a mis une jolie robe.

Teaching Resource Options

PRINT

Workbook PE, pp. 195–200
Unit 7 Resource Book
  Audioscript, pp. 102–103
  Communipak, pp. 148–170
  Video Activities, p. 94
  Videoscript, p. 100
  Workbook TE, pp. 75–80

AUDIO & VISUAL

Audio Program
CD 4 Track 13

VIDEO PROGRAM

  MODULE 23
VIDÉO   DVD

23.1 Dialogue: Pas de chance!
(13:24–14:40 min.)

---

10 **COMPREHENSION** describing what people did and did not do

1. Élodie a été à la montagne. Elle n'a pas nagé. Elle a fait du VTT.
2. Nous avons été à la campagne. Nous n'avons pas visité de monuments. Nous avons fait du camping.
3. Vous avez été à Paris. Vous n'avez pas parlé italien. Vous avez vu la tour Eiffel.
4. J'ai été à la mer. J'ai fait de la planche à voile. Je n'ai pas travaillé.
5. Mes parents ont été en Égypte. Ils ont vu les pyramides. Ils n'ont pas visité Paris.
6. Vous avez été dans un club de sport. Vous avez fait de la gymnastique. Vous n'avez pas grossi.
7. Christine a été à la plage. Elle a mis des lunettes de soleil. Elle n'a pas joué au tennis.

Realia note
Villages vacances

Most French employees get at least five weeks of paid vacation. One popular option is to go to a "vacation village" **(un village vacances).**

In this ad, the Viva group announces that they have a network **(un réseau)** of such "villages" and that, in addition to room and board, they offer sports instruction and numerous social events **(les villages sont "animés").**

Supplementary vocabulary
cette année *this year*
l'année dernière
l'année prochaine

---

10 **Vive les vacances!**

PARLER/ÉCRIRE Dites où les personnes suivantes ont été pendant les vacances. Dites aussi si oui ou non elles ont fait les choses entre parenthèses. Soyez logique *(Be logical)*.

▶ Christophe: à la piscine (étudier/nager)
Christophe a été à la piscine. Il n'a pas étudié. Il a nagé.

1. Élodie: à la montagne (nager/faire du VTT)
2. nous: à la campagne (visiter des monuments/faire du camping)
3. vous: à Paris (parler italien/voir la tour Eiffel)
4. moi: à la mer (faire de la planche à voile/travailler)
5. mes parents: en Égypte (voir les pyramides/visiter Paris)
6. vous: dans un club de sport (faire de la gymnastique/grossir)
7. Christine: à la plage (mettre des lunettes de soleil/jouer au tennis)

VOCABULAIRE *Quand?*

	maintenant	avant	après
le jour	aujourd'hui	hier	demain
le matin	ce matin	hier matin	demain matin
l'après-midi	cet après-midi	hier après-midi	demain après-midi
le soir	ce soir	hier soir	demain soir
le jour	samedi	samedi dernier *(last)*	samedi prochain *(next)*
le week-end	ce week-end	le week-end dernier	le week-end prochain
la semaine	cette semaine	la semaine dernière	la semaine prochaine
le mois	ce mois-ci	le mois dernier	le mois prochain

---

11 **Quand?**

PARLER Demandez à vos camarades quand ils ont fait les choses suivantes. Ils vont répondre en utilisant une expression du **Vocabulaire.**

▶ faire tes devoirs?

1. faire des achats?
2. ranger ta chambre?
3. rencontrer tes voisins?
4. voir ton copain?
5. voir un film?
6. avoir un examen?
7. faire une promenade à pied?
8. être en ville?
9. mettre *(set)* la table?

Quand est-ce que tu as fait tes devoirs?

J'ai fait mes devoirs hier après-midi.
(vendredi soir, le week-end dernier, …)

GAME Moi aussi

For homework, have students write out their answers to Act. 12.

In class, students share their responses with one another. The object of the game is to find ten classmates who wrote the same answers.
  One student reads the first statement, without showing the text to his/her partner.

The partner then reads his/her first statement.
X: Ce matin, j'ai regardé la télé. Et toi?
Y: Moi aussi. Ce matin, j'ai regardé la télé.

The answers match, so each one writes the other's name next to #1. Then they both read their responses to the next item.

12 Le passé et le futur

PARLER/ÉCRIRE Décrivez ce que vous avez fait (phrases 1 à 5) et ce que vous allez faire (phrases 6 à 10). Dites la vérité … ou utilisez votre imagination!

1. Ce matin, j'ai …
2. Hier matin, j'ai …
3. Samedi après-midi, j'ai …
4. La semaine dernière, j'ai …
5. Le mois dernier, j'ai …

6. Ce soir, je vais …
7. Demain soir, je vais …
8. Vendredi soir, je vais …
9. Le week-end prochain, je vais …
10. La semaine prochaine, je vais …

13 Questions personnelles PARLER/ÉCRIRE

1. En général, est-ce que tu étudies avant ou après le dîner?
2. En général, est-ce que tu regardes la télé avant ou après le dîner?
3. À quelle heure est-ce que tu as dîné hier soir?
4. Quel programme de télé est-ce que tu as regardé hier après-midi?
5. Qu'est-ce que tu vas faire le week-end prochain?
6. Où vas-tu aller le week-end prochain?

PRONONCIATION

gn = /ɲ/

Les lettres «gn»

The letters "**gn**" represent a sound similar to the "**ny**" in *canyon*. First, practice with words you know.

Répétez: **espagnol   gagner   mignon**
la montagne   la campagne

¡HOLA! ¿QUÉ TAL?

espagnol

Now try saying some new words. Make them sound French!

Répétez: **Champagne   Espagne** *(Spain)*   **un signe**
la vigne *(vineyard)*   **la ligne** *(line)*   **un signal**
la dignité   ignorer   magnétique   magnifique   Agnès

Agnès Mignard a gagné son match. C'est magnifique!

(L'alibi, p. 330)

LA RÉPONSE DE L'INSPECTEUR:

C'est Patrick Lescrot le cambrioleur. Samedi après-midi, il y a eu une panne d'électricité. Patrick Lescrot n'a pas pu *(was not able to)* regarder la télé. Son alibi n'est pas valable *(valid).*

trois cent trente-sept
Leçon 23 337

---

11 COMMUNICATION finding out when past events took place

Answers will vary.
1. —Quand est-ce que tu as fait des achats?
   —J'ai fait des achats (hier soir).
2. —Quand est-ce que tu as rangé ta chambre?
   —J'ai rangé ma chambre (hier matin).
3. —Quand est-ce que tu as rencontré tes voisins?
   —J'ai rencontré mes voisins (la semaine dernière).
4. —Quand est-ce que tu as vu ton copain?
   —J'ai vu mon copain (hier après-midi).
5. —Quand est-ce que tu as vu un film?
   —J'ai vu un film (samedi dernier).
6. —Quand est-ce que tu as eu un examen?
   —J'ai eu un examen (le mois dernier).
7. —Quand est-ce que tu as fait une promenade à pied?
   —J'ai fait une promenade à pied (dimanche dernier).
8. —Quand est-ce que tu as été en ville?
   —J'ai été en ville (le week-end dernier).
9. —Quand est-ce que tu as mis la table?
   —J'ai mis la table (hier soir).

12 COMMUNICATION describing past events and future plans

Answers will vary.
1. Ce matin, j'ai (été à l'école).
2. Hier matin, j'ai (eu un examen).
3. Samedi après-midi, j'ai (fait des achats).
4. La semaine dernière, j'ai (fait de l'escalade).
5. Le mois dernier, j'ai (acheté un vélo).
6. Ce soir, je vais (retrouver mes amis au café).
7. Demain soir, je vais (faire mes devoirs de français).
8. Vendredi soir, je vais (aller à un concert de rock).
9. Le week-end prochain, je vais (faire du ski).
10. La semaine prochaine, je vais (organiser une boum).

13 COMMUNICATION answering personal questions

Answers will vary.
1. En général, j'étudie après (avant) le dîner.
2. En général, je regarde la télé avant (après) le dîner.
3. Hier soir, j'ai dîné à (sept heures et demie).
4. Hier après-midi, j'ai regardé (un match de baseball).
5. Le week-end prochain, je vais (rendre visite à mes grands-parents).
6. Le week-end prochain, je vais aller (en ville).

Middle School Copymasters

Worksheet 3: *Quand?*, pp. 188–119

Often the answers will not be the same:
X: Hier matin, j'ai étudié. Et toi?
Y: Hier matin, j'ai joué au tennis.

Here the answers do not match, so they continue with #3. If time remains when they have shared the ten responses with one another, they may talk to another partner to try to find the missing matches.

At the end of the time limit, the student who has found the most matches wins.

À VOTRE TOUR

Main Topic
• Recapitulation and review

Teaching Resource Options

PRINT

Workbook PE, pp. 195–200
Unit 7 Resource Book
  Audioscript, p. 103
  Communipak, pp. 148–170
  Family Involvement, pp. 57–58
  Workbook TE, pp. 75–80

  Assessment
  Lesson 23 Quiz, pp. 107–108
  Portfolio Assessment, Unit 1 URB
    pp. 155–164
  Audioscript for Quiz 23, p. 106
  Answer Keys, pp. 213–xx

AUDIO & VISUAL

Audio Program
CD 4 Tracks 14, 15
CD 16 Track 3

TECHNOLOGY

Test Generator CD-ROM/eTest Plus
Online

1 COMPREHENSION

1. Tu as fini tes devoirs de français?
   (b) Non, je n'ai pas étudié cet après-midi.
2. Qu'est-ce que tu as fait alors?
   (d) J'ai joué au tennis avec Caroline.
3. Tu as gagné?
   (a) Non, j'ai perdu.
4. Mais d'habitude tu joues bien?
   (c) C'est vrai, mais aujourd'hui, je n'ai pas eu de chance …
5. Peut-être que Caroline a joué mieux que toi?
   (e) Tu as raison. Elle a joué comme une championne.

2 GUIDED ORAL EXPRESSION

Answers will vary.
• J'ai rencontré des amis au café. J'ai mangé une très bonne glace.
• La semaine dernière, j'ai été à un concert de rock. J'ai beaucoup aimé le concert.
• Samedi dernier, j'ai fait une promenade à la campagne avec des amis. Il a fait très beau.

Middle School Copymasters

Conversations: *L'après–midi au centre commercial*, p. 112

À votre tour!

❶  Allô!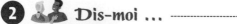

PARLER Reconstituez la conversation entre Robert et Julien. Pour cela, faites correspondre les réponses de Julien avec les questions de Robert.

1 Tu as fini tes devoirs de français?

2 Qu'est-ce que tu as fait alors?

3 Tu as gagné?

4 Mais d'habitude (*usually*) tu joues bien?

5 Peut-être que Caroline a joué mieux (*better*) que toi?

a Non, j'ai perdu!

b Non, je n'ai pas étudié cet après-midi.

c C'est vrai, mais aujourd'hui, je n'ai pas eu de chance …

d J'ai joué au tennis avec Caroline.

e Tu as raison. Elle a joué comme une championne.

❷ Dis-moi …

PARLER *I will tell you about some nice things that happened to me recently; then you will tell me about three nice things that happened to you.*

• J'ai réussi à mon examen d'anglais. (J'ai eu un «A».)
• J'ai eu un rendez-vous avec une personne très intéressante.
• J'ai vu un très bon film.

Et maintenant, dis-moi …

❸ Créa-dialogue

PARLER Avec vos camarades, discutez de ce que vous avez fait récemment (*recently*). Vous pouvez utiliser les expressions et les activités suggérées. Continuez la conversation avec des questions supplémentaires.

Quand?	
dimanche après-midi	lundi dernier
hier soir	la semaine dernière
samedi soir	le mois dernier
le week-end dernier	

Quoi?	
jouer aux jeux vidéo	dîner au restaurant
faire des achats	voir un film
faire du skate	avoir un rendez-vous
voir mes cousins	rendre visite à un copain
	faire du roller

▶ —Qu'est-ce que tu as fait <u>dimanche après-midi</u>?
  —<u>J'ai joué au tennis avec ma soeur.</u>
  —<u>Est-ce que tu as gagné?</u>
  —<u>Non, j'ai perdu.</u>
  —<u>Dommage!</u>

À VOTRE TOUR

Depending on your goals and objectives, you may or may not wish to assign all of the activities in the **À votre tour** section.

GROUP PRACTICE

In Act. 1 and 3, you may want to have students work in trios, with two performing and one acting as monitor.

④ Le week-end dernier

ÉCRIRE Write a short composition in which you describe what you did last weekend. You may adopt some of the following suggestions. Do not use **aller**.

- voir (qui? où? quand?)
- voir (quel film? où?)
- faire (de quel sport? de quelle activité? avec qui?)
- jouer (à quel jeu? à quel sport?)
- jouer (de quel instrument? où?)
- avoir un rendez-vous (avec qui?)
- faire une promenade (où? avec qui?)
- dîner (où? avec qui?)
- être (à quel endroit? avec qui? quand?)
- faire des achats (où? quand?)
- acheter (quoi? pourquoi?)
- regarder (quel programme de télé? quel DVD?)
- assister (à quel match? à quel concert?)

Vendredi soir, j'ai vu le film *Casablanca* au Palace avec mon copain …

COMMENT DIT-ON …?

How to wish someone good luck or give encouragement:

Bonne chance!

BONNE CHANCE!

Bon courage!

BON COURAGE!

LESSON REVIEW
CLASSZONE.COM

trois cent trente-neuf **339**
Leçon 23

PORTFOLIO ASSESSMENT

You will probably select only one speaking activity and one writing activity to go into the students' portfolios for Unit 7.

In this lesson, Act. 3 lends itself well to oral portfolio recordings.

---

③ GUIDED ORAL EXPRESSION

Answers will vary.
- —Qu'est-ce que tu as fait hier soir?
  —J'ai eu un rendez-vous.
  —Avec qui est-ce que tu as eu un rendez-vous?
  —Avec Thomas, mon meilleur ami.
  —C'est chouette!
- —Qu'est-ce que tu as fait samedi soir?
  —J'ai dîné au restaurant.
  —Est-ce que tu as aimé le dîner?
  —Oui, c'est un très bon restaurant.
  —Mmmh, j'ai faim.
- —Qu'est-ce que tu as fait le week-end dernier?
  —J'ai fait du skate.
  —Est-ce qu'il a fait bon?
  —Non, il a fait très froid.
  —Dommage!
- —Qu'est-ce que tu as fait lundi dernier?
  —J'ai vu mes cousins.
  —Est-ce que tu as dîné chez eux?
  —Oui, et on a joué aux jeux vidéo. J'ai gagné!
  —Super!
- —Qu'est-ce que tu as fait la semaine dernière?
  —J'ai fait des achats.
  —Qu'est-ce que tu as acheté?
  —J'ai acheté ce tee-shirt.
  —Il est extra!
- —Qu'est-ce que tu as fait le mois dernier?
  —J'ai rendu visite à un copain.
  —Est-ce que vous avez fait du sport?
  —Oui, on a joué au basket.
  —Super!

Culture note

Le tennis The French not only love to play tennis, they are avid tennis fans. It was a national event when France won the Davis Cup in 2001.

Roland Garros is the tennis stadium near Paris which hosts the annual French Open (**Les Internationaux de France**). The stadium was named in memory of Roland Garros (1888–1918), a World War I fighter pilot and the first aviator to cross the Mediterranean (1913).

④ WRITTEN SELF-EXPRESSION

Answers will vary.
Vendredi soir, j'ai vu le film *Casablanca* au Palace avec mon copain. Après, nous avons pris un chocolat au café.

Samedi matin, mes amis et moi, nous avons eu des cours. J'ai aussi étudié. Samedi après-midi, nous avons fait du roller au parc.

Dimanche après-midi, ma famille et moi, nous avons rendu visite à ma grand-mère. Nous avons dîné chez elle. Dimanche soir, j'ai fini mes devoirs.

Leçon 24

Main Topic Describing where people went

Teaching Resource Options

AUDIO & VISUAL

Audio Program
CD 4 Tracks 16, 17
CD 11 Tracks 19–25

TECHNOLOGY
Online Workbook

VIDEO PROGRAM

 VIDÉO   DVD

MODULE 24
Un bon week-end

TOTAL TIME: 6:23 min.
   DVD Disk 2
   Videotape 4 (COUNTER: 18:30 min.)

24.1 Dialogue: Un bon week-end
(18:41–20:19 min.)

24.2 Mini-scenes: Listening
   – Où êtes-vous allé? Et qu'est-ce que
   vous avez fait?
   (20:20–22:08 min.)

24.3 Mini-scenes: Speaking
   – Où est-ce qu'ils sont allés?
   (22:09–23:20 min.)

24.4 Vignette culturelle: La musique
(23:21–24:53 min.)

Comprehension practice Play the entire module through as an introduction to the lesson.

LEÇON 24

Qui a de la chance? 🎧 AUDIO

VENDREDI APRÈS-MIDI
Anne et Valérie parlent de leurs projets pour le week-end.

Anne:	Qu'est-ce que tu vas faire samedi soir?	
Valérie:	Je vais aller au cinéma avec Jean-Pierre.	
Anne:	Tu as de la chance! Moi, je dois rester à la maison.	
Valérie:	Mais pourquoi?	
Anne:	Les amis de mes parents viennent chez nous ce week-end. Mon père insiste <u>pour que</u> je reste pour le dîner. <u>Quelle barbe!</u>	*that / What a pain!*
Valérie:	C'est vrai! Tu n'as pas de chance!	

LUNDI MATIN
Anne et Valérie parlent de leur week-end.

Anne:	Alors, tu as passé un bon week-end?	
Valérie:	Euh non, pas très bon.	
Anne:	Mais tu <u>es sortie</u> avec Jean-Pierre!	*went out*
Valérie:	C'est vrai. Je <u>suis allée</u> au cinéma avec lui …	*went*

Nous avons vu un très, très mauvais film! Après le film, j'ai eu une <u>dispute</u> avec Jean-Pierre. Et, <u>en plus</u>, j'ai perdu mon <u>porte-monnaie</u> … et je suis rentrée chez moi à pied! Et toi, tu <u>es restée</u> chez toi?

quarrel
in addition
wallet / went back
stayed

Anne:	Non.	
Valérie:	Comment? Les amis de tes parents <u>ne sont pas venus</u>?	*didn't come*
Anne:	Si, si, ils sont venus … avec leur fils!	
Valérie:	Et alors?	
Anne:	Eh bien, c'est un garçon très <u>sympa</u> et très amusant …	*sympa = sympathique*

Après le dîner, nous <u>sommes allés</u> au Zénith.* Nous avons assisté à un concert de rock absolument extraordinaire. Après, nous sommes allés dans un café et nous avons fait des projets pour le week-end prochain.

went

Valérie:	Qu'est-ce que vous allez faire?
Anne:	Nous allons faire une promenade à la campagne dans la nouvelle voiture de sport de Thomas. (C'est le nom de mon nouveau copain!)
Valérie:	Toi, vraiment, tu as de la chance!

*Une salle *(hall)* de concert à Paris, parc de la Villette.

340 trois cent quarante
Unité 7

CLASSROOM MANAGEMENT Pair reading

Since this is a longer story, you may want to use it as a recapitulation at the end of the lesson.

Have students read the title. Then, in pairs, have them read the story and write out brief answers to the following questions:

   Qui a de la chance? Pourquoi?
   Qui n'a pas de chance? Pourquoi?

Compréhension

1. Qu'est-ce que Valérie va faire samedi soir?
2. Pourquoi est-ce qu'Anne doit *(must)* rester à la maison?
3. Est-ce que Valérie a aimé le film?
4. Qu'est-ce qu'elle a perdu?
5. Comment est-ce qu'elle est rentrée chez elle?
6. Où et avec qui est-ce qu'Anne a dîné?
7. Où est-ce qu'elle est allée après le dîner?
8. Qu'est-ce qu'elle va faire le week-end prochain?
9. Comment s'appelle son nouveau copain?

Et toi?

Dis si oui ou non tu as fait les choses suivantes samedi dernier.

1. (Je suis/Je ne suis pas) … allé(e) en ville.
2. (Je suis/Je ne suis pas) … allé(e) au cinéma.
3. (Je suis/Je ne suis pas) … allé(e) à un concert.
4. (Je suis/Je ne suis pas) … rentré(e) chez moi pour le dîner.
5. (Je suis/Je ne suis pas) … resté(e) chez moi le soir.

Les jeunes Français et la musique

«Pour moi, la musique c'est tout!»° déclare Anne, une jeune Française de quinze ans. Sa copine Hélène est d'accord: «Aujourd'hui, on ne peut pas° vivre° sans° musique.»

Comme les jeunes Américains, les jeunes Français sont des «fanas°» de la musique. Ils aiment particulièrement le rock, le rap français ou américain, la techno, le pop, le reggae et le ska, mais certains préfèrent la musique classique. En semaine, ils écoutent leur musique préférée sur leurs baladeurs et leurs chaînes hi-fi. Le week-end, ils vont au concert écouter les stars de la chanson° française, anglaise ou américaine.

Le 21 juin de chaque année, les jeunes célèbrent la «Fête de la Musique» avec tous° les Français. C'est une grande fête nationale avec des concerts publics gratuits° dans toutes les villes et tous les villages de France. Ce jour-là, 800 000 musiciens jouent pour 60 millions de spectateurs. Pour la «Fête de la Musique» tout le monde° fait de la musique.

COMPARAISONS CULTURELLES

- Do you think American teenagers would agree with Anne: "**On ne peut pas vivre sans musique?**" Explain.
- Do French and American teenagers listen to the same types of music?
- Do you think that the United States should declare a national music day like the French "**Fête de la Musique**"? Why or why not?

tout *everything*   **ne peut pas** *cannot*   **vivre** *live*   **sans** *without*   **fanas = fanatiques**   **chanson** *song*   **tous** *all* **gratuits** *free*   **tout le monde** *everyone*

SETTING THE SCENE

The opening scene of **Video Module 24** presents two girls who are at a café talking about where they went last Saturday. At the end, the conversation takes an unexpected twist.

The **Vignette culturelle** of the video expands on the culture note in the text. French young people are interviewed about their tastes in music.

Compréhension
Answers
1. Elle va aller au cinéma avec Jean-Pierre.
2. Des amis de ses parents viennent chez eux.
3. Non, elle n'a pas aimé le film.
4. Elle a perdu son porte-monnaie.
5. Elle est rentrée chez elle à pied.
6. Anne a dîné à la maison avec ses parents, les amis de ses parents et leur fils.
7. Elle est allée au Zenith (à un concert de rock) et dans un café.
8. Le week-end prochain, elle va faire une promenade à la campagne avec Thomas (dans sa nouvelle voiture de sport).
9. Il s'appelle Thomas.

Et toi? describing what one did last weekend

Answers will vary.
1. Je suis allé(e) en ville. (Je ne suis pas allé(e) en ville.)
2. Je suis allé(e) au cinéma. (Je ne suis pas allé(e) au cinéma.)
3. Je suis allé(e) au concert. (Je ne suis pas allé(e) au concert.)
4. Je suis rentré(e) chez moi pour le dîner. (Je ne suis pas rentré(e) chez moi pour le dîner.)
5. Je suis resté(e) chez moi le soir. (Je ne suis pas resté(e) chez moi le soir.)

Teaching Resource Options

PRINT

Workbook PE, pp. 201–208
Unit 7 Resource Book
 Communipak, pp. 148–170
 Video Activities, pp. 132–133
 Videoscript, pp. 137–138
 Workbook TE, pp. 109–116

TECHNOLOGY
Power Presentations

VIDEO PROGRAM

 VIDÉO DVD **MODULE 24**

24.2 Mini-scenes: Où êtes-vous allé? Et qu'est-ce que vous avez fait?
(20:20–22:08 min.)

24.3 Où est-ce qu'ils sont allés?
(22:09–23:20 min.)

Pronunciation In spoken French, the four forms of **allé** sound the same.

 1 **PRACTICE** describing who went where

1. Claire est
2. Olivier est
3. Éric et Jacques sont
4. Anne et Monique sont
5. Olivier est
6. Éric et Jacques sont
7. Olivier est
8. Anne et Monique sont

A Le passé composé avec *être*

Note the forms of the passé composé of **aller** in the sentences below, paying attention to the endings of the past participle **(allé).**

Jean-Paul **est allé** au cinéma. *Jean-Paul **went** to the movies.*
Mélanie **est allée** à la plage. *Mélanie **went** to the beach.*
Éric et Patrick **sont allés** en ville. *Éric and Patrick **went** downtown.*
Mes copines **sont allées** à la campagne. *My friends **went** to the country.*

The passé composé of **aller** and certain verbs of motion is formed with **être** according to the pattern:

> PRESENT of **être** + PAST PARTICIPLE

→ When the passé composé of a verb is conjugated with **être** (and not with **avoir**), the PAST PARTICIPLE *agrees* with the SUBJECT in gender and number.

INFINITIVE	aller	
PASSÉ COMPOSÉ	je **suis** allé tu **es** allé il **est** allé nous **sommes** allé s vous **êtes** allé s ils **sont** allé s	je **suis** allé e tu **es** allé e elle **est** allé e nous **sommes** allé es vous **êtes** allé es elles **sont** allé es
NEGATIVE	je **ne suis pas** allé	je **ne suis pas** allé e
INTERROGATIVE	est-ce que tu **es** allé? tu **es** allé? (**es**-tu allé?)	est-ce que tu **es** allé e ? tu **es** allé e ? (**es**-tu allé e ?)

→ When **vous** refers to a single person, the past participle is in the singular:
Mme Mercier, est-ce que vous êtes **allée** au concert hier soir?

WARM-UP AND REVIEW

As a preparation for the passé composé of **aller,** have students review the forms of **être,** together with the expression **chez.**

You will indicate what people are doing, and the students will let you know whether those people are at home or not.
Paul joue au foot. [Il n'est pas chez lui.]

Je regarde la télé. [Je suis chez moi.]
Nous étudions. [Nous sommes chez nous.]
Mes copains dînent. [Ils sont chez eux.]
Tu fais de la voile. [Tu n'es pas chez toi.]
Sophie nettoie sa chambre. [Elle est chez elle.]
Elles font du ski. [Elles ne sont pas chez elles.]
Vous voyagez. [Vous n'êtes pas chez vous.]

1 À Paris

PARLER/ÉCRIRE Des amis sont allés à Paris samedi dernier. Chacun est allé à un endroit différent. Dites qui est allé aux endroits suivants. Complétez chaque phrase avec le sujet approprié et la forme correspondante du verbe **aller**.

Olivier

Éric et Jacques

Claire

Anne et Monique

▶ **Anne et Monique** sont allées au Louvre.

1. ... allée à la tour Eiffel.
2. ... allé au Centre Pompidou.
3. ... allés au Stade de France.
4. ... allées aux Galeries Lafayette.
5. ... allé à la Villette.
6. ... allés au Zénith.
7. ... allé au musée d'Orsay.
8. ... allées au Quartier latin.

2 Conversation

PARLER Demandez à vos camarades s'ils sont allés aux endroits suivants.

▶ ce matin/à la bibliothèque?

1. hier matin/à l'école?
2. hier soir/au cinéma?
3. dimanche dernier/au restaurant?
4. samedi dernier/dans les magasins?
5. l'été dernier/chez tes cousins?
6. le week-end dernier/à la campagne?
7. le mois dernier/à un concert?
8. la semaine dernière/chez le coiffeur *(barber, hairdresser)*?
9. les vacances dernières/à la mer?

> Ce matin, est-ce que tu es allé à la bibliothèque?

> Oui, je suis allé à la bibliothèque.
> (Non, je ne suis pas allé à la bibliothèque.)

3 Le week-end dernier

PARLER/ÉCRIRE Dites ce que les personnes de la Colonne A ont fait en choisissant une activité de la Colonne B. Puis dites où ces personnes sont allées en choisissant un endroit de la Colonne C. Soyez logiques!

A	B	C
je	voir des clowns	à la campagne
tu	nager	au zoo
nous	dîner en ville	dans un magasin de chaussures
Catherine	regarder les éléphants	à la bibliothèque
vous	choisir des livres	à la plage
mon petit frère	faire un pique-nique	au restaurant
André et Thomas	acheter des sandales	au cirque *(circus)*
les filles	faire du roller	dans la rue

▶ **J'ai nagé. Je suis allé(e) à la plage.**

---

2 COMMUNICATION finding out where people went

1. —Hier matin, est-ce que tu es allé(e) à l'école.
   —Oui, je suis allé(e) à l'école. (Non, je ne suis pas allé(e) à l'école.)
2. —Hier soir, est-ce que tu es allé(e) au cinéma?
   —Oui, je suis allé(e) au cinéma. (Non, je ne suis pas allé(e) au cinéma.)
3. —Dimanche dernier, est-ce que tu es allé(e) au restaurant?
   —Oui, je suis allé(e) au restaurant. (Non, je ne suis pas allé(e) au restaurant.)
4. —Samedi dernier, est-ce que tu es allé(e) dans les magasins?
   —Oui, je suis allé(e) dans les magasins. (Non, je ne suis pas allé(e) dans les magasins.)
5. —L'été dernier, est-ce que tu es allé(e) chez tes cousins?
   —Oui, je suis allé(e) chez mes cousins. (Non, je ne suis pas allé(e) chez mes cousins.)
6. —Le week-end dernier, est-ce que tu es allé(e) à la campagne?
   —Oui, je suis allé(e) à la campagne. (Non, je ne suis pas allé(e) à la campagne.)
7. —Le mois dernier, est-ce que tu es allé(e) à un concert?
   —Oui, je suis allé(e) à un concert. (Non, je ne suis pas allé(e) à un concert.)
8. —La semaine dernière, est-ce que tu es allé(e) chez le coiffeur?
   —Oui, je suis allé(e) chez le coiffeur. (Non, je ne suis pas allé(e) chez le coiffeur.)
9. —Les vacances dernières, est-ce que tu es allé(e) à la mer?
   —Oui, je suis allé(e) à la mer. (Non, je ne suis pas allé(e) à la mer.)

Vocabulary update:

la bibliothèque *municipal library*
le CDI (Centre de documentation et d'information) *school library*
Students in school would say: "Je suis allé au CDI."

3 COMPREHENSION describing where people went to do certain things

Answers will vary.
1. J'ai vu des clowns. Je suis allé(e) au cirque.
2. Tu as nagé. Tu es allé(e) à la plage.
3. Nous avons dîné en ville. Nous sommes allé(e)s au restaurant.
4. Catherine a regardé les éléphants. Elle est allée au zoo.
5. Vous avez choisi des livres. Vous êtes allé(e)(s) à la bibliothèque.
6. Mon petit frère a fait une promenade. Il est allé à la campagne.
7. André et Thomas ont acheté des sandales. Ils sont allés dans un magasin de chaussures.
8. Les filles ont fait du roller. Elles sont allées dans la rue.

Pronunciation

clown /klun/
zoo /zo/ or /zoo/

Teaching note This activity may be done in a game format. See Teaching note, p. 272.

Teaching Resource Options

PRINT

Workbook PE, pp. 201–208
Unit 7 Resource Book
    Communipak, pp. 148–170
    Workbook TE, pp. 109–116

AUDIO & VISUAL

Overhead Transparencies
16 Subject pronouns

TECHNOLOGY

Power Presentations

---

4 **ROLE PLAY** talking about last weekend

1. —Où est-ce que tu es allé(e)?
   —Je suis allé(e) au stade.
   —Ah bon! Qu'est-ce que tu as fait?
   —J'ai regardé un match de foot.
2. —Où est-ce que tu es allé(e)?
   —Je suis allé(e) à la plage.
   —Ah bon! Qu'est-ce que tu as fait?
   —J'ai joué au volley.
3. —Où est-ce que tu es allé(e)?
   —Je suis allé(e) à une boum.
   —Ah bon! Qu'est-ce que tu as fait?
   —J'ai dansé.
4. —Où est-ce que tu es allé(e)?
   —Je suis allé(e) à la campagne.
   —Ah bon! Qu'est-ce que tu as fait?
   —J'ai fait une promenade à pied.
5. —Où est-ce que tu es allé(e)?
   —Je suis allé(e) au Bon Marché.
   —Ah bon! Qu'est-ce que tu as fait?
   —J'ai acheté un blouson.
6. —Où est-ce que tu es allé(e)?
   —Je suis allé(e) dans un restaurant italien.
   —Ah bon! Qu'est-ce que tu as fait?
   —J'ai mangé des spaghetti.

Looking ahead If you wish to present the other verbs conjugated with **être**, you can have students refer to the Appendix, page R11. These verbs will be formally introduced in Book Two.

Extra practice Use Transparency Subject pronouns to do rapid substitution drills. Give the model sentence and then point to various subject pronouns.

Je suis venu(e) hier.
[tu] Tu es venu(e) hier.
Je suis arrivé(e) à midi.
Je suis rentré(e) à minuit.

Realia note
This is an ad for **Sport Magazine**. The word **infos** is a shortened form of **informations**, meaning news and background information.

---

4  **Week-end**

PARLER Des amis parlent de leur week-end. Jouez ces dialogues.

Où est-ce que tu es allée?
Je suis allée en ville.
Ah bon! Qu'est-ce que tu as fait?
J'ai acheté des vêtements.

▶ en ville / acheter des vêtements

1. au stade / regarder un match de foot
2. à la plage / jouer au volley
3. à une boum / danser
4. à la campagne / faire une promenade à pied
5. au Bon Marché / acheter un blouson
6. dans un restaurant italien / manger des spaghetti

VOCABULAIRE Quelques verbes conjugués avec *être* au passé composé

INFINITIVE	PAST PARTICIPLE		
aller	allé	to go	Nous **sommes allés** en ville.
arriver	arrivé	to arrive	Vous **êtes arrivés** à midi.
rentrer	rentré	to return, go back, come back	Nous **sommes rentrés** à la maison à onze heures.
rester	resté	to stay	Les touristes **sont restés** à l'hôtel Ibis.
venir	venu	to come	Qui **est venu** hier?

---

5 **Qui est resté à la maison?**

PARLER/ÉCRIRE Samedi après-midi, les personnes suivantes ont fait certaines choses. Dites si oui ou non elles sont restées à la maison.

▶ Paul a regardé la télé.   **Il est resté à la maison.**
▶ Mélanie a fait des achats.   **Elle n'est pas restée à la maison.**

1. Mlle Joly a lavé sa voiture.
2. Nous avons fait une promenade à vélo.
3. Tu as nettoyé le garage.
4. Éric et Olivier ont joué aux jeux vidéo.
5. Christine et Isabelle ont travaillé dans le jardin.
6. Vous avez fait du roller.
7. Mes cousins ont fait de la voile.
8. J'ai fait du jogging.

JOGGING

INFOS *Sport* magazine

COMPREHENSION Destinations and arrival times

PROPS: Map (or transparency) of France, clock with movable hands

Imagine that the class is visiting France.
Je suis allé(e) à Nice. [point to Nice]
Je suis arrivé(e) à midi. [move clock to 12]

Have pairs of students come up to show where they went and when they arrived.

X et Y, vous êtes allé(e)s à Lyon.
Vous êtes arrivé(e)s à 1h20.
Venez nous montrer la ville et l'heure.

Follow-up questions:
Où est-ce que X et Y sont allé(e)s?
À quelle heure sont-ils(elles) arrivé(e)s?

6 La journée de Sandrine

PARLER/ÉCRIRE Pendant les vacances, Sandrine travaille dans une agence de tourisme. Le soir, elle raconte *(tells about)* sa journée à son père.

▶ aller au bureau *(office)*

1. arriver à neuf heures
2. téléphoner à un client anglais
3. parler avec des touristes japonais
4. aller au restaurant à midi et demi
5. rentrer au bureau à deux heures
6. copier des documents
7. préparer des billets *(tickets)* d'avion
8. rester jusqu'à *(until)* six heures
9. dîner en ville
10. rentrer à la maison à neuf heures

Je suis allée au bureau.

7 Une question de circonstances *(A matter of circumstances)*

PARLER/ÉCRIRE Nos activités dépendent souvent des circonstances.
Dites si oui ou non les personnes suivantes ont fait les choses indiquées.

▶ On est mardi aujourd'hui.
  • les élèves/rester à la maison?
  Les élèves ne sont pas restés à la maison.

1. On est dimanche.
  • M. Boulot/travailler?
  • nous/aller à l'école?
  • vous/dîner à la cantine *(school cafeteria)*?

2. Il fait très beau aujourd'hui.
  • moi/aller à la campagne?
  • mes copines/regarder la télé?
  • toi/venir à la piscine avec nous?

3. Il fait très mauvais!
  • Marc/faire un pique-nique?
  • Hélène et Juliette/rester à la maison?
  • ma mère/rentrer à la maison à pied?

4. Mes copains et moi, nous n'avons pas beaucoup d'argent.
  • toi/aller dans un restaurant cher?
  • mes copains/venir chez moi en taxi?
  • moi/acheter des vêtements?

---

5 COMPREHENSION concluding who stayed home and who did not

1. Elle est restée à la maison.
2. Nous ne sommes pas resté(e)s à la maison.
3. Tu es resté(e) à la maison.
4. Ils ne sont pas restés à la maison. (Ils sont restés à la maison.)
5. Elles sont restées à la maison.
6. Vous n'êtes pas resté(e)(s) à la maison.
7. Ils ne sont pas restés à la maison.
8. Je ne suis pas resté(e) à la maison.

Variation Have students respond using **chez** plus stress pronouns.

Paul est resté chez lui.
Mélanie n'est pas restée chez elle.

6 ROLE PLAY narrating the day's events

1. Je suis arrivée à neuf heures.
2. J'ai téléphoné à un client anglais.
3. J'ai parlé avec des touristes japonais.
4. Je suis allée au restaurant à midi et demi.
5. Je suis rentrée au bureau à deux heures.
6. J'ai copié des documents.
7. J'ai préparé des billets d'avion.
8. Je suis restée jusqu'à six heures.
9. J'ai dîné en ville.
10. Je suis rentré(e) à la maison à neuf heures.

Variation (using other subjects)

[elle] Elle est allée au bureau.
[nous] Nous sommes allés au bureau.
[Élisabeth et sa sœur Alice (elles)] Elles sont allées au bureau.

7 COMPREHENSION drawing conclusions about past actions

1. M. Boulot n'a pas travaillé.
   Nous ne sommes pas allé(e)s à l'école.
   Vous n'avez pas dîné à la cantine.
2. Je suis allé(e) à la campagne.
   Mes copines n'ont pas regardé la télé.
   Tu es venu(e) à la piscine avec nous.
3. Marc n'a pas fait de pique-nique.
   Hélène et Juliette sont restées à la maison.
   Ma mère n'est pas rentrée à la maison à pied.
4. Tu n'es pas allé(e) dans un restaurant cher.
   Mes copains ne sont pas venus chez moi en taxi.
   Je n'ai pas acheté de vêtements.

Teaching note Remind students to use **pas de** in items 3 and 4:

3. Marc n'a <u>pas</u> fait <u>de</u> pique-nique.
4. Je n'ai <u>pas</u> acheté <u>de</u> vêtements.

Expansion Have students write an original affirmative and negative sentence for each item.

Nous avons eu un examen de français.
Je n'ai pas regardé la télé ce matin.

SECTION B

Communicative function
Saying that one never does
something

Teaching Resource Options

PRINT

Workbook PE, pp. 201–208
Unit 7 Resource Book
  Audioscript, p. 139
  Communipak, pp. 148–170
  Video Activities, p. 131
  Videoscript, p. 137
  Workbook TE, pp. 109–116

AUDIO & VISUAL

Audio Program
CD 4 Track 18

TECHNOLOGY

Power Presentations

VIDEO PROGRAM

VIDÉO   DVD

MODULE 24

24.1 Dialogue: Un bon week-end
(18:41–20:19 min.)

Teaching strategy Point out that
the pattern with **ne ... jamais** in the
passé composé is the same as with
ne ... pas.

 PRACTICE talking about what
one never does

1. Le dimanche, elle n'étudie jamais.
2. Le dimanche, il ne travaille jamais.
3. Le dimanche, nous ne parlons jamais français.
4. Le dimanche, vous n'allez jamais à la bibliothèque.
5. Le dimanche, il ne va jamais en ville.
6. Le dimanche, ils ne mangent jamais à la cantine.
7. Le dimanche, tu ne rends jamais visite à tes copains.
8. Le dimanche, vous ne dînez jamais chez vous.
9. Le dimanche, je ne range jamais ma chambre.
10. Le dimanche, je ne lave jamais la voiture.

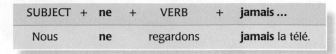

B La construction négative *ne ... jamais*

Compare the following negative constructions.

Éric **ne** parle **pas** à Paul.   Éric does **not** speak to Paul.
Éric **ne** parle **jamais** à Paul.   Éric **never** speaks to Paul.

Nous **n'**étudions **pas** le dimanche.   We do **not** study on Sundays.
Nous **n'**étudions **jamais** le dimanche.   We **never** study on Sundays.

To say that one NEVER does something, French speakers use the construction
ne ... jamais, as follows:

SUBJECT +	ne	+ VERB	+	jamais ...
Nous	ne	regardons		jamais la télé.

→ **Ne** becomes **n'** before a vowel sound.

Nous **n'**allons **jamais** à l'opéra.

→ Note the use of **ne ... jamais** in the passé composé:

Nous **n'**avons **jamais** visité Québec.   We **never** visited Quebec.
Je **ne** suis **jamais** allé à Genève.   I **never** went to Geneva.

8 Jamais le dimanche

PARLER/ÉCRIRE Le dimanche les personnes suivantes ne font jamais
ce qu'elles font pendant la semaine. Exprimez cette situation.

▶ François va à l'école.
Le dimanche, il ne va jamais à l'école.

1. Anne étudie.
2. Marc travaille.
3. Nous parlons français.
4. Vous allez à la bibliothèque.
5. M. Bernard va en ville.
6. Les élèves mangent à la cantine.
7. Tu rends visite à tes copains.
8. Vous dînez chez vous.
9. Je range ma chambre.
10. Je lave la voiture.

9 Et toi?

PARLER/ÉCRIRE Dites si vous avez jamais *(ever)* fait les choses suivantes.

▶ aller en France
Oui, je suis allé(e) en France.
Non, je ne suis jamais allé(e) en France.

1. aller en Chine?
2. visiter Paris?
3. voyager en limousine?
4. voir un opéra?
5. voir un fantôme *(ghost)*?
6. téléphoner au Président?
7. surfer sur l'Internet en français?
8. dîner dans un restaurant vietnamien?
9. jouer aux échecs?
10. faire une promenade en scooter?

C Les expressions *quelqu'un, quelque chose* et leurs contraires

Compare the affirmative and negative constructions in heavy print.

—Tu attends **quelqu'un?**   *Are you waiting for **someone (anyone)?***
—Non, je **n'**attends **personne.**   *No, I'm **not** waiting for **anyone.***

—Vous faites **quelque chose** ce soir?   *Are you doing **something (anything)** tonight?*
—Non, nous **ne** faisons **rien.**   *No, we're **not** doing **anything.***
     *No, we're doing **nothing.***

To refer to unspecified people or things, French speakers use the following expressions:

quelqu'un	someone, anyone somebody, anybody	**ne ... personne**	no one, not anyone nobody, not anybody
quelque chose	something, anything	**ne ... rien**	nothing, not anything

→ Like all negative expressions, **personne** and **rien** require **ne** before the verb.

→ In short answers, **personne** and **rien** may be used alone.

Qui est là? **Personne.**
Qu'est-ce que tu fais? **Rien.**

10 Florence est malade

PARLER Florence est malade *(sick)* aujourd'hui. Elle répond négativement aux questions de Paul.

▶ dîner avec quelqu'un?

Tu dînes avec quelqu'un?
Non, je ne dîne avec personne.

1. inviter quelqu'un?
2. faire quelque chose ce soir?
3. manger quelque chose à midi?
4. regarder quelque chose à la télé?
5. attendre quelqu'un ce matin?
6. voir quelqu'un cet après-midi?
7. préparer quelque chose pour le dîner?
8. rencontrer quelqu'un après le dîner?

PRONONCIATION   qu = /k/

Les lettres «qu»

The letters "**qu**" represent the sound /k/.

Répétez: **qui quand quelque chose quelqu'un quatre quatorze Québec Monique Véronique sympathique un pique-nique le ski nautique**

un bouquet

Véronique pense que Monique aime la musique classique.

---

9 COMMUNICATION answering personal questions

Answers will vary.
1. Oui je suis allé(e) en Chine. (Non, je ne suis jamais allé(e) en Chine.)
2. Oui, j'ai visité Paris. (Non, je n'ai jamais visité Paris.)
3. Oui, j'ai voyagé en limousine. (Non, je n'ai jamais voyagé en limousine.)
4. Oui, j'ai vu un opéra. (Non, je n'ai jamais vu d'opéra.)
5. Non, je n'ai jamais vu de fantôme. (Oui, j'ai vu un fantôme.)
6. Non, je n'ai jamais téléphoné au Président. (Oui, j'ai téléphoné au Président.)
7. Oui, j'ai surfé sur l'Internet en français. (Non, je n'ai jamais surfé sur l'Internet en français.)
8. Oui, j'ai dîné dans un restaurant vietnamien. (Non, je n'ai jamais dîné dans un restaurant vietnamien.)
9. Non, je n'ai jamais joué aux échecs. (Oui, j'ai joué aux échecs.)
10. Non, je n'ai jamais fait de promenade en scooter. (Oui, j'ai fait une promenade en scooter.)

SECTION C

Communicative function
Identifying people and things

Language note Word order with **ne... personne** and **ne... rien** is presented in Book Two. In general, **personne** and **rien** have the same position in the sentence as **quelqu'un** and **quelque chose:**
Quelqu'un a téléphoné?
Non, personne n'a téléphoné.

Exception: In the passé composé **rien** comes between the auxiliary and the past participle:
Tu as acheté quelque chose?
Non, je n'ai rien acheté.

Teaching strategy Point out that **pas** is never used together with **personne** or **rien.**

10 ROLE PLAY giving negative responses

1. —Tu invites quelqu'un?
 —Non, je n'invite personne.
2. —Tu fais quelque chose ce soir?
 —Non, je ne fais rien.
3. —Tu manges quelque chose à midi?
 —Non, je ne mange rien à midi.
4. —Tu regardes quelque chose à la télé?
 —Non, je ne regarde rien à la télé.
5. —Tu attends quelqu'un ce matin?
 —Non, je n'attends personne ce matin.
6. —Tu vois quelqu'un cet après-midi?
 —Non, je ne vois personne cet après-midi.
7. —Tu prépares quelque chose pour le dîner?
 —Non, je ne prépare rien pour le dîner.
8. —Tu rencontres quelqu'un après le dîner?
 —Non, je ne rencontre personne après le dîner.

Teaching Resource Options

PRINT

Workbook PE, pp. 201–208
Unit 7 Resource Book
  Audioscript, pp. 139–140
  Communipak, pp. 148–170
  Family Involvement, pp. 129–130
  Workbook TE, pp. 109–116

Assessment
Lesson 24 Quiz, pp. 144–145
Portfolio Assessment, Unit 1 URB
  pp. 155–164
Audioscript for Quiz 24, p. 143
Answer Keys, pp. 213–216

AUDIO & VISUAL

Audio Program
CD 4 Tracks 19, 20
CD 16 Track 4

TECHNOLOGY

Test Generator CD-ROM/eTest Plus
  Online

1 COMPREHENSION

1. Tu es restée chez toi samedi soir?
(e) Non! J'ai téléphoné à une copine et nous sommes allées au cinéma.
2. Qu'est-ce que vous avez vu?
(c) Un vieux western avec Gary Cooper.
3. Qu'est-ce que vous avez fait ensuite?
(d) Nous sommes allées dans un café sur le boulevard Saint Michel.
4. Vous avez mangé quelque chose?
(a) Oui, des sandwichs.
5. À quelle heure es-tu rentrée chez toi?
(b) À onze heures et demie.

2 GUIDED ORAL EXPRESSION

Answers will vary.
• Je suis allé(e) en France.
• J'ai vu l'Arc de Triomphe.
• J'ai visité Québec.
• Je suis allé(e) à Montréal.

Expansion I did not see you last weekend. Please answer my questions in French. Tell me:
• Did you stay home Saturday morning?
• What did you do?
• Where did you go Saturday afternoon?
• What did you do there?
• Did you meet your friends?
• If so, what did you do together?

À votre tour!

OBJECTIFS

Now you can …
• say where you went and when you came back
• talk about things you have never done

1 Allô!

PARLER Reconstituez la conversation entre Sophie et Charlotte. Pour cela, faites correspondre les réponses de Charlotte avec les questions de Sophie.

1. Tu es restée chez toi samedi soir?
2. Qu'est-ce que vous avez vu?
3. Qu'est-ce que vous avez fait ensuite?
4. Vous avez mangé quelque chose?
5. À quelle heure es-tu rentrée chez toi?

a. Oui, des sandwichs.
b. À onze heures et demie.
c. Un vieux western avec Gary Cooper.
d. Nous sommes allées dans un café sur le boulevard Saint Michel.
e. Non! J'ai téléphoné à une copine et nous sommes allées au cinéma.

2 Dis-moi …

PARLER *I will tell you about some places I have never visited. Then you will tell me about a few places where you have been.*

• Je ne suis jamais allée à la Martinique.
• Je n'ai jamais vu la Statue de la Liberté.
• Je n'ai jamais été à New York.
• Je n'ai jamais visité San Francisco.

Et maintenant, dis-moi …

3 Créa-dialogue

PARLER Avec vos copains, discutez de ce que vous avez fait récemment *(recently)*. Utilisez les suggestions suivantes.

▶ —Tu es resté(e) chez toi hier matin?
—Oui, je suis resté(e) chez moi.
—Qu'est-ce que tu as fait?
—J'ai rangé ma chambre.

▶ —Tu es resté(e) chez toi hier matin?
—Non, je ne suis pas resté(e) chez moi.
—Qu'est-ce que tu as fait?
—Je suis allé(e) à l'école.

▶ rester chez toi / hier matin / ??

1. aller en ville / samedi après-midi / ??
2. rentrer chez toi / vendredi soir / ??
3. rester à la maison / samedi matin / ??

À VOTRE TOUR

Depending on your goals and objectives, you may or may not wish to assign all of the activities in the À votre tour section.

GROUP PRACTICE

In Act. 1 and 3, you may want to have students work in trios, with two performing and one acting as monitor.

4 Composition: Samedi dernier

ÉCRIRE Read what Céline did last Saturday. Then write a short composition in the **passé composé** telling how a friend of yours (real or imaginary) spent the day. Use only familiar vocabulary.

Le matin, Céline est restée à la maison. Elle a rangé sa chambre et après elle a fini ses devoirs.

L'après-midi, elle est allée au cinéma avec son copain Trinh. Ils ont vu une comédie. Ensuite ils sont allés dans un magasin de vêtements. Céline a acheté un tee-shirt et Trinh a acheté une nouvelle casquette. Finalement, Céline est rentrée chez elle.

Le soir, elle a dîné avec ses parents. Après, elle est restée dans sa chambre. Elle a surfé sur l'Internet et elle a téléchargé de la musique reggae. Elle adore la musique reggae!

```
Samedi dernier
Le matin, mon ami
Kevin n'est pas
resté à la maison.
Il a fait du jogging
et après ...
```

4. aller à la plage			
dimanche dernier	5. aller à la campagne	6. aller à une boum	
??	le week-end dernier	la semaine dernière	8. travailler
	??	??	l'été dernier
		7. faire un voyage	??
		le mois dernier	
		??	

STRATEGY Writing

Narration in the *passé composé* Read the description of Céline's activities again. Note that the author wrote **Céline est restée, elle est allée,** and **Céline est rentrée,** adding a final "e" to the past participles because the subject, **Céline/elle** is feminine. In referring to Céline and Trinh, the author wrote **ils sont allés** and added a final "s" to **allé** because the subject, **ils,** is plural.

When you are writing in the passé composé, it is important to go back over your composition and check all the verb forms. If you have used the verbs **aller, venir, arriver, rester,** or **rentrer,** look to be sure that you formed the passé composé with **être,** rather than **avoir,** and that in each case the past participle agrees with the subject.

COMMENT DIT-ON ...?

How to celebrate a happy occasion:

Bon anniversaire!

Bonne année!

LESSON REVIEW
CLASSZONE.COM

PORTFOLIO ASSESSMENT

You will probably select only one speaking activity and one writing activity to go into the students' portfolios for Unit 7.

In this lesson, Act. 4 offers an excellent writing portfolio topic.

TESTS DE CONTRÔLE

Teaching Resource Options

PRINT

Unit 7 Resource Book
    Communipak, pp. 148–170

Assessment
Unit 7 Test, pp. 179–187
Portfolio Assessment, Unit 1 URB
    pp. 155–164
Multiple Choice Test Items,
    p. 200–208
Listening Comprehension
    Performance Test, pp. 188–189
Reading Performance Test,
    pp. 194–196
Speaking Performance Test,
    pp. 190–193
Writing Performance Test,
    pp. 197–199
Test Scoring Tools, p. 209
Audioscript for Tests,
    pp. 210–212
Answer Keys, pp. 213–216

AUDIO & VISUAL
Audio Program
CD 16 Tracks 5–8

TECHNOLOGY
Test Generator CD-ROM/eTest Plus
    Online

1 COMPREHENSION

1.	c	7.	c
2.	a	8.	a
3.	b	9.	b
4.	a	10.	b
5.	c	11.	b
6.	b	12.	a

2 COMPREHENSION

1.	avons loué	6.	a eu
2.	ont joué	7.	ont fait
3.	a rangé	8.	ai été
4.	avez fini	9.	as vu
5.	as vendu	10.	a mis

Tests de contrôle

By taking the following tests, you can check your progress in French and also prepare for the unit test. Write your answers on a separate sheet of paper.

Review...
new words and
expressions
• verbs: p. 310
• sports: pp. 312, 313
• expressions with
  avoir: p. 320
• expressions of time:
  p. 336
• **quelqu'un** and
  quelque chose: p. 347

1 **The right choice** ---

Choose the expressions (a), (b), or (c) which best complete the following sentences.

1. Céline va au cinéma. Elle va — une comédie.
   a. aider   **b.** rencontrer   **c.** voir
2. Thomas va au stade. Il va — un match de foot.
   a. assister à   **b.** attendre   **c.** nettoyer
3. Mathieu va rester à la maison. Il va — la voiture de sa mère.
   a. aider   **b.** laver   **c.** rencontrer
4. Charlotte va au café. Elle va — ses copines.
   a. rencontrer   **b.** assister à   **c.** louer

5. Julien est à la mer. Il fait —.
   a. du ski   **b.** du roller   **c.** de la planche à voile
6. Léa est à la montagne. Elle fait —.
   a. de la voile   **b.** de l'escalade   **c.** ses devoirs

7. Clément met un pull parce qu'il a —.
   a. faim   **b.** chaud   **c.** froid
8. Mélanie commande (*orders*) un soda parce qu'elle a —.
   a. soif   **b.** tort   **c.** de la chance

9. Je suis allé au cinéma—.
   a. demain   **b.** hier soir   **c.** samedi prochain
10. Je vais aller à une boum —.
    a. hier matin   **b.** demain après-midi   **c.** la semaine dernière

11. Catherine est au café. Elle attend —.
    a. un   **b.** quelqu'un   **c.** personne
12. Pierre n'a pas faim. Il ne mange —.
    a. rien   **b.** quelque chose   **c.** une pizza

Review...
the **passé composé**
• **-er** verbs: p. 321
• **-ir** and **-re** verbs:
  p. 333
• irregular verbs: p. 335

2 **The right verb** ---

Complete the following sentences with the appropriate forms of the **passé composé** of the verbs in parentheses.

1. **(louer)**   La semaine dernière, nous — un DVD.
2. **(jouer)**   Hier après-midi, Céline et Thomas — au tennis.
3. **(ranger)**   Samedi matin, Pauline — sa chambre.

4. (finir)   Est-ce que vous — les exercices?

5. (vendre)   À qui est-ce que tu — ton vélo?

6. (avoir)   Monsieur Lescure — un accident avec sa nouvelle voiture.

7. (faire)   Pendant les vacances, les élèves — un voyage au Canada.

8. (être)   Moi, j'— à Paris l'année dernière.

9. (voir)   Quel film est-ce que tu — mardi soir?

10. (mettre)   Mathieu — un CD de rock.

③ Être or avoir?

Complete the following sentences with the **passé composé** forms of the verbs in parentheses. Be sure to use the appropriate forms of **être** or **avoir.**

1. (acheter)   Nous — un livre sur Paris.

2. (aller)   Marie — à la tour Eiffel.

3. (rester)   Mes copains — à l'hôtel.

4. (téléphoner)   Ils — à des amis.

5. (arriver)   Pierre — à l'aéroport.

6. (rentrer)   Nous — le 15 août.

7. (visiter)   Tu — le musée d'Orsay.

8. (venir)   Mes amis — avec nous.

> **Review...**
> • passé composé with être: pp. 342 and 344

④ Non!

Transform the statements below into **negative** sentences. Replace the underlined words with the expressions in parentheses.

1. Léa a voyagé <u>en bus</u>. **(en train)**

2. J'ai joué <u>au foot</u> hier. **(au basket)**

3. Tu es resté <u>à l'hôtel</u>. **(chez tes cousins)**

4. Éric a invité <u>sa cousine</u>. **(son copain)**

> **Review...**
> • the negative passé composé: p. 324

⑤ Composition: Thanksgiving

Write a short paragraph of five or six sentences about what you and your family did last Thanksgiving. Did you travel somewhere or did people come to your house? What did you do together? Use the **passé composé,** limiting yourself to words and expressions that you know in French.

STRATEGY Writing

a Make a list of the verbs you will use to describe your activities. Review which ones use **avoir** in the **passé composé** and which use **être.**

	avoir	être
<u>dîner</u> chez mes cousins	x	

b Organize your ideas and write your paragraph.

c Check the **passé composé** forms of all the verbs in your composition.

③ COMPREHENSION

1. avons acheté

2. est allée

3. sont restés

4. ont téléphoné

5. est arrivé

6. sommes rentré(e)s

7. as visité

8. sont venus

④ COMPREHENSION

1. Léa n'a pas voyagé en train.

2. Je n'ai pas joué au basket hier.

3. Tu n'es pas resté chez tes cousins.

4. Éric n'a pas invité son copain.

⑤ WRITTEN SELF-EXPRESSION

Answers will vary.
Le Thanksgiving dernier, ma famille est restée dans notre ville. Le matin, mon frère et moi, nous avons assisté au match de football américain de notre lycée. Notre équipe a gagné!

L'après-midi, mes parents, mon frère et moi, nous sommes allés chez ma tante. Nous avons mangé un grand dîner. J'ai joué aux jeux vidéo avec mon cousin.

Le soir, nous avons regardé un DVD. Ma famille est rentrée chez nous à dix heures.

Vocabulaire

POUR COMMUNIQUER

Talking about past activities

Qu'est-ce que tu as fait hier?	What did you do yesterday?
J'ai vu un film.	I saw a film.
Je suis allé au cinéma.	I went to the movies.
Je n'ai pas travaillé.	I didn't work.
Je ne suis pas allé à l'école.	I didn't go to school.

Explaining why

Pourquoi est-ce que tu es allé en ville?	Why did you go downtown?
Je suis allé en ville pour louer un DVD.	I went downtown to rent a DVD.

Talking about one's activities

Est-ce que tu fais	du roller?	Do you do	in-line skating?
	de la voile?		sailing?
	de l'escalade?		rock climbing?
Marc ne fait pas de sport.		Marc doesn't do sports.	

MOTS ET EXPRESSIONS

Activités sportives

le jogging	jogging	l'escalade	rock climbing
le roller	in-line skating	la natation	swimming
le skate	skateboarding	la planche à voile	windsurfing
le ski	skiing	la voile	sailing
le ski nautique	water-skiing		
le snowboard	snowboarding		
le sport	sport(s)		
le VTT	mountain biking		

Équipement sportif

des rollers	in-line skates
un skate	skateboard
un snowboard	snowboard
un VTT	mountain bike

Vacation travel

un autocar, un car	touring bus
un avion	plane
un bateau	boat, ship
un train	train

Vacation destinations

la campagne	countryside
la mer	ocean, shore
la montagne	mountains

Les contraires

souvent	often	ne ... jamais	never
quelque chose	something, anything	ne ... rien	nothing, not anything
quelqu'un	someone, anyone, somebody	ne ... personne	no one, not anyone, nobody

Verbes en -er

aider	to help
assister à	to go to, to attend
laver	to wash
louer	to rent
nettoyer	to clean
passer	to spend
préparer	to prepare
ranger	to clean, to pick up
rencontrer	to meet
réparer	to fix

Verbes irréguliers

avoir chaud/froid	to be (feel) hot/cold
avoir faim/soif	to be hungry/thirsty
avoir raison/tort	to be right/wrong
avoir de la chance	to be lucky
faire des achats	to go shopping
faire les devoirs	to do homework
faire un pique-nique	to have a picnic
voir	to see

Le passé composé avec *avoir*

parler	j'ai parlé	I spoke
finir	j'ai fini	I finished
vendre	j'ai vendu	I sold
avoir	j'ai eu	I had
être	j'ai été	I was, I have been
faire	j'ai fait	I did
mettre	j'ai mis	I put
voir	j'ai vu	I saw

Le passé composé avec *être*

aller	je suis allé(e)	I went
arriver	je suis arrivé(e)	I arrived
rentrer	je suis rentré(e)	I came back
rester	je suis resté(e)	I stayed
venir	je suis venu(e)	I came

Le calendrier

Noël	Christmas		Pâques	Easter
un jour	day		une semaine	week
un mois	month		les vacances	vacation
			les grandes vacances	summer vacation
l'après-midi	afternoon			
le matin	morning			
le soir	evening			
le week-end	weekend			

Expressions pour indiquer quand

aujourd'hui	today		d'abord	first
hier	yesterday		avant	before
demain	tomorrow		pendant	during
			après	after, afterwards
prochain(e)	next		ensuite	then, after that
dernier (dernière)	last		enfin	at last
			finalement	finally

Expressions utiles

pour	in order to
seul(e)	alone

TEST PREP CLASSZONE.COM FLASHCARDS AND MORE!

CONTENT
- Understand and convey information about leisure activities pp. 311, 314-315
- Understand and convey information about travel p. 315

ASSESSMENT
- Communicate effectively with some hesitation and errors, which do not hinder comprehension pp. 317, 339, 349, 351
- Demonstrate culturally acceptable behavior for engaging in conversations pp. 317, 328, 339
- Demonstrate culturally acceptable behavior for obtaining information pp. 317, 348
- Demonstrate culturally acceptable behavior for understanding some ideas and familiar details p. 317
- Demonstrate culturally acceptable behavior for providing information pp. 317, 339, 348
- Understand most important information pp. 316, 328, 338, 348

ENTRACTE 7

Objectives
- Reading skills development
- Re-entry of materials in the unit
- Development of cultural awareness

Le roller: un sport qui roule!
Objectives
- Reading at the paragraph level

Teaching Resource Options

PRINT

Workbook PE, pp. 209–212
Activités pour tous PE, pp. 127–129
Unit 7 Resource Book
   Activités pour tous TE, pp. 171–173
   Workbook TE, pp. 175–178

Le roller: un sport qui roule!°

Beaucoup de jeunes Français participent aux sports d'équipe° comme° le foot, le basket et le volley, mais certains préfèrent les sports individuels comme le jogging ou la natation. Aujourd'hui, beaucoup de jeunes pratiquent aussi les «sports de glisse»° comme le roller, le skate, la planche à voile (en été) et le ski et le snowboard (en hiver).

Le roller est particulièrement populaire parce qu'il peut être pratiqué en toute° saison et par les gens de tout âge. Deux millions de Français font régulièrement du roller, principalement dans les grandes villes et surtout° dans la région parisienne. «Pour moi,» dit Clément, 15 ans, «le roller est l'occasion° de me faire des nouveaux copains.» Mélanie, 17 ans, dit qu'elle fait du roller «parce que j'ai l'impression de vitesse,° d'indépendance et de liberté. Je suis libre° comme un oiseau.» Pour Charlotte, 21 ans, «le roller est un excellent moyen° de faire de l'exercice et de rester en bonne forme° physique.»

Pour certaines personnes qui habitent dans les grandes villes, le roller est un nouveau moyen de transport urbain. Philippe Tardieu, un jeune avocat° de la région parisienne, va à son bureau° en roller. «Le roller est plus économique, moins polluant° et souvent plus rapide que l'auto. Le roller, ça roule...!»

Le roller a beaucoup d'avantages, mais c'est aussi un sport qui peut être dangereux si on ne fait pas attention. Pour faire du roller, on doit être en bonne forme physique et avoir l'équipement nécessaire. On doit toujours porter un casque pour se protéger° la tête. On doit aussi porter des genouillières pour se protéger les genoux° et des protège-poignets pour se protéger les poignets.°

On peut faire du roller dans la rue ou sur toute surface plane, mais il est préférable de pratiquer ce sport dans les endroits réservés pour cette activité. Dans les grandes villes, il y a des «rollerparks» où les jeunes peuvent aussi faire du roller acrobatique et jouer au hockey sur roller.

À Paris, une association sportive nommée Pari-Roller organise tous les vendredis soirs° une grande randonnée° en roller dans les rues de la ville. Cette randonnée commence à dix heures du soir et finit à une heure du matin. Il y a souvent 12 000 (douze mille) participants de tout âge accompagnés de policiers en roller. Pendant cet événement, les rues du circuit sont interdites° aux voitures. Pour beaucoup de Parisiens, cet événement est l'occasion de redécouvrir° leur ville dans une ambiance° d'amitié, de bonne humeur et de fête populaire.

---

roule *rolls* **équipe** *team* **comme** *like* **glisse** *gliding* **toute** *any* **surtout** *above all* **occasion** *opportunity* **vitesse** *speed* **libre** *free* **moyen** *means* **forme** *shape* **avocat** *lawyer* **bureau** *office* **polluant** *polluting* **protéger** *to protect* **genoux** *knees* **poignets** *wrists* **tous les vendredis soirs** *every Friday evening* **randonnée** *long ride* **interdites** *closed* **redécouvrir** *to rediscover* **ambiance** *atmosphere*

PRE-READING

Have students look at the illustrations. Can they guess what the reading is about ? [in-line skating]

L'équipement du roller

le casque
(pour protéger la tête)

le protège-coude
(pour protéger les coudes)

le protège-poignet
(pour protéger les poignets)

les genouillières
(pour protéger les genoux)

les rollers

Compréhension

Faites correspondre *(Match)* les personnes et leurs opinions.

> **a.** Clément
> **b.** Mélanie
> **c.** Charlotte
> **d.** Philippe

1. «Le roller, ça roule!»
2. «Le roller est moins polluant que l'auto.»
3. «Quand je fais du roller, je suis libre comme un oiseau.»
4. «Le roller est l'occasion de me faire des nouveaux copains.»
5. «Le roller est un excellent moyen de faire de l'exercice.»
6. «Quand je fais du roller, j'ai l'impression de vitesse.»
7. «En ville, le roller est un bon moyen de transport.»

Et vous?

Classez *(Rank)* les avantages du roller par ordre d'importance personnelle — de 6 (plus important) à 1 (moins important). Comparez votre classement avec vos camarades.

Le roller, c'est ...

- un moyen de faire de l'exercice
- un moyen de rester en forme
- un moyen de rencontrer des copains
- un moyen de transport urbain
- l'impression d'indépendance
- l'impression de vitesse

trois cent cinquante-cinq **355**
Lecture et Culture

Compréhension
Answers
1. d
2. d
3. b
4. a
5. c
6. b
7. d

POST-READING

Using the advantages of in-line skating listed in **Et vous?**, have each student create a chart listing the six advantages vertically on the left and numbers 1–6 horizontally across the top. Have them rank the order of importance for themselves by writing **moi** in the corresponding boxes. Then, have them compare their rankings with a classmate's, writing the name of the classmate in the corresponding box.

Les activités du week-end
Objectives
• Reading at the paragraph level
• Building reading skills

Teaching Resource Options

PRINT

Workbook PE, pp. 209–212
Activités pour tous PE, pp. 127–129
Unit 7 Resource Book
  Activités pour tous TE, pp. 171–173
  Workbook TE, pp. 175–178

Pronunciation Karim /karim/

Questions sur le texte
Pierre: Qu'est-ce que Pierre a fait le week-end dernier? (Il a fait un match de foot.)

Est-ce qu'il a gagné le match? (Non, il a perdu.)

Qu'est-ce qu'il a fait le soir? (Il est allé chez des copains et il a dansé.)

Aïcha: Où est allée Aïcha le week-end dernier? (Elle est allée chez son oncle Karim.)

Qui est-ce qu'elle a vu là-bas? (Elle a vu tous ses cousins et cousines.)

Élisabeth: Pourquoi est-ce qu'Élisabeth a acheté un cadeau? (Elle a acheté un cadeau pour l'anniversaire de son père.)

Où est-ce qu'elle est allée l'après-midi? (Elle est allée au ciné-club.)

Quel film est-ce qu'elle a vu? (Elle a vu *Les temps modernes.*)

Qu'est ce-qu'elle a fait après le film? (Elle est allée dans un café.)

Yvan: Qu'est-ce qu'Yvan a fait le matin? (Il est allé au rollerpark et il a joué au hockey avec des copains.)

À quelle heure est-ce qu'il est rentré chez lui? (Il est rentré chez lui à midi.)

Où est-ce qu'il a dîné? (Il a dîné au restaurant.)

Les activités du week-end

Qu'est-ce que vous faites le week-end? Qu'est-ce que vous avez fait le week-end dernier? Voici les réponses de quatre jeunes du monde° francophone.

Pierre
(16 ans)
Basse Terre, Guadeloupe

Le samedi, je joue généralement au foot. Je fais partie° de l'équipe° junior de mon village. Le week-end dernier, nous avons fait un match. Nous avons bien joué, mais nous avons perdu! Après le match, je suis allé à la plage. Le soir, je suis allé chez des copains. Nous avons mis de la musique et nous avons dansé.

Aïcha
(14 ans)
Casablanca, Maroc

Samedi dernier, nous avons eu une grande réunion de famille chez mon oncle Karim. Une centaine° de personnes sont venues. Nous avons fait un «méchoui». (C'est un repas° où on rôtit° un mouton° entier à la broche.°) J'ai eu l'occasion° de voir tous° mes cousins et cousines. On s'est bien amusé.°

Élisabeth
(15 ans)
Bruxelles, Belgique

Samedi matin, j'ai fait des achats. J'ai choisi un cadeau pour l'anniversaire de mon père. (J'ai acheté une cravate en soie.°) L'après-midi, je suis allée au ciné-club avec un copain. Nous avons vu *Les Temps modernes,* un vieux film de Charlie Chaplin. Après, nous sommes allés dans un café et nous avons rencontré d'autres° copains. J'ai passé la soirée° en famille.

monde *world*   **fais partie** *am a member*   **équipe** *team*
soie *silk*   **d'autres** *other*   **soirée** *evening*

Yvan
(14 ans)
Montréal, Québec

Le matin, je suis allé à un rollerpark avec des copains et nous avons joué au hockey. À midi, je suis rentré chez moi. L'après-midi, j'ai aidé mes parents à repeindre° la cuisine. Pour le dîner, nous sommes allés au restaurant.

une centaine *about 100*   **repas** *meal*   **rôtit** *roasts*   **mouton** *sheep*
à la broche *on the spit*   **occasion** *opportunity*   **tous** *all*
On s'est bien amusé. *We had a good time.*   **repeindre** *repaint*

CONNEXIONS

Pick one of the above French-speaking cities, and find out more about it on the Internet. Imagine that you will be spending a week in that city.

• What kinds of things would you like to do?
• What places would you like to visit?
• What would be the best season to go?

PRE-READING ACTIVITY

Have students glance over the reading quickly. What are the questions that were asked in the interview?

POST-READING ACTIVITY

Ask each student to decide which of the four people they would like to spend a weekend with and why.

Imaginez que vous avez la possibilité de passer un week-end avec un de ces jeunes. Qui allez-vous choisir? Pourquoi?

STRATEGY Reading

More cognate patterns
Here are two important cognate patterns that will help you read French more easily.

• French verbs in **-er** sometimes correspond to English verbs in *-ate*.

FRENCH	ENGLISH	FRENCH	ENGLISH
situer	*situate*	**situé**	*situated*
indiquer	*indicate*	**indiqué**	*indicated*

• The ending **-ment** usually corresponds to the English ending *-ly*.
généralement *generally*

Activité écrite: Une carte postale

Imaginez que vous avez passé le week-end avec l'une des quatre personnes: Pierre, Yvan, Élisabeth ou Aïcha. Dans une carte postale, décrivez ce week-end de votre point de vue personnel.

Chers amis,

J'ai passé le week-end avec Yvan. Nous avons ....

Writing Hint Be sure to use the **passé composé.**

★ Rabat
Le Maroc

EN BREF: LE MAROC

Population: 30 millions
Capitale: Rabat
Langues: arabe, français, espagnol

Le Maroc est un pays° d'Afrique du Nord° situé entre la Méditerranée au nord, l'Atlantique à l'est° et le Sahara au sud.° Autrefois° administré par la France, ce pays est maintenant gouverné par un roi,° le roi Mohammed VI. Le sud du pays est habité par les Touareg, un peuple nomade qui traverse le Sahara en caravanes de chameaux.°

De culture islamique, le Maroc est un pays moderne avec une longue tradition intellectuelle et artistique. Les artisans marocains créent° des produits d'excellente qualité: textiles, céramiques et objets de cuir° et de cuivre.°

Il y a aujourd'hui un million de Marocains qui habitent en France où ils ont introduit le couscous, le thé à la menthe° et d'autres° spécialités de leur pays.

---

pays *country* **nord** *north* **est** *east* **sud** *south* **Autrefois** *In the past* **roi** *king* **chameaux** *camels* **créent** *create* **cuir** *leather* **cuivre** *copper* **menthe** *mint* **d'autres** *other*

Words with several meanings
passer *to pass [by], to spend time*
gagner *to earn, to win*
l'anniversaire *anniversary, birthday*

Activité écrite: Une carte postale

Answers will vary.

Chers amis,

J'ai passé le week-end avec Yvan. Nous avons joué au hockey avec ses copains à un rollerpark. À midi, nous sommes rentrés chez lui. L'après-midi, nous avons aidé ses parents à repeindre la cuisine. Pour le dîner, nous sommes allés au restaurant.

À la semaine prochaine!

Paul

Bruxelles

Brussels is an important center for the 15-member European Union (**l'Union européenne**). It is the seat of the Council of Ministers and houses the working committees of the European Parliament.

Photo cultural note

The photo shows typical goods found at the Marrakesh market in Morocco.

Les quatre erreurs de Sophie

Objectives
• Reading for fun
• Logical thinking: finding errors of fact

Teaching Resource Options

PRINT

Workbook PE, pp. 209–212
Activités pour tous PE, pp. 127–129
Unit 7 Resource Book
   Activités pour tous TE
   Workbook TE

Le quatre erreurs de Sophie: Answers

Marrakech, le 10 juillet
Erreur: Le Maroc est un pays d'Afrique du nord.

Québec, le 25 juillet
Erreur: Ottawa est la capitale du Canada.

Fort-de-France, le 3 août
Erreur: La Martinique est une île de la mer des Caraïbes.

Port-au-Prince, le 14 août
Erreur: Les gens d'Haïti parlent créole et français.

Photo culture notes

Leather market Leather bags at the market "Souq" in the medina of "Fès El-Bali" (old town).

Citadelle Massive entry gate at the Citadel with Sentry guard.

Les quatre erreurs de Sophie

Pendant les vacances, Sophie Lambert, une jeune Française, a fait un grand voyage dans les pays° francophones. Dans chaque° pays où elle est allée, elle a écrit° des cartes postales à ses copains. Dans chaque carte postale, Sophie a fait une erreur.° Quelle est cette erreur? (Les erreurs de Sophie concernent la géographie ou les gens.) Lisez attentivement chaque carte et cherchez l'erreur que Sophie a faite.

pays *countries*   **chaque** *each*   **a écrit** *wrote*   **erreur** *error, mistake*

> *Marrakech, le 10 juillet*
> Ma chère Pauline,
>   Je suis au Maroc. C'est un pays d'Afrique du Sud° où on parle arabe et où beaucoup de gens parlent aussi français. Samedi, je suis allée à la «médina» qui est le vieux quartier° de Marrakech. Là, j'ai acheté un beau sac de cuir° à un artisan local.
>   Amitiés,
>   Sophie

Sud *south*   **quartier** *district*   **cuir** *leather*

> *Québec, le 25 juillet*
> Mon cher Guillaume,
>   Je passe une semaine à Québec, la capitale du Canada. Hier j'ai téléphoné à une copine et nous sommes allées dans la vieille ville. Ensuite, nous sommes allées à la Citadelle et nous avons vu le changement de la garde.° Ici, les gens parlent un français un peu ancien.° Par exemple, pour dire «au revoir», on dit° «bonjour». C'est amusant, non?
>   Amicalement,
>   Sophie

changement de la garde *changing of the guard*   **ancien** *old*   **dit** *says*

358 trois cent cinquante-huit
Unité 7

PRE-READING ACTIVITY

Have students look at each of the postcards and read the descriptions of the places pictured. Then have them locate the four cities on a map.

POST-READING ACTIVITY

Have students imagine that they had been able to accompany Sophie on one part of her trip. Which part would they have chosen and why?

Fort-de-France, le 3 août

Ma chère Élodie,

Un grand bonjour de la Martinique qui est une petite île° de l'Océan Pacifique. Je suis arrivée ici la semaine dernière. Ici, il fait toujours chaud et les gens vont à la plage toute l'année!° Hier j'ai acheté un maillot de bain et des lunettes de soleil dans une boutique de l'hôtel. Ensuite, j'ai nagé et j'ai fait de la planche à voile et de la plongée sous-marine.° J'ai vu des poissons de toutes les couleurs!

Affectueusement,
Sophie

île *island*   toute l'année *all year long*
plongée sous-marine *scuba diving*

Port-au-Prince, le 14 août

Mon cher Mathieu,

Je suis arrivée à Haïti dimanche dernier. J'ai trouvé une chambre dans une pension° à Port-au-Prince, la capitale du pays. Les gens d'ici parlent créole et espagnol. Hier soir, je suis allée écouter un orchestre de musique «compas». Génial! J'aime aussi la cuisine créole. C'est épicé,° mais c'est très bon!

Amitiés,
Sophie

pension *boarding house*   épicé *spicy, hot*

Les 4 erreurs:

1. *Le Maroc est en Afrique du Nord (et non pas en Afrique du Sud).*
2. *La capitale du Canada est Ottawa (et non pas Québec).*
3. *La Martinique est dans l'Océan Atlantique (et non pas dans l'Océan Pacifique).*
4. *À Haïti, on parle créole et français (et non pas espagnol).*

CLASSROOM MANAGEMENT Pair writing practice

Ask students to bring in local postcards. Divide the class into small groups.

Each group of students writes a postcard in French. In the text, however, they introduce an error of history or geography.

Then let groups exchange cards and try to find the errors.

Expansion activities PLANNING AHEAD

Games

• Dessinez!

Have students work in small groups. Each student will draw a table place setting, with all the items in the wrong place. Then, students will describe their drawings to the other players, who will try to reproduce the drawing as best they can. Award points for the most accurate reproduction at each round.

Pacing Suggestion: Upon completion of Leçon 25.

Projects

• Au marché

Have students work in pairs or small groups to write and perform a shopping scene at a French market. In each scene, students will ask for several items, inquire about the price, and pay for their items. Encourage students to incorporate props into their scenes to make them more realistic. Have groups exchange dialogues and proofread one another's work. Students should rehearse the finished dialogues and present them to the class. As an alternative, you could change the setting to a restaurant or cafeteria and have students practice using verbs with the partitive.

Pacing Suggestion: Upon completion of Leçon 26.

• Un menu

Each student will create a menu for a French restaurant. First, have students research on the Internet to identify items they would typically find on the menu of a French restaurant. Have them make a list of appetizers, main dishes, desserts, and beverages. Then have students name their restaurant and design their menu, choosing the dishes that will be served in it. Each student will ask a classmate to proofread the first draft of his or her menu. Finally, students will create a final draft of their respective menus. You may want to grade the menus on accuracy, variety of vocabulary used, creativity, neatness, and visual appeal. As an alternative, students might create menus for a francophone restaurant.

Pacing Suggestion: Upon completion of Leçon 27.

Bulletin Boards

• La nourriture

Students will work in small groups to create a poster for a certain category of food: *les fruits, les légumes, les boissons, la viande, les desserts,* and so on. Assign these a day or two in advance so that each group can find photographs or create illustrations of items that fit their category. Have students lay out the images on a poster board, making sure to leave room for a title and descriptive captions for each item. You may also want to have students show where their category of food is located in a standard food pyramid.

Pacing Suggestion: Upon completion of Leçon 25.

• Les articles partitifs, les articles indéfinis

Students will make posters illustrating the use of the partitive article and the indefinite article. See pages 378–379 for examples. First, have each student select a food item to illustrate. Then, have students create an illustration of the whole item and caption it using the indefinite article. Next to the first illustration and caption, have students create an illustration of a portion of the food item (a slice, a piece, and so on) and caption it using the partitive article.

Pacing Suggestion: Upon completion of Leçon 26.

Music

• L'hymne national

Teach your students *La Marseillaise,* the national anthem of France. You can download the music from the Internet. The lyrics are provided below in French. You may also want to give students a list of vocabulary words from the song in English.

• *La Marseillaise* was written during the French Revolution by an engineer and amateur musician, Rouget de Lisle. It was first adopted as the French national anthem in 1795.

La Marseillaise

Allons enfants de la patrie,	(Refrain)
Le jour de gloire est arrivé	Aux armes, citoyens!
Contre nous de la tyrannie	Formez vos bataillons!
L'étendard sanglant est levé	Marchons! Marchons!
Entendez vous dans les campagnes,	Qu'un sang impur
Mugir ces féroces soldats?	Abreuve nos sillons!
Ils viennent jusque dans nos bras	
Egorger nos fils, nos compagnes!	

Pacing Suggestion: Upon completion of Leçon 28.

Storytelling

• Une mini-histoire

Create a brief story in dialogue format about a funny or a difficult customer in a restaurant or at a market. Pass out copies of your scripted dialogue to students. Repeat the conversation with pauses, allowing students to repeat after you, or to fill in the words. Then have them work in pairs to develop their own conflict based on the scripted tale. Ask students to write out their expanded conversations, practice them aloud for intonation, and perform them for the class.

Pacing Suggestion: Upon completion of Leçon 28.

Recipe

• Tapioca banane

Many recipes from the islands of the Caribbean incorporate the tropical fruits that are native to the area. This simple dessert uses bananas and coconut milk.

Pacing Suggestion: Upon completion of Leçon 27.

Hands-on Crafts

• Un paysage créole

Students will create a three dimensional tableau representing a Caribbean scene. First have students decide what kind of scene they want to create. They may wish to look for photographs or videos of Martinique, Guadeloupe, and Haiti for inspiration. Have them bring in small cardboard boxes and cut away all but the bottom and one side of their box. They should paint or color the background before they begin attaching items to the bottom, or "floor." Students can use pieces of the rest of the box as backing to stand up human figures and whatever else they want to place in their tableau. Have them cut these figures out of construction paper and decorate them with seashells, toothpicks, and other items, each to a cardboard backing, and place them at intervals on the "floor" of the box in order to create a multi-layered image.

Pacing Suggestion: Upon completion of Leçon 28.

Mangez chaque jour ...
du fromage, de la viande,
des fruits et du pain.

Santé et Bien-être social   Health and Welfare
Canada   Canada

End of Unit

• Le dîner français

Students will prepare and eat a typical French meal. Have the class vote and select several courses: 1–2 appetizers, 1–2 main dishes, and 1–2 desserts. Then, divide the class into groups, one group for each dish. Have each group prepare a dish and bring it to class. Remind students that all conversation during the meal should be in French! Encourage everyone to sample all the dishes. This would be a great time to discuss differences in French and American mealtime behavior. As an alternative, students could bring simple, inexpensive dishes (crêpes, salads, and so on) from a local French restaurant.

Tapioca banane

Ingrédients
- 1 litre d'eau
- 200 g de tapioca
- 2 bananes, coupées en rondelles
- 1/2 bol de lait de coco
- 1/2 bol de sucre
- 100 g de cacahuètes pilées

Préparation
1. Faites bouillir l'eau.
2. Ajoutez le tapioca.
3. Mélangez bien et puis ajoutez les bananes.
4. Ajoutez le sucre et le lait de coco.
5. Remuez et cuisez pendant quelques minutes à feu doux.
6. Servez lorsque le tapioca est gonflé.
7. Si vous voulez, saupoudrez avec des cacahuètes pilées.

Ingredients
- approx. 4 cups water
- approx. 7 oz. tapioca
- 2 bananas, cut up
- approx. 3/4 cups coconut milk
- approx. 3/4 cups sugar
- approx. 3.5 oz. crushed peanuts

Directions
1. Boil the water.
2. Add the tapioca.
3. Mix well and add the banana slices.
4. Add the sugar and coconut milk.
5. Stir and cook for several minutes at low heat.
6. The tapioca is ready to serve when it puffs up.
7. Serve topped with crushed peanuts.

Rubric
A = 13–15 pts. **B** = 10–12 pts. **C** = 7–9 pts. **D** = 4–6 pts. **F** = < 4 pts.

Criteria	Scale				
Vocabulary Use	1	2	3	4	5
Grammar/Spelling Accuracy	1	2	3	4	5
Creativity	1	2	3	4	5

Planning Guide CLASSROOM MANAGEMENT

OBJECTIVES

Communication
- Talk about your favorite foods *pp. 366–367, 370–371*
- Describe the different meals of the day *pp. 364, 375*
- Prepare a shopping list and do the grocery shopping *pp. 366–367, 370–371, 376, 378–379*
- Order a meal in a restaurant *pp. 376, 378–379*
- Set the table *p. 364*
- Ask people to do things for you *pp. 389, 392*

Grammar
- Le verbe *vouloir p. 376*
- Le verbe *prendre p. 377*
- L'article partitif: *du, de la pp. 378–379*
- L'article partitif dans les phrases négatives *p. 381*
- Le verbe *boire p. 383*
- Les pronoms compléments *me, te, nous, vous p. 388*
- Les pronoms compléments à l'impératif *p. 390*
- Les verbes *pouvoir* et *devoir p. 392*
- Le verbe connaître *p. 398*
- Les pronoms compléments: *le, la, les p. 399*
- La place des pronoms à l'impératif *p. 401*
- Les pronoms compléments: *lui, leur p. 402*
- Les verbes *dire* et *écrire p. 404*

Vocabulary
- Les repas et la table *p. 364*
- La nourriture et les boissons *pp. 366–367*
- Les fruits et les légumes *pp. 370–371*
- Verbes comme *prendre p. 377*
- Les services personnels *p. 389*
- Verbes suivis d'un complément indirect *p. 403*

Pronunciation
- Les lettres «ou» et «u» *p. 383*
- Les lettres «s» et «ss» *p. 393*
- Les lettres «on» et «om» *p. 405*

Culture
- Le marché *p. 371*
- À la cantine *p. 375*
- Les restaurants français et la cuisine française *p. 387*
- Un pique-nique français *p. 397*
- La cuisine créole *p. 415*

PROGRAM RESOURCES

 Print
- Workbook PE, *pp. 213–249*
- *Activités pour tous* PE, *pp. 131–149*
- Block Scheduling Copymasters *pp. 193–224*
- Teacher to Teacher Copymasters
- Unit 8 Resource Book
  Lessons 25–28 Resources
    Workbook TE
    Activités pour tous TE
    Lesson Plans
    Block Scheduling Lesson Plans
    Family Letter
    Absent Student Copymasters
    Family Involvement
    Video Activities
    Videoscripts
    Audioscripts
    Assessment Program
  Unit 8 Resources
    Communipak
    Activités pour tous TE Reading
    Workbook TE Reading and
      Culture Activities
    Assessment Program
    Answer Keys

 Audiovisual
- Audio Program PE CD 4
  Tracks 21–43
- Audio Program Workbook CD 12
  Tracks 1–27
- *Chansons* Audio CD
- Video Program Modules 25, 26, 27, 28
- Overhead Transparencies
  45 Table setting;
  46a, 46b *La nourriture et les boissons;*
  47 *Les fruits et les légumes*
  48 *Au marché*
  49 *Le partitif (du, de la)*

 Technology
- Online Workbook
- ClassZone.com
- eTest Plus Online/Test Generator CD-ROM
- EasyPlanner Plus Online/EasyPlanner CD-ROM
- Power Presentations on CD-ROM

✓ **Assessment Program Options**

Lesson Quizzes
Portfolio Assessment
Unit Test Form A
Unit Test Form B
Unit Test Part III (Alternate)
  Cultural Awareness
Listening Comprehension
  Performance Test
Speaking Performance Test
Reading Comprehension
  Performance Test
Writing Performance Test
Multiple Choice Test Items
Test Scoring Tools
Audio Program CD 16 Tracks 9–16
Answer Keys
eTest Plus Online/Test Generator
  CD-ROM

Pacing Guide SAMPLE LESSON PLAN

DAY	DAY	DAY	DAY	DAY
1 **Unité 8 Opener** **Leçon 25** • Vocabulaire et Culture– Les repas et la nourriture • Vocabulaire–Les repas et la table	**2** **Leçon 25** • Vocabulaire–La nourriture et les boissons	**3** **Leçon 25** • Vocabulaire–Les fruits et les légumes • Note culturelle–Le marché	**4** **Leçon 25** • À votre tour!	**5** **Leçon 26** • Conversation et Culture– À la cantine • Note culturelle– À la cantine • Le verbe *vouloir*
6 **Leçon 26** • Le verbe *prendre* • Vocabulaire–Verbes comme *prendre* • L'article partitif: *du, de la*	**7** **Leçon 26** • L'article partitif dans les phrases négatives	**8** **Leçon 26** • Le verbe *boire* • Prononciation–Les lettres «ou» et «u»	**9** **Leçon 26** • À votre tour!	**10** **Leçon 27** • Conversation et Culture– Un client difficile • Note culturelle– Les restaurants français et la cuisine française • Les pronoms compléments *me, te, nous, vous*
11 **Leçon 27** • Vocabulaire–Les services personnels • Les pronoms compléments à l'impératif	**12** **Leçon 27** • Les verbes *pouvoir* et *devoir* • Prononciation– Les lettres «s» et «ss»	**13** **Leçon 27** • À votre tour!	**14** **Leçon 28** • Conversation et Culture– Pique-nique • Note culturelle– Un pique-nique français • Le verbe *connaître*	**15** **Leçon 28** • Les pronoms compléments: *le, la, les*
16 **Leçon 28** • La place des pronoms à l'impératif	**17** **Leçon 28** • Les pronoms compléments: *lui, leur* • Vocabulaire–Verbes suivis d'un complément indirect	**18** **Leçon 28** • Vocabulaire–Verbes suivis d'un complément indirect *(continued)* • Les verbes *dire* et *écrire* • Prononciation–Les lettres «on» et «om»	**19** **Leçon 28** • À votre tour!	**20** • Tests de contrôle
21 • Unit 8 Test	**22** • Entracte–Lecture et culture			

Student Text Listening Activity Scripts
AUDIO PROGRAM

▶ **LEÇON 25 LE FRANÇAIS PRATIQUE** Les repas et la nourriture
À votre tour!
• **Écoutez bien!** *p. 372* CD 4, TRACK 21

Pauline et Thomas ont fait les courses dans deux supermarchés différents. Écoutez bien les phrases. Si vous entendez le nom d'un produit acheté par Pauline, marquez A. Si vous entendez le nom d'un produit acheté par Thomas, marquez B. Écoutez bien. Chaque phrase va être répétée. Commençons.

1. Où est la mayonnaise? #
2. Est-ce que tu as acheté des pommes de terre? #
3. J'aime bien le jus de pomme. #
4. Il y a un poulet pour le dîner. #
5. Les tomates coûtent deux euros la livre. #
6. Est-ce que tu aimes le gâteau? #
7. Le thon est mon poisson préféré. #
8. Passe-moi la confiture, s'il te plaît. #
9. Est-ce que tu aimes le saucisson? #
10. Pour le dessert, il y a une tarte. #
11. Les pommes sont bon marché. #
12. Au petit déjeuner, nous mangeons des céréales. #
13. Voici les oeufs. #
14. Où as-tu mis le lait? #
15. L'eau minérale est sur la table. #
16. Combien coûte la salade? #
17. Où as-tu acheté les poires? #
18. Combien de pamplemousses as-tu acheté? #
19. Passe-moi le jus d'orange, s'il te plaît. #
20. Mets le jambon au réfrigérateur. #
21. Mon petit frère n'aime pas les carottes. #
22. Tiens, voilà le pain. #

• **Conversation dirigée** *p. 372* CD 4, TRACK 22

Listen to the conversation. Écoutez la conversation entre Marc et Juliette.

Marc:	Est-ce que tu as faim, Juliette?
Juliette:	Oui, j'ai très faim.
Marc:	Est-ce que tu veux déjeuner?
Juliette:	Oui, je veux déjeuner, merci.
Marc:	Est-ce que tu aimes la cuisine italienne?
Juliette:	Je préfère la cuisine française.
Marc:	Est-ce que tu aimes la viande?
Juliette:	Oui, j'aime la viande, mais j'aime aussi les légumes.
Marc:	Est-ce que tu veux aller à La Campagne?
Juliette:	Oui, d'accord.

• **Créa-dialogue** *p. 373* CD 4, TRACK 23

Listen to the sample *Créa-dialogues.* Écoutez les conversations.
Modèle: —Tu aimes la viande?   —Non, je n'aime pas la viande.
　　　—Tu aimes les légumes?   —Non, je n'aime pas les légumes.
　　　—Tu aimes le poisson?   —Oui, j'aime beaucoup le poisson.
　　　—On déjeune à La Marine?   —D'accord.

Maintenant écoutez le dialogue numéro 1.
—Tu aimes le poisson?   —Non, je n'aime pas beaucoup le poisson.
—Tu aimes la viande?   —J'aime un peu la viande.
—Tu aimes les spaghetti?   —Oui, j'aime beaucoup les spaghetti!
—Alors, on déjeune Chez Rigoletto?   —D'accord!

▶ **LEÇON 26** À la cantine

• **À la cantine** *p. 374*

A. Compréhension orale CD 4, TRACK 24

Please turn to page 374 for complete *Compréhension orale* text.

B. Écoutez et répétez. CD 4, TRACK 25

You will now hear a paused version of the dialog. Listen to the speaker and repeat right after he or she has completed the sentence.

• **Grammaire** *p. 376* CD 4, TRACK 26

Le verbe *vouloir*
Repeat the sentences after the speaker.

Je **veux** aller au café. #   Tu **veux** déjeuner. #
Il **veut** dîner. #   Nous **voulons** une glace. #
Vous **voulez** des spaghetti. #   Elles **veulent** des frites. #
J'**ai voulu** dîner chez Maxim's. #

• **Grammaire** *p. 377* CD 4, TRACK 27

Le verbe *prendre*
Je **prends** une pizza. #   Tu **prends** un sandwich. #
Elle **prend** une salade. #   Nous **prenons** le train. #
Vous **prenez** l'avion. #   Ils **prennent** des photos. #
J'**ai pris** un steak. #

• **Prononciation** *p. 383* CD 4, TRACK 28

Les lettres «ou» et «u»
Écoutez: la p**ou**le   le p**u**ll
The letters "**ou**" always represent the sound /u/.
Répétez: /u/ #   v**ou**s # n**ou**s # p**ou**let # s**ou**pe # f**ou**rchette # c**ou**teau #
　　　　　　　　　d**ou**zaine #
The letter "**u**" always represents the sound /y/.
Répétez: /y/ #   t**u** # d**u** # **u**ne # lég**u**me # j**u**s # s**u**cre # bien s**û**r # aven**u**e #
　　　　　　　　　m**u**sée #

Now distinguish between the two vowel sounds:
Répétez: /u/ – /y/ #   p**ou**le–p**u**ll # r**ou**e–r**u**e # v**ou**s–v**u**e # je j**ou**e–le j**u**s #
　　　　　　　　　V**ou**s b**u**vez d**u** j**u**s de pamplem**ou**sse. Je v**ou**drais de la s**ou**pe,
　　　　　　　　　d**u** p**ou**let et d**u** j**u**s de raisin. #

À votre tour!
• **Allô!** *p. 384* CD 4, TRACK 29

Listen to the conversation. Écoutez la conversation entre Frédéric et Sandrine.

Frédéric:	Tu dînes au restaurant ce soir?
Sandrine:	Non, j'ai invité mon copain Fabien à dîner chez moi.
Frédéric:	Tu as fait les courses?
Sandrine:	Oui, je suis allée au supermarché ce matin.
Frédéric:	Qu'est-ce que tu as acheté?
Sandrine:	Du riz, des oeufs, de la salade et du fromage.
Frédéric:	Tu n'as pas acheté de viande?
Sandrine:	Mais non, tu sais bien que Fabien est végétarien.
Frédéric:	C'est vrai. Et pour le dessert, tu as acheté de la glace?
Sandrine:	Non, j'ai pris un gâteau au chocolat.

• **Créa-dialogue** *p. 384* CD 4, TRACK 30

Listen to some sample *Créa-dialogues.* Écoutez les conversations.
Modèle: —Où es-tu allée?   —Je suis allée au supermarché.
　　　—Qu'est-ce que tu as acheté?   —J'ai acheté du pain, du lait et
　　　　　　　　　　　　　　　　　de la confiture.

Maintenant, écoutez le dialogue numéro 1.
—Où es-tu allé?   —Je suis allé à la cantine.
—Qu'est-ce que tu as mangé?   —J'ai mangé du rosbif, de la salade et
　　　　　　　　　　　　　　　　　de la glace.

▶ LEÇON 27 Un client difficile

• Un client difficile *p. 386*

A. Compréhension orale CD 4, TRACK 31

Please turn to page 386 for complete *Compréhension orale* text.

B. Écoutez et répétez. CD 4, TRACK 32

You will now hear a paused version of the dialog. Listen to the speaker and repeat right after he or she has completed the sentence.

• Vocabulaire *p. 389* CD 4, TRACK 33

Les services personnels

Repeat the sentences after the speaker. Répétez les phrases.

aider quelqu'un #   J'**aide** mes copains avec les devoirs. #
amener quelqu'un #   Le taxi **amène** les touristes à la gare. #
apporter quelque chose **à** quelqu'un #   Le serveur **apporte** le menu **aux** clients. #
donner quelque chose **à** quelqu'un #   Mme Marin **donne** 10 euros **à** sa fille. #
montrer quelque chose **à** quelqu'un #   Est-ce que tu **montres** tes photos à ton copain? #
prêter quelque chose **à** quelqu'un #   Est-ce que tu **prêtes** tes disques à tes amis? #

• Grammaire *p. 392* CD 4, TRACK 34

Les verbes *pouvoir* et *devoir*

Repeat the sentences after the speaker. Répétez les phrases.

Je **peux** venir. #   Je **dois** rentrer avant midi. #
Tu **peux** travailler. #   Tu **dois** gagner de l'argent. #
Elle **peut** voyager. #   Elle **doit** visiter Paris. #
Nous **pouvons** dîner ici. #   Nous **devons** regarder le menu. #
Vous **pouvez** rester. #   Vous **devez** finir vos devoirs. #
Ils **peuvent** aider. #   Ils **doivent** mettre la table. #
J'**ai pu** étudier. #   J'**ai dû** faire mes devoirs. #

• Prononciation *p. 393* CD 4, TRACK 35

Les lettres «s» et «ss»

Écoutez: poi**s**on   poi**ss**on

Be sure to distinguish between "s" and "ss" in the middle of a word.

Répétez: /z/ #   mauvai**s**e # cui**s**ine # frai**s**e # mayonnai**s**e # quelque cho**s**e # maga**s**in #
/s/ # poi**ss**on # sauci**ss**on # de**ss**ert # boi**ss**on # a**ss**iette # pamplemou**ss**e #
/z/ – /s/ # poi**s**on–poi**ss**on # dé**s**ert–de**ss**ert #
Comme de**ss**ert nou**s** choi**s**i**ss**ons une tarte aux frai**s**es. #

À votre tour!

• Allô! *p. 394* CD 4, TRACK 36

Listen to the conversation. Écoutez la conversation entre Corinne et Philippe.

Corinne: Dis, Philippe, j'ai besoin d'un petit service.
Philippe: Qu'est-ce que je peux faire pour toi?
Corinne: Prête-moi ta mobylette, s'il te plaît.
Philippe: Ah, je ne peux pas. Je dois aller en ville cet après-midi.
Corinne: Dans ce cas, apporte-moi *Paris-Match.*
Philippe: D'accord! Je vais aller à la librairie Duchemin.
Corinne: Alors, achète-moi aussi le nouvel album d'Astérix.
Philippe: Écoute, je n'ai pas assez d'argent.
Corinne: Je t'ai prêté vingt euros hier!
Philippe: C'est vrai . . . Bon, je t'achète tout ça.

• Créa-dialogue *p. 394* CD 4, TRACK 37

Listen to the sample *Créa-dialogues.* Écoutez les conversations.

Modèle: —S'il te plaît, prête-moi ton vélo!
—Pourquoi?
—Parce que je voudrais faire une promenade à la campagne.
—D'accord, je te prête mon vélo.

Maintenant, écoutez le dialogue numéro 1.

—S'il te plaît, prête-moi ta raquette!
—Pourquoi?
—Parce que je voudrais jouer au tennis.
—D'accord, je te prête ma raquette.

▶ LEÇON 28 Pique-nique

• Pique-nique *p. 396* CD 4, TRACK 38

A. Compréhension orale

Please turn to page 396 for complete *Compréhension orale* text.

B. Écoutez et répétez. CD 4, TRACK 39

You will now hear a paused version of the dialog. Listen to the speaker and repeat right after he or she has completed the sentence.

• Grammaire *p. 398* CD 4, TRACK 40

Le verbe *connaître*

Écoutez et répétez.

Je **connais** Stéphanie. #   Tu **connais** son cousin? #
Elle **connaît** ces garçons. #   Nous **connaissons** Paris. #
Vous **connaissez** Montréal? #   Ils **connaissent** ce café. #
J'**ai connu** ton frère pendant les vacances. #

• Prononciation *p. 405* CD 4, TRACK 41

Les lettres «on» et «om»

Écoutez: li**on**   li**onn**e

Be sure to distinguish between the nasal and non-nasal vowel sounds.

REMEMBER: Do not pronounce an /n/ or /m/ after the nasal vowel /ɔ̃/.

Répétez: /ɔ̃/ #   m**on** # t**on** # s**on** # b**on** # avi**on** # m**on**trer # rép**on**dre # invit**ons** # blous**on** #
/ɔn/ # télépho**nn**e # Simo**n**e # do**nn**er # co**nn**ais # mayo**nn**aise # perso**nn**e # bo**nn**e #
/ɔm/ # fro**m**age # pro**m**enade # to**m**ate # po**mm**e # do**mm**age # co**mm**ent #
/ɔ̃/ – /ɔn/ # lion–lio**nn**e # bon–bo**nn**e # Simon–Simo**n**e # Yvon–Yvo**nn**e # Moniqu**e** do**nn**e une po**mm**e à Raym**on**d. # Simo**n**e co**nn**aît m**on** oncle Lé**on**. #

À votre tour!

• Allô! *p. 406* CD 4, TRACK 42

Listen to the conversation. Écoutez la conversation entre Olivier et Sophie.

Olivier: Qu'est-ce que tu fais ce week-end?
Sophie: J'organise une fête.
Olivier: Tu m'invites?
Sophie: Bien sûr, je t'invite.
Olivier: Et Catherine? Tu l'invites aussi?
Sophie: Catherine? Je ne la connais pas. Qui est-ce?
Olivier: C'est ma nouvelle copine.
Sophie: Ah oui, je vois qui c'est maintenant. Eh bien, d'accord! Je l'invite.
Olivier: Tu veux son numéro de téléphone?
Sophie: Oui, je ne l'ai pas.
Olivier: C'est le 01.44.32.28.50.
Sophie: Je lui téléphone tout de suite.

• Créa-dialogue *p. 406* CD 4, TRACK 43

Listen to some sample *Créa-dialogues.* Écoutez les conversations.

Modèle: —Tu regardes la télé?   —Oui, je la regarde.
—À quelle heure est-ce que tu la regardes?   —À huit heures.

Maintenant, écoutez le dialogue numéro 1.

—Tu invites tes amis?   —Oui, je les invite.
—Quand est-ce que tu les invites?   —Je les invite ce week-end.
—À quelle occasion est-ce que tu les invites?   —Je les invite pour mon anniversaire.

> Complete videoscripts, plus Workbook and Assessment audioscripts, are available in the Unit Resource Books.

Main Theme
• Food and Meals

COMMUNICATION
• Talking about favorite foods
• Describing meals
• Preparing a shopping list
• Doing the grocery shopping
• Ordering a meal in a restaurant
• Setting the table
• Asking people to do things for you

CULTURES
• Learning about French meals
• Learning about the market
• Learning about French school cafeterias and what they serve
• Learning about French restaurants
• Learning about French cuisine
• Learning about French picnics
• Learning about creole cuisine

CONNECTIONS
• Connecting to Math: Calculating quantities and prices
• Connecting to English: Recognizing English cooking terms that were borrowed from French
• Connecting to Cooking: Making crêpes

COMPARISONS
• Comparing school cafeterias in France and the U.S.
• Comparing meals in France and the U.S.

COMMUNITIES
• Finding French foods at the local supermarket
• Using French to order in a restaurant

UNITÉ
8

Les repas

LEÇON 25 LE FRANÇAIS PRATIQUE: Les repas et la nourriture

LEÇON 26 À la cantine

LEÇON 27 Un client difficile

LEÇON 28 Pique-nique

THÈME ET OBJECTIFS

Food and meals

Eating well is not only essential for our health, it should be an enjoyable experience as well.

In this unit, you will learn ...
• to talk about your favorite foods
• to describe the different meals of the day
• to prepare a shopping list and do the grocery shopping
• to order a meal in a restaurant
• to set the table

You will also be able ...
• to ask people to do things for you

WEBQUEST
CLASSZONE.COM

UNIT OVERVIEW

▶ **Communication Goals:** Students will be able to buy food and order a meal.

▶ **Linguistic Goals:** Students will learn to express quantities and use object pronouns.

▶ **Critical Thinking Goals:** Students will begin to understand the concept of the partitive and to observe the differences between object pronouns in French and English.

▶ **Cultural Goals:** Students will learn about French meals, restaurants, and cafeterias as well as grocery shopping habits in France.

trois cent soixante et un
Unité 8 361

Teaching Resource Options

PRINT

Unit 8 Resource Book
　Family Letter

AUDIO & VISUAL

Audio Program
Chansons CD

TECHNOLOGY

EasyPlanner CD-ROM/EasyPlanner
Plus Online

Middle School Copymasters

Unité 8: Conversations, *Des conseils*
drill, Blue Notes Sweepstakes game,
puzzles, worksheets, *Un banquet*
project, pp. T39–T46

Pacing

Your pacing of Unit 8 will depend
on where you are in the academic
year.

Since this material is reintroduced
in ***Discovering French, Nouveau!--
Blanc,*** you may want to present
the material primarily for student
recognition. However, if you have
the time, present all four lessons of
Unit 8
so that students have a solid
introduction to object pronouns.

For further suggestions on pacing,
see p. 359D.

Leçon 25

Main Topic Meals and foods

Teaching Resource Options

PRINT

Workbook PE, pp. 213–220
Activités pour tous PE, pp. 131–133
Block Scheduling Copymasters,
    pp. 193–200
Unit 8 Resource Book
    Activités pour tous TE, pp. 9–11
    Audioscript, pp. 33–34
    Communipak, pp. 152–173
    Lesson Plans, pp. 12–13
    Block Scheduling Lesson Plans, pp. 14–16
    Absent Student Copymasters, pp. 18–21
    Video Activities, pp. 24–29
    Videoscript, pp. 30–31
    Workbook TE, pp. 1–8

AUDIO & VISUAL

Audio Program
CD 12 Tracks 1–7

TECHNOLOGY

Online Workbook

VIDEO PROGRAM

MODULE 25
Le français pratique:
Les repas et la nourriture

TOTAL TIME: 6:53 min.
    DVD Disk 2
    Videotape 4 (COUNTER: 25:07 min.)

25.1 Introduction: Listening
    – Où allez-vous quand vous avez
    faim? (25:17–26:10 min.)

25.2 Mini-scenes: Listening
    – Qu'est-ce que vous aimez
    manger? (26:11–27:09 min.)

25.3 Mini-scenes: Listening
    – Vous préférez les frites ou les
    spaghetti? (27:10–27:35 min.)

25.4 Mini-scenes: Speaking
    – Qu'est-ce que vous préférez?
    (27:36–28:26 min.)

25.5 Dialogue: Au marché
    (28:27–30:03 min.)

25.6 Vignette culturelle: Les courses
    (30:04–32:00 min.)

Comprehension practice Play
the entire module through as an
introduction to the lesson.

LEÇON 25

Les repas et la nourriture

LE FRANÇAIS PRATIQUE
VIDÉO · DVD · AUDIO

Accent sur … Les repas français

For the French, a meal is more than just food served on a plate. It is a happy social occasion where people gather around a table to enjoy one another's company. Dinner is the most important family time of the day. Parents and children sit down together and talk about the day's events and topics of common interest. Special events are celebrated by more elaborate meals.

In traditional homes, children do not go to the refrigerator to fix their own sandwiches nor do they help themselves to snacks. They are expected to sit down at the table with everyone else at mealtime, eat what is served, join in the conversation, and not ask to be excused until the adults are finished.

Le petit déjeuner *(breakfast)*

Le petit déjeuner français traditionnel est un repas simple: tartines° de pain avec du beurre° et de la confiture° et un grand bol de café au lait ou de chocolat chaud. Dans les familles modernes, les enfants mangent «à l'américaine»: ils prennent° des céréales et du jus d'orange.

tartines *slices* **beurre** *butter* **confiture** *jam*
prennent *have*

Le déjeuner *(lunch)*

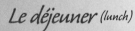

Le déjeuner est généralement servi entre° midi et demi et une heure et demie. Il se compose de hors-d'oeuvre divers (saucisson,° radis,° salade de concombres, etc.), d'un plat principal (viande° ou poisson° avec des légumes°), d'une salade verte, d'un fromage° et d'un dessert (gâteau,° fruits ou glace). Le café est toujours servi à la fin du repas.

entre *between* **saucisson** *salami* **radis** *radishes*
viande *meat* **poisson** *fish* **légumes** *vegetables*
fromage *cheese* **gâteau** *cake*

USING THE VIDEO

Ask students whether they prefer to eat in restaurants, cafés, or fast-food places. What do they usually order there? What kinds of foods do they eat at home? Where do their families shop for groceries?

Then show the Video Module 25 and have students look for similarities and differences in eating and grocery shopping habits in France and the U.S.

In the first part, French people are eating out in cafés and restaurants. Then diners express their preferences for various foods in an interview situation. The *Vignette culturelle* shows French shoppers purchasing fruits and vegetables at an open-air market.

Le goûter *(afternoon snack)*

Après les cours, beaucoup de jeunes vont à la pâtisserie. Là, ils achètent un pain au chocolat,° un croissant ou un éclair.

pain au chocolat *chocolate croissant*

Le dîner *(dinner)*

Le dîner est le repas familial principal. Il est servi entre huit heures et neuf heures avec tout le monde° présent. C'est un repas simple qui se compose d'une soupe, d'un plat principal (viande ou poisson, omelette ou pâtes°), d'une salade et d'un dessert léger° (yaourt ou fruit).

tout le monde *everybody*
pâtes *pasta* **léger** *light*

Photo culture notes

Le petit déjeuner
This French breakfast mixes traditional elements (**des biscottes, du pain, du beurre, de la confiture**) with modern foods (**des céréales**).

Note that the coffee is served in deep bowls (**un bol**).

Note also the open cupboard (**le buffet**) in the back of the room. It is used to display decorative dishes.

Le déjeuner
In summer, lunches are lighter and may consist of cold cuts (**des viandes froides**), salad, and fruit.

Note the bottle of mineral water which is almost always present on a French table.

Le goûter
Many department stores have snack counters where one can buy sandwiches, croissants, mini-pizzas, and light pastries.

Le dîner
Note the basket of fruit on the table. In France, it is typical to serve fruit at the end of the meal.

Note also the wardrobe (**l'armoire**) against the wall.

Cultural note

Eating habits in Quebec are a blend between those in France and English-speaking Canada. Like other Canadians, the **Québécois** have bacon, eggs, toast, and cereal for breakfast. But, like the French, they enjoy wine, mineral water, and croissants at a sidewalk café. Ethnic food, particularly in Montreal, is also very popular. People eat out in cafés, restaurants, and fast-food places. **Le casse-croûte** *(snack bar)* is a favorite place for a quick lunch.

SECTION A

Communicative function
Discussing meals and food

Teaching Resource Options

PRINT

Workbook PE, pp. 213–220
Unit 8 Resource Book
    Communipak, pp. 152–173
    Video Activities, p. 24
    Videoscript, p. 30
    Workbook TE, pp. 1–8

AUDIO & VISUAL

Overhead Transparencies
45 Table setting

VIDEO PROGRAM

VIDÉO   DVD

 MODULE 25

25.1 Introduction: Où allez-vous quand vous avez faim?
(25:17–26:10 min.)

Looking ahead The verb **prendre** is formally presented in Lesson 26. Here students will be using only the **je** and **tu** forms.

Language notes
• Remind students that **la cuisine** is also *the kitchen.*

• In Quebec, meals of the day are:
le déjeuner *(breakfast)*
le dîner *(lunch)*
le souper *(dinner)*

• **Un fast-food** (in official French, **un restaurant rapide**) is a restaurant that serves hamburgers, pizza, etc.

Cultural note In setting the table in France, the spoon is usually placed above the plate.

Supplementary vocabulary
une nappe *tablecloth*
une soucoupe *saucer*
le couvert *place setting*
mettre le couvert *to set the table*
(putting out the dishes, glasses, silverware)

A VOCABULAIRE Les repas et la table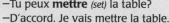

▶ *How to talk about meals:*

—En général, à quelle heure est-ce que tu **prends le petit déjeuner** *(have breakfast)*?
—Je prends le petit déjeuner à sept heures et demie.
—Où est-ce que tu vas **déjeuner** *(to have lunch)* aujourd'hui?
—Je vais déjeuner à **la cantine de l'école** *(school cafeteria)*.

Les repas et la nourriture

NOMS		VERBES	
un repas	meal		
le petit déjeuner	breakfast	prendre le petit déjeuner	to have breakfast
le déjeuner	lunch	déjeuner	to have lunch
le dîner	dinner	dîner	to have dinner
la nourriture	food		
la cuisine	cooking, cuisine		

—Tu peux **mettre** *(set)* la table?
—D'accord. Je vais mettre la table.

COMPREHENSION Table setting

PROPS: Plastic dishes and place settings
Present the new vocabulary.
Voici une cuillère. Voici une assiette. ...
X, viens ici. Montre-nous la serviette.

Have students pass around the items.
X, donne le verre à Y et la tasse à Z.

Have students manipulate the items.
X, mets la tasse sur l'assiette.
Puis, mets le couteau sur l'assiette et la cuillère dans la tasse.
Ouvre la serviette et mets-la sur la tasse. ...

❶ Et toi?

PARLER/ÉCRIRE Exprime tes préférences. Pour cela complète les phrases suivantes.

1. Mon repas préféré est …

   • le petit déjeuner   • le déjeuner
   • le dîner

2. Je préfère déjeuner …

   • chez moi   • dans un fast-food
   • à la cantine de l'école   • …?

3. En général, la nourriture de la cantine de l'école est …

   • excellente   • mauvaise
   • bonne   • …?

4. Je préfère dîner …

   • chez moi   • au restaurant
   • chez mes copains   • …?

5. Je préfère la nourriture …

   • mexicaine   • chinoise
   • italienne   • …?

6. Quand je dois aider pour le dîner, je préfère …

   • préparer la salade   • laver les assiettes
   • mettre la table   • …?

❷ Questions personnelles   **PARLER/ÉCRIRE**

1. À quelle heure est-ce que tu prends ton petit déjeuner le lundi? Et le dimanche?
2. En général, à quelle heure est-ce que tu dînes?
3. Où est-ce que tu déjeunes pendant la semaine? le samedi? le dimanche?
4. Où est-ce que tu as déjeuné hier? Avec qui?
5. Où est-ce que tu vas dîner ce soir? Avec qui?

6. Est-ce que tu vas souvent au restaurant? Quand? Avec qui? Quel est ton restaurant préféré?
7. Est-ce que tu as jamais *(ever)* déjeuné dans un restaurant français? (dans un restaurant mexicain? dans un restaurant italien? dans un restaurant chinois? dans un restaurant vietnamien?) Quand et avec qui?
8. Est-ce que tu mets la table chez toi? Qui a mis la table pour le petit déjeuner? Et pour le dîner?

❸ 👥 Au restaurant

PARLER Vous êtes dans un restaurant français. Vous avez commandé *(ordered)* les choses suivantes. Le serveur a oublié *(forgot)* d'apporter le nécessaire (les ustensiles, etc.).

Monsieur, je voudrais un verre pour le jus d'orange.

Pardon. Voici un verre.

▶ pour le jus d'orange

1. pour l'eau minérale *(mineral water)*
2. pour le thé
3. pour la soupe
4. pour les frites
5. pour le steak
6. pour le gâteau *(cake)*

---

❶ **COMMUNICATION** expressing opinions about food

Answers will vary.
1. Mon repas préféré est (le petit déjeuner).
2. Je préfère déjeuner (chez mes copains).
3. En général, la nourriture de la cantine de l'école est (bonne).
4. Je préfère dîner (chez ma grand-mère).
5. Je préfère la nourriture (française).
6. Quand je dois aider avec le dîner, je préfère (préparer la salade).

---

❷ **COMMUNICATION** answering personal questions

Answers will vary.
1. Le lundi, je prends mon petit déjeuner à (sept heures et demie). Le dimanche, je prends mon petit déjeuner à (neuf heures et demie).
2. En général, je dîne à (sept heures).
3. Pendant la semaine, je déjeune (à la cantine de l'école). Le samedi, je déjeune (chez des copains). Le dimanche, je déjeune (chez mes grands-parents).
4. Hier, j'ai déjeuné (à la cantine de l'école, avec mes copains Paul et Anne).
5. Ce soir, je vais dîner (à la maison, avec mes parents et ma sœur).
6. Oui, je vais souvent au restaurant. (Non, je ne vais pas souvent au restaurant.) Je vais au restaurant (le dimanche, avec mes parents). (Je vais au restaurant pour mon anniversaire, avec mes grands-parents.) Mon restaurant préféré est (un restaurant français, Chez Nous).
7. (Oui, j'ai déjeuné dans un restaurant français. (Le mois dernier, avec mes parents) (Non, je n'ai jamais déjeuné dans un restaurant français.)
   • (Oui, j'ai déjeuné dans un restaurant mexicain. (Samedi dernier, avec mes amis) (Non, je n'ai jamais déjeuné dans un restaurant mexicain.)
   • (Oui, j'ai déjeuné dans un restaurant italien. (Vendredi dernier, avec mes copains) (Non, je n'ai jamais déjeuné dans un restaurant italien.)
   • (Oui, j'ai déjeuné dans un restaurant chinois. (Le mois dernier, avec mes cousins) (Non, je n'ai jamais déjeuné dans un restaurant chinois.)
   • (Oui, j'ai déjeuné dans un restaurant vietnamien. (La semaine dernière, avec ma copine) (Non, je n'ai jamais déjeuné dans un restaurant vietnamien.)
8. Oui, je mets la table chez moi. (Non, je ne mets pas la table chez moi.) (Ma mère) a mis la table pour le petit déjeuner. (Mon frère et moi) avons mis la table pour le dîner.

---

❸ **ROLE PLAY** asking for missing utensils

—Monsieur, je voudrais …
—Pardon. Voici …
1. un verre pour l'eau minérale/un verre
2. une tasse (une cuillère) pour le thé/une tasse (une cuillère)
3. une cuillère pour la soupe/une cuillère
4. une fourchette pour les frites/une fourchette
5. un couteau (une fourchette) pour le steak/un couteau (une fourchette)
6. une fourchette pour le gâteau/une fourchette

SECTION B

Communicative function
Talking about food and beverages

Teaching Resource Options

PRINT

Workbook PE, pp. 213–219
Unit 8 Resource Book
  Communipak, pp. 152–173
  Video Activities, pp. 25–26
  Videoscript, pp. 30–31
  Workbook TE, pp. 1–8

AUDIO & VISUAL

Overhead Transparencies
46a, 46b *La nourriture et les boissons*
(a), (b)

VIDEO PROGRAM

VIDÉO   DVD   **MODULE 25**

25.2 Mini-scenes: Qu'est-ce que vous aimez manger?
(26:11–27:09 min.)

25.3 Mini-scenes: Vous préférez les frites ou les spaghetti?
(27:10–27:35 min.)

25.4 Mini scenes: Qu'est-ce que vous préférez? (27:36–28:26 min.)

Pronunciation

• l'oeuf /lœf/
• les oeufs /lezø/

Supplementary vocabulary

LE PETIT DÉJEUNER
les oeufs brouillés *scrambled eggs*
les oeufs sur le plat *fried eggs*
le beurre de cacahuète *peanut butter*

LA VIANDE
le rôti *roast*
l'agneau *lamb*
le boeuf *beef*
le porc *pork*
une côtelette *chop, cutlet*

LE POISSON
le saumon *salmon*
la morue *cod*
la perche *perch*

B **VOCABULAIRE La nourriture et les boissons**

▶ *How to express food preferences:*

—Est-ce que tu aimes **le poisson** *(fish)*?
—Oui, j'aime le poisson mais je préfère **la viande** *(meat)*.
—Quelle viande est-ce que tu aimes?
—J'aime **le rosbif** *(roast beef)* et **le poulet** *(chicken)*.

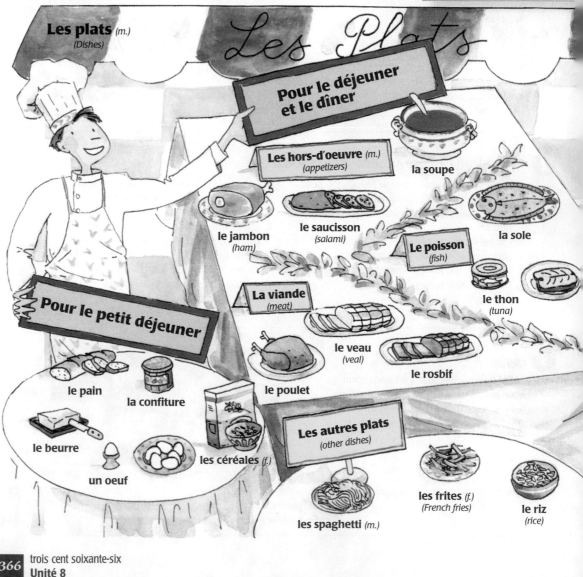

Les plats (m.)
(Dishes)

Les Plats

Pour le déjeuner et le dîner

Les hors-d'oeuvre (m.)
(appetizers)

la soupe

le jambon
(ham)

le saucisson
(salami)

Le poisson
(fish)

la sole

La viande
(meat)

le thon
(tuna)

Pour le petit déjeuner

le veau
(veal)

le rosbif

le pain

la confiture

le poulet

Les autres plats
(other dishes)

le beurre

les céréales (f.)

un oeuf

les spaghetti (m.)

les frites (f.)
(French fries)

le riz
(rice)

TEACHING STRATEGY Foods and beverages

Use Transparencies 46a and 46b, *La nourriture et les boissons,* to present the various foods and beverages. Since the partitive will not be introduced until Lesson 26, ask questions about students' likes and dislikes using the definite article.

X, est-ce que tu préfères le poulet ou le jambon?
Y, est-ce que tu aimes les céréales?
Z, est-ce que W aime la confiture?, etc.

Quelle viande est-ce que tu aimes?

J'aime le rosbif et le poulet.

aimer	*to like*	Alice **aime** le poulet.
préférer	*to prefer*	Philippe **préfère** le rosbif.
détester	*to hate*	Paul **déteste** le poisson.

Les Plats

Les ingrédients (m.)

la mayonnaise

le ketchup

le sucre
(sugar)

le sel
(salt)

Le dessert

le gâteau
(cake)

la glace
(ice cream)

la tarte
(pie)

La salade et le fromage

le fromage
(cheese)

la salade
(lettuce)

le yaourt

**Les boissons
(une boisson)**
(drink, beverage)

l'eau (f.)
(water)

**le jus
d'orange**

**le thé
glacé**
(iced tea)

le lait
(milk)

**l'eau
minérale**

**le jus
de pomme**
(apple juice)

Photo culture note

Le rayon de charcuterie
Many French supermarkets have a deli counter **(un rayon de charcuterie)** where one can buy salami **(du saucisson)**, sausages **(des saucisses)**, slices of ham **(des tranches de jambon)**, and all types of **pâtés**.

Looking ahead Vegetables and fruits are activated in the next section of this lesson.

Pronunciation

• **le yaourt** /jaurt/

• **la mayonnaise** /majɔnɛz/

• **le ketchup** /kɛtʃœp/

Supplementary vocabulary

LES INGRÉDIENTS
le poivre *pepper*
l'huile *oil*
le vinaigre *vinegar*
la moutarde *mustard*
la sauce tomate
la margarine

At your discretion, you may want to introduce some common adult beverages:
le vin *wine*
la bière *beer*
le cidre *cider*

Cultural note Soft drinks are usually ordered by brand name. All are masculine.

Language note

In Quebec:
le yogourt /yogurt/ *yogurt*
un breuvage *beverage*
la crème glacée *ice cream*

CRITICAL THINKING The French connection

Ask students: Which of the above food names have English cognates?

dessert < **dessert**	juice < **jus**
salad < **salade**	sole < **sole**
poultry < **poulet**	soup < **soupe**
tart < **tarte**	

Which food names has English borrowed from French? [hors d'oeuvre, mayonnaise]

Which food names has French borrowed from English? **[le rosbif, le ketchup]**

Teaching Resource Options

PRINT

Workbook PE, pp. 213–220
Unit 8 Resource Book
   Communipak, pp. 152–173
   Workbook TE, pp. 1–8

4 **COMMUNICATION** expressing food preferences

Answers will vary.
1. (J'aime [beaucoup]) le poulet. (Je n'aime pas/Je déteste le poulet.)
2. (J'aime [beaucoup]) les frites. (Je n'aime pas/Je déteste les frites.)
3. (J'aime [beaucoup] l'eau minérale.) (Je n'aime pas/Je déteste l'eau minérale.)
4. (J'aime [beaucoup] les oeufs.) (Je n'aime pas/Je déteste les oeufs.)
5. (J'aime [beaucoup] le yaourt.) (Je n'aime pas/Je déteste le yaourt.)
6. (J'aime [beaucoup] les spaghetti.) (Je n'aime pas/Je déteste les spaghetti.)
7. (J'aime [beaucoup] le jambon.) (Je n'aime pas/Je déteste le jambon.)
8. (J'aime [beaucoup] le thon.) (Je n'aime pas/Je déteste le thon.)
9. (J'aime [beaucoup] le gâteau.) (Je n'aime pas/Je déteste le gâteau.)
10. (J'aime [beaucoup] le thé glacé.) (Je n'aime pas/Je déteste le thé glacé.)
11. (J'aime [beaucoup] le poisson.) (Je n'aime pas/Je déteste le poisson.)
12. (J'aime [beaucoup] le riz.) (Je n'aime pas/Je déteste le riz.)
13. (J'aime [beaucoup] les céréales.) (Je n'aime pas/Je déteste les céréales.)
14. (J'aime [beaucoup] le rosbif.) (Je n'aime pas/Je déteste le rosbif.)

♻ **Re-entry and review** You may wish to review the use of the definite article in the general sense; see page 158.

5 **ROLE PLAY** asking a friend to pass you food

—S'il te plaît, André, passe-moi ...
—Tiens. Voilà ...
—Merci.
1. le sel   5. le fromage
2. le sucre   6. la confiture
3. le beurre   7. l'eau
4. le lait

6 **ROLE PLAY** choosing food

Answers will vary.
—Vous avez choisi?
—Oui, j'ai choisi ...
• la viande (le poisson)
• le poulet (le veau)
• la sole (le thon)
• les frites (les spaghetti)
• le fromage (la salade)
• le yaourt (la glace)
• la tarte (le gâteau)
• le thé (le café)

---

4 **Vous aimez ça?**

PARLER/ÉCRIRE Dites si oui ou non vous aimez les choses suivantes.

• J'aime …
• J'aime beaucoup …
• Je n'aime pas …
• Je déteste …

▶ J'aime le fromage.
(Je n'aime pas le fromage.)

5 **Dîner avec André**

PARLER Vous dînez avec André, un ami canadien. Demandez à André de vous passer les choses suivantes.

▶ —S'il te plaît, André, passe-moi le pain.
—Tiens. Voilà le pain.
—Merci.

6 **La Petite Marmite**

PARLER Vous dînez au restaurant français La Petite Marmite. Le garçon demande ce que vous préférez. Répondez-lui.

La Petite Marmite
menu

■ soupe / saucisson
■ viande / poisson
■ poulet / veau
■ sole / thon
■ frites / spaghetti
■ fromage / salade
■ yaourt / glace
■ tarte / gâteau
■ thé / café

Vous avez choisi?

Oui, j'ai choisi la soupe.

7 Dans le réfrigérateur ou sur la table?

PARLER Choisissez un produit et demandez à vos camarades où est le produit. Ils vont dire si le produit est dans le réfrigérateur ou sur la table.

> Où est la confiture?

> Elle est sur la table.

8 Les préférences

PARLER/ÉCRIRE Indiquez les préférences culinaires des personnes suivantes en complétant les phrases.

1. J'aime …
2. Je déteste …
3. Ma mère aime …
4. Mon petit frère (ma petite soeur) déteste …
5. Mon copain aime …
6. Ma copine déteste …
7. Les enfants aiment …
8. En général, les Italiens aiment …
9. En général, les Japonais aiment …

9 Les courses (Food shopping)

ÉCRIRE Vous passez les vacances en France avec votre famille. Faites la liste des courses pour les repas suivants.

▶ un repas végétarien

1. un pique-nique à la campagne
2. un bon petit déjeuner
3. un repas d'anniversaire
4. le dîner de ce soir
5. le déjeuner de demain
6. un repas de régime (diet)

LISTE

Un repas végétarien:
— oeufs
— salade
— fromage
— pain
— yaourt
— eau minérale

CLASSROOM MANAGEMENT Groups

Have groups of 3 or 4 students work together to compose a shopping list for one of the meals suggested in Act. 9.

Each recorder (**secrétaire**) then reads aloud the shopping list that the group has prepared. The rest of the class tries to guess the corresponding menu.

---

7 EXCHANGES asking where certain foods are

- —Où sont les oeufs?
  —Ils sont dans le réfrigérateur.
- —Où est le yaourt?
  —Il est dans le réfrigérateur.
- —Où est le beurre?
  —Il est dans le réfrigérateur.
- —Où est le lait?
  —Il est dans le réfrigérateur.
- —Où est le jambon?
  —Il est dans le réfrigérateur.
- —Où est la mayonnaise?
  —Elle est dans le réfrigérateur.
- —Où est le gâteau?
  —Il est dans le réfrigérateur.
- —Où est le poulet?
  —Il est sur la table.
- —Où est l'eau minérale?
  —Elle est est sur la table.
- —Où sont les céréales?
  —Elles sont sur la table.
- —Où est le sel?
  —Il est sur la table.
- —Où est le riz?
  —Il est sur la table.
- —Où est le pain?
  —Il est sur la table.
- —Où est le ketchup?
  —Il est sur la table.
- —Où est la confiture?
  —Elle est sur la table.

Language note In France, a refrigerator is often referred to as **un frigo** or **un frigidaire.**

8 COMMUNICATION expressing preferences

Answers will vary.
1. la glace
2. le saucisson
3. le fromage
4. le poisson
5. le rosbif
6. la sole
7. les gâteaux
8. les spaghetti
9. le riz/le poisson

9 COMMUNICATION writing shopping lists

Answers will vary.
1. Un pique-nique à la campagne: oeufs, pain, jambon, thon, rosbif, salade, saucisson, jus de pomme, eau minérale
2. Un bon petit déjeuner: céréales, lait, jambon, oeufs, pain, fromage, confiture, jus d'orange, thé
3. Un repas d'anniversaire: gâteau, glace, jus de pomme, thé glacé, pain, jambon, fromage, moutarde, thon, rosbif
4. Le dîner de ce soir: soupe, sole, salade, spaghetti, fromage, jus de pomme, tarte
5. Le déjeuner de demain: salade, yaourt, poulet, frites, fromage, glace
6. Un repas de régime: soupe, salade, yaourt, poulet, jus d'orange, eau minérale

Middle School Copymasters

Conversation 1: *La boum*, p. 125

C VOCABULAIRE Les fruits et les légumes *(Fruits and vegetables)*

▶ *How to shop for food:*

À la maison
–Où vas-tu?
–Je vais au **marché.**
  Je vais **faire les courses** *(to do the food shopping).*
–Qu'est-ce que tu vas acheter?
–Je vais acheter des **tomates** et des **oranges.**

Au marché
–Pardon, madame. Combien coûtent les **pommes?**
–Elles coûtent un euro cinquante le kilo.
–Donnez-moi deux **kilos de** pommes, s'il vous plaît.
–Voilà. Ça fait trois euros.

10 Qu'est-ce que vous préférez?

PARLER/ÉCRIRE Indiquez vos préférences.

▶ pour le petit déjeuner: (un oeuf ou des céréales?)   **Je préfère des céréales.**

1. pour le petit déjeuner: (un pamplemousse ou une banane?)
2. après le déjeuner: (une pomme ou une poire?)
3. avec le poulet: (des haricots verts ou des petits pois?)
4. avec le steak: (des pommes de terre ou des carottes?)
5. comme *(as)* salade: (une salade de tomates ou une salade de concombres *(cucumbers)*?)
6. pour le dessert: (une tarte aux cerises ou une tarte aux poires?)
7. comme glace: (une glace à la vanille ou une glace à la fraise?)

11 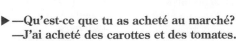 **Les achats**

PARLER Vos copains reviennent du marché. Demandez ce qu'ils ont acheté.

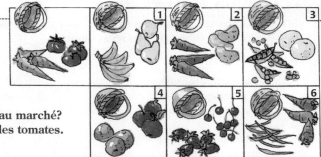

▶ —Qu'est-ce que tu as acheté au marché?
    —J'ai acheté des carottes et des tomates.

COMPREHENSION Fruits and vegetables

PROPS: Plastic fruits and vegetables

Place the items on a desk ("market stand").
Have students "buy" and distribute them.
**X, viens au marché et achète une pomme.
Maintenant, donne la pomme à Y.**

Frequently ask who has what.
Qui a la pomme? [Y] Qui a l'orange? [Z]

Optional: If the fruits and vegetables are light in weight and if the class is well behaved, manipulate the props as follows:
**Y, donne-moi la pomme, s'il te plaît.
Attention, je vais lancer la pomme à X.**

[Toss the apple to X.]
Qui a l'orange? X? Bien, lance l'orange à Y.

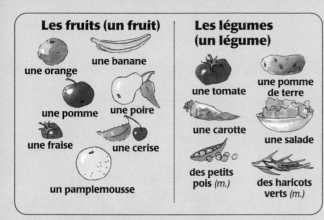

Les fruits (un fruit)

une orange
une banane
une pomme
une poire
une fraise
une cerise
un pamplemousse

Les légumes (un légume)

une tomate
une pomme de terre
une carotte
une salade
des petits pois *(m.)*
des haricots verts *(m.)*

NOTE culturelle

Le marché

In France, as in the United States, most people do their food shopping at the supermarket **(le supermarché).** However, to have fresher fruits and vegetables, many people still go to the local open-air market **(le marché)** where farmers come to sell their produce.

LES QUANTITÉS

une livre (de)	*pound*	**Donnez-moi**
un kilo (de)	*kilo (2.2 pounds)*	
une douzaine (de)	*dozen*	

une livre de tomates.
un kilo de pommes.
une douzaine d'oeufs.

⑫ 👥 *Au marché*

PARLER Vous êtes au marché. Demandez au vendeur combien coûtent certaines choses. Dites aussi quelle quantité vous voulez acheter.

Supplementary vocabulary

Les fruits
un ananas /anana/ or /ananas/
un citron
un melon
le raisin *grapes*
une cerise
une pastèque *watermelon*
une pêche

Les légumes
un champignon *mushroom*
un chou-fleur *cauliflower*
un concombre
des épinards *(m.) spinach*
un oignon *onion*
un poivron *pepper*
une aubergine *eggplant*
une laitue
une salade

Cultural notes

- In general, farmers come to sell their produce on a given day of the week **(le jour du marché).** These open-air markets exist in large cities as well as in small villages.

- French people often buy food in speciality shops, such as:
  la boulangerie *(bakery)*
  la pâtisserie *(pastry shop)*
  la boucherie *(butcher shop)*
  la charcuterie *(delicatessen)*
  la crémerie *(dairy shop)*
  l'épicerie *(grocery store)*

- In the metric system, a pound **(une livre)** equals 500 grams or 1.1 U.S. pounds.

⑫ ROLE PLAY Purchasing food at the market

Teaching note The cues for this activity are written on the ends of the "boxes" at the bottom of the illustration.

—Pardon, monsieur. Combien coûtent les ...
—... coûtent ...
—Alors, donnez-moi ..., s'il vous plaît.
—Voici. Ça fait ...

- oeufs/trois euros la douzaine/une douzaine d'oeufs/trois euros
- fraises/trois euros la livre/une livre de fraises/trois euros
- oranges/deux euros le kilo/trois kilos d'oranges/six euros
- haricots verts/deux euros cinquante le kilo/deux kilos d'haricots verts/cinq euros
- petits pois/deux euros vingt-cinq la livre/une livre de petits pois/deux euros vingt-cinq
- pommes/un euro cinquante le kilo/trois kilos de pommes/quatre euros cinquante
- poires/un euro cinquante le kilo/un kilo de poires/un euro cinquante
- cerises/trois euros la livre/une livre de cerises/trois euros

Teaching Resource Options

PRINT

Workbook PE, pp. 213–220
Unit 8 Resource Book
    Audioscript, p. 32
    Communipak, pp. 152–173
    Family Involvement, pp. 22–23
    Workbook TE, pp. 1–8

    Assessment
    Lesson 25 Quiz, p. 36–37
    Portfolio Assessment, Unit 1 URB
      pp. 155–164
    Audioscript for Quiz 25, p. 35
    Answer Keys, p. 218–221

AUDIO & VISUAL

Audio Program
CD 4 Tracks 21, 22, 23
CD 16 Track 9

TECHNOLOGY

Test Generator CD-ROM/eTest Plus
   Online

1 LISTENING COMPREHENSION

1. A	2. B	3. A	4. B	5. B
6. A	7. A	8. B	9. A	10. B
11. A	12. B	13. B	14. B	15. B
16. B	17. B	18. A	19. A	20. A
21. A	22. A			

2 GUIDED ORAL EXPRESSION

M: Est-ce que tu as faim, Juliette?
J: Oui, j'ai très faim.
M: Est-ce que tu veux déjeuner?
J: Oui, je veux déjeuner, merci.
M: (Est-ce que) tu aimes la cuisine italienne?
J: Je préfère la cuisine française.
M: (Est-ce que) tu aimes la viande?
J: Oui, j'aime la viande, mais j'aime aussi les légumes.
M: Est-ce que tu veux aller (déjeuner) à La Campagne?
J: Oui, d'accord.

À votre tour!

1 🎧 *Écoutez bien!*

ÉCOUTER Pauline et Thomas ont fait les courses dans deux supermarchés différents. Écoutez bien les phrases. Si vous entendez le nom d'un produit acheté par Pauline, marquez A. Si vous entendez le nom d'un produit acheté par Thomas, marquez B.

	1	2	3	4	5	6
A: Pauline						
B: Thomas						

A. Pauline

B. Thomas

2 🎧 👥 *Conversation dirigée*

PARLER Avec un(e) camarade, composez un dialogue basé sur les instructions suivantes. C'est samedi aujourd'hui. Ce matin Marc et Juliette ont fait des achats en ville. Il est midi et demi maintenant.

Marc 				Juliette 
	asks Juliette if she is hungry	⇄	says she is very hungry	
	asks her if she wants to have lunch	→ ↙	answers yes	
	asks if she likes Italian cooking (**la cuisine italienne**)	→ ↙	says that she prefers French cooking	
	asks her if she likes meat	→ ↙	says she does, but that she also likes vegetables	
	suggests they go to La Campagne	→	accepts	

À VOTRE TOUR

Depending on your goals and objectives, you may or may not wish to assign all of the activities in the **À votre tour** section.

PAIR/GROUP PRACTICE

Act. 2 and 3 lend themselves to pair practice. They can also be done in trios, with two students performing and the third acting as monitor.

3 🎧 👥 *Créa-dialogue* ----------------------------

PARLER Vous êtes à Deauville avec un(e) ami(e).
Essayez de découvrir *(try to discover)* ce que votre ami(e)
aime manger. Proposez à votre ami(e) de déjeuner dans
le restaurant correspondant à ses préférences.

▶ —Tu aimes <u>la viande</u>?
—Non, je n'aime pas <u>la viande</u>.
—Tu aimes <u>les légumes</u>?
—Non, je n'aime pas <u>les légumes</u>.
—Tu aimes <u>le poisson</u>?
—Oui, j'aime beaucoup <u>le poisson</u>.
—On déjeune <u>à La Marine</u>?
—D'accord.

1  spécialités italiennes
CHEZ RIGOLETTO

2 AU PALAIS DES GLACES spécialités de glaces

3 À la Normandie spécialités de fromages

4 À LA CAMPAGNE Restaurant végétarien

5  L'Auvergnat spécialités de jambon

6  CHEZ OBÉLIX spécialités de bonnes viandes

7 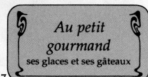 Au petit gourmand ses glaces et ses gâteaux

4 ✏️ *Comparaisons* ----------------------------

ÉCRIRE Avec un(e) camarade de classe, préparez
le menu de trois repas américains et trois repas
français typiques. Comparez ces menus.

Repas américains	Repas français
• petit déjeuner	• petit déjeuner
_____	_____
• déjeuner	• déjeuner
_____	_____
• dîner	• dîner

CONNEXIONS

La France exporte beaucoup de produits
alimentaires *(food products)*, en particulier des
fromages et des eaux minérales.

Allez dans votre supermarché local et visitez
le rayon *(department)* de ces produits.

• Est-ce qu'il y a des fromages français?
Quelles sortes de fromage?

• Est-ce qu'il y a des eaux minérales françaises?
Quelles marques *(brands)*?

 **LESSON REVIEW** CLASSZONE.COM

trois cent soixante-treize **373**
Leçon 25

3 **COMPREHENSION**

Answers will vary.
—Tu aimes ... ?
—Non, je n'aime pas ...
—Tu aimes ... ?
—Je ...
—Tu aimes ... ?
—Oui, j'aime ...
—Alors, on déjeune ... ?
—D'accord!

1. le poisson/beaucoup le poisson/la viande/J'aime un peu la viande/les spaghetti/beaucoup les spaghetti/Chez Rigoletto
2. le poisson/le poisson/la viande/n'aime pas la viande/les desserts/beaucoup les desserts/au Palais des Glaces
3. la glace/la glace/la salade/n'aime pas la salade/le fromage/beaucoup le fromage/Ah, enfin! Alors, on déjeune À la Normandie
4. les spaghetti/beaucoup les spaghetti/la viande/déteste la viande/la salade/j'adore la salade/À la Campagne
5. le poisson/le poisson/le poulet/n'aime pas le poulet/le jambon/beaucoup le jambon/à L'Auvergnat?
6. le fromage/le fromage/le poisson/déteste le poisson/la viande/j'adore la viande/Chez Obélix
7. la viande/la viande/les légumes/déteste les légumes/les desserts/j'adore les desserts/Au petit gourmand

Culture note La Marine
"La Marine" is a seafood restaurant
located in the harbor section of
Deauville, an Atlantic Ocean resort on
the coast of Normandy.

Teaching strategy As a
preparation for Act. 3, have students
name the types of foods that might be
on the menu in each of the restaurants.
This list of foods could function as a
point of departure for the dialogues.

4 **WRITTEN SELF-EXPRESSION**

Answers will vary.

Repas américains	Repas français
• petit déjeuner	• petit déjeuner
oeufs	pain
pain grillé	confiture
saucisson	café / chocolat chaud
café	• déjeuner
jus d'orange	hors-d'oeuvre
• déjeuner	viande
sandwich	légumes
pomme	salade verte
lait	fromage
• dîner	dessert
poulet	• dîner
pomme de terre	soupe
carottes	omelette / viande / poisson
	salade
	dessert léger (yaourt ou fruit)

Leçon 26

Main Topic Talking about food

Teaching Resource Options

PRINT

Workbook PE, pp. 221–228
Activités pour tous PE, pp. 135–137
Block Scheduling Copymasters,
  pp. 201–208
Unit 8 Resource Book
  Activités pour tous TE, 72–74
  Audioscript, pp. 71
  Communipak, pp. 152–173
  Lesson Plans, pp. 50–51
  Block Scheduling Lesson Plans,
    pp. 52–54
  Absent Student Copymasters,
    pp. 55–60
  Video Activities, pp. 63–68
  Videoscript, pp. 69–70
  Workbook TE, pp. 39–46

AUDIO & VISUAL

Audio Program
CD 4 Tracks 24, 25
CD 12 Tracks 8–17

TECHNOLOGY

Online Workbook

VIDEO PROGRAM

VIDÉO   DVD

MODULE 26
Les courses

TOTAL TIME: 6:48 min.
  DVD Disk 2
  Videotape 4 (COUNTER: 32:15 min.)

26.1 Dialogue: Le pique-nique
  (32:24–34:42 min.)

26.2 Mini-scenes: Listening
  – Voici du pain (34:43–36:06 min.)

26.3 Mini-scenes: Listening
  – Je prends du beurre?
  (36:07–36:32 min.)

26.4 Mini-scenes: Speaking
  – Tu veux du pain?
  (36:33–37:58 min.)

26.5 Vignette culturelle: Le petit déjeuner (37:59–39:03 min.)

Comprehension practice Play the entire module through as an introduction to the lesson.

LEÇON 26 À la cantine 🎧 AUDIO

Il est midi et demi. Suzanne va à la cantine. Elle rencontre Jean-Marc.

Suzanne:	Est-ce que tu veux déjeuner avec moi?
Jean-Marc:	Ça dépend. Qu'est-ce qu'il y a aujourd'hui?
Suzanne:	Il y a du poisson!
Jean-Marc:	Du poisson?
Suzanne:	Oui, du poisson.
Jean-Marc:	Quelle horreur! Bon, aujourd'hui, je ne veux pas déjeuner.
Suzanne:	Il y a aussi du gâteau.
Jean-Marc:	Du gâteau! Hm …
Suzanne:	Et de la glace!
Jean-Marc:	Une minute … je vais prendre un plateau.

How disgusting!

to take / tray

Compréhension

1. À quelle heure est-ce que Suzanne va déjeuner?
2. Qui est-ce qu'elle rencontre?
3. Est-ce que Jean-Marc aime le poisson?
4. Qu'est-ce qu'il aime?
5. Est-ce qu'il va déjeuner avec Suzanne? Pourquoi?

SETTING THE SCENE

Language note

Ask questions about the school cafeteria.
Est-ce que vous déjeunez à la cantine de l'école? Si oui, levez la main.
Est-ce que vous aimez la nourriture?
Qu'est-ce que vous aimez particulièrement?
Qu'est-ce que vous détestez?

Then have students read the opening text and the *Note culturelle* to find out what foods and beverages French students are served at school and what their reactions are.

Et toi?

1. En général, où est-ce que tu déjeunes?
2. À quelle heure est-ce que tu déjeunes?
3. En général, est-ce que tu aimes la nourriture de la cantine?
4. Qu'est-ce que tu fais quand tu n'aimes pas la nourriture de la cantine?

NOTE *culturelle*

À la cantine

Où est-ce que tu déjeunes pendant la semaine? Quand on habite près de l'école, on peut° rentrer à la maison. Quand on habite loin, on déjeune à la cantine. À midi, beaucoup de jeunes Français déjeunent à la cantine de leur école.

À la cantine, chacun° prend° un plateau et va chercher° sa nourriture. Cette nourriture est généralement bonne, abondante° et variée. Le menu change chaque° jour de la semaine. Un repas typique inclut° les plats suivants:

- **un hors-d'oeuvre**
  salade de concombres,
  salade de pommes de terre,
  carottes râpées,° jambon …

- **un plat principal° chaud**
  poulet, steak, côtelette de porc°

- **une garniture°**
  spaghetti, frites, petits pois,
  purée de pommes de terre°

- **une salade verte**

- **du fromage**

- **un dessert**
  glace ou fruit

- **une boisson**
  eau minérale, limonade, jus de fruit

Où est-ce que tu préférerais° déjeuner?
À ton école ou dans une école française?

peut *can* **chacun** *each one* **prend** *takes* **chercher** *to get*
abondante *plentiful* **chaque** *each* **inclut** *includes*
râpées *grated* **principal** *main* **côtelette de porc** *pork chop*
garniture *side dish* **purée de pommes de terre** *mashed potatoes*
est-ce que tu préférerais *would you prefer*

trois cent soixante-quinze 375
Leçon 26

USING THE VIDEO

In the opening segment of Video Module 26, a father and son are sent to the supermarket to get food for a picnic. Students will see what a French supermarket looks like.

In the middle segments, people talk about various foods, often in contexts where they naturally use the partitive article.

The *Vignette culturelle* is filmed at Nathalie Aubin's house. The family members each explain what they usually have for breakfast.

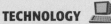
A Le verbe *vouloir*

Note the forms of the irregular verb **vouloir** *(to want)*.

INFINITIVE	vouloir	
PRESENT	Je **veux** aller au café.	Nous **voulons** une glace.
	Tu **veux** déjeuner.	Vous **voulez** des spaghetti.
	Il/Elle/On **veut** dîner.	Ils/Elles **veulent** des frites.
PASSÉ COMPOSÉ	J'**ai voulu** dîner chez Maxim's.	

→ When making a request, French speakers often use **je voudrais** *(I would like)*, which is more polite than **je veux** *(I want)*.

  Je voudrais un café.   *I would like a cup of coffee.*
  Je voudrais dîner.   *I would like to have dinner.*

→ When accepting an offer, French speakers often use the expression **je veux bien**.

  — Est-ce que tu veux déjeuner avec moi? *Do you want to have lunch with me?*
  — Oui, **je veux bien.**   *Yes, I do. (Yes, I want to.)*

Où vous voulez.
Quand vous voulez.

1 Vive la différence!

PARLER/ÉCRIRE Nous sommes samedi. Des amis vont en ville. Pour le déjeuner, chacun veut faire des choses différentes.

▶ Cécile/aller dans un café
  Cécile veut aller dans un café.

1. nous/manger des frites
2. toi/manger une pizza
3. vous/aller dans un restaurant italien
4. moi/aller dans un restaurant chinois
5. Patrick et Alain/déjeuner à midi
6. Isabelle/déjeuner à une heure

2 Oui ou non?

PARLER/ÉCRIRE Dites si oui ou non les personnes entre parenthèses veulent faire les choses indiquées.

▶ Il est midi. (nous/déjeuner?)
  Oui, nous voulons déjeuner.
▶ C'est samedi. (les élèves/étudier?)
  Non, les élèves ne veulent pas étudier.

1. Il fait froid. (Éric/jouer au foot?)
2. Il fait beau. (mes copains/aller à la plage?)
3. La nourriture est mauvaise. (vous/déjeuner à la cantine?)
4. Il y a des spaghetti. (moi/dîner?)
5. Il y a une excellente comédie. (toi/regarder la télé?)
6. C'est dimanche. (nous/travailler?)

3 Expression personnelle

PARLER/ÉCRIRE Complétez les phrases suivantes avec une expression personnelle.

1. Ce week-end, je voudrais …
   Je ne veux pas …
2. Cet été, je voudrais …
   Je ne veux pas …
3. Après l'école, je voudrais …
   Je ne veux pas …
4. Dans la vie *(life)*, je voudrais …
   Je ne veux pas …

B Le verbe *prendre*

Note the forms of the irregular verb **prendre** *(to take)*.

INFINITIVE	prendre	
PRESENT	Je **prends** une pizza.	Nous **prenons** le train.
	Tu **prends** un sandwich.	Vous **prenez** l'avion.
	Il/Elle/On **prend** une salade.	Ils/Elles **prennent** des photos.
PASSÉ COMPOSÉ	J'**ai pris** un steak.	

➔ The singular forms follow the pattern of regular **-re** verbs. The plural forms are irregular.

VOCABULAIRE Verbes comme *prendre*

prendre	*to take*	Nous **prenons** le métro.
	to have (food)	Est-ce que tu **prends** un café?
apprendre	*to learn*	Nous **apprenons** le français.
apprendre à + *infinitive*	*to learn how to*	Sophie **apprend à** jouer de la guitare.
comprendre	*to understand*	Est-ce que vous **comprenez** l'espagnol?

4 *Qu'est-ce qu'ils prennent?*

PARLER/ÉCRIRE Dites ce que les personnes suivantes prennent.
Pour cela, choisissez une expression logique de la liste.

> un bateau   une salade
> un taxi   une limonade
> le bus   un steak-frites
> des photos

▶ Philippe a faim.   **Il prend un steak-frites.**

1. J'ai très soif.
2. Vous n'avez pas très faim.
3. Hélène a un nouvel appareil-photo.
4. Tu vas à l'aéroport.
5. Nous allons à l'école.
6. Les touristes vont à la Statue de la Liberté.

5 *Questions personnelles* PARLER/ÉCRIRE

1. À quelle heure est-ce que tu prends le petit déjeuner le lundi? Et le dimanche?
2. Est-ce que tu prends le bus pour aller à l'école? Et tes copains?
3. Est-ce que tu prends des photos? Avec quel appareil?
4. Quand tu fais un grand voyage, est-ce que tu prends l'autocar? le train? l'avion?
5. Est-ce que tu apprends le français? l'italien? l'espagnol? Et ton copain?
6. Est-ce que tu apprends à jouer du piano? à jouer de la guitare? à faire du snowboard? à faire de la planche à voile?
7. Où as-tu appris à nager? À quel âge?
8. Est-ce que tu comprends quand le prof parle français? Et les autres *(other)* élèves?
9. À ton avis, est-ce que les adultes comprennent les jeunes? Est-ce que les jeunes comprennent les adultes?

SECTION B

Communicative function
Describing daily activities

Pronunciation You may point out that **prendre** has three stems, all pronounced differently:
prend- /prã/
je prends, tu prends, il prend
pren- /prən/
nous prenons, vous prenez
prenn- /prɛn/
ils prennent
Note: The "d" is silent in all the singular forms, and is dropped in the plural forms.

Language note Remind students that *to take* a person somewhere is **amener**. (Also: *to take* a test is **passer** un examen.)

4 COMPREHENSION describing what people are doing

1. Je prends une limonade.
2. Vous prenez une salade.
3. Elle prend des photos.
4. Tu prends un taxi.
5. Nous prenons le bus.
6. Ils prennent un bateau.

5 COMMUNICATION answering personal questions

Answers will vary.
1. Le lundi, je prends le petit déjeuner à (sept heures et demie). Le dimanche, je prends le petit déjeuner à (neuf heures et demie).
2. Oui, je prends le bus pour aller à l'école. (Non, je ne prends pas le bus pour aller à l'école.) Oui, mes copains prennent le bus pour aller à l'école. (Non, ils ne prennent pas le bus pour aller à l'école.)
3. Oui, je prends des photos avec l'appareil-photo (de mon frère). (Non, je ne prends pas de photos.)
4. Quand je fais un grand voyage, je prends (le train / l'avion / l'autocar).
5. Oui, j'apprends le français (l'espagnol / l'italien). (Non, je n'apprends pas [l'italien / l'espagnol].) Oui, mon copain apprend le français (l'espagnol / l'italien). (Non, mon copain n'apprend pas le français [l'espagnol / l'italien].)
6. Oui, j'apprends à jouer (du piano / de la guitare). (Non, je n'apprends pas à [jouer du piano / de la guitare].) Oui, j'apprends à faire (du snowboard / de la planche à voile). (Non, je n'apprends pas à faire [du snowboard / de la planche à voile].)
7. J'ai appris à nager (à la plage à l'âge de 5 ans).
8. Oui, je comprends quand le prof parle français. (Non, je ne comprends pas quand le prof parle français.) Oui, les autres élèves comprennent quand le prof parle français. (Non, ils ne comprennent pas quand le prof parle français.)
9. À mon avis, les adultes ne comprennent pas les jeunes. (À mon avis, les adultes comprennent les jeunes.) Non, les jeunes ne comprennent pas les adultes. (Oui, les jeunes comprennent les adultes.)

COMPREHENSION Choosing foods

PROPS: Pictures of various foods: salad, hamburger, sandwich, ice cream, etc.

Hold up the foods and pick one.
J'ai faim. Qu'est-ce que je vais prendre?
Bien, je prends un hamburger.

Have individual students select foods.
X, viens ici. Qu'est-ce que tu prends?

[X picks ice cream] **Ah, X prend une glace.**
Similarly present plural forms of prendre.
Y et Z, qu'est-ce que vous prenez? [salad] **Ah bon, ils prennent une salade.**
Tiens, Y et Z prennent une salade.
Moi aussi, je vais prendre une salade.
Nous trois, nous prenons une salade.

Teaching Resource Options

PRINT

Workbook PE, pp. 221–228
Unit 8 Resource Book
 Communipak, pp. 152–173
 Video Activities, pp. 63–65
 Videoscript, pp. 69–70
 Workbook TE, pp. 39–46

AUDIO & VISUAL

Overhead Transparencies
49 *Le partitif (du, de la)*

TECHNOLOGY

Power Presentations

Looking ahead This section introduces the forms and basic uses of the partitive article. This concept is further developed in Book Two.

VIDEO PROGRAM

 **MODULE 26**

26.1 Dialogue: Le pique-nique
(32:24–34:42 min.)

26.2 Mini-scenes: – Voici du pain
(34:43–36:06 min.)

26.3 Mini-scenes: – Je prends du beurre? (36:07–36:32 min.)

26.4 Mini-scenes: – Tu veux du pain?
(36:33–37:58 min.)

C L'article partitif: *du, de la*

LEARNING ABOUT LANGUAGE

The pictures on the left represent *whole* items: a whole chicken, a whole cake, a whole head of lettuce, a whole fish. The nouns are introduced by INDEFINITE ARTICLES: **un, une.**

The pictures on the right represent a *part* or *some quantity* of these items: a serving of chicken, a slice of cake, some leaves of lettuce, a piece of fish. The nouns are introduced by PARTITIVE ARTICLES: **du, de la.**

Voici …

Voilà …

un poulet — du poulet

un gâteau — du gâteau

une salade — de la salade

une sole — de la sole

FORMS

The PARTITIVE ARTICLE is used to refer to A CERTAIN QUANTITY or A CERTAIN AMOUNT OF SOMETHING and corresponds to the English *some* or *any*. It has the following forms:

MASCULINE	du	some	**du** fromage, **du** pain
FEMININE	de la	some	**de la** salade, **de la** limonade

→ Note that **du** and **de la** become **de l'** before a vowel sound.

 de l'eau minérale

Mangez chaque jour …
du fromage, de la viande,
des fruits et du pain.
 Santé et Bien-être social Health and Welfare
Canada Canada

TEACHING STRATEGY

PROP: Transparency 49: *Le partitif*

Use Transparency 49 *Le partitif* to present the differences between the indefinite article and the partitive article.

Help students notice the difference between *a whole item* (**un/une**) and *a part or amount of something* (**du/de la**).

Voici un poulet. [pointing to transparency]
Voici du poulet. [pointing to transparency]

Then have various students come up and point to the corresponding items as you mention them randomly in sentences. Meanwhile, students at their desks point to the illustrations in their books. Begin slowly, and then speak more rapidly.

 Voici un poulet.
 Je voudrais du gâteau.

USES

Note how the partitive article is used in the sentences below.

Philippe mange **du** fromage.	*Philippe is eating (some) cheese.*
Nous prenons **de la** salade.	*We are having (some) salad.*
—Est-ce que tu veux **du** lait?	*Do you want (any, some) milk?*
—Non, mais je voudrais **de l'**eau.	*No, but I would like some water.*

→ While the words *some* or *any* are often omitted in English, the articles **du** and **de la** must be used in French.

→ Partitive articles may also be used with nouns designating things other than foods and beverages. For example:

Tu as **de l'argent?**	*Do you have (any) money?*

Partitive articles are often, but not always, used after the following expressions and verbs.

voici	**Voici du** pain.	*Here is (some) bread.*
voilà	**Voilà de la** mayonnaise.	*Here is (some) mayonnaise.*
il y a	Est-ce qu'**il y a de la** salade?	*Is there (any) salad?*
acheter	Nous **achetons du** fromage.	*We are buying (some) cheese.*
avoir	Est-ce que tu **as de la** limonade?	*Do you have (any) lemon soda?*
manger	Marc **mange du** rosbif.	*Marc is eating (some) roast beef.*
prendre	Est-ce que vous **prenez du** café?	*Are you having (any) coffee?*
vouloir	Est-ce que tu **veux de la** glace?	*Do you want (any) ice cream?*

Voici un gâteau.   **Voici du gâteau.**

6 Le menu

PARLER/ÉCRIRE Vous avez préparé un dîner pour le Club Français.
Dites à un(e) camarade ce qu'il y a au menu.

▶ la viande   **Il y a de la viande.**

1. le rosbif	3. la salade	5. la glace	7. l'eau minérale
2. le poulet	4. le fromage	6. la tarte	8. le jus d'orange

Nous achetons du poulet.
Voilà une sole.
Tu prends de la sole?
Il y a une salade sur la table.
Je vais prendre de la salade.
Maman va faire un gâteau.

If students ask

The plural partitive article **des** is used with plural "mass nouns":

des spaghetti
des épinards (spinach)
des oeufs brouillés (scrambled eggs)
des carottes râpées (grated carrots)

Language notes

• Depending on the context, these expressions (**voici, voilà, il y a,** etc.) can also be followed by definite and indefinite articles:
Voici **le gâteau.**
Voici **un gâteau.**
Voici **du gâteau.**

Since these distinctions sometimes tend to be confusing, they are not developed until Book Two. At this point, the important thing is that students become familiar with the partitive and its uses.

• The partitive article is also used with **boire,** which is taught in section E of this lesson.

Middle School Copymasters

Worksheet 1: Shopping, p. 130

6 PRACTICE describing a menu

1. Il y a du rosbif.
2. Il y a du poulet.
3. Il y a de la salade.
4. Il y a du fromage.
5. Il y a de la glace.
6. Il y a de la tarte.
7. Il y a de l'eau minérale.
8. Il y a du jus d'orange.

Teaching Resource Options

PRINT

Workbook PE, pp. 221–228
Unit 8 Resource Book
   Communipak, pp. 152–173
   Workbook TE, pp. 39–46

TECHNOLOGY

Power Presentations

---

7 EXCHANGES offering food and beverages

Answers will vary.
1. –Tu veux de la soupe ou de la salade?
   –Je voudrais de la soupe (de la salade).
2. –Tu veux du poisson ou de la viande?
   –Je voudrais du poisson (de la viande).
3. –Tu veux du rosbif ou du poulet?
   –Je voudrais du rosbif (du poulet).
4. –Tu veux du ketchup ou de la mayonnaise?
   –Je voudrais du ketchup (de la mayonnaise).
5. –Tu veux du fromage ou du yaourt?
   –Je voudrais du fromage (du yaourt).
6. –Tu veux du beurre ou de la margarine?
   –Je voudrais du beurre (de la margarine).
7. –Tu veux du gâteau ou de la tarte?
   –Je voudrais du gâteau (de la tarte).
8. –Tu veux du jus d'orange ou du jus de pomme?
   –Je voudrais du jus d'orange (du jus de pomme).

---

8 COMPREHENSION/ PRACTICE using the partitive

Answers will vary.
1. du sucre (du lait, de la crème)
2. du sucre (du lait, de la crème)
3. du sel
4. de la mayonnaise (de la moutarde, du jambon)
5. du ketchup
6. de la moutarde (du ketchup)
7. du lait (du sucre)
8. du beurre (de la confiture)

Variation (dialogue format)

– Qu'est-ce que tu mets sur le pain?
– Je mets du beurre (de la confiture).

---

9 DESCRIPTION describing food purchases

1. Il a acheté de la confiture.
2. Il a acheté de l'eau minérale.
3. Il a acheté du beurre.
4. Il a acheté du café.
5. Il a acheté du fromage.
6. Il a acheté du poisson.
7. Il a acheté du lait.

---

7 👥 **Au choix**

PARLER Vous déjeunez avec votre famille. Offrez aux membres de votre famille le choix entre les choses suivantes. Ils vont indiquer leurs préférences.

▶ le jus ou l'eau minérale?

1. la soupe ou la salade?
2. le poisson ou la viande?
3. le rosbif ou le poulet?
4. le ketchup ou la mayonnaise?
5. le fromage ou le yaourt?
6. le beurre ou la margarine?
7. le gâteau ou la tarte?
8. le jus d'orange ou le jus de pomme?

Tu veux du jus ou de l'eau minérale?

Je voudrais de l'eau minérale.

---

8 **Qu'est-ce qu'on met?**

PARLER/ÉCRIRE Dites quels produits de la liste on met dans ou sur les choses suivantes.

▶ On met **du beurre (de la confiture)** sur le pain.

1. On met … dans le café.
2. On met … dans le thé.
3. On met … dans la soupe.
4. On met … dans un sandwich.
5. On met … sur un hamburger.
6. On met … sur un hot dog.
7. On met … dans les céréales.
8. On met … sur un toast.

> le fromage
> le jambon
> le beurre
> la confiture
> le ketchup
> la mayonnaise
> le sel
> la crème
> le sucre
> la moutarde (mustard)
> le lait

---

9 **Les courses**

PARLER/ÉCRIRE M. Simon a fait les courses. Dites ce qu'il a acheté.

▶ Il a acheté de la viande.

---

10 **Le Cochon d'Or**

LIRE/PARLER Émilie est allée au restaurant. Voici l'addition. Dites ce qu'elle a pris.

▶ Émilie a pris de la salade de tomates.

RESTAURANT Le Cochon d'Or

salade de tomates	3€
poulet	4€
salade	3€
fromage	3€
glace	3€50
eau minérale	2€50
	19 €

TEACHING PROJECT Les repas

PROPS: One large paper plate per student

Have students illustrate their paper plates with drawings or pictures of at least five food items for one meal of the day. (They should write their names on the back of the plate.) Then in small groups, students take turns telling what they have for the particular meal.

As a follow-up activity, collect the plates and redistribute them so that each student has another student's plate. Then have them write what this person is having. For example:

Pierre prend un hot dog, des frites avec du ketchup et de la salade. Comme dessert, il prend du gâteau et de la glace.

11 🏃 *Au café*

PARLER Au café, une cliente commande *(orders)* les choses suivantes. Le serveur apporte ces choses.

▼

> S'il vous plaît, monsieur, je voudrais de la limonade.

> Voici de la limonade, mademoiselle.

12 *Menus*

PARLER/ÉCRIRE Préparez des menus pour les personnes suivantes. Dites ce que vous allez acheter pour chaque personne.

▶ une personne qui aime manger
  Je vais acheter du rosbif, du fromage, de la glace …

1. une personne malade *(sick)*
2. un(e) athlète
3. un petit enfant
4. un végétarien (une végétarienne)
5. une personne qui veut maigrir
6. un invité *(guest)* japonais
7. une invitée française
8. un invité américain

D L'article partitif dans les phrases négatives

Note the forms of the partitive articles in the negative sentences below.

AFFIRMATIVE	NEGATIVE	
Tu manges **du jambon?**	Non, je **ne** mange **pas de** jambon.	*No, I don't eat ham.*
Tu veux **de la salade?**	Non, merci, je **ne** veux **pas de** salade.	*Thanks, I don't want any salad.*
Il y a **de l'eau minérale?**	Non, il **n'y** a **pas d'eau** minérale.	*No, there is no mineral water.*

In negative sentences, the PARTITIVE ARTICLE follows the pattern:

du, de la (de l')	→	**ne … pas de (d')**
Marc prend **du** café.		Éric **ne** prend **pas de** café.
Sophie prend **de la** limonade.		Alain **ne** prend **pas de** limonade.
Anne prend **de l'**eau.		Nicole **ne** prend **pas d'**eau.

GAME Menus

Prepare slips of paper numbered 1 to 8. Divide the class into eight groups, and distribute the numbered slips.

Each group prepares a menu for the corresponding guest in Act. 12 (e.g., group 2 sets up a menu for **un(e) athlète**).

The recorder (**secrétaire**) of each group then reads the menu:

Nous allons servir du rosbif, …

The rest of the class tries to identify the guest.

---

10 DESCRIPTION describing food purchases

1. Émilie a pris du poulet.
2. Émilie a pris de la salade.
3. Émilie a pris du fromage.
4. Émilie a pris de la glace.
5. Émilie a pris de l'eau minérale.

Expansion Have students say how much was paid for each item. **Jacqueline a pris une salade de tomates. Elle a payé 3 euros.**

Variation Have students choose only three items at the **Cochon d'Or** and say how much they paid.

J'ai pris du fromage, de la salade et de l'eau minérale. J'ai payé 8 euros 50.

11 ROLE PLAY asking for things in a restaurant

—S'il vous plaît, monsieur, je voudrais …
—Voici …, mademoiselle.
1. du pain/du pain
2. du sucre/du sucre
3. du beurre/du beurre
4. du yaourt/du yaourt
5. du thé/du thé
6. de l'eau/de l'eau
7. du jus d'orange/du jus d'orange
8. du sel/du sel
9. de la glace/de la glace

12 COMPREHENSION preparing special menus

1. Je vais acheter (du riz, du pain, de la soupe).
2. Je vais acheter (de la viande, des légumes, du poisson, des fruits).
3. Je vais acheter (de la soupe, des hamburgers, de la salade, de la glace).
4. Je vais acheter (de la salade, des oeufs, du pain, de la confiture, du yaourt, des fruits).
5. Je vais acheter (du yaourt, de la salade, de la soupe).
6. Je vais acheter (des spaghetti, du riz, du poisson, de la viande).
7. Je vais acheter (du pain, de la sole, de la salade, des légumes, du fromage, un dessert).
8. Je vais acheter (du pain, de la salade, du rosbif, des carottes, des pommes de terre, un gâteau).

SECTION D

Communicative function
Making negative statements

Language note The same pattern occurs with **ne… jamais**. **Je ne prends jamais de** sucre avec le café.

Teaching Resource Options

PRINT

Workbook PE, pp. 221–228
Unit 8 Resource Book
  Audioscript, p. 71
  Communipak, pp. 152–173
  Workbook TE, pp. 39–46

AUDIO & VISUAL

Audio Program
CD 4 Track 28

TECHNOLOGY
Power Presentations

13 ROLE PLAY explaining one doesn't have certain foods

—Est-ce que vous avez ...
—Je regrette, mademoiselle, mais nous n'avons pas de (d')...
1. du jambon/jambon
2. du melon/melon
3. du thon/thon
4. de la sole/sole
5. du veau/veau
6. du yaourt/yaourt
7. du jus de pamplemousse/jus de pamplemousse
8. de l'eau minérale/eau minérale
9. de la tarte aux pommes/tartes aux pommes
10. du gâteau au chocolat/gâteau au chocolat

14 PRACTICE negative sentences with the partitive

1. Non, il ne prend pas de mayonnaise.
2. Non, elle ne veut pas de gâteau.
3. Non, il ne mange pas de glace.
4. Non, elle ne prend pas de beurre.
5. Non, il ne veut pas de tarte.
6. Non, elle ne met pas de crème dans son café.

15 EXCHANGES talking about what one does and does not eat

—Est-ce que tu manges souvent ...
—Oui, je mange souvent ... (Non, je ne mange pas souvent de ...
1. de la confiture/de la confiture/confiture
2. du veau/du veau/veau
3. du pain français/du pain français/pain français
4. du fromage français/du fromage français/fromage français
5. de la tarte aux fraises/de la tarte aux fraises/tarte aux fraises
6. de la soupe/de la soupe/soupe
7. du rosbif/du rosbif/rosbif
8. du poulet/du poulet/poulet
9. du thon/du thon/thon
10. de la glace/de la glace/glace

Photo culture note
À la cantine In the cafeteria, French students eat directly from the tray. On the table you will note a pitcher of water **(un pichet).**

---

13 **Un mauvais restaurant**

PARLER Une cliente demande au serveur s'il y a certaines choses au menu. Le serveur répond négativement.

▶ le rosbif

Est-ce que vous avez du rosbif?

Je regrette mademoiselle, mais nous n'avons pas de rosbif.

1. le jambon	6. le yaourt
2. le melon	7. le jus de pamplemousse
3. le thon	8. l'eau minérale
4. la sole	9. la tarte aux pommes
5. le veau	10. le gâteau au chocolat

14 **Au régime** (On a diet)

PARLER Les personnes suivantes sont au régime parce qu'elles veulent maigrir. Répondez négativement aux questions suivantes.

▶ —Est-ce qu'Anne mange du pain?
  —Non, elle ne mange pas de pain.

1. Est-ce que Marc prend de la mayonnaise?
2. Est-ce que Pauline veut du gâteau?
3. Est-ce que Jean-Pierre mange de la glace?
4. Est-ce qu'Alice prend du beurre?
5. Est-ce que Monsieur Ledodu veut de la tarte?
6. Est-ce que Mademoiselle Poix met de la crème dans son café?

15 **Conversation**

PARLER Demandez à vos camarades s'ils mangent souvent les choses suivantes.

▶ du poisson

Est-ce que vous mangez souvent du poisson?

Oui, je mange souvent du poisson.

Non, je ne mange pas souvent de poisson.

1. de la confiture	6. de la soupe
2. du veau	7. du rosbif
3. du pain français	8. du poulet
4. du fromage français	9. du thon
5. de la tarte aux fraises	10. de la glace

16 **Dans le réfrigérateur**

PARLER Vous préparez le dîner. Demandez à un(e) camarade s'il y a les choses suivantes dans le réfrigérateur.

▶ le lait   —Est-ce qu'il y a du lait?
           —Non, il n'y a pas de lait.

1. le jus d'orange?	6. l'eau minérale?
2. le pain?	7. le jus de pomme?
3. la glace?	8. le fromage?
4. le beurre?	9. la mayonnaise?
5. le jambon?	10. le ketchup?

GAME Qu'est-ce qu'il y a?

PROPS: Vocabulary cards of food items
Divide the class in half—Team A and Team B. Place 5 cards backwards on the chalkledge so that students cannot see the pictures. Player A-1 guesses a food item:

Est-ce qu'il y a du pain?
[Oui, il y a du pain. (Non, ...)]

If A-1 guesses correctly, his/her team wins a point. The teacher replaces the appropriate card with another one and the student guesses again. If not, player B-1 gets a chance to guess, etc. The team with the most points at the end of the game wins.

Note: It is easier to remember the position of the cards if you alphabetize them as you place them on the chalk ledge.

E Le verbe *boire*

Note the forms of the irregular verb **boire** *(to drink)*.

INFINITIVE	boire	
PRESENT	Je **bois** du lait.	Nous **buvons** du café.
	Tu **bois** de l'eau.	Vous **buvez** du thé glacé.
	Il/Elle/On **boit** du soda.	Ils/Elles **boivent** du jus d'orange.
PASSÉ COMPOSÉ	J'**ai bu** du jus de tomate.	

17 Les boissons

PARLER/ÉCRIRE Philippe et ses amis ont soif. Chacun *(Each person)* boit quelque chose de différent.

▶ **Philippe boit de l'eau.**

| Philippe | 1. nous | 2. toi | 3. vous | 4. Cécile | 5. mes copains | 6. moi |

18 Expression personnelle

PARLER/ÉCRIRE Complétez les phrases suivantes avec la forme appropriée du verbe **boire** et une expression de votre choix. Attention: utilisez le passé composé dans les phrases 6 à 8.

1. Au petit déjeuner, je …
2. Au petit déjeuner, mes parents …
3. À la cantine de l'école, nous …
4. Quand il fait chaud, on …
5. Quand il fait froid, on …
6. Hier soir au dîner, j' …
7. Hier matin, au petit déjeuner, ma mère …
8. À la dernière boum, nous …

PRONONCIATION

ou = /u/   **u** = /y/

Les lettres «ou» et «u»

The letters "ou" always represent the sound /u/.
Répétez: /u/   **vous nous poulet soupe**
fourchette couteau douzaine

la poule   **le pull**

The letter "u" always represents the sound /y/.
Répétez: /y/   **tu du une légume jus sucre bien sûr avenue musée**

Now distinguish between the two vowel sounds:
Répétez: /u/ – /y/   **poule** *(hen)* – **pull   roue** *(wheel)* – **rue   vous** – **vue** *(view)*   **je joue** – **le jus**

Vous buvez du jus de pamplemousse. Je voudrais de la soupe, du poulet et du jus de raisin.

COMPREHENSION Drinking beverages

PROPS: Vocabulary cards of beverages
Hold up the beverages and pick one.
J'ai soif. Qu'est-ce que je vais boire? [gesture "drinking" milk]
Normalement je bois du lait.

Have individual students select beverages.
X, viens ici. Qu'est-ce que tu bois?
[X picks water] **Ah, X boit de l'eau.**

Similarly present plural forms of **boire**.
Y et Z, qu'est-ce que vous buvez? [coffee]
Tiens, Y et Z boivent du café.
Moi aussi, je vais boire du café.
Nous trois, nous buvons du café.

---

16 EXCHANGES describing which foods are available and which are not

1. —Est-ce qu'il y a du jus d'orange?
   —Oui, il y a du jus d'orange.
2. —Est-ce qu'il y a du pain?
   —Non, il n'y a pas de pain.
3. —Est-ce qu'il y a de la glace?
   —Oui, il y a de la glace.
4. —Est-ce qu'il y a du beurre?
   —Non, il n'y a pas de beurre.
5. —Est-ce qu'il y a du jambon?
   —Oui, il y a du jambon.
6. —Est-ce qu'il y a de l'eau minérale?
   —Non, il n'y a pas d'eau minérale.
7. —Est-ce qu'il y a du jus de pomme?
   —Oui, il y a du jus de pomme.
8. —Est-ce qu'il y a du fromage?
   —Non, il n'y a pas de fromage.
9. —Est-ce qu'il y a de la mayonnaise?
   —Non, il n'y a pas de mayonnaise.
10. —Est-ce qu'il y a du ketchup?
    —Non, il n'y a pas de ketchup.

Variation Ask students whether these items are in their refrigerators at home.
– **Et chez toi, est-ce qu'il y a du lait dans le réfrigérateur?**
– **Oui, il y a du lait. (Non, il n'y a pas de lait.)**

SECTION E

Communicative function
Talking about what one is drinking

17 PRACTICE describing what people are drinking

1. Nous buvons du jus de raisin.
2. Tu bois de la limonade.
3. Vous buvez du thé glacé.
4. Cécile boit de l'eau minérale.
5. Mes copains boivent du jus de pomme.
6. Je bois du jus d'orange.

Variation Have students give sentences in the negative.
Philippe ne boit pas d'eau.

18 COMMUNICATION describing beverage choices

Answers will vary.
1. Au petit déjeuner, je bois (du lait).
2. … mes parents boivent (du thé).
3. … nous buvons (de l'eau).
4. Quand il fait chaud, on boit (du thé glacé).
5. … on boit (du chocolat chaud).
6. … j'ai bu (du jus de pomme).
7. … ma mère a bu (du café au lait).
8. … nous avons bu (du jus de raisin).

PRONUNCIATION

Teaching strategy If your students still have trouble pronouncing /y/, be sure they pronounce the vowel as /i/.

Then have them repeat the word, rounding their lips as if to whistle.

For example, to pronounce **du**, first say **di**. Then repeat **di** with rounded lips. The resulting word will be quite close to **du**.

Teaching Resource Options

PRINT

Workbook PE, pp. 221–228
Unit 8 Resource Book
   Audioscript, p. 72
   Communipak, pp. 152–173
   Family Involvement, pp. 61–62
   Workbook TE, pp. 39–46

Assessment
Lesson 26 Quiz, pp. 76–77
Portfolio Assessment, Unit 1 URB
  pp. 155–164
Audioscript fpr Quiz 26, p. 75
Answer Keys, pp. 218–221

AUDIO & VISUAL

Audio Program
CD 4 Tracks 29, 30
CD 16 Track 10

TECHNOLOGY

Test Generator CD-ROM/eTest Plus
Online

VIDEO PROGRAM

VIDÉO   DVD
  MODULE 26

26.5 Vignette culturelle: Le petit déjeuner (37:59–39:03 min.)

1 COMPREHENSION

1. Tu dînes au restaurant ce soir?
  (d) Non, j'ai invité mon copain Fabien à dîner chez moi.
2. Tu as fait les courses?
  (a) Oui, je suis allée au supermarché ce matin.
3. Qu'est-ce que tu as acheté?
  (b) Du riz, des oeufs, de la salade et du fromage.
4. Tu n'as pas acheté de viande?
  (e) Mais non, tu sais bien que Fabien est végétarien.
5. C'est vrai. Et pour le dessert, tu as acheté de la glace?
  (c) Non, j'ai pris un gâteau au chocolat.

Middle School Copymasters

Worksheet 2: *Au régime,*
  pp. 131–132;
Worksheet 3: *Une pyramide importante,* pp. 133–135

À votre tour!

1  Allô!

PARLER Reconstituez la conversation entre Frédéric et Sandrine. Pour cela, faites correspondre les réponses de Sandrine avec les questions de Frédéric.

1 Tu dînes au restaurant ce soir?

2 Tu as fait les courses?

3 Qu'est-ce que tu as acheté?

4 Tu n'as pas acheté de viande?

5 C'est vrai. Et pour le dessert, tu as acheté de la glace?

a. Oui, je suis allée au supermarché ce matin.
b. Du riz, des oeufs, de la salade et du fromage.
c. Non, j'ai pris un gâteau au chocolat.
d. Non, j'ai invité mon copain Fabien à dîner chez moi.
e. Mais non, tu sais *(know)* bien que Fabien est végétarien.

2 Dis-moi …

I will tell you about my breakfast this morning.

• J'ai pris le petit déjeuner à sept heures.
• J'ai mangé du pain avec du beurre et de la confiture.
• J'ai bu du jus d'orange.

PARLER *Now choose one of the meals you had yesterday and tell me …*

• *at what time you had that meal*
• *what you ate*
• *what you drank*

3  Créa-dialogue

PARLER Avec vos camarades, décrivez où vous êtes allé(e)s et ce que vous avez fait aux endroits suivants.

▶
au supermarché
acheter

Où es-tu allée?

Je suis allée au supermarché.

Qu'est-ce que tu as acheté?

J'ai acheté du pain, du lait et de la confiture.

À VOTRE TOUR

Depending on your goals and objectives, you may or may not wish to assign all of the activities in the **À votre tour** section.

PAIR/GROUP PRACTICE

Act. 1 and 2 lend themselves to pair practice. Act. 3 can be done in trios, with two students performing and the third acting as monitor.

4. Composition: Un bon repas

Imaginez que vous êtes allé(e) *(went)* dans un bon restaurant pour une occasion spéciale. Décrivez le repas. Voici quelques suggestions:

- Dans quel restaurant êtes-vous allé(e)?
- Avec qui et pour quelle occasion?
- Qu'est-ce que vous avez mangé comme *(as)* hors d'oeuvre?
- Comme plat principal?
- Comme dessert?
- Qu'est-ce que vous avez bu?
- Qu'est-ce que les autres *(other)* personnes ont mangé et bu?
- Est-ce que tout le monde *(everyone)* a aimé le repas?

STRATEGY Writing

Writing about food When you are writing in French about what you ate and drank at a recent meal, you have to decide whether you had a whole item (for example, **une pizza**) or whether you had a portion of that item (for example, **de la pizza**).

Before you begin your composition, make a list of the foods and beverages that you and your friends had. Then, next to each item, write the appropriate article (**un/une** or **du/de la/de l'**). Use this list as you write your composition.

un steak
du poulet

COMMENT DIT-ON ...?

How to show your appreciation for good food:

Hm ... C'est délicieux!

C'est exquis!

C'est fameux!

1. à la cantine manger	2. au restaurant manger	3. au marché acheter	4. à la boum boire

5. à la cuisine prendre	6. au café boire	7. dans un restaurant chinois ??

LESSON REVIEW
CLASSZONE.COM

PORTFOLIO ASSESSMENT

You will probably select only one speaking activity and one writing activity to go into the students' portfolios for Unit 8.

In this lesson, Act. 2 and 3 can be adapted as oral portfolio recordings.

Act. 4 is an excellent topic for a written portfolio piece.

---

2 GUIDED ORAL EXPRESSION

Answers will vary.
- J'ai dîné à (sept heures).
- J'ai mangé (du poulet, des frites, et de la salade). J'ai aussi mangé (une pomme et de la glace).
- J'ai bu (du jus de pomme).

3 GUIDED ORAL EXPRESSION

Answers will vary.
1. —Où es-tu allé(e)?
   —Je suis allé(e) à la cantine.
   —Qu'est-ce que tu as mangé?
   —J'ai mangé du rosbif, de la salade et de la glace.
2. —Où es-tu allé(e)?
   —Je suis allé(e) au restaurant.
   —Qu'est-ce que tu as mangé?
   —J'ai mangé du poulet, du fromage et du yaourt.
3. —Où es-tu allé(e)?
   —Je suis allé(e) au marché.
   —Qu'est-ce que tu as acheté?
   —J'ai acheté du fromage, du lait et du thon.
4. —Où es-tu allé(e)?
   —Je suis allé(e) à la boum.
   —Qu'est-ce que tu as bu?
   —J'ai bu de l'eau minérale et du jus de raisin.
5. —Où es-tu allé(e)?
   —Je suis allé(e) à la cuisine.
   —Qu'est-ce que tu as pris?
   —J'ai pris de la glace et du jus d'orange.
6. —Où es-tu allé(e)?
   —Je suis allé(e) au café.
   —Qu'est-ce que tu as bu?
   —J'ai bu (du chocolat chaud).
7. —Où es-tu allé(e)?
   —Je suis allé(e) dans un restaurant chinois.
   —Qu'est-ce que tu as (mangé)?
   —J'ai (mangé du poulet et du riz).

4 WRITTEN SELF-EXPRESSION

Answers will vary.
Pour mon anniversaire, ma famille et moi, nous sommes allés au restaurant Le Bon Repas. Comme hors d'oeuvre, j'ai mangé de la salade et ma soeur a mangé de la soupe. Comme plat principal, ma soeur et moi, nous avons pris du poulet, mais nos parents ont pris du rosbif. Comme dessert, tout le monde a mangé du gâteau au chocolat avec de la glace. J'ai bu du lait, ma soeur a bu de l'eau minérale, et mes parents ont bu du café au lait. Tout le monde a aimé le repas!

Teaching strategy You may suggest supplementary vocabulary, such as:

la dinde *(turkey)*
le maïs /mais/ *(corn)*
le homard *(lobster)*
le rôti *(roast)*

Leçon 27

Main Topic Ordering food in a restaurant

Teaching Resource Options

AUDIO & VISUAL

Audio Program
CD 4 Tracks 31, 32
CD 12 Tracks 18–21

TECHNOLOGY

Online Workbook

VIDEO PROGRAM

 MODULE 27
 Un client difficile

TOTAL TIME: 7:34 min.
 DVD Disk 2
 Videotape 4 (COUNTER: 39:16 min.)

27.1 Dialogue: Un client difficile
 (39:41–41:57 min.)

27.2 Mini-scenes: Listening
 – Apportez-moi du poulet
 (41:58–43:21 min.)

27.3 Mini-scenes: Speaking
 – Qu'est-ce que tu veux?
 (43:22–44:13 min.)

**27.4 Vignette culturelle: La recette
 des crêpes** (44:14–46:50 min.)

Comprehension practice Play
the entire module through as an
introduction to the lesson.

Language note Tell the students
the meaning of **un ronchon** (grouch).

LEÇON 27

Un client difficile

VIDÉO DVD AUDIO

M. Ronchon a beaucoup d'appétit … mais pas beaucoup de
patience. En fait, M. Ronchon est rarement de bonne humeur.
Et quand il est de mauvaise humeur, c'est un client difficile.
Aujourd'hui, par exemple, au restaurant …

*As a matter of fact / in
a good mood*
for instance

—Garçon! — *Waiter!*
—J'arrive! — *I'm coming!*
—Qu'est-ce que vous avez comme — *as, for*
 hors-d'oeuvre?
—Nous avons du jambon et du saucisson.
—Apportez-moi tout ça … avec du pain — *all of that*
 et du beurre!
—Bien, monsieur.

—Et comme boisson, qu'est-ce que
 je vous apporte?
—Donnez-moi de l'eau minérale …
 Dépêchez-vous! J'ai soif! — *Hurry up!*

—Apportez-moi du poulet et des frites …
 Vite! J'ai très faim! — *Fast!*
—Je vous apporte ça tout de suite. — *right away*

—Et apportez-moi aussi du fromage,
 de la glace, de la tarte aux pommes et
 de la tarte aux abricots … Mais, qu'est-ce — *apricots*
 que vous attendez?
—Tout de suite, monsieur, tout de suite.

—Mais qu'est-ce que vous m'apportez?
—Je vous apporte l'addition! — *check*

SETTING THE SCENE

This comic scene is much more effective if presented
by video. If this is not possible, play the corresponding audio segment which has been taken from the
video soundtrack.

MAKING CRÊPES

The *Vignette culturelle,* Part 4 of Video Module 27,
shows how to make **crêpes**. If students ask, a **crêpe**
recipe can be found at the end of Entracte 8, pp.
416–417.

Compréhension

1. En général, est-ce que M. Ronchon est de bonne humeur ou de mauvaise humeur?
2. Qu'est-ce qu'il va prendre comme hors-d'oeuvre?
3. Qu'est-ce qu'il va prendre comme plat principal *(main course)*?
4. Qu'est-ce qu'il va boire?
5. Qu'est-ce qu'il va manger comme dessert?
6. Qu'est-ce que le garçon apporte après le dessert?
7. Quelle est la réaction de M. Ronchon? Est-ce qu'il est de bonne humeur ou de mauvaise humeur?

Et toi?

1. En général, est-ce que tu es de bonne humeur?
2. Et aujourd'hui, est-ce que tu es de bonne ou de mauvaise humeur?
3. En général, est-ce que tu as beaucoup d'appétit?
4. Est-ce que tu es une personne patiente?
5. Quand tu vas au restaurant avec un copain (une copine), qui paie l'addition?

NOTE *culturelle*

Les restaurants français et la cuisine française

Les Français aiment manger chez eux, mais ils aiment aussi aller au restaurant. Pour les gens pressés,° il y a la restauration rapide° et les pizzerias.

Pour les gens qui veulent faire un bon repas, il y a toutes° sortes de restaurants spécialisés: auberges,° restaurants régionaux, restaurants de poisson, … Il y a aussi les «grands restaurants» où la cuisine est extraordinaire … et très chère!

La cuisine française a une réputation internationale. Pour beaucoup de personnes, c'est la meilleure° cuisine du monde.°

Les Américains ont emprunté° un grand nombre de mots° au vocabulaire de la cuisine française. Est-ce que tu connais les mots suivants: **soupe, sauce, mayonnaise, omelette, filet mignon, tarte, purée, soufflé?** Est-ce que tu aimes **les croissants? les crêpes? la mousse au chocolat?**

INTERNET ACTIVITY

Go to the sites of restaurants in France and read their menus. Which menu/restaurant do you find tempting?

pressés *in a hurry* **restauration rapide** *fast food* **toutes** *all* **auberges** *country inns* **meilleure** *best* **du monde** *in the world* **ont emprunté** *have borrowed* **mots** *words*

trois cent quatre-vingt-sept
Leçon 27 387

Compréhension
Answers
1. Il est de mauvaise humeur.
2. Comme hors d'oeuvre, il va prendre du jambon, du saucisson, du pain et du beurre.
3. Comme plat principal, il va prendre du poulet et des frites.
4. Il va boire de l'eau minérale.
5. Comme dessert, il va manger du fromage, de la glace, de la tarte aux pommes et de la tarte aux abricots.
6. Après le dessert, le garçon apporte l'addition.
7. Il est de mauvaise humeur.

Et toi?
Answers will vary.
1. Oui, en général, je suis de bonne humeur. (Non, en général, je ne suis pas de bonne humeur.)
2. Aujourd'hui, je suis de bonne humeur (de mauvaise humeur).
3. Oui, en général, j'ai beaucoup d'appétit. (Non, en général, je n'ai pas beaucoup d'appétit.)
4. Oui, je suis une personne patiente. (Non, je ne suis pas une personne patiente.)
5. Quand je vais au restaurant avec un copain (une copine), je paie l'addition (ma copine/mon copain paie l'addition).

Note culturelle

Teaching strategy First, have the students pronounce the borrowed French words in boldface type as we do in English. Then have them try to pronounce the words "sounding French."

Photo culture notes

La cuisine française
Most people who appreciate fine cooking consider French cuisine to be the best in the world. French chefs (**un chef**) like to create new dishes that will enhance their reputations. In France the top chefs enjoy the status of superstars.

① EXCHANGES asking friends to do things for you

1. –Tu me téléphones demain?
   –D'accord, je te téléphone demain.
2. –Tu m'attends après la classe?
   –D'accord, je t'attends après la classe.
3. –Tu m'invites à ta fête (soirée)?
   –D'accord, je t'invite à ma fête (soirée).
4. –Tu m'invites à dîner?
   –D'accord, je t'invite à dîner.
5. –Tu me rends visite ce week-end?
   –D'accord, je te rends visite ce week-end.
6. –Tu me rends visite cet été?
   –D'accord, je te rends visite cet été.
7. –Tu m'achètes une glace?
   –D'accord, je t'achète une glace.
8. –Tu m'apportes un sandwich?
   –D'accord, je t'apporte un sandwich.
9. –Tu me vends ton baladeur?
   –D'accord, je te vends mon baladeur.
10. –Tu m'écoutes?
   –D'accord, je t'écoute.

Variation (response in the negative)

Non, je ne te téléphone pas.

Variation (in the plural)

– Tu nous téléphones?
– Oui, je vous téléphone.

Realia note
Le cahier de texte
French students are often required to buy special notebooks of the type pictured on page 389 (**un cahier de texte**) in which they write down their daily homework assignments.

388 · Langue et Communication
Unité 8 LEÇON 27

Ⓐ Les pronoms compléments *me, te, nous, vous*

In the sentences below, the pronouns in heavy print are called OBJECT PRONOUNS. Note the form and the position of these pronouns in the sentences below.

Anne **me** parle.	Elle **m'**invite.	*Anne talks **to me**.*	*She invites **me**.*
Mes amis **te** parlent.	Ils **t'**invitent.	*My friends talk **to you**.*	*They invite **you**.*
Tu **nous** parles.	Tu **nous** invites.	*You talk **to us**.*	*You invite **us**.*
Je **vous** parle.	Je **vous** invite.	*I am talking **to you**.*	*I invite **you**.*

FORMS

The OBJECT PRONOUNS that correspond to the subject pronouns **je, tu, nous, vous** are:

me ↓ m´ (+ VOWEL SOUND)	*me, to me*	**nous**	*us, to us*
te ↓ t´ (+ VOWEL SOUND)	*you, to you*	**vous**	*you, to you*

Cette carte **vous** donne l'accès à 60 musées.

CARTE
MUSÉES ET MONUMENTS

POSITION

In French, object pronouns usually come before the verb, according to the following patterns:

AFFIRMATIVE			NEGATIVE				
SUBJECT + OBJECT PRONOUN + VERB …			SUBJECT + **ne** + OBJECT PRONOUN + VERB + **pas** …				
Paul	**nous**	invite.	Éric	**ne**	**nous**	invite	**pas**.

① D'accord!

PARLER Demandez à vos camarades de faire les choses suivantes pour vous. Ils sont d'accord pour faire ces choses.

▶ téléphoner ce soir?

1. téléphoner demain?
2. attendre après la classe?
3. inviter à ta fête/soirée?
4. inviter à dîner?
5. rendre visite ce week-end?
6. rendre visite cet été?
7. acheter une glace?
8. apporter un sandwich?
9. vendre ton baladeur?
10. écouter?

Tu me téléphones ce soir?

D'accord, je te téléphone ce soir.

TEACHING STRATEGY Object pronouns

The introduction of **me, te, nous, vous** before **le, la, les, lui, leur** serves two purposes:

▶ These pronouns are very useful in conversation.

▶ Students can practice sentence word order with these pronouns without having to make the distinction between direct and indirect objects. The third person pronouns are presented in Lesson 28.

2 Pauvre Chloé!

PARLER Charlotte a de la chance.
Sa copine Chloé n'a pas de chance.
Jouez les deux rôles.

▶ mon copain/inviter

1. ma tante/inviter au restaurant
2. mes cousins/téléphoner souvent
3. mon frère/écouter
4. mes parents/comprendre
5. mes voisins/inviter à dîner
6. ma copine/aider avec mes devoirs
7. mon grand-père/acheter
   des cadeaux *(gifts)*
8. mes amis/attendre après la classe

Mon copain m'invite.

Tu as de la chance.
Mon copain
ne m'invite pas.

VOCABULAIRE Les services personnels

aider quelqu'un	*to help*	J'**aide** mes copains avec les devoirs.
amener quelqu'un	*to bring*	Le taxi **amène** les touristes à la gare *(train station).*
apporter quelque chose à quelqu'un	*to bring*	Le serveur **apporte** le menu **aux** clients.
donner quelque chose à quelqu'un	*to give*	Mme Marin **donne** 10 euros **à** sa fille.
montrer quelque chose à quelqu'un	*to show*	Est-ce que tu **montres** tes photos **à** ton copain?
prêter quelque chose à quelqu'un	*to lend, loan*	Est-ce que tu **prêtes** tes CD **à** tes amis?

3 Questions personnelles

PARLER/ÉCRIRE Réponds affirmativement ou négativement aux questions suivantes.

1. Est-ce que tes copains t'aident avec tes devoirs?
2. Est-ce que ta mère ou ton père t'aide avec les devoirs de français?
3. Est-ce que ton père ou ta mère te prête sa voiture?
4. Est-ce que ton frère ou ta soeur te prête ses CD?
5. Est-ce que tes profs te donnent des conseils *(advice)*?
6. Est-ce que ton copain te montre ses photos?
7. Est-ce que tes cousins t'apportent des cadeaux *(gifts)* quand ils viennent chez toi?
8. Est-ce que tes parents t'amènent au restaurant pour ton anniversaire?

trois cent quatre-vingt-neuf
Leçon 27 389

---

1. —Ma tante m'invite au restaurant.
   —Tu as de la chance. Ma tante ne m'invite pas au restaurant.
2. —Mes cousins me téléphonent souvent.
   —Tu as de la chance. Mes cousins ne me téléphonent pas souvent.
3. —Mon frère m'écoute.
   —Tu as de la chance. Mon frère ne m'écoute pas.
4. —Mes parents me comprennent.
   —Tu as de la chance. Mes parents ne me comprennent pas.
5. —Mes voisins m'invitent à dîner.
   —Tu as de la chance. Mes voisins ne m'invitent pas à dîner.
6. —Ma copine m'aide avec mes devoirs.
   —Tu as de la chance. Ma copine ne m'aide pas avec mes devoirs.
7. —Mon grand-père m'achète des cadeaux.
   —Tu as de la chance. Mon grand-père ne m'achète pas de cadeaux.
8. —Mes amis m'attendent après la classe.
   —Tu as de la chance. Mes amis ne m'attendent pas après la classe.

Teaching note Remind students to use **pas de** in item 7.

Variation (with ne... jamais) Mon copain ne m'invite jamais.

Language note The verbs **donner, montrer,** and **prêter** are new.

Re-entry and review You may want to review the conjugation of **amener**:
  j'**amène, nous amenons,** etc.
Remind students of the distinction between **amener** *(to bring people)* and **apporter** *(to bring things).*

3 **COMMUNICATION** answering personal questions

Answers will vary.
1. Oui, mes copains m'aident avec mes devoirs. (Non, mes copains ne m'aident pas avec mes devoirs.)
2. Oui, ma mère (mon père) m'aide avec mes devoirs de français. (Non, ma mère [mon père] ne m'aide pas avec mes devoirs de français.)
3. Oui, mon père (ma mère) me prête sa voiture. (Non, mon père [ma mère] ne me prête pas sa voiture.)
4. Oui, mon frère (ma soeur) me prête ses CD. (Non, mon frère [ma soeur] ne me prête pas ses CD.)
5. Oui, mes profs me donnent des conseils. (Non, mes profs ne me donnent pas de conseils.)
6. Oui, mon copain me montre ses photos. (Non, mon copain ne me montre pas ses photos.)
7. Oui, mes cousins m'apportent des cadeaux quand ils viennent chez moi. (Non, mes cousins ne m'apportent pas de cadeaux quand ils viennent chez moi.)
8. Oui, mes parents m'amènent au restaurant pour mon anniversaire. (Non, mes parents ne m'amènent pas au restaurant pour mon anniversaire.)

Teaching Resource Options

PRINT

Workbook PE, pp. 229–236
Unit 8 Resource Book
   Communipak, pp. 152–173
   Video Activities, pp. 101–102
   Videoscript, pp. 106–107
   Workbook TE, pp. 79–86

TECHNOLOGY

Power Presentations

VIDEO PROGRAM

  MODULE 27

27.2 Mini-scenes: Apportez-moi du poulet (41:58–43:21 min.)

27.3 Mini-scenes: Qu'est-ce que tu veux? (43:22–44:13 min.)

4 **PRACTICE** describing what people do for others

1. nous
2. t'
3. vous
4. me
5. te
6. nous
7. vous
8. nous
9. m'

SECTION B

Communicative function
Giving orders

Language note The only time the pronoun follows the verb is the affirmative imperative:

Téléphone-moi.

5 **EXCHANGES** borrowing things from friends

1. —Prête-moi ton appareil-photo!
  —Tiens, voilà mon appareil-photo.
  —Merci.
2. —Prête-moi ta veste!
  —Tiens, voilà ma veste.
  —Merci.
3. —Prête-moi ton ordinateur!
  —Tiens, voilà mon ordinateur.
  —Merci.
4. —Prête-moi ta raquette!
  —Tiens, voilà ma raquette.
  —Merci.
5. —Prête-moi ton vélo!
  —Tiens, voilà mon vélo.
  —Merci.
6. —Prête-moi ton skate!
  —Tiens, voilà mon skate.
  —Merci.

---

4 **Bons services**

PARLER/ÉCRIRE Informez-vous sur les personnes suivantes. Dites ce que leurs amis ou leurs parents font pour eux. Pour cela, complétez les phrases avec les pronoms **me (m'), te (t'), nous** ou **vous**.

▶ J'organise une boum.   **Ma soeur me prête ses CD.**
▶ Nous avons faim.   **Cécile nous apporte des sandwichs.**

1. Nous organisons un pique-nique. Nos copains … aident.
2. Tu as soif. Je … apporte un soda.
3. Vous préparez l'examen. Le prof … donne des conseils *(advice)*.
4. J'ai besoin d'argent. Mon cousin … prête vingt euros.
5. Tu es chez les voisins. Ils … montrent leur appartement.
6. Nous sommes à l'hôpital. Nos amis … rendent visite.
7. Vous êtes sympathiques. Je … invite chez moi.
8. Nous allons prendre l'avion. Le taxi … amène à l'aéroport.
9. Je nettoie le garage. Mon frère … aide.

B **Les pronoms compléments à l'impératif**

Compare the position and the form of the object pronouns when the verb is in the imperative.

AFFIRMATIVE	NEGATIVE
Téléphone-**moi** ce soir!	Ne **me** téléphone pas demain!
Invite-**moi** samedi!	Ne **m'**invite pas dimanche!
Apporte-**nous** du thé!	Ne **nous** apporte pas de café!

When the IMPERATIVE verb is AFFIRMATIVE, the object pronouns come *after* the verb.

→ **me** becomes **moi**

When the imperative verb is negative, the object pronouns come *before* the verb.

5 **Prêts** *(Loans)*

PARLER Demandez à vos copains de vous prêter les choses suivantes. Ils vont accepter.

Prête-moi ton portable!

Tiens, voilà mon portable.

Merci.

COMPREHENSION Showing and distributing things

PROPS: Miscellaneous objects from Lesson 25 (plastic fruits and vegetables; picnicware)

Place the objects on a table. Show and give the class certain items but not others.

  Je vous montre une tasse. [hold up cup]
  Je ne vous montre pas le verre. [hide glass]

Then call on students.

  X, viens ici. Montre-nous la pomme.
  Ne nous montre pas l'orange.
  Y, viens ici et donne-moi le couteau.
  Ne me donne pas la fourchette.
  Donne la fourchette à Z.
  Z, ne me montre pas la fourchette.
  Passe la fourchette à W. ...

6 À Paris

PARLER/ÉCRIRE Vous visitez Paris. Demandez certains services aux personnes suivantes.

▶ au garçon de café *(waiter)*
  • apporter un sandwich
  S'il vous plaît, apportez-moi un sandwich.

1. au garçon de café
  • apporter de l'eau
  • apporter une limonade
  • donner un croissant

2. à la serveuse *(waitress)* du restaurant
  • montrer le menu
  • donner du pain
  • apporter l'addition *(check)*

3. au chauffeur de taxi *(cab driver)*
  • amener au musée d'Orsay
  • montrer Notre-Dame
  • aider avec les bagages

4. à un copain parisien
  • téléphoner ce soir
  • donner ton adresse
  • prêter ton plan *(map)* de Paris

7 Quel service?

PARLER Demandez à vos camarades certains services. Pour cela complétez les phrases en utilisant ces verbes.

aider	amener	apporter
donner	montrer	prêter

▶ J'ai soif. … de la limonade.
  S'il te plaît, apporte-moi (donne-moi) de la limonade.

1. Je ne comprends pas les devoirs de maths.
2. Je voudrais téléphoner à ta cousine.
3. Je n'ai pas d'argent pour aller au cinéma.
4. Je voudrais voir tes photos.
5. J'ai soif.
6. J'organise une boum.
7. Je vais peindre *(to paint)* ma chambre.
8. Je vais à l'aéroport.
9. Je ne sais pas où tu habites.

▶ J'ai faim. … un sandwich
  S'il te plaît, apporte-moi (donne-moi) un sandwich.

… avec le problème.
… son numéro de téléphone.
… dix dollars.
… tes photos.
… de l'eau minérale.
… tes CD.
… avec ce projet.
… là-bas avec ta voiture.
… ton adresse.

8 Non!

PARLER Proposez à vos camarades de faire les choses suivantes pour eux. Ils vont refuser et donner une explication.

▶ téléphoner ce soir (Je ne suis pas chez moi.)

1. téléphoner demain soir (Je dois faire mes devoirs.)
2. inviter ce week-end (Je vais à la campagne.)
3. inviter dimanche (Je dîne chez mes cousins.)
4. attendre après la classe (Je dois rentrer chez moi.)
5. prêter mes CD (Je n'ai pas de chaîne hi-fi.)
6. acheter un sandwich (Je n'ai pas faim.)
7. rendre visite ce soir (Je vais au cinéma.)

> Je te téléphone ce soir?

> Non, ne me téléphone pas. Je ne suis pas chez moi.

trois cent quatre-vingt-onze
Leçon 27 391

---

6 ROLE PLAY asking for services

1. S'il vous plaît, apportez-moi de l'eau.
   S'il vous plaît, apportez-moi une limonade.
   S'il vous plaît, donnez-moi un croissant.
2. S'il vous plaît, montrez-moi le menu.
   S'il vous plaît, donnez-moi du pain.
   S'il vous plaît, apportez-moi l'addition.
3. S'il vous plaît, amenez-moi au musée d'Orsay.
   S'il vous plaît, montrez-moi Notre-Dame.
   S'il vous plaît, aidez-moi avec les bagages.
4. S'il te plaît, téléphone-moi ce soir.
   S'il te plaît, donne-moi ton adresse.
   S'il te plaît, prête-moi ton plan de Paris.

Teaching note Have students use the **vous** form in items 1, 2, and 3; and the **tu** form in item 4.

Expansion Have students make original requests to the people in items 1–4. Sample answers:
1. S'il vous plaît, apportez-moi le menu.
2. S'il vous plaît, apportez-moi (donnez-moi) du beurre.
3. S'il vous plaît, amenez-moi au musée du Louvre.
4. S'il te plaît, montre-moi la tour Eiffel.

---

7 COMPREHENSION asking for appropriate services

Answers will vary.
1. S'il te plaît, aide-moi avec le problème.
2. S'il te plaît, donne-moi (montre-moi) son numéro de téléphone.
3. S'il te plaît, prête-moi (donne-moi) dix dollars.
4. S'il te plaît, montre-moi tes photos.
5. S'il te plaît, donne-moi (apporte-moi) de l'eau minérale.
6. S'il te plaît, prête-moi tes CD.
7. S'il te plaît, aide-moi avec ce projet.
8. S'il te plaît, amène-moi là-bas avec ta voiture.
9. S'il te plaît, donne-moi ton adresse.

---

8 EXCHANGES asking friends not to do things

1. —Je te téléphone demain soir?
   —Non, ne me téléphone pas. Je dois faire mes devoirs.
2. —Je t'invite ce week-end?
   —Non, ne m'invite pas. Je vais à la campagne.
3. —Je t'invite dimanche?
   —Non, ne m'invite pas. Je dîne chez mes cousins.
4. —Je t'attends après la classe?
   —Non, ne m'attends pas. Je dois rentrer chez moi.
5. —Je te prête mes CD?
   —Non, ne me prête pas tes CD. Je n'ai pas de chaîne hi-fi.
6. —Je t'achète un sandwich?
   —Non, ne m'achète pas de sandwich. Je n'ai pas faim.
7. —Je te rends visite ce soir?
   —Non, ne me rends pas visite. Je vais au cinéma.

Teaching note Remind students to use **pas de** in item 6.

Middle School Copymasters

Drill 2: *Savoir-faire à une boum,* pp. T40–T41

Langue et Communication • **391**
Unité 8 LEÇON 27

Teaching Resource Options

PRINT

Workbook PE, pp. 229–236
Unit 8 Resource Book
  Audioscript, pp. 108–109
  Communipak, pp. 152–173
  Workbook TE, pp. 79–86

AUDIO & VISUAL

Audio Program
CD 4 Tracks 34, 35

TECHNOLOGY

Power Presentations

SECTION C

Communicative function
Saying what one can and must do

 Review and expansion
The **je** form of **devoir** and the **je** and **tu** forms of **pouvoir** were introduced in Lesson 5.

Teaching strategy Have students note how the forms of **pouvoir** are similar to those of **vouloir**.

Language notes

• In writing, the accent circonflexe appears on the past participle **dû** to distinguish it from the partitive article **du**.

• **Devoir** + noun means *to owe*.
Je dois dix euros à Hélène.

9 **COMPREHENSION**
determining shopping options

Answers will vary.
1. Elles peuvent acheter un CD. (des lunettes de soleil)
2. Je peux acheter une veste (un appareil-photo, une raquette).
3. Tu peux acheter un pantalon. (des lunettes de soleil, des livres, et un CD).
4. Vous pouvez acheter un appareil-photo.
5. Elle peut acheter des chaussures.
6. Nous pouvons acheter une raquette.
7. Il peut acheter des livres.

C Les verbes *pouvoir* et *devoir*

FORMS

Note the forms of the irregular verbs **pouvoir** *(can, may, be able)* and **devoir** *(must, have to)*.

INFINITIVE	pouvoir	devoir
PRESENT	Je **peux** venir. Tu **peux** travailler. Il/Elle/On **peut** voyager. Nous **pouvons** dîner ici. Vous **pouvez** rester. Ils/Elles **peuvent** aider.	Je **dois** rentrer avant midi. Tu **dois** gagner de l'argent. Il/Elle/On **doit** visiter Paris. Nous **devons** regarder le menu. Vous **devez** finir vos devoirs. Ils/Elles **doivent** mettre la table.
PASSÉ COMPOSÉ	J'**ai pu** étudier.	J'**ai dû** faire mes devoirs.

USES

• **Pouvoir** has several English equivalents.

can	Est-ce que tu **peux** venir au pique-nique?	*Can you come to the picnic?*
may	Est-ce que je **peux** prendre la voiture?	*May I take the car?*
to be able	Jacques ne **peut** pas réparer sa mobylette.	*Jacques is not able to fix his moped.*

• **Devoir** is used to express an OBLIGATION.

must	Vous **devez** faire vos devoirs.	*You must do your homework.*
to have to	Est-ce que je **dois** ranger ma chambre?	*Do I have to pick up my room?*

→ **Devoir** is usually followed by an infinitive. It cannot stand alone.

Est-ce que tu **dois étudier** ce soir?   *Do you have to study tonight?*
Oui, je **dois étudier.**   *Yes, I have to (study).*
Non, je **ne dois pas étudier.**   *No, I don't have to (study).*

9 **Le coût de la vie** *(The cost of living)*

PARLER/ÉCRIRE Décrivez ce que les personnes suivantes peuvent acheter avec leur argent.

▶ Philippe a quinze euros.
 Il peut acheter des lunettes de soleil.

1. Alice et Françoise ont vingt euros.
2. J'ai cent euros.
3. Tu as soixante euros.
4. Vous avez quatre-vingts euros.
5. Ma copine a soixante-cinq euros.
6. Nous avons cinquante euros.
7. Mon frère a vingt-cinq euros.

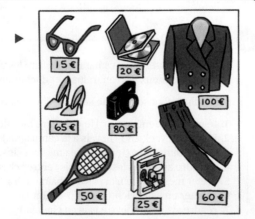

10   Obligations?

PARLER Demandez à vos camarades s'ils doivent faire les choses suivantes.

▶ étudier?

1. étudier ce soir?
2. ranger ta chambre?
3. mettre la table?
4. réussir à l'examen?
5. aller chez le dentiste cette semaine?
6. parler au professeur après la classe?

Est-ce que tu dois étudier?

Oui, je dois étudier.
(Non, je ne dois pas étudier.)

7. être poli(e) *(polite)* avec tes voisins?
8. rentrer chez toi après la classe?

11   Excuses

PARLER/ÉCRIRE Thomas demande à ses amis de repeindre *(to repaint)* sa chambre avec lui, mais chacun a une excuse. Dites que les personnes suivantes ne peuvent pas aider Thomas. Dites aussi ce qu'elles doivent faire.

▶ Hélène (étudier)
  Hélène ne peut pas aider Thomas.
  Elle doit étudier.

1. nous (faire les courses)
2. Lise et Rose (acheter des vêtements)
3. moi (aider ma mère)
4. toi (nettoyer le garage)
5. Alice (rendre visite à sa grand-mère)
6. vous (déjeuner avec vos cousins)
7. mon frère et moi (laver la voiture)
8. Nathalie et toi (préparer l'examen)

12   Expression personnelle

PARLER/ÉCRIRE Complétez les phrases suivantes avec vos idées personnelles.

1. Chez moi, je peux …
  Je ne peux pas …
2. À l'école, nous devons …
  Nous ne devons pas …
3. À la maison, je dois …
  Mes frères (Mes sœurs) doivent …

4. Quand on est riche, on peut …
  On doit …
5. Quand on est malade *(sick)*, on doit …
  On ne doit pas …
6. Quand on veut maigrir, on doit …
  On ne peut pas …

PRONONCIATION   s = /z/   ss = /s/

Les lettres «s» et «ss»

Be sure to distinguish between "**s**" and "**ss**" in the middle of a word.

poison   poisson

Répétez: /z/   **mauvaise cuisine fraise mayonnaise**
              quelque chose magasin

        /s/   **poisson saucisson dessert boisson assiette pamplemousse**

     /z/–/s/   **poison – poisson   désert** *(desert)* **– dessert**

             Comme dessert nous choisissons une tarte aux fraises.

---

10   EXCHANGES finding out what friends have to do and don't have to do

1. —Est-ce que tu dois étudier ce soir?
  —Oui, je dois étudier ce soir. (Non, je ne dois pas étudier ce soir.)
2. —Est-ce que tu dois ranger ta chambre?
  —Oui, je dois ranger ma chambre. (Non, je ne dois pas ranger ma chambre.)
3. —Est-ce que tu dois mettre la table?
  —Oui, je dois mettre la table. (Non, je ne dois pas mettre la table.)
4. —Est-ce que tu dois réussir à l'examen?
  —Oui, je dois réussir à l'examen. (Non, je ne dois pas réussir à l'examen.)
5. —Est-ce que tu dois aller chez le dentiste cette semaine?
  —Oui, je dois aller chez le dentiste cette semaine. (Non, je ne dois pas aller chez le dentiste cette semaine.)
6. —Est-ce que tu dois parler au professeur après la classe?
  —Oui, je dois parler au professeur après la classe. (Non, je ne dois pas parler au professeur après la classe.)
7. —Est-ce que tu dois être poli(e) avec tes voisins?
  —Oui, je dois être poli(e) avec mes voisins. (Non, je ne dois pas être poli[e] avec mes voisins.)
8. —Est-ce que tu dois rentrer chez toi après la classe?
  —Oui, je dois rentrer chez moi après la classe. (Non, je ne dois pas rentrer chez moi après la classe.)

11   PRACTICE making excuses

1. Nous ne pouvons pas aider Thomas. Nous devons faire les courses.
2. Lise et Rose ne peuvent pas aider Thomas. Elles doivent acheter des vêtements.
3. Je ne peux pas aider Thomas. Je dois aider ma mère.
4. Tu ne peux pas aider Thomas. Tu dois nettoyer le garage.
5. Alice ne peut pas aider Thomas. Elle doit rendre visite à sa grand-mère.
6. Vous ne pouvez pas aider Thomas. Vous devez déjeuner avec vos cousins.
7. Mon frère et moi, nous ne pouvons pas aider Thomas. Nous devons laver la voiture.
8. Nathalie et toi, vous ne pouvez pas aider Thomas. Vous devez préparer l'examen.

Teaching note Help students choose correct pronouns for items 7 and 8: **nous lavons …, vous préparez …**

12   COMMUNICATION talking about what one can and should do

Answers will vary.
1. Chez moi, je peux (écouter la radio). Je ne peux pas (regarder la télé après onze heures).
2. À l'école, nous devons (écouter le prof). Nous ne devons pas (lire des bandes dessinées en classe).
3. À la maison, je dois (ranger ma chambre). Mes frères (Mes soeurs) doivent (laver la voiture).
4. Quand on est riche, on peut (faire de grands voyages). On doit (aider les pauvres).
5. Quand on est malade, on doit (rester au lit). On ne doit pas (faire de promenade à vélo).
6. Quand on veut maigrir, on doit (manger beaucoup de salade). On ne peut pas (manger beaucoup de glace).

Teaching Resource Options

PRINT

Workbook PE, pp. 229–236
Unit 8 Resource Book
   Audioscript, p. 109
   Communipak, pp. 152–173
   Family Involvement, pp. 98–99
   Workbook TE, pp. 79–86

Assessment
Lesson 27 Quiz, pp. 112–113
Portfolio Assessment, Unit 1 URB
   pp. 155–164
Audioscript for Quiz 27, p. 111
Answer Keys, pp. 218–221

AUDIO & VISUAL

Audio Program
CD 4 Tracks 36, 37
CD 16 Track 11

TECHNOLOGY

Test Generator CD-ROM/eTest Plus
Online

1 COMPREHENSION

1. Dis, Philippe, j'ai besoin d'un petit service.
  (e) Qu'est-ce que je peux faire pour toi?
2. Prête-moi ta mobylette, s'il te plaît.
  (d) Ah, je ne peux pas. Je dois aller en ville cet après-midi.
3. Dans ce cas, apporte-moi *Paris Match*.
  (b) D'accord, je vais aller à la librairie Duchemin.
4. Alors, achète-moi aussi le nouvel album d'Astérix.
  (c) Écoute, je n'ai pas assez d'argent.
5. Je t'ai prêté vingt euros hier.
  (a) C'est vrai ... Bon, je t'achète tout ça.

Culture note

In addition to bookstores **(des librairies)** many French cities have a **Maison de la presse** that sells magazines and newspapers as well as books.

Middle School Copymasters

Conversation 2: *Un garçon pénible*, p. 126; Drill 1: *Des conseils*, pp. T39–T40; Game: Blue Notes Sweepstakes, pp. T42–T43, 136–138

À votre tour!

OBJECTIFS

Now you can ...
• ask people for favors
• say what your friends do for you

1 Allô!

PARLER Reconstituez la conversation entre Corinne et Philippe. Pour cela, faites correspondre les réponses de Philippe avec ce que dit Corinne.

Corinne

1 Dis, Philippe, j'ai besoin d'un petit service.

2 Prête-moi ta mobylette, s'il te plaît.

3 Dans ce cas, apporte-moi *Paris-Match*.

4 Alors, achète-moi aussi le nouvel album d'Astérix.

5 Je t'ai prêté vingt euros hier!

Philippe

a C'est vrai ... Bon, je t'achète tout ça *(all that)*.

b D'accord! Je vais aller à la librairie *(bookstore)* Duchemin.

c Écoute, je n'ai pas assez d'argent.

d Ah, je ne peux pas. Je dois aller en ville cet après-midi.

e Qu'est-ce que je peux faire pour toi?

2 *Créa-dialogue*

PARLER Demandez certains services à vos camarades. Ils vont vous demander pourquoi. Répondez à leurs questions. Ils vont accepter le service.

▶ —S'il te plaît, <u>prête-moi ton vélo</u>!
—Pourquoi?
—Parce que je voudrais <u>faire une promenade à la campagne</u>.
—D'accord, je te <u>prête mon vélo</u>.

	▶ prêter	1. prêter	2. prêter	3. apporter	4. prêter	5. donner	6. donner
QUEL SERVICE?					$1.00	$5.00	??
POURQUOI?	faire une promenade à la campagne	jouer au tennis	organiser une boum	prendre des photos	acheter une glace	??	??

À VOTRE TOUR

Depending on your goals and objectives, you may or may not wish to assign all of the activities in the **À votre tour** section.

PAIR/GROUP PRACTICE

Act. 1 and 2 lend themselves to pair practice. They can also be done in trios, with two students performing and the third acting as monitor.

3  Au restaurant

PARLER Avec un(e) camarade, préparez un dialogue original correspondant à la situation suivante.

You are having dinner at a French restaurant called Sans-Souci. You have a friendly but inexperienced waiter/waitress (played by your classmate) who forgets to bring you what you need. However, whenever you mention something, he/she agrees to bring it right away **(tout de suite).**

Tell your waiter/waitress …

- to please show you the menu **(le menu)**
- to please give you some water
- to bring you a napkin
- to give you a beverage (of your choice)
- to bring you a dessert (of your choice)
- to bring you the silverware that you need for eating the dessert

COMMENT DIT-ON …?

How to show your reaction to bad food:

Pouah! … C'est infect! … C'est dégoûtant! C'est infâme!

4 ✍ Composition: Bonnes relations

ÉCRIRE Select a person you like (a friend, a neighbor, a relative, a teacher) and write a short paragraph mentioning at least four things this person does for you. You may want to use some of the following verbs:

acheter	amener	aider
donner	inviter	montrer
prêter	rendre visite	téléphoner

> J'ai une bonne copine.
> Elle s'appelle Stéphanie.
> Elle est très sympathique.
> Elle me téléphone souvent
> et le week-end, elle m'invite
> chez elle. Elle est très
> intelligente et quand je ne
> comprends pas, elle m'aide
> avec mes devoirs de français.
> Elle me donne toujours
> des conseils (advice) excellents.

Now tell me about a friend of yours and let me know some of the things this friend does for you.

LESSON REVIEW
CLASSZONE.COM

---

2 GUIDED ORAL EXPRESSION

1. —S'il te plaît, prête-moi ta raquette!
   —Pourquoi?
   —Parce que je voudrais jouer au tennis.
   —D'accord, je te prête ma raquette.
2. —S'il te plaît, prête-moi ta chaîne hi-fi!
   —Pourquoi?
   —Parce que je voudrais organiser une boum.
   —D'accord, je te prête ma chaîne hi-fi.
3. —S'il te plaît, apporte-moi ton appareil-photo!
   —Pourquoi?
   —Parce que je voudrais prendre des photos.
   —D'accord, je t'apporte mon appareil-photo.
4. —S'il te plaît, prête-moi un dollar!
   —Pourquoi?
   —Parce que je voudrais acheter une glace.
   —D'accord, je te prête un dollar.
5. —S'il te plaît, donne-moi cinq dollars!
   —Pourquoi?
   —Parce que je voudrais (acheter un magazine).
   —D'accord, je te donne cinq dollars.
6. —S'il te plaît, donne-moi (ton livre de français)!
   —Pourquoi?
   —Parce que je voudrais (faire mes devoirs).
   —D'accord, je te donne (mon livre de français).

3 GUIDED ORAL EXPRESSION

- —Mademoiselle (Monsieur), montrez-moi le menu, s'il vous plaît.
  —Je vous apporte le menu tout de suite, monsieur (mademoiselle).
- —Mademoiselle (Monsieur), donnez-moi (apportez-moi) de l'eau (minérale), s'il vous plaît.
  —Je vous donne (apporte) de l'eau (minérale) tout de suite, monsieur (mademoiselle).
- —Mademoiselle (Monsieur), apportez-moi une serviette, s'il vous plaît.
  —Je vous apporte une serviette tout de suite, monsieur (mademoiselle).
- —Mademoiselle (Monsieur), apportez-moi (du jus de pomme), s'il vous plaît.
  —Je vous apporte (du jus de pomme) tout de suite, monsieur (mademoiselle).
- —Mademoiselle (Monsieur), apportez-moi (du gâteau).
  —Je vous apporte (du gâteau) tout de suite, monsieur (mademoiselle).
- —Mademoiselle (Monsieur), donnez-moi (apportez-moi) (une fourchette) pour le dessert, s'il vous plaît.
  —Je vous donne (apporte) (une fourchette) tout de suite, monsieur (mademoiselle).

4 WRITTEN SELF-EXPRESSION

Answers will vary.
Ma meilleure amie s'appelle Karine. Elle habite à Montréal. Elle me téléphone souvent et j'aime beaucoup parler avec elle. Quand elle me rend visite, je l'amène au parc et au stade. Elle me prête ses CD. Elle m'aide avec les devoirs de maths, et elle me montre comment faire un très bon gâteau au chocolat. Mmm … Vous aimez le gâteau au chocolat?

Leçon 28

Main Topic Talking about friends and acquaintances

Teaching Resource Options

PRINT

Workbook PE, pp. 237–243
Activités pour tous PE, pp. 143–145
Block Scheduling Copymasters,
  pp. 217–224
Unit 8 Resource Book
  Activités pour tous TE, pp. 123–125
  Audioscript, pp. 144, 145–147
  Communipak, pp. 152–173
  Lesson Plans, pp. 126–127
  Block Scheduling Lesson Plans,
    pp. 128–130
  Absent Student Copymasters,
    pp. 131–135
  Video Activities, pp. 138–141
  Videoscript, pp. 142–143
  Workbook TE, pp. 115–121

AUDIO & VISUAL

Audio Program
CD 4 Tracks 38, 39
CD 12 Tracks 22–27

TECHNOLOGY

Online Workbook

VIDEO PROGRAM

VIDÉO   DVD

MODULE 28
Sur la plage

TOTAL TIME: 5:48 min.
  DVD Disk 2
  Videotape 4 (COUNTER: 47:05 min.)

28.1 Dialogue: Sur la plage
  (48:16–49:30 min.)

28.2 Mini-scenes: Listening
  – Tu le connais? (49:31–50:32 min.)

28.3 Mini-scenes: Listening
  – On va lui parler?
  (50:33–51:34 min.)

**28.4 Vignette culturelle: À la plage
de Deauville**
  (51:35–52:53 min.)

Comprehension practice Play the entire module through as an introduction to the lesson.

---

28 Pique-nique  AUDIO

Mélanie et Jean-Marc organisent un pique-nique ce week-end. Ils préparent la liste des <u>invités</u>. Qui vont-ils inviter?   *guests*

Mélanie: Tu connais Stéphanie?
Jean-Marc: Oui, je la connais. C'est une copine.
Mélanie: Je l'invite au pique-nique?
Jean-Marc: Bien sûr. Invite-la.
Mélanie: Et son cousin Frédéric, tu le connais?
Jean-Marc: Oui, je le connais un peu.
Mélanie: Je l'invite aussi?
Jean-Marc: Non, ne l'invite pas. Il est trop snob.
Mélanie: <u>Comment</u>? Tu le trouves snob? Moi, je le trouve intelligent et sympathique. Et <u>puis</u>, il a une voiture et nous avons besoin d'une voiture pour transporter <u>tout le monde</u> …   *What?* / *also* / *everyone*
Jean-Marc: Mélanie, tu es <u>géniale</u> … C'est vrai, Frédéric n'est pas <u>aussi snob que ça</u> … Téléphonons-lui <u>tout de suite</u> et invitons-le au pique-nique!   *brilliant* / *that snobbish* / *right away*

396 trois cent quatre-vingt-seize
Unité 8

SETTING THE SCENE

Ask students if they go on picnics with family or friends.
Est-ce que vous faites des pique-niques avec votre famille /vos copains?

Where do they go? What do they do?
Où allez-vous? Qu'est-ce que vous faites?

And what do they eat and drink?
Qu'est-ce que vous mangez? Qu'est-ce que vous buvez?

NOTE culturelle

Un pique-nique français

Quand ils vont à la campagne, les Français adorent faire des pique-niques. Un pique-nique est un repas froid assez simple. Il y a généralement du poulet froid et des oeufs durs° et aussi du jambon, du saucisson ou du pâté* pour les sandwichs. Quand on a l'équipement nécessaire, on peut aussi faire des grillades° sur un barbecue. Comme dessert, il y a des fruits (bananes, oranges, pommes, poires, raisin°). Comme boisson, il y a de l'eau minérale, des sodas et des jus de fruit.

*The French have created dozens of varieties of **pâté**, ranging from the expensive and refined **foie gras** (made from the livers of fattened geese) to the everyday **pâté de campagne** (a type of cold meat loaf served in thin slices with bread).

durs *hard-boiled* **grillades** *grilled meat* **raisin** *grapes* (Note that **raisin** is always in the singular.)

Compréhension

1. Qui est Stéphanie?
2. Qui est Frédéric?
3. Est-ce que Jean-Marc a une bonne ou une mauvaise opinion de Frédéric? Pourquoi?
4. Et Mélanie, comment est-ce qu'elle trouve Frédéric?
5. Finalement, est-ce que Jean-Marc va inviter Frédéric au pique-nique? Pourquoi?

Et toi?

1. Est-ce que tu aimes faire des pique-niques?
2. Quand tu fais un pique-nique avec des copains, où allez-vous?
3. Qui invites-tu?
4. En général, qu'est-ce qu'on mange à un pique-nique américain?
5. Qu'est-ce qu'on boit?
6. Dans ta famille, est-ce qu'on fait des barbecues? Où? Qui est le «chef»? Qu'est-ce qu'on mange et qu'est-ce qu'on boit?

trois cent quatre-vingt-dix-sept **397**
Leçon 28

USING THE VIDEO

Video Module 28 was filmed in Normandy at the resort town of Deauville. In the dialogue scenes, two boys on vacation are trying to figure out how to introduce themselves to a girl at the beach.

In the *Vignette culturelle,* other young people are interviewed about their vacation activities. The theme

of the module provides an appropriate point for wishing your students a relaxing summer vacation.

Photo cultural note

In the photo, French youngsters are having a picnic on the grass (**un pique-nique sur l'herbe**) in a park. Note that they have simply spread a tablecloth (**une nappe**) on the ground. In France, public picnic grounds with tables are mainly found at the rest areas along the superhighways (**les autoroutes**).

Compréhension
Answers
1. C'est une copine de Jean-Marc.
2. C'est le cousin de Stéphanie.
3. Il a une mauvaise opinion de Frédéric. Il pense qu'il est trop snob.
4. Elle le trouve intelligent et sympathique.
5. Oui, parce qu'il a une voiture.

Et toi?
Answers will vary.
1. Oui, j'aime faire des pique-niques. (Non, je n'aime pas faire de pique-niques.)
2. Quand je fais un pique-nique avec des copains, nous allons (à la plage, à la campagne).
3. J'invite (ma soeur, mes amis).
4. En général, on mange (des sandwichs, de la salade et des fruits).
5. On boit (de l'eau minérale, du soda, du jus de fruits).
6. Dans ma famille, on fait des barbecues (dans le jardin). (Mon père) est le chef. On mange (des hamburgers, du poulet, et des hot dogs). On boit (du soda et du jus de raisin). (Non, on ne fait pas de barbecues dans ma famille.)

Pronunciation The expression **un barbecue** /barb kju/ has been borrowed from the English. It refers to the meal as well as to the grill on which it was cooked.

Supplementary vocabulary

PICNIC FOODS
du poulet frit *fried chicken*
du poulet rôti *roast chicken*
des chips (m.) /ʃip/ or /ʃips/
des côtes (f.) **de porc** *spare ribs*
de la salade de pommes de terre *potato salad*
de la salade de chou *cole slaw*

SECTION A

Communicative function
Talking about whom one knows

Teaching Resource Options

PRINT

Workbook PE, pp. 237–243
Unit 8 Resource Book
   Audioscript, p. 144
   Communipak, pp. 152–173
   Video Activities, pp. 138–139
   Videoscript, p. 142
   Workbook TE, pp. 115–121

AUDIO & VISUAL

Audio Program
CD 4 Track 40

TECHNOLOGY

Power Presentations

VIDEO PROGRAM

VIDÉO   DVD
  MODULE 28

28.2 Mini-scenes: Tu le connais?
  (49:31–50:32 min.)

Spelling hint The circumflex appears on the "î" of **connaître** <u>only</u> when the next letter is a "t."

Supplementary vocabulary The verb **reconnaître** (to recognize) is conjugated like **connaître**.

Teaching strategy This is a simplified explanation of the distinction between **connaître** and **savoir**. The more complex differences are presented formally in, e.g., **Je connais la leçon** (I know which one it is) vs. **Je sais la leçon** (I know it because I have studied it). For the complete conjugation of **savoir**, see Appendix, p. R10.

1 **PRACTICE** describing whom or what people know

1. Nous connaissons Paul. Nous ne connaissons pas ses copains.
2. Vous connaissez le prof d'anglais. Vous ne connaissez pas le prof de maths.
3. Je connais les voisins. Je ne connais pas leurs amis.
4. Tu connais Paris. Tu ne connais pas Bordeaux.
5. Les touristes connaissent le Louvre. Ils ne connaissent pas le musée d'Orsay.
6. Mon copain connaît ce café. Il ne connaît pas ce restaurant.

A Le verbe *connaître*

Note the forms of the irregular verb **connaître** *(to know)*.

INFINITIVE	connaître	
PRESENT	Je **connais** Stéphanie.	Nous **connaissons** Paris.
	Tu **connais** son cousin?	Vous **connaissez** Montréal?
	Il/Elle/On **connaît** ces garçons.	Ils/Elles **connaissent** ce café.
PASSÉ COMPOSÉ	J'**ai connu** ton frère pendant les vacances.	

→ In the passé composé, **connaître** means *to meet for the first time*.

→ The French use **connaître** to say that they *know* or *are acquainted with people or places*. To say that they *know information*, they use **je sais, tu sais.** Compare:

PEOPLE/PLACES
Je **connais** Éric.
Tu **connais** Frédéric.
Je **connais** un bon restaurant.

INFORMATION
Je **sais** où il habite.
Tu **sais** à quelle heure il vient?
Je **sais** qu'il est près du théâtre.

Je connais Éric.   Je sais où il habite.

1 **On ne peut pas tout connaître**

PARLER/ÉCRIRE Les personnes suivantes connaissent la première personne ou la première chose entre parenthèses. Elles ne connaissent pas la deuxième.

▶ Philippe (Isabelle/sa soeur)
  Philippe connaît Isabelle.
  Il ne connaît pas sa soeur.

1. nous (Paul/ses copains)
2. vous (le prof d'anglais/le prof de maths)
3. moi (les voisins/leurs amis)
4. toi (Paris/Bordeaux)
5. les touristes (le Louvre/le musée d'Orsay)
6. mon copain (ce café/ce restaurant)

2 **Questions personnelles** **PARLER/ÉCRIRE**

1. Est-ce que tu connais New York? Chicago? San Francisco? Montréal? Quelles villes est-ce que tu connais bien?
2. Dans ta ville est-ce que tu connais un bon restaurant? Comment est-ce qu'il s'appelle? Est-ce que tu connais un supermarché? un centre commercial? un magasin de CD? Comment est-ce qu'ils s'appellent?
3. Est-ce que tu connais des monuments à Paris? Quels monuments?
4. Est-ce que tu connais bien tes voisins? Est-ce qu'ils sont sympathiques? Est-ce que tu connais personnellement le directeur (la directrice) de ton école? Est-ce qu'il (elle) est strict(e)?
5. Quels acteurs de cinéma est-ce que tu connais? Quelles actrices? Quels musiciens? Quels athlètes professionnels?

COMPREHENSION   Direct object pronouns

PROPS: 3 pictures of known personalities: a man, a woman, a couple

Tape the 3 pictures on the chalkboard.

Point to the picture of the man:
Vous le connaissez? [write **le** on board]
Bien sûr, vous le connaissez. C'est ...

Present the other 2 pictures (writing **la, les**).

Have students point to the right picture.
X, tu le connais? [X points to man]
Tu ne la connais pas? [X points to woman]
Tu les connais? [X points to couple]

B Les pronoms compléments: *le, la, les*

In the questions below, the nouns in heavy type follow the verb directly. They are the DIRECT OBJECTS of the verb. Note the forms and position of the DIRECT OBJECT PRONOUNS which are used to replace those nouns in the answers.

Tu connais **Éric?**	Oui, je **le** connais. Je **l'**invite souvent.	*Yes, I know **him**.* *I invite **him** often.*
Tu connais **Stéphanie?**	Oui, je **la** connais. Je **l'**invite aussi.	*Yes, I know **her**.* *I invite **her** also.*
Tu connais **mes copains?**	Je **les** connais bien. Je **les** invite.	*I know **them** well.* *I invite **them**.*
Tu connais **mes amies?**	Je **les** connais aussi. Je **les** invite souvent.	*I know **them** too.* *I invite **them** often.*

FORMS AND USES

Direct object pronouns have the following forms:

	SINGULAR		PLURAL
MASCULINE	**le** ↓ **l'** (+ VOWEL SOUND)	*him, it*	
FEMININE	**la** ↓ **l'** (+ VOWEL SOUND)	*her, it*	**les** *them*

Qui le vend?
Qui le répare?

On le trouve
dans les pages
jaunes!

LA POSTE ▰

→ The direct object pronouns **le, la, l', les** can refer to either people or things.

Tu vois **Nicole?**	Oui, je **la** vois.	*Yes, I see **her**.*
Tu vois **ma voiture?**	Oui, je **la** vois.	*Yes, I see **it**.*
Tu comprends **le professeur?**	Oui, je **le** comprends.	*Yes, I understand **him**.*
Tu comprends **ce mot** *(word)*?	Oui, je **le** comprends.	*Yes, I understand **it**.*

POSITION

Direct object pronouns generally come *before* the verb according to the following patterns:

	AFFIRMATIVE			NEGATIVE				
	SUBJECT	+ **le/la/les**	+ VERB ...	SUBJECT	+ **ne** +	**le/la/les**	+ VERB	+ **pas** ...
Éric?	Je	**le**	connais bien.	Tu	**ne**	**le**	connais	**pas.**
Ces filles?	Nous	**les**	invitons.	Vous	**ne**	**les**	invitez	**pas.**

Vary the verbs (beginning with consonants).
Y, tu la vois souvent? [Y points to woman]
Tu les trouves intéressants? [points to couple]

Once students are comfortable with **le, la, les,** you may wish to introduce verbs beginning with vowels.
Z, tu les admires? [Z points to couple]
Tu l'admires aussi? [Z is confused]
Point to the man, addressing the entire class:
Cet homme, est-ce que vous l'admirez?

Write **l'** under the man's picture.
Et cette femme, vous l'admirez? Oui?

Write **l'** under the woman's picture.

---

2 COMMUNICATION answering personal questions

Answers will vary.
1. Oui, je connais (New York). Je connais bien (New York).
2. Oui, je connais un bon restaurant dans ma ville. Il s'appelle (Chez Nous). Oui, je connais un supermarché. Il s'appelle (Shopi). Non, je ne connais pas de centre commercial. Non, je ne connais pas de magasin de CD.
3. Oui, je connais des monuments à Paris. Je connais (l'Arc de Triomphe et le musée d'Orsay).
4. Oui, je connais bien mes voisins. Oui, ils sont sympathiques. Non, je ne connais pas personnellement la directrice de mon école. Oui, elle est stricte.
5. Je connais (Matt Damon et Ben Affleck). Je connais (Reese Witherspoon). Je connais (Dave Matthews et John Mayer). Je connais (Tom Brady et Nomar Garciaparra).

Language note In item 5, **connaître** means *to know* in the sense of *to know of* or *to know by reputation.* Students should be able to name one person in each category.

SECTION B

Communicative function
Talking about people and things

Pronunciation Be sure students make the liaison when the next word begins with a vowel sound.

Language notes
• Point out that direct object pronouns, in French as in English, replace the entire noun group: article (possessive, demonstrative, number), noun, adjective.
• Direct object pronouns are NOT used to replace nouns introduced by **un, une, des, du, de la.**
• The pronoun **en** is introduced in Book Two.

Teaching strategy The following common verbs take direct objects in French. You may want to write them on the board.
• with people: **aider, inviter, rencontrer,**
• with things: **acheter, avoir, laver, nettoyer, prendre, vendre**
• with people or things: **aimer, connaître, trouver, voir**
Point out that while **attendre, écouter,** and **regarder** take direct objects in French, the English equivalents have prepositions: *to wait for, to listen to, to look at.*

Teaching Resource Options

PRINT

Workbook PE, pp. 237–244
Unit 8 Resource Book
   Communipak, pp. 152–173
   Workbook TE, pp. 115–121

TECHNOLOGY

Power Presentations

3 **ROLE PLAY** indicating whether one knows people

–Tu connais ... ?
–Oui, je ... connais.
–Et toi, Lise?
–Non, je ne ... connais pas.
1. Christophe/le/le
2. Jacqueline/la/la
3. Anne et Valérie/les/les
4. Jérôme et Jean-François/les/les
5. la fille là-bas/la/la
6. cette étudiante/la/la
7. ma cousine/la/la
8. les cousins de Véronique/les/les
9. la copine de Jacques/la/la
10. ses frères/les/les

---

4 **EXCHANGES** answering questions using pronouns

–Tu prends ... ?
–Oui, je ... prends. (Non, je ne ... prends pas.)
1. tes CD/les/les
2. ton livre de français/le/le
3. ta guitare/la/la
4. ton baladeur/le/le
5. ta chaîne hi-fi/la/la
6. ton maillot de bain/le/le
7. ton skate/le/le
8. tes tee-shirts/les/les
9. tes sandales/les/les

---

5 **ROLE PLAY/COMPREHENSION** asking about activities

Answers will vary.
- –Quand est-ce que tu vois ta cousine?
  –Je la vois pendant les vacances.
- –Où est-ce que tu regardes la télé?
  –Je la regarde dans le salon.
- –À quelle heure est-ce que tu regardes la télé?
  –Je la regarde à neuf heures du soir.
- – Quand est-ce que tu regardes la télé?
  –Je la regarde le week-end (pendant les vacances, le samedi matin).
- – Quand est-ce que tu ranges ta chambre?
  –Je la range le samedi matin.
- –À quelle heure est-ce que tu ranges ta chambre?
  –Je la range à huit heures du matin.
- –Où est-ce que tu fais les courses?
  –Je les fais dans un supermarché.
- –Quand est-ce que tu fais les courses?
  –Je les fais le week-end.
- –À quelle heure est-ce que tu fais les courses?
  –Je les fais à neuf heures du matin.
- –Où est-ce que tu achètes tes CD?
  –Je les achète à la Boîte à Musique.
- –Quand est-ce que tu achètes tes CD?
  –Je les achète le week-end (pendant les vacances).
- –Où est-ce que tu achètes tes vêtements?
  –Je les achète à Mod'Shop.
- –Quand est-ce que tu achètes tes vêtements?
  –Je les achète le week-end (le samedi matin).
- –Où est-ce que tu prends le petit déjeuner?
  –Je le prends dans la cuisine.

---

3 À la boum de Delphine

PARLER Pierre connaît tous les invités *(all the guests)* à la boum de Delphine, mais Lise ne les connaît pas. Jouez les trois rôles.

▶ ces garçons?

Tu connais ces garçons?
Et toi, Lise?
Oui, je les connais.
Non, je ne les connais pas.

1. Christophe?
2. Jacqueline?
3. Anne et Valérie?
4. Jérôme et Jean-François?
5. la fille là-bas?
6. cette étudiante?
7. ma cousine?
8. les cousins de Véronique?
9. la copine de Jacques?
10. ses frères?

---

4 Un choix difficile

PARLER Vous allez passer le mois de juillet en France. Vous êtes limité(e) à 20 kilos de bagages. Un(e) camarade demande si vous allez prendre les choses suivantes. Répondez affirmativement ou négativement.

▶ ta raquette?
   —Tu prends ta raquette?
   —Oui, je la prends.
      (Non, je ne la prends pas.)
1. tes CD?
2. ton livre de français?
3. ta guitare?
4. ton baladeur?
5. ta chaîne hi-fi?
6. ton maillot de bain?
7. ton skate?
8. tes tee-shirts?
9. tes sandales?

---

5 Questions et réponses

PARLER Julien pose des questions à Luc en utilisant les éléments des colonnes A et B. Jérôme répond logiquement en utilisant les éléments des colonnes B et C et un pronom complément. Avec un(e) camarade, jouez les deux rôles.

A	B	C
où	rencontrer tes copains	le samedi matin
quand	voir ta cousine	à 8 heures du matin
à quelle heure	regarder la télé	à 9 heures du soir
	ranger ta chambre	à la Boîte à Musique
	faire les courses	à Mod' Shop
	acheter tes CD	au café Le Pont Neuf
	acheter tes vêtements	dans un supermarché
	prendre le petit déjeuner	le week-end
		pendant les vacances
		dans la cuisine
		dans le salon

Où est-ce que tu rencontres tes copains?

Je les rencontre au café Le Pont Neuf.

C La place des pronoms à l'impératif

Note the position of the object pronoun when the verb is in the imperative.

	AFFIRMATIVE COMMAND	NEGATIVE COMMAND
J'invite **Frédéric?**	Oui, invite-**le!**	Non, ne **l'**invite pas!
Je prends **la guitare?**	Oui, prends-**la!**	Non, ne **la** prends pas!
J'achète **les sandales?**	Oui, achète-**les!**	Non, ne **les** achète pas!

In AFFIRMATIVE COMMANDS, the object pronoun comes *after* the verb and is joined to it by a hyphen.
In NEGATIVE COMMANDS, the object pronoun comes *before* the verb.

6 Invitations

PARLER/ÉCRIRE Vous préparez une liste de personnes à inviter à une boum. Vous êtes limité(e)s à quatre *(4)* des personnes suivantes. Faites vos suggestions d'après les modèles.

▶ Caroline est sympathique.
Invitons-la!
▶ Jean-Louis est pénible.
Ne l'invitons pas!

1. Sylvie est très sympathique.
2. Cécile et Anne aiment danser.
3. Jacques est stupide.
4. Robert joue bien de la guitare.
5. Ces filles sont intelligentes.
6. Martin et Thomas sont snobs.
7. Nicolas n'est pas mon ami.
8. Ces garçons sont pénibles.
9. Cette fille est gentille.
10. Tes copains sont méchants.

7 Le pique-nique

PARLER Élodie demande à Mathieu si elle doit prendre certaines choses pour le pique-nique.

▶ ma guitare (oui)

Est-ce que je prends ma guitare?
Oui, prends-la!

1. la limonade (oui)
2. les sandwichs (non)
3. la salade (oui)
4. le lait (non)
5. le gâteau (non)
6. mon appareil-photo (oui)
7. mes lunettes de soleil (oui)
8. les impers (non)

8 Oui ou non?

PARLER Votre petit cousin de Québec passe deux semaines chez vous. Il vous demande s'il doit ou peut faire les choses suivantes. Répondez affirmativement ou négativement.

1. Je fais les courses?
2. Je regarde tes photos?
3. Je range ma chambre?
4. J'achète le journal *(newspaper)*?
5. J'invite les voisins à déjeuner?
6. Je prépare le dîner?
7. Je prends ton vélo?
8. Je loue les DVD?
9. J'aide ta mère?
10. Je mets la télé?

Je fais les devoirs?
Oui, fais-les. (Non, ne les fais pas.)

SECTION C
Communicative function
Giving orders

6 COMPREHENSION making suggestions about whom to invite

1. Invitons-la!
2. Invitons-les!
3. Ne l'invitons pas!
4. Invitons-le!
5. Invitons-les!
6. Ne les invitons pas!
7. Ne l'invitons pas!
8. Ne les invitons pas!
9. Invitons-la!
10. Ne les invitons pas!

Variation (dialogue format) With a classmate, decide if you will invite the following people.

Caroline est sympathique.
– J'invite Caroline?
– Oui, invite-la.

Jean-Louis est pénible.
– J'invite Jean-Louis?
– Non, ne l'invite pas.

7 ROLE PLAY offering and accepting or refusing services

1. —Est-ce que je prends de la limonade?
—Oui, prends-la!
2. —Est-ce que je prends les sandwichs?
—Non, ne les prends pas!
3. —Est-ce que je prends la salade?
—Oui, prends-la!
4. —Est-ce que je prends le lait?
—Non, ne le prends pas!
5. —Est-ce que je prends le gâteau?
—Non, ne le prends pas!
6. —Est-ce que je prends mon appareil-photo?
—Oui, prends-le!
7. —Est-ce que je prends mes lunettes de soleil?
—Oui, prends-les!
8. —Est-ce que je prends les impers?
—Non, ne les prends pas!

8 ROLE PLAY telling a friend what to do and not to do

1. Oui, fais-les. (Non, ne les fais pas.)
2. Oui, regarde-les. (Non, ne les regarde pas.)
3. Oui, range-la. (Non, ne la range pas.)
4. Oui, achète-le. (Non, ne l'achète pas.)
5. Oui, invite-les à déjeuner. (Non, ne les invite pas à déjeuner.)
6. Oui, prépare-le. (Non, ne le prépare pas.)
7. Oui, prends-le. (Non, ne le prends pas.)
8. Oui, loue-les. (Non, ne les loue pas.)
9. Oui, aide-la. (Non, ne l'aide pas.)
10. Oui, mets-la. (Non, ne la mets pas.)

Communicative function
Talking about others

Teaching Resource Options

PRINT
Workbook PE, pp. 237–243
Unit 8 Resource Book
  Communipak, pp. 152–173
  Video Activities, p. 139
  Videoscript, pp. 142–143
  Workbook TE, pp. 115–121

TECHNOLOGY
Power Presentations

VIDEO PROGRAM

VIDÉO   DVD
 MODULE 28

28.3 Mini-scenes: On va lui parler?
(50:33–51:34 min.)

9 **EXCHANGES** asking friends
whom they're telephoning

1. –Tu téléphones à ton copain?
   –Oui, je lui téléphone. (Non, je ne lui téléphone pas.)
2. –Tu téléphones à tes cousins?
   –Oui, je leur téléphone. (Non, je ne leur téléphone pas.)
3. –Tu téléphones à ta grand-mère?
   –Oui, je lui téléphone. (Non, je ne lui téléphone pas.)
4. –Tu téléphones à ton prof de français?
   –Oui, je lui téléphone. (Non, je ne lui téléphone pas.)
5. –Tu téléphones à tes voisins?
   –Oui, je leur téléphone. (Non, je ne leur téléphone pas.)
6. –Tu téléphones à ta tante favorite?
   –Oui, je lui téléphone. (Non, je ne lui téléphone pas.)

Variation (in the plural)

– Vous téléphonez à votre copine?
– Oui, nous lui téléphonons. (Non, nous ne lui téléphonons pas.)

D Les pronoms compléments *lui, leur*

In the questions below, the nouns in heavy type are INDIRECT OBJECTS. These nouns represent PEOPLE and are introduced by **à**.

Note the forms and position of the corresponding INDIRECT OBJECT PRONOUNS in the answers on the right.

Tu téléphones **à Philippe?**	Oui, je **lui** téléphone.
Tu parles **à Juliette?**	Non, je ne **lui** parle pas.
Tu téléphones **à tes amis?**	Oui, je **leur** téléphone.
Tu prêtes ton vélo **à tes cousines?**	Non, je ne **leur** prête pas mon vélo.

FORMS

INDIRECT OBJECT PRONOUNS replace **à** + <u>noun representing people</u>. They have the following forms:

	SINGULAR		PLURAL	
MASCULINE/FEMININE	**lui**	*to him, to her*	**leur**	*to them*

POSITION

Like other object pronouns, **lui** and **leur** come before the verb, except in affirmative commands.

Voici Henri.   Parle-**lui**!   Prête-**lui** ton vélo!

→ In negative sentences, **lui** and **leur,** like other object pronouns, come between **ne** and the verb.

Voici Éric.	Je ne **lui** téléphone pas.
Voici mes voisins.	Je ne **leur** parle pas.

9 **Au téléphone**

PARLER Demandez à vos camarades s'ils téléphonent aux personnes suivantes.

▶ ta copine

1. ton copain
2. tes cousins
3. ta grand-mère
4. ton prof de français
5. tes voisins
6. ta tante favorite

Tu téléphones à ta copine?

Oui, je lui téléphone.
(Non, je ne lui téléphone pas.)

VOCABULAIRE Verbes suivis *(followed)* d'un complément indirect

parler à	*to speak, talk (to)*	Je **parle à** mon copain.
rendre visite à	*to visit*	Nous **rendons visite à** nos voisins.
répondre à	*to answer*	Tu **réponds au** professeur.
téléphoner à	*to phone, call*	Jérôme **téléphone à** Juliette.
demander à	*to ask*	Je ne **demande** pas d'argent **à** mes frères.
donner à	*to give (to)*	Tu **donnes** ton adresse **à** ta copine.
montrer à	*to show (to)*	Nous **montrons** nos photos **à** nos amis.
prêter à	*to lend, loan (to)*	Je ne **prête** pas mon baladeur **à** ma soeur.

➔ **Répondre** is a regular **-re** verb.
   Je réponds à François.   **J'ai répondu** à Catherine.

➔ The verbs **téléphoner**, **répondre**, and **demander** take indirect objects in French, but not in English. Compare:

téléphoner	Nous **téléphonons**	à	Paul.	Nous **lui téléphonons.**	
	*We **are calling***	…	*Paul.*	*We **are calling him.***	

répondre	Tu **réponds**	à	tes parents.	Tu **leur réponds.**	
	*You **answer***	…	*your parents.*	*You **answer them.***	

demander	Je **demande**	à	Sylvie	…	son stylo.	Je **lui demande** son stylo.
	*I **am asking***	…	*Sylvie*	*for*	*her pen.*	*I **am asking her** for her pen.*

---

10 **Les copains de Léa**

PARLER/ÉCRIRE Léa a beaucoup de copains. Décrivez ce que chacun fait pour elle. Complétez les phrases avec **Léa** ou **à Léa.**

▶ Françoise invite <u>Léa</u>.
   Patrick rend visite <u>à Léa</u>.

1. Marc téléphone …
2. Jean-Paul voit … samedi prochain.
3. Sophie prête son vélo …
4. Mélanie écoute …
5. François donne son adresse …
6. Philippe regarde … pendant la classe.
7. Antoine attend … après la classe.

8. Nathalie parle …
9. Pauline invite … au concert.
10. Pierre répond …
11. Céline montre ses photos …
12. Thomas demande … son numéro de téléphone.
13. Éric rend visite …

Language note Point out that **rendre visite** takes an indirect object because the expression literally means *render a visit to someone*.

Extra practice Have students reword the sample sentences using object pronouns.

Je lui parle.

Nous leur rendons visite. etc.

10 PRACTICE distinguishing between direct and indirect objects

1. à Léa	8. à Léa
2. Léa	9. Léa
3. à Léa	10. à Léa
4. Léa	11. à Léa
5. à Léa	12. à Léa
6. Léa	13. à Léa
7. Léa	

Expansion (using object pronouns)

Léa, C'est une fille!
Françoise l'invite.
Patrick lui rend visite.

Teaching Resource Options

PRINT

Workbook PE, pp. 237–243
Unit 8 Resource Book
  Audioscript, p. 144
  Communipak, pp. 152–173
  Workbook TE, pp. 115–121

AUDIOVISUAL

Audio Program
CD 4 Track 41

TECHNOLOGY

Power Presentations

11 **EXCHANGES** talking about giving presents

Answers will vary.
1. Je lui donne …
2. Je lui donne …
3. Je lui donne …
4. Je lui donne …
5. Je leur donne …
6. Je lui donne …
7. Je leur donne …

12 **COMMUNICATION** answering personal questions

Answers will vary.
1. Oui, le week-end, je leur rends visite. Non, je ne lui rends pas visite.
2. Oui, je lui prête mes CD. (Non, je ne lui prête pas mes CD.) Oui, je leur prête mes CD. (Non, je ne leur prête pas mes CD.)
3. Oui, je lui demande de l'argent. (Non, je ne lui demande pas d'argent.)
4. Oui, je leur demande des conseils. (Non, je ne leur demande pas de conseils.)
5. Oui, je leur donne de bons conseils.
6. Oui, je lui montre mes photos. (Non, je ne lui montre pas mes photos.) Oui, je leur montre mes photos. (Non, je ne leur montre pas mes photos.)
7. Oui, je lui réponds en français. (Non, je ne lui réponds pas en français.)
8. Oui, je leur parle de mon problème. (Non, je ne leur parle pas [de mon problème].) Oui, je lui parle. (Non, je ne lui parle pas.)

SECTION E

Communicative function
Describing what people say and write

♻ **Re-entry and review** Ask students which two other verbs have **vous** forms ending in **-tes**: **vous êtes, vous faites.**

Looking ahead The verb **lire** is not introduced until Book Two. If you wish to present the forms quickly for recognition, have students turn to the Appendix, page R10.

---

11 **Joyeux anniversaire!**

PARLER Choisissez un cadeau d'anniversaire pour les personnes suivantes. Un(e) camarade va vous demander ce que vous donnez à chaque personne.

▶ à ton copain

1. à ton petit frère
2. à ta mère
3. à ta grand-mère
4. à ta copine
5. à tes cousins
6. à ton (ta) prof
7. à tes copains

Qu'est-ce que tu donnes à ton copain?

Je lui donne un livre.

Cadeaux
un pull
un jeu vidéo
une cravate
un livre
des billets *(tickets)* de théâtre
un magazine
ma photo
une boîte *(box)* de chocolats
un gâteau
??

12 **Questions personnelles**

PARLER/ÉCRIRE Réponds aux questions suivantes. Utilise **lui** ou **leur** dans tes réponses.

1. Le week-end, est-ce que tu rends visite à tes copains? à ton oncle?
2. Est-ce que tu prêtes tes CD à ta soeur? à ton frère? à tes copains?
3. Est-ce que tu demandes de l'argent à ton père? à ta mère?
4. Est-ce que tu demandes des conseils *(advice)* à tes parents? à tes professeurs?
5. Est-ce que tu donnes de bons conseils à tes copains?
6. Est-ce que tu montres tes photos à ton frère? à ta soeur? à ta copine? à ton copain? à tes cousins?
7. En classe, est-ce que tu réponds en français à ton professeur?
8. Quand tu as un problème, est-ce que tu parles à tes copains? à ton professeur? à tes grands-parents? à tes parents?

E **Les verbes *dire* et *écrire***

Note the forms of the irregular verbs **dire** *(to say, tell)* and **écrire** *(to write)*.

INFINITIVE	dire	écrire
PRESENT	je **dis**	j' **écris**
	tu **dis**	tu **écris**
	il/elle/on **dit**	il/elle/on **écrit**
	nous **disons**	nous **écrivons**
	vous **dites**	vous **écrivez**
	ils/elles **disent**	ils/elles **écrivent**
PASSÉ COMPOSÉ	j'ai **dit**	j'ai **écrit**

→ Note the use of **que/qu'** *(that)* after **dire** and **écrire**.
  Florence **dit que** Frédéric est sympathique.   *Florence **says (that)** Frédéric is nice.*
  Alain **écrit qu'**il est allé à un pique-nique.   *Alain **writes (that)** he went on a picnic.*

→ **Décrire** *(to describe)* follows the same pattern as **écrire**.

13 Correspondance

PARLER/ÉCRIRE Pendant les vacances, on écrit beaucoup de lettres. Dites à qui les personnes suivantes écrivent.

▶ Juliette/à Marc
Juliette écrit à Marc.

1. nous/à nos copains
2. toi/à ta cousine
3. moi/à ma grand-mère
4. Nicolas/à ses voisins
5. vous/à vos parents
6. les élèves/au professeur

14 La boum

PARLER/ÉCRIRE Des amis sont à une boum. Décrivez ce que chacun dit.

▶ toi/la musique est super
Tu dis que la musique est super.

1. Nicole/les sandwichs sont délicieux
2. nous/les invités *(guests)* sont sympathiques
3. Pauline/Jérôme danse bien
4. moi/ces garçons dansent mal
5. vous/vous n'aimez pas ce CD
6. mes copains/ils vont organiser une soirée le week-end prochain

15 Questions personnelles **PARLER/ÉCRIRE**

1. Est-ce que tu aimes écrire?
2. Pendant les vacances, est-ce que tu écris à tes copains? à tes voisins? à ton(ta) meilleur(e) *(best)* ami(e)?
3. À Noël, est-ce que tu écris des cartes *(cards)*? À qui?
4. À qui as-tu écrit un mail récemment *(recently)*?
5. Est-ce que tu dis toujours la vérité *(truth)*?
6. À ton avis, est-ce que les journalistes disent toujours la vérité? Et les politiciens?

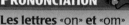

PRONONCIATION

Les lettres «on» et «om»

on = /ɔ̃/   on(n)e = /ɔ/

Be sure to distinguish between the nasal and non-nasal vowel sounds.

REMEMBER: Do not pronounce an /n/ or /m/ after the nasal vowel /ɔ̃/.

lion   lionne

Répétez:
/ɔ̃/ **mon ton son bon avion montrer répondre invitons blouson**

/ɔn/ **téléphone Simone donner connais mayonnaise personne bonne**

/ɔm/ **fromage promenade tomate pomme dommage comment**

/ɔ̃/–/ɔn/ **lion–lionne bon–bonne Simon–Simone Yvon–Yvonne**

Monique donne une pomme à Raymond.
Simone connaît mon oncle Léon.

---

13 PRACTICE telling whom people are writing

1. Nous écrivons à nos copains.
2. Tu écris à ta cousine.
3. J'écris à ma grand-mère.
4. Nicolas écrit à ses voisins.
5. Vous écrivez à vos parents.
6. Les élèves écrivent au professeur.

Variation (dialogue format, reviewing **lui, leur**)

– Est-ce que Juliette écrit à Marc?
– Oui, elle lui écrit.

Variation (in the passé composé)
Juliette a écrit à Marc.

14 PRACTICE describing what people are saying

1. Nicole dit que les sandwichs sont délicieux.
2. Nous disons que les invités sont sympathiques.
3. Pauline dit que Jérôme danse bien.
4. Je dis que ces garçons dansent mal.
5. Vous dites que vous n'aimez pas ce CD.
6. Mes copains disent qu'ils vont organiser une soirée le week-end prochain.

15 COMMUNICATION answering personal questions

Answers will vary.
1. Oui, j'aime écrire. (Non, je n'aime pas écrire.)
2. Oui, pendant les vacances, j'écris à mes copains (à mes voisins, à mon [ma] meilleur[e] ami[e]). (Non, pendant les vacances, je n'écris pas à mes copains [à mes voisins, à mon (ma) meilleur(e) ami(e)].)
3. Oui, à Noël, j'écris des cartes. J'écris à (mes grands-parents, mes amis, mes professeurs, mes cousins, et mes voisins). (Non, à Noël, je n'écris pas de cartes.)
4. J'ai écrit un mail à (ma tante Marie) récemment.
5. Oui, je dis toujours la vérité. (Non, je ne dis pas toujours la vérité.)
6. Oui, à mon avis, les journalistes disent toujours la vérité. (Non, à mon avis, les journalistes ne disent pas toujours la vérité.) Oui, à mon avis, les politiciens disent toujours la vérité. (Non, à mon avis, les politiciens ne disent pas toujours la vérité.)

PRONUNCIATION

Remind students that the letters "on" and "om" represent a nasal vowel when they occur at the end of a word or when they are followed by a consonant. When these letters are followed by a vowel, they do not represent a nasal sound.

Additional practice

/ɔ̃/	/ɔn/
champion	**championne**
mignon	**mignonne**

Langue et Communication • **405**
Unité 8 LEÇON 28

① COMPREHENSION

1. Qu'est-ce que tu fais ce week-end?
  (d) J'organise une fête.
2. Tu m'invites?
  (c) Bien sûr, je t'invite.
3. Et Catherine? Tu l'invites aussi?
  (e) Catherine? Je ne la connais pas. Qui est-ce?
4. C'est ma nouvelle copine.
  (f) Ah oui, je vois qui c'est maintenant. Eh bien, d'accord! Je l'invite.
5. Tu veux son numéro de téléphone?
  (b) Oui, je ne l'ai pas.
6. C'est le 01.44.32.28.50.
  (a) Je lui téléphone tout de suite.

OBJECTIFS
Now you can …
• talk about people you know and don't know
• use pronouns to refer to people and things

À votre tour!

① 🎧 👥 Allô!

PARLER Reconstituez la conversation entre Olivier et Sophie. Pour cela, faites correspondre les réponses de Sophie avec les questions d'Olivier.

1. Qu'est-ce que tu fais ce week-end?
2. Tu m'invites?
3. Et Catherine? Tu l'invites aussi?
4. C'est ma nouvelle copine.
5. Tu veux son numéro de téléphone?
6. C'est le 01.44.32.28.50.

a. Je lui téléphone tout de suite (*right away*).
b. Oui, je ne l'ai pas.
c. Bien sûr, je t'invite.
d. J'organise une fête.
e. Catherine? Je ne la connais pas. Qui est-ce?
f. Ah oui, je vois qui c'est maintenant. Eh bien, d'accord! Je l'invite.

② 🎧 👥 Créa-dialogue

PARLER Avec vos camarades, discutez de certaines choses que vous faites. Posez plusieurs questions sur chaque activité.

Tu regardes la télé?
Oui je la regarde.
À quelle heure est-ce que tu la regardes?
À huit heures.

regarder la télé?	1. inviter tes amis?	2. voir tes cousins?
à quelle heure?	quand? à quelle occasion?	quand? où?

3. faire les courses?	4. aider ta mère?	5. faire tes devoirs?	6. téléphoner à tes copains?	7. rendre visite à ta grand-mère?	8. écrire à ton cousin?
quand? où?	quand? comment?	quand? où?	quand? pourquoi?	quand? pourquoi?	pourquoi?

À VOTRE TOUR

Depending on your goals and objectives, you may or may not wish to assign all of the activities in the **À votre tour** section.

PAIR/GROUP PRACTICE

Act. 1 lends itself to pair practice. It can also be done in trios, with two students performing and the third acting as monitor.

3 ✎ Composition: Les personnes dans ma vie *(life)*

Select three people from the list and write a short paragraph about each one. Give their names, say when you see them, and describe several things you do for them as well as one thing that you can't do. In your descriptions use the suggested verbs … and your imagination!

- un cousin/une cousine
- un frère/une soeur
- un copain/une copine
- un voisin/une voisine
- mon meilleur *(best)* ami
- ma meilleure amie
- un professeur de français (d'anglais, de maths, d'histoire)

téléphoner	voir	prêter	inviter
écrire	connaître	donner	rendre visite
répondre	parler	aider	

Ma cousine s'appelle Denise. Je la vois pendant les vacances de Noël. Je lui écris des mails et elle me répond toujours. …

COMMENT DIT-ON …?

How to tell someone to leave you alone:

Laisse-moi tranquille!

Fiche-moi la paix!

ⓘ LESSON REVIEW
CLASSZONE.COM

PORTFOLIO ASSESSMENT

You will probably select only one speaking activity and one writing activity to go into the students' portfolios for Unit 8.

In this lesson, Act. 3 can be used as the basis for a written portfolio entry.

---

2 GUIDED ORAL EXPRESSION

Answers will vary.
1. —Tu invites tes amis?
   —Oui, je les invite.
   —Quand est-ce que tu les invites?
   —Je les invite (ce week-end).
   —À quelle occasion est-ce que tu les invites?
   —Je les invite (pour mon anniversaire).
2. —Tu vois tes cousins?
   —Oui, je les vois (souvent).
   —Quand est-ce que tu les vois?
   —Je les vois (le dimanche).
   —Où est-ce que tu les vois?
   —Je les vois (chez ma grand-mère).
3. —Tu fais les courses?
   —Oui, je les fais.
   —Quand est-ce que tu les fais?
   —Je les fais (samedi matin).
   —Où est-ce que tu les fais?
   —Je les fais (au supermarché).
4. —Tu aides ta mère?
   —Oui, je l'aide.
   —Quand est-ce que tu l'aides?
   —Je l'aide (le soir).
   —Comment est-ce que tu l'aides?
   —Je (mets la table).
5. —Tu fais tes devoirs?
   —Oui, je les fais.
   —Quand est-ce que tu les fais?
   —Je les fais (avant le dîner).
   —Où est-ce que tu les fais?
   —Je les fais (dans ma chambre).
6. —Tu téléphones à tes copains?
   —Oui, je leur téléphone.
   —Quand est-ce que tu leur téléphones?
   —Je leur téléphone (le soir et le week-end).
   —Pourquoi est-ce que tu leur téléphones?
   —Je leur téléphone (pour organiser le week-end).
7. —Tu rends visite à ta grand-mère?
   —Oui, je lui rends visite.
   —Quand est-ce que tu lui rends visite?
   —Je lui rends visite (le dimanche).
   —Pourquoi est-ce que tu lui rends visite?
   —Parce que (j'aime lui parler).
8. —Tu écris à ton cousin?
   —Oui, je lui écris.
   —Pourquoi est-ce que tu lui écris?
   —(Pour lui parler de mon nouveau copain.)

3 WRITTEN SELF-EXPRESSION

Answers will vary.
- Mon copain s'appelle Thomas. Je lui téléphone souvent. Il veut maigrir, alors je ne lui apporte jamais de glace. Je lui apporte des fruits!
- Mes voisins s'appellent Georges et Céline. Je les vois le matin et le soir. Je leur parle beaucoup. Je les aide dans leur jardin de temps en temps. Je ne leur rends pas visite le dimanche parce qu'ils vont en ville le dimanche.
- Mon amie s'appelle Rénée. Je déjeune toujours avec elle. On est dans la même classe, mais je ne lui parle jamais pendant la classe. Je l'aide avec ses devoirs.

Teaching Resource Options

PRINT

Unit 8 Resource Book
  Communipak, pp. 252–273

Assessment
Unit 8 Test, pp. 184–192
Portfolio Assessment, Unit 1 URB
  pp. 155–164
Multiple Choice Test Items,
  pp. 205–213
Listening Comprehension
  Performance Test, pp. 193–194
Reading Performance Test,
  pp. 199–201
Speaking Performance Test,
  pp. 195–198
Writing Performance Test,
  pp. 202–204
Test Scoring Tools, p. 214
Audioscript for Tests, pp. 215–217
Answer Keys, pp. 218–221

AUDIO & VISUAL
Audio Program
CD 16 Tracks 13–16

TECHNOLOGY
Test Generator CD-ROM/eTest Plus
Online

1 COMPREHENSION

1. de l'eau	6. du fromage
2. du lait	7. du beurre
3. du poulet	8. de la glace
4. du jambon	9. du pain
5. du thé glacé	10. du gâteau

2 COMPREHENSION

1. montre	6. écrit
2. déjeune	7. comprends
3. fait	8. bois
4. apprend	9. prend
5. donnent	10. prête

Tests de contrôle

By taking the following tests, you can check your progress in French and also prepare for the unit test. Write your answers on a separate sheet of paper.

Review...
• foods and beverages:
  pp. 366-367
• partitive article:
  pp. 378-379

1 Foods and beverages

Give the names of the foods and beverages you see on the table. With each one, be sure to use the appropriate partitive article: **du, de la,** or **de l'**.

Sur la table, il y a ...

1. —	3. —	5. —	7. —	9. —
2. —	4. —	6. —	8. —	10. —

Review...
• new verbs:
  pp. 364, 370, 377,
  383, 389, and 404

2 The right choice

Complete each of the following sentences with the appropriate forms of the verbs in the box. Be logical in your choice of verbs and do not use the same word more than once.

1. Caroline — ses photos de vacances à sa copine.
2. Madame Durand — au restaurant La Marmite.
3. Monsieur Lemaire — les courses au supermarché Prisunic.
4. À la piscine, mon petit frère — à nager.
5. Les gens généreux — de l'argent aux pauvres *(poor people)*.
6. Nicolas — un mail à sa cousine.
7. Est-ce que tu — bien quand le professeur parle français?
8. Au petit déjeuner, je — du jus d'orange.
9. Pauline — des photos avec son nouvel appareil-photo.
10. Catherine — souvent son vélo à sa soeur.

apprendre
boire
comprendre
déjeuner
donner
écrire
faire
montrer
prendre
prêter

3 The right verb

Complete the following sentences with the appropriate forms of the present tense of the verb in parentheses.

(vouloir)   **1.** Cécile — voyager. Ses copines — visiter Paris.

(prendre)   **2.** Les touristes — le train. Nous — le bus.

(apprendre) **3.** Élodie — l'anglais. Ses copains — l'espagnol.

(boire)   **4.** Nous — du thé. Les enfants — du lait.

(pouvoir)   **5.** Mes amis — venir à la boum. Est-ce que vous — rester?

(devoir)   **6.** Éric — étudier. Nous — aider nos parents.

(connaître) **7.** Isabelle — Céline. Nous — ses copains.

(écrire)   **8.** Tu — une lettre. Mes cousins — un mail.

(dire)   **9.** Je — «oui». Mais vous, vous — «non».

> **Review...**
> • irregular verbs:
>   pp. 376, 377, 383,
>   392, 398, and 404

4 The right pronoun

Complete the following sentences with the appropriate pronoun in parentheses that replaces the underlined words.

▶ Je connais <u>Céline</u>.   Je **la** connais. **(le, la)**

1. Nous invitons <u>Pierre</u>.   Nous — invitons à la boum. **(l', le)**
2. Tu écris <u>à Charlotte</u>.   Tu — écris. **(la, lui)**
3. J'aide <u>mes parents</u>.   Je — aide. **(l', les)**
4. Vous téléphonez <u>à Mathieu</u>.   Vous — téléphonez souvent. **(le, lui)**
5. J'écoute <u>mes CD</u>.   Je — écoute. **(les, leur)**
6. Nous parlons <u>à nos amis</u>.   Nous — parlons. **(les, leur)**
7. Tu regardes <u>ces photos</u>.   Tu — regardes avec Léa. **(les, leur)**
8. Vous lavez <u>la voiture</u>.   Vous — lavez. **(la, lui)**

> **Review...**
> • object pronouns:
>   pp. 399 and 402

5 Composition: Mon repas d'anniversaire

Write a short paragraph of five or six sentences describing what you would like for a special birthday dinner. Use only vocabulary and expressions that you know in French.

STRATEGY Writing

a First write out your menu.

b Then plan your paragraph, perhaps explaining why you are choosing certain items.

c Read over your composition to check that you are using the correct article with each food item.

hors d'oeuvre: _____

viande ou poisson: _____

autres plats: _____

_____

dessert: _____

boissons: _____

---

3 COMPREHENSION

1. veut / veulent
2. prennent / prenons
3. apprend / apprennent
4. buvons / boivent
5. peuvent / pouvez
6. doit / devons
7. connaît / connaissons
8. écris / écrivent
9. dis / dites

4 COMPREHENSION

1. l'   5. les
2. lui   6. leur
3. les   7. les
4. lui   8. la

5 WRITTEN SELF-EXPRESSION

Answers will vary.
Pour mon anniversaire, je veux dîner au restaurant Le Bon Temps. Comme hors d'oeuvre, je voudrais de la salade et de la soupe. Comme viande, je voudrais du poulet parce que j'aime le poulet! Comme autres plats, je voudrais des petits pois et des carottes. Je vais boire du lait. Après le dîner, je vais manger de la tarte aux pommes parce que c'est mon dessert préféré!

Vocabulaire

Language Learning Benchmarks

FUNCTION

- Engage in conversations pp. 370, 380, 390
- Express likes and dislikes pp. 368, 369
- Make requests pp. 365, 367, 371, 381, 391
- Begin to provide information pp. 365, 377, 398

CONTEXT

- Converse in face-to-face social interactions pp. 390, 391, 400, 402
- Listen to audio and video texts pp. 362-363, 374, 386, 396
- Use authentic materials when reading: schedules p. 389
- Use authentic materials when reading: signs p. 373
- Use authentic materials when reading: short narratives p. 412
- Write notes p. 395
- Write lists pp. 369, 373, 409

TEXT TYPE

- Use short sentences when speaking pp. 376, 383, 405
- Use short sentences when writing pp. 376, 383
- Use learned words and phrases when speaking pp. 365, 379
- Use learned words and phrases when writing pp. 365, 380
- Use simple questions when speaking pp. 369, 382, 393, 404
- Use simple questions when writing p. 389
- Use commands when speaking p. 401
- Use commands when writing p. 401
- Understand some ideas and familiar details presented in clear, uncomplicated speech when listening pp. 372, 397
- Understand short texts enhanced by visual clues when reading pp. 375, 387, 416–417

POUR COMMUNIQUER

Saying where you will eat

Je vais déjeuner	à la maison.	I will have lunch	at home.
	à la cantine (de l'école)		at the (school) cafeteria
	au restaurant		at the restaurant

Planning a meal

Il faut …	
aller au marché	go to the market
faire les courses	do the food shopping
acheter la nourriture	buy the food
choisir les boissons	choose the beverages
préparer le repas	fix the meal
faire la cuisine	do the cooking
mettre le couvert	set the table

Saying what foods you like and dislike

J'aime [le rosbif].	I like roast beef.
Je préfère [la glace].	I prefer ice cream.
Je déteste [les frites].	I detest French fries.

Shopping for food, asking for certain quantities

Je voudrais …		une livre de beurre	a pound of butter
du beurre	(some) butter	un kilo de sole	a kilo (2.2 pounds) of sole
de la sole	(some) sole	une douzaine d'oeufs	a dozen eggs
des oeufs	(some) eggs		

MOTS ET EXPRESSIONS

Les repas (Meals)

le petit déjeuner	breakfast	prendre le petit déjeuner	to have breakfast
le déjeuner	lunch	déjeuner	to have lunch
le dîner	dinner	dîner	to have dinner

Le couvert (Place settings)

un couteau	knife	une assiette	plate
un verre	glass	une cuillère	spoon
		une fourchette	fork
		une serviette	napkin
		une tasse	cup

La nourriture et les plats

un dessert	dessert	le poulet	chicken	les céréales	cereal
le fromage	cheese	le riz	rice	les frites	French fries
le gâteau	cake	le rosbif	roast beef	la glace	ice cream
un hors-d'oeuvre	appetizer	le saucisson	salami	la nourriture	food
le jambon	ham	les spaghetti	spaghetti	la salade	salad
le pain	bread	le thon	tuna	la sole	sole
un plat	dish	le veau	veal	la soupe	soup
le poisson	fish	le yaourt	yogurt	la tarte	pie
				la viande	meat

Les fruits et les légumes

un fruit	*fruit*	une banane	*banana*	une poire	*pear*
des haricots verts	*green beans*	une carotte	*carrot*	une pomme	*apple*
un légume	*vegetable*	une cerise	*cherry*	une pomme de terre	*potato*
un pamplemousse	*grapefruit*	une fraise	*strawberry*	une salade	*(head of) lettuce*
des petits pois	*peas*	une orange	*orange*	une tomate	*tomato*

Les ingrédients

le beurre	*butter*	la confiture	*jam*
le ketchup	*ketchup*	la mayonnaise	*mayonnaise*
un oeuf	*egg*		
le sel	*salt*		
le sucre	*sugar*		

Les boissons

le jus d'orange	*orange juice*	une boisson	*beverage*
le jus de pomme	*apple juice*	l'eau	*water*
le lait	*milk*	l'eau minérale	*mineral water*
le thé glacé	*iced tea*		

Interacting with others

Est-ce que Paul	me te nous vous le la les	connaît?	Does Paul know	me? you? us? you? him? her? them?	
Est-ce que Sophie	me te nous vous lui leur	parle?	Is Sophie talking	to me? to you? to us? to you? to him/her? to them?	

Verbes réguliers

aider	*to help*
amener	*to bring (people)*
apporter	*to bring (things)*
demander (à)	*to ask*
donner (à)	*to give (to)*
montrer (à)	*to show (to)*
prêter (à)	*to lend, to loan (to)*
répondre (à)	*to answer*

Verbes irréguliers

apprendre	*to learn*
apprendre à + *infinitive*	*to learn how to*
boire	*to drink*
comprendre	*to understand*
connaître	*to know*
décrire	*to describe*
devoir	*must, to have to*
dire	*to say, to tell*
écrire (à)	*to write (to)*
pouvoir	*can, may, to be able*
prendre	*to take, to have (a meal)*
vouloir	*to want*

TEST PREP
CLASSZONE.COM

FLASHCARDS
AND MORE!

ENTRACTE 8

Objectives
- Reading skills development
- Re-entry of material in the unit
- Development of cultural awareness

Teaching Resource Options

PRINT

Workbook PE, pp. 245–249
Activités pour tous PE, pp. 147–149
Unit 8 Resource Book
   Activités pour tous TE, pp. 175–177
   Workbook TE, pp. 179–183

Bon appétit, Aurélie!
Objectives
- Reading at the paragraph level
- Reading for cultural information about French foods and eating habits

----

Questions sur le texte

1. Où est-ce qu'Aurélie mange à midi? le soir? [à la cantine de l'école/ à la maison]
2. Qui fait les courses chez Aurélie? [sa mère]
3. Qui prépare le dîner chez Aurélie? [son père]
4. Qu'est-ce qu'il y a comme dessert chez Aurélie? [du yaourt ou un fruit]
5. Quel type de restaurant est-ce qu'il y a dans le quartier d'Aurélie? [vietnamien]
6. Quel type de pizza est-ce qu'Aurélie préfère? [une pizza avec du fromage, des olives et des anchois]
7. Qu'est-ce qu'Aurélie boit avec la pizza? [un soda]

Comparaisons culturelles

- À la maison, Aurélie mange une salade de concombres ou de tomates, de la viande (un bifteck ou du poulet), des légumes (des haricots verts ou des pommes de terre), parfois du cassoulet en boîte, une salade verte et des fromages et un dessert (du yaourt ou un fruit).

- Au restaurant avec la famille, Aurélie mange du riz avec des crevettes et des petits pois.

- Au restaurant avec les copains, Aurélie mange une pizza avec du fromage, des olives et des anchois.

412 • **Entracte**
Unité 8

Bon appétit, Aurélie!

Nous avons demandé à Aurélie de décrire ses repas. Voici sa réponse.

À midi, je mange à la cantine de l'école et le soir à la maison. C'est ma mère qui fait les courses et c'est mon père qui prépare le dîner. J'adore ça! Il fait une cuisine assez traditionnelle, mais bien équilibrée.° En général, on commence par une salade de concombres ou de tomates. Ensuite, il y a de la viande, par exemple, un bifteck ou du poulet, avec des haricots verts ou des pommes de terre. Parfois, on mange du cassoulet° en boîte.° Après, il y a une salade verte et des fromages divers. Comme dessert, il y a du yaourt ou un fruit. Avec le repas, on boit de l'eau minérale.

Quand mon père n'a pas envie de faire la cuisine, on va au restaurant. Dans notre quartier, il y a un restaurant vietnamien que nous aimons bien. Mon plat préféré, c'est le riz avec des crevettes° et des petits pois.

Quand je sors avec mes copains, on va dans les fast-food. J'aime bien aller dans les pizzerias parce qu'on peut choisir ses ingrédients. En général, je prends une pizza avec du fromage, des olives et des anchois. Avec la pizza, je bois souvent un soda.

COMPARAISONS CULTURELLES

Comparez les repas d'Aurélie avec vos repas. Qu'est-ce que vous mangez pour le dîner? Faites une liste des similarités et des différences.

	AURÉLIE	LES SIMILARITÉS AVEC MOI	LES DIFFÉRENCES AVEC MOI
À la maison	_____	_____	_____
Au restaurant avec la famille	_____	_____	_____
Au restaurant avec les copains	_____	_____	_____

équilibrée *balanced*
cassoulet *bean stew with pork or duck*
en boîte *canned* **crevettes** *shrimp*

ALLOpizza

MENU

		26 cm. 1 pers.	31 cm. 2/3 pers.	40 cm. 3/4 pers.
ITALIENNE	sauce tomate, origan, mozzarella, anchois, olives	7,50 €	12 €	15 €
4 SAISONS	sauce tomate, mozzarella, crème, olives, tomates fraîches, champignons	7,50 €	12 €	15 €
3 FROMAGES	sauce tomate, mozzarella, origan, chèvre, Roquefort	8 €	13 €	17 €
PESCATORE	sauce tomate, mozzarella, origan, oignons, saumon, champignons	8 €	13 €	17 €
ANGLAISE	sauce tomate, mozzarella, origan, bacon, oeuf, pommes de terre	9 €	14 €	20 €
TEXANE	sauce tomate, mozzarella, origan, boeuf épicé, pepperoni, oignons	9 €	14 €	20 €

02-47-66-89-89

Petit dictionnaire

anchois	*anchovies*
frais/fraîche	*fresh*
boeuf épicé	*spicy beef*
oignon	*onion*
champignon	*mushroom*
origan	*oregano*
chèvre	*goat cheese*
saumon	*salmon*

Et vous?

Formez un groupe de 4 à 5 personnes. Imaginez que vous êtes en France. Vous voulez dîner et vous avez décidé de commander des pizzas. Faites une liste de ce que chacun veut commander.

NOM	TYPE DE PIZZA	DIMENSION	PRIX
John	Texane	31 cm.	14 €
•			
•			
•			
•			
•			

ALLOpizza

Objectives
• Reading authentic documents
• Vocabulary expansion

Et vous?
Answers will vary.

Sara	Italienne	26 cm.	7,50 euros
Josh	Pescatore	31 cm.	13 euros
Emma	Anglaise	26 cm.	9 euros
Noah	4 Saisons	40 cm.	15 euros
Alex	3 Fromages	31 cm.	13 euros

Supplementary vocabulary

Here are some other popular toppings on pizzas in France:

de l'ananas *pineapple*
des artichauts *artichokes*
de l'aubergine *eggplant*
des câpres *capers*
du jambon *ham*
des lardons *diced bacon*
du maïs *corn*
de la persillade *parsley vinaigrette*
des poivrons *peppers*
du poulet fumé *smoked chicken*
du saumon *salmon*
du thon *tuna*

Culture notes

• The French often have an egg on their pizza. The egg **(l'oeuf)** is broken on top of the pizza just before baking.

• Pizza in France generally does not come sliced as it does here in the United States. It arrives as a complete pizza, and the cutting is left to the customer.

• Many pizzerias in France have websites from which customers can order pizza to be picked up **(pizza à emporter)** or to be delivered **(la livraison)**.

PRE-READING

Have students look quickly at the menu and decide what meal is presented.

How can they tell?

Le petit déjeuner

Objectives
- Reading at the paragraph level
- Building reading skills

Teaching Resource Options

PRINT

Workbook PE, pp. 245–249
Activités pour tous PE, pp. 147–149
Unit 8 Resource Book
    Activités pour tous TE, pp. 175–177
    Workbook TE, pp. 179–183

Questions sur le texte

1. Qu'est-ce que Fabrice met sur son pain?
   (Il met du beurre et de la confiture sur son pain.)
2. Qu'est-ce qu'il boit?
   (Il boit un grand bol de café au lait.)
3. Pourquoi est-ce que Mathieu dit qu'il prend le petit déjeuner «à l'américaine»?
   (Parce qu'il prend des céréales et il boit du jus d'orange.)
4. Qu'est-ce que Sandrine boit au petit déjeuner?
   (Elle boit du lait chaud ou du chocolat avec beaucoup de sucre.)
5. Quel jour est-ce qu'elle mange des croissants?
   (Elle mange des croissants le dimanche.)
6. Pourquoi est-ce que Sylvie ne mange pas beaucoup au petit déjeuner?
   (Elle n'a pas très faim le matin.)
7. Qu'est-ce qu'elle prend avec elle pour manger avant la première classe?
   (Elle prend une barre de céréales ou une barre chocolatée.)
8. De quelle origine est Stéphanie?
   (Elle est martiniquaise.)
9. En général, qu'est-ce qu'elle mange au petit déjeuner?
   (Elle mange du pain et de la confiture.)
10. Qu'est-ce qu'elle mange avec le blaff de poisson?
    (Elle mange des bananes vertes cuites.)

Comparaisons culturelles

Answers will vary.
- Mathieu a le petit déjeuner le plus semblable parce qu'il mange des céréales et il boit du jus d'orange.
- Stéphanie a le petit déjeuner le plus different parce qu'elle mange du poisson!

Activité écrite

Answers will vary.
Pendant la semaine, le petit déjeuner est normal. Je mange des céréales et je bois du jus d'orange ou du chocolat chaud. Mais, le dimanche matin, ma famille et moi, nous allons dans un restaurant. Je mange une omelette avec du fromage et des champignons et du pain grillé. J'aime le dimanche!

Le petit déjeuner *en France*

«Qu'est-ce que vous prenez au petit déjeuner?» Aux États-Unis, le petit déjeuner est généralement un repas abondant.° En France, c'est un repas simple.

Fabrice (13 ans)

Chez nous, nous sommes très traditionnels. Je mange du pain avec du beurre et de la confiture. Je bois un grand bol° de café au lait.

Mathieu (16 ans)

Chez nous, on prend le petit déjeuner «à l'américaine». Je mange des céréales et je bois du jus d'orange.

Sandrine (16 ans)

Je mange des tartines de pain° grillé° et je bois du lait chaud ou du chocolat avec beaucoup de sucre. Le dimanche, il y a parfois° des croissants. (Ça dépend si quelqu'un veut faire les courses!)

Sylvie (15 ans)

Le matin, je n'ai pas très faim. En général, je mange une tartine, c'est tout.° Je prends avec moi une barre de céréales ou une barre chocolatée que je mange avant° la première classe.

---

abondant *abundant, copious*   **bol** *deep bowl*   **tartines de pain** *slices of bread*   **grillé** *toasted*   **parfois** *sometimes*   **tout** *all*   **avant** *before*

COMPARAISONS CULTURELLES

Comparez le petit déjeuner des cinq jeunes Français avec votre petit déjeuner.

- Qui a le petit déjeuner le plus semblable *(most similar)*? Expliquez.
- Qui a le petit déjeuner le plus différent? Expliquez.

Activité écrite

Décrivez le petit déjeuner chez vous:

- pendant la semaine
- le dimanche matin

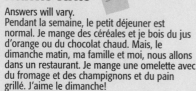

414   quatre cent quatorze
Unité 8

PRE-READING

Have students glance over the reading quickly. What is the question that was asked in the interview?

POST-READING

Ask each student to decide which of the five people they would like to have breakfast with and why.

Chez qui veux-tu prendre le petit déjeuner? Pourquoi?

Stéphanie (13 ans)

Je suis martiniquaise. En général, je mange du pain et de la confiture
comme° tout le monde.° Parfois ma mère prépare un petit déjeuner martiniquais
typique. On mange du blaff de poisson° et des bananes vertes cuites.°
On mange aussi des ananas,° des papayes et de la gelée de goyave.°
C'est délicieux!

---

comme *like*   **tout le monde** *everyone*   **blaff de poisson** *fish stew*   **cuites** *cooked*
ananas *pineapple*   **gelée de goyave** *guava jelly*

NOTE *culturelle*

La cuisine créole

La cuisine créole est une cuisine régionale typique de la Martinique et
de la Guadeloupe. C'est une cuisine assez épicée° qui utilise les produits
locaux,° principalement les produits de la mer° et les fruits exotiques.

Voici certaines spécialités:

boudin créole	*spicy sausage*
colombo	*rice with spicy meat sauce*
blaff de poisson	*fish stew*
matoutou crabes	*stewed crabs served with rice*
crabes farcis	*stuffed crabs*
langoustes grillées	*(small) lobsters, broiled*

épicée *hot (spicy)*   **locaux** *local*   **mer** *sea*

DÉCOUVREZ
LA MARTINIQUE
au
TYPIC BELLEVUE
LE PLUS TYPIQUE DES RESTAURANTS
UN CHOIX UNIQUE DE SPÉCIALITÉS CRÉOLES
Boulevard de la Marne Tél. 05.96.71.68.87
FORT-DE-FRANCE
Parking Boulevard de Verdun
★★ **RELAIS CRÉOLE** ★★
Menu du jour et à la carte
Ouvert midi et soir sauf dimanche

LA VILLA CRÉOLE
La Bonne Cuisine Française et Créole
ANSE-MITAN
TROIS-ÎLETS
☎ 66.05.53

CONNEXIONS

Haitian people have their own creole cuisine which is somewhat
different from that of Martinique. Find out about Haitian cuisine by
visiting a local Haitian restaurant or by surfing the Internet.

• What products do Haitians use in their cooking?

• What are some typical dishes?

quatre cent quinze
Lecture et Culture 415

Questions personnelles

Answers will vary.
1. Est-ce que tu bois du jus de fruit le matin?
    Quel jus de fruit?
    Oui, je bois du jus de fruit. Je bois du jus
    d'orange. (Non, je ne bois pas de jus de fruit.)
2. Est-ce que tes parents boivent du café?
    Sinon, qu'est-ce qu'ils boivent?
    Oui, mes parents boivent du café. (Non,
    mes parents ne boivent pas de café. Ils
    boivent du thé.)
3. Est-ce que tu manges souvent des
    croissants? Quand? Oui, je mange souvent
    les croissants. Je les mange des croissants le
    week-end.
    (Non, je ne mange pas souvent de
    croissants. Je les mangent quand je suis à
    Paris.)
4. Est-ce que tu aimes la confiture? Quelle est
    ta confiture préférée?
    Oui, j'aime la confiture. Ma confiture
    préférée est la confiture aux fraises. (Non, je
    n'aime pas la confiture.)
5. Est-ce que tu manges des céréales? De
    quelles sortes?
    Oui, je mange des céréales. Je mange des
    céréales sucrées. (Non, je ne mange pas de
    céréales.)
6. Est-ce que tu préfères le petit déjeuner
    français ou le petit déjeuner américain?
    Pourquoi?
    Je préfère le petit déjeuner américain parce
    que j'aime les omelettes. (Je préfère le petit
    déjeuner français parce qu'il est plus léger.)

Realia note
Le menu
At the **Typic Bellevue** one can either
select the **prix fixe** menu (**le menu du
jour**) or order dishes from the main
menu (**à la carte**).

Realia note
La Villa Créole is a small Martinique
restaurant on the beach at Anse-Mitan
(**anse** = bay) in the town of Trois–Îlets
(**îlet** = small island)

Les crêpes
Objectives
- Reading for information
- Understanding and following instructions

Teaching Resource Options

PRINT

Workbook PE, pp. 245–249
Activités pour tous PE, pp. 147–149
Unit 8 Resource Book
  Activités pour tous TE, pp. 175–177
  Workbook TE, pp. 179–183

VIDEO PROGRAM

VIDÉO DVD

 MODULE 28

28.4 Vignette culturelle:
La recette des crêpes
(51:35–52:53 min.)

Photo culture note

Une cuisine française
French kitchens are smaller than American kitchens, but they are usually equipped in the same way.

Note in the background:
- the counter (**le comptoir**)
- the cabinets (**les placards**)
- the sink (**l'évier**)
- pots and pans (**les casseroles**)
- the microwave oven (**le four à micro-ondes**)

Les crêpes

Les crêpes sont d'origine bretonne.° Aujourd'hui, on vend les crêpes dans les «crêperies». On peut aussi faire des crêpes à la maison. Voici une recette° très simple.

les ingrédients

3 oeufs
3 cuillères à soupe de sucre
une pincée° de sel
2 tasses de lait
1 tasse de farine°
1 cuillère à soupe d'huile°
du beurre

les ustensiles

un petit bol   un grand bol

un fouet   une poêle

STRATEGY Reading

Using illustrations When you are reading, the context is not only the printed word. Sometimes the illustrations can help you understand the text. As you read the recipe, try guessing the meanings of the new words by studying the pictures.

D'abord: Pour faire la pâte°

Mettez les oeufs dans le petit bol. Battez-les° bien avec le fouet.

Ajoutez° le sucre, le sel et un peu de lait.

Mettez la farine dans le grand bol. Versez° le contenu° du petit bol dans le grand bol.

Ajoutez l'huile et le reste du lait. Mélangez° bien la pâte. Attendez deux heures.

---

bretonne *from Brittany*   **recette** *recipe*   **pincée** *pinch*   **farine** *flour*
huile *oil*   **pâte** *batter*   **Battez-les** *Beat them*   **Ajoutez** *Add*   **Versez** *Pour*
contenu *contents*   **Mélangez** *Mix, Stir*

PRE-READING

Have students identify the type of reading. [a recipe: **une recette**]

  What kinds of verb forms are used in this recipe? [commands]

Optional: Show the *Vignette culturelle* of Video Module 28 which demonstrates the making of crêpes.

Ensuite: Pour faire les crêpes

Chauffez° la poêle. Mettez du beurre dans la poêle.

Mettez une cuillère de pâte dans la poêle.

Agitez° la poêle pour étendre° la pâte.

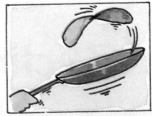

Retournez° la crêpe quand elle est dorée.°

**Si vous êtes adroit(e), faites sauter° la crêpe en l'air.
Si vous n'êtes pas adroit(e), abstenez-vous!°**

Enfin: Pour servir les crêpes

**Mettez la crêpe sur une assiette chaude.
Faites les autres° crêpes.**

Mettez du sucre ou de la confiture sur chaque° crêpe.

Au choix, roulez-la° ou pliez-la° en quatre.

Chauffez *Heat* **Agitez** *Shake* **étendre** *spread* **Retournez** *Turn over* **dorée** *golden brown* **faites sauter** *flip*
abstenez-vous *don't try* **autres** *other* **chaque** *each* **roulez-la** *roll it* **pliez-la** *fold it*

TEACHING STRATEGY Les crêpes

You might want to cooperate with the home economics department and let the students learn to make **crêpes** in the school kitchen.

Reference Section

CONTENTS

I Les noms, les articles et les adjectifs

Les noms et les articles

In French, all nouns are MASCULINE or FEMININE, SINGULAR or PLURAL.
Nouns are often introduced by ARTICLES.

Definite Article *(the)*

	SINGULAR	PLURAL		
MASCULINE	le (l')	les	le garçon, l'ami	les garçons, les amis
FEMININE	la (l')	les	la fille, l'amie	les filles, les amies

Indefinite Article *(a, an; some)*

	SINGULAR	PLURAL		
MASCULINE	un	des	un copain	des copains
FEMININE	une	des	une copine	des copines

→ **Des** often corresponds to the English *some.*
Although the word *some* is often omitted in
English, the article **des** must be used in French.

J'ai **des** cousins à Paris.
*I have **(some)** cousins in Paris.*

→ After a NEGATIVE verb, **un, une,** and **des**
become **de (d').**

J'ai **une** soeur.   Je n'ai pas **de** frères.

Note also:

	MASCULINE	FEMININE
my	mon	ma (mon)
	mon frère mon ami	ma soeur mon amie
your	ton	ta (ton)
	ton frère ton ami	ta soeur ton amie

Les adjectifs de description

FORMS

In French, descriptive adjectives AGREE with the nouns they modify.
REGULAR adjectives have the following endings:

	SINGULAR	PLURAL		
MASCULINE	–	-s	intelligent	intelligents
FEMININE	-e	-es	intelligente	intelligentes

→ Adjectives that end in **-e** in the masculine remain the same in the feminine.
un garçon **timide**   une fille **timide**
→ Adjectives that end in **-s** in the masculine singular remain the same in the masculine plural.
un ami **français**   des amis **français**

POSITION

Most adjectives come AFTER the noun they modify.   A few adjectives come before the noun.
une fille **intelligente**   *an intelligent girl*   une **petite** voiture   *a small car*

APPENDIX A

Les personnes

VOCABULAIRE La famille

un frère	brother	une soeur	sister
un père	father	une mère	mother
un grand-père	grandfather	une grand-mère	grandmother
un cousin		une cousine	
un oncle	uncle	une tante	aunt

Les animaux domestiques (Pets)

un chien   un chat

VOCABULAIRE D'autres personnes (Other people)

un garçon	boy	une fille	girl
un ami	friend	une amie	
un copain	friend	une copine	
un camarade	classmate	une camarade	
un élève	high school student	une élève	
un étudiant	college student	une étudiante	
un prof	professor, teacher	une prof	
un homme	man	une femme	woman
un monsieur	man, gentleman	une dame	lady
un voisin	neighbor	une voisine	
des gens	people	une personne	

Adjectifs de description

VOCABULAIRE La nationalité

américain	espagnol	japonais
anglais	français	mexicain
canadien (canadienne)	italien (italienne)	suisse
chinois		

VOCABULAIRE La description physique

blond	brun	jeune*	young
grand*	petit	beau (belle)*	good-looking, beautiful, handsome
		joli	pretty

VOCABULAIRE La personnalité

amusant	bon (bonne)*	good	mauvais*	bad
intéressant	gentil (gentille)	nice, kind	bête	not smart, stupid
intelligent	mignon (mignonne)	cute	méchant	nasty
timide	sportif (sportive)	athletic		
	sympathique	nice, pleasant		

→ Adjectives marked with an asterisk [*] usually come before the noun.
   Cécile est une **jolie** fille.

Quelques objets (A few objects)

VOCABULAIRE Dans le garage

un vélo	bike		une auto	
un scooter	motorscooter		une bicyclette	
			une mobylette	moped
			une moto	motorcycle
			une voiture	car

VOCABULAIRE À la maison

un objet		une chose	thin
un crayon	pencil	une affiche	poster
un stylo	pen		
un livre	book		
un ordinateur	computer	une calculatrice	pocket calculator
un sac		une raquette	
un appareil-photo	camera	une montre	watch
un téléphone		une guitare	
un portable	cell phone		
un baladeur	portable player	une chaîne hi-fi	
un CD		une radio	
		une radiocassette	boombox
		une télé	TV

VOCABULAIRE Une chambre (bedroom)

APPENDIX A

VOCABULAIRE Au café

Les plats *(dishes)*

un croissant	une crêpe
un hamburger	une glace *(ice cream)*
un hot-dog	une omelette
un sandwich	une pizza
un steak	une salade
un steak-frites	

Les boissons *(drinks, beverages)*

un café	une limonade
un chocolat *(cocoa)*	
un thé *(tea)*	
un jus de pomme *(apple juice)*	
un jus d'orange	
un jus de raisin *(grape juice)*	
un jus de tomate	
un soda *(soft drink)*	

VOCABULAIRE Les couleurs

De quelle couleur…?　　*What color…?*

— **De quelle couleur** est la moto?
— Elle est rouge.

| blanc (blanche) | noir (noire) | bleu (bleue) | rouge (rouge) | jaune (jaune) | vert (verte) | marron (marron) | orange (orange) |

→ Colors are adjectives and take adjective endings.
　un vélo **vert**　　une voiture **verte**

NOTE: The colors **marron** and **orange** are INVARIABLE: they have the same form in the masculine and feminine.

II *Les verbes*

Les verbes réguliers en -er: formes affirmatives et négatives

INFINITIVE	AFFIRMATIVE		NEGATIVE			ENDINGS
	parler					
STEM	**parl-**					
	je	parle	je	**ne** parle	**pas**	-e
	tu	parles	tu	**ne** parles	**pas**	-es
	il / elle	parle	il / elle	**ne** parle	**pas**	-e
PRESENT	nous	parl**ons**	nous	**ne** parl**ons**	**pas**	-ons
	vous	parl**ez**	vous	**ne** parl**ez**	**pas**	-ez
	ils / elles	parl**ent**	ils / elles	**ne** parl**ent**	**pas**	-ent

▶ For verbs ending in **-ger**, the **nous-** form is written with **-geons:**
  nous man**geons**, nous na**geons**

Les verbes irréguliers *être, avoir, faire*

être *(to be)*	**avoir** *(to have)*	**faire** *(to do, make)*
je **suis**	j′ **ai**	je **fais**
tu **es**	tu **as**	tu **fais**
il/elle **est**	il/elle **a**	il/elle **fait**
nous **sommes**	nous **avons**	nous **faisons**
vous **êtes**	vous **avez**	vous **faites**
ils/elles **sont**	ils/elles **ont**	ils/elles **font**

APPENDIX A

VOCABULAIRE Quelques activités

aimer		to like, love	manger		to eat
chanter		to sing	marcher		to walk
danser		to dance	nager		to swim
dîner		to have supper, dinner	organiser une boum		to organize a party
écouter	le professeur	to listen to the teacher	parler		to speak
	la radio	to listen to the radio	regarder	un magazine	to look at a magazine
étudier		to study		la télé	to watch TV
habiter à		to live in	téléphoner		to phone, call
jouer	au basket	to play basketball	travailler		to work
	au foot	to play soccer	visiter		to visit (a place)
	au tennis		voyager		to travel
	aux jeux vidéo	to play video games			

→ When referring to things, **marcher** means *to work, to function.*

Je **marche** parce que ma voiture ne marche pas.

VOCABULAIRE Expressions avec *être, avoir* et *faire*

être

être d'accord	to agree	Pourquoi est-ce que tu n'**es** pas **d'accord** avec moi?

avoir

avoir … ans	to be … [years old]	Ma cousine **a quinze ans.**
avoir faim	to be/feel hungry	Je mange un sandwich parce que j'**ai faim.**
avoir soif	to be/feel thirsty	Tu **as soif**? Voici une limonade.

faire:

faire attention	to pay attention	Les élèves **font attention** en classe.
faire un match	to play a game	Mes cousins **font un match** de tennis.
faire une promenade	to go for a walk	Nous **faisons une promenade** en ville.
faire un voyage	to take a trip	Cécile **fait un voyage** à Québec.

III *Les nombres, la date, l'heure et le temps*

A VOCABULAIRE Les nombres

▶ *How to count:*

0 to 19

0	zéro	10	dix
1	un	11	onze
2	deux	12	douze
3	trois	13	treize
4	quatre	14	quatorze
5	cinq	15	quinze
6	six	16	seize
7	sept	17	dix-sept
8	huit	18	dix-huit
9	neuf	19	dix-neuf

20 to 59

20	vingt	30	trente
21	vingt et un	31	trente et un
22	vingt-deux	32	trente-deux
23	vingt-trois		…
24	vingt-quatre	40	quarante
25	vingt-cinq	41	quarante et un
26	vingt-six	46	quarante-six
27	vingt-sept		…
28	vingt-huit	50	cinquante
29	vingt-neuf	51	cinquante et un
		59	cinquante-neuf

60 to 100

60	soixante	80	quatre-vingts
61	soixante et un	81	quatre-vingt-un
62	soixante-deux	82	quatre-vingt-deux
63	soixante-trois	88	quatre-vingt-huit
	…		…
70	soixante-dix	90	quatre-vingt-dix
71	soixante et onze	91	quatre-vingt-onze
72	soixante douze	99	quatre-vingt-dix-neuf
76	soixante-seize	100	cent

→ Note the use of **et** in the numbers 21, 31, 41, 51, 61, 71.

B VOCABULAIRE La date

▶ *How to give the date:*

Quel jour est-ce aujourd'hui?
  C'est jeudi.

Quelle est la date?
  C'est le trois janvier.
  C'est le dix-sept mai.

Quand est-ce, ton anniversaire?
  C'est le vingt-deux novembre.

Les jours de la semaine:

lundi	mercredi	vendredi	dimanche
mardi	jeudi	samedi	

Les mois de l'année:

janvier	avril	juillet	octobre
février	mai	août	novembre
mars	juin	septembre	décembre

→ The first of the month is **le premier.**   Demain, c'est **le premier** juillet.

APPENDIX A

C VOCABULAIRE L'heure

▶ **How to tell time:**

Quelle heure est-il?
Il est ...

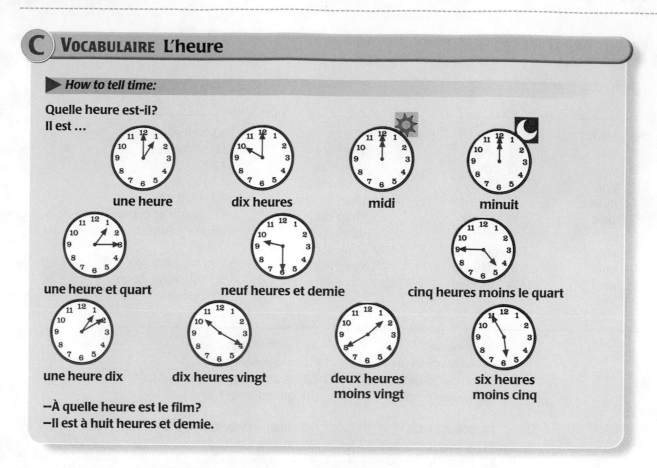

une heure   dix heures   midi   minuit

une heure et quart   neuf heures et demie   cinq heures moins le quart

une heure dix   dix heures vingt   deux heures moins vingt   six heures moins cinq

—À quelle heure est le film?
—Il est à huit heures et demie.

→ In French, official time is given on a 24-hour clock. Compare:

	CONVERSATIONAL TIME	OFFICIAL TIME
10 A.M.	Il est **dix heures du matin.**	Il est **dix heures.**
1 P.M.	Il est **une heure de l'après-midi.**	Il est **treize heures.**
9 P.M.	Il est **neuf heures du soir.**	Il est **vingt et une heures.**

D VOCABULAIRE Le temps

▶ **How to talk about the weather:**

Quel temps fait-il?

	beau.	It's nice.
	bon.	It's fine, pleasant.
Il fait	chaud.	It's hot.
	froid.	It's cold.
	mauvais.	It's bad.
Il pleut.		It's raining.
Il neige.		It's snowing.

Les saisons:

le printemps	spring
l'été	summer
l'automne	fall
l'hiver	winter

[1] Also known as Île-de-France
[2] Also known as Nord-Pas-de-Calais
[3] Also known as Provence-Alpes-Côte d'Azur *(Bottin 1989)*

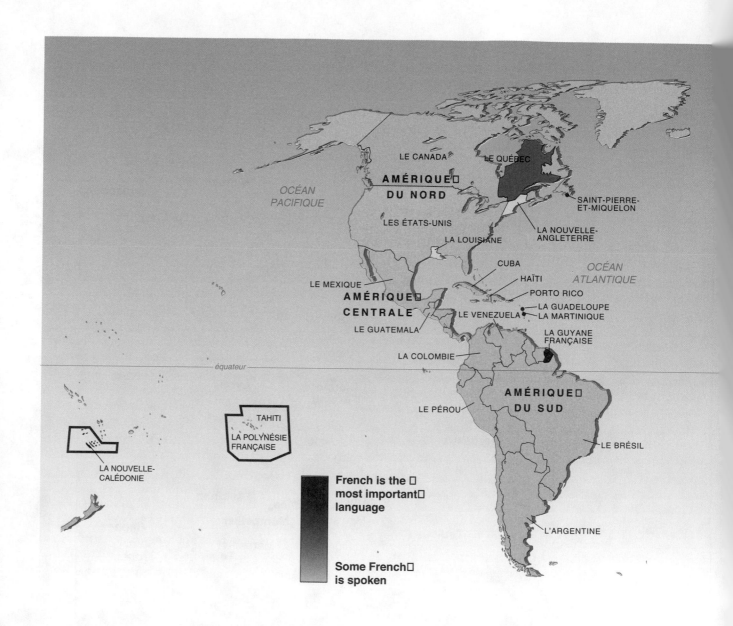

LE CANADA
LE QUÉBEC
AMÉRIQUE DU NORD
OCÉAN PACIFIQUE
SAINT-PIERRE-ET-MIQUELON
LES ÉTATS-UNIS
LA NOUVELLE-ANGLETERRE
LA LOUISIANE
CUBA
HAÏTI
OCÉAN ATLANTIQUE
LE MEXIQUE
PORTO RICO
AMÉRIQUE CENTRALE
LA GUADELOUPE
LE VENEZUELA
LA MARTINIQUE
LE GUATEMALA
LA GUYANE FRANÇAISE
LA COLOMBIE
équateur
AMÉRIQUE DU SUD
LE PÉROU
TAHITI
LA POLYNÉSIE FRANÇAISE
LE BRÉSIL
LA NOUVELLE-CALÉDONIE

French is the most important language

Some French is spoken

L'ARGENTINE

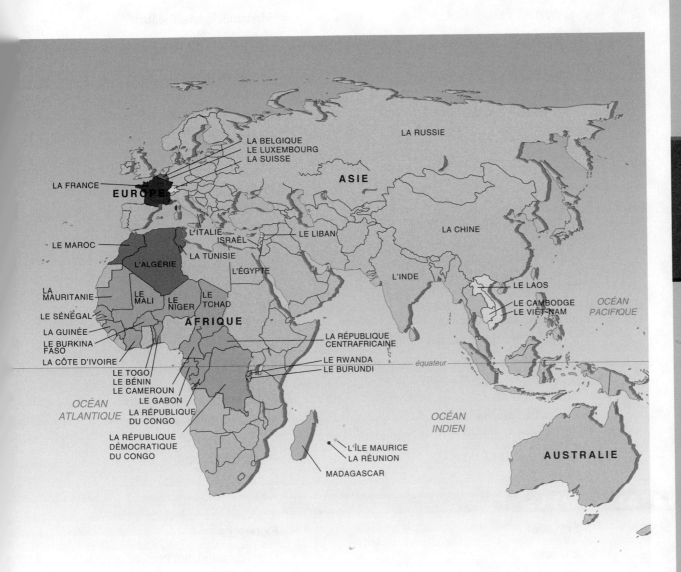

LA BELGIQUE
LE LUXEMBOURG
LA SUISSE

LA RUSSIE

ASIE

LA FRANCE

EUROPE

L'ITALIE

LE LIBAN

LA CHINE

LE MAROC

ISRAËL

L'ALGÉRIE

LA TUNISIE

L'ÉGYPTE

L'INDE

LA
MAURITANIE

LE
MALI

LE
NIGER

LE
TCHAD

LE LAOS

OCÉAN
PACIFIQUE

LE SÉNÉGAL

AFRIQUE

LE CAMBODGE
LE VIÊT-NAM

LA GUINÉE

LE BURKINA
FASO

LA RÉPUBLIQUE
CENTRAFRICAINE

LA CÔTE D'IVOIRE

LE RWANDA
LE BURUNDI

équateur

LE TOGO
LE BÉNIN
LE CAMEROUN

OCÉAN
ATLANTIQUE

LE GABON
LA RÉPUBLIQUE
DU CONGO

OCÉAN
INDIEN

AUSTRALIE

LA RÉPUBLIQUE
DÉMOCRATIQUE
DU CONGO

L'ÎLE MAURICE
LA RÉUNION

MADAGASCAR

APPENDIX 2

VOWELS

SOUND	SPELLING	EXAMPLES
/a/	a, à, â	Madame, là-bas, théâtre
/i/	i, î	visite, Nice, dîne
	y (initial, final, or between consonants)	Yves, Guy, style
/u/	ou, où, oû	Toulouse, où, août
/y/	u, û	tu, Luc, sûr
/o/	o (final or before silent consonant)	piano, idiot, Margot
	au, eau	jaune, Claude, beau
	ô	hôtel, drôle, Côte d'Ivoire
/ɔ/	o	Monique, Noël, jolie
	au	Paul, restaurant, Laure
/e/	é	Dédé, Québec, télé
	e (before silent final z, t, r)	chez, et, Roger
	ai (final or before final silent consonant)	j'ai, mai, japonais
/ɛ/	è	Michèle, Ève, père
	ei	seize, neige, tour Eiffel
	ê	tête, être, Viêt-nam
	e (before two consonants)	elle, Pierre, Annette
	e (before pronounced final consonant)	Michel, avec, cher
	ai (before pronounced final consonant)	française, aime, Maine
/ə/	e (final or before single consonant)	je, Denise, venir
/φ/	eu, oeu	deux, Mathieu, euro, oeufs
	eu (before final se)	nerveuse, généreuse, sérieuse
/œ/	eu (before final pronounced consonant except /z/)	heure, neuf, Lesieur
	oeu	soeur, coeur, oeuf
	oe	oeil

NASAL VOWELS

SOUND	SPELLING	EXAMPLES
/ɑ̃/	an, am	France, quand, lampe
	en, em	Henri, pendant, décembre
/ɔ̃/	on, om	non, Simon, bombe
/ɛ̃/	in, im	Martin, invite, impossible
	yn, ym	syndicat, sympathique, Olympique
	ain, aim	Alain, américain, faim
	(o) + in	loin, moins, point
	(i) + en	bien, Julien, viens
/œ̃/	un, um	un, Lebrun, parfum

Sound-Spelling Correspondences

SEMI-VOWELS

Sound	Spelling	Examples
/j/	**i, y** (before vowel sound)	bien, piano, Lyon
	-il, -ill (after vowel sound)	oeil, travaille, Marseille, fille
/ɥ/	**u** (before vowel sound)	lui, Suisse, juillet
/w/	**ou** (before vowel sound)	oui, Louis, jouer
/wa/	**oi, oî**	voici, Benoît
	oy (before vowel)	voyage

CONSONANTS

Sound	Spelling	Examples
/b/	**b**	Barbara, banane, Belgique
/k/	**c** (before **a, o, u,** or consonant)	casque, cuisine, classe
	ch(r)	Christine, Christian, Christophe
	qu, q (final)	Québec, qu'est-ce que, cinq
	k	kilo, Kiki, ketchup
/ʃ/	**ch**	Charles, blanche, chez
/d/	**d**	Didier, dans, médecin
/f/	**f**	Félix, franc, neuf
	ph	Philippe, téléphone, photo
/g/	**g** (before **a, o, u,** or consonant)	Gabriel, gorge, légumes, gris
	gu (before **e, i, y**)	vague, Guillaume, Guy
/ɲ/	**gn**	mignon, champagne, Allemagne
/ʒ/	**j**	je, Jérôme, jaune
	g (before **e, i, y**)	rouge, Gigi, gymnastique
	ge (before **a, o, u**)	orangeade, Georges, nageur
/l/	**l, ll**	Lise, elle, cheval
/m/	**m**	Maman, moi, tomate
/n/	**n**	banane, Nancy, nous
/p/	**p**	peu, Papa, Pierre
/r/	**r, rr**	arrive, rentre, Paris
/s/	**c** (before **e, i, y**)	ce, Cécile, Nancy
	ç (before **a, o, u**)	ça, garçon, déçu
	s (initial or before consonant)	sac, Sophie, reste
	ss (between vowels)	boisson, dessert, Suisse
	t (before **i** + vowel)	attention, Nations Unies, natation
	x	dix, six, soixante
/t/	**t**	trop, télé, Tours
	th	Thérèse, thé, Marthe
/v/	**v**	Viviane, vous, nouveau
/gz/	**x**	examen, exemple, exact
/ks/	**x**	Max, Mexique, excellent
/z/	**s** (between vowels)	désert, Louise, télévision
	z	Suzanne, zut, zéro

APPENDIX 3

Numbers

A. CARDINAL NUMBERS

0 zéro	18 dix-huit	82 quatre-vingt-deux
1 un (une)	19 dix-neuf	90 quatre-vingt-dix
2 deux	20 vingt	91 quatre-vingt-onze
3 trois	21 vingt et un (une)	100 cent
4 quatre	22 vingt-deux	101 cent un (une)
5 cinq	23 vingt-trois	102 cent deux
6 six	30 trente	200 deux cents
7 sept	31 trente et un (une)	201 deux cent un
8 huit	32 trente-deux	300 trois cents
9 neuf	40 quarante	400 quatre cents
10 dix	41 quarante et un (une)	500 cinq cents
11 onze	50 cinquante	600 six cents
12 douze	60 soixante	700 sept cents
13 treize	70 soixante-dix	800 huit cents
14 quatorze	71 soixante et onze	900 neuf cents
15 quinze	72 soixante-douze	1 000 mille
16 seize	80 quatre-vingts	2 000 deux mille
17 dix-sept	81 quatre-vingt-un (une)	1 000 000 un million

Notes:
1. The word **et** occurs only in the numbers 21, 31, 41, 51, 61, and 71: **vingt et un** / **soixante et onze**
2. **Un** becomes **une** before a feminine noun: **trente et une filles**
3. **Quatre-vingts** becomes **quatre-vingt** before another number: **quatre-vingt-cinq**
4. **Cents** becomes **cent** before another number: **trois cent vingt**
5. **Mille** never adds an **-s:** **quatre mille**

B. ORDINAL NUMBERS

1$^{er\,(ère)}$ premier (première)	5e cinquième	9e neuvième
2e deuxième	6e sixième	10e dixième
3e troisième	7e septième	11e onzième
4e quatrième	8e huitième	12e douzième

Note: Premier becomes **première** before a feminine noun: **la première histoire**

C. METRIC EQUIVALENTS

1 gramme	= 0.035 ounces		1 ounce	= **28,349 grammes**
1 kilogramme	= 2.205 pounds		1 pound	= **0,453 kilogrammes**
1 litre	= 1.057 quarts		1 quart	= **0,946 litres**
1 mètre	= 39.37 inches		1 foot	= **30,480 centimètres**
1 kilomètre	= 0.62 miles		1 mile	= **1,609 kilomètres**

A. REGULAR VERBS

INFINITIVE	PRESENT		PASSÉ COMPOSÉ	
parler *(to talk, speak)*	je **parle** tu **parles** il **parle**	nous **parlons** vous **parlez** ils **parlent**	j'ai **parlé** tu as **parlé** il a **parlé**	nous **avons parlé** vous **avez parlé** ils **ont parlé**

IMPERATIVE: **parle, parlons, parlez**

finir *(to finish)*	je **finis** tu **finis** il **finit**	nous **finissons** vous **finissez** ils **finissent**	j'ai **fini** tu as **fini** il a **fini**	nous **avons fini** vous **avez fini** ils **ont fini**

IMPERATIVE: **finis, finissons, finissez**

vendre *(to sell)*	je **vends** tu **vends** il **vend**	nous **vendons** vous **vendez** ils **vendent**	j'ai **vendu** tu as **vendu** il a **vendu**	nous **avons vendu** vous **avez vendu** ils **ont vendu**

IMPERATIVE: **vends, vendons, vendez**

B. -er VERBS WITH SPELLING CHANGES

INFINITIVE	PRESENT		PASSÉ COMPOSÉ
acheter *(to buy)*	j'**achète** tu **achètes** il **achète**	nous **achetons** vous **achetez** ils **achètent**	j'ai **acheté**

Verb like **acheter:** amener *(to bring, take along)*

espérer *(to hope)*	j'**espère** tu **espères** il **espère**	nous **espérons** vous **espérez** ils **espèrent**	j'ai **espéré**

Verbs like **espérer:** célébrer *(to celebrate)*, préférer *(to prefer)*

commencer *(to begin, start)*	je **commence** tu **commences** il **commence**	nous **commençons** vous **commencez** ils **commencent**	j'ai **commencé**

manger *(to eat)*	je **mange** tu **manges** il **mange**	nous **mangeons** vous **mangez** ils **mangent**	j'ai **mangé**

Verbs like **manger:** nager *(to swim)*, voyager *(to travel)*

payer *(to pay, pay for)*	je **paie** tu **paies** il **paie**	nous **payons** vous **payez** ils **paient**	j'ai **payé**

Verbs like **payer:** nettoyer *(to clean)*

APPENDIX 4

C. IRREGULAR VERBS

INFINITIVE	PRESENT		PASSÉ COMPOSÉ
avoir *(to have, own)*	j'ai tu as il a	nous avons vous avez ils ont	j'ai eu
	IMPERATIVE: **aie, ayons, ayez**		
être *(to be)*	je suis tu es il est	nous sommes vous êtes ils sont	j'ai été
	IMPERATIVE: **sois, soyons, soyez**		
aller *(to go)*	je vais tu vas il va	nous allons vous allez ils vont	je suis allé(e)
	IMPERATIVE: **va, allons, allez**		
boire *(to drink)*	je bois tu bois il boit	nous buvons vous buvez ils boivent	j'ai bu
connaître *(to know)*	je connais tu connais il connaît	nous connaissons vous connaissez ils connaissent	j'ai connu
devoir *(to have to, should, must)*	je dois tu dois il doit	nous devons vous devez ils doivent	j'ai dû
dire *(to say, tell)*	je dis tu dis il dit	nous disons vous dites ils disent	j'ai dit
dormir *(to sleep)*	je dors tu dors il dort	nous dormons vous dormez ils dorment	j'ai dormi
écrire *(to write)*	j'écris tu écris il écrit	nous écrivons vous écrivez ils écrivent	j'ai écrit
	Verb like **écrire:** décrire *(to describe)*		
faire *(to make, do)*	je fais tu fais il fait	nous faisons vous faites ils font	j'ai fait

C. IRREGULAR VERBS

INFINITIVE	PRESENT		PASSÉ COMPOSÉ
lire *(to read)*	je **lis** tu **lis** il **lit**	nous **lisons** vous **lisez** ils **lisent**	j'ai **lu**
mettre *(to put, place)*	je **mets** tu **mets** il **met**	nous **mettons** vous **mettez** ils **mettent**	j'ai **mis**

Verb like **mettre:** promettre *(to promise)*

ouvrir *(to open)*	j'**ouvre** tu **ouvres** il **ouvre**	nous **ouvrons** vous **ouvrez** ils **ouvrent**	j'ai **ouvert**

Verbs like **ouvrir:** découvrir *(to discover)*, offrir *(to offer)*

partir *(to leave)*	je **pars** tu **pars** il **part**	nous **partons** vous **partez** ils **partent**	je **suis parti(e)**
pouvoir *(to be able, can)*	je **peux** tu **peux** il **peut**	nous **pouvons** vous **pouvez** ils **peuvent**	j'ai **pu**
prendre *(to take)*	je **prends** tu **prends** il **prend**	nous **prenons** vous **prenez** ils **prennent**	j'ai **pris**

Verbs like **prendre:** apprendre *(to learn)*, comprendre *(to understand)*

savoir *(to know)*	je **sais** tu **sais** il **sait**	nous **savons** vous **savez** ils **savent**	j'ai **su**
sortir *(to go out, get out)*	je **sors** tu **sors** il **sort**	nous **sortons** vous **sortez** ils **sortent**	je **suis sorti(e)**
venir *(to come)*	je **viens** tu **viens** il **vient**	nous **venons** vous **venez** ils **viennent**	je **suis venu(e)**

Verb like **venir:** revenir *(to come back)*

voir *(to see)*	je **vois** tu **vois** il **voit**	nous **voyons** vous **voyez** ils **voient**	j'ai **vu**

APPENDIX 4

C. IRREGULAR VERBS *continued*

INFINITIVE	*PRESENT*		*PASSÉ COMPOSÉ*
vouloir	je **veux**	nous **voulons**	j'ai voulu
(to want)	tu **veux**	vous **voulez**	
	il **veut**	ils **veulent**	

D. VERBS WITH *ÊTRE* IN THE *PASSÉ COMPOSÉ*

aller *(to go)*	je **suis allé(e)**	**passer** *(to go by, through)*	je **suis passé(e)**
arriver *(to arrive, come)*	je **suis arrivé(e)**	**rentrer** *(to go home)*	je **suis rentré(e)**
descendre *(to go down)*	je **suis descendu(e)**	**rester** *(to stay)*	je **suis resté(e)**
entrer *(to enter, go in)*	je **suis entré(e)**	**revenir** *(to come back)*	je **suis revenu(e)**
monter *(to go up)*	je **suis monté(e)**	**sortir** *(to go out, get out)*	je **suis sorti(e)**
mourir *(to die)*	il/elle **est mort(e)**	**tomber** *(to fall)*	je **suis tombé(e)**
naître *(to be born)*	je **suis né(e)**	**venir** *(to come)*	je **suis venu(e)**
partir *(to leave)*	je **suis parti(e)**		

French-English Vocabulary

The French-English vocabulary contains active and passive words from the text, as well as the important words of the illustrations used within the units. Obvious passive cognates have not been listed.

The numbers following an entry indicate the lesson in which the word or phrase is activated. R1, 2, or 3 indicates vocabulary from one of the **Rappel** sections in the **Reprise Unit**; (**I** stands for the list of classroom expressions at the end of the first **Images** section in Book 1A; **E** stands for **Entracte**, and **AX** stands for **Appendix**.)

Nouns: If the article of a noun does not indicate gender, the noun is followed by *m. (masculine)* or *f. (feminine)*. If the plural *(pl.)* is irregular, it is given in parentheses.

Adjectives: Adjectives are listed in the masculine form. If the feminine form is irregular, it is given in parentheses. Irregular plural forms *(pl.)* are also given in parentheses.

Verbs: Verbs are listed in the infinitive form. An asterisk (*) in front of an active verb means that it is irregular. (For forms, see the verb charts in Appendix 4C.) Irregular present tense forms are listed when they are used before the verb has been activated. Irregular past participle *(p.p.)* forms are listed separately.

Words beginning with an **h** are preceded by a bullet (•) if the **h** is aspirate; that is, if the word is treated as if it begins with a consonant sound.

A

a: **il y a** there is, there are [9]
à at, in, to [6], **14**
　à côté next door; next to
　à demain see you tomorrow [4B]
　à droite on (to) the right [13]
　à gauche on (to) the left [13]
　à la mode popular; in fashion; fashionable **17**
　à mon avis in my opinion **19**
　à partir de as of, beginning
　à pied on foot **14**
　à quelle heure? at what time? **R3**
　à qui? to whom? **R3**
　à samedi! see you Saturday! [4B]
　à vélo by bicycle **14**
abolir to abolish
abondant plentiful, copious, large
abord: d'abord (at) first **22**
un **abricot** apricot
absolument absolutely
un **accent** accent mark, stress
accepter to accept
des **accessoires** *m.* accessories **17**
un **accord** agreement
　d'accord okay, all right [5]
　être d'accord to agree [6], **AX**
un **achat** purchase
　faire des achats to go shopping **21**
acheter to buy **17, 18**
　acheter + du, de la *(partitive)* to buy (some) **26**

un **acteur, une actrice** actor, actress
une **activité** activity
l' **addition** *f.* check
adorer to love
une **adresse** address [13]
　quelle est ton adresse? what's your address? [13]
adroit skilled, skillful
un(e) **adulte** adult
aéronautique aeronautic, aeronautical
un **aéroport** airport
affectueusement affectionately *(at the end of a letter)*
une **affiche** poster [9]
affirmativement affirmatively
l' **Afrique** *f.* Africa
l' **âge** *m.* age
　quel âge a-t-il/elle? how old is he/she? [9], **R1**
　quel âge as-tu? how old are you? [2C], **R1**
　quel âge a ton père/ta mère? how old is your father/your mother? [2C]
âgé old
une **agence** agency
une **agence de tourisme** tourist office
une **agence de voyages** travel agency
agiter to shake
agité agitated
ah! ah!, oh!
ah bon? oh? really? [8]
ah non! ah, no!
ai *(see* **avoir***)*: **j'ai** I have [9]

j'ai… ans I'm … (years old) [2C]
aider to help **21, 27**
une **aile** wing
aimer to like [7], **25**
　est-ce que tu aimes…? do you like …? [5], **R3**
　j'aime… I like … [5], **R3**
　j'aimerais I would like
　je n'aime pas… I don't like … [5], **R3**
ainsi thus
aîné older
　un frère aîné older brother
　une soeur aînée older sister
ajouter to add
l' **Algérie** *f.* Algeria *(country in North Africa)*
　algérien (algérienne) Algerian
l' **Allemagne** *f.* Germany
allemand German
* **aller** to go **14**
　aller + inf. to be going to + *inf.* **14**
　allez *(see* **aller***)*: **allez-vousen** go away!
　allez-y come on!, go ahead!, do it!
　comment allez-vous? how are you? [1C]
allô! hello! *(on the telephone)*
allons *(see* **aller***)*: **allons-y** let's go! **14**
alors so, then [11]
une **alouette** lark
les **Alpes** *f.* (the) Alps
l' **alphabet** *m.* alphabet

French-English Vocabulary

l' **Alsace** f. Alsace (province in eastern France)
amener to bring (a person) 18, 27
américain American [1B, 11]
à l'américaine American-style
un **Américain, une Américaine** American person
l' **Amérique** f. America
un **ami, une amie** (close) friend [2A], **AX**
amicalement love (at the end of a letter)
l' **amitié** f. friendship
amitiés best regards (at the end of a letter)
amusant funny, amusing [11]
amuser to amuse
s'amuser to have fun
on s'est bien amusé! we had a good time!
un **an** year
avoir… ans to be … (years old) [10]
il/elle a… ans he/she is … (years old) [2C], **R1**
j'ai… ans I'm … (years old) [2C], **R1**
l'an dernier last year
par an per year
un **ananas** pineapple
ancien (ancienne) former, old, ancient
un **âne** donkey
un **ange** angel
anglais English [1B, 11]
un **Anglais, une Anglaise** English person
un **animal** (pl. **animaux**) animal
les **animaux domestiques** pets **AX**
une **animation** live entertainment
animé animated, lively
une **année** year [4B]
bonne année! Happy New Year! 24
toute l'année all year long
un **anniversaire** birthday [4B]
bon anniversaire! happy birthday! 24
c'est quand, ton anniversaire? when is your birthday? [4B], **AX**
mon anniversaire est le (2 mars) my birthday is (March 2nd) [4B], **AX**
un **annuaire** telephone directory
un **anorak** ski jacket
les **antiquités** f. antiquities, antiques

août m. August [4B], **AX**
un **appareil-photo** (pl. **appareils-photo**) (still) camera [9]
un **appartement** apartment [13]
s' **appeler** to be named, called
comment s'appelle…? what's …'s name? [2B]
comment s'appelle-t-il/elle? what's his/her name? [9]
comment t'appelles-tu? what's your name? [1A], **R1**
il/elle s'appelle… his/her name is … [2B]
je m'appelle… my name is … [1A], **R1**
apporter to bring (things) 18
apporter quelque chose à quelqu'un to bring something to someone 27
apporte-moi (apportez-moi) bring me [I]
* **apprendre (à)** + inf. to learn (to) 26
apprécier to appreciate
approprié appropriate
après after 21; after, afterwards 22, 23
d'après according to
l' **après-midi** m. afternoon 21
cet après-midi this afternoon 23
de l'après-midi in the afternoon, P.M. [4A]
demain après-midi tomorrow afternoon 23
hier après-midi yesterday afternoon 23
l' **arabe** m. Arabic (language)
un **arbre** tree
un arbre généalogique family tree
l' **arche** f. **de Noé** Noah's Ark
l' **argent** m. money 20
l'argent de poche allowance, pocket money
arrêter to arrest; to stop
arriver to arrive, come 14
j' arrive! I'm coming!
une arrivée arrival
un **arrondissement** district
un **artifice: le feu d'artifice** fireworks
un **artiste, une artiste** artist
as (see **avoir**): **est-ce que tu as…?** do you have …? [9]
un **ascenseur** elevator
un **aspirateur** vacuum cleaner
asseyez-vous! sit down! [I]
assez rather [11]; enough
assieds-toi! sit down! [I]

une **assiette** plate 25
assister à to go to, attend 21
associer to associate
athlétique athletic **AX**
l' **Atlantique** m. Atlantic Ocean
attendre to wait, wait for 20
attention f.: **faire attention** to be careful, pay attention [8]
attentivement carefully
au (à + le) to (the), at (the), in (the) [6], 14
au revoir! good-bye! [1C]
une **auberge** inn
une auberge de campagne country inn 27
aucun: ne… aucun none, not any
aujourd'hui today [4B], 23
aujourd'hui, c'est… today is … [4B]
aussi also, too [1B, 7]
aussi… que as … as 19
une **auto (automobile)** car, automobile [9]
une auto-école driving school
un autobus bus
un autocar touring bus 21
l' **automne** m. autumn, fall **AX**
en automne in (the) autumn, fall [4C]
autre other 25
d'autres others
un(e) autre another
aux (à + les) to (the), at (the), in (the) 14
avant before 21
avant hier the day before yesterday
en avant let's begin
avantageux (avantageuse) reasonable, advantageous
avec with [6]
avec moi, avec toi with me, with you [5]
avec qui? with who(m)? [8], **R3**
une **avenue** avenue [13]
un **avion** airplane, plane 21
en avion by airplane 21
un **avis** opinion
avis de recherche missing person's bulletin
à mon avis in my opinion 19
à votre avis in your opinion
* **avoir** to have [10]
avoir… ans to be … (years old) [10], **AX**
avoir besoin de to need 20

avoir chaud to be warm, hot 22

avoir de la chance to be lucky 22

avoir envie de to feel like, want 20

avoir faim to be hungry [10], **AX**

avoir froid to be cold 22

avoir lieu to take place

avoir raison to be right 22

avoir soif to be thirsty [10], 22, **AX**

avoir tort to be wrong 22

avril *m.* April [4B] , **AX**

le baby-foot tabletop soccer game

le babysitting: faire du babysitting to baby-sit

les bagages *m.* bags, baggage

bain: un maillot de bain bathing suit 17

un baladeur portable player [9], **AX**

une banane banana 25

une bande dessinée comic strip

des bandes dessinées comics

la Bannière étoilée Star-Spangled Banner

une banque bank

une barbe: quelle barbe! what a pain! *(colloq.)*

bas: en bas downstairs [13]

au bas at the bottom

le baseball baseball 15

basé based

le basket (basketball) basketball 15

jouer au basket to play basketball [5]

des baskets *m.* hightops (sneakers) 17

un bateau boat, ship 21

un bateau-mouche sightseeing boat

la batterie drums 15

battre to beat

bavard talkative

beau (bel, belle; *m.pl.* beaux) handsome, good-looking, beautiful [9, 12], 19

il est beau he is good-looking, handsome [9]

il fait beau it's beautiful (nice) out [4C]

un beau-frère stepbrother, brother-in-law

un beau-père stepfather, father-in-law

beaucoup (de) much, very much, many, a lot [7]

la beauté beauty

un bec beak

bel (*see* beau) beautiful, handsome 19

la Belgique Belgium

belle (*see* beau) beautiful [9, 12], 19

elle est belle she is beautiful [9]

une belle-mère stepmother, mother-in-law

une belle-soeur stepsister, sister-in-law

les Bermudes *f.* Bermuda

le besoin need

avoir besoin de to need, to have to 20

des besoins d'argent money needs

bête dumb, silly [11], **AX**

le beurre butter 25

une bibliothèque library [13]

une bicyclette bicycle [9], **AX**

bien well, very well, carefully [7]

bien sûr of course [5]

ça va bien everything's fine (going well) [1C]

ça va très bien I'm (everything's) very well [1C]

c'est bien that's good (fine) [12]

eh bien! well! 18

je veux bien (…) I'd love to (…), I do, I want to [5], 26

oui, bien sûr… yes, of course … [5]

très bien very well [7]

bientôt: à bientôt! see you soon!

bienvenue welcome

le bifteck steak

un bifteck de tortue turtle steak

bilingue bilingual

un billet bill, paper money 20; ticket

la biologie biology

une biscotte dry toast

blaff de poisson *m.* fish stew

blanc (blanche) white [E1, 12], **AX**

Blanche-Neige Snow White

blanchir to blanch, turn white

bleu blue [E1, 12], **AX**

blond blonde [9], **AX**

il/elle est blond(e) he/she is blond [9]

un blouson jacket 17

* boire to drink 26

une boisson drink, beverage [3B], 25

une boîte box

un bol deep bowl

bon (bonne) good [12]

bon marché *(inv.)* inexpensive 17

ah bon? oh, really? [8]

de bonne humeur in a good mood

il fait bon the weather's good (pleasant) [4C]

le bonheur happiness

bonjour hello [1A, 1C]

une botte boot 17

une bouche mouth [E2]

une boucherie butcher shop

le boudin sausage

une boulangerie bakery

un boulevard boulevard [13]

une boum party *(colloq.)* 14

une boutique boutique, shop 17

boxe: un match de boxe boxing match

un bras arm [E2]

brésilien (brésilienne) Brazilian

la Bretagne Brittany *(province in northwestern France)*

bricoler to do things around the house

broche: à la broche on the spit

bronzé tan

un bruit noise

brun brown, dark-haired [9], **AX**

il/elle est brun(e) he/she has dark hair [9]

brunir to turn brown

Bruxelles Brussels

le bulletin de notes report card

un bureau desk [I, 9]; office

un bus bus

en bus by bus 14

un but goal; end

ça that, it

ça fait combien? ça fait… how much is that (it)? that (it) is … [3C]

ça, là-bas that (one), over there [9]

FRENCH-ENGLISH VOCABULARY

ça va? how's everything? how are you? [1C]

ça va everything's fine, I'm OK [1C]

ça va (très) bien, ça va bien everything's going very well, everything's fine (going well) [1C]

ça va comme ci, comme ça everything's (going) so-so [1C]

ça va (très) mal things are going (very) badly [1C]

regarde ça look at that [9]

une **cabine d'essayage** fitting room

les **cabinets** *m.* toilet

un **cadeau** (*pl.* **cadeaux**) gift, present

cadet (cadette) younger

un **frère cadet** (a) younger brother

une **soeur cadette** (a) younger sister

le **café** coffee [3B]

un **café au lait** coffee with hot milk

un **café** café (*French coffee shop*) [6]

au **café** to (at) the café [6]

un **cahier** notebook [I, 9]

une **calculatrice** calculator [9]

un **calendrier** calendar

un **camarade, une camarade** classmate [9], **AX**

le **Cambodge** Cambodia (*country in Asia*)

un **cambriolage** burglary

un **cambrioleur** burglar

une **caméra** movie camera

la **campagne** countryside 21

à la **campagne** to (in) the countryside 21

une **auberge de campagne** country inn

le **Canada** Canada

canadien (canadienne) Canadian [1B, 11], **AX**

un **Canadien, une Canadienne** Canadian person

un **canard** duck

la **cantine de l'école** school cafeteria 25

un **car** touring bus 21

un **car scolaire** school bus

une **carotte** carrot 25

des **carottes râpées** grated carrots

un **carré** square

le **Vieux Carré** *the French Quarter in New Orleans*

une **carte** map [I]; card

une **carte postale** postcard

les **cartes** *f.* (playing) cards 15

jouer aux cartes to play cards 15

un **cas** case

en cas de in case of

une **casquette** (baseball) cap 17

une **cassette** cassette tape

une **cassette vidéo** videotape [9]

le **catch** wrestling

une **cathédrale** cathedral

une **cave** cellar

un **CD** CD, compact disc [9], **AX**

ce (c') this, that, it

ce n'est pas that's/it's not [12]

ce que what

ce sont these are, those are, they are [12]

c'est it's, that's [2A, 9, 12]

c'est + *day of the week* it's … [4B], **AX**

c'est + *name or noun* it's … [2A]

c'est bien/mal that's good/bad [12]

c'est combien? how much is that/it? [3C]

c'est le ([12] octobre) it's (October [12]) [4B], **AX**

qu'est-ce que c'est? what is it? what's that? [9]

qui est-ce? who's that/this? [9]

ce (cet, cette; ces) this, that, these, those 18

ce… -ci this… (over here) 18

ce mois-ci this month 23

ce n'est pas it's (that's) not [12]

ce soir this evening, tonight 23

un **cédérom (un CD-ROM)** CD-ROM

une **cédille** cedilla

une **ceinture** belt 17

cela that

célèbre famous

cent one hundred [2B], 17, **AX**

cent un, cent deux 101, 102, 17, **AX**

deux cents, trois cents, … neuf cents 200, 300, … 900 17

une **centaine** about a hundred

un **centime** centime (*1/100 of a euro*)

un **centre** center

un **centre commercial** shopping center [13]

les **céréales** *f.* cereal 25

une **cerise** cherry 25

certain certain

certains some of them

ces (*see* **ce**) these, those 18

c'est (*see* **ce**)

cet (*see* **ce**) this, that 18

cette (*see* **ce**) this, that 18

chacun each one, each person

une **chaise** chair [I, 9]

une **chaîne** (TV) channel

une **chaîne hi-fi** stereo set [9], **AX**

une **mini-chaîne** compact stereo

la **chaleur** heat, warmth

une **chambre** bedroom [9, 13]

un **champion, une championne** champion

la **chance** luck

avoir de la chance to be lucky 22

bonne chance! good luck! 23

une **chanson** song

chanter to sing [5, 7], **AX**

un **chanteur, une chanteuse** singer

un **chapeau** (*pl.* **chapeaux**) hat 17

chaque each, every

charmant charming

un **chat** cat [2C, E4]

un **château** (*pl.* **châteaux**) castle

chatter to chat (online)

chaud warm, hot

avoir chaud to be warm (hot) (*people*) 22

il fait chaud it's warm (hot) (*weather*) [4C]

chauffer to warm, heat up

un **chauffeur** driver

une **chaussette** sock 17

une **chaussure** shoe 17

un **chef** boss; chef

une **chemise** shirt 17

un **chemisier** blouse 17

cher (chère) expensive; dear 17

chercher to look for, to get, to find 17

je cherche… I'm looking for…17

un **cheval** (*pl.* **chevaux**) horse [E4]

les **cheveux** *m.* hair [E2]

chez + *person* at (to) someone's house 14; at (to) the office of

chez moi (toi, lui…) (at) home 15

chic (*inv.*) nice; elegant, in style

une **chic fille** a great girl

un **chien** dog [2C], **AX**

la **chimie** chemistry
chinois Chinese [11], **AX**
le **chinois** Chinese (language)
le **chocolat** hot chocolate, cocoa
[3B]
  une glace au chocolat
  chocolate ice cream
choisir to choose **19**
un **choix** choice
  au choix choose one, your
  choice
une **chorale** choir
une **chose** thing [9], **AX**
  quelque chose something
  24
chouette great, terrific [12], **17**
le **cidre** cider
un **cinéaste, une cinéaste** film
maker
un **cinéma** movie theater [13]
  au cinéma to (at) the movies,
  movie theater [6]
cinq five [1A]
cinquante fifty [1C]
cinquième fifth **16**
une **circonstance** circumstance
cité: la Cité Interdite Forbidden
City
une **clarinette** clarinet **15**
une **classe** class
  en classe in class [6]
classique classical
un **clavier** keyboard **15**
un **client, une cliente** customer
un **clip** music video
un **cochon** pig
un **coiffeur, une coiffeuse**
hairdresser
un **coin** spot
une **coïncidence** coincidence
le **Colisée** the Coliseum (a large
stadium built by the Romans)
des **collants** m. (pair of) tights,
pantyhose **17**
un **collège** junior high school
une **colonie** colony
une **colonne** column
combien how much **20**
  combien coûte…? how
  much does…cost? [3C], **17**
  combien de how much, how
  many **20**
  combien de temps? how
  long?
  combien d'heures? how
  many hours?
  ça fait combien? how much
  is this (it)? [3C]
  c'est combien? how much is
  this (it)? [3C]

commander to order
comme like, as, for
comme ci, comme ça so-so
  ça va comme ci, comme ça
  everything's so-so [1C]
commencer to begin, start
comment? how? [8], **R3**; what?
  comment allez-vous? how
  are you? [1C]
  comment est-il/elle? what's
  he/she like? what does
  he/she look like? [9]
  **comment dit-on… en
  français?** how do you say
  … in French? [I]
  comment lire reading hints
  comment s'appelle…?
  what's…'s name? [2B], **R1**
  comment s'appelle-t-il/elle?
  what's his/her name? [9]
  comment t'appelles-tu?
  what's your name? [1A]
  comment trouves-tu…?
  what do you think of…?
  17
  comment vas-tu? how are
  you? [1C]
un **commentaire** comment,
commentary
**commercial: un centre
commercial** shopping
center [13]
le **commérage** gossip
communiquer to communicate
un **compact (disc), un CD** compact
disc, CD [9]
complément object
compléter to complete
* **comprendre** to understand **26**
  je (ne) comprends (pas) I
  (don't) understand [I]
compter to count (on); to
expect, intend
concerne: en ce qui concerne
as for
un **concert** concert **14**
un **concombre** cucumber
la **confiture** jam **25**
confortable comfortable [13]
une **connaissance** acquaintance
  faire connaissance (avec) to
  become acquainted (with)
* **connaître** to know, be
acquainted with; (in passé
composé) to meet for the
first time **28**
  tu connais…? do you
  know…? are you
  acquainted with…? [2B]

connu (p.p. of **connaître**)
knew, met **28**
un **conseil** piece of advice, counsel
des **conseils** m. advice
un **conservatoire** conservatory
une **consonne** consonant
se **contenter** to limit oneself
le **contenu** contents
continuer to continue [13]
une **contradiction** disagreement
une **contravention** (traffic) ticket
cool cool, neat
un **copain, une copine** friend, pal
[2A]
  **un petit copain, une petite
  copine** boyfriend,
  girlfriend
copier to copy
une **copine** friend [2A]
coréen (coréenne) Korean
un **corps** body
correspondant corresponding
correspondre to correspond,
agree
la **Corse** Corsica (French island off
the Italian coast)
un **costume** man's suit
la **Côte d'Azur** Riviera (southern
coast of France on the
Mediterranean)
la **Côte d'Ivoire** Ivory Coast
(French-speaking country in
West Africa)
côté: à côté (de) next door;
next to
une **côtelette de porc** pork chop
le **cou** neck [E2]
une **couleur** color [12]
  de quelle couleur …? what
  color …? [12]
un **couloir** hall, corridor
coup: dans le coup with it
courage: bon courage! good
luck! **23**
courageux (courageuse)
courageous
le **courrier électronique** e-mail,
electronic mail
une **course** race
  faire les courses to go
  shopping (for food) **25**
court short **17**
un **cousin, une cousine** cousin
[2C], **16**
le **coût: le coût de la vie** cost of
living
un **couteau** (pl. **couteaux**) knife **25**
coûter to cost
  combien coûte…? how
  much does…cost? [3C], **17**

French-English Vocabulary *continued*

il (elle) coûte... it costs... [3C]
un **couturier, une couturière** fashion designer
un **couvert** place setting 25
un **crabe** crab
  des matoutou crabes stewed crabs with rice
la **craie** chalk
  un morceau de craie piece of chalk [I]
une **cravate** tie 17
un **crayon** pencil [I, 9]
  créer to create
un **crétin** idiot
une **crêpe** crepe (pancake) [3A]
une **crêperie** crepe restaurant
une **crevaison** flat tire
une **croisade** crusade
un **croissant** crescent (roll) [3A]
une **cuillère** spoon 25
  une cuillère à soupe soup spoon
la **cuisine** cooking 25
une **cuisine** kitchen [13]
  cuit cooked
  culturel (culturelle) cultural
  curieux (curieuse) curious, strange
la **curiosité** curiosity
le **cybercafé** internet café
un **cyclomoteur** moped

D

d'abord (at) first 22
d'accord okay, all right
  être d'accord to agree [6]
  oui, d'accord yes, okay [5]
une **dame** lady, woman *(polite term)* [2A], **AX**
les **dames** *f.* checkers *(game)* 15
  dangereux (dangereuse) dangerous
  dans in [9]
  danser to dance [5, 7], **AX**
la **date** date [4B], **AX**
  quelle est la date? what's the date? [4B]
de (d') of, from, about [6], 15
  de l'après-midi in the afternoon [4A]
  de quelle couleur...? what color ...? [12], **AX**
  de qui? of whom? [8]
  de quoi? about what?
  de temps en temps from time to time
  pas de not any, no [10]
débarquer to land

décembre *m.* December [4B], **AX**
décider (de) to decide (to)
une **déclaration** statement
  décoré decorated
* **découvrir** to discover
* **décrire** to describe
  décrivez... describe...
un **défaut** shortcoming
un **défilé** parade
  dégoûtant: c'est dégoûtant! it's (that's) disgusting 27
  dehors outside
  en dehors de outside of
  déjà already; ever
  déjeuner to eat (have) lunch 25
le **déjeuner** lunch 25
le **petit déjeuner** breakfast 25
  délicieux (délicieuse) delicious 26
  demain tomorrow [4B], **AX**
  à demain! see you tomorrow! [4B]
  demain, c'est... (jeudi) tomorrow is ... (Thursday) [4B]
  demander (à) to ask 28
  demandez ... ask ...
  demi half
  un demi-frère half-brother
  une demi-soeur half-sister
  demi: ... heures et demie half past ... [4A], **AX**
  midi et demi half past noon [4A], **AX**
  minuit et demi half past midnight [4A]
  démodé out of style, unfashionable 17
un **démon** devil
une **dent** tooth
un **départ** departure
se **dépêcher: dépêchez-vous!** hurry up!
  dépend: ça dépend that depends
une **dépense** expense
  dépenser to spend (money) 20
  dernier (dernière) last 23
  derrière behind, in back of [9], **R2**
  des some, any [10]; of (the), from (the), about (the) 15
la **description physique** physical description **AX**
le **désert** desert
  désirer to wish, want
  vous désirez? what would you like? may I help you? [3B], 17

  désolé sorry
le **dessert** dessert 25
le **dessin** art, drawing
un **dessin animé** cartoon
  détester to hate, detest [1C]
  deux two [1A], **AX**
  deuxième second 16
  le deuxième étage third floor
  devant in front of [9], **R2**
  développer to develop
  deviner to guess
* **devoir** to have to, should, must 27
un **devoir** homework assignment [I]
les **devoirs** *m.* homework
  faire mes devoirs to do my homework 21
  d'habitude usually
  différemment differently
  différent different
  difficile hard, difficult [12]
la **dignité** dignity
  dimanche *m.* Sunday [4B], **AX**
le **dîner** dinner, supper 25
  dîner to have dinner [7], 25
  dîner au restaurant to have dinner at a restaurant [5]
* **dire** to say, tell 28
  que veut dire...? what does...mean? [I]
  directement straight
un **directeur, une directrice** director, principal
  dirigé directed, guided
  dis! (*see* **dire**) say!, hey! [12]
  dis donc! say there!, hey there! [12]
  discuter to discuss
une **dispute** quarrel, dispute
  dit (*p.p. of* **dire**) said
  dit (*see* **dire**): **comment dit-on... en français?** how do you say...in French? [I]
  dites... (*see* **dire**) say..., tell...
  dix ten [1A, 1B], **AX**
  dix-huit eighteen [1B], **AX**
  dixième tenth 16
  dix-neuf nineteen [1B], **AX**
  dix-sept seventeen [1B], **AX**
un **docteur** doctor
  dois (*see* **devoir**): **je dois** I have to (must) [5], **R3**
  domestique domestic
  les animaux *m.* **domestiques** pets [2C]
  dommage! too bad! [7]
  donner (à) to give (to) 27, 28
  donne-moi... give me... [3A], [I]

donnez-moi... give me [3B], [I]

s'il te plaît, donne-moi... please, give me... [3B]

doré golden brown

* **dormir** to sleep

le **dos** back [E2]

une **douzaine** dozen 25

douze twelve [1B]

douzième twelfth 16

droit: tout droit straight [13]

droite right à droite to (on) the right [13]

drôle funny [12]

du (de + le) of (the), from (the) 15; some, any 26

du matin in the morning, A.M. [4A]

du soir in the evening, P.M. [4A]

dû (*p.p. of* **devoir**) had to 27

dur hard

des oeufs (*m.*) **durs** hard-boiled eggs

durer to last

un **DVD** DVD [9]

dynamique dynamic

l' **eau** *f.* (*pl.* **eaux**) water 25

l' **eau minérale** mineral water 25

un **échange** exchange

les **échecs** *m.* chess 15

une **éclosion** hatching

une **école** school [13]

économiser to save money

écouter to listen to [I], [7]

écouter la radio to listen to the radio [5]

écouter des CD to listen to CDs 21

l' **écran** *m.* screen (computer)

* **écrire** to write 28

l' **éducation** *f.* education

l' **éducation civique** civics

l' **éducation physique** physical education

une **église** church [13]

égyptien (égyptienne) Egyptian

eh bien! well! 18

électronique: une guitare électrique electric guitar

élégant elegant 17

un **éléphant** elephant [E4]

un **élève, une élève** pupil, student [9], **AX**

élevé high

elle she, it [3C, 6, 10]; her 15

elle coûte... it costs ... [3C]

elle est (canadienne) she's (Canadian) [2B]

elle s'appelle... her name is ... [2B]

embrasser: je t'embrasse love and kisses (*at the end of a letter*)

un **emploi du temps** time-table (*of work*)

emprunter à to borrow from

en in, on, to, by

en avion by airplane, plane 21

en bas (haut) downstairs (upstairs) [13]

en bus (métro, taxi, train, voiture) by bus (subway, taxi, train, car) 14

en ce qui concerne as for

en face opposite, across (the street)

en fait in fact

en famille at home

en plus in addition

en scène on stage

en solde on sale

va-t'en! go away! 14

un **endroit** place 14

un **enfant, une enfant** child 16

enfin at last 22

ensuite then, after that 22

entendre to hear 20

entier (entière) entire

l' **entracte** *m.* interlude

entre between

une **entrée** entry (*of a house*)

un **entretien** discussion

envers toward

l' **envie** *f.* envy; feeling

avoir envie de to want; to feel like, want to 20

envoyer to send

envoyer un mail to send an e-mail

épicé hot (spicy)

une **épicerie** grocery store

les **épinards** *m.* spinach

une **équipe** team

une **erreur** error, mistake

es (*see* **être**)

tu es + *nationality* you are ... [1B]

tu es + *nationality*? are you ...? [1B]

tu es de...? are you from ...? [1B]

l' **escalade** *f.* rock climbing 21

faire de l'escalade to go rock climbing 21

un **escalier** staircase

un **escargot** snail

l' **Espagne** *f.* Spain

espagnol Spanish [11], **AX**

parler espagnol to speak Spanish [5]

espérer to hope 18

un **esprit** spirit

essayer to try on, to try

l' **essentiel** *m.* the important thing

est (*see* **être**)

est-ce que (qu')...? *phrase used to introduce a question* [6]

c'est... it's ..., that's ... [2A, 2C, 12]

c'est le + *date* it's ... [4B]

il/elle est + *nationality* he/she is ... [2B]

n'est-ce pas...? isn't it? [6]

où est...? where is ...? [6]

quel jour est-ce? what day is it? [4B]

qui est-ce? who's that (this)? [2A, 9]

l' **est** *m.* east

et and [1B, 6]

et demi(e), et quart half past, quarter past [4A]

et toi? and you? [1A]

établir to establish

un **étage** floor of a building, story

les **États-Unis** *m.* United States

été (*p.p. of* **être**) been, was 23

l' **été** *m.* summer, **AX**

en été in (the) summer [4C]

l'heure d'été daylight savings time

étendre to spread

une **étoile** star

étrange strange

étranger (étrangère) foreign

* **être** to be [6]

être à to belong to

être d'accord to agree [6], **AX**

une **étude** study

un **étudiant, une étudiant(e)** (college) student [9], **AX**

étudier to study [5, 7]

eu (*p.p. of* **avoir**) had 23

il y a eu there was

euh... er ..., uh ...

euh non... well, no

un **euro** euro; monetary unit of Europe

européen (européenne) European

eux they, them **15**

eux-mêmes themselves

un **événement** event **14**

un **examen** exam, test

　réussir à un examen to pass an exam, a test

excusez-moi excuse me [13]

un **exemple** example

　par exemple for instance

un **exercice** exercise

　faire des exercices to exercise

exiger to insist

expliquer to explain

　expliquez… explain …

exprimer to express

exquis: c'est exquis! it's exquisite! **26**

extérieur: à l'extérieur outside

extraordinaire extraordinary

　il a fait un temps extraordinaire! the weather was great!

—— **F** ——

face: en face (de) opposite, across (the street) from

facile easy [12]

faible weak

la **faim** hunger

　avoir faim to be hungry **22**

　j'ai faim I'm hungry [3A]

　tu as faim? are you hungry? [3A]

faire to do, make [8]

　faire attention to pay attention, be careful [8], **AX**

　faire de + *activity* to do, play, study, participate in **21**

　faire des achats to go shopping **21**

　faire beau *(weather)* to be nice out **AX**

　faire les courses to go shopping **25**

　faire mauvais *(weather)* to be bad out **AX**

　faire mes devoirs to do my homework **21**

　faire les magasins to go shopping (browsing from store to store)

　faire partie de to be a member of

　faire sauter to flip

faire un match to play a game *(match)* [8], **AX**

faire un pique-nique to have a picnic **21**

faire un voyage to take a trip [8], **AX**

faire une promenade to take a walk [8]

faire une promenade à pied (à vélo, en voiture) to take a walk (a bicycle ride, a drive) **14**

fait *(p.p. of* **faire***)* did, done, made **23**

fait: en fait in fact

fait *(see* **faire***)***: ça fait combien?** how much is that (it)? [3C]

　ça fait… euros that's (it's) … euros [3C]

　il fait (beau, etc.**)** it's (beautiful, etc.) *(weather)* [4C]

　quel temps fait-il? what (how) is the weather? [4C]

fameux: c'est fameux! it's superb! **26**

familial with the family

une **famille** family [2C], **16**

　en famille at home

un **fana, une fana** fan *(person)*

un **fantôme** ghost

la **farine** flour

fatigué tired

faux (fausse) false [12]

favori (favorite) favorite

les **félicitations** *f.* congratulations

une **femme** woman [9], **AX**; wife **16**

une **fenêtre** window [I, 9]

fermer to close [I]

une **fête** party, holiday

le **feu d'artifice** fireworks

une **feuille** sheet, leaf [I]

une **feuille** de papier sheet of paper [I]

un **feuilleton** series, serial story *(in newspaper)*

février *m.* February [4B], **AX**

fiche-moi la paix! leave me alone! *(colloq.)* **28**

la **fièvre** fever

une **fille** girl [2A], **AX**; daughter **16**

un **film** movie **14, 21**

　un film policier detective movie

un **fils** son **16**

la **fin** end

finalement finally **22**

fini *(p.p. of* **finir***)* over, finished **23**

finir to finish **19**

flamand Flemish

un **flamant** flamingo

une **fleur** flower

un **fleuve** river

un **flic** cop *(colloq.)*

une **flûte** flute **15**

une **fois** time

　à la fois at the same time

la **folie: à la folie** madly

folklorique: une chanson folklorique folksong

fonctionner to work, function

fondé founded

le **foot (football)** soccer **15**

　le football américain football

　jouer au foot to play soccer [5]

une **forêt** forest

formidable great!

fort strong

　plus fort louder [I]

un **fouet** whisk

une **fourchette** fork **25**

la **fourrure** fur

　un manteau de fourrure fur coat

frais: il fait frais it's cool *(weather)* [4C], **AX**

une **fraise** strawberry **25**

un **franc** franc *(former monetary unit of France)* [3C]

　ça fait… francs that's (it's) … francs [3C]

français French [1B, 11]

　comment dit-on… en français? how do you say… in French? [I]

　parler français to speak French [5]

le **français** French *(language)*

un **Français, une Française** French person

la **France** France [6]

　en France in France [6]

francophone French-speaking

un **frère** brother [2C], **16**

des **frites** *f.* French fries **25**

　un steak-frites steak and French fries [3A]

froid cold

　avoir froid to be (feel) cold *(people)* **22**

　il fait froid it's cold out *(weather)* [4C]

le **fromage** cheese **25**

　un sandwich au fromage cheese sandwich

un **fruit** fruit **25**

furieux (furieuse) furious

une **fusée** rocket

G

gagner to earn, to win **20**
un **garage** garage [13]
un **garçon** boy [2A], **AX**; waiter
une **gare** train station
une **garniture** side dish
un **gâteau** (*pl.* **gâteaux**) cake **25**
gauche left
à gauche to (on) the left [13]
une **gelée** jelly
généralement generally
généreux (généreuse)
generous
la **générosité** generosity
génial brilliant: terrific [12]
des **gens** *m.* people [10], **AX**
gentil (gentille) nice, kind [11];
sweet
la **géographie** geography
une **girafe** giraffe [E4]
une **glace** ice cream [3A], **25;** mirror,
ice
glacé iced
un thé glacé iced tea **25**
un **goûter** afternoon snack
une **goyave** guava
grand tall [9]; big, large [12];
big (*size of clothing*) **17**
un grand magasin
department store **17**
une grande surface big
store, self-service store
grandir to get tall; to grow up
une **grand-mère** grandmother [2C],
16
un **grand-père** grandfather [2C],
16
les **grands-parents** *m.*
grandparents **16**
grec (grecque) Greek
un **grenier** attic
une **grillade** grilled meat
une **grille** grid
grillé: le pain grillé toast
une tartine de pain grillé
buttered toast
la **grippe** flu
gris gray [12], **AX**
gros (grosse) fat, big
grossir to gain weight, get fat
19
la **Guadeloupe** Guadeloupe
(*French island in the West
Indies*)
une **guerre** war
une **guitare** guitar [9], **15**
un **gymnase** gym

H

habillé dressed
habiter (à) to live (in + *city*) [7]
Haïti Haiti (*French island in the
West Indies*)
un **hamburger** hamburger [3A]
les **haricots** *m.* **verts** green beans
25
la **hâte** haste
en hâte quickly
haut high
en.haut upstairs [13]
plus.haut above
hélas! too bad!
hésiter to hesitate
l' **heure** *f.* time, hour; o'clock [4A]
… heure(s) (dix) (ten) past …
[4A], **AX**
… heure(s) et demie half
past … [4A], **AX**
… heure(s) et quart quarter
past … [4A], **AX**
… heure(s) moins (dix) (ten)
of … [4A], **AX**
… heure(s) moins le quart
quarter to … [4A], **AX**
à… heures at … o'clock [6],
AX
à quelle heure…? at what
time …? [8], **AX**
à quelle heure est…? at
what time is …? [4A], **AX**
il est… heure(s) it's … o'clock
[4A], **AX**
par heure per hour, an hour
quelle heure est-il? what
time is it? [4A]
heureux (heureuse) happy
hier yesterday **23**
avant-hier the day before
yesterday
un **hippopotame** hippopotamus
[E4]
une **histoire** story, history
l' **hiver** *m.* winter [4C], **AX**
en hiver in (the) winter [4C]
hollandais Dutch
un **homme** man [9]
honnête honest
un **hôpital** (*pl.* **hôpitaux**) hospital
[13]
une **horreur** horror
quelle horreur! what a
scandal! how awful!
un **hors-d'oeuvre** appetizer **25**
un **hot dog** hot dog [3A]
un **hôte, une hôtesse** host, hostess

un **hôtel** hotel [13]
un **hôtel de police** police
department
l' **huile** *f.* oil
huit eight [1A], **AX**
huitième eighth **16**
l' **humeur** *f.* mood
de bonne humeur in a good
mood
un **hypermarché** shopping center

 I

ici here [6]
une **idée** idea
c'est une bonne idée! it's
(that's) a good idea! **20**
ignorer to be unaware of
il he, it [3C, 6, 10]
il est it is [12]
il/elle est + *nationality*
he/she is … [2B]
il y a there is, there are [9],
R2
il y a + du, de la (*partitive*)
there is (some) **26**
il y a eu there was
il n'y a pas de… there is/are
no … [10], **R2**
est-ce qu'il y a…? is there,
are there …? [9]
qu'est-ce qu'il y a…? what
is there …? [9]
une **île** island
illustré illustrated
un **immeuble** apartment building
[13]
un **imper (imperméable)** raincoat
17
l' **impératif** *m.* imperative
(command) mood
impoli impolite
l' **importance** *f.* importance
ça n'a pas d'importance it
doesn't matter
importé imported
impressionnant impressive
l' **imprimante** *f.* printer
inactif (inactive) inactive
inclure to include
l' **indicatif** *m.* area code
indiquer to indicate, show
indiquez… indicate …
infâme: c'est infâme! that's
(it's) awful! **27**
infect: c'est infect! that's
revolting! (*colloq.*) **27**

les **informations** *f.* news
l' **informatique** *f.* computer science
s' **informer (de)** to find out about
un **ingénieur** engineer
un **ingrédient** ingredient 25
un **inspecteur, une inspectrice** police detective
un **instrument** instrument 15
  intelligent intelligent [11], **AX**
  intéressant interesting [11], **AX**
l' **intérieur** *m.* interior, inside
l' **Internet** *m.* the Internet
    surfer sur l'Internet (sur le Net) to surf the Internet
  interroger to question
  interviewer to interview
  inutilement uselessly
un **inventaire** inventory
un **invité, une invitée** guest
  inviter to invite [7]
  israélien (israélienne) Israeli
  italien (italienne) Italian [11], **AX**
un **Italien, une Italienne** Italian person

j' (*see* **je**)
  jamais ever; never
  jamais le dimanche! never on Sunday!
    ne... jamais never 24
la **Jamaïque** Jamaica
une **jambe** leg [E2]
un **jambon** ham 25
  janvier *m.* January [4B], **AX**
  japonais Japanese [11], **AX**
un **jardin** garden [13]
  jaune yellow [E1, 12], **AX**
  jaunir to turn yellow
  je I [6]
un **jean** pair of jeans 15
un **jeu** (*pl.* **jeux**) game 17
    les jeux d'ordinateur computer games
    les jeux télévisés TV game shows
    les jeux vidéo video games
  jeudi *m.* Thursday [4B], **AX**
  jeune young [9], **AX**
les **jeunes** *m.* young people
un **job** (part-time) job
le **jogging** jogging 21
    faire du jogging to jog 21

un **jogging** jogging suit 25
  joli pretty (*for girls, women*) 17; (*for clothing*) 17
    plus joli(e) que prettier than
  jouer to play [7]
    jouer à + *game, sport* to play a game, sport 15
    jouer aux jeux vidéo to play video games [5]
    jouer au tennis (volley, basket, foot) to play tennis (volleyball, basketball, soccer) [5]
    jouer de + *instrument* to play a musical instrument 15
un **jour** day [4B], 21
    le Jour de l'An New Year's Day
    par jour per week, a week
    quel jour est-ce? what day is it? [8], **AX**
un **journal** (*pl.* **journaux**) newspaper
une **journée** day, whole day
    bonne journée! have a nice day!
  joyeux (joyeuse) happy
  juillet *m.* July [8], **AX**
    le quatorze juillet Bastille Day (*French national holiday*)
  juin *m.* June [4B], **AX**
un **jumeau** (*pl.* **jumeaux**), **une jumelle** twin
une **jupe** skirt 17
le **jus** juice
    le jus d'orange orange juice [3B], 25
    le jus de pomme apple juice [3B], 25
    le jus de raisin grape juice [3B], **AX**
    le jus de tomate tomato juice [3B], **AX**
  jusqu'à until
  juste right, fair
    le mot juste the right word

un **kangourou** kangaroo [E4]
le **ketchup** ketchup 25
un **kilo** kilogram
    un kilo (de) a kilogram (of) 25

l' (*see* **le, la**)
la **the** [2B], [10]; her, it 28
là **here, there** [6]
    là-bas over there [6]
    ça, là-bas that (one), over there [9]
    ce... -là that ... (over there) 18
    oh là là! uh, oh!; oh, dear!; wow!; oh, yes!
  laid ugly
  laisser (un message) to leave (a message)
    laisser: laisse-moi tranquille! leave me alone! 28
le **lait** milk 25
une **lampe** lamp [9]
une **langue** language
  large wide
  laver to wash 21
se **laver** to wash (oneself), wash up
le **the** [2B], [10]; him, it 28
    le + *number* + *month* the ... [4B]
    le (lundi) on (Mondays) [10]
une **leçon** lesson
un **légume** vegetable 25
  lent slow
  les the [10]; them 28
une **lettre** letter
    leur(s) their 16
    leur (to) them 28
se **lever: lève-toi!** stand up! [I]
    levez-vous! stand up! [I]
un **lézard** lizard [E4]
le **Liban** Lebanon (*country in the Middle East*)
    libanais Lebanese
    libéré liberated
une **librairie** bookstore
  libre free
un **lieu** place, area
    avoir lieu to take place
une **ligne** line
  limité limited
la **limonade** lemon soda [3B]
un **lion** lion [E4]
 • **lire** to read
    comment lire reading hints
    lisez... (*see* **lire**) read ... [I]
une **liste** list
    une liste des courses shopping list
un **lit** bed [9], **AX**
un **living** living room (*informal*)

un **livre** book [I, 9]
une **livre** metric pound **25**
local (*m.pl.* **locaux**) local
une **location** rental
logique logical
logiquement logically
loin far [13]
loin d'ici far (from here)
le **loisir** leisure, free time
un **loisir** leisure-time activity
Londres London
long (longue) long **17**
longtemps (for) a long time
moins longtemps que for a shorter time
le **loto** lotto, lottery, bingo
louer to rent **21**
un **loup** wolf [E4]
lui him **15**; (to) him/her **28**
lui-même: en lui-même to himself
lundi *m.* Monday [4B], **AX**
des **lunettes** *f.* glasses **17**
des lunettes de soleil sunglasses **17**
le **Luxembourg** Luxembourg
un **lycée** high school

m' (*see* **me**)
M. (monsieur) Mr. (Mister) [1C]
ma my [2C], **16**
et voici ma mère and this is my mother [2C]
ma chambre my bedroom [9]
une **machine** machine
une machine à coudre sewing machine
Madagascar Madagascar (*French-speaking island off of East Africa*)
Madame (Mme) Mrs., ma'am [1C]
Mademoiselle (Mlle) Miss [1C]
un **magasin** store, shop [13], **17**
faire les magasins to go shopping (browsing from store to store)
un grand magasin department store **17**
magnétique magnetic
un **magnétophone** tape recorder
un **magnétoscope** VCR (videocassette recorder)
magnifique magnificent
mai *m.* May [4B], **AX**
maigre thin, skinny

maigrir to lose weight, get thin **19**
un **mail** e-mail
un **maillot de bain** bathing suit **17**
une **main** hand [E2]
maintenant now [7], **23**
mais but [6]
j'aime…, mais je préfère… I like …, but I prefer … [5]
je regrette, mais je ne peux pas… I'm sorry, but I can't … [5]
mais oui! sure! [6]
mais non! of course not! [6]
une **maison** house [13]
à la maison at home [6]
mal badly, poorly [1C], [7]
ça va mal things are going badly [1C]
ça va très mal things are going very badly [1C]
c'est mal that's bad [12]
malade sick
malheureusement unfortunately
malin clever
manger to eat [7], **AX**
j'aime manger I like to eat [5]
manger + du, de la (*partitive*) to eat (some) **26**
une salle à manger dining room [13]
un **manteau** (*pl.* **manteaux**) overcoat **17**
un manteau de fourrure fur coat
un **marchand, une marchande** merchant, shopkeeper, dealer
un **marché** open-air market **25**
un marché aux puces flea market
bon marché (*inv.*) inexpensive **17**
marcher to work, to run (*for objects*) [9], **AX**; to walk (*for people*) [9], **AX**
il/elle (ne) marche (pas) bien it (doesn't) work(s) well [9]
est-ce que la radio marche? does the radio work? [9]
mardi *m.* Tuesday [4B], **AX**
le Mardi gras Shrove Tuesday
un **mari** husband **16**
le **mariage** wedding, marriage
marié married
une **marmite** covered stew pot

le **Maroc** Morocco (*country in North Africa*)
une **marque** brand (name)
une **marraine** godmother
marrant fun
marron (*inv.*) brown [12]
mars *m.* March [4B], **AX**
martiniquais from Martinique
la **Martinique** Martinique (*French island in the West Indies*)
un **match** game, (sports) match **14**
faire un match to play a game, (sports) match [8]
les **maths** *f.* math
le **matin** morning **21**; in the morning **AX**
ce matin this morning **23**
demain matin tomorrow morning **23**
du matin in the morning, A.M. [4A]
hier matin yesterday morning **23**, **AX**
des **matoutou crabes** *m.* stewed crabs with rice
mauvais bad [12]
c'est une mauvaise idée that's a bad idea
il fait mauvais it's bad (weather) [4C]
la **mayonnaise** mayonnaise **25**
me (to) me **27**
méchant mean, nasty [11]
un **médecin** doctor
un médecin de nuit doctor on night duty
la **Méditerranée** Mediterranean Sea
meilleur(e) better, best **19**
mélanger to mix, stir
même same; even
eux-mêmes themselves
les mêmes choses the same things
une **mémoire** memory
mentionner to mention
la **mer** ocean, shore **21**
à la mer to (at) the sea **21**
merci thank you [1C]
oui, merci yes, thank you [5]
mercredi *m.* Wednesday [4B], **AX**
une **mère** mother [2C], **16**
mériter to deserve
mes my **16**
la **messagerie vocale** voice mail
le **métro** subway
en métro by subway **14**

* **mettre** to put on, to wear **17**; to put, to place, to turn on **18**
  mettre la table to set the table **25**
mexicain Mexican [11], **AX**
midi *m.* noon [4A]
  il est midi it is noontime **AX**
mieux better
mignon (mignonne) cute [11], **AX**
militaire military
mille one thousand [2B], **17**
minérale: l'eau *f.* **minérale** mineral water **25**
une **mini-chaîne** compact stereo [9]
minuit *m.* midnight [4A]
  il est minuit it is midnight **AX**
mis (*p.p. of* **mettre**) put, placed **23**
mixte mixed
Mlle Miss [1C]
Mme Mrs. [1C]
une **mob (mobylette)** motorbike, moped [9], **AX**
moche plain, ugly **17**
la **mode** fashion
  à la mode popular; in fashion; fashionable **17**
moderne modern [13]
moi me [1A], **15**; (to) me **27**
  moi, je m'appelle (Marc) me, my name is (Marc) [1A]
  avec moi with me [5]
  donne-moi give me [3A]
  donnez-moi give me [3B]
  excusez-moi… excuse me … [13]
  prête-moi… lend me … [3C]
  s'il te plaît, donne-moi… please give me … [3B]
un **moine** monk
moins less
  moins de less than
  moins… que less … than **19**
  …heure(s) moins (dix) (ten) of … [4A]
  …heure(s) moins le quart quarter of … [4A]
un **mois** month [4B], **21**
  ce mois-ci this month **23**
  le mois dernier last month **23**
  le mois prochain next month **23**
  par mois per month, a month
mon (ma; mes) my [2C], **16**
  mon anniversaire est le… my birthday is the … [4B]

  voici mon père this is my father [2C]
le **monde** world
  du monde in the world
  tout le monde everyone
la **monnaie** money; change
Monsieur (M.) Mr., sir [1C]
  un monsieur (*pl.* **messieurs**) gentleman, man (*polite term*) [2A]
une **montagne** mountain **21**
  à la montagne to (at) the mountains **21**
une **montre** watch [9], **AX**
montrer à to show … to **27, 28**
  montre-moi (montrez-moi) show me [I]
un **morceau** piece
  un morceau de craie piece of chalk [I]
un **mot** word
une **moto** motorcycle [9]
la **moutarde** mustard
un **mouton** sheep
moyen (moyenne) average, medium
en **moyenne** on the average
un **moyen** means
muet (muette) silent
le **multimédia** multimedia
un **musée** museum [13]
la **musique** music **15**

n' (*see* **ne**)
nager to swim [7], **AX**
  j'aime nager I like to swim [5]
une **nationalité** nationality [1B], **AX**
nautique: le ski nautique water-skiing **21**
ne (n')
  ne… aucun none, not any
  ne… jamais never **24**
  ne… pas not [6]
  ne… personne nobody **24**
  ne… plus no longer
  ne… rien nothing **24**
  n'est-ce pas? right?, no?, isn't it (so)?, don't you?, aren't you? [6]
né born
nécessaire necessary
négatif (négative) negative
négativement negatively
la **neige** snow
  neiger to snow
  il neige it's snowing [4C], **AX**

le **Net** the Internet
nettoyer to clean **21**
neuf nine [1A]
neuvième ninth **16**
un **neveu** (*pl.* **neveux**) nephew
un **nez** nose [E2]
une **nièce** niece
un **niveau** (*pl.* **niveaux**) level
Noël *m.* Christmas
  à Noël at Christmas **21**
noir black [E1, 12]
un **nom** name; noun
un **nombre** number
nombreux (nombreuses) numerous
nommé named
non no [1B, 6]
  non plus neither
  mais non! of course not! [6]
le **nord** north
le **nord-est** northeast
normalement normally
nos our **16**
une **note** grade
notre (*pl.* **nos**) our **16**
la **nourriture** food **25**
nous we [6]; us **15**; (to) us **27**
nouveau (nouvel, nouvelle; m.pl. nouveaux) new **19**
la **Nouvelle-Angleterre** New England
la **Nouvelle-Calédonie** New Caledonia (*French island in the South Pacific*)
novembre *m.* November [4B], **AX**
  le onze novembre Armistice Day
la **nuit** night
un **numéro** number

objectif (objective) objective
un **objet** object [9], **AX**
une **occasion** occasion; opportunity
occupé occupied
un **océan** ocean
octobre *m.* October [4B], **AX**
une **odeur** odor
un **oeil** (*pl.* **yeux**) eye [E2]
un **oeuf** egg **25**
officiel (officielle) official
offert (*p.p. of* **offrir**) offered
* **offrir** to offer, to give
oh là là! uh, oh!, oh, dear!, wow!, oh, yes!
un **oiseau** (*pl.* **oiseaux**) bird
une **omelette** omelet [3A]

on one, they, you, people **20**
  on est… today is …
  on va dans un café? shall we
    go to a café?
  on y va let's go
  comment dit-on… en
    français? how do you say
    … in French? [I]
un **oncle** uncle [2C], **16**
  onze eleven [1B], **AX**
  opérer to operate
l' **or** m. gold
  orange (inv.) orange (color) [E1,
    12]
  une orange orange (fruit)
  le jus d'orange orange juice
    [3B], **25**
un **ordinateur** computer [9]
un **ordinateur portable** laptop
    computer
une **oreille** ear [E2]
  organiser to organize [7]
  organiser une boum to
    organize a party **AX**
  originairement originally
l' **origine** f. origin, beginning
  d'origine bretonne from
    Brittany
  orthographiques: les signes m.
    orthographiques spelling
    marks
  ou or [1B, 6]
  où where [6, 8], **R3**
  où est…? where is …? [6]
  où est-ce? where is it? [13]
  d'où? from where? **15**
  oublier to forget
l' **ouest** m. west
  oui yes [1B, 6]
  oui, bien sûr… yes, of course
    … [5]
  oui, d'accord… yes, okay …
    [5]
  oui, j'ai… yes, I have … [9]
  oui, merci… yes, thank you
    … [5]
  mais oui! sure! [6]
un **ouragan** hurricane
un **ours** bear [E4]
  ouvert open
• **ouvrir** to open
  ouvre… (ouvrez…) open … [I]

le **pain** bread **25**
  pâle pale
un **pamplemousse** grapefruit **25**
une **panne** breakdown

une **panne d'électricité**
    power failure
un **pantalon** pants, trousers **17**
une **panthère** panther
une **papaye** papaya
le **papier** paper
  une feuille de papier a sheet
    (piece) of paper [I]
  Pâques m. Easter **21**
  à Pâques at Easter **21**
  par per
  par exemple for example
  par jour per day
un **parc** park [13]
  un parc public city park
  parce que (parce qu') because
    [8]
  pardon excuse me [13], **17**
les **parents** m. parents, relatives **16**
  paresseux (paresseuse) lazy
  parfait perfect
  rien n'est parfait nothing is
    perfect
  parfois sometimes
  parisien (parisienne) Parisian
  parler to speak, talk [I, 7]
  parler à to speak (talk) to **28**
  parler (français, anglais,
    espagnol) to speak
    (French, English, Spanish)
    [5]
un **parrain** godfather
une **partie** part
• **partir** to leave
  à partir de as of, beginning
  partitif (partitive) partitive
  pas not
  ne… pas not [6]
  pas de not a, no, not any
    [10], **26**
  pas du tout not at all,
    definitely not **15**
  pas possible not possible
  pas toujours not always [5]
  pas très bien not very well
le **passé composé** compound
    past tense
  passer to spend (time) **21**; to
    pass by
  passionnément passionately
une **pâte** dough
  patient patient
le **patinage** ice skating, roller
    skating
une **patinoire** skating rink
une **pâtisserie** pastry, pastry shop
une **patte** foot, paw (of bird or
    animal)
  pauvre poor **20**
  payer to pay, pay for **20**

un **pays** country
un **PC portable** laptop computer
la **peau** skin, hide
• **peindre** to paint
  peint painted
une **pellicule** film (camera)
  pendant during **21**
  pénétrer to enter
  pénible bothersome, a pain
    [12]
  penser to think **17**
  penser de to think of **17**
  penser que to think that **17**
  qu'est-ce que tu penses
    de…? what do you think
    of …? **17**
une **pension** inn, boarding house
  Pentecôte f. Pentecost
  perdre to lose, to waste **20**
  perdu (p.p. of **perdre**) lost
un **père** father [2C], **16**
• **permettre** to permit
un **perroquet** parrot
la **personnalité** personality **AX**
  personne (de) nobody **24**
  ne… personne nobody, not
    anybody, not anyone **24**
  une personne person [2A]
  personnel (personnelle)
    personal
  personnellement personally
  péruvien (péruvienne)
    Peruvian
  petit small, short [9, 12], **17**
  il/elle est petit(e) he/she is
    short [9]
  un petit copain, une petite
    copine boyfriend,
    girlfriend
  plus petit(e) smaller
  le petit déjeuner breakfast
    25
  prendre le petit déjeuner to
    have breakfast **25**
  le petit-fils, la petite-fille
    grandson, granddaughter
  les petits pois m. peas **25**
  peu little, not much
  un peu a little, a little bit [7]
  un peu de a few
  peut (see **pouvoir**)
  peut-être perhaps, maybe [6]
  peux (see **pouvoir**)
  je peux I can **R3**
  je ne peux pas I cannot **R3**
  est-ce que tu peux…? can
    you …? [5], **R3**
  je regrette, mais je ne peux
    pas… I'm sorry, but I can't
    … [5]

French-English Vocabulary *continued*

la **photo** photography
une **phrase** sentence [I]
la **physique** physics
un **piano** piano 15
une **pie** magpie [E4]
une **pièce** coin 20; room
un **pied** foot [E2]
   à pied on foot 14
   faire une promenade à pied to take a walk 14
   piloter to pilot (a plane)
une **pincée** pinch
le **ping-pong** Ping-Pong 15
un **pique-nique** picnic 14
   faire un pique-nique to have a picnic 21
une **piscine** swimming pool [13]
une **pizza** pizza [3A]
un **placard** closet
une **plage** beach [13]
   plaît: s'il te plaît please *(informal)* [3A]; excuse me (please)
   s'il te plaît, donne-moi… please, give me … [3B]
   s'il vous plaît please *(formal)* [3B]; excuse me (please)
un **plan** map
la **planche à voile** windsurfing 21
   faire de la planche à voile to windsurf 21
une **plante** plant
un **plat** dish, course *(of a meal)* 25
le **plat** principal main course
un **plateau** tray
   pleut: il pleut it's raining [4C], **AX**
   plier to fold
   plumer to pluck
   plus more
   plus de more than
   plus joli que prettier than
   plus… que more … than, …-er than 19
   en plus in addition
   le plus the most
   ne… plus no longer, no more
   non plus neither
   plusieurs several
une **poche** pocket
   l'argent *m.* **de poche** allowance, pocket money
une **poêle** frying pan
un **point de vue** point of view
une **poire** pear 25
   pois: les petits pois *m.* peas 25
un **poisson** fish [E4], 25
   un poisson rouge goldfish
   blaff de poisson fish stew

   poli polite
un **politicien, une politicienne** politician
un **polo** polo shirt 17
une **pomme** apple
   le jus de pomme apple juice [3B], 25
une **pomme de terre** potato 25
   une purée de pommes de terre mashed potatoes
le **porc: une côtelette de porc** pork chop
un **portable** cell phone [9]
une **porte** door [I, 9]
un **porte-monnaie** change purse, wallet
   porter to wear 17
   portugais Portuguese
   poser: poser une question to ask a question
une **possibilité** possibility
la **poste** post office
   pouah! yuck! yech!
une **poule** hen [E4]
le **poulet** chicken 25
   pour for [6]; in order to 21
   pour que so that
   pour qui? for whom? [8], **R3**
le **pourcentage** percentage
   pourquoi why **R3**[8]
   * **pouvoir** to be able, can, may 27
   pratique practical
   pratiquer to participate in
des **précisions** *f.* details
   préféré favorite
   préférer to prefer 18; to like (in general)
   je préfère I prefer [5], **R3**
   tu préférerais? would you prefer?
   premier (première) first 16
   le premier de l'an New Year's Day
   le premier étage second floor
   le premier mai Labor Day *(in France)*
   c'est le premier juin it's June first [4B]
   * **prendre** to take, to have *(food)* [I], 26
   prendre + du, de la *(partitive)* to have (some) 26
   prendre le petit déjeuner to have breakfast 25
un **prénom** first name
   préparer to prepare; to prepare for 21
   près nearby [13]

   près d'ici nearby, near here
   tout près very close
une **présentation** appearance
   la présentation extérieure outward appearance
des **présentations** *f.* introductions
   pressé in a hurry
   prêt ready
un **prêt** loan
   prêter à to lend to, to loan 27, 28
   prête-moi… lend me… [3C]
   principalement mainly
le **printemps** spring [4C], **AX**
   au printemps in the spring [4C]
   pris *(p.p. of* **prendre***)* took 26
un **prix** price
   quel est le prix …? what's the price …? 17
un **problème** problem
   prochain next 21, 23
   le week-end prochain next weekend 21
un **produit** product
un **prof, une prof** teacher *(informal)* [2A, 9], **AX**
un **professeur** teacher [9]
   professionnel (professionnelle) professional
un **programme** program
un **projet** plan
une **promenade** walk
   faire une promenade à pied to go for a walk [8], 14
   faire une promenade à vélo to go for a ride (by bike) 14
   faire une promenade en voiture to go for a drive (by car) 14
   * **promettre** to promise
une **promo** special sale
   proposer to suggest
   propre own
un **propriétaire, une propriétaire** landlord/landlady, owner
la **Provence** Provence *(province in southern France)*
   pu *(p.p. of* **pouvoir***)* could, was able to 27
   n'a pas pu was not able to
   public: un parc public city park
   un jardin public public garden
la **publicité** commercials, advertising, publicity
une **puce** flea
   un marché aux puces flea market

puis then, also
puisque since
un **pull** sweater, pullover **17**
les **Pyrénées** (the) Pyrenees
   *(mountains between France
   and Spain)*

qu' *(see* que*)*
une **qualité** quality
quand when [8], **R3**
   **c'est quand, ton
   anniversaire?** when is
   your birthday? [4B], **AX**
une **quantité** quantity **25**
quarante forty [1C], **AX**
un **quart** one quarter
   ... heure(s) et quart
   quarter past ... [4A], **AX**
   **... heure(s) moins le
   quart** quarter of ... [4A], **AX**
un **quartier** district, neighborhood
   [13]
   un joli quartier a nice
   neighborhood [13]
quatorze fourteen [1B], **AX**
quatre four [1A], **AX**
quatre-vingt-dix ninety [2B],
   AX
quatre-vingts eighty [2B], **AX**
quatrième fourth **16**
que that, which
   que veut dire...? what does
   ... mean? [I]
   qu'est-ce que (qu') what
   *(phrase used to introduce a
   question)* [8]
   qu'est-ce que c'est? what is
   it? what's that? [9]
   **qu'est-ce que tu penses
   de...?** what do you think
   of ...? **17**
   qu'est-ce que tu veux? what
   do you want? [3A]
   qu'est-ce qu'il y a? what is
   there? [9], **R2**; what's the
   matter?
   qu'est-ce qui ne va pas?
   what's wrong?
un **Québécois, une Québécoise**
   person from Quebec
québécois from Quebec
quel (quelle) what, which, what
   a **18**
   quel (quelle)...! what a...!
   **quel âge a ta mère/ton
   père?** how old is your
   mother/your father? [2C]

quel âge a-t-il/elle? how old
   is he/she? [9]
quel âge as-tu? how old are
   you? [2C]
quel est le prix...? what is
   the price ...? **17**
quel jour est-ce? what day is
   it? [4B], **AX**
quel temps fait-il? what's
   (how's) the weather? [4C]
quelle est la date? what's the
   date? [4B], **AX**
quelle est ton adresse?
   what's your address? [13]
quelle heure est-il? what
   time is it? [4A], **AX**
à quelle heure? at what
   time? [4A], **AX**
à quelle heure est...? at
   what time is ...? [4A], **AX**
de quelle couleur...? what
   color is ...? [12], **AX**
quelqu'un someone **24**
quelque chose something **24**
quelques some, a few [9]
une **question** question
une **queue** tail
qui who, whom [8]
   qui est-ce? who's that (this)?
   [2A, 9]
   qui se ressemble... birds of a
   feather ...
   à qui? to whom? [8]
   avec qui? with who(m)? [8]
   c'est qui? who's that? *(casual
   speech)*
   de qui? about who(m)? [8]
   pour qui? for who(m)? [8]
qui? whom? **R3**
quinze fifteen [1B], **AX**
quoi? what? [9]
quotidien (quotidienne) daily
   la vie quotidienne daily life

raconter to tell about
une **radio** radio [9], **AX**
   écouter la radio to listen to
   the radio [5]
   une radiocassette boom box
   [9], **AX**
   une radiocassette/CD boom
   box with CD
raisin: le jus de raisin grape
   juice [3B]
une **raison** reason **avoir raison** to
   be right **22**
ranger to pick up **21**

rapidement rapidly
un **rapport** relationship
une **raquette** racket [9], **AX**
   une raquette de tennis
   tennis racket **15**
rarement rarely, seldom [7]
un **rayon** department *(in a store)*
réalisé made, directed
récemment recently
une **recette** recipe
**recherche: un avis de
   recherche** missing
   person's bulletin
un **récital** *(pl.* récitals*)* *(musical)*
   recital
reconstituer to reconstruct
un **réfrigérateur** refrigerator
refuser to refuse
regarder to look at, watch [I, 7]
   regarde ça look at that [9]
   regarder la télé to watch TV
   [5], **AX**
un **régime** diet
   être au régime to be on a
   diet
régional *(m.pl.* régionaux*)*
   regional
regretter to be sorry
   je regrette, mais... I'm sorry,
   but ... [5]
régulier (régulière) regular
une **reine** queen
rencontrer to meet **21**
une **rencontre** meeting, encounter
un **rendez-vous** date,
   appointment **14**
   j'ai un rendez-vous à... I
   have a date, appointment
   at ... [4A]
rendre visite à to visit, come to
   visit **20, 28**
la **rentrée** first day back at school
   in fall
rentrer to go back, come back
   22; to return, go back,
   come back **14**
réparer to fix, repair **21**
un **repas** meal **25**
* **repeindre** to repaint
répéter to repeat [I]
répondre (à) to answer,
   respond (to) [I], **28**
   répondez-lui (moi) answer
   him (me)
   répondre que oui to answer
   yes
une **réponse** answer
un **reportage** documentary
représenter to represent
réservé reserved

une **résolution** resolution
un **restaurant** restaurant [13]
   au restaurant to (at) the restaurant [6]
   dîner au restaurant to have dinner at a restaurant [5]
   un restaurant trois étoiles three star restaurant
  rester to stay **14, 24**
  retard: un jour de retard one day behind
   en retard late
  retourner to return; to turn over
  réussir to succeed **19**
   réussir à un examen to pass an exam **19**
* **revenir** to come back **15**
  revoir: au revoir! good-bye! [1C]
le **rez-de-chaussée** ground floor
un **rhinocéros** rhinoceros [E4]
  riche rich **20**
  rien (de) nothing **24**
   rien n'est parfait nothing is perfect
   ne... rien nothing **24**
une **rive** (river) bank
une **rivière** river, stream
le **riz** rice **25**
une **robe** dress **17**
le **roller** in-line skating **21**
   faire du roller to go in-line skating **21**
   des rollers in-line skates **21**
  romain Roman
le **rosbif** roast beef **25**
  rose pink [12], **AX**
  rosse nasty *(colloq.)*
une **rôtie** toast *(Canadian)*
  rôtir to roast
une **roue** wheel
  rouge red [E1, 12]
  rougir to turn red
  rouler to roll
  roux (rousse) red-head
une **rue** street [13]
   dans la rue (Victor Hugo) on (Victor Hugo) street [13]
  russe Russian

(S)

  sa his, her **16**
un **sac** book bag, bag [I]; bag, handbag [9], **AX**
  sais (*see* **savoir**)
je **sais** I know [I, 9], **28**

  je ne sais pas I don't know [I, 9]
  tu sais you know **28**
une **saison** season [4C]
   toute saison all year round (any season)
une **salade** salad [3A], **25**; lettuce **25**
un **salaire** salary
une **salle** hall, large room
   une salle à manger dining room [13]
   une salle de bains bathroom [13]
   une salle de séjour informal living room
un **salon** formal living room [13]
  salut hi!, good-bye! [1C]
une **salutation** greeting
  samedi Saturday [4B], **23**
   samedi soir Saturday night
   à samedi! see you Saturday! [4B]
   le samedi on Saturdays [10]
une **sandale** sandal **17**
un **sandwich** sandwich [3A], **AX**
  sans without
des **saucisses** *f.* sausages
le **saucisson** salami **25**
* **savoir** to know *(information)*
je **sais** I know [I, 9], **28**
   je ne sais pas I don't know [I, 9]
   tu sais you know **28**
un **saxo (saxophone)** saxophone **15**
une **scène** scene, stage
les **sciences** *f.* **économiques** economics
les **sciences** *f.* **naturelles** natural science
un **scooter** motor scooter [9], **AX**
  second second
  seize sixteen [1B]
un **séjour** stay; informal living room
le **sel** salt **25**
  selon according to
   selon toi in your opinion
une **semaine** week [4B], **21**
   cette semaine this week **23**
   la semaine dernière last week **23**
   la semaine prochaine next week **23**
   par semaine per week, a week
  semblable similar
le **Sénégal** Senegal *(French-speaking country in Africa)*

  sensationnel (sensationnelle) sensational
  séparer to separate
  sept seven [1A], **AX**
  septembre *m.* September [4B], **AX**
  septième seventh **16**
une **série** series
  sérieux (sérieuse) serious
un **serveur, une serveuse** waiter, waitress
  servi served
une **serviette** napkin **25**
  ses his, her **16**
  seul alone, only; by oneself **21**
  seulement only, just
un **short** shorts **17**
  si if, whether
  si! so, yes! *(to a negative question)* [10]
un **signal** (*pl.* **signaux**) signal
un **signe** sign
   un signe orthographique spelling mark
un **singe** monkey [E4]
  situé situated
  six six [1A], **AX**
  sixième sixth **16**
le **skate** skateboarding **21**
un **skate** skateboard **21**
   faire du skate to go skateboarding **21**
le **ski** skiing
   le ski nautique water-skiing **21**
   faire du ski to ski **21**
   faire du ski nautique to go water-skiing **21**
   skier to ski
  snob snobbish
le **snowboard** snowboarding **21**
   faire du snowboard to go snowboarding **21**
   un snowboard snowboard **21**
la **Société Nationale des Chemins de Fer (SNCF)** *French railroad system*
une **société** society
un **soda** soda [3B]
une **soeur** sister [2C], **16**
la **soie** silk
la **soif** thirst
   avoir soif to be thirsty **22**
   j'ai soif I'm thirsty [3B]
   tu as soif? are you thirsty? [3B]
un **soir** evening **21**
   ce soir this evening, tonight **23**

demain soir tomorrow night (evening) **21, 23**
du soir in the evening, P.M. [4A]
hier soir last night **23**
le soir in the evening
une soirée (whole) evening; (evening) party
soixante sixty [1C, 2A], **AX**
soixante-dix seventy [2A], **AX**
un **soldat** soldier
un **solde** (clearance) sale **en solde** on sale
la **sole** sole (*fish*) **25**
le **soleil** sun
les lunettes *f.* **de soleil** sunglasses **17**
sommes (*see* **être**)
nous sommes… it is, today is … (*date*)
son (sa; ses) his, her **16**
un **sondage** poll
une **sorte** sort, type, kind
* **sortir** to leave, come out
un **souhait** wish
la **soupe** soup **25**
une **souris** mouse (computer)
sous under [9], **R2**
le **sous-sol** basement
souvent often [7]
soyez (*see* **être**): soyez
les **spaghetti** *m.* spaghetti **25**
spécialement especially
spécialisé specialized
une **spécialité** specialty
le **sport** sports **15, 21**
faire du sport to play sports **21**
des vêtements *m.* **de sport** sports clothing **17**
une voiture de sport sports car **15**
sportif (sportive) athletic [11]
un **stade** stadium [13]
un **stage** sports training camp; internship
une **station-service** gas station
un **steak** steak [3A]
un steak-frites steak and French fries [3A]
un **stylo** pen [I, 9]
le **sucre** sugar **25**
le **sud** south
suggérer to suggest
suis (*see* **être**)
je suis + *nationality* I'm … [1B]
je suis de… I'm from… [1B]
suisse Swiss [11], **AX**
la **Suisse** Switzerland

suivant following
suivi followed
un **sujet** subject, topic
super terrific [7]; great [12], **17**
un **supermarché** supermarket [13]
supersonique supersonic
supérieur superior
supplémentaire supplementary, extra
sur on [9], **R2**; about
sûr sure, certain
bien sûr! of course! [6]
oui, bien sûr…! yes, of course …! [5]
tu es sûr(e)? are you sure? **16**
sûrement surely
la **surface: une grande surface** big store, self-service store
surfer to go snowboarding
surfer sur l'Internet (sur le Net) to surf the Internet
surtout especially
un **survêtement** jogging or track suit **17**
un **sweat** sweatshirt **17**
une **sweaterie** shop specializing in sweatshirts and sportswear
sympa nice, pleasant (*colloq.*)
sympathique nice, pleasant [11], **AX**
une **synagogue** Jewish temple or synagogue
un **synthétiseur** electronic keyboard, synthesizer

t' (*see* **te**)
ta your [2C], **16**
une **table** table [I, 9]
mettre la table to set the table **25**
un **tableau** (*pl.* **tableaux**) chalkboard [I]
Tahiti Tahiti (*French island in the South Pacific*)
une **taille** size
de taille moyenne of medium height or size
un **tailleur** woman's suit
se **taire: tais-toi!** be quiet!
une **tante** aunt [2C], **16**
la **tarte** pie **25**
une **tasse** cup **25**
un **taxi** taxi
en taxi by taxi **14**
te (to) you **27**
un **tee-shirt** T-shirt **17**

la **télé** TV [9], **AX**
à la télé on TV
regarder la télé TV [5]
télécharger to download
un **téléphone** telephone [9], **AX**
téléphoner (à) to call, phone [5], [7], **28, AX**
télévisé: des jeux *m.* **télévisés** TV game shows
un **temple** Protestant church
le **temps** time; weather
combien de temps? how long?
de temps en temps from time to time
quel temps fait-il? what's (how's) the weather? [4C]
tout le temps all the time
le **tennis** tennis **15**
jouer au tennis to play tennis [5]
des tennis *m.* tennis shoes, sneakers **17**
un **terrain de sport** (playing) field
une **terrasse** outdoor section of a café, terrace
la **terre** earth
une pomme de terre potato **25**
terrifiant terrifying
tes your **16**
la **tête** head [E2]
le **thé** tea [3B]
un thé glacé iced tea **25**
un **théâtre** theater [13]
le **thon** tuna **25**
tiens! look!, hey! [2A, 10]
un **tigre** tiger [E4]
timide timid, shy [11], **AX**
le **tissu** fabric
un **titre** title
toi you **15**
avec toi with you [5]
et toi? and you? [1A]
les **toilettes** *f.* bathroom, toilet [13]
un **toit** roof
une **tomate** tomato **25**
le jus de tomate tomato juice [3B]
un **tombeau** tomb
ton (ta; tes) your [2C], **16 c'est quand, ton anniversaire?** when's your birthday? [4B]
tort: avoir tort to be wrong **22**
une **tortue** turtle [E4]
un bifteck de tortue turtle steak
toujours always [7]
je n'aime pas toujours… I don't always like … [5]

un **tour** turn
    à votre tour it's your turn
la **Touraine** Touraine (*province in central France*)
    tourner to turn [13]
la **Toussaint** All Saints' Day (*November 1*)
    tout (toute; tous, toutes) all, every, the whole
    tous les jours every day
    tout ça all that
    tout le monde everyone
    tout le temps all the time
    toutes sortes all sorts, kinds
    tout completely, very
    tout droit straight [13]
    tout de suite right away
    tout près very close
    tout all, everything
    pas du tout not at all 15
un **train** train 21
    tranquille quiet
    laisse-moi tranquille! leave me alone! 28
un **travail** (*pl.* **travaux**) job
    travailler to work [5, 7], **AX**
une **traversée** crossing
    treize thirteen [1B], **AX**
    trente thirty [1C], **AX**
un **tréma** diaeresis
    très very [11]
    très bien very well [7]
    ça va très bien things are going very well [1C]
    ça va très mal things are going very badly [1C]
    trois three [1A], **AX**
    troisième third 16; *9th grade in France*
    trop too, too much 17
    trouver to find, to think of 17
    comment trouves-tu...? what do you think of ...? how do you find ...? 17
    s'y trouve is there
    tu you [6]
la **Tunisie** Tunisia (*country in North Africa*)

U

    un, une one [1A]; a, an [2A], [10]
    unique only
    uniquement only
une **université** university, college
l' **usage** *m.* use
un **ustensile** utensil
    utile useful

    utiliser to use
    en utilisant (by) using
    utilisez... use ...

V

    va (*see* **aller**)
    va-t'en! go away! 14
    ça va? how are you? how's everything? [1C]
    ça va! everything's fine (going well); fine, I'm OK [1C]
    on va dans un café? shall we go to a café?
    on y va let's go
les **vacances** *f.* vacation
    bonnes vacances! have a nice vacation!
    en vacances on vacation [6]
    les grandes vacances summer vacation 21
une **vache** cow
    vais (*see* **aller**): **je vais** I'm going 14
la **vaisselle** dishes
    faire la vaisselle to do the dishes
    valable valid
une **valise** suitcase
    vanille: une glace à la vanille vanilla ice cream
    varié varied
les **variétés** *f.* variety show
    vas (see **aller**)
    comment vas-tu? how are you? [1C]
    vas-y! come on!, go ahead!, do it! 14
le **veau** veal 25
une **vedette** star
un **vélo** bicycle [9], **AX**
    à vélo by bicycle 14
    faire une promenade à vélo to go for a bicycle ride 14
    un vélo tout terrain (un VTT) mountain bike
un **vendeur, une vendeuse** salesperson
    vendre to sell 20
    vendredi *m.* Friday [4B], **AX**
    vendu (*p.p. of* **vendre**) sold 23
*   **venir** to come 15
le **vent** wind
une **vente** sale
le **ventre** stomach [E2]
    venu (*p.p. of* **venir**) came, come 24
    vérifier to check

la **vérité** truth
un **verre** glass 25
    verser to pour
    vert green [E1, 12], **AX**
    les haricots *m.* **verts** green beans 25
une **veste** jacket 17
des **vêtements** *m.* clothing 17
    des vêtements de sport sports clothing 17
    veut (*see* **vouloir**): **que veut dire...?** what does ... mean? [I]
    veux (*see* **vouloir**)
    est-ce que tu veux...? do you want ...? [5], **R3**
    je ne veux pas... I don't want ... [5], **R3**
    je veux... I want ... [5], **26**, **R3**
    je veux bien... I'd love to, I do, I want to ... [5], **26**
    qu'est-ce que tu veux? what do you want? [3A]
    tu veux...? do you want ...? [3A]
la **viande** meat 25
la **vie** life
    la vie quotidienne daily life
    viens (*see* **venir**)
    viens... come ... [I]
    oui, je viens yes, I'm coming along with you
    vieux (vieil, vieille; *m.pl.* **vieux)** old 19
    le Vieux Carré *the French Quarter in New Orleans*
le **Viêt-nam** Vietnam (*country in Southeast Asia*)
    vietnamien (vietnamienne) Vietnamese
une **vigne** vineyard
un **village** town, village [13]
    un petit village small town [13]
une **ville** city
    en ville in town, [6]
    une grande ville big city, town [13]
le **vin** wine
    vingt twenty [1B, 1C], **AX**
    violet (violette) purple, violet [E1]
un **violon** violin 15
une **visite** visit
    rendre visite à to visit (*a person*) **20, 28**
    visiter to visit (*places*) **23, 20**
    vite! fast!, quick!

vive: vive les vacances! three cheers for vacation!

* **vivre** to live

le **vocabulaire** vocabulary

voici... here is, this is..., here come(s) ... [2A]
   voici + du, de la *(partitive)* here's some **26**
   voici mon père/ma mère here's my father/my mother [2C]

voilà... there is ..., there come(s) ... [2A]
   voilà + du, de la *(partitive)* there's some **26**

la **voile** sailing **21**
   faire de la voile to sail **21**
   la planche à voile windsurfing **21**

* **voir** to see **21, 23**
   voir un film to see a movie **21**

un **voisin, une voisine** neighbor [9], **AX**

une **voiture** car [9], **AX**
   une voiture de sport sports car **15**
   en voiture by car **14**
   faire une promenade en voiture to go for a drive by car **14**

une **voix** voice

le **volley (volleyball)** volleyball **15**

un **volontaire, une volontaire** volunteer
   comme volontaire as a volunteer

vos your **16**

votre *(pl.* **vos***)* your **16**

voudrais *(see* **vouloir***)*: **je voudrais** I'd like [3A, 3B, 5], **26**

* **vouloir** to want **26**
vouloir + du, de la *(partitive)* to want some (of something) **26**
vouloir dire to mean **26**
voulu *(p.p. of* **vouloir***)* wanted **26**

vous you [6]; (to) you **27**
   vous désirez? what would you like? may I help you? [3B], **17**
   s'il vous plaît please [3B]

un **voyage** trip
   bon voyage! have a nice trip!
   faire un voyage to take a trip [8]

voyager to travel [5, 7], **AX**

vrai true, right, real [12]

vraiment really **15**

le **VTT** mountain biking **21**
   faire du VTT to go mountain biking **21**
   un VTT mountain bike **21**

vu *(p.p. of* **voir***)* saw, seen **23**

une **vue** view
   un point de vue point of view

W

---

les **WC** *m.* toilet

un **week-end** weekend **22, 23**
   bon week-end! have a nice weekend!
   ce week-end this weekend **21, 23**
   le week-end on weekends
   le week-end dernier last weekend **23**
   le week-end prochain next weekend **21, 23**

Y

---

y there
   il y a there is, there are [9]
   est-ce qu'il y a...? is there ...?, are there ...? [9]
   qu'est-ce qu'il y a? what is there? [9]
   allons-y! let's go! **14**
   vas-y! come on!, go ahead!, do it! **14**

le **yaourt** yogurt **25**

des **yeux** *m.* *(sg.* **oeil***)* eyes [E2]

Z

---

un **zèbre** zebra

zéro zero [1A], **AX**

zut! darn! [1C]

English-French Vocabulary

The English-French vocabulary contains only active vocabulary.

The numbers following an entry indicate the lesson in which the word or phrase is activated. (**I** stands for the list of classroom expressions at the end of the first **Images** section in Book 1A; **E** stands for **Entracte**, and **AX** stands for **Appendix**.)

Nouns: If the article of a noun does not indicate gender, the noun is followed by *m. (masculine)* or *f. (feminine)*. If the plural *(pl.)* is irregular, it is given in parentheses.

Verbs: Verbs are listed in the infinitive form. An asterisk (*) in front of an active verb means that it is irregular. (For forms, see the verb charts in Appendix 4C.)

Words beginning with an **h** are preceded by a bullet (•) if the **h** is aspirate; that is, if the word is treated as if it begins with a consonant sound.

 A

a, an un, une [2A], [10]
  a few quelques 25
  a little (bit) un peu [7]
  a lot beaucoup [7]
able: to be able (to) *pouvoir 27
about de 15
  about whom? de qui? [8], **AX**
accessories des accessoires *m.* 17
acquainted: to be acquainted with *connaître 28
  are you acquainted with …? tu connais…? [2B]
address une adresse [13]
  what's your address? quelle est ton adresse? [13]
after après 21, 22
  after that ensuite 22
  afterwards après 22
afternoon l'après-midi *m.* 21
  in the afternoon de l'après-midi [4A]
  this afternoon cet après-midi 23
  tomorrow afternoon demain après-midi 23
  yesterday afternoon hier après-midi 23
to agree *être d'accord [6]
airplane un avion 21
  by airplane en **avion** 21
all tout
  all right d'accord [5]
  not at all pas du tout 15
alone seul 21
  leave me alone! laisse-moi tranquille! 28
also aussi [1B, 7]

always toujours [7]
  not always pas toujours [5]
A.M. du matin **[4A]**
am (*see* **to be**)
  I am … je suis + *nationality* [1B]
American américain 2, 19, **AX**
  I'm American je suis américain(e) [1B, 11]
amusing amusant [11]
an un, une [2A, 10]
and et [1B, 6]
  and you? et toi? [1A]
annoying pénible [12]
another un(e) autre
to answer répondre (à) 28
any des [10]; du, de, la, de l', de 26
  not any pas de [10], 26
anybody: not anybody ne… personne 24
anyone quelqu'un 24
anything quelque chose 24
  not anything ne… rien 24
apartment un appartement [13]
  apartment building un immeuble [13]
appetizer un • hors-d'oeuvre 25
apple une pomme
  apple juice le jus de pomme [3B], 25
appointment un rendez-vous 14
  I have an appointment at… j'ai un rendez-vous à… [4A]
April avril *m.* [4B], **AX**
are (*see* **to be**)
  are there? est-ce qu'il y a? [9]
  are you…? tu es +

  nationality? [1B]
  there are il y a [9]
  these/those/they are ce sont [12]
arm un bras [E2]
to arrive arriver 14
as … as aussi… que 19
to ask demander (à) 28
at à [6]; chez 14
  at (the) au, à la, à l', aux 14
  at …'s house chez … 14
  at … o'clock à … heure(s) [6], **AX**
  at home à la maison [6]
  at last enfin 22
  at the restaurant au restaurant [6]
  at what time? à quelle heure? [4A, 8], **R3**
  at what time is …? à quelle heure est …? [4A], **AX**
athletic sportif (sportive) [11]
to attend assister à 21
  attention: to pay attention *faire attention [8]
August août *m.* [4B], **AX**
aunt une tante [2C], 16
automobile une auto, une voiture [9], **AX**
autumn l'automne *m.*, **AX**
  in (the) autumn en automne [4C]
avenue une avenue [13]
away: go away! va-t'en! 14

 B

back le dos [E2]
back: to come back rentrer 14, 24; *revenir 15

to go back rentrer **14, 24**
in back of derrière [9]
bad mauvais [12], **AX**
   I'm/everything's (very) bad
     ça va (très) mal [1C]
   it's bad (weather) il fait
     mauvais [4C]
   that's bad c'est mal [12]
   too bad! dommage! [7]
   badly mal [1C]
   things are going (very) badly
     ça va (très) mal [1C]
bag un sac [I, 9], **AX**
banana une banane **25**
banknote un billet **20**
baseball le baseball **15**
basketball le basket
   (basketball) **15**
bathing suit un maillot de bain
   17
bathroom une salle de bains
   [13]
to **be** *être [6]
   to be … (years old) *avoir…
     ans [10]
   to be able (to) *pouvoir **27**
   to be acquainted with
     *connaître **28**
   to be active in *faire de +
     activity **21**
   to be careful *faire attention
     [8]
   to be cold (*people*) *avoir
     froid **22**; (*weather*) il fait
     froid [4C]
   to be going to (*do something*)
     *aller + *inf.* **14**
   to be hot (*people*) *avoir
     chaud **22**
   to be hungry *avoir faim
     [10], **22**
   to be lucky *avoir de la
     chance **22**
   to be present at assister à **21**
   to be right *avoir raison **22**
   to be supposed to *devoir **27**
   to be thirsty *avoir soif [10],
     22
   to be warm (*people*) *avoir
     chaud **22, 23**
   to be wrong *avoir tort **22**
beach une plage [13]
beans: green beans les
   •haricots *m.* verts **25**
beautiful beau (bel, belle; *m.pl.*
   beaux) [9]
   it's beautiful (nice) weather il
     fait beau [4C]

because parce que (qu') [8]
bed un lit [9], **AX**
bedroom une chambre [9, 13]
been été (*p.p. of* *être) **23**
before avant **21, 23**
behind derrière [9]
below en bas [13]
belt une ceinture **17**
best meilleur **19**
better meilleur **19**
beverage une boisson [3B], **25**
bicycle un vélo, une bicyclette
   [9], **AX**
   by bicycle à vélo **14**
   take a bicycle ride *faire une
     promenade à vélo **14**
big grand [9, 12]
bill (*money*) un billet **20**
birthday un anniversaire [4B]
   my birthday is (March 2)
     mon anniversaire est le
     (2 mars) [4B]
   when is your birthday? c'est
     quand, ton anniversaire?
     [4B]
bit: a little bit un peu [7]
black noir [E1, 12], **AX**
blond blond [9], **AX**
blouse un chemisier **17**
blue bleu [E1, 12], **AX**
boat un bateau (*pl.* bateaux) **21**
book un livre [I, 9], **AX**
boom box une radiocassette
   [9]
boots des bottes *f.* **17**
bothersome pénible [12]
boulevard un boulevard [13]
boutique une boutique **17**
boy le garçon [2A, 2B], **AX**
bread le pain **25**
breakfast le petit déjeuner **25**
   to have breakfast prendre
     le petit déjeuner **25**
to **bring** (*a person*) amener **18**;
   (*things*) apporter **27**
   to bring something to
     someone apporter
     quelque chose à quelqu'un
     27
brother un frère [2C], **16**, **AX**
brown brun [9]; marron (*inv.*)
   [12]
building: apartment building
   un immeuble [13]
bus un bus
   by bus en bus **14**
   touring bus un autocar,
     un car **21**

but mais [5]
butter le beurre **25**
to **buy** acheter **33, 34**
   to buy (some) acheter + du,
     de la (*partitive*) **26**
by: by airplane, plane en avion
   21
   by bicycle à vélo **14**
   by bus en bus **14**
   by car en voiture **14**
   by oneself seul(e) **21**
   by subway en métro **14**
   by taxi en taxi **14**
   by train en train **14**

café un café [6]
   at (to) the café au café [6]
cafeteria: school cafeteria
   la cantine de l'école **25**
cake un gâteau (*pl.* gâteaux) **25**
calculator une calculatrice [9]
to **call** téléphoner [7]
came venu (*p.p. of* *venir) **23**
camera un appareil-photo
   (*pl.* appareils-photo) [9], **AX**
can *pouvoir **27**
   can you …? est-ce que tu
     peux…? [5], **R3**
   I can't je ne peux pas [5]
Canada le Canada
Canadian canadien
   (canadienne) [1B, 11], **AX**
   he's/she's (Canadian) il/elle
     est (canadien/canadienne)
     [2B]
cannot: I cannot je ne peux
   pas [5]
   I'm sorry, but I cannot je
     regrette, mais je ne peux
     pas [5]
cap (baseball) une casquette **17**
car une auto, une voiture [9], **AX**
   by car en voiture **14**
card une carte **(playing) cards**
   des cartes *f.* **15**
careful: to be careful *faire
   attention [8]
carrot une carotte **25**
cat un chat [2C], **AX**
cell phone un portable [9], **AX**
cereal les céréales *f.* **25**
chair une chaise [I, 9], **AX**
chalk la craie [I]
   piece of chalk un morceau
     de craie [I]

English-French Vocabulary *continued*

chalkboard un tableau (*pl.* tableaux) [I]
checkers les dames *f.* 15
cheese le fromage 25
cherry une cerise 25
chess les échecs *m.* 15
chicken le poulet 25
child un (une) enfant 16
children des enfants *m.* 16
Chinese chinois [11], **AX**
chocolate: hot chocolate un chocolat [3B]
to **choose** choisir 19
chose, chosen choisi (*p.p. of* choisir) 23
Christmas Noël 21
  at Christmas à Noël 21
church une église [13]
cinema le cinéma [6]
  to the cinema au cinéma [6]
city une ville [13]
  in the city en ville [6]
clarinet une clarinette 15
class une classe [6]
  in class en classe [6]
classmate un (une) camarade [9], **AX**
to **clean** nettoyer 21
clothing des vêtements *m.* 17
  sports clothing des vêtements *m.* de sport 17
coffee le café [3B, 13]
coin une pièce 20
cold le froid
  to be (feel) cold *avoir froid 22
  it's cold (*weather*) il fait froid [4C]
college student un étudiant, une étudiante [9], **AX**
color une couleur [12]
  what color? de quelle couleur? [12]
to **come** arriver 14; *venir 15
  come on! vas-y! 14
  here comes ... voici... [2A]
  to come back rentrer 14, 24; *revenir 15
  to come to visit rendre visite à 20, 28
comfortable comfortable [13]
compact disc un compact (disc), un CD [9], **AX**
computer un ordinateur, un PC [9], **AX**
computer game un jeu d'ordinateur (*pl.* les jeux d'ordinateur)

concert un concert 14
to **continue** continuer [13]
cooking la cuisine 25
cool: it's cool (*weather*) il fait frais [4C]
cost le coût 17
  to cost coûter
  how much does ... cost? combien coûte...? [3C], 17
  it costs ... il/elle coûte... [3C]
country(side) la campagne 21
  to (in) the country(side) à la campagne 21
course: of course! bien sûr! [5]; mais oui! [6]
  of course not! mais non! [6]
cousin un cousin, une cousine [2C], 16
crepe une crêpe [3A]
croissant un croissant [3A]
cuisine la cuisine 25
cup une tasse 25
cute mignon (mignonne) [11], **AX**

to **dance** danser [5, 7], **AX**
dark-haired brun [9]
darn! zut! [1C]
date la date [4B], **AX**; un rendez-vous 14
  I have a date at ... j'ai un rendez-vous à... [4A]
  what's the date? quelle est la date? [4B]
daughter une fille 16
day un jour [4B], 21
  what day is it? quel jour est-ce? [4B]
  whole day une journée
dear cher (chère) 17
December décembre *m.* [4B], **AX**
department store un grand magasin 17
desk un bureau [I, 9], **AX**
dessert le dessert 25
to **detest** détester 25
did fait (*p.p. of* *faire) 23
difficult difficile [12]
dining room une salle à manger [13]
dinner le dîner 25
  to have (eat) dinner dîner 7, 25
  to have dinner at a restaurant dîner au restaurant [5]

dish (*course of a meal*) un plat 25
to **do, to make** *faire [8], **AX**
  do it! vas-y! 14
  I do je veux bien 26
  to do + *activity* *faire de + *activity* 21
  to do my homework *faire mes devoirs 21
dog un chien [2C], **AX**
door une porte [I, 9], **AX**
done fait (*p.p. of* *faire) 23
downstairs en bas [13]
downtown en ville [6]
dozen une douzaine 25
dress une robe 17
drink une boisson [3B], 25
to **drink** *boire 26
drive: to take a drive *faire une promenade en voiture 14
drums une batterie 15
dumb bête [11]
during pendant 21
DVD un DVD [9]

ear une oreille [E2]
to **earn** gagner 20
Easter Pâques *m.* 21
  at Easter à Pâques 21
easy facile [12]
to **eat** manger [7], **AX**
  I like to eat j'aime manger [5]
  to eat breakfast *prendre le petit déjeuner 25
  to eat dinner dîner [7], 25
  to eat lunch déjeuner 25
  to eat (some) manger + du, de la (partitive) 26
egg un oeuf 25
eight •huit [1A], **AX**
eighteen dix-huit [1B], **AX**
eighth •huitième 16
eighty quatre-vingts [2B], **AX**
elegant élégant 17
elephant un éléphant [E4]
eleven onze [1B], [3C]
eleventh onzième 16
English anglais(e) [1B, 11], **AX**
errand: to run errands *faire les courses 25
evening un soir 21
  in the evening du soir [4A]
  this evening ce soir 23
  tomorrow evening demain soir 21, 23

event un événement **14**
everything tout
  everything's going (very) well ça va (très) bien [1C]
  everything's (going) so-so ça va comme ci, comme ça [1C]
  how's everything? ça va? [1C]
exam un examen
  to pass an exam réussir à un examen **19**
excuse me excusez-moi [13]
expensive cher (chère) **17**
eye un oeil (*pl.* yeux) [E2]

fall l'automne [4C], **AX**
  in (the) fall en automne [4C]
false faux (fausse) [12]
family une famille [2C], **16**
far (from) loin (de) [13]
fashion la mode
  in fashion (fashionable) à la mode **17**
fat: to get fat grossir **19**
father un père **16**
  this is my father voici mon père [2C]
February février *m.* [4B], **AX**
to **feel like** *avoir envie de + *inf.* **20**
few: a few quelques [9]
fifteen quinze [1B], **AX**
fifth cinquième **16**
fifty cinquante [1C], **AX**
film un film **14, 21**
finally finalement **22**
to **find** trouver **17**
fine ça va [1C]
  fine! d'accord [5]
  everything's fine ça va bien [1C]
  that's fine c'est bien [12]
to **finish** finir **19**
finished fini (*p.p. of* finir) **23**
first d'abord **22**; premier (première) **16**
  it's (June) first c'est le premier (juin) [4B]
fish un poisson **25**
five cinq [1A], **AX**
to **fix** réparer **21**
flute une flûte **15**
food la nourriture **25**
foot un pied [E2]

on foot à pied **14**
for pour [6]
  for whom? pour qui? [8]
fork une fourchette **25**
forty quarante [1C], **AX**
four quatre [1A], **AX**
fourteen quatorze [1B], **AX**
fourth quatrième **16**
franc (former monetary unit of France) un franc [3C]
  that's (it's) … francs ça fait…francs [3C]
France la France [6]
  in France en France [6]
French français(e) [1B, 11], **AX**
  how do you say … in French? comment dit-on… en français? [I]
  French fries des frites *f.* **25**
  steak and French fries un steak-frites [3A]
Friday vendredi *m.* [4B], **AX**
friend un ami, une amie [2A], un copain, une copine [2A], **AX**
  school friend un (une) camarade [9]
from de **22**
  from (the) du, de la, de l', des **15**
  from where? d'où? **15**
  are you from …? tu es de…? [1B]
  I'm from … je suis de… [1B]
front: in front of devant [9]
fruit(s) des fruits *m.* **25**
funny amusant [11]; drôle [12]

to **gain weight** grossir **19**
game un jeu (*pl.* jeux) **15**; un match **14**
  to play a game (match) *faire un match [8]
  to play a game jouer à + *game* **15**
garage un garage [13]
garden un jardin [13]
gentleman un monsieur (*pl.* messieurs) [2A]
to **get: to get fat** grossir **19**
  to get thin maigrir **19**
girl une fille [2A], **AX**
to **give (to)** donner (à) **27, 28**
  give me donne-moi, donnez-moi [3A, 3B]

please give me s'il te plaît donne-moi [3B]
glass un verre **25**
glasses des lunettes *f.* **17**
  sunglasses des lunettes *f.* de soleil **17**
to **go** *aller **14**
  go ahead! vas-y! **14**
  go away! va-t'en! **14**
  to go (come) back rentrer **14, 24**; *revenir **15**
  to go by bicycle *aller en vélo **14**
  to go by car, by train … *aller en auto, en train… **14**
  to go food shopping *faire les courses **25**
  to go rock climbing *faire de l'escalade **21**
  to go shopping *faire des achats **21**
  to go to assister à **21**
gone allé(e) (*p.p. of* *aller) **24**
good bon (bonne) [12]
  good morning (afternoon) bonjour [1A]
  that's good c'est bien [12]
  the weather's good (pleasant) il fait bon [4C]
  good-bye! au revoir!, salut! [1C]
  good-looking beau (bel, belle; *m.pl.* beaux) [9, 12], **19**
grandfather un grand-père [2C], **16**
grandmother une grand-mère [2C], **16**
grandparents les grands-parents *m.* **16**
grape juice le jus de raisin [3B]
grapefruit un pamplemousse **25**
gray gris [12], **AX**
great super [12], **17**
green vert [E1, 12], **AX**
  green beans les •haricots *m.* verts **25**
guitar une guitare [9], **15**

had eu (*p.p. of* *avoir) **23**
hair les cheveux *m.* [E2], **15**
  he/she has dark hair il/elle est brun(e) [9]

English-French Vocabulary *continued*

half: half past … … heure(s) et demie [4A], **AX**
 half past midnight minuit et demi [4A], **AX**
 half past noon midi et demi [4A], **AX**
ham le jambon **25**
hamburger un hamburger [3A]
hand une main [E2]
handbag un sac [9]
handsome beau (bel, belle; *m.pl.* beaux) [9, 12], **19**
hard difficile [12] **17**
to **hate** détester **25**
to **have** *avoir [10]; (*food*) *prendre **26**
 do you have …? est-ce que tu as…? [9]
 I have j'ai [9]
 I have to (must) je dois [5]
 to have (some) *avoir + du, de la (*partitive*); *prendre + du, de la (*partitive*) **26**
 to have a picnic *faire un pique-nique **21**
 to have breakfast *prendre le petit déjeuner **25**
 to have dinner dîner **25**
 to have dinner at a restaurant dîner au restaurant [5]
 to have to *avoir besoin de + *inf.* **20**; *devoir **27**
he il [3C, 6, 10]; lui **15**
 he/she is … il/elle est + *nationality* [2B]
head la tête [E2]
to **hear** entendre **20**
hello bonjour [1A, 1C]
to **help** aider **21, 27**
 may I help you? vous désirez? [3B], **17**
her elle **15**; son, sa; ses **16**; la **28**
 (to) her lui **28**
 her name is … elle s'appelle… [2B] **R1**
 what's her name? comment s'appelle-t-elle? [9]
here ici [6]
 here comes, here is voici [2A]
 here's my mother/father voici ma mère/mon père [2C]
 here's some voici + du, de la (*partitive*) **26**
 this … (over here) ce… -ci **18**

hey! dis! [12]; tiens! [2A, 10]
hey there! dis donc! [12]
hi! salut! [1C]
high school student un (une), élève [9], **AX**
him lui **15**; le **28**
 (to) him lui **28**
 his son, sa; ses **16**
 his name is … il s'appelle… [2B], **R1**
 what's his name? comment s'appelle-t-il? [9]
home, at home à la maison [6], **AX**; chez (moi, toi…) **15**
 to go home rentrer **14, 24**
homework les devoirs *m.* **21**
 homework assignment un devoir [I]
 to do my homework *faire mes devoirs **21**
to **hope** espérer **18**
horse un cheval (*pl.* chevaux) [E4]
hospital un hôpital [13]
hot chaud [4C], **23**
 hot chocolate un chocolat [3B]
 hot dog un •hot dog [3A]
 to be hot (*people*) *avoir chaud **22**
 it's hot (*weather*) il fait chaud [4C]
hotel un hôtel [13]
house une maison [13]
 at someone's house chez + *person* **14**
how? comment? [8]
 how are you? comment allez-vous?, comment vas-tu?, ça va? [1C]
 how do you find …? comment trouves-tu…? **17**
 how do you say … in French? comment dit-on… en français? [I]
 how much? combien (de)? **20**
 how much does … cost? combien coûte…? [3C], **17**
 how much is that/this/it? c'est combien?, ça fait combien? [3C]
 how old are you? quel âge as-tu? [2C], **R1**
 how old is he/she? quel âge a-t-il/elle? [9] **R1**
 how old is your father/mother? quel âge a ton père/ta mère? [2C]

 how's everything? ça va? [1C]
 how's the weather? quel temps fait-il? [4C]
 to learn how to *apprendre à **26**
hundred cent [2B], **17, AX**
hungry avoir faim [3A]
 are you hungry? tu as faim? [3A]
 I'm hungry j'ai [3A]
 to be hungry avoir faim [10], **22**
husband un mari **16**

I je [6], moi **15**
 I don't know je ne sais pas [I, 9]
 I have a date/appointment at … j'ai un rendez-vous à… [4A]
 I know je sais [I, 9], **28**
 I'm fine/okay ça va [1C]
 I'm (very) well/so-so/(very) bad ça va (très) bien/comme ci, comme ça/(très) mal [1C]
ice la glace [3A], **25**
 ice cream une glace [3A], **25**
 iced tea un thé glacé **25**
idea une idée **20**
 it's (that's) a good idea c'est une bonne idée **20**
if si
in à [6], **14**; dans [9]
 in (Boston) à (Boston) [6]
 in class en classe [6]
 in front of devant [9], **R2**
 in order to pour **21**
 in the afternoon de l'après-midi [4A]
 in the morning/evening du matin/soir [4A]
 in town en ville [6]
 in (the) au, à la, à l', aux **14**
inexpensive bon marché (*inv.*) **17**
ingredient un ingrédient **25**
in-line skating le roller **21**
 in-line skates des rollers **21**
 to go in-line skating faire du roller **21**
instrument un instrument **15**
 to play a musical instrument jouer de + *instrument* **15**

intelligent intelligent 25
interesting intéressant [11], **AX**
to **invite** inviter [7]
is (*see* **to be**)
  is there? est-ce qu'il y a? [9], **R2**
  isn't it (so)? n'est-ce pas? [6]
  there is il y a [9] **R2**
  there is (some) il y a + du, de
    la (*partitive*) 26
  it il, elle [6], [10]; le, la **28**
  it's … c'est… [2A]
  it's … (o'clock) il est…
    heure(s) [4A]
  it's … euros ça fait… euros [3C]
  it's fine/nice/hot/cool/cold/
  bad (*weather*) il fait
    beau/bon/chaud/frais/froid/
    mauvais [4C], **AX**
  it's (June) first c'est le
    premier (juin) [4B]
  it's not ce n'est pas [12]
  it's raining il pleut [4C], **AX**
  it's snowing il neige [4C], **AX**
  what time is it? quelle heure
    est-il? [4A]
  who is it? qui est-ce? [2A, 9]
  its son, sa; ses **16**
Italian italien, italienne [11], **AX**

jacket un blouson, une veste
  17
jam la confiture 25
January janvier *m.* [4B], **AX**
Japanese japonais(e) [11], **AX**
jeans: pair of jeans un jean 17
to **jog** *faire du jogging 21
jogging le jogging 21
  jogging suit un jogging, un
    survêtement 17
juice le jus
  apple juice le jus de pomme
    [3B], **25**
  grape juice le jus de raisin [3B]
  orange juice le jus d'orange
    [3B], **25**
  tomato juice le jus de
    tomate [3B]
July juillet *m.* [4B], **AX**
June juin *m.* [4B], **AX**

ketchup le ketchup 25
keyboard un clavier 15

---

kilogram un kilo (de) 25
kind gentil (gentille) [11]
kitchen une cuisine [13]
knife un couteau 25
to **know** *connaître 36
  do you know …? tu
    connais…? [2B]
  I (don't) know je (ne) sais
    (pas) [I, 9], **28**
  you know tu sais 28

lady une dame [2A], **AX**
lamp une lampe [9]
large grand [9], [12]
last dernier (dernière) 23
  last month le mois dernier
    23
  last night hier soir 23
  last Saturday samedi dernier
    23
  at last enfin 22
to **learn (how to)** *apprendre (à) +
  inf. 26
left gauche
  on (to) the left à gauche [13]
leg une jambe [E2]
lemon soda la limonade [3B]
to **lend** prêter (à) 27, **28**
  lend me prête-moi [3C]
less … than moins… que 19
let's go! allons-y! 14
lettuce la salade 25
library une bibliothèque [13]
like: what does he/she look
  like? comment est-il/elle? [9]
  what's he/she like?
    comment est-il/elle? [9]
  to like aimer [7]
  do you like? est-ce que tu
    aimes? [5]
  I also like j'aime aussi [5]
  I don't always like je n'aime
    pas toujours [5]
  I don't like je n'aime pas [5]
  I like j'aime [5]
  I like …, but I prefer …
    j'aime…, mais je préfère… [5]
  I'd like je voudrais [3A, 3B, 5]
  what would you like? vous
    désirez? [3B], 17
to **listen** écouter [7]
  to listen to CDs écouter des
    CD 21
  to listen to the radio écouter
    la radio [5], **AX**

---

little petit [9, 12], **17**
  a little (bit) un peu [7]
to **live** habiter [7]
living room (*formal*) un salon [13]
to **loan** prêter (à) 27, **28**
long long (longue) 17
to **look (at)** regarder [7], **AX**
  look! tiens! [2A, 10]
  look at that regarde ça [9]
  I'm looking for … je
    cherche… 17
to **look for** chercher 17
  what does he/she look like?
    comment est-il/elle? [9]
to **lose** perdre 20
  to lose weight maigrir 19
lot: a lot beaucoup [7]
to **love: I'd love to** je veux bien [5]
luck la chance 22
  to be lucky *avoir de
    la chance 22
lunch le déjeuner 25
  to have (eat) lunch déjeuner
    25

made fait (*p.p. of* *faire) 23
to **make** *faire [8]
man un homme [9]; un
  monsieur (*polite term*)
  [2A], **AX**
many beaucoup (de) [7]
  how many combien de 20
map une carte [I]
March mars *m.* [4B], **AX**
match un match [8]
  to play a match *faire un
    match [8]
May mai *m.* [4B], **AX**
may *pouvoir 27
maybe peut-être [6]
mayonnaise la mayonnaise 25
me moi [1A], 27
  excuse me pardon [13], 17
  (to) me me, moi 27
meal un repas 25
mean méchant [11], **AX**
  to mean *vouloir dire 26
  what does … mean? que
    veut dire…? [I]
meat la viande 25
to **meet** rencontrer 21
  to meet for the first time
    *connaître (*in passé
    composé*) 28
Mexican mexicain(e) [11], **AX**

midnight minuit *m.* [4A]
milk le lait 25
mineral water l'eau *f.* minérale 25
Miss Mademoiselle (Mlle) [1C]
modern moderne [13]
Monday lundi *m.* [4B], **AX**
money l'argent *m.* 21
month un mois [4B], 19
  last month le mois dernier 23
  next month le mois prochain 23
  this month ce mois-ci 23
moped une mob (mobylette) [9]
more … than plus… que 19
morning le matin 21
  good morning bonjour [1A]
  in the morning du matin [4A]
  this morning ce matin 21
  tomorrow morning demain matin 23
  yesterday morning hier matin 23
mother une mère [2C], 16
  this is my mother voici ma mère [2C]
motorbike une mob (mobylette) [9], **AX**
motorcycle une moto [9], **AX**
motorscooter un scooter [9], **AX**
mountain une montagne 21
  mountain bike un VTT 21
  mountain biking le VTT 21
  to do mountain biking faire du VTT 21
  to (at/in) the mountain(s) à la montagne 21
mouth une bouche [E2]
movie un film 14, 21
  movie theater un cinéma [6]
  movies le cinéma [13]
  at (to) the movies au cinéma [6]
Mr. Monsieur (M.) [1C]
Mrs. Madame (Mme) [1C]
much, very much beaucoup [7]
  how much? combien? 20
  how much does … cost? combien coûte…? [3C], 17
  how much is it? ça fait combien?, c'est combien? [3C]
  too much trop 17
museum un musée [13]

music la musique 15
must *devoir 27
  I must je dois [5]
my mon, ma; mes [2C], 16
  my birthday is (March 2) mon anniversaire est le (2 mars) [4B], **AX**
  my name is … je m'appelle… [1A], **R1**

name: his/her name is … il/elle s'appelle… [2B]
  my name is … je m'appelle… [1A]
  what's…'s name? comment s'appelle…? [2B]
  what's his/her name? comment s'appelle-t-il/elle? [9]
  what's your name? comment t'appelles-tu? [1A]
napkin une serviette 25
nasty méchant [11]
nationality la nationalité [1B], **AX**
nearby près [13]
neat chouette [12]
neck le cou [E2]
to **need** *avoir besoin de 20
neighbor un voisin, une voisine [9], **AX**
neighborhood un quartier [13]
  a nice neighborhood un joli quartier [13]
never ne… jamais 24
new nouveau (nouvel, nouvelle; *m.pl.* nouveaux) 19
next prochain 21, 23
  next week la semaine prochaine 23
nice gentil (gentille), sympathique [11], **AX**
  it's nice (beautiful) weather il fait beau [4C]
night: tomorrow night demain soir [4A]
  last night hier soir 23
nine neuf [1A], **AX**
nineteen dix-neuf [1B], **AX**
ninety quatre-vingt-dix [2B], **AX**
ninth neuvième 16
no non [1B], [6]
  no … pas de [10], 26

no? n'est-ce pas? [6]
nobody ne… personne, personne 24
noon midi *m.* [4A]
nose le nez [E2]
not ne… pas [6]
  not a, not any pas de [10], 26
  not always pas toujours [5]
  not anybody ne… personne 24
  not anything ne… rien 24
  not at all pas du tout 15
  it's (that's) not ce n'est pas [12]
  of course not! mais non! [6]
notebook un cahier [I, 9]
nothing ne… rien, rien 24
November novembre *m.* [4B], **AX**
now maintenant [7], 23

o'clock heure(s)
  at … o'clock à… heures [4A]
  it's … o'clock il est… heure(s) [4A]
object un objet [9], **AX**
ocean la mer 21; l'océan *m.*
  to (at) the oceanside à la mer 21
October octobre *m.* [4B], **AX**
of de [6]
  of (the) du, de la, de l', des 15
  of course not! mais non! [6]
  of course! bien sûr [5]
  of whom de qui [8]
often souvent [7]
oh: oh, really? ah, bon? [8]
okay d'accord [5]
  I'm okay ça va [1C]
old vieux (vieil, vieille; *m.pl.* vieux) 19
  he/she is … (years old) il/elle a… ans [2C]
  how old are you? quel âge as-tu? [2C]
  how old is he/she? quel âge a-t-il/elle? [9]
  how old is your father/mother? quel âge a ton père/ta mère? [2C]
  I'm … (years old) j'ai… ans [2C]
  to be … (years old) *avoir … ans [10]
omelet une omelette [3A]

on sur [9], **R2**
   on foot à pied **14**
   on Monday lundi [10]
   on Mondays le lundi [10]
   on vacation en vacances [6]
one un, une **1**; (*we, they, people*)
   on **20**
oneself: by oneself seul **21**
only seul **21**
open … ouvre… (ouvrez…) [I]
opinion: in my opinion à mon
   avis **19**
or ou [1B, 6]
orange (*color*) orange (in*v.*) [E1,
   12]
orange (*fruit*) une orange **25**
   orange juice le jus d'orange
      [3B], **25**
order: in order to pour **21**
to **organize** organiser [7], **AX**
other autre **25**
our notre; nos **16**
out of style démodé **17**
over: over (at) …'s house
   chez… **15**
   over there là-bas [6]
   that (one), over there ça,
      là-bas [9]
overcoat un manteau (*pl.*
   manteaux) **17**
to **own** *avoir [10]

P.M. du soir [4A]
pain: a pain pénible [12]
pants un pantalon **17**
pantyhose des collants *m.* **17**
paper le papier [I]
   sheet of paper une feuille de
      papier [I]
parents les parents *m.* **16**
park un parc [13]
party (*informal*) une fête, une
   soirée, une boum **14**
to **pass a test (an exam)** réussir à
   un examen **19**
past: half past … … heure(s) et
   demie [4A]
   quarter past … … heure(s) et
      quart [4A]
to **pay (for)** payer **20**
   to pay attention *faire
      attention [8], **AX**
pear une poire **25**
peas les petits pois *m.* **25**
pen un stylo [I, 9], **AX**

pencil un crayon [I, 9], **AX**
people des gens *m.* [10], **AX**;
   on **20**
perhaps peut-être [6]
person une personne [2A, 9]
pet un animal (*pl.* animaux)
   domestique [2C], **AX**
to **phone** téléphoner [7]
piano un piano **15**
to **pick up** ranger **21**
picnic un pique-nique **14**
   to have a picnic *faire
      un pique-nique **21**
pie une tarte **25**
piece: piece of chalk
   un morceau de craie [I]
ping-pong le Ping-Pong **15**
pink rose [12], **AX**
pizza une pizza [3A]
place un endroit **14**
place setting un couvert **25**
to **place** *mettre **18**
   placed mis (*p.p. of* *mettre)
      23
plain moche **17**
plane un avion **21**
   by plane en avion **21**
plate une assiette **25**
to **play** jouer [7]
   to play a game jouer à +
      game **15**
   to play a game (match) *faire
      un match [8], **AX**
   to play a musical instrument
      jouer de + *instrument* **15**
   **to play basketball (soccer,
      tennis, volleyball)** jouer au
      basket (au foot, au tennis,
      au volley) [5]
pleasant sympathique [11]
   it's pleasant (good) weather
      il fait bon [4C]
please s'il vous plaît (*formal*)
   [3B]; s'il te plaît (*informal*)
   [3A]
   please give me … s'il te plaît,
      donne-moi… [3B]
polo shirt un polo **17**
pool: swimming pool
   une piscine [13]
poor pauvre **20**
poorly mal [1C]
popular à la mode **17**
portable player un baladeur
   [9], **AX**
poster une affiche [9]
potato une pomme de terre **25**
pound une livre (de) **25**

to **prefer** préférer **18, 25**
   I prefer je préfère + *inf.* [5]
   I like …, but I prefer …
      j'aime…, mais je préfère…
      [5]
to **prepare** préparer **21**
pretty joli [9], **17, AX**
price un prix **17**
   what's the price? quel est
      le prix? **17**
pullover un pull **17**
pupil un (une) élève [9]
to **purchase** acheter **21**
purple violet (violette) [E1], **AX**
to **put** *mettre **18**
   to put on *mettre **18**

quantity une quantité **25**
quarter un quart
   quarter of … … heure(s)
      moins le quart [4A], **AX**
   quarter past … … heure(s) et
      quart [4A], **AX**

racket une raquette [9], **AX**
radio une radio [9], **AX**
   to listen to the radio écouter
      la radio [5]
rain: it's raining il pleut [4C], **AX**
raincoat un imper
   (imperméable) **17**
rarely rarement [7]
rather assez [11]
really: oh, really? ah, bon? [8]
really?! vraiment?! **15**
red rouge [E1, 12], **AX**
relatives les parents *m.* **16**
to **rent** louer **21**
to **repair** réparer **21**
to **respond** répondre **28**
restaurant un restaurant [13]
   at (to) the restaurant au
      restaurant [6]
   have dinner at a restaurant
      dîner au restaurant [5]
to **return** rentrer **24**; *revenir **15**
rice le riz **25**
rich riche **20**
ride: to take a bicycle ride
   *faire une promenade
   à vélo **14**
right vrai [12]; droite

ENGLISH-FRENCH VOCABULARY

right? n'est-ce pas? [6]
   all right d'accord [5]
   to be right *avoir raison **22**
   to (on) the right à droite [13]
roast beef le rosbif **25**
rock climbing l'escalade *f.* **21**
   to do rock climbing *faire de l'escalade **21**
room une chambre [9]; une salle [13]
   bathroom une salle de bains [13]
   dining room une salle à manger [13]
   formal living room un salon [13]
to **run** (*referring to objects*) marcher [9]

sailing la voile **21**
salad une salade [3A], **25**
salami le saucisson **25**
salt le sel **25**
sandal une sandale **17**
sandwich un sandwich [3A]
Saturday samedi *m.* [4B], **23**
   see you Saturday! à samedi! [4B]
   last Saturday samedi dernier **23**
   next Saturday samedi prochain **23**
saw vu (*p.p. of* *voir) **23**
saxophone un saxo (saxophone) **15**
say *dire **28**
   say ... dites...
   say! dis (donc)! [12]
   how do you say ... in French? comment dit-on... en français? [I]
school une école [13]
   school cafeteria la cantine de l'école **25**
   school friend un (une) camarade [9]
sea la mer **21**
   to (at) the sea à la mer **21**
season une saison [4C]
second deuxième **16**
to **see** *voir **21**
   see you tomorrow! à demain! [4B], **21**
seen vu (*p.p. of* *voir) **23**
seldom rarement [7]

to **sell** vendre **20**
September septembre *m.* 4B], **AX**
to **set the table** *mettre la table **25**
seven sept [1A], **AX**
seventeen dix-sept [1B], **AX**
seventh septième **16**
seventy soixante-dix [2A], **AX**
she elle [6, 10], **15**
sheet of paper une feuille de papier [I]
ship un bateau (*pl.* bateaux) **21**
shirt une chemise **17**
shoe une chaussure [2A]
   tennis shoes des tennis *m.* **17**
shop une boutique **17**
shopping: shopping center un centre commercial [13]
   to go food shopping *faire les courses **25**
   to go shopping *faire des achats **21**
shore la mer **21**
short court **17**; petit [9, 12], **17**
   he/she is short il/elle est petit(e) [9]
shorts un short **21**
should *devoir **35**
to **show** indiquer; montrer à **27, 28**
to **shut** fermer [I]
shy timide [11]
silly bête [11]
to **sing** chanter [5, 7], **AX**
sir Monsieur (M.) [1C]
sister une soeur [2C], **16**
six six [1A], **AX**
sixteen seize [1B], **AX**
sixth sixième **16**
sixty soixante [1C], [2A], **AX**
skateboard un skate
skateboarding le skate **21**
   to go skateboarding faire du skate **21**
to **ski** *faire du ski **21**
skiing le ski **21**
skirt une jupe **17**
small petit [9, 12], **17**
sneakers des tennis *m.* **17**
   hightop sneakers des baskets *m.* **17**
snow: it's snowing il neige [4C], **AX**
snowboard un snowboard, un surf (des neiges) **21**

snowboarding le snowboard, le surf (des neiges) **21**
   to go snowboarding faire du snowboard **21**
so alors [7]
   so-so comme ci, comme ça [1C]
   everything's (going) so-so ça va comme ci, comme ça [1C]
soccer le foot (football) **15**
sock une chaussette **17**
soda un soda [3B]
   lemon soda une limonade [3B]
sold vendu (*p.p. of* vendre) **23**
sole (*fish*) la sole **25**
some des [10]; du, de la, de l' **26**; quelques [9]
somebody quelqu'un **24**
someone quelqu'un **24**
something quelque chose **24**
son un fils **16**
sorry: to be sorry regretter
   I'm sorry, but (I cannot) je regrette, mais (je ne peux pas) [5]
soup la soupe **25**
spaghetti les spaghetti *m.* **25**
Spanish espagnol(e) [11], **AX**
to **speak** parler [7]
   to speak (French, English, Spanish) parler (français, anglais, espagnol) [5]
   to speak to parler à **28**
to **spend** (*money*) dépenser **20**; (*time*) passer **21**
spoon une cuillère **25**
sports le sport **21**
   to play a sport *faire du sport **21**; jouer à + *sport* **15**
   sports clothing des vêtements *m.* de sport **17**
spring le printemps [4C], **AX**
   in the spring au printemps [4C]
stadium un stade [13]
to stay rester **14**
steak un steak [3A]
   steak and French fries un steak-frites [3A]
stereo set une chaîne hi-fi [9], **AX**
stomach le ventre [E2]
store un magasin [13], **17**
   department store un grand magasin **17**
straight tout droit [13]

strawberry une fraise **25**
street une rue [13]
student (*high school*) un (une)
    élève [9]; (*college*) un
    étudiant, une étudiante [9]
to study étudier [5, 7], **AX**
stupid bête [11]
style: in style à la mode **17**
    out of style démodé **17**
subway le métro **14**
    by subway en métro **14**
to succeed réussir **19**
sugar le sucre **25**
summer l'été *m.* [4C]
    summer vacation les
        grandes vacances **21**
    in the summer en été [4C]
sun le soleil **17**
Sunday dimanche *m.* [4B], **AX**
sunglasses des lunettes *f.* de
    soleil **17**
supermarket un supermarché
    [13]
supper le dîner **25**
    to have (eat) supper dîner [7],
        25
sure bien sûr [5]
    sure! mais oui! [6]
    are you sure? tu es sûr(e)? **16**
sweater un pull **17**
sweatshirt un sweat **17**
to swim nager [7], **AX**
    I like to swim j'aime nager
        [5]
    swimming pool une piscine
        [13]
    swimsuit un maillot de bain
        17
Swiss suisse [11]

table une table [I, 9], **AX**
    to set the table *mettre la
        table **25**
to take *prendre [I], **26**
    to take along amener **18, 27**
    to take a bicycle ride *faire
        une promenade à vélo **14**
    to take a drive *faire une
        promenade en voiture **14**
    to take a trip *faire un
        voyage [8], **AX**
    to take a walk *faire une
        promenade à pied **14**
to talk parler [7]
    to talk to parler à **28**

tall grand [9, 12]
taxi un taxi **14**
    by taxi en taxi **14**
tea le thé [3B]
    iced tea un thé glacé **25**
teacher un (une) prof [2A, 9];
    un professeur [9]
telephone un téléphone
    [9], **AX**
    to telephone téléphoner
        [7], **AX**
television la télé [9]
    to watch television regarder
        la télé [5]
to tell *dire **28**
ten dix [1A, 1B], **AX**
tennis le tennis **15**
    tennis racket une raquette
        de tennis **15**
    tennis shoes des tennis *m.*
        17
    to play tennis jouer au
        tennis [5]
tenth dixième **16**
terrific génial [12]; super [12],
    17
test un examen
    to pass a test réussir à
        un examen **19**
than que **19**
thank you merci [1C]
that que **17**; ce, cet, cette **18**
    that is … c'est… [9, 12]
    that (one), over there ça, là-
        bas [9]
    that's … c'est… [2A, 9, 12];
        voilà [2A]
    that's … euros ça fait…
        euros [3C]
    that's bad c'est mal [12]
    that's a good idea! c'est une
        bonne idée! **20**
    that's good (fine) c'est bien
        [12]
    that's not … ce n'est pas…
        [12]
    what's that? qu'est-ce que
        c'est? [9]
the le, la, l' [2B, 10]; les [10]
theater un théâtre [13]
    movie theater un cinéma [13]
their leur, leurs **16**
them eux, elles **15**; les **28**
    (to) them leur **28**
themselves eux-mêmes
then alors [11]; ensuite **22**
there là [6]
    there is (are) il y a [9], **R2**

there is (here comes
    someone) voilà [2A]
there is (some) il y a + du,
    de la (*partitive*) **26**
there's some voilà + du,
    de la (*partitive*) **26**
over there là-bas [6]
that (one), over there ça,
    là-bas [9]; ce…-là **18**
what is there? qu'est-ce
    qu'il y a? [9]
these ces **18**
    these are ce sont [12]
they ils, elles [6]; eux **15**; on **20**
    they are ce sont [12]
thin: to get thin maigrir **19**
thing une chose
    things are going (very) badly
        ça va (très) mal [1C]
to think penser **17**
    to think of penser de,
        trouver **17**
    to think that penser que **17**
    what do you think of …?
        comment trouves-tu…?,
        qu'est-ce que tu penses
        de…? **17**
third troisième **16**
thirsty: to be thirsty *avoir soif
    22
    are you thirsty? tu as soif? [3B]
    I'm thirsty j'ai soif [3B]
thirteen treize [1B], **AX**
thirty trente [1C], **AX**
    3:30 trois heures et demie
        [4A]
this ce, cet, cette **18**
    this is … voici… [2A]
those ces **18**
    those are ce sont [12]
thousand mille [2B], **17**
three trois [1A], **AX**
Thursday jeudi *m.* [4B], **AX**
tie une cravate **17**
tights des collants *m.* **17**
time: at what time is …?
    à quelle heure est…? [4A]
    at what time? à quelle
        heure? [4A]
    what time is it? quelle heure
        est-il? [4A]
to à [6], **14**; chez **14, 15**
    to (the) au, à la, à l', aux **14**
    in order to pour **21**
    to class en classe [6]
    to someone's house chez +
        person **14**
    to whom à qui [8]

ENGLISH-FRENCH VOCABULARY

today aujourd'hui [4B], **23**
  today is (Wednesday)
    aujourd'hui, c'est
    (mercredi) [4B], **AX**
toilet les toilettes [13]
tomato une tomate
  tomato juice le jus de
    tomate [3B]
tomorrow demain [4B], **AX**
  tomorrow afternoon
    demain après-midi **23**
  tomorrow is (Thursday)
    demain, c'est (jeudi) [4B], **AX**
  tomorrow morning demain
    matin **23**
  tomorrow night (evening)
    demain soir **23**
  see you tomorrow! à
    demain! [4B], **21**
tonight ce soir **23**
too aussi [1B, 7]; trop **17**
  too bad! dommage! [7]
touring bus un autocar, un car
  21
town un village [13]
  in town en ville [6]
track suit un survêtement **17**
train un train **21**
  by train en train **14, 21**
to **travel** voyager [5, 7], **AX**
  trip: to take a trip *faire
    un voyage [8]
trousers un pantalon **17**
true vrai [12]
T-shirt un tee-shirt **17**
Tuesday mardi *m.* [4B], **AX**
tuna le thon **25**
to **turn** tourner [13]
to **turn on** *mettre **18**
  TV la télé [9]
to **watch TV** regarder la télé [5]
twelfth douzième **16**
twelve douze [1B], **AX**
twenty vingt [1B, 1C], **AX**
two deux [1A], **AX**

ugly moche **17**
uncle un oncle [2C], **16**, **AX**
under sous [9]
to **understand** *comprendre **26**
  I (don't) understand je (ne)
    comprends (pas) [I]
unfashionable démodé **17**
United States les États-Unis *m.*

upstairs en • haut [13]
us nous **15**
  (to) us nous **27**

vacation les vacances *f.* **21**
  on vacation en vacances [6]
  summer vacation les
    grandes vacances **21**
veal le veau **25**
vegetable un légume **25**
very très [11]
  very well très bien [7]
  very much beaucoup [7]
videotape une cassette vidéo
  [9]
violin un violon **15**
to **visit** (*place*) visiter [7], **20**, **AX**
  (*people*) rendre visite à **20,
  28**
volleyball le volley (volleyball)
  15

to **wait (for)** attendre **20**
walk une promenade **14**
  to take (go for) a walk *faire
    une promenade à pied **8,
    14**
  to walk *aller à pied **14**;
    marcher [9]
to **want** *avoir envie de **20**;
  *vouloir **26**
  do you want …? tu veux…? [3A]
  do you want to …? est-ce
    que tu veux…? [5]
  I don't want … je ne veux
    pas… [5]
  I want … je veux… [5], **26**
  I want to je veux bien **26**
  what do you want? qu'est-ce
    que tu veux? [3A]; vous
    désirez? [3B], **17**
  wanted voulu (*p.p. of*
    *vouloir) **26**
warm chaud [4C], **23**
  to be warm (*people*) *avoir
    chaud **22**
  it's warm (*weather*) il fait
    chaud [4C]
was été (*p.p. of* *être) **23**
to **wash** laver **21**

to **waste** perdre **20**
watch une montre [9]
to **watch** regarder [7]
  to watch TV regarder la télé [5]
water l'eau *f.* **25**
  mineral water l'eau minérale
    25
  to water-ski *faire du ski
    nautique **21**
  water-skiing le ski nautique
    21
we nous [6], **15**; on **20**
to **wear** *mettre **18**; porter **17**
**weather: how's (what's) the
  weather?** quel temps fait-il? [4C]
  it's … weather il fait… [4C]
Wednesday mercredi *m.*
  [4B], **AX**
week une semaine [4B], **21**
  last week la semaine
    dernière **23**
  next week la semaine
    prochaine **23**
  this week cette semaine **23**
weekend un week-end **21**
  last weekend le week-end
    dernier **23**
  next weekend le week-end
    prochain **21, 23**
  this weekend ce week-end
    23
weight: to gain weight grossir
  19
well bien [7]
  well! eh bien! **18**
  well then alors [11]
  **everything's going (very)
    well** ça va (très) bien [1C]
went allé (*p.p. of* *aller) **24, R2**
what comment? quoi? **17**;
  qu'est-ce que [8]
  what color? de quelle
    couleur? [12], **AX**
  what day is it? quel jour
    est-ce? [4B], **AX**
  what do you think of …?
    comment trouves-tu…?,
    qu'est-ce que tu penses
    de…? **17**
  what do you want? qu'est-ce
    que tu veux? [3A]; vous
    désirez? [3B], **17**
  what does … mean? que
    veut dire…? [I]
  what does he/she look like?
    comment est-il/elle? [9]
  what is it? qu'est-ce que
    c'est? [9]

what is there? qu'est-ce qu'il y a? [9], **R2**

what time is it? quelle heure est-il? [4A]

what would you like? vous désirez? [3B], **17**

what's ...'s name? comment s'appelle...? [2B]

what's he/she like? comment est-il/elle? [9]

what's his/her name? comment s'appelle-t-il/elle? [9]

what's that? qu'est-ce que c'est? [9]

what's the date? quelle est la date? [4B], **AX**

what's the price? quel est le prix? **17**

what's the weather? quel temps fait-il? [4C], **AX**

what's your address? quelle est ton adresse? [13]

what's your name? comment t'appelles-tu? [1A], **R1**

at what time is ...? à quelle heure est...? [4A]

at what time? à quelle heure? [4A, 8]

when quand [8], **R3**

when is your birthday? c'est quand, ton anniversaire? [4B], **AX**

where où [6, 8], **R3**

where is ...? où est...? [6]

where is it? où est-ce? [13]

from where? d'où? [13]

whether si

which quel (quelle) **18**

white blanc (blanche) [E, 12], **AX**

who qui [8]

who's that/this? qui est-ce? [2A], [9]

whom? qui? **R3**

about whom? de qui? [8]

for whom? pour qui? [8]

of whom? de qui? [8]

to whom? à qui? [8], **R3**

with whom? avec qui? [8], **R3**

why pourquoi [8]

wife une femme **16**

to **win** gagner **20**

window une fenêtre [I, 9], **AX**

to **windsurf** *faire de la planche à voile **21**

windsurfing la planche à voile **21**

winter l'hiver *m.* [4C], **AX**

in the winter en hiver [4C]

with avec [6]

with me avec moi [5]

with you avec toi [5]

with whom? avec qui? [8], **R3**

woman une dame (*polite term*) [2A]; une femme [9], **AX**

to **work** travailler [5, 7], **AX**; (*referring to objects*) marcher [9], **AX**

does the radio work? est-ce que la radio marche? [9]

it (doesn't) work(s) well il/elle (ne) marche (pas) bien [9]

would: I'd like je voudrais [3A, 3B, 5]

to **write** *écrire **28**

wrong faux (fausse) [12]

to be wrong *avoir tort **22**

year un an, une année [4B]

he/she is ... (years old) il/elle a... ans [2C]

I'm ... (years old) j'ai... ans [2C]

to be ... (years old) *avoir... ans [10]

yellow jaune [E1, 12]

yes oui [1B, 6]; (*to a negative question*) si! [10]

yes, of course oui, bien sûr [5]

yes, okay (all right) oui, d'accord [5]

yes, thank you oui, merci [5]

yesterday hier **23**

yesterday afternoon hier après-midi **23**

yesterday morning hier matin **23**

yogurt le yaourt **25**

you tu, vous [6], **15**; on **20**

you are ... tu es + *nationality* [1B]

and you? et toi? [1A]

(to) you te, vous **27**

your ton, ta; tes [2C]; votre; vos **16**

what's your name? comment t'appelles-tu? [1A]

young jeune [9], **AX**

zero zéro [1A], **AX**

Index

money (French), talking about how much things cost; borrowing money 285
Morocco 357
music, talking about 220

nationalities, adjectives describing R2
negation, in the **passé composé** 324, 342; **ne...jamais** 346; **ne...personne** 347; **ne...rien** 347; followed by **de** 381; position 212, 381
nouns, noun + **de** + noun 223; irregular plurals 258; number: singular/plural 258
nouveau, nouvelle 279
numbers, pronunciation of 33; ordinal 233; cardinal 262; summary chart R7

on 288
opinions, introducing personal opinions 281

parler forms of R5
partitive article 378-379; in negative phrases 381
passé composé 333; **-ir** verbs 278 (TE); **-re** verbs 290 (TE); **acheter (préférer)** 268-269; (TE) **aller** 206-207; (TE) **mettre** 272; (TE) **venir** 218; (TE) formed with **avoir** 321; formed with **être** 342, 344; in negative sentences 324; in questions 326; summary charts R15-R18
past events, talking about 321, 333, 335, 340
past participle, regular verbs 321, 333; irregular verbs 335; agreement with subject 342
personality traits, adjectives describing R2
physical traits, adjectives describing R2

plural, adjectives 230, 232, 270-271
possession, possessive adjectives 230, R2; with **de** 228
preferences, expressing 268, 367; telling someone to leave you alone 391
pouvoir 392
préférer 268
prendre present 364, 377, 379; past participle 377
prepositions with stress pronouns 221
present tense of regular verbs: *see* **-er, -ir, -re** verbs; summary charts R16; of irregular verbs: *see* individual verb listings; summary charts R16
pronouns, direct object 388, 390; indirect object 402; stress 221 subject 288
pronunciation 208, 213, 219, 223, 228, 232, 233, 270, 271, 272, 273, 279, 280, 281, 290, 293, 327, 337, 347, 378, 383, 393, 405; summary chart R12

quantity, expressions of 370, 371; partitive article to express 378-379
quand 336
quel, quelle 271
quelqu'un, quelque chose 347
questions, information 326; "yes-no" 326

-re verbs imperative 291; present 290, 403; past participle 333

savoir vs. **connaître** 398
sequence, how to talk about the order in which things take place 323
sound-spelling correspondence summary chart R12
sports, talking about 220

stress pronouns 221
subject pronouns 288
surprise, mild doubt, expressing 222, 231

time, telling R8

vacation, talking about 312
venir, in **passé composé** 344; present 218
verbs *see* **-er, -ir, -re** verbs; irregular: *see* individual verb listings; summary charts R15-R18; followed by indirect objects 403; stem-changing 218, 268, 286, 310
vieux, vieille 279
voici 379
voilà 379
voir past participle 335; present 332
vouloir 376; **je veux/ne veux pas, je voudrais** 376, 379

weather, talking about R8
weekend, talking about 310

Credits